# Learn Java with Projects

A concise practical guide to learning everything a Java
professional really needs to know

**Dr. Seán Kennedy**

**Maaike van Putten**

BIRMINGHAM—MUMBAI

# Learn Java with Projects

Copyright © 2023 Packt Publishing

**Associate Group Product Manager**: Kunal Sawant

**Book Project Manager**: Deeksha Thakkar

**Senior Editor**: Rounak Kulkarni

**Technical Editor**: Jubit Pincy

**Copy Editor**: Safis Editing

**Indexer**: Hemangini Bari

**Production Designer**: Vijay Kamble

**DevRel Marketing Coordinator**: Shrinidhi Manoharan and Sonia Chauhan

**Business Development Executive**: Kriti Sharma

First published: September 2023

Production reference: 2141223

Published by Packt Publishing Ltd.

Grosvenor House

11 St Paul's Square

Birmingham

B3 1RB, UK

ISBN 978-1-83763-718-8

www.packtpub.com

*To my wife Maria, and my daughters, Emily, Miriam, and Lilian.*

*– Dr. Seán Kennedy*


*To Adnane, for not distracting me.*

*– Maaike van Putten*

# Contributors

## About the authors

**Dr. Seán Kennedy** is a university lecturer with over 20 years of experience in teaching. He has a Ph.D. in IT and is Oracle-certified in Java at the Professional level (OCP). In his daily work, he has taught Java on Ericssons' bespoke Master's program for over a decade. He has several very popular Java courses on Udemy, one of which, *'Java 21, Java 17, Java 11, Advanced Java 8'*, has been selected for inclusion in their Udemy Business program (where only the top 3% of courses qualify). He has a YouTube channel called *Let's Get Certified* that teaches Java at all levels and prepares candidates for Java certification. Outside of work, he enjoys tennis, walking, reading, TV, and nature.

*I want to thank those who have always supported me, especially my wife, Maria, and my late parents.*

**Maaike van Putten** is a software consultant and trainer with a passion for empowering others in their careers. Her love for Java shows in numerous software development projects she participated in and the 5 Oracle Java certifications she obtained. She has designed and delivered a broad spectrum of training courses catering to beginners and seasoned developers in Java and many other languages and frameworks. Next to that, she has authored multiple books and online courses through multiple platforms reaching over 600,000 learners.

*I want to thank all my students for inspiring and motivating me.*

# About the reviewers

**Alejandro Duarte** is a Software Engineer, published author, and award winner. He currently works for MariaDB as a Developer Relations Engineer. Starting his coding journey at 13 with BASIC on a rudimentary black screen, Alejandro quickly transitioned to C, C++, and Java during his academic years at the National University of Colombia. He relocated first to the UK and then to Finland to foster his career in the open-source software industry. He's a recognized figure in Java circles, credited with articles amassing millions of views, as well as technical videos and presentations at international events. You can contact him on X (Twitter) *@alejandro_du*.

*Thanks to the global Java community for being part of such an amazing technology. Thanks to MariaDB plc for allowing me the flexibility to work on this project.*

**Thiago Braga Rodrigues**, a university lecturer, researcher, and Java specialist, has journeyed academically from Brazil to Ireland over the span of a decade. He holds a BEng in Biomedical Engineering and a Ph.D. in IT. Throughout his academic journey, Thiago's research endeavors have led him to globally recognized institutions, such as Harvard Medical School in the USA, and Athlone Institute of Technology in Ireland, where he delved into the intricacies of bioinformatics. His expertise encompasses programming, biomedical engineering, and software engineering, with a particular focus on developing hardware and software solutions for wearable systems. As both an author and reviewer for various academic journals and conferences, Thiago persistently contributes to the advancement of his field. Outside of academia and work, he is a classically trained violin teacher with experience playing in several orchestras. An avid gamer, Thiago seamlessly blends technology, arts, and leisure throughout his enriching journey.

**Giuseppe Pedullà** is a senior software developer and software architect, working since 2014. He has worked in some large companies and created some products for clients such as banks, insurance companies, and so on. He has developed complex solutions for his clients, making architectural decisions to improve software efficiency. He also teaches coding, conducts webinars, and so on.

*I thank my wife and my children who are very patient and push me to do things that realize me as a developer and so on. I thank them because they help me and they understand that I want to do something to help me improve in what I do.*

**Anurag Sharma** is a seasoned Integration Architect, boasting 11 years of rich experience in the IT realm, with deep-seated expertise in JAVA/J2EE and a broad suite of integration technologies, including a prominent presence in the Salesforce ecosystem as a MuleSoft Ambassador. As a JAVA-certified professional, Anurag has a track record of success in developing and designing solutions across diverse domains such as airlines, retail, and manufacturing, to name a few.

With a dual-level certification in JAVA and comprehensive certifications in MuleSoft, Anurag has been a vital asset to tech giants like Oracle and HCL, in both India and the UK. His thought leadership and insights have resonated on global stages such as Salesforce's London World Tour and Dreamforce, where he has been a sought-after speaker.

Anurag is known for his commitment to the Integration community, where he spearheads mentorship programs, nurturing both novices and seasoned professionals in the field. He solves problems on Tech helper forums. Beyond his mentorship roles, Anurag contributes to the vibrancy of the tech world through his writings, illuminating tech articles that decipher complex technical landscapes for a broader audience.

In the quieter moments, you will find Anurag immersed in literature, as reading and writing about technology are not just hobbies but gateways to staying ahead in the ever-evolving tech universe.

# Table of Contents

# 2

## Variables and Primitive Data Types                                            31

# 3

## Operators and Casting                                                         43

# 4

## Conditional Statements                                                        69

# 7

# Part 2: Object-Oriented Programming

# 8

# 9

# Inheritance and Polymorphism                                              213

# 10

## Interfaces and Abstract Classes                                        269

# 11

## Dealing with Exceptions                                               291

# 12

## Java Core API                                                               315

# Part 3: Advanced Topics

# 13

## Generics and Collections                                                    359

# 14

# Lambda Expressions                                 393

# 15

# Streams – Fundamentals                              427

# Preface

Welcome to the world of Java programming! Java is one of the most versatile and widely used programming languages in the world. Its platform independence, object-oriented nature, and extensive library support make it an ideal choice for developing a wide range of applications, from desktop to mobile and enterprise solutions.

Whether you are a novice eager to learn the fundamentals or an experienced developer seeking to enhance your skills, this book is designed to be your comprehensive guide to mastering the Java programming language. We start with the basics: how to get set up with an editor; and primitive data types; and progress systematically to more advanced concepts such as lambdas, streams, and concurrency.

This book is more than just a guide; it's a companion on your journey to master Java. Our goal is to make this journey enjoyable and effective. This book adopts a hands-on approach, combining theoretical concepts with lots of practical exercises and a capstone project. Whether you are a self-learner or part of a formal educational program, the hands-on exercises and capstone project will help solidify your knowledge, making the learning experience engaging and practical.

*Learning by doing* is critical in mastering any programming language and we have taken that to heart in this book. At the end of each chapter, you'll have a few exercises and a project that will help you get some experience with Java. The exercises are typically smaller tasks, and the project is a bit bigger. In all of them, you'll have quite some freedom to choose how to implement it specifically. Why? Well, because that's what it's going to be like in real life as well! We will provide you with a sample solution, but if ours is a bit different, that doesn't mean yours is bad. If you're in doubt, ask some AI assistants such as ChatGPT what they think about your solution. Still unclear? We're always willing to help you as well!

Alright, back to the exercises and projects. We wanted to choose a common theme for our exercises and projects. Believe it or not, but one of your writers (hint: it's the female one) is surrounded by miniature gigantic historic reptile replicas during the writing of the book. In fact, currently, it's hard to type because this enormous battery-powered Tyrannosaurus Rex tries to destroy my laptop.

I couldn't help but draw quite some inspiration from that. So yes, all the exercises and projects will be dinosaur-themed, based on the collection and vivid fantasy play of my 5-year-old son. (I wake up around 5-6 AM. Not by my alarm clock, and definitely not because I'm part of the 5 AM club. No, I have this (most amazing) excited kid telling me fun facts about dinosaurs. Might as well put this knowledge to use!)

So, here's your context: congratulations, you're hired! You are now working for our special dinosaur zoo: Mesozoic Eden. It's a unique blend of prehistoric wilderness and modern comfort, where humans and dinosaurs coexist. People can visit for a day, or camp here for several weeks.

At Mesozoic Eden, we house a rich variety of dinosaur species, each with its distinct behavior and lifestyle, ranging from the colossal Brachiosaurus to the swift-footed Velociraptor, the regal Tyrannosaurus Rex, and many more. We even have a state-of-the-art laboratory where we continue to discover and study new dinosaur breeds.

As part of our team, your role is not only about taking care of these majestic creatures and ensuring their well-being but also about maintaining the safety and security of our guests. Our park employs cutting-edge technology and stringent protocols to ensure a safe environment for all.

In the exercises and projects, you'll take on various software development tasks as an employee of Mesozoic Eden, from coding software for feeding schedules to the app that handles emergency alerts, ensuring park operations run smoothly, and above all, creating an unforgettable experience for our visitors.

## Who this book is for

This book is suitable for beginners looking to take their first steps into programming as well as experienced developers transitioning to Java. Whether you are a student or professional, the content is structured to cater to a diverse audience.

If you are interested in Java 8 OCA Oracle certification, then this book is extremely helpful as it covers many important fundamental concepts by going "under the hood" to explain what is happening in memory. It is no coincidence that both authors are Oracle OCP qualified.

## What this book covers

*Chapter 1, Getting Started with Java*, starts by discussing the main Java features, such as OOP. How to install Java on various operating systems and how to write your first Java program with and without an IDE are also explored.

*Chapter 2, Variables and Primitive Data Types*, explains what a variable is and the fact that Java uses "strong-typing" (you must declare a variables type). This chapter also covers Java's primitive data types, their sizes in bytes (needed to understand for later when discussing casting), and their ranges.

*Chapter 3, Operators and Casting*, explores how Java's operators cooperate using precedence and associativity. We discuss Java's various operators and explain both widening and narrowing when casting in Java.

*Chapter 4, Conditional Statements*, focuses on both scope and conditional statements. We initially examine Java's use of block scope. We then explain the various forms of the `if` statement; and conclude the chapter with both `switch` statements and `switch` expressions.

*Chapter 5, Understanding Iteration*, discusses loops, including `while`, `do-while`, `for`, and enhanced for. This chapter also explores the `break` and `continue` statements.

*Chapter 6, Working with Arrays*, describes why one needs arrays. We show how to declare and initialize arrays of various primitive types, including using the shorthand syntax. We discuss how to loop through an array, processing each element. Multi-dimensional arrays are also covered; as is the `Arrays` class.

*Chapter 7, Methods*, discusses the importance of methods and the difference between the method definition and method execution. Method overloading is discussed and the varargs format is explained. Lastly, the important concept of call-by-value is explained.

*Chapter 8, Classes, Objects, and Enums*, is a significant OOP chapter and details the following: the difference between classes and objects; the `this` reference; access modifiers; basic and advanced encapsulation; the object life cycle; the `instanceof` keyword; enums and records.

*Chapter 9, Inheritance and Polymorphism*, explains inheritance and polymorphism. We detail what overriding means and discuss the `super`, `protected`, `abstract`, and `final` keywords. We also explore `sealed` classes and upcasting/downcasting.

*Chapter 10, Interfaces and Abstract Classes*, covers both `abstract` classes and interfaces. We explain `static`, `default`, and `private` interface methods and also `sealed` interfaces.

*Chapter 11, Dealing with Exceptions*, explains exceptions and their purpose. We explain the difference between checked and unchecked exceptions. We delve into throwing exceptions and how to create your own custom exceptions. The important catch or declare principle is discussed; as are the try-catch, try-catch-finally, and try-with-resources blocks.

*Chapter 12, Java Core API*, introduces important classes/interfaces from the API, such as `Scanner`. We compare and contrast `String` and `StringBuilder` and discuss how to create a custom immutable type. We example the `List` interface and its popular implementation `ArrayList`. Lastly, we explore the Date API.

*Chapter 13, Generics and Collections*, discusses the collections framework and its interfaces `List`, `Set`, `Map`, and `Queue`. We examine several implementations of each and basic operations. We explain sorting using both the `Comparable` and `Comparator` interfaces. We finish by examining generics and basic hashing concepts.

*Chapter 14, Lambda Expressions*, explains what lambda expressions are and their relationship to functional interfaces. Several functional interfaces from the API are examined. Lastly, method references and the role of context in understanding them are outlined.

*Chapter 15, Streams: Fundamentals*, is our first chapter on streams. In this chapter, we discuss what a stream pipeline is and what stream laziness means. We show different ways to create both finite and infinite streams. We examine the terminal operations that start off the streaming process - including reductions such as `collect()` which is very useful for extracting information out of a stream.

*Chapter 16, Streams: Advanced Concepts*, starts by examining intermediate operations such as `filter()`, `map()`, and `sorted()`. We explore the primitive streams followed by how to map from one stream to another, regardless of type. The `Optional` type is explained and we conclude with a discussion of parallel streams.

*Chapter 17, Concurrency*, starts by explaining what concurrency is. We examine working with threads and present issues with concurrent access. Mechanisms to resolve these issues are discussed; namely: atomic classes, `synchronized` blocks, and the `Lock` interface. Concurrent collections and the `ExecutorService` are explored next. We finish with a discussion on threading problems such as data races, deadlock, and livelock.

## To get the most out of this book

While much of the code will work with earlier Java versions, we would recommend installing or upgrading to Java 21 to avoid version-related compiler errors.

If you currently have nothing on your system, the following setup would be great:

- JDK 21 or later (Oracle's JDK or OpenJDK)
- IntelliJ IDEA (community edition is good enough) or Eclipse or Netbeans

| Software/hardware covered in the book | Operating system requirements |
| --- | --- |
| Java 21+ | Windows, macOS, or Linux |

See *Chapter 1* for instructions on how to get both Java and an IDE installed on various operating systems.

If you are using the digital version of this book, we advise you to type the code yourself or access the code from the book's GitHub repository (a link is available in the next section). Doing so will help you avoid any potential errors related to the copying and pasting of code.

> **Disclaimer**
> With the intention of the Publisher and Author, certain graphics included in this title are displaying large screen examples where the textual content is not relevant to the graphic example. We encourage our readers to download the digital copy included in their purchase for magnified and accessible content requirements.

# Download the example code files

You can download the example code files for this book from GitHub at https://github.com/ PacktPublishing/Learn-Java-with-Projects. If there's an update to the code, it will be updated in the GitHub repository.

We also have other code bundles from our rich catalog of books and videos available at https:// github.com/PacktPublishing/. Check them out!

# Code in Action

The Code in Action videos for this book can be viewed at https://bit.ly/3GdtYeC

# Download the color images

We also provide a PDF file that has color images of the screenshots and diagrams used in this book. You can download it here: https://packt.link/gbp/9781837637188

# Conventions used

There are a number of text conventions used throughout this book.

Code in text: Indicates code words in text, database table names, folder names, filenames, file extensions, pathnames, dummy URLs, user input, and Twitter handles. Here is an example: " So, the main() method has now handed over control to the simpleExample() method, and control will not return to main() until simpleExample() exits"

A block of code is set as follows:

```
public class HelloWorld {
public static void main(String[] args) {
System.out.println("Hello world!");
}
}
```

When we wish to draw your attention to a particular part of a code block, the relevant lines or items are set in bold:

```
//          int age = 25;
            System.out.println(age);
```

Any command-line input or output is written as follows:

```
Enter a number (negative number to exit) -->
1
Enter a number (negative number to exit) -->
2
```

> Tips or important notes
> Appear like this.

# Get in touch

Feedback from our readers is always welcome.

**General feedback**: If you have questions about any aspect of this book, email us at `customercare@packtpub.com` and mention the book title in the subject of your message.

**Errata**: Although we have taken every care to ensure the accuracy of our content, mistakes do happen. If you have found a mistake in this book, we would be grateful if you would report this to us. Please visit `www.packtpub.com/support/errata` and fill in the form.

**Piracy**: If you come across any illegal copies of our works in any form on the internet, we would be grateful if you would provide us with the location address or website name. Please contact us at `copyright@packt.com` with a link to the material.

**If you are interested in becoming an author**: If there is a topic that you have expertise in and you are interested in either writing or contributing to a book, please visit `authors.packtpub.com`.

# Share Your Thoughts

Once you've read *Learn Java with Projects*, we'd love to hear your thoughts! Scan the QR code below to go straight to the Amazon review page for this book and share your feedback.

`https://packt.link/r/1837637180`

Your review is important to us and the tech community and will help us make sure we're delivering excellent quality content.

# Download a free PDF copy of this book

Thanks for purchasing this book!

Do you like to read on the go but are unable to carry your print books everywhere?

Is your eBook purchase not compatible with the device of your choice?

Don't worry, now with every Packt book you get a DRM-free PDF version of that book at no cost.

Read anywhere, any place, on any device. Search, copy, and paste code from your favorite technical books directly into your application.

The perks don't stop there, you can get exclusive access to discounts, newsletters, and great free content in your inbox daily

Follow these simple steps to get the benefits:

1.  Scan the QR code or visit the link below

https://packt.link/free-ebook/9781837637188

2.  Submit your proof of purchase
3.  That's it! We'll send your free PDF and other benefits to your email directly

# Part 1:
# Java Fundamentals

In this part, we will start by looking into the features of Java and how to get set up using Java and an IDE. We will examine variables and Java's eight primitive data types. Following that, we will discuss Java's operators and casting. We then move on to Java conditional statements and looping constructs. After that, we will look at using arrays, before finally finishing with methods.

This section has the following chapters:

- *Chapter 1, Getting Started with Java*
- *Chapter 2, Variables and Primitive Data Types*
- *Chapter 3, Operators and Casting*
- *Chapter 4, Conditional Statements*
- *Chapter 5, Understanding Iteration*
- *Chapter 6, Working with Arrays*
- *Chapter 7, Methods*

# 1

# Getting Started with Java

Welcome to the exciting world of Java! Java is a very popular programming language. It is a multipurpose, powerful, and popular programming language that has been used by millions of developers worldwide to create a wide variety of applications. And yes, it really is multipurpose since it can be used to create all sorts of applications, from web and mobile apps to game development and beyond.

So, you've done a great job choosing a (new) language. We're going to take you on a (hopefully) fascinating journey that will provide you with valuable skills and open new opportunities in the ever-evolving field of technology.

What are we waiting for? In this chapter, we're going to cover the following main topics:

- Java features

- Installing Java

- Compiling and running Java programs

- Working with an **integrated development environment** (IDE)

- Creating and running a program with an IDE

## Technical requirements

Before diving into the magical world of Java programming, let's ensure you have the right hardware. If your hardware doesn't meet these requirements, don't worry; online alternatives are discussed later in this chapter. If you are using your work laptop, make sure that you have download rights. Here's a brief overview of the requirements:

- **Operating system**: Java can run on various operating systems, including Windows, macOS, and Linux. Ensure that you have a recent version of one of these operating systems installed on your computer.

- **Java Development Kit (JDK)**: To compile and run Java programs, you'll need the JDK installed on your system. The JDK includes the **Java Runtime Environment (JRE)**, which contains the necessary libraries and components for running Java applications. We'll see how to install this later.

- **System resources**: More is always better, but Java isn't too demanding. It doesn't require high-end hardware, but it's still a good idea to have a system with sufficient resources for a smooth development experience. The following are the minimum and recommended system requirements:

  - **Minimum requirements**:

    - CPU: 1 GHz or faster processor

    - RAM: 2 GB

    - Disk space: 1 GB (for JDK installation and additional files)

  - **Recommended requirements**:

    - CPU: 2 GHz or faster multi-core processor

    - RAM: 4 GB or more

    - Disk space: 2 GB or more (for JDK installation, additional files, and projects)

Keep in mind that these requirements may change with future updates to the JDK and related tools. We have placed the files in a GitHub repository. You can clone the projects with the use of Git and import them to your computer this way. It's beyond the scope of explaining how to use Git here but it's recommended to look into it independently. You can access the files and examples used in this book here: `https://github.com/PacktPublishing/Learn-Java-with-Projects`.

## Exploring Java features

Java was developed by James Gosling at Sun Microsystems in the mid-1990s. When Java was created, it was originally designed as a language for consumer electronics. It attempted to support complex host architectures, focused on portability, and supported secure networking. However, Java outgrew its own ambitions. It quickly gained momentum as a versatile language for creating enterprise, web, and mobile applications. Today, Java no longer belongs to Sun Microsystems. Oracle Corporation acquired Sun Microsystems in 2010. And with that acquirement, Java became an integral part of Oracle's software ecosystem.

Java was very unique at the time it was created. The huge success of Java can be attributed to some of its core features. These features were very innovative at the time but are now found in many other (competing) languages. One of the core features is object-oriented programming. OOP allows us to structure our code in a neat way that helps with reusability and maintainability. We're going to start discussing the core features by having a look at **object-oriented programming (OOP)**.

## OOP in Java

Arguably the most important feature of Java is its support for OOP. If you ask any Java developer what Java is, the answer is often that it's an OOP language.

It's safe to say that OOP is a key feature. *What is this OOP thing?* you may wonder. OOP is a programming paradigm. It structures applications to model real-world objects and their interactions and behaviors. Let's go over the main concepts of OOP:

- **Objects**: This may be stating the obvious but, in OOP, **objects** are the main building blocks of your program. An object is a representation of a real-world entity, such as a user, an email, or a bank account. Each object has its own **attributes** (data fields) and behaviors (**methods**).

- **Classes**: Objects are created using their **class**. A class is a blueprint for creating objects. It defines the attributes and methods that objects of the class should have. For example, a `Car` class might define attributes such as color, make, and model, and methods such as start, accelerate, and brake.

- **Inheritance**: Another key feature is **inheritance**. Inheritance allows one class to inherit the attributes and methods of another class. For example, `Car` could inherit from a `Vehicle` class. We're not going to cover the details here, but inheritance helps to better structure the code. The code is more reusable, and the hierarchy of related classes opens doors in terms of what we can do with our types.

- **Encapsulation**: Encapsulation is giving a class control over its own data. This is done by bundling data (attributes) and methods that operate on that data. The attributes can only be accessed via these special methods from outside. Encapsulation helps to protect the internal state of an object and allows you to control how the object's data can be accessed or modified. Don't worry if this sounds tricky still, we'll deal with this in more detail later.

- **Polymorphism** and **Abstraction**: These are two key concepts of OOP that will be explained later when you're ready for them.

## Working with OOP

I can imagine this all sounds very abstract at this point, but before you know it, you'll be creating classes and instantiating objects yourself. OOP helps to make code more maintainable, better structured, and reusable. These things really help to be able to make changes to your application, solve problems, and scale up when needed.

OOP is just one key feature of Java. Another key feature is that it's a compiled language. Let's make sure you understand what is meant by that now.

## Compiled language

Java is a **compiled programming language**, which means that the source code you write must be transformed into a machine-readable format before it can be interpreted. This machine-readable format is called bytecode. This process is different from that of interpreted languages, where the source code is read, interpreted, and executed on the fly. During runtime, the computer interprets an interpreted language line by line. When a compiled language is running, the computer interprets the bytecode during runtime. We'll dive deeper into the compilation process in just a bit when we are going to compile our own code. For now, let's see what the benefits of compiled languages are.

### Benefits of Java being a compiled language

Compiling code first requires an extra step, and it takes time in the beginning, but it brings advantages. First of all, the performance of compiled languages is typically better than interpreted languages. This is because the bytecode gets optimized for efficient execution on the target platform.

Another advantage of compilation is the early detection of syntax errors and certain other types of errors before the code is executed. This enables developers to identify and fix issues before deploying the application, reducing the likelihood of runtime errors.

Java code is turned into bytecode – a form of binary code - by the compiler. This bytecode is platform-independent. This means that it allows Java applications to run on different operating systems without modification. Platform independence is actually the key feature that we're going to be discussing next.

## Write once, run anywhere

Java's **Write Once, Run Anywhere** (**WORA**) principle is another key feature. This used to set Java apart from many other programming languages, but now, this is rather common, and many competing languages also implemented this feature. This principle ensures that Java code can run on different platforms without requiring different versions of the Java code for each platform. This means that a Java program is not tied to any specific operating system or hardware architecture.

When you have different versions of the code for each platform, this means that you have to maintain all these versions of the code as well. Let's say you have a code base for Linux, macOS, and Windows. When a new feature or a change is required, you need to add this to three places! You can imagine that WORA was a game-changer at the time Java came out. And it leads to an increased reach of your application – any device that can run Java applications can run yours.

### Understanding the WORA elements

The WORA principle is made possible by bytecode and the **Java Virtual Machine** (**JVM**). Bytecode is the compiled Java program. The compiler turns the Java code into this bytecode, and this bytecode is platform-independent. It can run on any device that can run the bytecode executer.

This bytecode executer is called the JVM. Each platform (Windows, macOS, Linux, and so on) has its own JVM implementation, which is specifically designed to translate bytecode into native machine code for that platform. Since the bytecode remains the same across platforms, the JVM handles the differences between operating systems and hardware architectures. The WORA principle is explained in *Figure 1.1*.

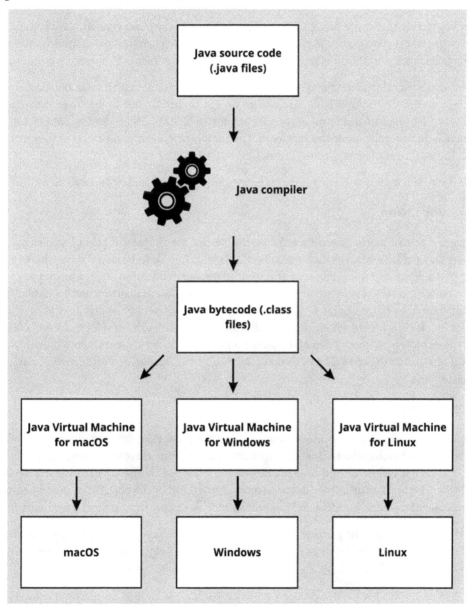

Figure 1.1 – The WORA principle in a diagram

You can see that the compiler creates bytecode and that this bytecode can be picked up by the JVM. The JVM is platform-specific and does the translation to the platform it's on. There's more that the JVM does for us, and that is automatic memory management. Let's explore this next.

## Automatic memory management

Another key feature that made Java great is its **automatic memory management**, which simplifies development and prevents common memory-related errors. Java handles memory allocation and garbage collection for you. The developer doesn't need to take care of manually managing the memory.

Nowadays, this is the rule and not the exception. Most other modern languages have automatic memory management as well. However, it is important to know what automatic memory management means. The memory allocation and deallocation are done automatically. This actually leads to simplifying the code. There is no boilerplate code that just focuses on the allocation and deallocation of the memory. This also leads to fewer memory-related errors.

Let's make sure you understand what is meant by memory allocation and deallocation.

### Memory allocation

In code, you create variables. Sometimes, these variables are not simple values but complex objects with many data fields. When you create an object, this object needs to be stored somewhere in the memory of the device that it's running on. This is called **memory allocation**. In Java, when you create an object, device memory is automatically allocated to store the object's attributes and associated data. This is different from languages such as C and C++, where developers must manually allocate and deallocate memory. Java's automatic memory allocation streamlines the development process and reduces the chances of memory leaks or dangling pointers, which can cause unexpected behavior or crashes. It also makes the code cleaner to read, since you don't need to deal with any allocation or deallocation code.

### Garbage collection

When a memory block is no longer used by the application, it needs to be deallocated. The process Java uses for this is called **garbage collection**. Garbage collection is the process of identifying and reclaiming memory that is no longer in use by a program. In Java, when an object is no longer accessible or needed, the garbage collector automatically frees up the memory occupied by the object. This process ensures that the memory is efficiently utilized and prevents memory leaks and the problems that come with it.

The JVM periodically runs the garbage collector to identify and clean up unreachable objects. Java's garbage collection mechanism uses many different sophisticated algorithms to determine when an object is no longer needed.

Now that we've covered the basics, let's move on to installing Java.

# Installing Java

Before you can start writing and running Java programs, you'll need to set up the JDK on your computer. The JDK contains essential tools and libraries required for Java development, such as the Java compiler, the JRE, and other useful utilities that help development.

We will guide you through the process of installing Java on Windows, macOS, and Linux, and we'll give you some suggestions for when you don't have access to either one of those. But before proceeding with the installation of Java, it's a good idea to check whether it's already installed on your system.

## Checking whether Java is installed on your system

Java may have been pre-installed, or you may have installed it previously without realizing it. To check whether Java is installed, follow these simple steps. The first one depends on your operating system.

### Step 1 – Open a terminal

For Windows, press the *Windows* key, type `cmd`, and press *Enter* to open the **Command Prompt**.

For macOS, press *Command + Space* to open the **Spotlight** search, type `Terminal`, and press *Enter* to open **Terminal**.

For Linux, open a Terminal window. The method for opening the Terminal window varies depending on your Linux distribution (for example, in Ubuntu, press *Ctrl + Alt + T*).

### Step 2 – Check for the Java version

In the Command Prompt or Terminal window, type the following command and press *Enter*:

```
java -version
```

### Step 3 – Interpret the response

If Java is installed, you will see the version information displayed. If not, the Command Prompt will display an error message, indicating that Java is not recognized or found.

If you find that Java is already installed on your system, make sure it's version 21 or later to ensure compatibility with modern Java features. If it's an older version or not installed, proceed with the installation process for your specific platform, as described in the following sections. If an older version is installed, you may want to uninstall this first to avoid having an unnecessarily complicated setup. You can install this the common way of uninstalling programs for your operating system.

In *Figure 1.2* and *Figure 1.6*, you'll see examples of the output you can expect when Java is installed.

```
Last login: Tue Mar 14 11:18:00 on ttys000

The default interactive shell is now zsh.
To update your account to use zsh, please run `chsh -s /bin/zsh`.
For more details, please visit https://support.apple.com/kb/HT208050.
Maaikes-MBP:~ maaikevanputten$ java --version
openjdk 19.0.1 2022-10-18
OpenJDK Runtime Environment (build 19.0.1+10-21)
OpenJDK 64-Bit Server VM (build 19.0.1+10-21, mixed mode, sharing)
Maaikes-MBP:~ maaikevanputten$ 
```

Figure 1.2 – The macOS terminal output where Java 19 is installed

Now, let's see how to install Java on each operating system.

## Installing Java on Windows

To install Java on a Windows operating system, follow these steps:

1.  Visit the **Oracle Java SE Downloads** page at `https://www.oracle.com/java/technologies/downloads/`. This software can be used for educational purposes for free, but requires a license in production. You can consider switching to **OpenJDK** to run programs in production without a license: `https://openjdk.org/install/`.

2.  Select the appropriate installer for your Windows operating system (for example, **Windows x64 Installer**).

3.  Download the installer by clicking on the file link.

4.  Run the downloaded installer (the `.exe` file) and follow the on-screen instructions to complete the installation.

5.  To add Java to the system's `PATH` environment variable, search for **Environment Variables** in the **Start** menu and select **Edit the system environment variables**. You should see a screen similar to *Figure 1.3*.

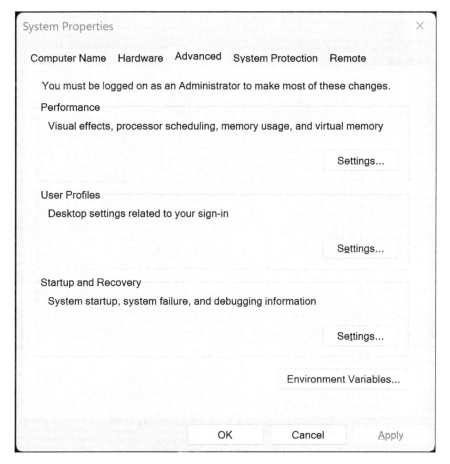

Figure 1.3 – The System Properties window

6.  In the **System Properties** window, click on the **Environment Variables…** button. A screen like the one in *Figure 1.4* will pop up.

7.  Under **System variables**, find the **Path** variable, select it, and click **Edit**. You can see an example of which one to select in the following *Figure 1.4*:

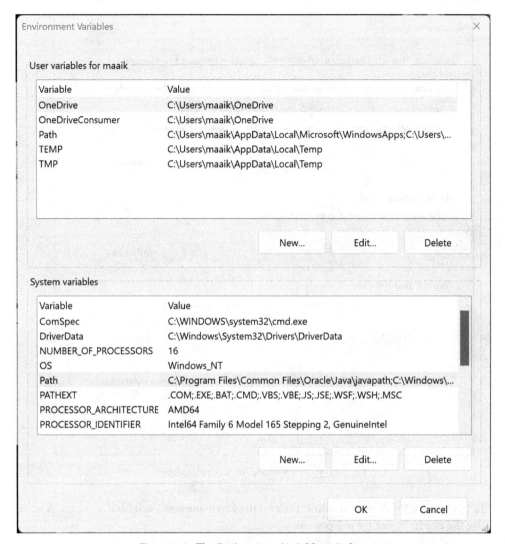

Figure 1.4 – The Environment Variables window

8.  Click **New…** and add the path to the bin folder of your Java installation (for example, `C:\Program Files\Java\jdk-21\bin`). In *Figure 1.5*, this has been done already.

Figure 1.5 – Adding the path to Java to the Path variable

9.  Click **OK** to save the changes and close the **Environment Variables** windows.

10. Verify Java is installed by opening the Command Prompt (reopen it if you have it open already) and then typing the following:

```
java -version
```

11. The output should look as shown in *Figure 1.6*. However, your version should be 21 or higher to keep up with all the snippets in this book.

Figure 1.6 – Command Prompt after Java version check after installing Java

## Installing Java on macOS

To install Java on a macOS operating system, follow these steps:

1. Visit the **Oracle Java SE Downloads** page at `https://www.oracle.com/java/technologies/javase-jdk16-downloads.html`.

2. Select the macOS installer (for example, **macOS x64 Installer**).

3. Download the installer by clicking on the file link.

4. Run the downloaded installer (the `.dmg` file) and follow the on-screen instructions to complete the installation.

5. Java should be automatically added to your system's `PATH` environment variable. To verify the installation, open the Terminal and run the following command:

```
java -version
```

6. You should see the version of Java you just installed, similar to *Figure 1.2*.

## Installing Java on Linux

Installing on Linux can be a little bit tricky to explain in a few steps. Different Linux distributions require different installation steps. Here, we will see how to install Java on a Linux Ubuntu system:

1. Open the **Terminal** and update your package repository by running the following command:

```
sudo apt-get update
```

2.   Install the default JDK package by running the following command:

```
sudo apt install default-jdk
```

3.   To verify the installation, run the `java -version` command. You should see the version of Java you just installed.

4.   If you need to set the `JAVA_HOME` environment variable (which you won't need for working your way through this book but will need for doing more complex Java projects), you first need to determine the installation path by running the following command:

```
sudo update-alternatives --config java
```

5.   Take note of the path displayed (for example, `/usr/lib/jvm/java-19-openjdk-amd64/bin/java`).

6.   Open the `/etc/environment` file in a text editor with root privileges:

```
sudo nano /etc/environment
```

7.   Add the following line at the end of the file, replacing the path with the path you noted in *Step 4* (excluding the `/bin/java` part):

```
JAVA_HOME="/usr/lib/jvm/java-19-openjdk-amd64"
```

8.   Save and close the file. Then, run the following command to apply the changes:

```
source /etc/environment
```

Now, Java should be installed and configured on your Linux operating system.

## Running Java online

If you don't have access to a computer with macOS, Linux, or Windows, there are online solutions out there. The free options are not perfect but, for example, the **w3schools** solution for trying Java in the browser is not bad at all. There are quite a few of these out there.

In order to work with multiple files there might be free tools out there, but most of them are paid. A currently free one that we would recommend is on `replit.com`. You can find it here: `https://replit.com/languages/java`.

You need to sign up, but you can work for free with multiple files and save them on your account. This is a good alternative if you would for example only have a tablet to follow along with this book.

Another option would be to use GitHub Codespaces: `https://github.com/codespaces`. They have the opportunity to enter a repository (for example the one we use for this book) and directly try the examples that are available in the repo and adjust them to try new things.

Having navigated through the installation of Java, it's time to talk about compiling and running programs.

# Writing our first program

Before diving into the process of compiling and running Java programs, let's create a simple Java program using a basic text editor. This will help you understand the structure of a Java program and how to write and save a Java source code file. For this example, we will create a **"Hello world!" program** that will be used to demonstrate the process of compilation and execution.

## Hello world

You may have heard of **"Hello world!" programs**. They are a common way to start learning a new programming language. It's a simple program that prints the message `"Hello world!"` to the console. Writing this program will provide you with a very basic understanding of Java syntax, and it will help you to become familiar with the process of writing, compiling, and running Java code.

## Steps to create the program

Alright, let's start coding. Here are the steps:

1. First, open a basic text editor on your computer. **Notepad** on Windows, **TextEdit** on macOS, or **Gedit** on Linux are suitable options.

2. Write the following Java code in your text editor:

   ```
   public class HelloWorld {
       public static void main(String[] args) {
           System.out.println("Hello world!");
       }
   }
   ```

3. Save the file as `HelloWorld.java` in a directory of your choice. Don't forget the `.java` extension when saving the file. This indicates that the file contains Java source code. The code should not have `.txt` after `.java`. This happens sometimes in Windows, so make sure to not select the text file in the filetype dropdown.

---

**TextEdit – file extension issues**

The later versions of macOS have some issues with **TextEdit**. You can't save it as a Java file by default. In order to enable this, you need to go to **Format | Make Plain Text** and select **UTF-8**.

After this, you can save it as a `.java` file. You may still run into encoding errors; the problem is with the encoding, and fixing it might be a lot of effort missing the goal of this exercise. It might be better to download **Notepad++**, **TextPad**, or **Sublime** for this part. Or go ahead and download the `HelloWorld.java` file from our GitHub repository.

---

## Understanding the program

Let's have a look at the code we just used. First of all, be aware that this is *case-sensitive*. That means that when you look at the code, most things will not work as you expect if you mix up lowercase and uppercase.

First, we created a class named `HelloWorld` with a `main` method. We'll cover classes and methods in a lot more detail, of course. But a class is the fundamental building block of Java applications, and it can contain methods. Methods can be executed to do things – *things* being executing statements.

The `main` method is a special method. It is the entry point of our Java program and contains the code that will be executed when the program is run. The line with `System.out.println("Hello world!")`; writes the `Hello world!` message to the console. Please note, that `println` stands for print line, so it uses a lowercase *L* and not an uppercase *i*.

With the `HelloWorld.java` file saved, we are now ready to move on to the next section, where we will learn how to compile and run the Java program using the command line and an IDE.

# Compiling and running Java programs

Now that we have our first program written, let's discuss how we can compile and run it. We will cover the basics of the compilation process, the role of the JVM, and how to compile and run Java code using the command line and an IDE.

## Understanding the compilation process

The source code is written in a human-readable format using the Java programming language. Or at least, we hope that this is your opinion after this book. Before the code can be executed, it must be transformed into a format that the computer can understand. You already know that Java is a compiled language and that this process is called compilation.

During compilation, the **Java compiler (javac)** converts the source code (`.java` files) into bytecode (`.class` files). Once the bytecode is generated, it can be executed by the JVM. We have already learned that the JVM is the bytecode executer and that every platform has its own custom JVM enabling the WORA feature of Java.

## Compiling the code with javac on the command line

To compile a Java program using the command line, follow these steps:

1.  Open a terminal (Command Prompt on Windows, Terminal on macOS or Linux).

2.  Navigate to the directory containing your Java source code file (for example, the directory of your previously created `HelloWorld.java` file). In case you don't know how to do that, this can be done with the `cd` command, which stands for *change directory*. For example, if I'm in a directory called `documents` and I want to step into the subfolder called `java programs`, I'd run the `cd "java programs"` command. The quotes are only needed when there are spaces in the directory name. It's beyond the scope of this book to explain how to change directories for any platform. There are many excellent explanations for every platform on how to navigate the folder structure using the command line on the internet.

3.  Once you're in the folder containing the Java file, enter the following command to compile the Java source code:

    ```
    javac HelloWorld.java
    ```

    If the compilation is successful, a new file with the same name but a `.class` extension (for example, `HelloWorld.class`) will be created in the same directory. This file contains the bytecode that can be executed by the JVM.

Let's see how we can run this compiled code.

## Running the compiled code with Java on the command line

To run the compiled Java program, follow these steps:

1.  In the terminal, make sure you are still in the directory containing the `.class` file.

2.  Enter the following command to execute the bytecode:

    ```
    java HelloWorld
    ```

The JVM will load and run the bytecode, and you should see the output of your program. In this case, the output will be as follows:

```
Hello world!
```

It's pretty cool that we can write Java in Notepad and run it on the command line, but the life of a modern-day Java developer is a lot nicer. Let's add IDEs to the mix and see this for ourselves.

# Working with an IDE

Creating files in text editors is a little old-fashioned. Of course, you can still do it this way – it's actually an excellent way of becoming an amazing programmer, but it's also a very frustrating way. There are tools available to do quite a bit of the heavy work for us and to assist us while writing our code. These tools are called IDEs.

## What is an IDE?

An IDE is a software application that comes with everything you need to write, compile, run, and test your code. Using an IDE can make it easier to develop all sorts of programs. Not only that but also debugging and managing your code is easier. Comparatively, you can think of an IDE somewhat like Microsoft Office Word for me as I write this book. While I could have written it using Notepad, using Word provides significant advantages. It assists in checking for spelling errors and allows me to easily add and visualize layouts, among other helpful features. This analogy paints a picture of how an IDE doesn't just provide a platform to write code but also offers a suite of tools to streamline and enhance your coding experience.

## Choosing an IDE

When it comes to Java development, there are several IDEs available, each with its own set of features and capabilities. In this section, we will discuss the factors to consider when choosing an IDE and help you set up some popular Java IDEs. Throughout this book, we'll be working with **IntelliJ**. Alternatives that are also great would be **VS Code** and **Eclipse**.

### *Factors to consider when choosing an IDE*

Most modern IDEs have features such as code completion, debugging, version control integration, and support for third-party tools and frameworks. Some of them have better versions of these than others. Compare and contrast what you prefer when choosing or switching IDEs.

Some IDEs require a heavier system to run on than others. For example, VS Code is rather lightweight and IntelliJ is rather heavy. Also, VS Code can be used for many languages, including Java. It is uncommon to do a lot of other things with IntelliJ rather than Java. Choose an IDE that provides a balance between features and performance, especially if you have limited system resources.

And of course, it's possible that the IDE you'd prefer is not available for the platform you're using. Make sure that it's available and stable for your system.

Lastly, and very importantly, think about the costs. Some IDEs are free and others require a paid license. Luckily, many of the ones that require a paid license have a free edition for non-commercial use. So, make sure to also consider your budget and the licensing you need when choosing an IDE.

In the following subsections, we'll walk you through the steps of setting up the three (currently) most common IDEs for Java development:

- IntelliJ
- Eclipse
- Visual Studio Code

> **Note**
> We'll be working with IntelliJ for the rest of this book.

## Setting up IntelliJ

So, let's start with that one. IntelliJ IDEA is a popular Java IDE that was developed by **JetBrains**. It offers both a free **Community Edition** and a paid **Ultimate Edition**. It provides a wide range of features, including intelligent code completion, debugging tools, version control integration, and support for various Java frameworks.

Here are the steps for installing IntelliJ:

1.  Visit the IntelliJ IDEA download page at `https://www.jetbrains.com/idea/download/`.
2.  Choose the edition you prefer: the free **Community Edition** or the paid **Ultimate Edition**. For beginners, the Community Edition is truly great already.
3.  Download the installer for your operating system (Windows, macOS, or Linux).
4.  Run the installer and follow the instructions to complete the installation.
5.  Launch **IntelliJ IDEA**. If you're using the Ultimate Edition, you may need to enter your JetBrains account credentials or a license key.
6.  On the **Welcome** screen, you can create a new **project**, import an existing **project**, or explore the available tutorials and documentation.

## Setting up Eclipse

Eclipse is a free, open source Java IDE that is widely used in the Java community. It has been around for a really long time already and quite a lot of companies work with it still. It offers a variety of features, just like IntelliJ. Eclipse can be customized to suit your needs, but its interface may be less intuitive than other IDEs.

To set up Eclipse, follow these steps:

1.  Visit the Eclipse download page at `https://www.eclipse.org/downloads/`.

2.  Download the Eclipse installer for your operating system (Windows, macOS, or Linux).

3.  Run the installer and select **Eclipse IDE for Java Developers** from the list of available packages.

4.  Choose an installation folder and follow the instructions to complete the installation.

5.  Launch **Eclipse** and select a workspace directory. This is where your projects and settings will be stored.

6.  On the **Welcome** screen, you can create a new Java **project**, import an existing **project**, or explore the available tutorials and documentation.

### Setting up Visual Studio Code

Visual Studio Code, often referred to as VS Code, is a lightweight, free, and open source code editor developed by Microsoft. It's incredibly popular for all sorts of tasks because it supports a wide range of programming languages. It is a popular choice for developers who prefer a more minimalist and fast-performing environment. All sorts of additions can be added with the use of extensions.

Here are the steps for installing VS Code and preparing it for Java development:

1.  Visit the Visual Studio Code download page at **https://code.visualstudio.com/download**.

2.  Download the installer for your operating system (Windows, macOS, or Linux).

3.  Run the installer and follow the on-screen instructions to complete the installation.

4.  Launch Visual Studio Code.

5.  Open the **Extensions** view by clicking on the *Extensions* icon (four squares) on the left side of the window.

6.  Search for **Java Extension Pack** in the *Extensions Marketplace* and click the **Install** button. This extension pack includes various extensions for Java development, such as **Language Support for Java (TM) by Red Hat**, **Debugger for Java**, and **Maven for Java**.

7.  With the **Java Extension Pack** installed, you can now create or import Java projects. If it doesn't load directly, you may need to reopen VS Code.

Now that you've set up an IDE, let's create and run a program with it.

# Creating and running a program with an IDE

Working with an IDE such as IntelliJ as compared to working with a plain text editor is a breeze. We're now going to guide you through creating, running, and debugging a program with the use of IntelliJ. We'll create the same program as we did when we were using the text editor.

## Creating a program in an IDE

When you use an IDE to type code, you'll see that it helps you to complete your code constantly. This is considered very helpful by most people, and we hope you'll enjoy this feature too.

In order to get started with IntelliJ, we first need to create a project. Here are the steps for creating our `Hello World` program again:

1.  Launch IntelliJ IDEA and click on **New Project** from the **Welcome** screen or go to **File | New | Project**.

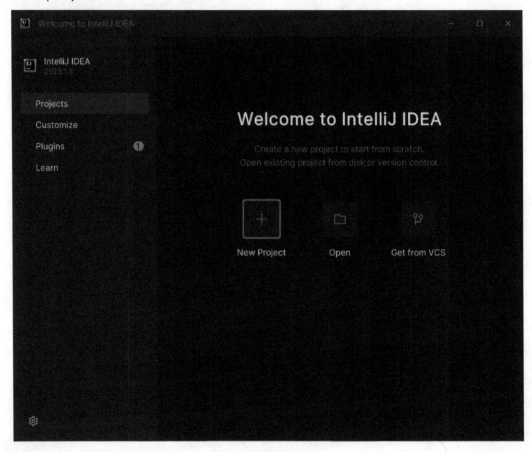

Figure 1.7 – Initial screen of IntelliJ

2.  Name the project `HelloWorld`.
3.  Select **Java** for the language and make sure that the correct project SDK is selected. Click **Next**.
4.  Don't tick the **Create Git repository** box and don't tick the **Add sample code** box.

5.  Click **Create** to create the project.

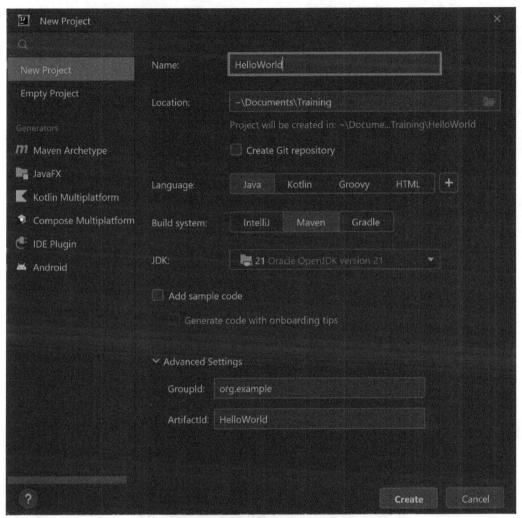

Figure 1.8 – Wizard to create a new project

6.  Once the project is created, expand the `src` folder in the **Project** view on the left. If there is no other folder underneath it, right-click on the `src` folder and select **New | Java Class**. If there is another folder underneath it, there is probably a main folder with a Java folder in there. Right-click on the Java folder and select **New | Java Class**. If it's called something differently, just right-click on the blue folder.

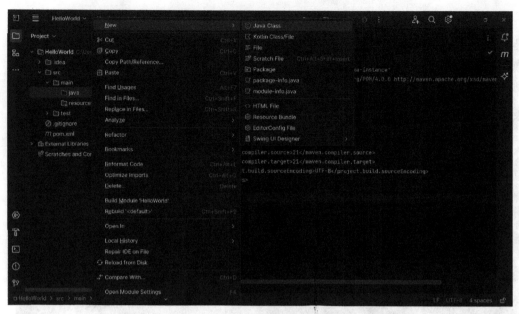

Figure 1.9 – Create a new Java Class

7.    Name the new class `HelloWorld` and click **OK**. IntelliJ will create a new `.java` file with the class definition.

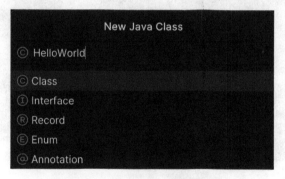

Figure 1.10 – Call the class "HelloWorld"

8. In the `HelloWorld` class, write our `main` method:

```java
public class HelloWorld {
    public static void main(String[] args) {
        System.out.println("Hello world!");
    }
}
```

```
HelloWorld.java  ×

 1  ▶    public class HelloWorld {
 2
 3  ▶        public static void main(String[] args) {
 4
 5            System.out.println("Hello world!");
 6
 7        }
 8
 9    }
```

Figure 1.11 – Code in HelloWorld.java

Now that we've written our first program, make sure that it is saved. By default, IntelliJ automatically saves our files. Let's see whether we can run the program as well.

## Running your program

Admittedly, we had to take a few extra steps to create our program. We had to create a project first. The good news is, running the program is easier! Here's how to do it:

1. If you haven't done so, make sure your changes are saved by pressing *Ctrl + S* (Windows/Linux) or *Cmd + S* (macOS). By default, auto-save is enabled.

2. To run the program, right-click anywhere in the `HelloWorld` class and select Run `'HelloWorld.main()'`. Alternatively, you can click the green triangle icon next to the main method and select Run `'HelloWorld.main()'`. IntelliJ will compile and run the program.

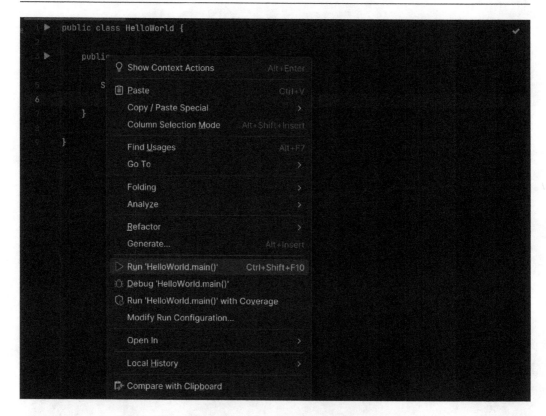

Figure 1.12 – Running the program

3.  Verify that the output of the program, `"Hello world!"`, is displayed in the **Run tool** window at the bottom of the screen.

```
"C:\Program Files\Java\jdk-21\bin\java.exe" "-
Hello world!

Process finished with exit code 0
```

Figure 1.13 – Output of the program

**Saved and unsaved files**

In most IDEs, you can tell whether a file is saved or not by looking at the tab of the open file. It has a dot or an asterisk next to it if it isn't saved. The dot is missing if it has been saved.

## Debugging a program

Our program is quite easy right now, but we may want to step through our program line by line. We can do that by debugging the program. Let's give our file a little extra content for debugging. This way we can see how to inspect variables, understand the execution flow, and, this way, find the flaws in our code:

1.  Update the `HelloWorld.java` file with the following code:

    ```java
    public class HelloWorld {
        public static void main(String[] args) {
            String greeting = "Hello, World!";
            System.out.println(greeting);

            int number = 5;
            int doubled = doubleNumber(number);
            System.out.println("The doubled number is: " +
                doubled);
        }

        public static int doubleNumber(int input) {
            return input * 2;
        }
    }
    ```

2.  In this updated version of the program, we added a new method called `doubleNumber`, which takes an integer as input and returns its double. In the `main` method, we call this method and print the result. Don't worry if you don't fully get this – we just want to show you how you can step through your code.

3.  Save your changes by pressing *Ctrl* + *S* (Windows/Linux) or *Cmd* + *S* (macOS).

    Now, let's debug the updated program.

4.  Set a breakpoint on the line you want to pause the execution at by clicking in the gutter area next to the line number in the editor. A red dot will appear, indicating a breakpoint. For example, set a breakpoint at the line `int doubled = doubleNumber(number);`. An example is shown in *Figure 1.7*.

```
1  ▶  public class HelloWorld {
       no usages
2  ▶      public static void main(String[] args) {
3              String greeting = "Hello, World!";
4              System.out.println(greeting);
5
6              int number = 5;
7  ●          int doubled = doubleNumber(number);
8              System.out.println("The doubled number is: " + doubled);
9          }
10
       1 usage
11         public static int doubleNumber(int input) {
12             return input * 2;
13         }
14     }
15
```

Figure 1.14 – Adding a breakpoint on line 7

5.  Start the debugger by right-clicking in the HelloWorld class and selecting Debug 'HelloWorld.main()' or you can click the green play icon next to the main method and select the **debug** option. IntelliJ will compile and start the program in debug mode.

6.  When the line with the breakpoint is going to be executed, the program will pause. During the pause, you can use the **Debug** tool window, which will appear at the bottom of the screen. Here, you can view the state of the program, including the values of local variables and fields. An example is shown in *Figure 1.8*.

Figure 1.15 – Debug tool window in IntelliJ. The intent of this screenshot
is to show the layout and text readability is not required.

7.  Use the step controls in the **Debug** tool window to step through the code (blue arrow with the angle in *Figure 1.8*), step into the method that is being called (blue arrow down), or continue the execution (green arrow on the left in *Figure 1.8*).

By following these steps, you can debug Java programs using IntelliJ IDEA and step through the code to see what is happening. This is something that will come in handy to understand what is going on in your code. This process will be similar in other Java IDEs, although the specific steps and interface elements may vary.

## Exercises

And that's all theory for this chapter! So, roll up those sleeves, and let's dive into your first day at Mesozoic Eden. Welcome aboard! Mesozoic Eden is a famous zoo where dinosaurs live that have been brought to live with high end genetic manipulation techniques. Here are some exercises for you to test your knowledge so far:

1.  Your first task involves welcoming our guests. Modify the following code snippet so that it outputs "Welcome to Mesozoic Eden":

    ```
    public class Main {
        public static void main(String[] args) {
            System.out.println("Hello world");
        }
    }
    ```

2.  Complete the following programs by filling out the blanks so that it prints out your name and the position you want to have in Mesozoic Eden 5 years from now:

    ```
    public class Main {
        public static void main(String[] args) {
            _____;
            String position = "Park Manager";
            System.out.println("My name is " + name + "
                and I want to be a " _____ " in Mesozoic
                Eden.");
        }
    }
    ```

3.  We've received some questions about opening hours. Complete the following program so that it prints the park's opening and closing hours:

    ```
    public class Main {
        public static void main(String[] args) {
            String openingHours = "08:00";
            String closingHours = "20:00";
        }
    }
    ```

4.  Create a Java project with a package named `dinosaur`. You can create a package by right-clicking on the `src/main/java` folder, selecting "new" and choosing "package".

5.  Modify the code from exercise 1 so that it prints out `"Welcome, [YourName] to Mesozoic Eden!"`, where `[YourName]` is replaced by, surprise surprise, your name. Bonus: try to create a separate String variable as shown in the second and third exercises.

6.  Some guests reported feeling unsafe near the T-Rex. Let's solve this by adding another `System.out.println` to the program of exercise 5. It should print the phrase `"Mesozoic Eden is safe and secure."` after the welcome message.

## Project

Create a program that simulates a sign at the entrance of Mesozoic Eden. The sign is simulated by printing output to the console. The sign should display a welcome message, the opening and closing hours, and a short safety message.

## Summary

You've made it through the first chapter! And we've done a lot already. We kicked off by exploring Java's key features, such as its OOP approach, the (once unique) WORA principle, its compiled nature, and the super-helpful automatic memory management. These features make Java an incredibly versatile and powerful language – a great choice for different programming tasks, such as web development, desktop apps, mobile apps, and so much more!

Next, we walked you through the process of installing Java on various platforms: Windows, macOS, and Linux. We also discussed how to check whether Java is already installed on your system. After this part, you can be sure that you have all the essential tools to kick off your Java programming adventure.

After you had Java all setup, we demystified the compilation process and introduced you to the JVM, a vital component of the Java ecosystem that enables the portability of Java code. We then demonstrated how to compile and run Java code using the `javac` and `java` command-line tools. These tools lay the groundwork for working with Java programs at their core.

Of course, using the command line for this is great. But nowadays, we more often work with an IDE, and we can just press a button to do all this. So, we mentioned several advantages and nice features of working with an IDE, such as code completion, debugging, and project management. We discussed the factors to weigh up when choosing an IDE and provided guidance on setting up popular IDEs such as IntelliJ IDEA, Eclipse, and VS Code. In this book, we'll be using IntelliJ throughout for the examples.

After covering the essentials of IDEs, we delved into creating and running a Java program using an IDE. We explained the structure of a typical Java program and guided you, step by step, through the process of creating, running, and debugging your very first Java program.

After this, you were ready for the first hands-on project. And now you're here! All set and ready to take the next step on your Java journey. This next step will be working with variables and primitive data types. Good luck!

# 2

# Variables and Primitive Data Types

In *Chapter 1*, we introduced the compiler and the JVM. We learned how to use both of them from the command line when we wrote our first Java program, *Hello World*. We also introduced **IntelliJ**, a powerful and friendly IDE, and we ran *Hello World* from there as well.

All programming languages require variables and provide in-built primitive data types. They are essential for the operation of even the simplest programs. By the end of this chapter, you will be able to declare variables using Java's primitive types. In addition, you will understand the differences between the various primitive data types and which ones to use in a given situation.

In this chapter, we are going to cover the following main topics:

- Understanding and declaring variables
- Exploring Java's primitive data types

## Technical requirements

The code for this chapter can be found on GitHub at `https://github.com/PacktPublishing/Learn-Java-with-Projects/tree/main/ch2`.

## Understanding and declaring variables

If you want to store a value for later use, you need a variable. Therefore, every programming language provides this feature via variables. In this section, we will learn what a variable is and how to declare one. The area in your code where you can use a particular variable is known as the variable's *scope*. This is a very important concept and will be covered in detail in *Chapter 4*.

## What is a variable?

Variables are locations in memory that have a *name* (called an identifier) and a *type*. They resemble named pigeonholes or post office boxes (see *Figure 2.1*). The variable's name is required so that we can refer to the variable and distinguish it from other variables.

A variable's *type* specifies the sort of values it can store/hold. For example, is the variable to be used for storing whole numbers such as 4 or decimal numbers such as 2.98? The answer to that question determines the variable's *type*.

## Declaring a variable

Let's suppose we want to store the number 25 in a variable. We will assume that this number represents a person's age, so we will use the `age` identifier to refer to it. Introducing a variable for the first time is known as "declaring" the variable.

A whole number (positive or negative) is an integer and Java provides an in-built primitive type especially for integers called `int`. We will discuss primitive data types in more detail in the next section. When declaring a variable in Java, we must specify the variables type. This is because Java is known as a *strongly typed* language, which means you must specify the variable's type immediately upon declaring it.

Let's declare a variable, give it a type, and initialize it:

```
int age;
age = 25;
```

The first line declares `age` as an `int` and the second line assigns it a value of 25.

Note that the semi-colons ( ; ) at the end of the lines are delimiters that tell the compiler where a Java statement ends. The = sign is the assignment operator and will be covered in *Chapter 3*. For now, just realize that 25 is "assigned into" the `age` variable.

---

**Assignment operator**

The = sign in Java is not the same as the equals sign, =, in mathematics. Java uses the == sign for equals, which is called equivalence.

---

We can write the previous two lines of code in one line:

```
int age = 25;
```

*Figure 2.1* shows the in-memory representation of both code segments:

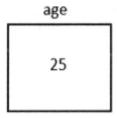

age

25

Figure 2.1 – An integer variable named age with a value of 25

As can be seen in *Figure 2.1*, **age** is the name of the variable and **25** is the integer value stored in the variable's *location*.

## Naming a variable

An identifier is simply a name that you give to the Java construct you are coding; for example, identifiers (names) are required for naming variables, methods, classes, and so forth.

> **Identifiers**
>
> An identifier consists of letters, digits, underscores, and currency symbols. Identifiers cannot begin with a number and cannot contain whitespace (spaces, tabs, and newlines). In the following examples, the commas separate the various identifiers.
>
> Examples of unusual but *valid* identifiers are a£€_23, _29, Z, thisIsAnExampleOfAVeryLongVariableName, €2_, and $4 ;.
>
> Examples of *invalid* identifiers are 9age and abc def;.

Name your variables carefully. This helps make code more readable, which results in fewer bugs and easier maintenance. *Camel case* is a very popular technique in this regard. Concerning variable names, camel case means that *all* of the first word is lowercase. In addition, the first letter in each subsequent word in the variable name starts with an uppercase letter. Here's an example:

```
int ageOfCar;
int numberOfChildren;
```

In this code segment, we have two integer variables whose names/identifiers follow camel casing.

## Accessing a variable

To access a variable's value, just type in the variable's name. When we type in a variable's name in Java, the compiler will first ensure that a variable with that name exists. Assuming there is, the JVM will, at runtime, return the *value inside* that variable's pigeonhole. Therefore, the following code will output 25 to the screen:

```
int age = 25;
System.out.println(age);
```

The first line declares the age variable and initializes it to 25. The second line accesses the variable's location and outputs its value.

> **System.out.println()**
>
> System.out.println() displays whatever is inside the round brackets, (), on the screen.

## Accessing a variable that you have not declared

As stated previously, Java is known as a *strongly typed* language. This means that you have to specify the variable's type immediately upon declaring it. If the compiler comes across a variable and does not know its type, it generates an error. For example, consider the following line of code:

```
age = 25;
```

Assuming no other code declares age, the compiler generates an error stating cannot resolve symbol 'age'. This is because the compiler is looking for the *type* to associate with *age* and it cannot find it (as we did not specify the type).

Here is a slightly different example. In this example, we are attempting to output the age variable to the screen:

```
int length = 25;
System.out.println(age);
```

In this example, we have declared a variable named length and thus, there is no declaration of age. When we attempt to access the age variable in System.out.println(), the compiler goes looking for age. The compiler cannot find age and generates an error stating cannot resolve symbol 'age'. In effect, what the compiler is saying is that we have attempted to use a variable named age that the compiler cannot find. This is because we did not even declare the variable, not to mention specify its type.

> **Comments**
>
> Comments are very useful as they help us explain what is happening in the code.
>
> // is a single-line comment. When the compiler sees //, it ignores the rest of the line.
>
> ./* some text */ is a multi-line comment. Anything between the opening /* and the closing */ is ignored. This format saves inserting // at the start of each line.
>
> Here are some examples:
>
> ```
> int age; // from here to the rest of the line is ignored
> // this whole line is ignored
> /*     all
> of
> these lines
> are
> ignored    */
> ```

Given that Java, as a strongly typed language, requires all variables to have a data type, we will now discuss Java's support for primitive data types.

# Understanding Java's primitive data types

Java provides eight in-built data types. In-built means that these data types come with the language. These primitive data types are the topic of this section.

## Java's primitive data types

All of the primitive data types are named using lowercase letters only; for example, int and double. When we create our own data types later on, namely classes, records, and interfaces, we will follow a different naming convention. For example, we may have a class named Person or Cat. This is simply a widely adopted coding convention and the compiler does not distinguish between naming conventions. However, it is very easy to recognize any of the primitive data types as they are always in lowercase letters only. Before we discuss the primitive data types themselves, there are a few important points to make.

### Numeric primitive data types are signed

In Java, all numeric primitive data types are represented as a series of bits. In addition, they are also signed. The most significant bit (leftmost bit) is used for the sign; 1 means negative and 0 means positive.

**Integer literals**

A literal value is one that's typed in at the keyboard (as opposed to a computed value). An integer literal can be expressed in various numbering systems: decimal (base 10), hexadecimal (base 16), octal (base 8), and binary (base 2). However, it is no surprise that decimal is by far the most commonly used representation. For information purposes, all of the following declarations represent the decimal number 10:

```
int a = 10;      // decimal, the default
int b = 0b1010; // binary, prefixed by 0b or 0B
int c = 012;     // octal, prefixed by 0
int d = 0xa;     // hexadecimal, prefixed by 0x or 0X
```

## The sign bit affects the range

The presence of the sign bit means that byte has a range of $-2^7$ to $2^7-1$ (-128 to +127 inclusive). The -1 in the positive range is to allow for the fact that, in Java, 0 is considered a positive number. There is *not* one less positive number in any of the ranges. For example, with byte, you have 128 negative numbers (-1 to -128) and 128 positive numbers (0 to +127), resulting in 256 representations ($2^8$). To reinforce this point with a simple example, -1 to -8 is 8 numbers and 0 to 7 (inclusive) is 8 numbers also.

With these points discussed, let's look at the various primitive types. *Table 2.1* lists the eight primitive data types, their byte sizes, and their ranges (all of which are inclusive):

| primitive type | number of bytes | range |
|:---:|:---:|:---:|
| **byte** | 1 | -128..+127 ($-2^7$ to $2^7-1$) |
| **short** | 2 | -32,768..+32,767 ($-2^{15}$ to $2^{15}-1$) |
| **int** | 4 | $-2^{31}$ to $2^{31}-1$ |
| **long** | 8 | $-2^{63}$ to $2^{63}-1$ |
| **float** | 4 | 3.4e-38 to 3.4e+38 |
| **double** | 8 | 1.7e-308 to 1.7e+308 |
| **boolean** | 1 | **true** or **false** |
| **char** | 2 (unsigned) | 0..65,535 ($0..2^{16}-1$) |

Table 2.1 – Java's primitive types

Here are some interesting points from the preceding table:

- `byte`, `short`, `char`, `int`, and `long` are known as *integral* types as they have integer values (whole numbers, positive or negative). For example, -8, 17, and 625 are all integer numbers.

- `char` is used for characters – for example 'a', 'b', '?' and '+'. Note that single quotes surround the character. In code, `char c = 'a';` means that the variable c represents the letter a. As computers ultimately store all characters (on the keyboard) as numbers internally (binary), we need an encoding system to map the characters to numbers and vice versa. Java uses the Unicode encoding standard, which ensures a unique number for every character, regardless of platform, language, script, and so on. This is why `char` uses 2 bytes as opposed to 1. In fact, from the computer's perspective, `char c = 'a';` is the same as `char c = 97;` where 97 is the decimal value for 'a' in Unicode. Obviously, we as humans prefer the letter representation.

- `short` and `char` both require 2 bytes but have different ranges. Note that `short` can represent negative numbers, whereas `char` cannot. In contrast, `char` can store numbers such as 65,000, whereas `short` cannot.

- `float` and `double` are for floating-point numbers – in other words, numbers that have decimal places, such as 23.78 and -98.453. These floating-point numbers can use scientific notation – for example, 130000.0 can be expressed as `double d1=1.3e+5;`, and 0.13 can be expressed as `double d2=1.3e-1;`.

### Representation of the various types

Expanding from the previous callout, we can express integer literals using the following numbering systems:

- `Decimal`: Base 10; numbers 0..9. This is the default.

- `Hexadecimal`: Base 16; numbers 0..9 and letters a..f (or A..F). Prefix the literal with *0x* or *0X* to indicate that this is a hexadecimal literal.

- `binary`: Base 2; numbers 0..1. Prefix the literal with *0b* or *0B* to indicate that this is a binary literal.

Here are some sample code fragments that initialize `int` variables to 30 using the various numbering systems. Firstly, decimal is used; then hexadecimal, and finally, binary:

```
// decimal
int dec = 30;

// hexadecimal = 16 + 14
int hex = 0x1E;

// binary = 16 + 8 + 4 + 2
int bin = 0b11110;
```

Although there are several ways to initialize an `int`, using decimal is by far the most common.

A literal number, such as 22, is considered an `int` by default. If you want to have 22 treated as `long` (instead of `int`), you must suffix either an uppercase or lowercase *L* to the literal. Here's an example:

```
int x  = 10;
long n = 10L;
```

As per *Table 2.1*, using a `long` as opposed to an `int`, gives you access to much bigger and much smaller numbers. Use of uppercase L as opposed to lowercase l to signify `long` is preferred, as the lowercase l is similar to the number 1 (one).

Floating-point numbers behave similarly. A decimal number is, by default, `double`. To have any decimal number treated as `float` (as opposed to `double`), you must suffix the literal with either an uppercase or lowercase F. Assuming range is not an issue then one reason for using `float` as opposed to `double` is memory conservation (as `float` requires 4 bytes whereas `double` requires 8 bytes). Here's an example:

```
double d = 10.34;
float f  = 10.34F;
```

Variables of the `char` type are initialized with single quotes around the literal. Here's an example:

```
char c = 'a';
```

Variables of the `boolean` type can store only `true` or `false`. These `boolean` literals are in lowercase only as they are reserved words in Java, and Java is case-sensitive:

```
boolean b1 = true;
boolean b2 = false;
```

That concludes this section on Java's primitive type system, where we examined the various types, their sizes/ranges, and some code segments.

Now, let's put the theory of variables and primitive types into practice! But before that, here's a bit of a cheat code to help you with the exercises.

## Screen output

As we know, `System.out.println()` outputs what is inside the `()`. To do the exercises, we want to expand on that. Firstly, here's some code:

```
String name = "James";     // line 1
int age = 23; // line 2
double salary = 50_000.0; // line 3
String out = "Details: "  +  name  +  ", "  +  age  +  ",
```

```
"  +  salary;//line 4
System.out.println(out);   // line 5
```

Line 1 declares a string literal `"James"` and initializes the name variable with it. A string literal is a sequence of characters (including numbers), enclosed in double quotes. We will discuss the `String` class in detail in *Chapter 12*.

Lines 2 and 3 should be fine. We are declaring an `int` type called `age` and a `double` type called `salary` and using literal values to initialize them. The underscore used in line 3, enables us to make large numbers easier to read.

Line 4 builds the string to be output, namely `out`. We want to output the variables values, along with some helpful text to explain the output. Java builds the string from left to right.

Here, + is not the regular mathematical addition. We will discuss this in detail in *Chapter 3*, but for the moment, realize that when you have a string variable or literal on the left or the right of +, the operation becomes a `String` append (as opposed to mathematical addition).

One property this append shares with addition is that both sides of + must be of the same type. Since not all the variables in this example are string variables (or literals), Java has some work to do in the background (to get them all to the same type). Java copies the numeric variable values into new string locations to use them in building the string. For example, there is a location somewhere in memory that's been created for a string literal, "23" (in addition to the `int` location for `age`). This also happens for the `double` type's `salary` variable. Now, Java is ready to construct the string and assign it to `out` (line 4).

In the background, Java performs the following:

```
"Details: " + "James" => "Details: James"
"Details: James" + ", " => "Details: James, "
"Details: James, " + "23" => "Details: James, 23"
"Details: James, 23" + ", " => "Details: James, 23,
"Details: James, 23, " + "50000.0" => "Details: James, 23,
  50000.0"
```

So, `"Details: James, 23, 50000.0"` is used to initialize `out`, which is what is displayed on the screen when executing line 5.

## Exercises

All is going great in our lovely dinosaur park. However, we do need to do some administrative tasks:

1.  We need to keep track of the dinosaurs in the park. Declare variables to represent the breed, height, length, and weight of one dinosaur in the main method. Give the variables a value and print them.

2.   Now, we want to do something similar to the program of exercise 1 and print the dinosaur's age, name, and whether it's a carnivore or not. This needs to happen in the main method. Give the variables a value and print them.

3.   Our park is doing great! But it gets a bit too busy at times. The fire department advised us to introduce a maximum number of visitors that are allowed at any given time. Declare a variable to represent the maximum number of visitors allowed in the park per day. You can choose a reasonable value for the variable. Then, print it in the sentence: "There's a maximum of [x] people allowed in Mesozoic Eden."

4.   Our team is an integral part of Mesozoic Eden. Let's create a profile for an employee. Declare variables to represent the name and age of a Mesozoic Eden employee. Assign values and print them.

5.   We would like to know how many dinosaurs we have at any time. Declare a variable to represent the number of dinosaurs in the park. Assign it a value and print it.

6.   Safety is our priority. We maintain a safety rating scale to ensure our standards. Declare a variable to represent the park's safety rating on a scale from 1 to 10. Assign a value to it and print it.

7.   Now, let's bring together some dinosaur information in one statement. Create a program that uses string concatenation to print out a dinosaur's name, age, and diet (a string with a value of `carnivore` or `herbivore`).

8.   Each dinosaur species has a unique name. For a quick referencing system, we use the first letter of a dinosaur species. Declare a character variable that represents the first letter of a dinosaur species, assign a value, and print it.

# Project – dinosaur profile generator

As part of your responsibilities in Mesozoic Eden, you are tasked with creating an extensive database of all the dinosaurs living in the park. For now, you only need to complete the first step: a profile generator. These profiles will not only help in keeping track of our prehistoric residents but also provide essential data for scientific study, healthcare, diet management, and visitor engagement.

In this project, we will focus on developing a program that can model an individual dinosaur's profile.

The profile should include the following characteristics:

- Name
- Age
- Species
- Diet (carnivore or herbivore)
- Weight

Each characteristic should be stored as a variable within the program. Here's your chance to get creative and think about the kind of dinosaur you want to describe. Is it a towering T-Rex or a friendly Stegosaurus? Maybe it's a swift, scary Velociraptor or a mighty Triceratops?

Once you have declared and assigned values to these variables, the program should print out a complete profile of the dinosaur. The output can be something like `"Meet [Name], a [Age]-year-old [Species]. As a [Diet], it has a robust weight of [Weight] kilograms."`.

## Summary

In this chapter, we learned that a variable is simply a memory location with a name and a value. To utilize variables, we have to know how to declare and access them.

To declare a variable, we specify the variable's name and its type – for example, `int countOfTitles=5;`. This line of code declares an `int` variable named `countOfTitles` with a value of 5. Naming them properly using camel case, is a great aid in making your code more readable and maintainable. To access the variable, we just specify the variable's name – for example, `System.out.println(countOfTitles);`.

As Java is a strongly typed language, we have to specify a variables' type when we declare it. Java provides eight in-built primitive data types for our use. They are easily recognizable due to their lowercase letters. In the preceding line of code, `int` is the primitive data type for the `countOfTitles` variable. We saw the sizes in bytes of the primitive types, which determines their range of values. All numeric types are signed, with the most significant bit being used for the sign. The `char` type is unsigned and is 2 bytes in size so that Java can support any character in any language anywhere in the world. Using code snippets, we saw variables of the different types in use.

Now that we know how to declare and use variables, let's move on to operators that enable us to combine variables.

# 3

# Operators and Casting

In *Chapter 2*, we learned that variables are simply named pigeonholes and contain values. These values vary and Java provides eight primitive data types accordingly. These primitive types cater for whole numbers (`byte`, `char`, `short`, `int`, and `long`), decimal numbers (`float` and `double`), and the literals true and false (`boolean`).

We also learned how to declare a variable. As Java is a strongly typed language, this means you must give every variable a data type immediately upon declaration. This is where primitive data types are very useful.

Now that we know how to declare variables, let's do something interesting with them. By the end of this chapter, you will be able to combine variables using Java's various operators. In addition, you will understand Java casting, including what it is, and when and why it occurs.

In this chapter, we are going to cover the following main topics:

- Learning how Java's operators cooperate

- Understanding Java's operators

- Explaining Java casting

## Technical requirements

The code for this chapter can be found on GitHub at `https://github.com/PacktPublishing/Learn-Java-with-Projects/tree/main/ch3`.

## Learning how Java's operators cooperate

Java provides numerous operators for us to work with. By way of definition, if we have an expression 3 + 4, the + is the *operator*, whereas 3 and 4 are the *operands*. Since + has *two* operands, it is known as a *binary* operator.

Before we discuss the operators themselves, we must first discuss two important features relating to Java operators, namely **order of precedence** and **associativity**.

## Order of precedence

Order of precedence specifies how operands are grouped with operators. This becomes important when you have shared operands in a complex expression. In the following code segment, we have an expression of 2 + 3 * 4, where * represents multiplication and + represents addition:

```
int a = 2 + 3 * 4;
System.out.println(a);
```

In the preceding code, 3 is shared by both 2 and 4. So, the question arises, do we group 3 with 2, where the expression is (2 + 3) * 4, giving us 20; or do we group 3 with 4, where the expression is 2 + (3 * 4), giving us 14? This is where the order of precedence applies. As * has higher precedence than +, 3 is grouped with 4 and therefore the expression evaluates to 2 + (3 * 4). Note that the evaluation order is still left to right; it is just that 3 is grouped with 4 rather than with 2.

> **Parentheses in an expression**
>
> Note that parentheses can change the default order of operator precedence. As we have seen, the default order of precedence, where * has higher precedence than +, means that 2 + 3 * 4 is 14. This is the same as 2 + (3 * 4).
>
> However, (2 + 3) * 4 is 20. In this case, the parentheses grouped 3 with 2, so the expression evaluated to 5 * 4 = 20.

This begs the question, what if you are evaluating an expression that contains operators at the same level of precedence? This is where associativity applies.

## Associativity

When an expression has two operators with the same level of precedence, operator associativity determines the groupings of operators and operands. For example, in the following code segment, we are evaluating a simple expression involving two divisions (which have the same level of precedence):

```
int x =  72 / 6 / 3;
```

As division associates left to right, 6 will be grouped with 72 and not 3. Thus, the expression is the same as (72 / 6) / 3, which evaluates to 12 / 3 = 4. Parentheses can also be used to change the default associativity order. Take, for example, the following code:

```
int x =  72 / (6 / 3);
```

In this case, 6 is now grouped with 3 and the expression evaluates to 72 / 2 = 36.

*Table 3.1* outlines the order of precedence and associativity rules:

| Operator Description | Operator | Associativity |
|---|---|---|
| Parentheses | () | left-to-right |
| Post-increment, post-decrement | x++, y-- | left-to-right |
| Pre-increment, pre-decrement, negation | ++x, --y, !b | right-to-left |
| Cast | (int) | right-to-left |
| Multiplication/Division/Modulus | *, /, % | left-to-right |
| Addition/Subtraction | +, - | left-to-right |
| Relational Operators | <, >, <=, >=, instanceof | left-to-right |
| Equality | ==, != | left-to-right |
| Bitwise Operators | & | left-to-right |
|  | ^ | |
|  | \| | |
| Logical Operators | && | left-to-right |
|  | \|\| | |
| Ternary Operator | ? : | right-to-left |
| Assignment Operators | =, +=, -=, *=, /= | right-to-left |

Table 3.1 – Order of precedence and associativity rules

Note that *Table 3.1* is simplified in that it refers to the operators that are commonly used. For example, the unsigned right shift operator, >>>, is omitted as it is rarely used. Also, note that the `instanceof` operator will be discussed in *Chapter 8*.

It is interesting to note that the assignment operator, namely =, is at the bottom of the precedence table. This means that regardless of the expression on the right-hand side of the assignment, the assignment will always be done last. This makes sense. Also, while most of the operators associate left to right, the assignment associates right to left. This is demonstrated in the following code segment:

```
boolean b1 = false;
boolean b2;
boolean b3;
b3 = b2 = b1;
System.out.println(b1);
System.out.println(b2);
System.out.println(b3);
```

The preceding code segment outputs `false` three times. The crucial line is `b3 = b2 = b1;`. Since the assignment associates right to left, the value in `b1`, which is `false`, is assigned to `b2`; then, the value in `b2`, which is now `false`, is assigned to `b3`.

Now that we understand these properties, let's examine the operators themselves.

# Understanding Java's operators

Operators can be grouped into the following categories:

- Unary operators

- Arithmetic operators

- Relational operators

- Logical operators

- Ternary operator

- Compound assignment operators

We will now discuss each category in turn.

## Unary operators

Unary operators have only one operand, hence the term *unary*. Let's examine them.

### Prefix and postfix unary operators

++ and -- denote these operators and they increment and decrement by 1, respectively. If the operator appears before the variable, it is known as *prefix*, while if the operator appears after the variable, it is called *postfix*. For example, ++x is prefix increment, whereas y-- is postfix decrement.

Depending on whether ++ or -- appears before or after the variable can, in some situations, affect the overall expression. This is best explained with a code sample, as shown in *Figure 3.1*:

```
25          int x=3;
26          ++x;
27          System.out.println(x);   // 4
28          System.out.println(x++);// 4
29          System.out.println(x);   // 5
30
31          int y=4;
32          y--;
33          System.out.println(y);   // 3
34          System.out.println(--y);// 2
35          System.out.println(y);   // 2
```

Figure 3.1 – Prefix and postfix increment and decrement operators

In *Figure 3.1*, on line 25, we can see that x is initialized to 3. On line 26, x is incremented by 1 to 4. Line 26 is a simple statement and because of that, whether it is prefix or postfix notation does not matter. Line 27 outputs the value of x to show that it is 4 at this point.

Line 28 is where things get interesting. The postfix notation on line 28 has a real effect on the screen output. As it is the postfix notation in the System.out.println command, the current value of x is output, and *afterwards*, x is incremented by 1. So, the output to the screen is 4, and afterwards, x is incremented to 5. Line 29 demonstrates that x is 5.

On line 31, y is initialized to 4. On line 32, y is decremented by 1 to 3. Again, as line 32 is a simple statement, prefix or postfix notation makes no difference. Line 33 outputs the value of y to show that it is 3 at this point.

The prefix notation on line 34 has no real effect on the screen output. As it is the prefix notation in the System.out.println command, the current value of y is decremented **before** being output. Thus, the value of y and the output to the screen match (both are 2). Lastly, line 35 demonstrates that the current value of y is 2.

### *Unary plus/minus operators*

Now that we have discussed the prefix and postfix operators, let's discuss other unary operators. The code in *Figure 3.2* will help:

```
37          int x = +6;
38          int y = -x;
39          System.out.println(x);   // 6
40          System.out.println(y);   // -6
41
42          int z = (int)3.45;
43          System.out.println(z);   // 3
44
45          boolean b = true;
46          System.out.println(!b);  // false
47          System.out.println(b);   // true
```

Figure 3.2 – Other unary operators

In *Figure 3.2*, line 37 uses the unary plus sign, +, to initialize x to 6. Here, + is the default as numbers without a sign are assumed to be positive numbers. Line 38 uses the unary minus sign, -, to initialize y to be the negative of x. Lines 39 and 40 demonstrate that x and y are 6 and -6, respectively.

## Cast operator

In *Figure 3.2*, line 42 uses the cast operator. We will discuss casting in greater detail later in this chapter. For now, 3.45 is a `double` literal (8 bytes) and cannot be stored in an `int` variable, z, as `int` variables are 4 bytes in size. The compiler spots this and generates an error. To get around this error, we can use a cast, which takes the form of *(cast type)*. This cast enables us to override the compiler error. In this case, we are casting 3.45 to an `int` variable, which means we lose the decimal places. Thus, we store 3 in z, as shown by the output from line 43.

## Logical NOT operator

In *Figure 3.2*, on line 45, we declare a boolean, b, and initialize it to `true`. On line 46, we output the inverted value of b by using the logical NOT operator. Note that we are not changing the value of b meaning, the value of b is still `true`. This is shown by the output from line 47.

Now, let's examine the arithmetic operators.

# Arithmetic operators

There are five arithmetic operators, all of which we will examine now.

## Addition/subtraction operators

As in mathematics, the + operator represents addition and the - operator represents subtraction. Both are binary operators; in other words, there are two operands, one on either side of the operator. The following code example demonstrates this:

```
int res = 6 + 4 - 2;
System.out.println(res); // 8
```

In this code segment, res has been assigned a value of 6 + 4 - 2, which is 8.

## Multiplication/division operators

The * operator represents multiplication and the / operator represents division. Both are binary operators. Note that *integer division truncates*. The following code segment demonstrates this:

```
System.out.println(10/3); // 3
```

This code segment outputs 3 because integer division truncates. We are dividing one integer, 10, by another integer, 3. The remainder is simply discarded.

## Modulus operator

The % operator is used for calculating the modulus (remainder). The following code example demonstrates the modulus operator in action:

```
int mod1 = 10 % 3;
System.out.println(mod1); // 1
int mod2 = 0 % 3;
System.out.println(mod2); // 0
```

The first line initializes mod1 to be the remainder of 10 divided by 3, which is 1. In other words, 3 goes into 10 three times and 1 is left over. Therefore, 1 is assigned to mod1.

The initialization of mod2 is interesting: 3 goes into 0 zero times and there is 0 (or nothing) left over. Hence, 0 is assigned to mod2.

## The precedence of arithmetic operators

As per *Table 3.1*, *, /, and % have higher precedence than the + and − operators, and assignment has the lowest precedence. *Figure 3.3* shows how this affects the evaluation of expressions in code:

```
61    int res = 3 + 2 * 4;
62    System.out.println(res); // 11
63    res = (3 + 2) * 4;
64    System.out.println(res); // 20
65    res = 6 + 4 - 2;
66    System.out.println(res); // 8
67    res = 10 / 4 * 6 % 10;
68    System.out.println(res); // 2
```

Figure 3.3 – Arithmetic operators precedence

Lines 61 demonstrates that * has higher precedence than +, in that the expression evaluates to 3 + (2 * 4) = 3 + 8 = 11.

Line 63 demonstrates that parentheses change the grouping. Now, the shared value, 2, is grouped with 3 (as opposed to 4, which was the case on line 61). The expression now evaluates to 5 * 4 = 20.

Line 65 demonstrates that + and - associate left to right. The expression evaluates to

10 - 2 = 8.

Lines 67 demonstrates that *, /, and % also associate left to right. The expression evaluates to 2 * 6 % 10, which, in turn, evaluates to 12 % 10, which is 2.

> **Math operations involving int variables or smaller result in an int**
>
> It is interesting to note that any math operation involving an int type or smaller results in int. This is demonstrated in the following code segment:
>
> ```
> byte b1=2, b2=3;
> byte b3 = b1 + b2; // compiler error
> byte b4 = (byte)(b1 + b2);// Ok
> ```
>
> The first line declares 2 bytes, namely b1 and b2. Notice that, even though 2 and 3 are integer literals, the compiler is aware that these values are within the range of byte (-128 to +127) and, consequently, allows the declarations.
>
> However, the next line is a problem. The compiler has a rule that all math operations involving int types or smaller result in an int. Therefore, even though the sum of the two bytes, 5, is well within the byte range, the compiler complains saying "possible loss of data converting from int to byte".
>
> The last line fixes this issue by casting the result of the addition (an int type) to a byte before the assignment. What this means is that the extra 3 bytes from the int (that do not fit into the byte) are simply discarded. Thus, the sum of b1 + b2 is cast from int to byte and the resultant byte is assigned to b4. Casting is discussed in more detail later in the chapter.

We will finish our discussion on arithmetic operators by examining + in a different context.

## String append

As we have seen, Java uses + for mathematical addition. However, this occurs only if both operands are numbers. For example, 3 + 4 results in 7 because both operands, 3 and 4, are numbers.

However, if either operand (or both) are strings, Java performs a String append. A String literal is enclosed in double quotes – for example, "abc", "123", "Sean", and "Maaike" are all String literals. So, just to be clear on what operation is performed and when, let's take a look at some examples:

- 3 + 4 is mathematical addition. Thus, the result is 7.

- "3" + 4 is a string append as there is a string on the left of +. The result is the string "34."

- 3 + "4" is a string append as there is a string on the right of +. Again, the result is the string "34."

- "3" + "4" is a string append as there is a string on both sides of +. The result is also the string "34."

So, what exactly happens during a string append? *Java cannot perform any mathematical operations when the operands are of different types.* Let's examine this with an example piece of code:

```
String s = "3" + 4;
System.out.println(s); // "34"
```

The first thing to note is that the first line of code only compiles because "3" + 4 results in a String literal. When Java encounters a string on the left/right/both sides of +, it performs string concatenation (append). Essentially, as + associates left to right, Java appends (adds) the string on the right of + to the end of the string on the left of +.

In this example, Java sees the String literal "3" and the + operator and realizes it must perform a String append. To do this, in memory, it creates a string version of 4 – in other words, "4". The integer 4 literal is not touched. Thus, a new variable is created under the hood – it is a String variable, and "4" is its value. The expression is now "3" + "4". As both operands on either side of + are now of the same type (both are strings), Java can perform the append. The new string is the result of "3" + "4", which is "34". This is what is assigned to s. The second line demonstrates this by outputting "34" for s.

In *Figure 3.4*, a more substantial example is presented:

```
78      int a=3, b=2;
79      int res = a + b;
80      System.out.println(res); // 5
81      String s = "abc";
82      String s1 = a + s;   // "3abc"
83      String s2 = s + a;   // "abc3"
84      System.out.println(s1 + " " + s2); // "3abc abc3"
85
86      System.out.println("Output is "+ a + b); // "Output is 32"
87      System.out.println("Output is "+ (a + b)); // "Output is 5"
```

Figure 3.4 – String append in action

On line 79, as both operands, a and b, are integers, Java initializes res to 5 (the sum of 3 and 2).

Line 82 is evaluated as follows: 3 + "abc" = "3" + "abc" = "3abc". In other words, Java realizes that it must do a string append due to the presence of "abc" on the right-hand side of +. Thus, somewhere in memory, a string version of the value of a is created. In other words, a variable with "3" is created. Note that a *remains an int with 3 as its value*. Now, Java can proceed since both operands are the same type (strings): "3" + "abc" results in "3abc".

Line 83 demonstrates that it does not matter which side of + the string is on. Plus, it does not matter if the string is a string literal or a string variable. The expression on line 83 is evaluated as follows: "abc" + 3 = "abc" + "3" = "abc3". This is what s2 is initialized to. Line 84 outputs the values of both s1 and s2 with a space between them. Note that System.out.println expects a string. The string output on line 84 is constructed as follows: "3abc" + " " = "3abc " + "abc3" = "3abc abc3".

Lines 86 and 87 require special mention. The problem with line 86 is that the output string is constructed as follows: `"Output is "+ 3 = "Output is " + "3" = "Output is 3" + 2 = "Output is 3" + "2" = "Output is 32"`. This is not what we wanted.

Line 87 rectifies this by using parentheses to ensure that a + b is grouped. Thus, the string is constructed as follows: `"Output is "+ 5 = "Output is "+ "5" = "Output is 5"`.

That finishes the arithmetic operators. We will now examine relational operators.

## Relational operators

Java has six relational operators, all of which result in a `boolean` value of `true` or `false`. They are as follows:

- `==` is the equivalence operator
- `!=` is the not equivalent operator
- `>` is the greater than operator
- `>=` is the greater than or equal to operator
- `<` is the less than operator
- `<=` is the less than or equal to operator

*Figure 3.5* shows the relational operators in action in code:

```
89    int x=3, y=4;
90    System.out.println(x == y); // false
91    System.out.println(x != y); // true
92    System.out.println(x > y);  // false
93    System.out.println(x >= y); // false
94    System.out.println(x < y);  // true
95    System.out.println(x <= y); // true
```

Figure 3.5 – Relational operators in code

Line 89 declares two `int` variables, namely x and y, and initializes them to 3 and 4, respectively. Line 90 uses Java's equivalence operator, `==`, to check if x and y are equivalent. As they are not, line 90 outputs `false`. Line 91 checks the exact opposite. As x is not equivalent to y, line 91 outputs `true`.

Line 92 outputs whether x is greater than y. This is, of course, `false` as 3 is not greater than 4. Similarly, line 93 outputs whether x is greater than or equal to y. Again, this is `false`.

Line 94 outputs whether x is less than y. This is `true` as 3 is less than 4. Line 95 outputs whether x is less than or equal to y. Again, this is `true`.

The relational operators and their boolean return values are going to be extremely useful going forward, particularly when we look at conditional statements in *Chapter 4*.

---

**Implicit promotion**

While Java's operators do not require the operands to be exactly the same type, the operands must be compatible. Consider the following code snippet:

```
System.out.println(3 + 4.0);  // 7.0
System.out.println(4 == 4.0); // true
```

The first line tries to add an `int` variable of 3 to a `double` variable. Java realizes that the types are not the same. However, Java can figure out a safe solution without bothering us. This is where *implicit promotion* comes in. `int` requires 4 bytes of storage whereas `double` requires 8 bytes. In the background, somewhere in memory, Java declares a temporary `double` variable and promotes `int` 3 to `double` 3.0, and stores 3.0 in this temporary location. Now, Java can add 3.0 to 4.0 (as both are `double`s), resulting in the answer 7.0.

The second line compares `int` 4 with `double` 4.0. The same process happens. Java implicitly promotes 4 to 4.0 (in a new temporary location) and then compares 4.0 with 4.0. This results in `true` being output.

---

Now, we will turn our attention to logical operators.

## Logical operators

Logical operators enable us to build complex `boolean` expressions by combining sub-expressions. These operators are as follows:

- `&&` is the logical AND
- `||` is the logical OR
- `&` is the bitwise AND
- `|` is the bitwise OR
- `^` is the bitwise eXclusive OR (XOR)

We will examine these in turn with code examples to help explain how they operate. But before we do that, it is worthwhile refreshing our truth tables, as shown in *Table 3.2*:

| P | Q | P && Q | P \|\| Q | P & Q | P \| Q | P ^ Q |
|---|---|--------|---------|-------|--------|-------|
| T | T | T | T | T | T | F |
| T | F | F | T | F | T | T |
| F | T | F | T | F | T | T |
| F | F | F | F | F | F | F |

Table 3.2 – Boolean truth tables

In *Table 3.2*, the first two columns, **P** and **Q**, represent two expressions, where **T** means true and **F** means false. For example, the logical AND column (the **P && Q** column) represents the result of the overall expression, **P && Q**, depending on the values of **P** and **Q**. So, if **P** is true and **Q** is T, then **P && Q** is also true.

With this table in mind, let's examine the operators in turn.

### Logical AND (&&)

The logical AND states that both boolean operands must be true for the overall expression to be true. This is represented by the **P && Q** column in *Table 3.2*.

Note that this operator is known as a short-circuiting operator. For example, in an expression P && Q, if P evaluates to false, then && will *not* evaluate the expression Q because the overall expression will evaluate to false regardless. This is because F && F is false and F && T is also false. In effect, Java knows that once the expression P is false on the left-hand side of an && expression, the overall expression must be false. So, there is no need to evaluate the Q expression on the right-hand side, so it *short-circuits*. This is better explained with a code example:

```
boolean b1 = false, b2 = true;
boolean res = b1 && (b2=false); // F &&
System.out.println(b1 + " " + b2 + " " + res);// false true
    false
```

The first line initializes two boolean variables, b1 and b2, to `false` and `true`, respectively. The second line is the important one. Note that the parentheses are required around the `b2=false` sub-expression to get the code to compile (otherwise, you will get a syntax error). So, when we plug in `false` for b1, the expression evaluates to `F && (b2=false)`. As the evaluation order is left to right, this will lead `&&` to short-circuit, because, regardless of what remains in the expression, there is no way the overall expression can evaluate to true. This means that the `(b2=false)` sub-expression is **not** executed.

The last line outputs the values of the variables. The output is `false`, `true`, and `false` for b1, b2, and res, respectively. Crucially, b2 is `true`, demonstrating that `&&` short-circuited.

## Logical OR (||)

The logical OR states that either or both boolean operands can be true for the overall expression to be true. This is represented by the **P || Q** column in *Table 3.2*.

This operator is also a short-circuiting operator. For example, in an expression P || Q, if P evaluates to true, then || will *not* evaluate the expression Q because the overall expression will evaluate to true regardless. This is because T || F is true and T || T is also true. In effect, Java knows that once the expression P is true on the left-hand side of an || expression, the overall expression must be true. So, there is no need to evaluate the expression, Q, and hence it *short-circuits*. Again a code example will help:

```
boolean b1=false, b2=true;
boolean res = b2 || (b1=true);   // T ||
System.out.println(b1 + " "+ b2 + " "+res);// false true
   true
```

The first line initializes two boolean variables, b1 and b2, to `false` and `true`, respectively. The second line is the important one. Note again that the parentheses are required around the `b1=true` sub-expression to get the code to compile. So, when we plug in `true` for b2, the expression evaluates to `T || (b1=true)`. As the evaluation order is left to right, this will lead || to short-circuit because, regardless of what remains in the expression, there is no way the overall expression can evaluate to false.

The last line outputs the values of the variables. The output is `false`, `true`, and `true` for b1, b2, and res, respectively. Crucially, b1 is `false`, demonstrating that || short-circuited.

**Order of evaluation versus precedence**

This topic often causes confusion and is best explained with some sample pieces of code. Let's start with an example that can be deceptively simple:

```
int x=2, y=3, z=4;
int res = x + y * z;      // x + (y * z)
System.out.println(res);// 14
```

As * has higher precedence than +, the common element y, is grouped with z and not x. Thus, the overall expression is x + (y * z) = 2 + 12 = 14.

What is important to note here is that the evaluation order is left to right and as evaluation order trumps precedence, x is evaluated first before the (y * z) sub-expression. While this makes no difference in this example, let's look at an example where it does make a difference:

```
boolean a=false, b=false, c=false;
// a || (b && c)
// The next line evaluates to T ||
boolean bool = (a = true) || (b = true) && (c = true);
System.out.print(a + ", " + b + ", " + c); // true, false, false
```

As && has higher precedence than ||, the expression evaluates to (a = true) || ( (b = true) && (c = true) ).

In other words, the common sub-expression (b = true) is grouped with (c = true) rather than (a = true). Now comes the crucial bit: *evaluation order trumps precedence*. Therefore, (a = true) is evaluated first, resulting in T || ((b = true) && (c = true)).

As || is a short-circuit operator, the rest of the expression (to the right of ||) is **not** evaluated. This is demonstrated by the output on the last line, where it outputs true, false, false, for a, b, and c, respectively. The crucial thing to note here is that b and c are still false!

Now that we have discussed the logical operators, we will move on to bitwise operators.

## Bitwise operators

Although some of the bitwise operators look very similar to the logical operators, they operate quite differently. The principle differences are that the bitwise operators can work with both boolean and integral (byte, short, int, long, and char) operands. In addition, bitwise operators do *not* short-circuit.

Let's examine the boolean bitwise operators first.

## Bitwise AND (&)

Comparing the bitwise AND (&) with the logical AND (&&), the difference is that the bitwise AND will *not* short-circuit. This is represented by the **P & Q** column in *Table 3.2*. If we take the sample code that we used for the logical AND but change it to use the bitwise AND operator, you will see the difference in the output:

```
boolean b1 = false, b2 = true;
boolean res = b1 & (b2=false); // F & F
System.out.println(b1 + " " + b2 + " " + res);// false
   false false
```

In this case, the (b2=false) sub-expression is executed because & did not short-circuit. So we had false & false, which is false. Thus, the output is false for all the variables.

## Bitwise OR (|)

Comparing the bitwise OR (|) with the logical OR (||), the difference is that the bitwise OR will *not* short-circuit. This is represented by the **P | Q** column in *Table 3.2*. If we take the sample code that we used for the logical OR but change it to use the bitwise OR operator, you will see the difference in the output:

```
boolean b1=false, b2=true;
boolean res = b2 | (b1=true);  // T | T
System.out.println(b1 + " "+ b2 + " "+res);// true true
   true
```

In this case, the (b1=true) sub-expression is executed because | did not short-circuit. So, we had: true | true, which is true. Thus, the output is true for all the variables.

## Bitwise XOR (^)

This is another non-short-circuiting operator. The bitwise XOR, represented by the ^ operator, evaluates to true, if and only if one of the operands is true but *not* both. This is represented by the **P ^ Q** column in *Table 3.2*. Let's look at some examples in terms of code:

```
boolean b1 = (5 > 1)  ^ (10 < 20);  // T ^ T == F
boolean b2 = (5 > 10) ^ (10 < 20);  // F ^ T == T
boolean b3 = (5 > 1)  ^ (10 < 2);   // T ^ F == T
boolean b4 = (5 > 10) ^ (10 < 2);   // F ^ F == F
// false true true false
System.out.println(b1 + " " + b2 + " " + b3 + " " + b4);
```

The `boolean` variable, b1, is initialized to `false` because both of the sub-expressions – (5 > 1) and (10 < 20) – are `true`. Similarly, b4 is also initialized to `false` because both (5 > 10) and (10 < 2) are `false`.

However, b2 is `true` because even though (5 > 10) is `false`, (10 < 20) is `true`, and F ^ T is `true`. Likewise, b3 is `true` because (5 > 1) is `true`, (10 < 2) is F, and T ^ F is `true`.

Now that we have examined the bitwise operators when used with `boolean` operands, we will now briefly examine how the same operators work when the operands are integral numbers.

### Bitwise operators (integral operands)

Though not commonly used, we have included them for completeness. A code example is useful here:

```
byte b1 = 6 & 8;        // both bits must be 1
byte b2 = 7 | 9;        // one or the other or both
byte b3 = 5 ^ 4;        // one or the other but not both
System.out.println(b1 + ", " + b2 + ", "+b3); // 0, 15, 1
```

When the operands are integrals (as opposed to booleans), the bit patterns become important in evaluating the result. For the & operator, both bits must be 1 for that bit to be 1 in the result:

```
6 & 8 (in binary) = 0110 & 1000 = 0000 = 0
```

For the | operator, one of the bits, or both, must be 1 for that bit to be 1 in the result:

```
7 | 9 (in binary) = 0111 | 1001 = 1111 = 15
```

For the ^ operator, one of the bits, but not both, must be 1 for that bit to be 1 in the result:

```
5 ^ 4 (in binary) = 0101 ^ 0100 = 0001 = 1
```

That completes the bitwise operators. Now, let's cover the ternary operator.

## Ternary operator

The ternary operator, as its name suggests, is an operator that takes three operands. The ternary operator is used to evaluate boolean expressions and assign values accordingly to a variable. In other words, as boolean expressions evaluate to `true` or `false` only, the goal of the ternary operator is to decide which of the two values to assign to the variable.

The syntax is of the following form:

```
variable = boolean expression ? value to assign if true :
value to assign if false
```

Let's look at an example:

```
int x = 4;
String s = x % 2 == 0 ? " is an even number" : " is an odd
    number";
System.out.println(x + s); // 4 is an even number
```

In this example, the boolean expression to be evaluated is x % 2==0, which, because x = 4, evaluates to true. Thus, is an even number is assigned to the string, s, and is output. Had x been 5, then the boolean expression would have been false, and therefore, is an odd number would have been assigned to s and output.

The last group of operators we will examine are compound assignment operators.

## Compound assignment operators

These operators exist as a shorthand for more verbose expressions. For example, assuming x and y are both integers, x = x + y can be written as x += y. There are compound assignment operators for all of the mathematical operators:

- += Example: x += y is the same as x = x + y

- -= Example: x -= y is the same as x = x - y

- *= Example: x *= y is the same as x = x * y

- /= Example: x /= y is the same as x = x / y

- %= Example: x %= y is the same as x = x % y

Indeed, there are compound assignment operators for the bitwise operators – for example, x &= 3 is the same as x = x & 3 but they are so rarely used that we will just mention that they exist.

There are one or two subtleties to be aware of. As mentioned earlier, any mathematical operation involving an int type or smaller results in int. This can result in a cast being required to get the code to compile. With the compound assignment operators, the cast is in-built, so the explicit cast is not required. Take the following code for example:

```
byte b1 = 3, b2 = 4;
//   b1 = b1 + b2;          // compiler error
b1 = (byte)(b1 + b2);       // ok
b1 += b2;            // ok, no cast required
```

The first line initializes 2 bytes, b1 and b2, to 3 and 4, respectively. The second line is commented out as it generates a compiler error. The addition of b1 and b2 results in an int type that cannot be directly assigned to a byte variable, unless you cast it down from int to byte. This is what the third line is doing – using the cast (byte) to override the compiler error. We'll cover casting very soon but for now, just realize that with the cast, you are overriding the compiler error, effectively saying "I know what I am doing, proceed."

The last line is interesting in that, in the background, it is the same as the third line. In other words, the compiler translates `b1 += b2` into `b1 = (byte) (b1 + b2)`.

Another subtlety to be aware of is that whatever is on the right-hand side of the compound assignment operator is going to be grouped, regardless of precedence. An example will help here. Consider the following:

```
int x = 2;
x *= 2 + 5;                    // x = x * (2 + 5) = 2 * 7 = 14
System.out.println(x); // 14
```

We know that * has higher precedence than + and that the order of evaluation is left to right. That said, what is on the right-hand side of *= is grouped by the compiler by surrounding 2 + 5 with parentheses (in the background). Thus, the expression becomes 2 * (2 + 5) = 2 * 7 = 14. To further this point, had the compiler *not* inserted parentheses, the expression would have been evaluated to 9. In other words, due to operator precedence, the expression would have been (2 * 2) + 5 = 4 + 5 = 9. However, as we have seen, this is **not** the case.

Let's look at another more complicated example:

```
int k=1;
k += (k=4) * (k+2);
System.out.println(k); // 25
```

In this example, the right-hand side is, once again, enclosed in parentheses:

```
k += (right hand side) where the right hand side is (k=4) *
  (k+2)
```

Translating += into its longer form gives us the following output:

```
k = k + (right hand side)
```

The order of evaluation is left to right, so plugging in the current value of k, which is 1, results in:

```
k = 1 + (right hand side)
```

Now, by plugging in the right-hand side expression, we get the following:

```
k = 1 + ( (k=4) * (k+2) )
```

As the order of evaluation is left to right, k is changed to 4 before we add 2:

```
k = 1 + ( 4 * 6 )
k = 1 + 24
k = 25
```

That concludes our treatment of Java operators. Now, let's examine Java casting, a topic we have touched on already in this chapter.

# Explaining Java casting

To discuss casting properly, we need to explain both the widening and narrowing of Java's primitive data types. With this in mind, it is helpful to remember the sizes of the primitive data types in bytes. *Table 3.3* represents this information:

| Primitive Data Type | Size in Bytes |
|:---:|:---:|
| byte | 1 |
| short | 2 |
| char | 2 |
| int | 4 |
| long | 8 |
| float | 4 |
| double | 8 |

Table 3.3 – The sizes of Java's primitive types

The preceding table presents the sizes in bytes of Java's various primitive data types. This will help us as we discuss both widening and narrowing.

## Widening

Widening is done automatically; in other words, a cast is not needed. As the promotion is done in the background, widening is also known as *implicit promotion*. With *Table 3.3* in mind, the widening rules are as follows:

byte → short/char → int → long → float → double

Given the sizes from *Table 3.3*, most of these rules should make sense. For example, a `byte` can automatically fit into a `short` because 1 byte fits into 2 bytes automatically. The only interesting one is `long` → `float`, which is *widening* from 8 bytes to 4 bytes. This is possible because even though a `long` requires 8 bytes and a `float` requires only 4 bytes, their ranges differ – that is, a `float` type can accommodate any `long` value but not vice versa. This is shown in the following code snippet:

```
System.out.println("Float: " + Float.MAX_VALUE);// Float:
   3.4028235E38
System.out.println("Float: " + Float.MIN_VALUE);// Float:
   1.4E-45
System.out.println(Long.MAX_VALUE);   //    9223372036854775807
System.out.println(Long.MIN_VALUE);   //    -9223372036854775808
```

Note the scientific notation E used for floating point. `float` takes up less space, but due to its representation, it can hold larger and smaller numbers than `long`.

---

**Scientific notation**

Scientific notation is a shorthand way to represent decimal numbers and can be useful for representing very large and/or very small numbers. Here are some examples:

```
double d1 = .00000000123;

double d2 = 1.23e-9;

System.out.println(d1==d2); // true

double d3 = 120_000_000;

double d4 = 1.2e+8;

System.out.println(d3==d4); // true
```

As the comparisons both return `true`, this means that d1 is the internal representation of d2. Similarly, both d3 and d4 are equivalent.

---

Let's examine widening in code. *Figure 3.6* demonstrates this:

```
14    char c   = 'a'; // normal
15    int i    = c;   // widening, char to int
16    float f  = i;   // widening, int to float
17    double d = f;   // widening, float to double
18    float f2 = 1L;  // widening, long to float
```

Figure 3.6 – Implicit widening examples

Line 14 is a regular char assignment – in other words, no widening is involved. Note that characters (represented by char) are simply small numbers (0..65,535). To represent a character, we enclose the character in single quotes. In contrast, a String, which is a sequence of characters, is represented in double quotes. Therefore, "a" is a String, whereas 'a' is a character.

Line 15 is a widening from char (2 bytes) to int (4 bytes). Line 16 is a widening from int to float. Although both int and float require 4 bytes, as discussed earlier with long, float has a greater range, so there is no issue here. Line 17 is a widening from float to double. Lastly, line 18 is a widening from long to float. Note that there are no compiler errors anywhere and that the cast operator is not needed in any of the assignments.

Now, let's discuss narrowing, where the cast operator *is* required.

## Narrowing

The cast operator is a type enclosed in parentheses – for example, (int) and (byte) are both cast operators that cast to int and byte, respectively. With *Table 3.3* in mind, the following figure, *Figure 3.7*, presents assignments that require casting:

```
22      // Narrowing
23      int i   = (int)3.3;                          // narrowing, double to int
24      byte b  = (byte) 233;                        // narrowing, int to byte
25      float f = (float) 3.5;                       // narrowing, double to float
26      System.out.println(i + " " + b + " " +f);    // 3 -23 3.5
```

Figure 3.7 – Casting examples

In the preceding figure, line 23 is attempting to assign 3.3, a double type (8 bytes), to an int type (4 bytes). Without the cast, this would be a compiler error. With the cast, you are overriding the compiler error. So, on line 23, we are casting 3.3 to int and assigning this int to the i variable. Therefore, after the assignment completes, i has a value of 3.

Line 24 is casting the int type, 233, into the byte variable, b. This literal value is outside the range of byte (-128 to +127), so a cast is required. Line 25 is casting the double type, 3.5, to float. Remember that, by default, a decimal number is double; to have it considered as a float as opposed to a double, you must suffix f or F. For example, 3.3f is float.

The output on line 26 is 3, -23, and 3.5 for i, b, and f, respectively. Note that in the output, the float variable appears without f.

How we arrived at -23 is explained in the following callout.

**Overflowing the byte**

Remember that the range of byte is -128 (10000000) to +127 (01111111). The leftmost bit is the sign bit, with 1 representing negative and 0 representing positive.

In the preceding example, we did the following:

```
byte b  = (byte) 233;
```

The literal value of 233 (an integer) is too big for byte but how was b assigned the value of -23? Mapping 233 as an int type gives us the following bit pattern:

```
11101001 = 1 + 8 + 32 + 64 + 128 = 233 (int)
```

Note that as an int is 4 bytes, 233 is 00000000000000000000000011101001. Mapping that bit pattern as a **byte** (the high order 3 bytes are truncated) gives us the following output:

```
11101001 = 1 + 8 + 32 + 64 + (-128) = -23 (byte)
```

Remember that the leftmost bit is the sign bit. That is why $-128$ is in the calculation. It is $-(2^7) = -128$.

We will conclude this section by looking at some unusual examples where casting is/is not required.

### *To cast or not to cast, that is the question*

There are certain situations where, because the compiler applies rules in the background, a cast is *not* required. Let's examine some of these situations with code examples. *Figure 3.8* presents the code:

```
32    char c = 12;
33    char c2 = 90_000;
34    short s = 12;
35    s = c;
36    s = (short) c;
37    c = s;
38    c = (char) s;
39
40    final char c1 = 12;
41    short s1 = 12;
42    s1 = c1;
```

Figure 3.8 – Situations where casting is not always necessary

Line 32 declares and initializes a char variable c, to an int value of 12. Remember that char variables are essentially small positive numbers. Although we are assigning an int value (4 bytes) to a char variable (2 bytes), because the literal value is within the range of char (0 to 65,535), the compiler allows it. Had the literal value been out of the range of char, the compiler would have generated an error – this is what is happening on line 33.

Line 34 declares and initializes a `short` variable, s, to an `int` value of `12`. Again, although `short` can hold only 2 bytes, the compiler realizes it can store the literal value, `12`, and allows it.

Note that, from the compiler's perspective, assigning literal values into variables is different to assigning *variables* to variables. For example, lines 32 and 37 are quite different. This will become apparent as we discuss the next few lines in the figure.

Lines 35 to 38 demonstrate that while both `char` and `short` require 2 bytes, they have different ranges: `char` (0 to 65,535) and `short` (-32,768 to +32,767). This means that a `short` variable can hold a negative value such as -15, whereas a `char` variable cannot. Conversely, a `char` variable can hold a value such as 65,000 but a `short` variable cannot. Therefore, as lines 35 and 37 demonstrate, you cannot directly assign a `char` variable to a `short` variable and vice versa. You need a cast in both scenarios. Lines 36 and 38 demonstrate this.

### Compile-time constants

However, lines 40 to 42 show a way around the requirement for the cast we just outlined. If you declare your variable as a *compile-time constant* (and assuming the value is in range), the compiler will allow the variable-to-variable assignment. Line 40 uses the `final` keyword to declare a compile-time constant. We will discuss `final` in detail in *Chapter 9*, but in this context, it means that c1 will always have a value of `12`. The value is fixed (or *constant*) for c1 and this is done at *compile time*. If you try to change the value of c1, you will get a compiler error. Now that the compiler knows that c1 will always have `12` as its value, the compiler can apply the same rules that it applies to literal values; in other words, is the value in range? This is why line 42 does *not* generate a compiler error.

This concludes our discussion on operators. Now, let's apply them!

# Exercises

Mesozoic Eden is doing great. The dinosaurs are healthy and the guests are happy. Now that you have some new skills, let's go ahead and perform slightly more complicated tasks!

1.  The caretakers want to be able to keep track of dinosaur weights. It's your task to write a program that calculates the average weight of two dinosaurs. This will help our team of nutritionists in planning the correct food portions.

2.  Proper nutrition is essential for the health of our dinosaurs. The caretakers want to have a rough guideline of how much to feed a dinosaur. Write a program that determines the amount of food required for a dinosaur based on its weight. You can come up with the amount of food needed per weight unit of the dinosaurs.

3.  For our park, we need to have a leap year checker. In our commitment to scientific accuracy, use the modulus operator to determine if the current year is a leap year. We want to make sure our calendar-themed exhibits are always up to date.

4.  Create a program that checks whether the park's maximum capacity has been reached. The program only needs to print true or false after the words "Max capacity reached:". This is crucial in maintaining safety standards and ensuring a positive visitor experience.

5.  Sometimes visitors want to compare dinosaurs' ages. And we get it – this could be interesting for educational purposes. Write a program that calculates the age difference between two dinosaurs.

6.  In Mesozoic Eden, we have a very strong safety-first policy. Write a program that checks whether the park's safety rating is above a certain threshold. Maintaining a good safety rating is our utmost priority.

## Project – Dino meal planner

As a zookeeper in Mesozoic Eden, the crucial tasks include planning the meals for our beloved dinosaurs. While we're not using conditionals and loops yet, we can still calculate some basic requirements!

Develop a simple program to help the zookeepers plan the meal portions for different dinosaurs. The program should use the dinosaur's weight to calculate how much food it needs to eat per meal.

If you need a bit more guidance, here's how you can do it:

- Declare variables for the dinosaur's weight and the proportion of its weight it needs to eat per day. For instance, if a dinosaur needs to eat 5% of its body weight daily, and it weighs 2,000 kg, it would need to eat 100 kg of food.

- Now, let's say you feed the dinosaur twice a day. Declare a variable for the number of feedings and calculate how much food you need to serve per feeding. In this example, it would be 50 kg per feeding.

- Print out the result in a meaningful way – for example, "Our 2,000 kg dinosaur needs to eat 100 kg daily, which means we need to serve 50 kg per feeding."

## Summary

In this chapter, we learned about how Java's operators work and how they cooperate. In addition, we learned how to cast in Java.

Initially, we discussed two important properties relating to operators: precedence and associativity. We saw that precedence dictates how common terms are grouped. Associativity comes into play when the operators have the same order of precedence.

We then examined the operators themselves. We started by looking at unary operators, which have one operand such as the prefix/postfix increment/decrement operators, ++ and --.

We then moved on to the arithmetic operators: +, -, *, /, and %. We noted that integer division truncates. In addition, we discussed that any math operations involving `int` types or smaller results in `int`. Lastly, we discussed in detail how the + operator works when one or both operands are strings. In these cases, a string append is performed.

Next, we discussed relational operators. The results of these operators are always boolean values and will be used when we construct conditional statements in *Chapter 4*.

As Java cannot perform operations where the types are different, where possible, Java performs implicit promotion. This is where Java promotes the smaller type to the larger type somewhere in memory. This is Java's way of invisibly continuing with the operation.

We then discussed the logical operators: &&, ||, &, |, and ^. Truth tables were presented to aid in understanding. Both the logical && and logical || operators are short-circuiting operators. Understanding this is important because the order of evaluation trumps precedence.

The bitwise operators, bitwise AND (&) and bitwise OR (|), are similar except that in contrast to && and ||, both & and | never short-circuit and can also work with integral operands.

The ternary operator takes three operands. It evaluates a boolean expression and assigns one of two values to a variable, depending on whether the boolean expression was `true` or `false`.

Regarding operators, the last group we covered were the compound assignment operators, of which there is one for each mathematical operator.

In our discussion on casting, we covered both widening and narrowing. Widening is done in the background and is often called *implicit promotion*. There is no risk here as the type being promoted fits easily into the target type.

Narrowing is where the cast is required. This is because, given that you are going from a type that requires more storage space to a type that requires less, there is a potential loss of data.

Now that we know how to use operators, in the next chapter, we will move on to conditional statements, where operators are commonly used.

# 4

# Conditional Statements

In *Chapter 3*, we learned about Java operators. We discussed two important properties of operators, namely, precedence and associativity. Precedence helps group shared operands. When precedence levels match, associativity is then used for grouping.

We discussed the unary operators – prefix and postfix increment/decrement, cast, and logical NOT. We also covered the binary operators – arithmetic, relational, logical, bitwise, and compound assignment. We learned about the behavior of the + symbol when one (or both) operands is a string. We discussed the logical AND (&&) and logical OR (||) and their short-circuiting property. Finally, the ternary operator, with its three operands, was covered.

We also learned about Java casting. This can be done implicitly, known as **implicit promotion** or **widening**. The other alternative is explicit casting, known as **narrowing**. When narrowing, we must cast to the target type in order to remove the compiler error. Lastly, we discussed compile-time constants, which, because their values never change, enable the compiler to apply different rules.

Now that we know about operators, let us do something interesting with them. By the end of this chapter, you will be able to use Java's operators to create conditional statements. Conditional statements enable us to make decisions. In addition, you will understand a fundamental concept in Java, namely, scope.

In this chapter, we are going to cover the following main topics:

- Understanding scope
- Exploring if statements
- Mastering switch statements and expressions

## Technical requirements

The code for this chapter can be found on GitHub at https://github.com/PacktPublishing/Learn-Java-with-Projects/tree/main/ch4.

# Understanding scope

In programming, scope defines where a variable is/is not usable within a program. This is often referred to as the visibility of the variable. In other words, where in the code is the variable "visible". Java uses **block scope**. In order to explain Java's scope, we must first understand what a block is.

## What is a block?

Curly braces delimit a block of code. In other words, a block starts with the opening curly brace, {, and ends with the closing curly brace, }. Note that the braces face each other, as in {   }. A variable is visible and available for use, from where it is declared in the block, to the closing } of that block. *Figure 4.1* presents a code example to help explain:

```java
3  public class Scope {
4      public static void main(String[] args) {
5          int x = 1;
6          x++;
7
8          { // start of block
9              int y = 2;
10             y++;
11             x++;
12         } // end of block
13         x++;
14         y++; // out of scope
15     }
16 }
```

Figure 4.1 – Block scope in Java

In the preceding figure, we declare an int variable, x, on line 5 and initialize it to 1. The current block of code is the group of Java statements surrounded by {   }. Therefore, the x variable's block of code starts on line 4, where the opening curly brace is, and ends on line 15, where the closing curly brace is. Thus, the scope of x is from line 5, where it is declared, to line 15 (the closing curly brace of the current scope). When we refer to x on line 6, there is no issue, as x is in scope.

On line 8, we start a new block/scope with {. Though somewhat unusual, as there is no code preceding { on line 8, lines 8 to 12 define a valid code block. Note that variables from the outer scope are visible within this inner (nested) scope. This is shown on line 11 where, in the inner scope, we refer to a variable declared in the outer scope, namely x, without any issue.

The inverse is not true, however; a variable defined in an inner scope is not visible in the outer scope. The y variable is in scope from where it is declared (line 9 of the inner scope) to line 12 (the closing curly brace of that scope). Thus, we get a compiler error on line 14 where, in the outer scope, we refer to the y variable.

---

### Indentation

Indentation really helps with the identification of code blocks and, consequently, scopes. The style we use is to start the code block at the end of the line. For example, in *Figure 4.1*, note the opening curly brace { on line 3. The closing curly brace } for that code block (and thus the scope) is on line 16. From an indentation point of view, the closing curly brace } is directly under the public keyword from line 3. More specifically, the closing curly brace is directly under the 'p' in public. While not necessary for compilation, it does make your code easier to read and maintain – the scope starts on line 3 and to find where the scope ends, one just scans down the program to find the matching curly brace } which lines up under public (from line 3).

Line 4 also defines a block and thus a scope. Line 15 contains the matching curly brace } for that scope – note that the closing curly brace is lined up under the keyword public (from line 4). Thankfully, the editors are a great help in keeping your code properly indented.

---

In summary, blocks are defined with { }. As Java uses block scope, the code blocks define the scope of where a variable can be used. Variables are visible in nested scopes, but not vice versa.

Now that we understand scope in Java, let us examine conditional logic in Java. We will start with if statements.

## Exploring if statements

As their name suggests, conditional statements are based on the evaluation of a condition. The result of this condition is either true or false – in other words, a boolean. *Figure 4.2* introduces the syntax of the overall if statement:

if (booleanExpression) statement/block

[ else if (booleanExpression) statement/block ] ...

[ else statement/block ]

Figure 4.2 – The if statement syntax

The square brackets [] in the preceding figure denote something as optional. For example, both the else if statements and the else statement are optional. The if statement itself is mandatory. The three ellipses, . . ., indicate that you can have as many else if statements as you like (or none at all).

Now that we have the overall syntax, let us break it down into smaller pieces.

## The if statement itself

As stated earlier, an `if` statement evaluates a `boolean` expression. This `boolean` expression is enclosed in parentheses. Curly braces that delimit a block of code are optional if there is only one statement after the `if` clause. However, it is considered good practice to always explicitly declare a block of code. *Figure 4.3* demonstrates both styles:

```
8      int x=5, y=4;
9      if(x > y)
10         System.out.println(x + " > "+y);
11     if(x < y)
12         System.out.println(x + " < "+y);
13     if(x == y){
14         String s = x + " == "+y;
15         System.out.println(s);
16     }
```

Figure 4.3 – Simple if statements

First, let us explain the code. Note the indentation, which is automatically facilitated by the code editors. This makes it easier to see the statements that are governed by the various `if` statements. Both lines 9 and 11 demonstrate simple `if` statements that control just one statement. Line 9 controls line 10. This means that if line 9 is true, line 10 is executed. If line 9 is false then line 10 is skipped. Similarly, if line 11 is true: line 12 is executed; if line 11 is false, line 12 is skipped.

However, if you wish to execute two or more statements when an `if` statement is true, a code block is required. This is demonstrated by lines 13 to 16. If the boolean expression on line 13 evaluates to true, then both of the statements on lines 14 and 15 will be executed. This is because they are in a code block.

As regards the running program, with x initialized to 5 and y to 4, when line 9 executes, it is true (as 5 > 4). Therefore, line 10 executes and therefore the output from *Figure 4.3* is 5 > 4. Lines 11 and 13 are both executed but as they both evaluate to false, nothing else is output to the screen.

What if, on line 8, we initialized the variables as follows:

```
int x=4, y=5;
```

Now, if (x > y) is false and line 10 is not executed; if (x < y) is true and line 12 outputs 4 < 5 to the screen; if (x == y) is also false, so lines 14 and 15 are not executed.

Lastly, let us make the variables equal by changing line 8 as follows:

```
int x=4, y=4;
```

Now, if (x > y) is false so line 10 is not executed; if (x < y) is also false so line 12 is not executed; however, if (x == y) is true, so line 14 builds up the string s to be "4 == 4" and line 15 outputs it.

Note the indentation, which is automatically facilitated by the code editors. This makes it easier to see the statements that are governed by the various if statements.

## else if statements

In *Figure 4.3*, there is no code to cater to the situations where an if expression evaluates to false. This is where the else if statement comes in. *Figure 4.4* shows an else if in code:

```
19          int x=4, y=5;
20          if(x > y) {
21              System.out.println(x + " > " + y);
22          } else if(x < y) {
23              System.out.println(x + " < " + y);
24          } else if(x == y){
25              System.out.println(x + " == " + y);
26          }
27          System.out.println("Here");
```

Figure 4.4 – else if statements

As x is 4 and y is 5 (line 19), the if expression on line 20 evaluates to false and thus control jumps to line 22 where the first else if is evaluated. As this evaluates to true, line 23 is executed. *Now, no other branch will be evaluated.* In other words, the next line of code executed after line 23 is line 27. Note that, as per good coding practice, each branch is coded as a block, even though there is only one statement in each block.

Had x been initialized to 5, then lines 20 and 22 would both have evaluated to false. Line 24 would be true, and thus, line 25 would be executed.

For situations where the if and else if statements do not match, we can use the else statement. Let us discuss that now.

## else statements

The code in *Figure 4.4* evaluates all possible scenarios when comparing x and y. Either x is greater than, less than, or equal to y. This logic lends itself nicely to introducing the else statement. The else statement is a *catch-all*. As per [] in *Figure 4.2*, the else clause is optional. If present, it must be coded at the end after any if and/or else if clauses. *Figure 4.5* is *Figure 4.4* refactored using an else clause, except that the values of x and y in *Figure 4.5* are now the same.

```
30          int x=4, y=4;
31          if(x > y) {
32              System.out.println(x + " > " + y);
33          } else if(x < y) {
34              System.out.println(x + " < " + y);
35          } else {
36              System.out.println(x + " == " + y);
37          }
38          System.out.println("Here");
```

Figure 4.5 – else statement

In *Figure 4.5*, as both x and y are 4, lines 31 and 33 evaluate to `false`. However, there is no condition on line 35 as it is simply an `else` statement (as opposed to `else if`). This means that the code block beginning on line 35 is executed automatically and line 36 is executed.

With regard to `if else` statements, it is important to understand a subtle problem that can arise known as the "dangling `else`" problem.

### Dangling else

Consider the following unindented code, which uses no code blocks:

```
boolean flag=false;                    // line 1
if (flag)                              // line 2
if (flag)                              // line 3
System .out.println("True True");      // line 4
else                                   // line 5
System.out.println("True False");      // line 6
```

This code has two `if` statements but only one `else` statement. Which `if` statement does `else` match with? The rule is: when an `else` statement is looking to match with `if`, it will match with the nearest *unmatched* `if` as it progresses back up through the code.

Following this rule, the `else` statement matches with the second `if` (line 3) as that `if` statement has not yet been matched. This means that the `if` statement on line 2 remains unmatched. The code, when written using proper indentation, is much clearer:

```
if (flag)                          // line 2
    if (flag)                      // line 3
        System.out.println("True True");     // line 4
    else                           // line 5
        System.out.println("True False");    // line 6
```

This is confirmed by the output. If `flag` is true, the output is `"True  True"`; if `flag` is false, however, nothing is output to the screen. Interestingly, there is no way line 6 can now be reached (as `boolean` variables have only two values: `true` and `false`).

Using code blocks makes the code even easier to understand, as can be seen as follows:

```
if (flag) {
    if (flag) {
        System.out.println("True True");
    }
    else {
        System.out.println("True False");
    }
}
```

This is why using code blocks, even for one statement, is very helpful. Throughout the book, we will use proper indentation and code blocks to aid clarity and ease of understanding.

Now, let us look at a more involved example. This example (and others to follow) use the pre-defined `Scanner` class from the Java **Application Programming Interface** (**API**). The API is a suite of pre-defined types (for example classes) that are available for our use. We will cover these topics as we progress through the book but suffice to say that the API is extremely useful as it provides pre-defined and well-tested code for our use.

The `Scanner` class resides in the `java.util` package. Therefore, we need to briefly discuss both packages and the `Scanner` class.

## Packages

A package is a group of related types, such as classes, that we can use. Conveniently, many are already available for us to use in the API.

To gain access to these types, we need to "import" them into our code. For this purpose, Java provides the `import` keyword. Any `import` statements go at the top of your file. We can import a whole package using the * wildcard; for example: `import java.util.*;`. We can also import a particular type explicitly by naming it in the `import` statement; for example: `import java.util.Scanner;`.

When you precede the type with its package name, such as `java.util.Scanner`, this is known as the "fully qualified name". We could omit the `import` statement and simply refer each time to `Scanner` using its fully qualified name; in other words, everywhere `Scanner` is mentioned, replace it with `java.util.Scanner`. Generally speaking, however, importing the type and using its non-qualified name is preferred.

There is one package that is automatically available (imported) for us and that is the `java.lang` package. For example, the `String` class resides in `java.lang` and that is why we never have to import anything to get access to the `String` class.

## Scanner class

It is helpful to know that while `Scanner` is a versatile class, for our purposes, we will simply use `Scanner` to enable us to retrieve keyboard input from the user. With this in mind, note that `System.in` used in the examples refers to the standard input stream which is already open and ready to supply input data. Typically, this corresponds to the keyboard. `System.in` is therefore perfect for getting input data from the user via the keyboard. The `Scanner` class provides various methods for parsing/interpreting the keyboard input. For example, when the user types in a number at the keyboard, the method `nextInt()` provides that number to us as an `int` primitive. We will avail of these methods in our examples.

## Nested if statements

Now that we have discussed packages and `Scanner`, in *Figure 4.6* and *Figure 4.7*, we discuss a more involved `if-else` example that deals with input from the user (via the keyboard). Both figures relate to the one example. *Figure 4.6* focuses on the declaration of constants to make the code more readable. In addition, *Figure 4.6* also focuses on declaring and using `Scanner`. On the other hand, *Figure 4.7* focuses on the subsequent `if-else` structure.

```
11          final int JAN = 1;  final int FEB = 2;   final int MAR = 3; // constants
12          final int APR = 4;  final int MAY = 5;   final int JUN = 6;
13          final int JUL = 7;  final int AUG = 8;   final int SEP = 9;
14          final int OCT = 10; final int NOV = 11;  final int DEC = 12;
15
16          Scanner sc = new Scanner(System.in);     // import java.util.Scanner;
17          System.out.print("Enter month --> ");
18          int month = sc.nextInt();
```

Figure 4.6 – Using Scanner to get input from the keyboard

Lines 11 to 14 define constants using the keyword `final`. This means that their values cannot change. It is good practice to use uppercase identifiers for constants (where words are separated by underscores). This will make the code in *Figure 4.7* more readable; in other words, instead of comparing `month` with 1 (which, in this context, means January), we will compare `month` with `JAN`, which reads better. For brevity's sake, we have declared three constants per line but you can easily declare one per line also.

Line 16 in *Figure 4.6* creates our `Scanner` object reference, `sc`. Essentially, we are creating a reference, namely `sc`, which refers to the `Scanner` object created using the new keyword. As stated previously, `System.in` means that `sc` is looking at the keyboard. This reference is what we will use to interact with `Scanner`, much like a remote control is used to interact with a television.

Line 17 prompts the user to enter a month (1..12) on the keyboard. This is actually very important because, without the prompt, the cursor will just blink and the user will wonder what they should type in. Line 18 is where `Scanner` really comes into its own. Here we use the `nextInt()` method to get in a number. For the moment, just know that when we call `sc.nextInt()`, Java does not return to our code until the user has typed in something and hit the return key. For the moment, we will make the (convenient) assumption that it is an integer. We will store the `int` primitive returned in our own `int` primitive, `month`. Now, in our code, we can use what the user typed in. *Figure 4.7* shows this in action.

```
20      int numDays=0;
21      if(month == JAN || month == MAR || month == MAY || month == JUL
22              || month == AUG || month == OCT || month == DEC) {
23          numDays=31;
24      } else if (month == APR || month == JUN || month == SEP || month == NOV) {
25          numDays=30;
26      } else if (month == FEB) {
27          System.out.print("Enter year --> ");
28          int year = sc.nextInt();
29
30          if( (year % 400 == 0) || (year % 4 == 0 && !(year % 100 == 0)) ){
31              numDays = 29; // leap year e.g. 2000, 2012, 2016
32          }else{
33              numDays = 28;    // 1900 (divisible by 100)
34          }
35      } else {
36          System.out.println("Invalid month: "+month);
37      }
38      if(numDays > 0){
39          System.out.println("Number of days is: "+numDays);
40      }
```

Figure 4.7 – A complex if statement

Note that the code presented in the preceding image is a *continuation* of *Figure 4.6*. On line 20, we declare an `int` variable, namely numDays, and initialize it to 0. Lines 21 to 22 are the start of the `if` statement. Using the `boolean` logical OR operator, the `if` statement checks to see whether the month value matches any of the constants defined in *Figure 4.6*. In the background, the constant values are used, so in reality, the `if` statement is as follows:

```
if(month == 1 || month == 3 || month == 5 || month == 7 ||
    month == 8 || month == 10 || month == 12)
```

Note that the `month` variable must be specified each time. In other words, `if (month == JAN || MAR || MAY || JUL || AUG || OCT || DEC)` will *not* compile.

So, assuming that the user typed in 1 (representing January), `month` becomes 1 and, as a result, lines 21 to 22 evaluate to true and numDays is set to 31 on line 23. The logic is the same if the user types in 3, 5, 7, 8, 10, and 12, representing March, May, July, August, October, and December, respectively.

If the user types in 4 (representing April), lines 21 to 22 evaluate to false and the `else if` statement on line 24 is evaluated. Line 24 evaluates to true and `numdays` is set to 30 on line 25. The logic is the same if the user types in 6, 9, and 11, representing June, September, and November, respectively.

Now, let us deal with the user typing in 2, representing February. The `if` condition on lines 21 to 22 and the `else if` condition on line 24 both evaluate to false. Line 26 evaluates to true. Now, we need to review the leap year logic. Of course, February has 28 days every year (as do all the months!) but has one extra day when the year is a leap year. The logic for determining whether a year is a leap year is as follows:

- **Scenario A**: `year` is a multiple of 400 => leap year
- **Scenario B**: `year` is a multiple of 4 AND `year` is *not* a multiple of 100 => leap year

The following are all leap years: 2000 (satisfies scenario A), 2012, and 2016 (both satisfy scenario B).

As the leap year algorithm depends on the year, we first need the year from the user. Lines 27 to 28 accomplish this. We then encounter a nested `if` statement from lines 30 to 34, which determines, according to the logic just outlined, whether the year entered by the user is a leap year. Line 30 implements the logic for both scenarios A and B. Whether `year` is a multiple of 400 is achieved with `(year % 400 == 0)`. The condition of `year` being a multiple of 4 and not a multiple of 100 is achieved with

`(year % 4 == 0 && !( year % 100 == 0))`. The fact that either condition satisfies the leap year calculation is achieved by using the logical OR operator between them. Assuming a year of 2000, line 30 would be true and `numDays` is set to 29. Assuming a year of 1900, the `if` statement on line 30 is false and, as there is no condition on line 32 (it is just an `else` statement), line 33 is executed, setting `numDays` to 28.

An invalid `month` value of, for example, 25 or -3 would result in the `else` branch on line 35 being executed. An error message would be output to the screen on line 36 as a result.

Lines 38 to 40 output the number of days provided that `numDays` was changed from its initial value of 0. The `if` statement on line 38 prevents the message `"Number of days is: 0"` from appearing on the screen if the user typed in an invalid `month` value.

That concludes our treatment of the `if` statement. Now, let us examine both `switch` statements and expressions, which can, in certain situations, be a more elegant option.

## Mastering switch statements and expressions

Complicated `if` statements, with many `else if` branches and an `else` branch can be verbose. The `switch` structure can, in many situations, be more concise and elegant. Let us start with `switch` statements.

## switch statements

Firstly, let us examine the syntax of the switch statement. *Figure 4.8* introduces the syntax.

```
switch (expression){
    [case label:
        statement(s);
        break;] ...
    [default:
        statement(s);
        break;]
}
```

Figure 4.8 – The switch statement syntax

A switch statement evaluates an expression. As of Java 21, the expression can be an integral primitive (excluding long) or any reference type. This means that we can switch on primitive variables of type byte, char, short, or int and also switch on class types, enum types, record types and array types. The case labels can now include a null label. Java 21 also brought in *pattern matching for switch*. We will present another switch example demonstrating this feature when we have those topics covered (*Chapter 9*). Until then, we will focus on the more traditional switch.

> **Wrapper types**
>
> For each of the primitive types, there is a corresponding class, known as a "wrapper type": byte (wrapped by Byte), short (Short), int (Integer), long (Long), float (Float), double (Double), boolean (Boolean), and char (Character). They are so called because they represent objects that encapsulate the primitive. As they are class types, useful methods are available. For example, int val = Integer.parseInt("22"); converts the String "22" into the number 22, stored in val, where we can perform arithmetic.

The expression just evaluated is compared against the case labels. The case labels are compile-time constants of the same type as the switch expression. If there is a match with a case label, the associated block of code is executed (note: no need for curly braces in the case or default blocks). To exit the case block, ensure you insert a break statement. The break statement exits the switch block. However, the break statement is optional. If you omit the break statement, the code *falls through* to the next case label (or default), even though there is no match.

The default keyword is used to specify a code block to execute if none of the case labels match. Typically, it is coded at the end of the switch block but this is not mandatory. In effect, default can appear anywhere in the switch block with similar semantics (this is a poor programming practice, however).

*Figure 4.9* presents an example.

```
18              Scanner sc = new Scanner(System.in);
19              System.out.print("Enter a sport --> ");
20              String sport = sc.next();
21              switch(sport){
22                  case "Soccer":
23                      System.out.println("I play soccer");
24                      break;
25                  case "Rugby":
26                      System.out.println("I play Rugby");
27                      break;
28                  default:// can be moved around
29                      System.out.println("Unknown sport");
30                      break;
31              }
```

Figure 4.9 – switch on a String example

Using the `Scanner` class, lines 18 to 20 ask and retrieve from the user a sport. Note that the `Scanner` method used on this occasion is `next()`, which returns a `String` type (as opposed to a primitive type).

Lines 21 to 31 present the `switch` block. Note that the `case` labels on lines 22 and 25 are both `String` compile-time constants. If the user types in `"Soccer"`, the `case` label on line 22 matches, and both lines 23 and 24 will execute. Interestingly, even though there are two statements to be executed, there is no need for curly braces here. This is a feature of `switch` blocks. As line 22 matched, line 23 will execute, and `"I play soccer"` will be echoed to the screen. The `break` statement on line 24 ensures that the `switch` block is exited and that the `"Rugby"` section is not executed.

If, on the other hand, the user types in `"Rugby"`, line 25 matches, and `"I play Rugby"` is echoed to the screen. Again, the `break` statement, this time on line 27, ensures that the `switch` block is exited and that the `default` section is not executed.

If the user typed in `"Tennis"`, then neither of the `case` labels on lines 22 and 25 will match. This is when the `default` section comes into play. When there are no matches with any `case` label, the `default` section is executed. Typically, the `default` section is coded at the end of the `switch` block and the `break` statement is traditionally inserted for completeness.

**Case labels are case-sensitive**

Note that the `case` labels are case-sensitive. In other words, in *Figure 4.9*, if the user types in `"soccer"`, the `case` label on line 22 will *not* match. The `"Rugby"` case label will not match either, naturally. Thus, the default section will execute, and `"Unknown sport"` will echo (print) to the screen.

Let us look at another example. *Figure 4.10* is a `switch` statement based on integers.

```
34          Scanner sc = new Scanner(System.in);
35          System.out.print("Enter a number (1..10) --> ");
36          int number = sc.nextInt();
37          final int two = 2; // compile-time constant
38          switch(number){
39              case 1:
40              case 3:
41              case 5:
42              case 7:
43              case 9:
44                  System.out.println(number + " is odd.");
45                  break;
46              case two:
47              case 4: case 6: case 8: case 10:
48                  System.out.println(number + " is even.");
49                  break;
50              default:
51                  System.out.println( number + " is outside range (1..10).");
52                  break;
53          }
```

Figure 4.10 – switch on an integer example

In the preceding figure, line 37 declares a compile-time constant, `two`, and initializes it to the integer literal, 2. Line 38 starts the `switch` block by switching on an `int` variable named `number`, which was declared and initialized based on user input, on line 36. All of the `case` labels in the `switch` block must now be integers – be they literal values as on lines 39 to 43 and line 47, or compile-time constants as on line 46. Note that if the `two` variable is not *final*, a compile-time error is generated (as it is no longer a constant).

In this example, we have multiple labels together, such as, lines 39-43. This section of code can be read as *if number is 1 or 3 or 5 or 7 or 9, then do the following*. So, for example, if the user types in 1, the `case` label on line 39 matches. This is known as the *entry point* of the `switch` statement. As there is no `break` statement on line 39, the code *falls through* to line 40, even though line 40 has a `case` label for 3. Again, line 40 has no `break` statement and the code *falls through* to line 41. In fact, the code keeps executing from the entry point until it reaches a `break` statement (or the end of the `switch` statement itself). This *fall-through* behavior is what enables the *if it's 1 or 3 or 5 or 7 or 9* type logic to work. If this *fall-through* behavior were not present, we would have to duplicate lines 44 to 45 for each of the `case` labels! Line 44 uses the `String` append to output that the number entered is odd, by appending `"is odd"` to the number – for example, `"7 is odd"`. Line 45 is the `break` statement that ensures we exit the `switch` block.

Line 46 is just to demonstrate that compile-time constants work for case labels. Line 47 shows that the case labels can be organized in a horizontal fashion if so desired. Remember, the use of indentation and spacing is just for human readability – the compiler just sees one long sequence of characters. So, lines 46 to 47 match for the numbers 2, 4, 6, 8, and 10. Again, the *fall-through* logic is used to keep the code concise. Lines 48 to 49 output that that number is even and break out of the switch block.

Line 50 is the default section, which caters to any numbers outside of the 1..10 range. Line 51 outputs that the number entered is out of range, and line 52 is the break statement. While the break statement is not strictly needed here (as default is at the bottom of the switch statement), it is considered good practice to include it.

Let us rewrite the code in *Figure 4.7* using a switch statement instead of a complicated if-else statement. Note that *Figure 4.6* is still relevant in declaring Scanner and the constants used; this is why we separated *Figure 4.6* (so we could use it with both the if and switch code). *Figure 4.11* represents *Figure 4.7* refactored using a switch statement.

```
22          int numDays=0;
23          switch(month){
24              case JAN:case MAR:case MAY:case JUL: case AUG:case OCT:case DEC:
25                  numDays=31;
26                  break;
27              case APR:case JUN:case SEP:case NOV:
28                  numDays=30;
29                  break;
30              case FEB:
31                  System.out.print("Enter year --> ");
32                  int year = sc.nextInt();
33      //          if( (A)        || (      B        &&      C)    ){
34                  if( (year % 400 == 0) || (year % 4 == 0 && !(year % 100 == 0)) ){
35                      numDays = 29; // leap year e.g. 2000, 2012, 2016
36                  }else{
37                      numDays = 28;   // 1900 (divisible by 100)
38                  }
39                  break;
40              default:
41                  System.out.println("Invalid month: "+month);
42                  break;
43
44          }
45          if(numDays > 0){
46              System.out.println("Number of days is: "+numDays);
47          }
```

Figure 4.11 – Refactoring an if statement with a switch statement

In the preceding figure, we can see the `switch` statement starts on line 23. The first group of `case` labels is on line 24 and the second group is on line 27. February, the odd one out, has a `case` label to itself (line 30). Finally, the `default` label is on line 40. Personally speaking, I find the use of `switch` in this example preferable due to the absence of the multiple logical OR expressions required in *Figure 4.7* (lines 21 to 22 and 24).

Now that we have covered valid `switch` statements, let us examine, in *Figure 4.12*, a few scenarios where compiler errors can arise.

```
58          byte b = 3;
59          switch(b){
60              case 127: case -128:
61                  System.out.println("ok");
62                  break;
63              case 128:
64              case 12:
65              case 12:
66          }
```

Figure 4.12 – Some switch compiler errors

In the preceding figure, we are switching on a `byte` variable, b. Recall that the valid `byte` range is -128 to +127. Line 60 demonstrates that the minimum and maximum values are fine. Line 63 shows that, as 128 is out of range for our `byte` type b, the `case` labels that are out of range of the `switch` variable cause a compiler error. Line 64 was fine until line 65 used the same `case` label – `case` label duplicates are not allowed.

We will finish our discussion on `switch` by discussing `switch` expressions.

## switch expressions

Like all expressions, `switch` expressions evaluate to a single value and, therefore, enable us to return values. All the `switch` examples so far have been `switch` *statements*, which return nothing. Note that in a `switch` expression, `break` statements are not allowed.

On the other hand, `switch` *expressions* return something – either implicitly or explicitly (using `yield`). We will explain `yield` shortly, but note that `yield` cannot be used in a `switch` statement (as they do not return anything). In addition, `switch` statements can *fall through*, whereas `switch` expressions do not. These differences are encapsulated in *Table 4.1*.

| | break | Returns a value | yield | Fall through | New case label | Regular case label |
|---|---|---|---|---|---|---|
| switch statement | Yes | No | No | Yes | Yes | Yes |
| switch expression | No | Yes | Yes | No | Yes | Yes |

Table 4.1 – Comparison of switch statements versus switch expressions

Let us look at some example code to demonstrate the differences. *Figure 4.13* is the traditional switch statement.

```
16      int nLetters=0;
17      String name="Jane";
18      switch(name){
19          case "Jane":
20          case "Sean":
21          case "Alan":
22          case "Paul":
23              nLetters = 4;
24              break;
25          case "Janet":
26          case "Susan":
27              nLetters = 5;
28              break;
29          case "Maaike":
30          case "Alison":
31          case "Miriam":
32              nLetters = 6;
33              break;
34          default:
35              System.out.println("Unrecognized name: "+name);
36              nLetters = -1;
37              break;
38      }
39      System.out.println(nLetters);
```

Figure 4.13 – A traditional switch statement

In the preceding figure, we are switching on the String variable, name. As it is initialized to "Jane", line 19 is true and line 23 sets nLetters to 4 (the number of letters in "Jane"). The break statement on line 24 ensures that there is no fall-through to line 27. Line 39 outputs 4 to the screen.

Notice that the code is quite verbose and requires the correct use of the break statement to prevent fall through. Plus, these break statements are tedious to write and easy to forget. *Figure 4.14* represents *Figure 4.13* written using a switch expression.

```
41        nLetters = switch(name){
42            case "Jane", "Sean", "Alan", "Paul" -> 4;
43            case "Janet", "Susan" -> 5;
44            case "Maaike", "Alison" , "Miriam" -> 6;
45            default -> {
46                System.out.println("Unrecognized name: "+name);
47                yield -1; // 'nLetters' initialized to -1
48            }
49        };
50        System.out.println(nLetters);
```

Figure 4.14 – A switch expression

The preceding figure shows the new case label where the labels are comma-delimited and an arrow token separates the labels from the expression (or code block). There is no break statement required anywhere as there is no fall-through behavior to worry about. As name is still "Jane" (from *Figure 4.13*, line 17), line 42 is executed, which initializes/returns 4 into nLetters. Thus, line 50 outputs 4. Note that the list of case labels in a switch expression must be exhaustive. In almost all cases, this means that a default clause is required. The default clause in this example executes a code block (lines 45-48), where an error is output to the screen and using the yield keyword, nLetters is initialized to (an error value of) -1.

We can omit the need for the nLetters variable by returning the expression value straight into the System.out.println() statement. *Figure 4.15* demonstrates this.

```
53        System.out.println(switch(name){
54            case "Jane", "Sean", "Alan", "Paul" -> 4;
55            case "Janet", "Susan" -> 5;
56            case "Maaike", "Alison" , "Miriam" -> 6;
57            default -> "Unrecognized name: "+name;
58        });
```

Figure 4.15 – A switch expression returning straight to System.out.println()

In the preceding figure, there is no variable used to store the result of the switch expression. This makes the code even more concise. The result of the switch expression is returned straight into the System.out.println() statement. Again, 4 is output to the screen.

## The yield keyword

*Figure 4.14* and *Figure 4.15* were simple `switch` expressions, where (for the most part), to the right of the arrow token was the value to be returned. However, instead of simply returning a value, what if you wished to execute a code block? This is where `yield` is used. *Figure 4.16* shows the use of `yield` in a `switch` expression.

```
60      nLetters = switch(name){
61          case "Jane", "Sean", "Alan", "Paul" -> {
62              System.out.println("There are 4 letters in: " + name);
63              yield 4;
64          }
65          case "Janet", "Susan" -> {
66              System.out.println("There are 5 letters in: "+name);
67              yield 5;
68          }
69          case "Maaike", "Alison" , "Miriam" -> {
70              System.out.println("There are 6 letters in: "+name);
71              yield 6;
72          }
73          default -> {
74              System.out.println("Unrecognized name: "+name);
75              yield -1;
76          }
77      };
78      System.out.println(nLetters);
```

Figure 4.16 – A switch expression using yield

The preceding figure highlights the fact that, if you need to execute more than one statement in a `switch` expression, you must provide a code block. This is shown with the curly braces for lines 61-64, 65-68, 69-72 and 73-76. To return an expression result from a code block we use `yield`. This is what is done on lines 63, 67, 71 and 75, where 4, 5, 6 and –1 are returned, respectively. As name is still `"Jane"`, line 63 returns 4 from the `switch` expression, initializing nLetters to 4. Therefore, line 78 outputs 4.

To aid flexibility, you can, up to a point, mix the syntaxes. In other words, regular `case` labels can be used in `switch` expressions, and the new `case` labels syntax can be used in `switch` statements. However, as stated earlier, `break` only appears in `switch` *statements* and `yield` only appears (if required) in switch *expressions*. *Figure 4.17* is a refactor of the verbose `switch` statement in *Figure 4.13*, where the new `case` labels are used in a `switch` statement.

```
82        switch(name){
83            case "Jane", "Sean", "Alan", "Paul" -> nLetters = 4;
84            case "Janet", "Susan" -> nLetters = 5;
85            case "Maaike", "Alison" , "Miriam" -> nLetters = 6;
86            default -> {
87                System.out.println("Unrecognized name: "+name);
88                nLetters = -1;
89            }
90        }
91        System.out.println(nLetters);
```

Figure 4.17 – A switch statement using new case labels and an arrow token

In the preceding figure, the labels are comma-delimited and the arrow token is present. As before, on the right of the arrow token, we have the initialization of nLetters to the number of letters in the name. However, in contrast to *Figure 4.13*, as we are using the arrow token, no break statements are required. Note however that curly braces are required for a code block as per the default clause (lines 86-89).

We can also use the regular case labels with switch expressions. This is shown in *Figure 4.18*, which is a refactored version of *Figure 4.16*.

```
94        nLetters = switch(name){
95            case "Jane":
96            case "Sean":
97            case "Alan":
98            case "Paul":
99                System.out.println("There are 4 letters in: " + name);
100               yield 4;
101           case "Janet":
102           case "Susan":
103               System.out.println("There are 5 letters in: "+name);
104               yield 5;
105           case "Maaike":
106           case "Alison":
107           case "Miriam":
108               System.out.println("There are 6 letters in: "+name);
109               yield 6;
110           default:
111               System.out.println("Unrecognized name: "+name);
112               yield -1;
113       };
114       System.out.println(nLetters);
```

Figure 4.18 – A switch expression using old-style case labels

In the preceding figure, the old-style `case` labels are used. This means that the keyword `case` must precede each label. The curly braces for the code blocks can, however, be omitted. As it is a `switch` expression, where there is more than one statement to be executed when a match is found, we need to use `yield` to return the expression result. As the `name` variable has never been changed from `"Jane"` throughout all the examples, a match is made on line 95, resulting in line 99 outputting `"There are 4 letters in: Jane"` to the screen. The `yield` on line 100 returns 4, and thus, `nLetters` is initialized to 4. Finally, line 114 outputs 4 to the screen.

This completes our treatment of `switch` expressions and, indeed, `switch` statements in general. We will now put what we have learned into practice.

## Exercises

We finally have the coding capability to make decisions. Mesozoic Eden is going to be benefiting from this so much. Let's show off our newly acquired skills, shall we?

1.  We need to determine whether a dinosaur is a carnivore or herbivore. Write an `if` statement that prints whether a dinosaur is a carnivore or herbivore based on a `boolean` variable. This information is critical for feeding and care guidelines.

2.  Different species require different care strategies and exhibit unique behavior traits. Write a `switch` statement that prints a description of a dinosaur based on its species. This will help educate both the staff and park visitors.

3.  Some dinosaurs are tougher to handle than others. Write an `if` statement that checks whether a number of years of experience is enough experience to work with a certain type of dinosaur. This ensures the safety of both our dinosaurs and employees.

4.  We are working with beautiful but dangerous creatures. So, safety first. Write a program that prints a warning message if the park's safety rating falls below a certain threshold. We must always be alert to potential issues that could harm our staff, visitors, or dinosaurs.

5.  Proper housing is essential for the dinosaurs' well-being. Write a `switch` statement that assigns a dinosaur to a specific enclosure based on its size (XS, S, M, L, or XL).

6.  Proper nutrition is crucial for maintaining our dinosaurs' health. Write an `if` statement that determines the number of feeds a dinosaur requires per day based on its weight.

7.  It is important to delegate tasks properly to keep operations running smoothly. Create a program that assigns different duties to employees based on their job titles using a `switch` statement.

8.  The park is not open to day visitors 24/7. Write an `if` statement that checks whether the park is open for them based on the time. They are open for day visitors from 10 A.M. to 7 P.M. This helps in managing visitor expectations and staff schedules.

# Project – Task allocation system

The manager of Mesozoic Eden needs a systematic way of managing the team and ensuring all tasks are efficiently accomplished.

Design a simple program that assigns tasks to the Mesozoic Eden employees based on their roles (for example, feeding, cleaning, security, and tour guiding). The program should decide tasks based on time, the employee's role, and other factors, such as the park's safety rating.

This program would not only help streamline operations but also ensure the safety and satisfaction of our staff, visitors, and, most importantly, our dinosaurs!

# Summary

In this chapter, we started by explaining that Java uses block scope. A block is delimited by { }. A variable is visible from the point of declaration to the closing } of that block. As blocks (and therefore, scopes) can be nested, this means that a variable defined in a block is visible to any inner/nested blocks. The inverse is not true, however. A variable declared in an inner block is not visible in an outer block

Conditional statements enable us to make decisions and are based on the evaluation of a condition resulting in true or false. The `if` statement allows several branches to be evaluated. Once one branch evaluates to true and is executed, no other branch is evaluated. An `if` statement can be coded on its own without any `else if` or `else` clause. The `else if` and `else` clauses are optional. However, if an `else` clause is present, it must be the last clause. We saw how a complex `if` example can lead to code verbosity.

We briefly discussed packages and the `Scanner` class. The `Scanner` class resides in the `java.util` package and is very useful for retrieving keyboard input from the user.

We also discussed both `switch` statements and `switch` expressions. An expression can return a value but a statement cannot. We saw how `switch` statements can make complicated `if` statements more concise and elegant. The expression you `switch` on (typically, a variable) can be a primitive `byte`, `char`, `short`, or `int` type ; or a reference type. The `case` labels must be compile-time constants and must be in range for the `switch` variable. `switch` statements have a fall-through feature, which enables multiple `case` labels to use the same section of code without repetition. However, this fall-through behavior requires a `break` statement to exit the `switch` statement. This requires care, as `break` statements are easy to forget.

`switch` expressions can return a value. They have no fall-through logic so `break` statements are not required. This makes the code more concise and less error-prone. If you wish to execute a code block in a `switch` expression, use `yield` to return the value.

`switch` statements do not support `yield` (as they do not return anything), and `switch` expressions do not support `break` (as they must return something). However, both of the `case` labels, namely the old-style `case X:` and the newer style `case A, B, C ->`, can be used with either `switch` statements or `switch` expressions.

Now that we know how to make decisions, we will move on to iteration in the next chapter, where we will examine the Java structures that enable us to repeat statements.

# 5

# Understanding Iteration

In *Chapter 4*, we learned about scope and conditional statements in Java. Scope determines the visibility of identifiers – in other words, where you can use them. Java uses block scope, which is defined by curly braces, { }. Scopes can be nested but not vice versa.

We discussed variations of the `if` statement. Each of these statements evaluates a boolean condition, resulting in true or false. If true, then that branch is executed and no other branch is evaluated. If false, then the next branch is evaluated. Unless an else clause is present, it is possible that no branch at all will be executed.

For complex `if` statements, Java supports the more elegant `switch` structure. We examined `switch` statements, with their *fall-through* behavior, and the use of the `break` statement. In addition, we discussed `switch` expressions, where a value can be returned, and their use of `yield`.

Now that we understand conditional logic, let us examine iteration (looping). Looping constructs enable us to repeat statements and/or blocks of code a finite number of times while a boolean condition is true or while there are more entries in the array/collection. By the end of this chapter, you will be able to use Java's looping constructs.

In this chapter, we are going to cover the following main topics:

- `while` loops
- `do-while` loops
- `for` loops
- Enhanced `for` (`for-each`) loops
- `break` and `continue` statements

## Technical requirements

The code for this chapter can be found on GitHub at `https://github.com/PacktPublishing/Learn-Java-with-Projects/tree/main/ch5`.

# while loops

An important feature of any programming language is the ability to perform an action repeatedly. This is known as "looping". We may want to repeat a piece of code a finite number of times or until some condition is met; for example, the user typing in a value that signifies that the loop should terminate. In most cases, a boolean expression can be used to determine whether the loop continues or not.

A `while` loop is one such looping construct. It repeatedly executes a statement or a block of code as long as a boolean expression is true. As soon as the boolean expression is false, the loop exits, and the next statement after the `while` loop executes.

```
while (booleanExprIsTrue) {

    // do something

}
```

Figure 5.1 – The while loop syntax

In the preceding figure, we are assuming a block of code, hence the curly braces { }. You could, of course, omit the curly braces { } and the loop will just repeatedly execute one statement (which ends with a semi-colon). Interestingly, as the boolean expression could be false to begin with, the `while` loop may not execute at all. More formally, a `while` loop executes *zero* or more times. Let us look at some examples. *Figure 5.2* presents a simple `while` loop:

```
9     int x=1;
10
11    while (x <= 3){
12        System.out.println("Loop: "+x); // 1, 2, 3
13        x++;
14    }
15    System.out.println("Final x value is: "+x); // 4
```

Figure 5.2 – A simple while loop

On line 9 in the preceding figure, a local variable, x, is initialized to 1. Line 11 evaluates the boolean expression, x <= 3. As x is 1, the boolean expression is true and the loop executes. Line 12 outputs "Loop: 1" and line 13 increments x to 2. The } symbol on line 14 is reached and the loop condition (on line 11) is automatically rechecked to see whether it still holds. As x is 2 and 2 <= 3, the condition is true and we re-enter the loop. Line 12 outputs "Loop: 2" and line 13 increments x to 3. The end of the block is reached on line 14, and again, the loop continuation expression is re-evaluated. As the expression 3 <= 3 is true, the loop is executed again. Line 12 outputs "Loop: 3" and line 13 increments x to 4. Once again, the end of the code block is reached and the loop continuation expression is re-evaluated. As x is now 4 and as 4 `<=` 3 is false, the loop exits. This is shown by line 15 outputting `"Final x value is: 4"`.

Note that if, on line 9, x had been initialized to `11` (as opposed to `1`), then the initial boolean expression on line 11 would have been evaluated to false and the loop would never have been executed at all.

A `while` loop can be very useful when you do *not* know how many times the loop is going to iterate. For example, the loop continuation expression may be predicated on user input. *Figure 5.3* is one such loop.

```
19    int sum = 0;
20    boolean keepGoing=true;
21    while(keepGoing){
22        Scanner sc = new Scanner(System.in);
23        System.out.println("Enter a number (negative number to exit) --> ");
24        int n = sc.nextInt();
25        if(n < 0){
26            keepGoing = false;
27        } else{
28            sum = sum + n; // sum += n
29        }
30    }
31    System.out.println("Sum of numbers is: "+sum);
```

Figure 5.3 – A while loop that ends based on user input

In the preceding figure, an algorithm for summing up a sequence of positive, user-inputted numbers is presented. The loop will keep going, totaling up the numbers entered by the user, until a negative number is entered. This negative number is naturally, not part of the total. Let us discuss it in more detail.

Line 19 declares a local `int` variable, `sum`, and initializes it to `0`. Line 20 declares a local boolean variable, `keepGoing`, and sets it to true. The boolean expression on line 21 evaluates to true (due to line 20) and, as a result, the loop block executes. Line 22 declares our `Scanner` reference, `sc`, pointing at the keyboard. Line 23 prompts the user to enter a number while informing the user that any negative number terminates the loop. Line 24 uses the `Scanner` method, `nextInt()`, to get an integer (whole number) from the user. This number is stored in the local variable, n. Line 25 checks to see whether a negative number has been entered. If so, line 26 sets the `keepGoing` flag to false so that the loop will not execute again. If a non-negative integer was entered by the user, then the number entered, n, is added to the running total, `sum`.

Let us walk through an example. We will add the following numbers: 1, 2, and 3, totaling 6. This is what the screen output looks like:

```
Enter a number (negative number to exit) -->
1
```

```
Enter a number (negative number to exit) -->
2
Enter a number (negative number to exit) -->
3
Enter a number (negative number to exit) -->
-1
Sum of numbers is: 6
```

Let us examine what is happening in the code. The loop (line 21) is entered because the keepGoing boolean was set to true on line 20. We are then prompted for our first number (line 23). We type in 1, resulting in n being initialized to 1 on line 24. As n is 1, the if statement on line 25 is false and the else block (lines 27-29) is executed; setting sum to 1 (0 + 1).

The loop block end is reached (line 30) and the loop continuation expression is automatically re-evaluated (line 21). As keepGoing is still true, the loop continues. We are prompted for our second number; we enter 2 and sum is changed to 3 (1 + 2).

The loop block end is reached again and, as keepGoing is still true, the loop continues. We are prompted for our next number; we enter 3 and sum is changed to 6 (3 + 3).

Again, the loop block end is reached and, as keepGoing is still true, the loop continues. We are prompted for our next number. This time we enter -1. As n is now negative, the if statement on line 25 is true and keepGoing is set to false (line 26). Now, when the loop continuation expression is next evaluated, as keepGoing is false, the loop exits.

Lastly, line 31 outputs "Sum of numbers is: 6".

Now that we have covered the while loop, let us examine its close relative, the do-while loop.

## do-while loops

As we have seen with the while loop, the boolean loop continuation expression is at the start of the loop. Though similar to the while loop, the do-while loop is different in one critical aspect: in the do-while loop, the loop continuation expression is at the *end* of the loop. Thus, the do-while loop is executed at least *once*. More formally, a do-while loop executes *one* or more times.

*Figure 5.4* presents the syntax of the do-while loop.

```
do {

    // do something

} while (booleanExprIsTrue);
```

Figure 5.4 – The do-while loop syntax

As can be seen in the preceding figure, the loop continuation expression is at the end of the loop, after one loop iteration. Also note the semi-colon, ; after ).

*Figure 5.5* presents a do-while version of the while loop in *Figure 5.2.*

```
19          int sum = 0;
20          boolean keepGoing=true;
21          do {
22              Scanner sc = new Scanner(System.in);
23              System.out.println("Enter a number (negative number to exit) --> ");
24              int n = sc.nextInt();
25              if(n < 0){
26                  keepGoing = false;
27              } else{
28                  sum = sum + n; // sum += n
29              }
30          } while(keepGoing);
31          System.out.println("Sum of numbers is: "+sum);
```

Figure 5.5 – A do-while loop that ends based on user input

In the preceding figure, the only differences with *Figure 5.2* are lines 21 and 30. On line 21, we simply enter the loop as, unlike in the while loop, there is no condition preventing us from doing so. Line 30 checks to see whether it is okay to re-enter the loop. The rest of the code is the same and the execution is the same.

While (pardon the pun) the two examples given have no material difference in the outcome, let us examine a situation where using a while loop as opposed to a do-while loop is preferable.

## while versus do-while

As already stated, a do-while loop executes at least once, whereas a while loop may not execute at all. This can be very useful in certain situations. Let us look at one such example. *Figure 5.6* presents a while loop that checks to see whether a person is of the legal age to purchase alcohol (which is 18 in Ireland).

```
49          Scanner sc = new Scanner(System.in);
50          System.out.println("Please enter your age -- > ");
51          int age = sc.nextInt();
52          while(age >= 18){
53              // purchase alcohol...
54              System.out.println("As you are "+age+" years of age, " +
55                      "you can purchase alcohol.");
56
57              System.out.println("Please enter your age -- > ");
58              age = sc.nextInt();
59          }
```

Figure 5.6 – A while loop to prevent underage purchasing of alcohol

In the preceding figure, line 49 declares the Scanner and points it at the keyboard so we can get user input. Line 50 prompts the user to enter their age. Line 51 takes in the user input and stores it in a local variable, namely age. Line 52 is important. The condition prevents the loop from being executed with an invalid age. The loop itself is trivial and simply outputs a message that includes the age so we can validate that the loop is executing properly.

Lines 57 to 58 are very important in that they enable us to prompt and get a new age from the user. The code deliberately overwrites the age variable. If we did not, then age would remain as the first value entered by the user and we would have an infinite loop. So, the first age is entered before the while loop is entered and every other age is entered at the end of the loop. This is a common pattern in while loops. The condition on line 52 prevents any age inputthat is < 18, from entering the loop.

Here is the first run of the code in *Figure 5.6*:

```
Please enter your age -- >
21
As you are 21 years of age, you can purchase alcohol.
Please enter your age -- >
12
```

The first two lines: the prompt and user input, are before the while loop and, as 21 >= 18, we enter the loop. The message As you are 21 years of age, you can purchase alcohol. is perfectly correct. The last two lines: repeating the prompt and user input, are from the bottom of the loop. We have entered 12, which causes the while loop to terminate.

The following is the output if, when prompted for the first age, we enter 12:

```
Please enter your age -- >
12
Process finished with exit code 0
```

Importantly, the message about purchasing alcohol does *not* appear.

Now, let us look at the do-while version. *Figure 5.7* presents the do-while version of the while loop in *Figure 5.6*.

```
49              Scanner sc = new Scanner(System.in);
50              System.out.println("Please enter your age -- > ");
51              int age = sc.nextInt();
52              do{
53                  // purchase alcohol...
54                  System.out.println("As you are "+age+" years of age, " +
55                          "you can purchase alcohol.");
56
57                  System.out.println("Please enter your age -- > ");
58                  age = sc.nextInt();
59              }while (age >= 18);
```

Figure 5.7 – A do-while loop to prevent underage purchasing of alcohol

In the interests of having as much of the code as similar as possible, lines 49 to 51 are untouched. Lines 52 and 59 are all that have changed. The condition is now at the end of the loop, after one iteration of the loop. This has implications when we start with an age of 12, as can be seen in the output:

```
Please enter your age -- >
12
As you are 12 years of age, you can purchase alcohol.
Please enter your age -- >
12
Process finished with exit code 0
```

The third line in the output is the issue. Obviously, 12 is too young to buy alcohol but the do-while loop would require an if statement to protect its code, whereas the while loop provides that protection automatically. Therefore, in this example, there is a material advantage in using the while loop over the do-while loop.

Now that we have covered while and do-while loops, let us now discuss for loops.

# for loops

The for loop comes in two styles: the *traditional* for loop and the *enhanced* for loop. The enhanced for loop is also known as the for-each loop and is specifically designed to work with arrays and collections. We will start by examining the traditional for loop.

## Traditional for loop

This type of for loop is extremely useful when you know how many iterations you wish to perform beforehand. Its syntax is detailed in *Figure 5.8*.

```
for (initialization; booleanExpression; incr/decr) {

    // do something

}
```

Figure 5.8 – The traditional for loop

The code block in the preceding figure is optional. We could simply control one statement, such as System.out.println("Looping");, and omit { }. The for header is the section inside (). It consists of three parts, delimited by semi-colons:

- **Initialization section**: This is where you initialize your loop control variables. The variables declared here have the scope of the loop block *only*. Traditionally, the variables declared here are named i, j, k, and so forth.

- **Boolean expression**: This determines whether the loop should be executed and is checked before every iteration, including the first one. Sound familiar? Yes, you are correct, a while loop and a traditional for loop are interchangeable.

- **Increment/decrement section**: This is where you increment/decrement your loop control variables (declared in the initialization section) so that the loop terminates.

We must understand the order of execution of the loop. In other words, which part is executed and when. *Figure 5.9*, which presents a simple for loop, will help in this regard.

```java
11    // for(init; booleanExpr; incr/decr)
12    for(int i=1; i<=3; i++){
13        System.out.println(i); // 1,2,3
14    }
```

Figure 5.9 – A simple traditional for loop

In this figure, the order of execution of the code is represented in numerical order as follows:

1. **Initialization section**: The loop control variable, i, is declared and initialized to 1.

2. **Boolean expression**: Evaluate the boolean expression to see whether it is okay to execute the loop. As 1 <= 3, it is okay to enter the loop.

3. **Execute the loop block**: This outputs 1 to the screen.

4. **Increment/Decrement section**: i is incremented (by 1) from 1 to 2 and then execution pops over to the boolean expression.

5. **Evaluate the boolean expression**: As 2 <= 3, the loop is executed.

6. **Execute the loop block**: This outputs 2 to the screen.

7. **Increment i from 2 to 3**: and then pop over to the boolean expression.

8. **Evaluate the boolean expression**: As 3 <= 3, the loop is executed.

9. **Execute the loop block**: This outputs 3 to the screen.

10. **Increment i from 3 to 4**: and then pop over to the boolean expression.

11. **Evaluate the boolean expression**: As 4 is not <= 3, the loop exits.

In summary, the initialization section is executed only once, at the start of the loop. The boolean expression is evaluated and, assuming it is true, the loop body is executed, followed by the increment/decrement section. The boolean expression is again evaluated and, again, assuming it is true, the loop body is executed, followed by the increment/decrement section. This repetition of the execution of the loop body followed by the increment/decrement section continues until the boolean expression fails and the loop exits.

*Figure 5.10* presents a for loop that goes from 3 down to 1 in decrements of 1:

```
16      for(int i=3; i>=1; i--){
17          System.out.println(i); // 3,2,1
18      }
```

Figure 5.10 – A simple for loop that operates in descending order

In the preceding figure, we initialize i to 3 and check the boolean expression. As 3 >= 1, we enter the loop and output 3. We then decrement i by 1 to 2 and check the boolean expression again. As 2 >= 1, we output 2 and then decrement i to 1. As the boolean expression is still true; we output 1 and i is decremented to 0. At this point, as i is 0, the boolean expression is false and the loop terminates.

*Figure 5.11* presents some code samples enabling us to discuss this looping construct further.

```
20      for(int i=1; i<=3; i++);{
21          System.out.println("Looping"); // only appears once!
22      }
23
24      for(int i=10; i<=50; i+=10){
25          System.out.println(i); // 10, 20, 30, 40, 50
26      }
27      System.out.println(i); // i is out of scope
28
29      for(int i=0, j=0; i<1 && j<1; i++, j++){
30          System.out.println(i + " " + j); // 0 0
31      }
```

Figure 5.11 – Additional traditional for loops

In the first loop of the preceding figure (lines 20-22), the important thing to notice is the ; symbol, which is just after the ) symbol of the `for` header. This loop controls an empty statement! Even though the indentation may suggest otherwise, the block of code that follows has nothing to do with the loop at all, and as a result, `"Looping"` appears only once in the output. In effect, the loop iterates three times, doing nothing each time. The block of code surrounding line 21 is not predicated on any condition and just executes once (as normal).

In the second loop (lines 24-26), the loop control variable, i, starts out at 10 and goes up in increments of 10 until it reaches 60, at which point the loop terminates. Each valid value of i is output to the screen – in other words, 10, 20, 30, 40, and 50. Note that line 27 does *not* compile, as each of the i variables declared in the preceding loops only have the scope of their individual loop. For example, the i variable declared on line 20 is only available until line 22; similarly, the i variable declared on line 24 is only available until line 26. Note: obviously, line 27 must be commented out for the code to compile and run.

The last loop (lines 29-31) shows that we can declare multiple loop control variables and use them throughout the loop. In this loop, we declare i and j and initialize them both to 0. The boolean expression is true as both i < 1 and j < 1 are true (true && true == true). Thus, we execute the loop and output 0 and 0. Both i and j are then incremented to 1. The loop condition fails and the loop terminates.

While arrays will be discussed in detail in *Chapter 6*, `for` loops are such a natural fit for arrays that we have inserted some examples here as well. Let us first examine how a traditional `for` loop can be used to process an array.

## Processing an array

Any `for` loop is useful for iterating over an array. An array is simply an area of memory set aside and given an identifier name for ease of reference. An array consists of elements which are organized in consecutive memory locations – in other words, the array elements are right beside each other in memory. This makes it easy to process arrays using loops.

Each element in an array is accessed by an index. Crucially, array indices start at 0 and go up in steps of 1. Therefore, the last valid index is the size of the array minus one. For example, an array of size 5 has valid indices of 0, 1, 2, 3, and 4. *Figure 5.12* is a loop processing an array.

```
33    int[] ia = {1,2,3};
34    for(int i=0; i<ia.length; i++){
35        System.out.println(ia[i]); // 1, 2, 3
36    }
```

Figure 5.12 – Processing an array using a traditional for loop

In this figure, line 33 declares an `int` array containing the values 1, 2, and 3 in indices 0, 1, and 2, respectively. The length of the array, accessible using the `length` property, is 3. The `for` loop (lines 34-35) processes the array, outputting each location one by one. Thus, when i is 0, `ia[0]` outputs 1 to the screen; when i is 1, `ia[1]` outputs 2, and when i is 2, `ia[2]` outputs 3.

Now that we have covered the traditional `for` loop, let us examine the enhanced `for` loop.

## Enhanced for loop

As stated earlier, the enhanced `for` loop, also known as the `for-each` loop, is ideal for processing arrays and/or collections. We will discuss collections is detail in *Chapter 13*. For the moment, just imagine a collection as a *list* of items. The enhanced `for` loop enables you to iterate over the list one element at a time. The syntax of the enhanced `for` loop is outlined in *Figure 5.13*.

```
for (dataType variableName : array or collection){

    // do something

}
```

Figure 5.13 – Enhanced for loop syntax

In the preceding figure, we can see that a variable is declared. The variables type matches the type of array/collection. For example, if the array is an array of `String`, then `String` is the data type of the variable. The variable name is of course, up to us. Again, the code block is optional.

Let us look at an example to help explain further. *Figure 5.14* is an enhanced `for` loop version of the traditional `for` loop presented in *Figure 5.12*.

```
38          int[] ia = {1,2,3};
39          for(int n:ia){
40              System.out.println(n); // 1, 2, 3
41          }
```

Figure 5.14 – Processing an array using an enhanced for loop

In this figure, line 38 reads as follows: *for each int n in (the array) ia.* Thus, on the first iteration, n is 1; on the second iteration, n is 2, and on the last iteration, n is 3. In the enhanced `for` loop, we do not have to keep track of a loop control variable ourselves. While this is useful, be aware that you are limited to starting at the beginning of the array/collection and progressing one element at a time, until you reach the end. With the traditional `for` loop, none of these restrictions apply.

However, with the traditional `for` loop, if you code the increment/decrement section incorrectly, you could end up in an infinite loop. This is not possible in the enhanced `for` version.

## Nested loops

Loops can, of course, be nested. In other words, loops can be coded within other loops. *Figure 5.15* presents one such example.

```
12          int[] data = {9, 3, 5, 7};
13
14          System.out.println("[]\t[n]\tHistogram");
15          for (int i=0; i<data.length; i++){
16              System.out.print(i + "\t" + data[i] + "\t");
17              for(int j=1; j<=data[i]; j++) { // write out data[i] stars
18                  System.out.print("*");        // print() not println()
19              }
20              System.out.println();             // go onto next line
21          }
```

Figure 5.15 – Nested for loops

The output from this program is presented in *Figure 5.16*. In the preceding figure, we are representing an array of `int` values, namely `data`, as a histogram (represented as a row of stars). The array is declared on line 12. Line 14 outputs a line of text so the output from the program is easier to interpret. The output has three columns: the current array index, the value in the `data` array at that index, and the histogram. Note that the output is tab-delimited. This is achieved by the use of the `\t` escape sequence.

**Escape sequences**

An escape sequence is a character preceded by a backslash. For example, \t is a valid escape sequence. When the compiler sees \, it peeks ahead at the next character and checks to see whether the two characters together form a valid escape sequence. Popular escape sequences are as follows:

\t: Insert a tab at this point in the text

\b: Insert a backspace at this point in the text

\n: Insert a newline at this point in the text

\": Insert a double quote at this point in the text

\\: Insert a backslash at this point in the text

They can be very useful in certain situations. For example, if we wanted to output the text *My name is "Alan"* (including the double quotes) to the screen, we would say:

```
System.out.println("My name is \"Alan\"");
```

If we did not escape the double quote before the A in Alan (in other words, if we tried System.out.println("My name is "Alan"");), then the double quote before the A would have been matched with the first " at the start of the string. This would have resulted in a compiler error with the A in Alan.

By escaping the double quote before the A in Alan, the compiler no longer treats that double quote as an end-of-string double quote and instead inserts " into the string to be output. The same happens to the double quote after the n in Alan–it is also escaped and therefore ignored as an end-of-string double quote and inserted into the string to be output. The double quote just before the ) is not escaped however, and is used to match the opening double quote for the string, namely the one just after the (.

The outer loop (lines 15-21) loops through the data array. As the array has 4 elements, the valid indices are 0, 1, 2, and 3. These are the values that the i loop control variable, declared on line 15, will represent. Line 16 outputs two of the columns: the current array index and the value at that index in the data array. For example, when i is 0, data[0] is 9, so "0\t9\t" is output; when i is 1, data[1] is 3, so "1\t3\t" is output, and so forth.

The inner loop (lines 17-19) outputs the actual histogram as a horizontal row of stars. The inner loop control variable, j, goes from 1 to the value of data[i]. So, for example, if i is 0, data[i] is 9; therefore, j goes from 1 to 9, outputting a star each time. Note that the print() method is used as opposed to println() – this is because println() automatically brings you on to the next line, whereas print() does not. As we want the stars to output horizontally, print() is exactly what we need. When we have our row of stars output, we execute System.out.println() (line 20), which brings us on to the next line.

*Figure 5.16* represents the output from the code in *Figure 5.15*.

```
[]    [n]  Histogram
0     9    ********
1     3    ***
2     5    *****
3     7    *******
```

Figure 5.16 – Output from the code in Figure 5.15

In this figure, you can see that the first column is the array index. The second column is the value in the data array at that index, and the third column is the histogram of stars based on the second column. So, for example, when i is 2, data[2] is 5, and we output a histogram of 5 stars.

Now that we understand loops, we will move on to two keywords that are particularly relevant to loops, namely break and continue.

# break and continue statements

Both the break and continue statements can be used in loops but with very different semantics. In the code examples presented, nested loops will be used to contrast the labeled versions with the non-labeled versions. We will start with the break statement.

## break statements

We have already encountered break in switch statements. When used in a loop, the loop exits immediately. *Figure 5.17* presents nested for loops with a break in the inner loop.

```
13    System.out.println("i, j");
14    for (int i = 1; i <= 3; i++) {
15        for (int j = 1; j <= 5; j++) {
16            if (j == 3) {
17                break; // breaks out of inner loop
18            }
19            System.out.println(i + ", " + j);
20        }
21    }
```

Figure 5.17 – Showing break inside a loop

In this figure, the outer loop, controlled by i, loops from 1 to 3 in steps of 1. The inner loop, controlled by j, loops from 1 to 5 in steps of 1.

The if statement on line 16 becomes true when j is 3. At this point, the break statement on line 17 is executed. A break without a label exits the nearest enclosing loop. In other words, the break on line 17 refers to the loop on line 15 (controlled by j). As there is no code between the closing } of both loops (lines 20 and 21), when break is executed in this program, the next line of code executed is the } for the outer loop (line 21). Automatically, the next iteration of the outer loop, i++ (line 14), starts. In effect, there is never any j value of 3 or higher in the output because, when j is 3, we break out of the inner loop and start with the next value of i. The output reflects this:

```
i, j
1, 1
1, 2
2, 1
2, 2
3, 1
3, 2
```

Without any break statement, in other words, if we had commented out lines 16 to 18, the output would be as follows (note the values of j go from 1 to 5):

```
i, j
1, 1
1, 2
1, 3
1, 4
1, 5
2, 1
2, 2
2, 3
2, 4
2, 5
3, 1
3, 2
3, 3
3, 4
3, 5
```

Before we discuss the labeled break, we will quickly discuss the label itself.

## Label

A label is a case-sensitive identifier followed by a colon that immediately precedes the loop being identified. For example, the following code defines a valid label, OUTER, for the loop controlled by i:

```
OUTER:
for (int i = 1; i <= 3; i++) {
    for (int j = 1; j <= 5; j++) {
```

Now let us look at the labeled break itself.

## Labeled break

A break that uses a label exits the loop identified by that label. The labeled break statement must be in the scope of the loop identified. In other words, you cannot break to a loop somewhere else in the code, completely unrelated to the current scope. *Figure 5.18* is closely related to the code in *Figure 5.17*, except this time, a label and a labeled break are used.

```
25    System.out.println("i, j"); // placed BEFORE label!!
26    OUTERLOOP:
27    for (int i = 1; i <= 3; i++) {
28        for (int j = 1; j <= 5; j++) {
29            if (j == 3) {
30                break OUTERLOOP;// case sensitive
31            }
32            System.out.println(i + ", " + j);
33        }
34    }
35    System.out.println("here");
```

Figure 5.18 – Labeled break

In the preceding figure, we have labeled, on line 26, the outer loop as OUTERLOOP. Yes, it took a while to come up with that identifier! Note that it is a compiler error to have any code between the label and the loop. That is why line 25 precedes the label.

The loop control variables, i and j, behave as before; i goes from 1 to 3 in steps of 1, and within each step of i, j goes from 1 to 5 in steps of 1. This time, however, when j is 3 in the inner loop, rather than breaking out of the inner loop, we are breaking out of the outer loop. After the labeled break (line 30) is executed, there are no more iterations of i and the next line executed is System.out. println("here") on line 35. As a result, the output is as follows:

```
i, j
1, 1
```

```
1, 2
here
```

As can be seen, once j reaches 3, the outer loop exits, and here is output.

Now, let us look at continue statements.

## continue statements

A continue statement can only occur inside a loop. When executed, continue says "skip to the *next* iteration" of the loop. Any other statements remaining in the current iteration are bypassed. There is a labeled version also. We will examine the unlabeled version first. *Figure 5.19* presents an example of continue.

```
32    System.out.println("i, j");
33    for (int i = 1; i <= 3; i++) {
34        for (int j = 1; j <= 5; j++) {
35            if (j == 3) {
36                continue; // next iteration
37            }
38            System.out.println(i + ", " + j);
39        }
40    }
```

Figure 5.19 – A continue example

In the preceding figure, the nested loops are the same as before – the outer loop iterates from 1 to 3; within that, the inner loop iterates from 1 to 5. On this occasion, when j is 3, we execute continue. What that means is that we jump to the end of the loop and the next statement executed is j++. This means that as line 38 is skipped, j with a value of 3 will never be output. The output demonstrates this:

```
i, j
1, 1
1, 2
1, 4
1, 5
2, 1
2, 2
2, 4
2, 5
3, 1
3, 2
3, 4
3, 5
```

As can be seen, j with a value of 3 is never output. Now, let us examine the labeled continue.

## labeled continue

A continue that uses a label continues the next iteration of the loop identified by that label. All other statements are bypassed. As with the labeled break, the labeled continue must be in the scope of the loop identified. *Figure 5.20* is closely related to the code in *Figure 5.19*, except this time, a label and a labeled continue are used.

```
28          System.out.println("i, j\n===="); // placed BEFORE label!!
29          OUTERLOOP:
30          for (int i = 1; i <= 3; i++) {
31              for (int j = 1; j <= 5; j++) {
32                  if (j == 3) {
33                      continue OUTERLOOP;// continues with OUTERLOOP
34                  }
35                  System.out.println(i + ", " + j);
36              }
37          }
```

Figure 5.20 – A labeled continue example

In this figure, line 29 gives the OUTERLOOP label to the outer loop starting on line 30. Now, when j is 3 and continue OUTERLOOP executes, the next line to code to execute is i++. Thus, every time j reaches 3, we start with the next value of i. So, there are no values of j greater than 2 output, as can be seen in the output:

```
i, j
1, 1
1, 2
2, 1
2, 2
3, 1
3, 2
```

That completes our explanations on the various looping constructs and the break and continue statements used with them. Let us now put that knowledge into practice to reinforce the concepts.

# Exercises

Now that we can iterate, it's time to do some similar tasks to the chapters before but iterate for multiple values!

Be creative on how to implement these ones and add context where you need it. As always, there's not one right answer:

1.  All of our dinosaurs are unique. Okay, we cloned their DNA, but still. Let's say they have unique personalities. That's why the IDs of all our dinosaurs are unique too: they are called `dino1`, `dino2`, `dino3`, and so on. Write a `for` loop that prints out the IDs of the first 100 dinosaurs in the park.

2.  Some of our dinosaurs have large appetites! Write a `do-while` loop that continues to feed a dinosaur until it is no longer hungry.

3.  We all love the thrill of waiting for the park to open. Use a `while` loop to print out a countdown to the park's opening time.

4.  For planning purposes, it's essential to know the total weight of all dinosaurs in a specific enclosure. Write a `for` loop that calculates this.

5.  Ticket selling can get hectic during the peak season. Write a `while` loop that simulates the park's ticket-selling process until tickets are sold out.

6.  Security is our topmost priority. Use a `do-while` loop to simulate a security check process that continues until all security measures are met.

# Project – Dino meal planner

Dinosaurs are not easy animals to keep. This is very advanced pet ownership. The right nutrition is difficult to manage, but it's vital to their health and well-being. Therefore, you are asked to create a system that can manage the feeding schedule of our various dinosaur residents.

The project's primary goal is to create a program that calculates the meal portions and feeding times for each dinosaur. Since we haven't covered arrays yet, we'll focus on a single dinosaur for now.

Here's how we can do it:

1.  Start by declaring a variable to hold the current time; let's say it's an integer and it goes from 0 (midnight) to 23 (last hour of the day).

2.  Define variables for each dinosaur species with different feeding times. For example, T-Rex could eat at 8 (morning), 14 (afternoon), and 20 (evening), while the Brachiosaurus could eat at 7 (morning), 11 (mid-morning), 15 (afternoon), and 19 (evening).

3. Next, establish a conditional statement (such as an `if-else` block) to check whether it's feeding time for each species, comparing the current time with their feeding times.

4. Now, let's define the feeding portions for our dinosaurs. We can assume that each species requires a different amount of food, depending on their sizes. For instance, the T-Rex requires 100 kg of food per meal, while the Brachiosaurus requires 250 kg of food per meal.

5. Similarly, using an `if-else` block, check which species you are dealing with and assign the food portions accordingly.

6. Finally, print the result. For instance, `"It's 8:00 - Feeding time for T-Rex with 100kg of food"`.

7. Wrap all of the preceding information inside a loop that runs from `0` to `23`, simulating the 24 hours in a day.

On behalf of the hungry dinosaurs in the park: thank you so much for putting your Java skills to use!

## Summary

In this chapter, we discussed how Java implements iteration (looping). We started with the `while` loop, which, because the condition is at the start of the loop, will execute zero or more times. In contrast, the `do-while` loop, where the condition is at the end of the loop, will execute one or more times. The `while` and `do-while` loops are very useful when you do not know how many times a loop will iterate.

In contrast, the traditional `for` loop is extremely useful when you do know how often you want a loop executed. The traditional `for` loop's header consists of three parts: the initialization section, the boolean expression, and the increment/decrement section. Thus, we can iterate a discrete number of times. This makes the traditional `for` loop ideal for processing arrays.

The enhanced `for` (`for-each`) loop is even more suitable for processing arrays (and collections), provided you are not interested in the current loop iteration index. Being concise, succinct, and easy to write, it is a more elegant `for` loop.

In effect, if you need to loop a specific number of times, use the traditional `for` loop. If you need to process an array/collection from the beginning all the way through to the end, with no concern for the loop index, use the enhanced `for` version.

All loops can, of course, be nested, and we looked at one such example. We defined a label as a case-sensitive identifier followed by a colon that immediately precedes a loop.

Nested loops and labels prepared us for our discussion regarding the `break` and `continue` keywords. Where `break` can also be used in a `switch` statement, `continue` can only be used inside loops. There are labeled and non-labeled versions of both. Regarding `break`, the unlabeled version exits the current loop, whereas the labeled version exits the identified loop. With regard to `continue`, the unlabeled version continues with the next iteration of the current loop, whereas the labeled version continues with the next iteration of the identified loop.

That completes our discussion on iteration. In this chapter, we touched upon arrays. Moving on to our next chapter, *Chapter 6*, we will cover arrays in detail.

# 6

# Working with Arrays

Arrays are an essential data structure that you can use to store multiple values in one variable. Mastering arrays will not only make your code more organized and efficient but also open the door to more advanced programming techniques. Once you add arrays to the mix, you can level up the data structures of your applications.

In this chapter, we'll explore arrays and equip you with the skills needed to effectively work with this fundamental data structure. You'll learn how to create, manipulate, and iterate over arrays to solve a wide range of programming challenges.

Here's an overview of what we'll cover in this chapter:

- What arrays are and how to use them
- Declaring and initializing arrays
- Accessing array elements
- Getting the length of an array and understanding the bounds
- Different ways to loop through arrays and process their elements
- Working with multidimensional arrays
- Performing common operations with arrays using the `Arrays` class

By the end of this chapter, you'll have a solid foundation in working with arrays, enabling you to tackle more complex programming tasks with confidence. So, let's dive in!

## Technical requirements

The code for this chapter can be found on GitHub at `https://github.com/PacktPublishing/Learn-Java-with-Projects/tree/main/ch6`.

# Arrays – what, when, and why?

So far, we've only seen single values, such as `int`, `double`, and `String`. Imagine we want to calculate an average result. That would look something like this:

```
double result1 = 7.0;
double result2 = 8.6;
double result3 = 9.0;

double total = result1 + result2 + result3;
double average = total / 3;
System.out.println(average);
```

This code isn't very scalable. If we were to add a fourth result, we would need to do three things in order to make this work:

- Declare and initialize a fourth variable

- Add this fourth variable to the total

- Divide by 4 instead of 3

This is a hassle, and it is error-prone. If we knew arrays, we could alter this by only changing one element of our code. Let's see what arrays are. Then, we will rewrite this example once we get to iterate over arrays.

---

**Java can't do basic math?!**

If you were to run the previous code snippet, you'd see something interesting. If I asked you to calculate the average, you'd say 8.2, and you would be right. If we ask Java to do it, it says 8.200000000000001.

You may wonder whether there is any use in learning Java at all if it can't do basic calculations. This is not just a Java problem; this is a general computer problem. It has to translate decimal numbers into binary numbers – much like you can't express ⅓ in decimal numbers exactly (0.33333).

---

## Arrays explained

Alright, so **arrays** can be a solution to structure our code better in specific situations. But what are they? An array is a data structure that can store a fixed-size, ordered collection of elements of the same data type. The elements in an array are stored in contiguous memory locations, making it easier for the computer to access and manipulate the data.

So far, we haven't seen a lot of situations yet where we would need them. We are really going to level up the complexity of our logic now as we learn how to work with arrays.

## When to use arrays

So, let's talk about when to use arrays. In our example earlier, where we calculated the average, an array would mean we wouldn't need three separate variables to store our three results. We would store them in one variable of the double array type instead. This makes it easier to handle the data.

Arrays (as well as other types of ways to store multiple values in one variable, which we'll see later) are used for various reasons:

- **Organizing data**: Arrays can help organize and manage large amounts of data in a structured way
- **Simplifying code**: Using arrays can simplify your code by reducing the number of variables needed to store and manipulate data
- **Improving performance**: Accessing and modifying elements in an array is faster than using other data structures because elements are stored in contiguous memory locations

Being able to work with arrays is going to be a great tool in your Java toolbox! Let's see how we can declare and initialize them.

# Declaring and initializing arrays

There are different ways to declare and initialize arrays in Java. What you'll need will depend a lot on the specific situation. So, let's just start with the basics of declaring arrays.

## Declaring arrays

To declare an array in Java, you need to specify the data type of the elements, followed by square brackets ( [] ) and the array's name. Take the following example:

```
int[] ages;
```

Here, int [] is the data type of the array, and ages is the name of the array. Right now, we can't add any values to the array, because it hasn't been initialized yet. This is different from initializing variables, which we have seen so far. Let's see how to initialize arrays next.

## Initializing arrays

After declaring an array, it needs to be initialized. We do this by specifying its size and allocating memory for the elements. We can use the new keyword to do this, followed by the data type, and then specify the size of the array inside the square brackets. Take the following example:

```
ages = new int[5];
```

This code initializes the ages variable to hold an array of integers with a size of 5.

We can also declare and initialize an array in a single line of code:

```
int[] ages = new int[5];
```

Here, we first declare the array on the left-hand side and initialize it on the right-hand side. We can also assign its values directly with a special short syntax, which we will explore next.

## Short syntax for array initialization

We can use Java's shortcut syntax for declaring and initializing arrays with specific values. Instead of declaring and initializing the array separately, we can use curly braces ({ }) to specify the elements directly. Take a look at the following example:

```
int[] ages = {31, 7, 5, 1, 0};
```

This code creates an array of integers and initializes it with the specified values. The size of the array is determined by the number of elements inside the curly braces.

Actually, our previous arrays had values already as well, because when you create an array using the new keyword, Java automatically initializes the elements with default values based on their data type. The default values are as follows:

- Numeric types (byte, short, int, long, float, double): 0 or 0.0
- char: '\u0000' (the Unicode null character)
- boolean: false
- Reference types (objects and arrays): null

For example, say you create an array of integers with a size of 3:

```
int[] results = new int[3];
```

Java initializes the elements with the default value of 0, because int is numeric. So far, we have seen how to declare and initialize arrays. It's now time to learn how to access the elements in an array and update the values.

## Accessing elements in an array

In order to access elements in an array, we need to use their **index**. The index represents the position in the array. This allows us to retrieve the value at a certain position and assign it a new value. Let's first talk about indexing.

## Understanding indexing

In Java, arrays use zero-based indexing, which means the first element has an index of 0, the second element has an index of 1, and so on. Take a look at our example of the `ages` array:

```
int[] ages = {31, 7, 5, 1, 0};
```

This means that the first element (`31`) has an index of 0 and the last element has an index of 4.

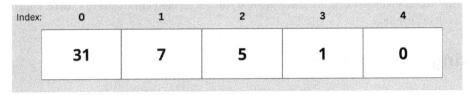

Figure 6.1 – Indexing explained with the ages array

We count the length of an array like we normally do, starting with 1. So, the length of this array would be 5. The last element in the array has an index equal to the array's length minus 1. For an array with a length of N, the valid indexes are in the range of 0 to N-1.

It is important to know how to use the index because that way we can access the elements in the array.

## Accessing array elements

To access an element in an array, you can use the array's name, followed by the index of the desired element inside square brackets. For example, to access the first element of our array named `ages`, you can use the following code:

```
int maaikesAge = ages[0];
```

This will store the value `31` in the age variable. In order to access the second element, you'd have to do the following:

```
int gaiasAge = ages[1];
```

We can also access the element and store another value in the element using the index.

---

**Printing arrays**

If we print the variable holding the array, we can get something like this: `[I@28a418fc`

This is not going to be very helpful. So, mind that you're printing what the `toString()` method is returning. This is not customized for the array and is not very useful. What we most likely want to see is the elements inside the array. There is a way to print the content of arrays. We'll see this when we cover the built-in methods for dealing with arrays.

## Modifying array elements

Modifying the elements is also done with the index. It looks a lot like assigning a variable as we did before. For example, to change the value of the last element in our array, named `ages`, we can use the following code:

```
ages[4] = 37;
```

We can only access elements that are there. If we try to get an element that is not there, we get an exception (error) message.

# Working with length and bounds

To avoid getting exceptions, we need to stay within the bounds of the array. Indexes always start at 0, and they end at the length of the array minus 1. If you try to access an element outside this range, you'll get `ArrayIndexOutOfBoundsException`. The key to avoiding this is working with the length of the array.

## Determining the length of an array

We can determine the length of an array using the `length` property. The `length` property returns the number of elements in the array. For example, to get the length of our `ages` array, we can use the following code:

```
int arrLength = ages.length;
```

The length of the array starts counting at 1. Therefore, the length of our `ages` array is 5. The maximum index is 4.

## Dealing with the bounds of an array

If you try to access or modify an array element using an invalid index (an index that is less than 0 or greater than or equal to the array's length), Java throws `ArrayIndexOutOfBoundsException`. This exception is a runtime error, which means it occurs when the program is running, not when we compile it. We'll learn more about exceptions in *Chapter 11*.

To prevent `ArrayIndexOutOfBoundsExceptions`, we should always validate array indexes before using them to access or modify array elements. We can do this by checking whether the index is within the valid range (0 to array length - 1). Here's an example that demonstrates how to validate an array index:

```
String[] names = {"Maria", "Fatiha", "Pradeepa", "Sarah"};
int index = 5;
if (index >= 0 && index < names.length) {
```

```
    System.out.println("Element at index " + index + ": " +
        names[index]);
} else {
    System.out.println("Invalid index: " + index);
}
```

The output will be as follows:

```
Invalid index: 5
```

This code snippet checks whether the index is within the valid range before accessing the array element. If the index is invalid, the program prints an error message instead of throwing an exception.

We can also use the loops we learned about in the previous chapter to iterate over the elements in an array and access or modify their values.

# Iterating over arrays

There are different methods to iterate over arrays. We will have a look at the use of the traditional `for` loop and the enhanced `for` loop (also known as the `for-each` loop).

## Using the for loop

We can use the traditional `for` loop to iterate over an array by using an index variable. The loop starts at index 0 and continues until the index reaches the length of the array. Here's an example that demonstrates how to use a `for` loop to iterate over an array and print its elements:

```
int[] results = {10, 20, 30, 40, 50};
for (int i = 0; i < results.length; i++) {
    System.out.println("Element at " + i + ": " +
        results[i]);
}
```

The output will be as follows:

```
Element at 0: 10
Element at 1: 20
Element at 2: 30
Element at 3: 40
Element at 4: 50
```

At this point, we know enough to revisit the example that we saw at the beginning of the chapter, calculating the average of several results. Instead of having separate primitives, we're now going to have an array. Here is what it will look like:

```
double[] results = {7.0, 8.6, 9.0};
double total = 0;
for(int i = 0; i < results.length; i++) {
    total += results[i];
}
double average = total / results.length;
System.out.println(average);
```

If we now want to add a result, we only need to alter it in one place. We just add the result to the results array. Since we loop over all the elements, we don't need to add an extra variable to calculate the total result. Also, since we use the length, we don't need to change 3 to 4.

We can also use loops to modify the values of the array. Here's an example that demonstrates how to double the value of each element in an array using a for loop:

```
int[] results = {10, 20, 30, 40, 50};
// Double the value of each element
for (int i = 0; i < results.length; i++) {
    results[i] = results[i] * 2;
}
// Print the updated array elements
for (int i = 0; i < results.length; i++) {
    System.out.println("Element at " + i + ": " +
        results[i]);
}
```

The output will be as follows:

```
Element at 0: 20
Element at 1: 40
Element at 2: 60
Element at 3: 80
Element at 4: 100
```

As you can see, the elements in the array are doubled in the first for loop. In the second for loop, they are printed. As you can tell by the output, the values did double!

Let's have a look at the enhanced for loop and how we can use that to iterate over arrays.

## Using the for each loop

We can also the `for-each` loop, also known as the enhanced for loop, to iterate over arrays. This special `for` loop simplifies the process of iterating over arrays (and other iterable objects). The `for-each` loop automatically iterates over the elements in the array and does not require an index variable. Here's an example that demonstrates how to use the `for-each` loop to iterate over an array and print its elements:

```java
int[] results = {10, 20, 30, 40, 50};
for (int result : results) {
    System.out.println("Element: " + result);
}
```

The output will be as follows:

```
Element: 10
Element: 20
Element: 30
Element: 40
Element: 50
```

The `for-each` loop requires a temporary variable that is used to store the current element during each iteration. In our example, this is `int result`. It is logical to call it `result`, since it is one element in the `results` array. But this is not necessary for the functionality; I could have also called it x, as follows:

```java
int[] results = {10, 20, 30, 40, 50};
for (int x : results) {
    System.out.println("Element: " + x);
}
```

The output would have been exactly the same. I like to read the line of code that says `for (int x : results)` in my head like this: for every element x in `results`, do whatever is in the code block.

So there are two ways to loop over arrays, let's talk about which one to choose when.

## Choosing between the regular loop and the enhanced for loop

We can use the regular `for` loop and the (enhanced) `for-each` loop to iterate over an array. These two approaches have some differences and there's a reason for choosing one or the other.

When you need to have the index available, you should use the traditional `for` loop since this uses an index variable to access the elements in the array, while the `for-each` loop directly accesses the elements without using an index variable.

The `for-each` loop does not allow you to modify the array elements during iteration, as it does not provide access to the index variable. If you need to modify the array elements during iteration, you should use the traditional `for` loop.

If you only want to read the variables and you don't need the index, you typically want to go for the `for-each` loop because the syntax is easier.

Alright, so now we know how to iterate over arrays. Let's make the data structure slightly more complicated and learn about multidimensional arrays.

# Handling multidimensional arrays

A **multidimensional array** is an array of arrays. In Java, you can create arrays with two or more dimensions. The most common type of multidimensional array is the two-dimensional array, also known as a matrix or a table, where the elements are arranged in rows and columns.

Let's see how to create multidimensional arrays.

## Declaring and initializing multidimensional arrays

To declare a two-dimensional array, you need to specify the data type of the elements, followed by two sets of square brackets ( [] [] ) and the name of the array. Take the following example:

```
int [] [] matrix;
```

Just like the one-dimensional array, we initialize a two-dimensional array with the use of the `new` keyword, followed by the data type and the size of each dimension inside the square brackets, like this:

```
matrix = new int [3] [4] ;
```

This code initializes a matrix of 3 rows and 4 columns. The type is `int`, so we know that the values of the matrix are integers.

We can also declare and initialize a multidimensional array in a single line:

```
int [] [] matrix = new int [3] [4] ;
```

We can use the short syntax as well. To initialize a multidimensional array with specific values, we use the nested curly braces ( { } ):

```
int [] [] matrix = {
    {1, 2, 3, 4},
    {5, 6, 7, 8},
    {9, 10, 11, 12}
};
```

Just like the one-dimensional arrays, Java determines the length by the provided values. This matrix has three inner arrays (three rows) each with four elements (four columns). Accessing and modifying the elements in a multidimensional array is similar, but we now need to provide two indices.

## Accessing and modifying elements of multidimensional arrays

To access or modify the elements of a multidimensional array, you need to specify the indexes of each dimension inside square brackets. For example, to access the element in the first row and second column of a two-dimensional array named `matrix`, you can use the following code:

```
int element = matrix[0][1];
```

To modify the same element, you can use the following code:

```
matrix[0][1] = 42;
```

*Figure 6.2* shows how the indexing works for our two-dimensional array, `matrix`.

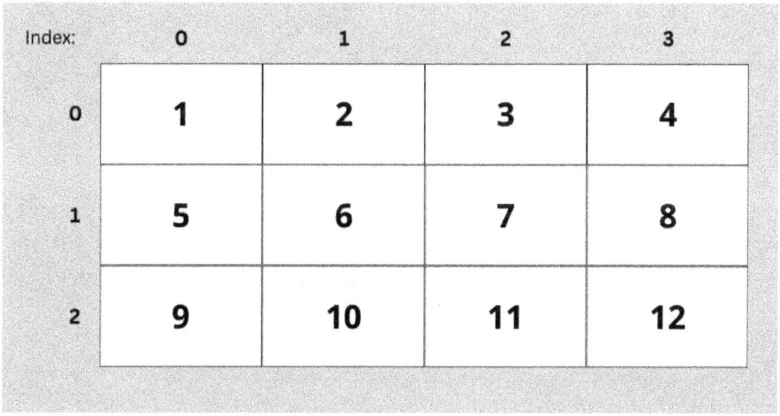

Figure 6.2 – The index of the rows and columns for array matrix

So, if we want to get to the element with value 12 and store it in a `last` variable, our code will be as follows:

```
int last = matrix[2][3];
```

We can also iterate over all the variables in a multidimensional array. Let's see how that is done.

## Iterating over multidimensional arrays

Since a multidimensional array is just an array in an array, we can use nested loops to iterate over multidimensional arrays. Here's an example that demonstrates how we can use a nested `for` loop to iterate over a two-dimensional array:

```
int[][] matrix = {
    {1, 2, 3, 4},
    {5, 6, 7, 8},
    {9, 10, 11, 12}
};

for (int i = 0; i < matrix.length; i++) {
    for (int j = 0; j < matrix[i].length; j++) {
        System.out.print(matrix[i][j] + " ");
    }
    System.out.println();
}
```

The output will be as follows:

```
1  2  3  4
5  6  7  8
9  10 11 12
```

All we do at this point is just print the element. This is something we can also do with the enhanced `for` loop to iterate over multidimensional arrays. Here's an example that demonstrates how to do that:

```
int[][] matrix = {
    {1, 2, 3, 4},
    {5, 6, 7, 8},
    {9, 10, 11, 12}
};

for (int[] row : matrix) {
    for (int element : row) {
        System.out.print(element + " ");
    }
    System.out.println();
}
```

The output will be the same as in the previous example:

```
1  2  3  4
5  6  7  8
9  10 11 12
```

As you can see, the outer `for-each` loop iterates over the rows of the two-dimensional array. The row is an array itself as well, which is why the type is `int []`. The inner `for-each` loop iterates over the elements within each row. These are integers.

Both traditional nested `for` loops and nested `for-each` loops can be used to iterate over multidimensional arrays. It's a matter of preference and whether you need to access the index of the elements.

Arrays can go very many levels deep, but that doesn't really change the basic principles. For example, for a four-dimensional array, you'll have `[] [] [] []` behind the type and you need a nested loop of four levels to iterate over all the elements.

Java helps us deal with arrays in different ways. Let's look at some built-in methods for arrays that we can use.

# Using Java's built-in methods for arrays

Working with arrays is very common. Usually, for very common things, Java has built-in functionality. We can do many common things we'd like to do with arrays with the use of the methods on the built-in `Arrays` class.

## Built-in Arrays class for working with arrays

The built-in `Arrays` class is a helper class in the `java.util` package. It offers many utility methods to help us efficiently work with arrays. We'll explore some common array manipulation tasks using the `Arrays` class.

### The toString() method

A highly useful operation you may want to perform on an array is to convert it into a `String`, which can be invaluable for debugging and logging purposes. To achieve this, the `Arrays` class offers a dedicated method called `toString()`. It's important to note that this method is static, allowing us to call it directly on the `Arrays` class.

```
import java.util.Arrays;

public class ArrayHelperMethods {
    public static void main(String[] args) {
```

```
        int[] results = {30, 10, 50, 20, 40};

        // Convert the array to a string representation
        String arrayAsString = Arrays.toString(results);
        System.out.println("Array: " + arrayAsString);
    }
}
```

The output will be as follows:

```
Array: [30, 10, 50, 20, 40]
```

As you can see, the `results` array is converted to a string that represents the array's elements, enclosed by square brackets and separated by commas. There are many such methods on the `Arrays` class! Let's explore the `sort` method next.

### The sort() method

A common operation you want to do on an array is to sort the array. Here's an example that shows how to sort the values of an array with the `sort` method from the `Arrays` class:

```
import java.util.Arrays;

public class ArrayHelperMethods {
    public static void main(String[] args) {
        int[] results = {30, 10, 50, 20, 40};

        // Sort the array
        Arrays.sort(results);
        System.out.println(Arrays.toString(results));
    }
}
```

The output will be as follows:

```
[10, 20, 30, 40, 50]
```

As you can see, the `results` array is unsorted at first. We can call the methods on the `Arrays` class directly on the `Arrays` class because they're static. For integer values, it sorts them from low to high by default. We can alter this behavior, but we don't have the knowledge we need to do that just yet.

We print the array with another built-in method, namely `toString`. This translates the array into something that we can understand.

When the array is sorted, we can use the `binarySearch` method to find a value.

## The binarySearch() method

We can also search for a value in an array. We are going to use the built-in `binarySearch` method to do this. Very importantly, this can only be done with sorted arrays because of how the search algorithm works. Here's an example of how to do this:

```java
import java.util.Arrays;

public class ArrayHelperMethods {
    public static void main(String[] args) {
        int[] results = {10, 20, 30, 40, 50};

        int target = 30;
        int index = Arrays.binarySearch(results, target);
        System.out.println("Index of " + target + ": " +
            index);
    }
}
```

The output will be as follows:

```
Index of 30: 2
```

The `binarySearch` method requires the input array to be sorted beforehand. The `binarySearch` algorithm is meant for finding a target value within a sorted array. Instead of searching the array element by element, it divides the array into halves repeatedly until it finds the target or the remaining portion to search becomes empty. When the value at the half is bigger, it knows it needs to move towards the left side of the array, when it's smaller it knows it needs to move towards the right. That's why it's a must that the array is sorted. The `binarySearch` method returns the index of the target value if found. If the target wasn't found, it returns a negative value, which represents the insertion point. So, say we updated our code to this:

```java
int[] results = {10, 20, 30, 40, 50};

int target = 31;
int index = Arrays.binarySearch(results, target);
System.out.println("Index of " + target + ": " +
    index);
```

This would result in the following:

```
Index of 31: -4
```

This is because it would have been at the fourth position in the array (not the fourth index!).

Let's see how we can give all the elements in the array a specific value with the `fill` method.

## The fill() method

Sometimes, you want to create an array of the same values programmatically. Here's an example of how this can be done. We use the `fill` method from the `Arrays` class. Here's how to do it:

```java
import java.util.Arrays;

public class ArrayHelperMethods {
    public static void main(String[] args) {
        int[] results = new int[5];

        Arrays.fill(results, 42);
        System.out.println(Arrays.toString(results));
    }
}
```

The output will be as follows:

```
[42, 42, 42, 42, 42]
```

The `fill` method sets all elements in the array to the specified value. Sometimes we need to create a copy of our array or resize it. In that case, we can use the `copyOf` method.

## The copyOf() method

Sometimes you need to create a copy of an array, for example, when you want to end it to another location in the application, but you don't want this to affect your original array.

This is an example of how we can create a copy of an array:

```java
import java.util.Arrays;

public class ArrayHelperMethods {
    public static void main(String[] args) {
        int[] results = {10, 20, 30, 40, 50};

        int[] copiedResults = Arrays.copyOf(results,
            results.length);
        System.out.println(Arrays.toString(copiedResults));
    }
}
```

The output will be as follows:

```
[10, 20, 30, 40, 50]
```

We can prove we copied the array with the following code:

```
copiedResults[0] = 1000;
System.out.println(Arrays.toString(copiedResults));
System.out.println(Arrays.toString(results));
```

If we didn't create a copy but just stored it in another variable instead, it would alter both arrays. The preceding code snippet will give the following output:

```
[1000, 20, 30, 40, 50]
[10, 20, 30, 40, 50]
```

But say we have this code:

```
int[] copiedResults = results;


copiedResults[0] = 1000;
System.out.println(Arrays.toString(copiedResults));
System.out.println(Arrays.toString(results));
```

It will give us this output:

```
[1000, 20, 30, 40, 50]
[1000, 20, 30, 40, 50]
```

As you can see, this alters both the variables holding the array. This is because both variables, `copiedResults` and `results`, have the same array object that they're pointing to. So, if you change it in one place, it changes for both. That's why you sometimes need to create copies of arrays.

So, the `copyOf` method creates a new array with the same elements as the original array, whereas this second method just creates a new variable that points to the same array object. We can also use it to resize the array by passing in a second argument.

### Resizing arrays with copyOf()

Arrays have a fixed size, but sometimes you need to alter the size nonetheless. The `Arrays.copyOf()` method that we just saw is also useful for resizing arrays. To resize an array, you can create a new array with the desired size and copy the elements from the original array to the new array. All you need to do is give it a second argument.

Here's an example that demonstrates how to resize:

```
import java.util.Arrays;
int[] originalArray = {10, 20, 30, 40, 50};
int newLength = 7;
```

```
int[] resizedArray = Arrays.copyOf(originalArray, newLength);

System.out.println("Original array: " + Arrays.
toString(originalArray));
System.out.println("Resized array: " + Arrays.toString(resizedArray));
```

The output will be as follows:

```
Original array: [10, 20, 30, 40, 50]
Resized array: [10, 20, 30, 40, 50, 0, 0]
```

In this example, we resized `originalArray`, which had a length of 5, to a new length of 7. The new array contains the elements of the original array, followed by default values (0 for `int`) to fill the remaining positions.

This is not something you should be doing constantly. It can be inefficient in terms of performance. If you would need to resize your array a lot, it's worth having a look at *Chapter 13* where we learn about **collections**.

### The equals() method

The last built-in method we're going to discuss is the `equals()` method. This method can determine whether two arrays have the same values. With this built-in method, you can compare two arrays for equality. Here's how to go about it:

```
import java.util.Arrays;

public class ArrayHelperMethods {
    public static void main(String[] args) {
        int[] results1 = {10, 20, 30, 40, 50};
        int[] results2 = {10, 20, 30, 40, 50};

        boolean arraysEqual = Arrays.equals(results1,
            results2);
        System.out.println("Are the arrays equal? " +
            arraysEqual);
    }
}
```

The output will be as follows:

```
Are the arrays equal? true
```

The `equals()` method compares two arrays element by element to check whether they have the same values in the same order. It returns `true` if the arrays are equal; otherwise, it returns `false`.

> **Well done!**
>
> You've done a great job learning arrays! At this point, you're ready to understand this programming joke:
>
> Why did the Java developer quit their job?
>
> Because they couldn't get "arrays!"

# Exercises

Arrays are incredibly useful for storing and managing similar types of data, such as a list of dinosaur names, dinosaur weights, and visitors' favorite snacks. Arrays are helpful and they enable us to manage more complex data in Mesozoic Eden. Try out the following:

1.  The unique appeal of our park lies in the diversity of our dinosaur species. (And also in that we have dinosaurs at all.) Create an array that holds the names of all the dinosaur species in the park. This list will help us in inventory management.

2.  Every visitor has their favorite dinosaur, and for many, it's the heaviest one. Write a program that finds this star's weight in an array of dinosaur weights. This information can then be highlighted in our park tours and educational programs.

3.  Dinosaurs come in all sizes, and the smallest ones hold a special place in the hearts of children. Write a program that finds this smallest dinosaur in an array of dinosaur weights.

4.  Running a dinosaur park is not a one-man show and requires a dedicated team of employees. Create an array of park employee names and print out the names using an enhanced `for` loop. This will help us to appreciate and manage our staff more effectively.

5.  To ensure the well-being of our dinosaur inhabitants, it's essential to monitor their average age. This data can help inform our care and feeding programs to better suit the age profile of our dinosaurs. Write a program that calculates this using an array of dinosaur ages.

6.  Our park is meticulously divided into various sections to facilitate visitor navigation and dinosaur housing. Create a two-dimensional array representing the park map, with each cell containing an array of Strings indicating an enclosure or facility for a certain section.

7.  The enjoyment of a park tour depends significantly on comfortable seating arrangements. Use nested loops to print out a seating chart for a park tour bus from a two-dimensional array. This will help us ensure that every guest has a pleasant journey throughout the park.

# Project – Dino tracker

Safety always comes first. That's why keeping track of all our dinosaur residents is of utmost importance. The park managers need to have an easy-to-use system for managing information about their slightly exotic pets.

For this project, you'll be creating a Dino tracker. This is a simple tracking system that maintains records of each dinosaur's name, age, species, and enclosure number. This will be done using fixed arrays – four arrays in total, one for each attribute.

Assume you have room for 10 dinosaurs in your park for now, so each array should have a length of 10. Each dinosaur will correspond to an index in the array. For example, if the dinosaur "Rex" is in the first position of the name array, his age, species, and enclosure number will also be in the first position of their respective arrays.

You're going to print information about all the dinosaurs and print their average age and weight after that.

I realize this might be a lot. If you need some extra guidance, here are some steps to guide you through the process:

1. **Initialization**: Start by creating four arrays: `dinoNames`, `dinoAges`, `dinoSpecies`, and `dinoEnclosures`. Each should have a size of 10.

2. **Data entry**: Manually enter the details for ten dinosaurs into the arrays. This is to populate your arrays with some initial data. If you're feeling lazy, like the Brachiosaurus, you could have `Dinosaur1`, `Dinosaur2`, and so on as names.

3. **Displaying details**: Write a loop that goes through the arrays and prints out the details of each dinosaur in a readable format.

4. **Average calculations**: Add the end, print the average age and weight of the dinosaurs. For the ages, you will need to sum up all the ages in the `dinoAges` array and divide by the number of dinosaurs. And, of course, this process is similar for weight, but using the weight array.

## Summary

In this chapter, we have explored arrays in Java. Arrays are data structures that allow us to store multiple values of the same data type in a contiguous block of memory. They provide an efficient way to organize lists of data.

We began by discussing the declaration and initialization of arrays. We learned about different ways to declare and initialize arrays, including using the shortcut syntax for array initialization. We also covered how to initialize arrays with default values.

After that, we discussed how to access and modify array elements using indexes. We learned about the importance of the array length and that we can find out the length by using the `length` property. We also talked about avoiding `ArrayIndexOutOfBoundsExceptions` by validating array indexes.

We then looked at iterating over arrays using both the traditional `for` loop and the enhanced `for` loop (the `for-each` loop).

After this, we explored multidimensional arrays, which are arrays of arrays, and learned how to declare, initialize, and access their elements. We also discussed how to iterate over multidimensional arrays.

Finally, we covered common array operations with the use of the `Arrays` class and its built-in methods. We saw how to sort arrays, search for elements in a sorted array, fill an array with a specific value, copy and resize an array, and compare arrays.

By mastering these concepts, you now have a solid foundation for working with arrays in Java. This understanding will help you store and manipulate data more efficiently in your Java programs. We ended by looking at some built-in methods. In the next chapter, you're going to learn how to write your own methods.

# 7
# Methods

In *Chapter 6*, we learned about arrays in Java. We learned that arrays are data structures that are fixed in size. They are stored in contiguous memory locations where each location is of the same type. We also saw how to declare, initialize, and process arrays. Both the traditional and enhanced `for` loops are ideal for processing arrays.

In addition, we discussed multi-dimensional arrays, including how they are organized and how to process them. Lastly, as arrays are very common, we discussed the `Arrays` class, which has several useful methods for processing arrays.

In this chapter, we will cover methods. Methods enable us to create a named block of code that can be executed from elsewhere in the code. Firstly, we will explain why methods are so commonplace. You will learn the difference between the method definition and the method invocation. We will explore what a method signature is and how method overloading enables methods to have the same name, without conflict. We will also explain variable arguments (`varargs`), which enable a method to be executed with 0 or more arguments. Lastly, Javas' principle of call-by-value for passing arguments (and returning values) will be outlined. By the end of this chapter, you will be well able to code and execute methods. In addition, you will understand method overloading, `varargs`, and Javas' call-by-value mechanism.

This chapter covers the following main topics:

- Explaining why methods are important
- Understanding the difference between method definition and method execution
- Exploring method overloading
- Explaining `varargs`
- Mastering call by value

## Technical requirements

The code for this chapter can be found on GitHub at `https://github.com/PacktPublishing/Learn-Java-with-Projects/tree/main/ch7`.

# Explaining why methods are important

Methods are code blocks that are given a name for ease of reference. They can accept inputs and return an output. Both the inputs and output are optional. A method should do one task and do it well. It is considered good practice to keep your methods short (less than 20 lines). The longer the method, the more likely it is that the method is doing too much. The maxim of "keep it simple" applies here.

## Flow of control

Simply put, when a method is called (executed), the normal flow of control of execution is changed. Let us discuss a simple example that will help demonstrate this. This is an important point to appreciate, especially for inexperienced developers. *Figure 7.1* presents the code:

```
3    public class Methods {
4        public static void main(String[] args) {
5            System.out.println("main: before call to simpleExample()");
6            simpleExample(); // method call
7            System.out.println("main: after call to simpleExample()");
8        }
9        public static void simpleExample(){ // method definition
10           System.out.println("\tExecuting simpleExample() method...");
11       }
12   }
```

Figure 7.1 – A very simple method

In this example, we have two methods: the main() method (lines 4 to 8) and the simpleExample() method (lines 9 to 11). Both exist inside the Methods class (lines 3 to 12).

In Java, every program starts with the main() method. The JVM calls it on our behalf; we do not have to call (or execute) it ourselves. Therefore, in this example, the first line in main(), line 5, is the first line to execute.

Line 6 is important – it is what we refer to as a method call. There is a direct correlation between the simpleExample() method definition on line 9 and the method call on line 6. We will discuss this relationship shortly. For the moment, just understand that the method call changes the order of execution of the program. Normally, Java executes lines of code from top to bottom and this is true. However, *method calls alter that*. In this example, when line 6 executes, the next line to execute is line 10 (inside the simpleExample() method).

So, the `main()` method has now handed over control to the `simpleExample()` method, and control will not return to `main()` until `simpleExample()` exits. This can occur when execution hits the closing `}` at the end of the `simpleExample()` method (line 11). This is what happens in this example. Alternatively, a method can exit by using the `return` keyword.

So, line 6 calls the `simpleExample()` method, causing its code to execute. Line 10 outputs some text to the screen. The closing `}` on line 11 causes `simpleExample()` to exit and control now returns to `main()`, where execution resumes at line 7.

In summary, the order of execution in this program is illustrated by the output:

```
main: before call to simpleExample()
    Executing simpleExample() method...
main: after call to simpleExample()
```

Here, you can see that `println()`, inside the `simpleExample()` method, is sandwiched between the two `println()` statements from `main()`. This demonstrates that the flow of control was altered by the method call on line 6.

### The stack

So, how can a caller method, such as `main()`, simply *resume* where it left off after the `simpleExample()` method returns? What about the local variables of `main()`?

The ability of a method to resume exactly where it left off, after the method it called returns, requires the use of a memory structure called the *stack*. We will discuss the stack later in this chapter.

Returning to our *why methods are important' discussion*, two major advantages of methods are that they provide abstraction and avoid code duplication. Let's examine these in turn.

## Abstraction

Abstraction is a principle in software engineering where clients of a service, are abstracted from the service implementation. This decouples clients, who use the service, from knowing how the service is implemented. Thus, if the service implementation is changed, the clients are not impacted.

Take, for example, a McDonald's drive-thru where you drive up and place your order. In this situation, you are the client of the McDonald's service. You do not care how McDonald's process your order; you simply want to place an order and receive the food/drinks. If McDonald's changes its internal implementation, you are shielded (abstracted) from those changes. This is known as abstraction.

For our purposes, the method itself is the McDonald's service. The method call is the McDonald's customer. The method call is abstracted from internal changes to the method code.

# Code duplication

Methods can help us avoid code replication. This has the added benefit of easing debugging. Let's look at a simple example of this. *Figure 7.2* demonstrates duplicated code:

```
 6          Scanner sc = new Scanner(System.in);
 7
 8          System.out.print("Enter a number (1..10) --> ");
 9          int number = sc.nextInt();
10          if(number < 1 || number > 10){
11              System.out.println("Invalid number! "+number);
12          }
13
14          System.out.print("Enter a number (1..10) --> ");
15          number = sc.nextInt();
16          if(number < 1 || number > 10){
17              System.out.println("Invalid number! "+number);
18          }
19
20          System.out.print("Enter a number (1..10) --> ");
21          number = sc.nextInt();
22          if(number < 1 || number > 10){
23              System.out.println("Invalid number! "+number);
24          }
```

Figure 7.2 – Duplicated code

In the preceding figure, lines 8 to 12 are repeated on lines 14 to 18 and lines 20 to 24. Each of these sections prompts the user for a number, stores the user input in a variable named number, and checks to see if the number is in range. If the number is out of range, then an error is flagged. While a loop would be an obvious improvement, bear in mind that these lines of code could well be in separate parts of the program. In addition, for this simple example, we are only interested in highlighting code duplication. We simply prompt for a number, accept the user's input, and validate it. The result is five lines of code repeated three times.

Now, let's assume that we want to adjust the upper valid range from 10 to 100. We have to change the prompts on lines 8, 14, and 20. In addition, the if statements on lines 10, 16, and 22 need to change. Thus, a simple range adjustment has resulted in quite a few code changes and we could easily forget to make one or more of the changes required. Let's refactor the code into a method. *Figure 7.3* shows the refactored code:

```
 3  ▶   public class Methods {
 4  ▶       public static void main(String[] args) {
 5             int number = getNumber();
 6             number = getNumber();
 7             number = getNumber();
 8         }
 9         public static int getNumber(){
10             Scanner sc = new Scanner(System.in);
11             System.out.print("Enter a number (1..10) --> ");
12             int number = sc.nextInt();
13             if(number < 1 || number > 10){
14                 System.out.println("Invalid number! "+number);
15             }
16             return number;
17         }
18     }
```

Figure 7.3 – The code from Figure 7.2 refactored to use a method

In the preceding figure, the method itself is coded from lines 9 to 17 and will be explained in detail in the next section. The five lines of repeated code from *Figure 7.2* are coded only once, on lines 11 to 15. The execution calls of the method are on lines 5, 6, and 7; one execution call per line. If we want to change the upper valid range from 10 to 100, we just need to change the method – that is, lines 11 and 13. These two changes are *automatically* reflected throughout the code. In effect, the three method calls on lines 5, 6, and 7 automatically reflect the changes made in the method.

As you can imagine, this situation scales very well. For example, if, in *Figure 7.2*, we had duplicated the code 10 times, we would have to make changes in 10 areas of the code. However, with the method implementation, there is still *only one* location to make the change and that is in the method itself.

Now that we have justified why methods exist, let's examine the difference between the method itself and the method call.

## Understanding the difference between method definition and method execution

For those new to programming, it may surprise you to know that there are two parts to having a method *do* something. Firstly, we must code the method (the method definition). This is similar to a bank machine on the street – it just sits there, doing nothing, waiting to be used. Secondly, we must execute the method (the method execution). This is similar to a customer "using" the bank machine.

Remember that the main method is the only method that is automatically executed by the JVM. Any other method calls have to be explicitly coded.

Now, let's examine the method definition and method execution in turn.

## Method definition

The method definition (declaration) is the method code itself - this is the block of code that is executed when the method is called. *Figure 7.4* presents the syntax:

[access-modifier] [static] **return-type methodName([parameters])** [throws someException] {

   // method code

}

Figure 7.4 – The syntax of the method definition

In the preceding figure, as in other figures, square brackets signify optional elements. The access-modifier and static elements will be discussed in *Chapter 8*. The throws someException element will be covered in *Chapter 11*. In this chapter, we will focus on the elements in bold; namely, return-type (mandatory), methodName (mandatory), and parameters (optional).

The return type of the method can be a primitive type, a reference type, or void. The void keyword means that the method is not returning anything. If that is the case, you *cannot* simply leave out the return type; you must specify void. In addition, when you're not returning anything from a method, you can specify return; or simply leave out the return keyword altogether (which is what we have done for all the main() methods).

Let's examine a method that accepts input and returns a result. *Figure 7.5* presents such an example:

```
14      // method definition/declaration
15 @    public static int performCalc(int x, int y, String operation){  // "parameters"
16          int result = switch(operation){
17              case "+" -> x + y;
18              case "-" -> x - y;
19              case "*" -> x * y;
20              case "/" -> x / y;
21              case "%" -> x % y;
22              default -> {
23                  System.out.println("Unrecognized operation: "+operation);
24                  yield -1; // error
25              }
26          };
27          return result;
28      }
```

Figure 7.5 – Sample method definition

In the preceding figure, we have a method that takes in two integers and a mathematical operation to be performed using the two integers as operands. For example, if "+" is passed in, the two numbers are added and the result is returned. Let's review how the method does this.

Line 15 is very important. For the moment, as stated earlier, *Chapter 8* will explain both `public` (access-modifier) and `static`. The `return-type` is an `int` – meaning, this method returns whole numbers. The name of the method is `performCalc`. Method names often begin with verbs and follow camel casing style.

Note that round brackets follow the method name. The round brackets are delimiters for the optional input parameters to the method. For each parameter, you must specify the data type of the parameter (as Java is a strongly typed language) and the parameter's identifier name. If you have two or more parameters, comma-separate them. These parameters are how the method accepts input. In *Figure 7.5*, we have two integers namely `x` and `y`, followed by a `String` called `operation`. The scope of any method parameters, in this case, `x`, `y`, and `operation`, is the whole of the method.

Lines 16-26 encapsulate a `switch` expression. In effect, depending on the mathematical `operation` passed in, that operation is performed on the two inputs, `x` and `y`. The local `int` variable, `result`, is initialized accordingly. The `result` variable is returned on line 27. As the return type declared on line 15 is an `int`, returning `result`, which is also an `int`, is fine.

A method definition in and of itself does not do anything. It just defines a block of code. As stated previously, this is similar to a bank machine on the street – it just sits there, doing nothing, waiting to be used. For the bank machine to be useful, you must "use" it. Similarly, we must "use" the method – this is what we call executing the method.

## Method execution

Executing the method is also known as calling or invoking the method. The method that calls the method is known as the "calling" (or caller) method. So, you have the calling method and the called method. When you call a method, you pass down the required arguments, if there are any. The called method will execute at this point. When the called method finishes, control returns to the caller method. The called method's result, if there is one, is also returned. This enables the called method to return data to the caller method, where it can be output to the screen, stored in a variable, or simply ignored.

> **Method parameters versus method arguments**
> The method definition defines parameters, whereas the method call passes down arguments. These terms are often used interchangeably.

*Figure 7.6* presents a code example to help explain this further:

```java
public static void main(String[] args) {
    int result = performCalc( x: 10,  y: 2,   operation: "+"); // method call; passing down "arguments"
    System.out.println(result); // 12
    System.out.println(performCalc( x: 10,  y: 2,   operation: "-")); // 8
    System.out.println(performCalc( x: 10,  y: 2,   operation: "*")); // 20
    System.out.println(performCalc( x: 10,  y: 2,   operation: "/")); // 5
    performCalc( x: 10,  y: 2,   operation: "%");// return value ignored
    System.out.println(performCalc( x: 10,  y: 2,   operation: "&")); // Unrecognized operation: &, -1
}
public static int performCalc(int x, int y, String operation){  // "parameters"
    int result = switch(operation){
        case "+" -> x + y;
        case "-" -> x - y;
        case "*" -> x * y;
        case "/" -> x / y;
        case "%" -> x % y;
        default -> {
            System.out.println("Unrecognized operation: "+operation);
            yield -1; // error
        }
    };
    return result;
}
```

Figure 7.6 – Sample code demonstrating method calls

### IntelliJ IDEA inlay hints

Note that the IntelliJ editor inserts inlay hints when you are coding. In the previous figure, the `performCalc` method signature (line 13) specifies that the parameters are namely x, y, and `operation`. That is why on each method call, the inlay hint uses these parameter names. For example, on line 5, we typed in 10 as the first argument; however, IntelliJ, upon inspecting the method signature, realized that 10 was mapping to 'x' and that is why you see "**x:**" before the 10. We did not type in "x:" at all! It is not part of the Java language to do that (IntelliJ is just trying to help us). In actual fact, for line 5, we typed in `performCalc(10, 2, "+")` and IntelliJ converted that to `performCalc(x: 10, y: 2, operation: "+")`.

In *Figure 7.6*, the `performCalc` method (lines 13-26) is unchanged from *Figure 7.5*. However, we can now see the various method calls (lines 5 and 7-11).

Let's start with line 5. On the right-hand side of the assignment, we have the `performCalc(10, 2, "+")` method call. This method call has higher precedence than the assignment, so it is executed first. The IntelliJ IDE does a very nice job of highlighting that 10 will be passed into the method as x, 2 will be passed into the method as y, and "+" will be passed in as `operation`. It is very important to realize that once we get to the method call on line 5, the next line of code that's executed is line 14 – so, from line 5, we jump into the `performCalc` method and start executing the `switch` expression on line 14.

Since `operation` is `"+"` for this method invocation, line 15 assigns 10 + 2 (12) to `result`. Line 25 returns `result` back to the calling method (line 5), where the value 12 is assigned into `result`. Line 6 outputs the return value from the `performCalc` invocation on line 5, which is 12.

> **Different scopes**
>
> Note that the two `result` variables (lines 5 and 14) are completely different as they are in two separate scopes – one is in the `main()` method and the other is in the `performCalc` method. As a result, there is no conflict or ambiguity whatsoever.

Line 7 executes `System.out.println()` with a method call inside the `()` of `println`. In this scenario, Java will execute the method call inside the `()` of `println`, and whatever the method returns will then be output to the screen. So, for line 7, the arguments passed to `performCalc` are 10, 2, and `"-"`. Therefore, in `performCalc`, x is 10, y is 2, and `operation` is `"-"`. The `switch` expression now executes line 16, resulting in `result` becoming 8 (10 -2). This `result` is returned (line 25) back to the calling method (line 7), where 8 is output to the screen.

Lines 8 and 9 operate similarly to line 7 except that the lines of code executed in the `switch` expression are different. The method call on line 8 executes line 17 in the `switch` expression, resulting in `result` being initialized to 20. This value is returned to the calling method (line 8), where 20 is output to the screen. The method call on line 9 executes line 18 in the `switch` expression, resulting in `result` being initialized to 5, and thus 5 is output to the screen.

Line 10 causes line 19 in the `switch` expression to be executed, initializing `result` to 0 (10 % 2). This `result` is returned back to the calling method, where, because it is not stored in a variable, it is simply lost/ignored.

The `performCalc` call on line 11 passes in `"&"`, which executes the `default` branch of the `switch` expression. This results in the error message "Unrecognized operation: &" being displayed on the screen and -1 being returned. The -1 is then output on the screen.

Now that we know how to define and execute methods, we will move on to discussing method overloading, where distinct methods can have the same identifier name.

# Exploring method overloading

Consider a scenario where you have an algorithm, implemented by a method, that operates similarly on various input types – for example, `String` and `int`. It would be a shame to have two separately contrived method names, one for each input type, such as `doStuffForString(String)` and `doStuffForInt(int)`. It would be much better if both methods had the same name – that is, `doStuff` – differentiated by their input types, which are `doStuff(String)` and `doStuff(int)`. Thus, there will be no contrived method names. This is what method overloading provides. To discuss method overloading properly, we must first define the method signature.

## Method signature

The method signature consists of the method's name and the optional parameters. It does *not* consist of the return type. Let's look at an example to explain this further:

```
public static int performCalc(int x, int y, String operation){
```

method signature

Figure 7.7 – Method signature

In the preceding figure, the method signature is highlighted in a dashed rectangle. It consists of the name of the method, followed by both the type and the order of the parameters. What this means is that the signature for the method in *Figure 7.7* is `performCalc`, which takes in two integers and a `String`, *in that order*. Note that the parameter names do not matter. So, in effect, from the perspective of the compiler, the method signature is `performCalc(int, int, String)`.

## Overloading a method

A method is overloaded when two or more methods share the same name but the parameters are different in type and/or order. This makes sense if you consider this from the viewpoint of the compiler. If you call a method that has two or more definitions, how will the compiler know which one you are referring to? To locate the correct method definition, the compiler compares and matches the method call with the overloaded method signatures. *Figure 7.8* presents an overloaded method with various signatures:

```
6     public static void someMethod(){}
7     public static void someMethod(int x){}
8     public static void someMethod(double x){}
9     public static void someMethod(String x){}
10    public static void someMethod(double x, int y){}
11    public static void someMethod(int x, double y){}
12    public static void someMethod(int a, double b){}
13    public static int someMethod(int x, double b){ return 0;}
```

Figure 7.8 – The method signature's impact on overloading

In this figure, the someMethod method is overloaded several times. The method signatures on lines 6 to 10 are someMethod(), someMethod(int), someMethod(double), someMethod(String), and someMethod(double, int), respectively.

The interesting cases are the compiler errors on lines 11-13. The error on line 11 is a misleading error from the compiler. In other words, if we comment out lines 12 and 13, the compiler error on line 11 disappears. There is nothing wrong with line 11 as this is the first time the compiler has seen this particular method signature – that is, someMethod(int, double). The problem is that lines 12 to 13 have the same signatures and the compiler is flagging all lines with that signature.

Line 12 reinforces the point that the parameter names do not matter as they are not part of the method signature. Therefore, the fact that they are named x and y on line 11 and a and b on line 12 makes no difference whatsoever.

Similarly, line 13 demonstrates that the return type is not part of the method signature. Line 13 is a compiler error because its signature, someMethod(int, double), is the same as on lines 11 and 12, even though the two methods have different return types (int and void, respectively).

In summary, the return type and parameter names are *not* part of the method signature. Now that we understand what is (and what is not) part of the method signature, let's look at a simple example of method overloading. *Figure 7.9* presents the code:

```
3 ▶  public class Methods {
4 ▶      public static void main(String[] args) {
5            int sum = add( x: 3,  y: 4);
6            System.out.println(sum); // 7
7            double addition = add( x: 3.0,  y: 4.0);
8            System.out.println(addition); // 7.0
9        }
10       public static int add(int x, int y){
11           System.out.println("add(int,int)");
12           return x + y;
13       }
14       public static double add(double x, double y){
15           System.out.println("add(double,double)");
16           return x + y;
17       }
18   }
```

Figure 7.9 – Method overloading example

In this figure, we have an overloaded add method. The first version (lines 10 to 13) takes in two int parameters; the second version (lines 14-17) takes in two double parameters. Their respective signatures are captured on lines 10 and 14, respectively. Thus, when we call add on line 5 and pass down two integers, the compiler matches the call with the version of add on line 10 because that version of add takes two integers. Similarly, the call to add on line 7 matches add on line 14 because both the call and method signature match (two double types in both).

Now that we understand how method parameter types and their order affect method overloading, let's examine how Java enables us to execute methods where the number of arguments is variable.

## Explaining varargs

Consider the following situation: you want to call a method, m1, but the number of arguments may vary. Do you overload the method with each version of the method taking in one extra parameter? For example, assuming the argument types are of the String type, do you overload m1 when each new version takes in an extra String parameter? In this case, you would have to code m1(String), m1(String, String), m1(String, String, String), and so forth. This is not scalable.

This is where varargs comes in. varargs is a very flexible language feature in Java, specifically provided for this use case. The syntax is that the type name is followed by an ellipsis (three dots). *Figure 7.10* shows varargs in action:

```java
4    public static void main(String[] args) {
5        m1();                    // 0
6        m1( ...args: 1);         // 1
7        m1( ...args: 1, 2);      // 3
8        m1( ...args: 1, 2, 3);   // 6
9    }
10   public static void m1(int... args){ // varargs
11       int sum = 0;
12       for(int i:args){
13           sum += i;
14       }
15       System.out.println(sum);
16   }
```

Figure 7.10 – varargs example

In this figure, on line 10, m1(int...  ) defines a method signature for the m1 method, defining 0 or more int parameters. This is quite different from String[] defined on line 4 for main. In effect, you don't have to pass in any argument to m1 at all; or you can pass in 1, 2, 3, or more integers. This is shown by the method calls (lines 5-8). Internally, in the m1 method, varargs is treated as an array. The for loop (lines 12-14) demonstrate that.

The output from *Figure 7.10* is as follows:

```
0
1
3
6
```

Line 5 generates no output at all. Line 6 generates 1; line 7 generates 3; and line 8 generates 6.

Let's examine some edge cases with `varargs`. *Figure 7.11* will help:

```
3  ▶   public class Methods {
4  ▶       public static void main(String[] args) {
5              m1();
6              m1("A");
7              m1("A", "B");
8              m1( n: "A",  ...args: "B", "C");
9          }
10         public static void m1(int n, String... args){}
11         public static void m1(String... args, int n){}
12         public static void m1(String[] args){} // this is not varargs
13
14   //    public static void m1(String... args){ // varargs
15   //        for(int i=0; i<args.length; i++){
16   //            System.out.println(args[i]);
17   //        }
18   //        for(String s:args){
19   //            System.out.println(s);
20   //        }
21   //    }
22   }
```

Figure 7.11 – varargs compiler errors

In the preceding figure, we can see that `varargs` must be the last parameter in the method definition. Line 10 is fine as it defines the `varargs` parameter as the last parameter. However, line 11 is a compiler error because it attempts to define a parameter *after* the varargs parameter. This makes sense as all other parameters are mandatory; so, if `varargs` can define 0 or more arguments, it must be the last parameter.

Given that `varargs` is treated as an array, this begs the question, can we use an array instead of `varargs`? The answer is no. The compiler errors (lines 5-8) all relate to the fact that, despite the presence of `m1(int [] )` on line 12, the compiler cannot find the method definition that matches any of these method calls.

The last major topic for methods is an important one: call by value. We will discuss that now.

# Mastering call by value

Java uses call by value when passing arguments to methods and returning results from methods. Concisely, this means that Java *makes a copy of something*. Effectively, when you are passing an argument to a method, a copy is made of that argument and when you are returning a result from a method, a copy is made of that result. Why do we care? Well, depending on what you are copying – a primitive or a reference has **major** implications. An example of a primitive type is `int` and an example of a reference type is an array.

In a method, there is a clear difference between the effect of changes when the parameter is a primitive type versus when the parameter is a reference type. We will demonstrate this shortly with a code example but first, to appreciate the differences, we need to understand what is happening in memory.

## Primitives versus references in memory

An array is an object, whereas a primitive is not. We will discuss objects in detail in *Chapter 8*, but for now, let's examine the code in *Figure 7.12*:

```
3 ▶   public class Methods {
4 ▶       public static void main(String[] args) {
5             int x = 19;          // primitive
6             int[] arr = {1, 2}; // array
7         }
8     }
```

Figure 7.12 – Sample code containing a primitive and an array

To understand what the code in the preceding figure looks like in memory, we need to discuss the stack, the heap, and references.

### Stack

The stack is a special area of memory used by methods. Each time a new method A, is called, a new frame is *pushed* (created) onto the stack. The frame contains, among other things, A's local variables and their values. Each frame is stacked one on top of the other, like plates. If A calls another method, B, the existing frame for A is saved and a new frame for B is pushed onto the stack, creating a new context. When B finishes, its stack frame is *popped* (removed) from the stack, and the frame for A is restored (with all its local variables and their values as they were, prior to the call to B). This is why a stack is called a **Last-In, First Out** (**LIFO**) structure. For further detail on the stack and Java Memory Management in general, please see our previous book: `https://www.amazon.com/Java-Memory-Management-comprehensive-collection/dp/1801812853/ref=sr_1_1?crid=3QUEBKJP46CN7&keywords=java+memory+management+maaike&qid=1699112145&sprefix=java+memory+management+maaike%2Caps%2C148&sr=8-1`

For our discussion here, what we need to be aware of is that local variables (primitives and/or references) are stored on the stack. Objects are *not* stored on the stack; objects are stored on the heap.

## Heap

The heap is an area of memory reserved for objects and arrays are objects. This means that arrays are stored on the heap. To access an object, we use a reference.

## References

The named identifier used to access an object is known as a reference. A reference is similar to a pointer. Consider a TV that has no buttons on it to change the channel but does have a remote control. The reference is the remote control and the TV is the object.

With these definitions in mind, let's review the code in *Figure 7.12*. Line 5 declares a primitive `int` type called x and initializes it to 19. Line 6 declares an `int` array, namely `arr`, and initializes `arr[0]` to 1 and `arr[1]` to 2. The array reference is `arr`. *Figure 7.13* shows the in-memory representation of *Figure 7.12* as we reach line 7:

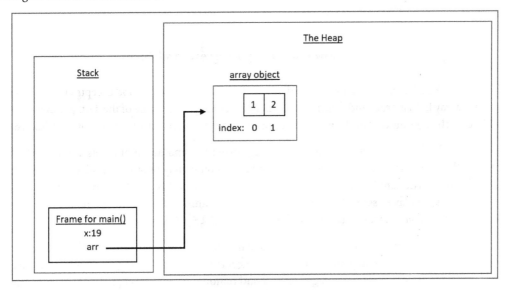

Figure 7.13 – In-memory representation of the code from Figure 7.12

In the preceding figure, we can see that there is a stack frame for the `main` method containing the local variables, `x` and `arr`. Note that, for simplicity, the `String[] args` parameter in `main` is omitted. Immediately, you can see the difference between the way primitives, namely `x`, and references, namely `arr`, are stored – `x` and its value are stored on the stack; whereas the value of `arr` refers to the object on the heap.

With this in mind, we are now in a position to examine a proper code example demonstrating the real impact of call by value when passing primitives versus passing references. *Figure 7.14* represents the code example we will be using:

```
3  ▶  public class Methods {
4  ▶      public static void main(String[] args) {
5              int x = 19;            // primitive
6              int[] arr = {1, 2}; // array
7              callByValue(x, arr);
8              System.out.println(x); // 19, unchanged
9              System.out.println(arr[0] + ", " + arr[1]); // -1, 2
10             x = callByValue(x, arr);
11             System.out.println(x); // -1, changed
12         }
13 @      public static int callByValue(int x, int[] arr){
14             x       = -1;
15             arr[0]  = -1;
16             return x;
17         }
18 }
```

Figure 7.14 – Call by value passing primitives and references

In this figure, the `callByValue` method is defined on lines 13-17: the method accepts an `int` type and an `int` array in that order and returns an `int`. Line 14 changes the value of the `int` parameter to -1 and line 15 changes index 0 of the array to -1. Lastly, the method returns the value of `x` on line 16.

Let us examine the first call to `callByValue`, passing down the `x` and `arr` arguments. It is important to note that the `x` and `arr` variables declared in `main` are completely separate variables from the `x` and `arr` parameters declared in the method `callByValue`. This is because they are in two separate scopes (methods). As Java uses call by value, copies of the primitive, `x`, and the reference, `arr`, are made and it is the *copies* that are passed into the method `callByValue`.

Making a copy of a primitive is like photocopying a blank sheet of paper - if you pass the photocopy to someone and they write on it, your original blank sheet is still blank. Making a copy of a reference is like copying a remote control – if you give the second remote control (the copied one) to someone else, they can change the channel on the TV. Crucially, there is only one TV in all of this – the copy is made of the remote control, *not the TV*.

> **Note**
>
> This saves memory as copying a reference has a much smaller memory footprint that copying a potentially large object.

*Figure 7.15* represents the in-memory representation of the code as we are about to `return` from the *first* invocation of `callByValue`:

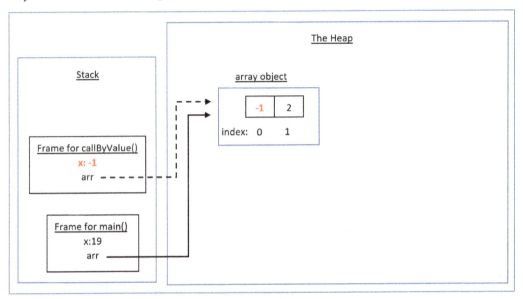

Figure 7.15 - In-memory view of Figure 7.14 (line 16) based on first call to callByValue (line 7)

As can be seen from the stack in the preceding figure, when we call `callByValue(x, arr)` from `main`, the existing frame for `main` is saved and a frame for `callByValue` is pushed onto the stack (on top of the frame for `main`). Then the code for `callByValue` is executed:

```
x = -1:
arr[0] = -1;
return x;
```

Firstly, x in changed in the `callByValue` frame. This is the copy of x from `main`. Note that the value of x in (the frame for) `main` remains untouched (still 19). Consequently, 19 is output for x in `main` (line 8). Thus, a called method cannot (directly) change the caller method's primitive values. We will revisit this point shortly.

However, the line `arr[0] = 1;` in `callByValue` does have a material impact on `main`. When `callByValue` uses its `arr` reference, which is a copy of the `arr` reference from `main`, it changes the one object that both methods share. In effect, the array object that `main` is looking at is changed. This is demonstrated in `main` after the `callByValue` method returns:

```
System.out.println(arr[0] + ", " + arr[1]); // -1, 2
```

Crucially, `-1` is output for the value at `arr[0]`. Therefore, be aware that when passing a reference to a method, the method can change the object that you are looking at.

Let's revisit the primitive situation. What if we wanted the called method to change the primitive value that's passed down? This is why `callByValue` is returning x. The first method call to `callByValue` completely ignores the return value:

```
callByValue(x, arr);
```

However, the second call does not:

```
x = callByValue(x, arr);
```

The -1 that's returned from `callByValue` is used to overwrite the value of x in `main`. As a result, -1 is output for x in `main` (line 11).

That completes our discussion on methods. Now, let's put that knowledge into practice to reinforce these concepts.

## Exercises

Maintaining a dinosaur park takes a lot more than just raw passion. It involves regular health check-ups for our dinosaurs, ensuring our guests are comfortable, and that the park is well-staffed. All these tasks involve methodical processes. Luckily, we now know about methods!

You can add these methods to the same class:

1.  The stage of life a dinosaur is in can significantly impact its behavior and needs. Write a method that takes a dinosaur's age and returns whether it's a hatchling, juvenile, or adult.

2.  It's important to remember that our dinosaurs aren't actually pets – they're large, often hefty creatures with large appetites. Write a method that accepts a dinosaur's weight and calculates how much food it needs daily.

3.  Being on top of our dinosaurs' average age helps us plan for the future. Design a method that accepts an array of dinosaur ages and calculates the average age.

4.  The park isn't open 24/7 to day visitors. We need some time to clean up the popcorn and repair any minor damages to the enclosures. Write a method that checks if the park is open or closed based on the current time. (Hint: this method doesn't require any input.)

5. Personalization is key to making our guests feel special. Create a method that uses a dinosaur's name and a visitor's name to craft a personal greeting message.

6. As you're well aware, safety is our top priority. We need a method to return whether we can let in another group of guests (a certain number of people) to the park based on the current number of visitors and the maximum number of visitors allowed.

# Project – Mesozoic Eden assistant

This is going to be our biggest project so far. So, buckle up!

Let's start with a high-level description. The Mesozoic Eden assistant is an interactive console application that assists in managing a dinosaur park. The assistant should have features to do the following:

- Add or remove dinosaurs
- Check the park's opening hours
- Greet guests and provide park information
- Track visitor counts to ensure the park isn't overcrowded
- Manage park staff details

Since we won't let you drown, if you need it, here is a step-by-step guide. A starting project will follow these steps:

1. **Create a data structure**: Create the necessary classes for `Dinosaur`, `Guest`, and `Employee`. Include appropriate properties and methods.

2. **Initialize the data**: You can choose to hardcode initial data or provide a mechanism to input data using the `Scanner` class.

3. **Implement interaction**: Implement a simple console-based interaction with the user using the `Scanner` class.

4. **Create a menu**: Create a menu that allows the user to interact with the park management system.

5. **Handle actions**: Each menu item should trigger a certain action, such as adding a dinosaur, checking park hours, or greeting a guest.

6. **Exit the program**: Provide an option for the user to exit the program.

Here is a code snippet to get you started:

```
import java.util.Scanner;

public class Main {
```

```java
// Use Scanner for reading input from the user
Scanner scanner = new Scanner(System.in);


public static void main(String[] args) {
    Main main = new Main();
    main.start();
}

public void start() {
    // This is the main loop of the application. It
      will keep running until the user decides to exit.
    while (true) {
        displayMenu();
        int choice = scanner.nextInt();
        handleMenuChoice(choice);
    }
}


public void displayMenu() {
    System.out.println("Welcome to Mesozoic Eden
      Assistant!");
    System.out.println("1. Add Dinosaur");
    System.out.println("2. Check Park Hours");
    System.out.println("3. Greet Guest");
    System.out.println("4. Check Visitors Count");
    System.out.println("5. Manage Staff");
    System.out.println("6. Exit");
    System.out.print("Enter your choice: ");
}

public void handleMenuChoice(int choice) {
    switch (choice) {
        case 1:
            // addDinosaur();
            break;
        case 2:
            // checkParkHours();
            break;
        case 3:
            // greetGuest();
            break;
```

```
            case 4:
                // checkVisitorsCount();
                break;
            case 5:
                // manageStaff();
                break;
            case 6:
                System.out.println("Exiting...");
                System.exit(0);
        }
    }
}
```

So, this is a great starting point! But it's not done. In the preceding code snippet, addDinosaur(), checkParkHours(), greetGuest(), checkVisitorsCount(), and manageStaff() are placeholders for methods you need to implement according to your data structures and functionality. The Scanner class is used to read the user's menu choice from the console.

You can make the project as sophisticated as you like by adding additional features and enhancements.

## Summary

In this chapter, we started our discussion on methods by stating that methods are simply code blocks that are given a name for ease of reference. Methods are important because they enable us to abstract away the implementation, while at the same time helping us to avoid unnecessary code duplication.

There are two parts to a method: the method definition (or declaration) and the method call (or invocation). The method definition declares (among other things) the method name, the input parameters, and the return type. The method name and the parameter types (including their order) constitute the method signature. The method call passes down the arguments (if any) to be used as inputs in the method. The return value from a method (if there is one) can be captured by assigning the method call to a variable.

Method overloading is where the same method name is used across several different methods. What distinguishes the various methods is that they have different signatures – the parameter types and/or their order will be different. The parameter names and return types do not matter.

A varargs (variable arguments) parameter is specified in a method declaration using an ellipsis (three dots). This means that when calling this method, the arguments corresponding to that parameter are variable – you can pass down 0 or more arguments for that parameter. Internally, in the method, the varargs parameter is treated as an array.

When passing arguments to a method, Java uses call by value. This means that a copy of the argument is made. Depending on whether you are passing down a primitive or a reference has major implications regarding the effect of the changes that are made by the called method on the calling method. If it's a primitive, the called method cannot change the primitive that the caller method has (unless the caller method deliberately overwrites the variable with the return value). If it's a reference, the called method can change the object that the caller method is looking at.

Now that we have finished looking at methods, let's move on to our first strictly **object-oriented programming (OOP)** chapter, where we will look at classes, objects, and enums.

# Part 2:
# Object-Oriented Programming

In this part, we will take a deep dive into **Object-Oriented Programming** (**OOP**). We will start by looking at classes and their relationship with objects. We will discuss the first core pillar of OOP, namely Encapsulation. Enums and records, both of which are closely related to classes, will also be covered. We will then move on to the remaining two major pillars in OOP, namely Inheritance and Polymorphism. Next up are `abstract` classes and the hugely important `interface` construct. Following that, we will examine Java's exception framework. Lastly, we will explore selected classes from the Java Core API, such as `String` and `StringBuilder`.

This section has the following chapters:

- *Chapter 8, Classes, Objects, and Enums*

- *Chapter 9, Inheritance and Polymorphism*

- *Chapter 10, Interfaces and Abstract Classes*

- *Chapter 11, Dealing with Exceptions*

- *Chapter 12, Java Core API*

# 8

# Classes, Objects, and Enums

In *Chapter 7*, we learned about methods in Java. After understanding why methods are useful, we learned that there are two parts to methods – the method definition and the method call. We saw that the method definition is the code that's executed when the method is invoked via the method call. We discussed how method signatures enable method overloading. We also learned how `varargs` helps us call a method with zero or more arguments. Finally, we discussed Java's call by value mechanism, where arguments that are passed to a method are copied in memory. Depending on the type of argument passed, primitive or reference, will have implications as to the effect of the changes made in the called method to those arguments passed from the caller method.

*Chapter 7* concluded the Java fundamentals section of this book. The topics in that section are common across many programming languages, including non-**object-oriented programming** (**OOP**) languages such as C. *Chapter 8* starts the OOP section of this book.

In this chapter, we will cover classes, objects, records and enums. Classes and objects are unique to OOP languages (such as Java); in other words, non-OOP languages (such as C) do not support them. Though closely related, understanding the difference between a class and an object is important. We will discuss the relationship between the class and objects of the class. To access an object, we must use a reference. Separating the reference from the object will prove very useful going forward. Instance versus class members will be discussed, as well as when to use either/both. This chapter will also explain the `'this'` reference and how it relates to the object responsible for the instance method currently executing.

We will also explain the access modifiers in Java. These access modifiers enable one of the key cornerstones in OOP, namely encapsulation. Though basic encapsulation can be easily achieved, properly encapsulating your class requires extra care. This will be covered in the Advanced encapsulation section.

Understanding the object life cycle, with regard to what is happening in memory as your program executes, is crucial to avoiding many subtle errors. This topic will be explained with the aid of diagrams.

Toward the end of the chapter, given our understanding (and separation!) of references from the objects they refer to, we will discuss the `instanceof` keyword. Lastly, we will cover a variation of classes, namely enums, whereby the number of object instances is restricted.

This chapter covers the following main topics:

- Understanding the differences between classes and objects

- Contrasting instance with class members

- Exploring the `'this'` reference

- Applying access modifiers

- Achieving encapsulation

- Mastering advanced encapsulation

- Delving into the object life cycle

- Explaining the `instanceof` keyword

- Understanding enums

- Appreciating records

# Technical requirements

The code for this chapter can be found on GitHub at `https://github.com/PacktPublishing/` `Learn-Java-with-Projects/tree/main/ch8`.

# Understanding the differences between classes and objects

As classes and objects are integral to OOP, it is vital to understand their differences. We will discuss the relationship between a class and its objects in this section. As creating objects requires the use of the `new` keyword, this will also be covered. Understanding constructors and what they do will also be examined. All of these topics are linked: objects are the in-memory representation of the class (template); to create an object, a constructor is used and to call the constructor, we use the `new` keyword. Let's examine these in turn.

## Classes

A class is so integral in Java that you cannot write any program without defining one! A class is a blueprint or template for your object. It is similar to a plan of a house – using a house plan, you can discuss the house all you want; however, you cannot go into the kitchen and make a cup of tea/coffee. The house plan is abstract in that regard and so is the class. The class defines fields (properties) and methods which operate on those fields. The fields are your data and the methods enable manipulation of that data.

## Objects

An object is your in-memory representation of your class. If the class is your house plan, then the object is your built house. Now, you can go into the kitchen and make that cup of tea/coffee. As with houses and house plans, you can create many objects based on the class. These objects are known as object *instances*, emphasizing that each object is its own unique instance.

In summary, the class is the template and the object is the in-memory representation of the class. You need an object (instance) if you want to execute its (instance) methods. So, how do we create an object? We use the new keyword.

## Getting familiar with the new keyword

The new keyword in Java enables us to create objects. The object is created on the heap, a special area of memory reserved for objects. A reference (similar to a pointer) to the object is returned. This reference enables us to manipulate the object; for example, to execute the instance methods. Let's examine the code example shown in *Figure 8.1*:

```
3       class Person{}
4  ▶    public class PersonExample {
5  ▶        public static void main(String[] args) {
6              Person p = new Person();
7          }
8      }
```

Figure 8.1 – Creating an object

In the preceding figure, line 3 defines a Person class. It contains nothing at the moment; we will expand it as we progress. Line 6 is important – we are creating a Person object using the new keyword. Apart from the new keyword, line 6 is very similar to any method call. The p reference (on the stack) is initialized to refer to an object of type Person (on the heap). **It is very important to separate the reference from the object**. For example, as we shall see when we discuss Inheritance (*Chapter 9*), a reference of type X does not have to refer to an object of type X; the reference can refer to an object of type Y, once Y is related to X. On line 6, the Person reference named p is referring to a Person object; however, going forward, that will rarely be the case. When "constructing" objects using the new keyword, the method that's invoked is a special method known called a *constructor*.

### Constructors

A constructor is a special method that's invoked by the `new` keyword. It has two distinct properties that differentiate it from other methods: it has the same name as the class and defines no return type, not even `void`. (Java returns the reference to the object in the background).

Every class contains a constructor, even if you do not code one yourself. If you do not code a constructor for your class, Java will synthesize (or define) a "default constructor" for you. The default constructor will have the same properties as regular constructors; namely, the same name as the class and no return type. However, the default constructor will not define any parameters; it will have the same access modifier as the class and will contain only one line of code, which is `super();`. We will discuss access modifiers later in this chapter and `super()` in *Chapter 9*.

Note that if you insert even one constructor, the default constructor is not synthesized. It's as if the compiler says, "Okay, you have a constructor(s), you know what you are doing, so I won't get involved."

Now that we know when default constructors are synthesized by the compiler, we can see that default constructors are required for both `Person` and `PersonExample` in *Figure 8.1*. *Figure 8.2* represents the code *after* the compiler has inserted the default constructors:

```
3    class Person{
4        Person(){
5            super();
6        }
7    }
8    public class PersonExample {
9        public PersonExample(){
10           super();
11       }
12       public static void main(String[] args) {
13           Person p = new Person();
14       }
15   }
```

Figure 8.2 – Default constructors inserted

The red rectangles in the preceding figure represent the default constructors inserted by the compiler. This happened to both classes because neither class defined any constructor at all and every class requires a constructor. The default constructors, in addition to having the same name as the class and not returning anything (not even `void`), define no parameters (lines 4 and 9) and simply call `super();`. As stated in the previous callout, `super()` will be discussed when we discuss Inheritance in *Chapter 9*.

We will discuss access modifiers in detail later but note that the access for the default constructors match the access for their respective classes. For example, `PersonExample` is a `public` class and so is its constructor (lines 8 and 9 respectively). The `Person` class mentions no *explicit* access modifier at all and neither does its constructor (lines 3 and 4 respectively).

Now, you can see why `new Person();` on line 13 does not generate a compiler error. To be clear, there is no compiler error on line 13 because the compiler inserted the default constructor for the `Person` class (lines 4 to 6) and thus `new Person()` was able to locate the constructor and therefore compile.

The default constructor for `PersonExample` (lines 9 to 11) has no material effect in this program. The JVM starts every program in the `main` method.

We will now move on to discuss instance members versus class members. Note that local variables (in a method) are neither.

## Contrasting instance with class members

An object can be more correctly termed an object *instance*. This is where *instance* members (methods/data) get their names: every object gets a copy of an instance member. Class members, however, are different in that there is only one copy per class, regardless of the number of object instances created. We'll discuss both of these topics now.

### Instance members (methods/data)

This is more easily explained by presenting a code example first. *Figure 8.3* presents a class with instance members:

```
3   class Person{
4       private String name;     // instance variable
5       private int count;       // instance variable
6
7       Person(String aName) { // constructor
8           name = aName;
9           count++;
10      }
11      public String getName() { // instance method
12          return name;
13      }
14      public void setName(String aName) { // instance method
15          name = aName;
16      }
17      public int getCount() { // instance method
18          return count;
19      }
20  }
21  public class PersonExample {
22      public static void main(String[] args) {
23          Person p1 = new Person( aName: "Maaike");
24          Person p2 = new Person( aName: "Sean");
25          System.out.println(p1.getName()); // Maaike
26          System.out.println(p2.getName()); // Sean
27          p1.setName("Maaike van Putten");
28          p2.setName("Sean Kennedy");
29          System.out.println(p1.getName()); // Maaike van Putten
30          System.out.println(p2.getName()); // Sean Kennedy
31      }
32  }
```

Figure 8.3 – A class with instance members

When you create an object using new, you are creating an object *instance*. Each instance gets a copy of the instance members (variables and methods). Regarding instance variables, we need to define where instance variables are declared and their resultant scope. An instance variable is defined within the class but outside every method coded in the class. Thus, the scope of an instance variable is the class itself; meaning, every instance method in the class can access the instance variables.

Now let us discuss the code example. In the preceding figure, the Person class defines both instance variables and instance methods. As the instance variables are declared outside every method, they have the scope of the class. The fact that the instance variables are marked private and the instance methods are marked public will be explained later in this chapter. The constructor is as follows:

```
Person(String aName) { // constructor
    name = aName;
    count++;
}
```

This constructor enables us to pass in a `String` and initialize the instance variable based on that `String`. For example, when we instantiate an object as follows:

```
Person p1 = new Person("Maaike");
```

we are passing `"Maaike"` into the constructor, so the `name` instance variable in the object referred to by `p1` refers to `"Maaike"`. The constructor is also keeping a count of the number of objects that are created by incrementing `count` each time the constructor is invoked. Note that no default `Person` constructor was inserted by the compiler in this example as a constructor was already coded in the class.

We also invoke the `getName()` instance method using the `p1` and `p2` references as follows:

```
System.out.println(p1.getName()); // Maaike
System.out.println(p2.getName()); // Sean
```

This syntax of `refName.instanceMethod()` is known as *dot notation*. As per the comments in the code, `"Maaike"` and `"Sean"` are output to the screen (in that order). *Figure 8.4* shows the in-memory representation of the code after we have created both objects, referenced by `p1` and `p2` respectively:

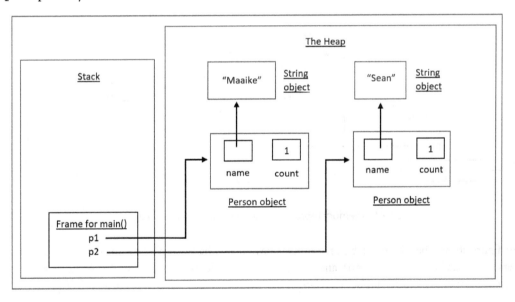

Figure 8.4 – In-memory representation of Figure 8.3 (start of line 27)

As the preceding figure shows, we have two references on the stack, namely p1 and p2. p1 refers to the first `Person` object on the heap – that is, the object that was created on line 23. The instance variable values of p1 (its "state") are `"Maaike"` and 1 for `name` and `count`, respectively. As strings are objects, `name` is a reference to another object, a `String` object, which has a value of `"Maaike"`. Similarly, the p2 reference refers to the object that was created on line 24. As can be seen from the diagram, the instance variable values of p2 are `"Sean"` and 1 for `name` and `count`, respectively.

Note that each `Person` object *instance* on the heap has a copy of the *instance* variables. That is why they are called instance variables.

Lines 27 and 28 change the values of the name instance variables to `"Maaike van Putten"` and `"Sean Kennedy"` for p1 and p2, respectively. *Figure 8.5* shows these changes:

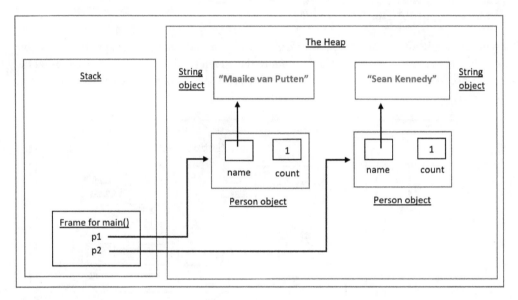

Figure 8.5 – In-memory representation of Figure 8.3 (start of line 29)

This figure shows that the two `String` objects have been changed: p1's instance variable name refers to `"Maaike van Putten"` and p2's instance variable name refers to `"Sean Kennedy"`. Consequently, lines 29 to 30 output `"Maaike van Putten"` and `"Sean Kennedy"`, respectively.

**String immutability**

Strings are immutable objects. This means that `String` objects, once created, cannot be changed. Ever. It may look like they have changed, as in the effect is created of a change, but a completely new object has been created and the original is left untouched. We will revisit `String` immutability in greater detail in *Chapter 12*.

So, the original `String` objects, `"Sean"` and `"Maaike"`, are still on the heap taking up space. They are of no use because, as we have no references to them, we have no way to get to them. Remember, the name instance variables for both `p1` and `p2` refer to the newly created `String` objects containing `"Maaike van Putten"` and `"Sean Kennedy"`, respectively.

So, what happens to these no-longer-used objects? They are "garbage collected." We will discuss this soon but for now, just know that the JVM runs a process called a garbage collector in the background to tidy up (reclaim) all the objects that can no longer be reached. We have no control over when this process runs but the fact that there is a garbage collector saves us from having to tidy up after ourselves (whereas in other OOP languages such as C++, you have to!).

The code in *Figure 8.3* has an issue – `count` is 1 and it should be 2. Instance variables that are integers are initialized to 0 by default. In each of the constructor calls, we increment `count` from 0 to 1. We would like the first constructor call to increment `count` from 0 to 1 and the second constructor call to increment `count` from 1 to 2. This is where class members come in.

## Class members (methods/data)

To mark a field and/or method as a class member, as opposed to an instance member, you can insert the `static` keyword into the declaration of the member. Class members are shared by all instances of the class. This means that you do not have to create an object instance to access the `static` members of the class.

The syntax for accessing a `static` member is different from accessing an instance member. Rather than use the reference, the class name is used, as in `className.staticMember`. This emphasizes the class nature of the member being accessed. For example, the JVM starts the program in *Figure 8.3* with `PersonExample.main()`. This is how the JVM starts every program as it saves on constructing an object and its resulting memory footprint.

Let's get back to our problem with `count` (which is 1 instead of 2). *Figure 8.6* represents the changes that must be made to fix this issue:

```java
3    class Person{
4        private String name;        // instance variable
5        private static int count;   // class variable
6
7        Person(String aName) { // constructor
8            name = aName;
9            Person.count++;
10       }
11       public String getName() { // instance method
12           return name;
13       }
14       public void setName(String aName) { // instance method
15           name = aName;
16       }
17       public static int getCount() { // class method
18           return Person.count;
19       }
20   }
21   public class PersonExample {
22       public static void main(String[] args) {
23           Person p1 = new Person( aName: "Maaike");
24           Person p2 = new Person( aName: "Sean");
25           System.out.println(Person.getCount()); // 2
26       }
27   }
```

Figure 8.6 – Making "count" static

Contrasting the code in *Figure 8.6* with the code in *Figure 8.3*, we can see that `count` is declared `static` (line 5). Thus, there is only one copy of *count*, which is shared across all instances of `Person`. Thus, p1 and p2 are looking at the same *count*.

In the constructor (line 9), while not necessary, we use the correct syntax to emphasize the `static` nature of `count`. Similarly, as `getCount` (line 17) is simply returning a `static` member, we marked it as `static`. In addition, we used the `Person.count` static syntax (line 18). Lastly, line 25 accesses the `static` method using the correct syntax, `Person.getCount`, to retrieve the `private` class variable, `count`. We can see that it outputs 2, which is correct. Comparing the other differences in code, some of the extra code in `main` (*Figure 8.3*) has been removed to help us focus on what we are discussing here.

**Instance to static but not vice versa**

If you are in an instance method, you can access a `static` member but not vice versa. We will discuss the reason why when we explain the `this` reference. This means that, in *Figure 8.6*, you could use the p1 reference to access the `getCount` method (line 25). As such, `p1.getCount()` is valid but this is a *poor* programming practice as it conveys the impression that `getCount` is an instance method when it is a `static` method - use `Person.getCount()` as per the code.

*Figure 8.7* shows the in-memory representation of the code in *Figure 8.6*:

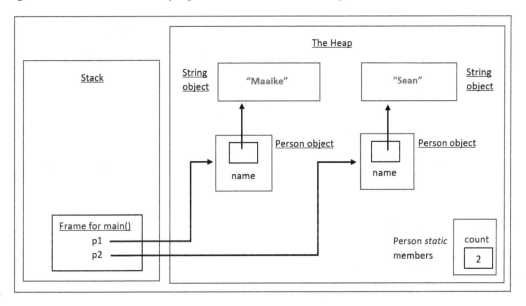

Figure 8.7 – In-memory representation of the code in Figure 8.6

As can be seen in the bottom-right corner of the preceding figure, the `static/class` members of the `Person` class are stored separately from the instances themselves. There is now only one copy of `count` and it is shared between p1 and p2. Thus, the `count` value of 2 is correct.

**Default values for class and instance variables**

Instance variables are initialized to default values every time a class is new'ed.

Class variables are initialized to default values the very first time a class is loaded. This could occur when using new or when referring to a class member (using the class syntax).

The default values for class and instance variables are as follows:

| Type | Default value |
| --- | --- |
| `byte, short, and int` | 0 |
| `long` | 0L |
| `float` | 0.0f |
| `double` | 0.0d |
| `char` | '\u0000' (Unicode zero) |
| `String` (or any reference to an object) | `null` |
| `boolean` | `false` |

Table 8.1 – Default values for class and instance variables

In a previous callout, we highlighted that you can access class members from an instance method but not vice versa. Let's delve into that now.

## Exploring the "this" reference

When you call an instance method, the compiler secretly passes into the method a copy of the object reference that invoked the method. This reference is available to the instance method as the `this` reference.

Class methods do not get a `this` reference. This is why, if you are in a `static` method (context) and you try to access an instance member directly (without an object reference), you will get a compiler error. In effect, every instance member requires an object reference when accessing it. This makes sense because instance members are instance-specific and therefore, you need an instance (reference) to say, *"I want to access this particular instance/object as opposed to that particular one."*

Let's refactor the code in *Figure 8.3* so that the `Person` class uses the `this` reference explicitly. In addition, all references to the incorrectly working `count` instance variable have been removed so that we can focus on the `this` reference. *Figure 8.8* includes the refactored `Person` class (the `PersonExample` class remains untouched):

```
3      class Person{
4          private String name;     // instance variable
5
6          Person(String aName) { // constructor
7      //       name = aName;
8              this.name = aName;
9          }
10         public String getName() { // instance method
11     //       return name;
12             return this.name;
13         }
14         public void setName(String aName) { // instance method
15     //       name = aName;
16             this.name = aName;
17         }
18     }
19 ▶  public class PersonExample {
20 ▶      public static void main(String[] args) {
21             Person p1 = new Person( aName: "Maaike");
22             Person p2 = new Person( aName: "Sean");
23             System.out.println(p1.getName()); // Maaike
24             System.out.println(p2.getName()); // Sean
25             p1.setName("Maaike van Putten");
26             p2.setName("Sean Kennedy");
27             System.out.println(p1.getName()); // Maaike van Putten
28             System.out.println(p2.getName()); // Sean Kennedy
29         }
30     }
```

Figure 8.8 – Using the "this" reference

In the preceding figure, lines 7, 11, and 15 are commented out and replaced by lines 8, 12, and 16, respectively. Let's contrast both the commented-out line 7 and the new line 8 more closely:

```
// name = aName; // line 7
this.name = aName; // line 8
```

Firstly, assume line 7 is uncommented. How does line 7 reconcile its variables? Initially, the compiler checks the current scope (the constructor block of code) and reconciles aName as a parameter to the constructor. However, the compiler still has not reconciled name, so it checks the next outer scope, the class scope, where the instance/class variables are defined. Here, it finds an instance variable called name, and therefore line 7 compiles.

Line 8 operates somewhat differently. Yes, it reconciles aName similarly but now, it comes across this.name (as opposed to name). Upon seeing *this*, the compiler immediately checks the instance variables that have been declared. It finds an instance variable called name, and therefore line 8 compiles. Lines 7 and 8 are, in effect, the same.

Line 16 is the same as line 8 as we used the same parameter identifier, aName. Line 12 is simply returning the name instance variable.

So, that covers how to use this in a class, but how do we associate the instance with this?

## Associating an instance with the "this" reference

Thankfully, the compiler does this automatically. As stated previously, the this reference is only passed (in secret) to instance methods and it refers to the instance that is invoking the method at that time. For example, when executing p1.getName(), the this reference in getName refers to p1, whereas when executing p2.getName(), the this reference in getName refers to p2. Thus, the this reference varies, depending on the instance that invokes the method. *Figure 8.9* represents the dynamic nature of the this reference in action:

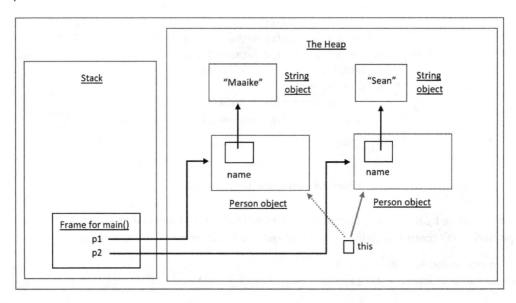

Figure 8.9 – The dynamic nature of the "this" reference

This figure represents the in-memory representation of the code in *Figure 8.8* as we execute line 12 from the method call on line 24. As getName on line 24 is invoked on p2 – in other words, p2.getName(); – the this reference inside getName refers to the same object that p2 is referring to. This is represented by the solid line from the this reference referring to the same object that p2 is referring to.

The dashed line represents what the this reference was referring to on line 12, from the method call on line 23, namely p1. Thus, the this reference is dynamically referring to the instances referred to by p1 or p2, depending on which invoked the instance method.

As we saw in the code in *Figure 8.8*, the this reference was not needed. Let's examine a situation where the this reference is needed.

## Shadowing or hiding an instance variable

Shadowing an instance variable occurs when a variable has the same identifier as the instance variable. *Figure 8.10* presents code where this occurs so that we can observe the issue it creates:

```java
class Person{
    private String name;    // instance variable

    Person(String name) { // constructor
        name = name; // shadowing/hiding the instance variable
    }
    public String getName() { // instance method
        return name;
    }
    public void setName(String aName) { // instance method
        name = aName;
    }
}
public class PersonExample {
    public static void main(String[] args) {
        Person p1 = new Person( name: "Maaike");
        System.out.println(p1.getName()); // null
    }
}
```

Figure 8.10 – Shadowing an instance variable

In the preceding figure, the constructor has a logical issue; in other words, the code compiles but the code is not working as expected. Line 7 is the issue. Remember that, if a variable is not qualified with this, the current scope is checked to see if the variable is declared there. On line 6, we have declared a constructor parameter that uses the name identifier, which is the same identifier as the instance variable on line 4. Thus, line 7 is essentially assigning the local variable to itself and the instance variable remains untouched. As the instance variable is a String type, its default value is null. As a result, null is output on line 19 instead of "Maaike".

To fix this issue, we have two options. The first option is to use a different identifier for the constructor parameter and use that new identifier. This is what setName does (lines 12-13): a method parameter called aName is used that does not shadow the name instance identifier. The second option is to use the this reference to specify that the variable being initialized is an instance variable. *Figure 8.11* shows this:

```
3   class Person{
4       private String name;    // instance variable
5
6       Person(String name) { // constructor
7           this.name = name;
8       }
9       public String getName() { // instance method
10          return name;
11      }
12      public void setName(String aName) { // instance method
13          name = aName;
14      }
15  }
16  public class PersonExample {
17      public static void main(String[] args) {
18          Person p1 = new Person( name: "Maaike");
19          System.out.println(p1.getName()); // Maaike
20      }
21  }
```

Figure 8.11 – Using "this" to fix the shadowing issue

In this figure, line 7 is important: this.name refers to the name instance variable, while name, on its own, refers to the method parameter. Thus, shadowing has been removed and line 19 now outputs "Maaike" as expected.

We know that only non-static (instance) methods receive the this reference. Let's examine how this issue can affect us and how to resolve it. *Figure 8.12* presents code where we are in a static context (method) and are trying to directly access an instance variable:

```
3  ▶   public class PersonExample {
4          int x;                 // instance variable
5          public void m(){}     // instance method
6  ▶       public static void main(String[] args) {
7              // Non-static field 'x' cannot be referenced
8              // from a static context
9              x = 9;   // same as 'this.x = 9;'
10             this.x = 99;
11             m();     // same as 'this.m();'
12             this.m();
13
14             // this works
15             PersonExample pe = new PersonExample();
16             pe.x=999;    // ok
17             pe.m();      // ok
18             System.out.println(pe.x);    // 999
19         }
20     }
```

Figure 8.12 – Accessing instance variables from a "static" context

In the preceding figure, we have an instance variable called x (line 4), an instance method called m (line 5), and a static method called main (lines 6–19). As we know, static methods such as main, do not get the this reference automatically (as they are class methods as opposed to instance methods).

There are compiler errors on lines 9, 10, 11, and 12. When you access an instance member directly, as on lines 9 and 11, the compiler inserts this before the member. In other words, by the time the compiler is finished with lines 9 and 11, internally, they look the same as lines 10 and 12. Consequently, as main does not have a this reference, the compiler complains about lines 9, 10, 11 and 12.

Lines 15-18 encapsulate how to resolve this issue. When you're in a static context and you want to access an instance member (variable or method), you need to create an object instance to refer to the instance member. Therefore, on line 15, we create an (object) instance of the class containing the instance member, namely PersonExample, and store the reference in an identifier, pe. Now that we have an instance, we can access the instance members, which we do on lines 16, 17 and 18. Line 16 successfully changes x from (its default value of) 0 to 999. This is what is output on line 18. Line 17 shows that access to m is not an issue either. Note that you must comment out lines 9-12 before the code will compile and run.

Throughout these examples, we have used the private and public access modifiers. Let's discuss these in more detail.

# Applying access modifiers

One of the cornerstones of OOP is the principle of *encapsulation* (data abstraction). Encapsulation can be achieved using access modifiers. Before we discuss encapsulation, we must understand the access modifiers themselves.

Access modifiers determine where a class, field, or method is visible and therefore available for use. The level you are annotating at, determines the available access modifiers:

- **Top level**: Classes, enums, records and interfaces – `public` or package-private (no keyword)
- **Member level**: The access modifiers are, in order from most restrictive to least restrictive, `private`, package-private, `protected`, and `public`

Let's discuss these in turn.

## private

A member marked as `private` is accessible within its own class only. In other words, the block scope of the class defines the boundary. When in a class (scope), you cannot access the `private` members of another class, even if you have an object reference to the class containing the `private` member.

## Package-private

There is no special keyword for `package-private`. If a type (class, interface, record, or enum) has no access modifier then `package-private` is applied. Types that are `package-private` are only visible within the same package. Recall that a package is simply a named group of related types.

The `Person` class (line 3) in *Figure 8.11* is a `package-private` class, meaning `Person` cannot be imported into another package. In addition, the `Person` constructor (line 6) is package-private, meaning that you cannot create an object of the `Person` type from within a different package.

At a **member** level, there are a few exceptions to the preceding text that you need to be aware of when you omit the access modifier:

- Class/record members are, as above, `package-private` by default.
- Interface members are `public` by default.
- Enum constants (members) are `public static` and `final` by default. Enum constructors are `private` by default. We will discuss enums later in the chapter.

> **The default package**
>
> The default package is also known as the package with no name or the unnamed package. Types that have no explicit package statement at the top of the file are put into this package. This is the package where the `Person` and `PersonExample` classes from *Figure 8.11* are placed.
>
> The implications of this are that, given the package has no name, if we are in a different (named) package, we have no way of importing `Person` and `PersonExample`. The fact that `PersonExample` is `public` (line 16) makes no difference. Therefore, only other types in the same (default) package can access them.

## protected

A member marked as `protected` means that it's visible within its own package (as with package-private) but also visible to subclasses outside of the package. We will discuss subclasses and `protected` in more detail when we cover inheritance in *Chapter 9*.

## public

A type or member marked as `public` is visible everywhere. Thus, no boundaries apply.

*Table 8.2* summarizes the access modifiers and their visibility:

| Access Modifier | Class | Package | Subclass (anywhere) | Everywhere |
|---|---|---|---|---|
| private | Y | N | N | N |
| package-private | Y | Y | N | N |
| protected | Y | Y | Y | N |
| public | Y | Y | Y | Y |

Table 8.2 – Access modifiers and their visibility

Let's examine *Table 8.2* horizontally. Only the class has access to members marked as `private`. If a class or member has no access modifier (package-private), then that class or member is only visible within the class and the package. If the member is marked as `protected`, then the member is visible to the class, package, and subclasses of that class, regardless of the package. Finally, if a class or member is marked as `public`, then the class or member is visible everywhere.

To further help explain *Table 8.2*, let's diagram an example suite of classes and their associated packages and draw up another visibility table specifically for it. *Figure 8.13* shows this:

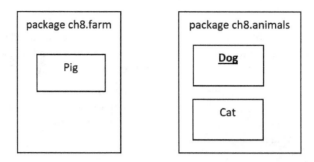

Figure 8.13 – Sample example access modifiers diagram

In this figure, the Dog class is in bold and underlined because the following table, *Table 8.3*, represents the visibility of *its* members. For example, when reading the `private` row, assume that we have marked a member in Dog as `private` and are determining its visibility in the other classes. Let's examine *Table 8.3*:

| Access Modifier | Dog | Cat | Pig |
|---|---|---|---|
| *private* | Y | N | N |
| *package-private* | Y | Y | N |
| *protected* (*) | Y | Y | N |
| *public* | Y | Y | Y |

Table 8.3 – Visibility when modifiers are applied to a Dog member

Thus, if a Dog member is `private`, only Dog can see it. If the Dog member is package-private, only Dog and Cat can see it. If the Dog member is `protected`, Dog and Cat can see it. Lastly, if the Dog member is `public`, every class can see it.

(*) We will complete this table when revisiting `protected` in the inheritance chapter.

> **How do access levels affect you?**
>
> Access levels will affect you in two ways. Firstly, you could be using an external class (from the Java API, for example) and want to know if you can use that class and/or its members in your code. Secondly, when writing a class, you will want to decide the access level each class and member will have. A good rule of thumb is to keep your members as `private` as possible to avoid misuse. Additionally, avoid `public` fields unless they are constants. We will discuss this further when we discuss encapsulation.

Let's look at these access modifiers in code. In particular, we will focus on the package and learn how to create one and how access is affected by its boundary.

## packages

Recall that the fully qualified type name includes the package name. *A package defines a namespace.* For example, in *Figure 8.13*, the Dog class in the ch8.animals package is fully qualified as ch8.animals.Dog. Therefore, a Dog class in a package named kennel would have a qualified name of kennel.Dog; which is completely different to ch8.animals.Dog. Thus, Java can distinguish between the two Dog types and no name collisions occur. As we shall see, the package structure is also used as a directory structure for your java files. Oracle gives very good guidelines (see https://docs.oracle.com/javase/tutorial/java/package/namingpkgs.html) on how to name your packages so that your types do not conflict with someone else's. Package names are written in all lowercase letters to differentiate them from type names. Following that, companies should use reverse internet domain names to begin their package names. For example, if you work at a company called somecompany.com and you are creating a package called somepackage, then the full package name should be com.somecompany.somepackage. Within a company, naming can then follow company conventions, such as including the region: com.somecompany.region.somepackage.

Let's examine the packages from *Figure 8.13*. We will start with ch8.animals:

```java
1     package ch8.animals;
2
3     public class Dog {
4         private String dogName;
5         protected int age;
6         public Dog(String dogName) { this.dogName = dogName; }
9         public String getDogName() { return dogName; }
12        void pkgPrivate(){}
13    }
14    class Cat{  // package private
15        Cat(){}
16        public void testDogAccess(){
17            Dog d = new Dog( dogName: "Rex");
18    //        d.dogName = "Abc"; // dogName is private to Dog
19            d.age = 2;
20            d.pkgPrivate(); //ok
21        }
22    }
```

Figure 8.14 – The "ch8.animals" package from Figure 8.13

In this figure, note that, for simplicity, we have grouped the two classes in the package into one Java file. This file is called Dog.java (as the public class is Dog). The first line is important: package ch8.animals states that the types (classes and so forth), that are defined here, go into this package. In addition, the file Dog.java will be put into a folder on the hard disk named ch8\animals.

In this figure, line 4 defines a private instance variable called dogName. This is accessible within the class only (as per lines 6 and 9) but not outside the class (as per line 18).

Line 5 defines a protected instance variable called age which we can access from another class within the package (line 19). Line 12 defines a package-private method called pkgPrivate() and line 20 shows that we can access it from another class in the same package. Note also that the Cat class and its constructor are both package-private (lines 14 and 15, respectively).

*Figure 8.15* shows the other package, ch8.farm:

```
1     package ch8.farm;
2
3     import ch8.animals.Dog; // class is public, ok
4     //import ch8.animals.Cat; // class is pkg-private, error
5
6     public class Pig{
7         void testDog(){
8             Dog d = new Dog( dogName: "Shep"); // constructor is public
9     //        d.pkgPrivate(); // package-private method, error
10        }
11    }
```

Figure 8.15 – The "ch8.farm" package from Figure 8.13

Again, note that line 1 states the package name – this is the ch8.farm package. The filename is Pig.java (as the public class is Pig) and the file will be put into a folder on the hard disk named ch\farm.

Note the use of the fully qualified names when importing (lines 3 and 4). As we want access to the Dog class which resides in a separate package, we must import it. There is no issue importing Dog since it is public. However, we are unable to import Cat as Cat is package-private (and we are in a different package).

Line 8 demonstrates that Pig can create a Dog object. Note that there are two access points here: the Dog class is public (so we can import it); and the Dog constructor is also public (so we can create an instance of Dog from code in a different package). This is why the access modifiers for the class and constructors should match. Line 9 shows that, when we are in a different package, we do not have access to package-private members from another package.

Now that we understand access modifiers, we are in a position to discuss encapsulation.

# Encapsulation

As previously stated, encapsulation is a key concept in OOP. The principle here is that you protect the data in your class and ensure that the data can only be manipulated (retrieved and/or changed) via your code. In other words, you have control over how external classes interact with your internal state (data). So, how do we do this?

## Achieving encapsulation

Basic encapsulation is very easy to achieve. You simply mark your data as `private` and manipulate the data via `public` methods. Thus, external classes cannot access the data directly (as it is `private`); these external classes must go through your `public` methods to retrieve or change the data.

These `public` methods make up the class's "interface"; in other words, how you interact with the class. This "interface" (group of `public` methods) is very different from and not to be confused with the `interface` language construct (*Chapter 10*). *Figure 8.16* presents a code example to help us further develop this topic:

```
1    package ch8;
2
3    class Adult{
4        private String name;
5        private int age;
6
7        Adult(String name, int age) {
8            this.age = age;
9            this.name = name;
10       }
11       public String getName() { return name; }
14       public void setName(String name) { this.name = name; }
17       public int getAge() { return age; }
20       public void setAge(int age) { this.age = age; }
23   }
24   public class BasicEncapsulation {
25       public static void main(String[] args) {
26           Adult john = new Adult( name: "John",  age: 20);
27           System.out.println(john.getName() + " "
28                   + john.getAge());    // John 20
29           //john.age = -99; // 'age' is private
30           john.setAge(-99); // uh-oh!
31           System.out.println(john.getName() + " "
32                   + john.getAge());    // John -99
33       }
34   }
```

Figure 8.16 – Basic encapsulation in action

In the preceding figure, the `Adult` class has two `private` instance variables, namely `name` and `age` (lines 4 and 5, respectively). Thus, these instance variables only have access within the `Adult` block of code. Note that even having an `Adult` object reference cannot bypass this access rule – the compiler error on (the commented out) line 29 demonstrates this.

---

**public class name and filename relationship**

In Java, the name of the `public` class must match the filename. In *Figure 8.16*, the `public` class is `BasicEncapsulation`. This means that the filename must be named `BasicEncapsulation.java`, which it is. This rule implies that you cannot have two `public` classes in the same file – that is why the `Adult` class is not `public`.

What if we were in a different package and we wanted to create an `Adult` object, as defined in *Figure 8.16*? This is an issue because `Adult` is package-private (line 3). To fix this issue, we need to make the `Adult` class `public` so that we can `import` it when in a different package. This means that we need to move the `Adult` class into a separate file, named `Adult.java`. In addition, both `Adult` and its constructor would need to be `public`. Why? Well, when we're in a different package, the class being `public` enables us to `import` the class and the constructor being `public` enables us to create objects of the `Adult` type.

---

The `Adult` constructor (line 7) has no access modifier and is therefore package-private. Thus, only classes within the same package can invoke this constructor. In other words, only classes in the `ch8` package (line 1) can create `Adult` objects. As `BasicEncapsulation` is also in `ch8`, the object creation on line 26 is fine.

The rest of the `Adult` class (lines 11-20) provides the getter/setter method pairs for manipulating the object state (the instance variables). These getter/setter methods are also known as accessor/mutator methods, respectively. There is usually a pair for each instance variable and they follow this format (note that this is just an example):

```
public int getAge(){
    return age;
}
public void setAge(int age){
    this.age = age;
}
```

After creating the `Adult` object on line 26 in *Figure 8.16*, we output the object state using the `public` accessor methods, `getName` and `getAge` (lines 27-28). As these accessor methods are `public`, these methods are available to any class in any package. Given that `'John'` and `20` are output, we know our object was created correctly.

Let's assume that we are the developers of the Adult class and require an adult to be 18 years or older. In addition, we will assume that the developer of the BasicEncapsulation class is unknown to us. Line 29 demonstrates that as our Adult data is private, it is protected from direct external corruption. This is exactly what encapsulation provides; it is its raison d'être!

Line 30 demonstrates that the object's state can still be corrupted. However, the corruption that's done via the set/mutator method on line 30 is very different from the direct corruption on line 29. As the author of the Adult class, we can control and therefore fix the corruption error in our set methods. The issue with our set (mutator) method is replicated in the constructor. *Figure 8.17* addresses this (internal) corruption issue in both the constructor and mutator methods:

```java
1    package ch8;
2
3    class Adult{
4        private String name;
5        private int age;
6
7        Adult(String name, int age) {
8            setAge(age);
9            this.name = name;
10       }
11       public String getName() { return name; }
14       public void setName(String name) { this.name = name; }
17       public int getAge() { return age; }
20       public void setAge(int age) {
21           if(isAgeOk(age)){
22               this.age = age;
23           }else{
24               this.age = -1; // error state
25           }
26       }
27       private boolean isAgeOk(int age){ // private
28           return age >= 18 ? true :false ; // ternary operator
29       }
30   }
```

Figure 8.17 – Ensuring "age" is at least 18

As `BasicEncapsulation` remains unchanged, it is not included in the preceding figure. Note that a new `isAgeOk` method has been introduced (lines 27-29). This method takes in an `int` parameter `age` and checks to see if it is `>= 18`. If so, the method returns `true`; otherwise, it returns `false`.

The `isAgeOk` method is invoked from the `setAge` mutator method (line 21). As the constructor calls `setAge` (line 8), it also avails of the age check logic. If an invalid age is passed into the constructor or `setAge`, an error value of –1 is set. Note that there are better ways to do this, but for now this is fine. When we run the program now, since the `age` value that is being passed into `setAge` is -99 (`john.setAge(-99)`), the instance variable `age` is set to the error value of –1.

That covers basic encapsulation. We will now discuss a particular issue with basic encapsulation and how advanced encapsulation resolves it.

# Mastering advanced encapsulation

The simple maxim of "private data, public methods" (where the `public` methods manipulate the data) goes a long way to ensuring proper encapsulation of your data. However, you are not completely safe just yet. In this section, we will review Java's call by value principle, which is used when passing arguments to and returning values from methods. We will examine how this can present a subtle issue. Lastly, we will examine how to protect your code from encountering this issue in the first place.

## Call By value revisited

In *Chapter 7*, we discussed how, when passing arguments to methods, Java's *call by value* mechanism creates *copies* of those arguments. We saw the need to be aware that when the argument is a reference, such as to an array, the called method can now manipulate the array object that the caller method is looking at.

Similarly, when a method is *returning* something, call by value applies again. In other words, a copy is made of what you are returning. Depending on what the copy is of, this can result in encapsulation being broken or not. If you are returning `private` primitive data, then there is no issue – a copy of the primitive is returned and the client can do whatever it likes to the copy; your `private` primitive data is safe. As you may recall from *Chapter 7*, copying primitives is like photocopying a sheet of paper. The photocopied sheet can be written on without it affecting the original copy.

## The issue

The issue arises if your `private` data is a reference (to an object). If the client receives a copy of the reference, then the client can manipulate your `private` object! From *Chapter 7*, you may recall that copying a reference is like copying a remote control to a TV. The new remote can change the channels on the same TV. *Figure 8.18* presents code that breaks encapsulation:

```
 5    class Seniors {
 6        private int[] ages = new int[2];
 7        private int num;
 8
 9        Seniors(){
10            num = 2;
11            ages[0] = 30;
12            ages[1] = 40;
13        }
14        public int getNum() { return num;}
15        public int[] getAges() { // breaks encapsulation
16            return ages;
17        }
18    }
19 ▶  public class AdvancedEncapsulation {
20 ▶      public static void main(String[] args) {
21            Seniors seniors = new Seniors();
22            // 1. Returning primitives is okay.
23            int num = seniors.getNum();
24            System.out.println(num); // 2
25            num = -100;
26            num = seniors.getNum();
27            System.out.println(num); // 2, ok, primitives are encapsulated once 'private'
28
29            // 2. Returning references requires care.
30            int[] copyAges = seniors.getAges(); // 'copyAges' and 'ages' refer to the same array object!
31            System.out.println(copyAges[0] + ", " + copyAges[1]);// 30, 40
32            // As we have a copy of the internal array reference, we can, from HERE
33            // change the "private" internal Seniors array! This breaks encapsulation.
34            copyAges[0] = -9;
35            copyAges[1] = -19;
36            int[] copyAges2 = seniors.getAges();
37            System.out.println(copyAges2[0] + ", " + copyAges2[1]);// -9, -19
38        }
39    }
```

Figure 8.18 – Code that breaks encapsulation

In the preceding figure, the Seniors class has two private instance variables (lines 6-7), namely ages and num. The constructor (lines 9-13) initializes the instance variables. We have a public getNum accessor method, which returns the private instance variable, num (line 14). Note that we have put this method on one line in the interest of space.

We have another accessor method called getAges (lines 15-17) that returns a private array called ages. *Line 16 is the problem* as it breaks encapsulation. We will explain why when we discuss the code in main.

In main, the first thing we do is create an instance of Seniors (line 21). This is so we can access the instance methods defined in Seniors. The rest of main is divided into two sections: one section (lines 23-27) demonstrates that returning private primitive data is fine; the other section (lines 30-37) demonstrates that simply returning private *references* breaks encapsulation.

Let's examine the first section. Line 23 initializes the local variable, num, based on the return value from seniors.getNum(). As the private Seniors instance variable, num, was initialized to 2 in the Seniors constructor (line 10), the (completely separate) local variable, num, is initialized to 2. We output this fact on line 24. We then change the local num variable's value to -100 (line 25). The question now is, when we changed the local variable num, was the private Seniors instance variable, num, changed also? To find out, we can simply retrieve num again using the public accessor method, getNum (line 26). Line 27 outputs 2, proving that the private primitive, num, was safe from changes made in main.

The second section is where things get interesting. Line 30 initializes a local variable called copyAges based on the return value from the public accessor method, seniors.getAges(). As getAges simply returns (a copy of) the private ages reference, we now have two references referring to the one array object. These references are the private instance variable, ages, and the local variable, copyAges. Line 31 outputs the values of copyAges, which are 30 and 40 for the indices 0 and 1, respectively. These are the same values that the private ages array was initialized to in the Seniors constructor (lines 11-12).

Now, on lines 34-35, we change the values of the copyAges array: index 0 is set to -9 and index 1 is set to -19. As with the first section, we are now wondering, did changing the local array have any effect on the private instance array in Seniors? The answer is yes! To prove this, we can retrieve the private array again using getAges (line 36) and output its values (line 37). The output values of -9 and -19 demonstrate that the client, AdvancedEncapsulation, was able to manipulate (change) the so-called private data of Seniors. Therefore, Seniors is not encapsulated after all.

*Figure 8.19* shows the situation in memory, shedding light on why Seniors is not encapsulated:

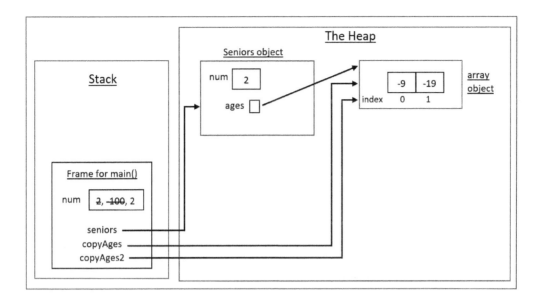

Figure 8.19 – In-memory representation of Figure 8.18 (at line 37)

In the preceding figure, the local variable, num, is on the stack. It is a copy of the private Seniors num instance variable, and its different values as we progress through main are reflected in strikethrough font. Line 25 (*Figure 8.18*) changes the local variable to -100. As can be seen, this change does not affect the private instance variable, num, in Seniors, which remains 2.

The issue is with the reference to the private array object, ages. Because getAges (line 15) simply returns the reference, a copy of that reference is stored in the local variable, copyAges (line 30). As the local reference, copyAges, and the private reference, ages, now refer to the same object, the copy reference can change the private array object. That is why the array object has values of -9 and -19 for indices 0 and 1, respectively. The copyAges2 reference is just there to prove that point.

## The solution

Now that we know the issue, fixing it is quite straightforward. The key is to, when returning a reference, ensure that you simply do not return the private reference (as call by value will return a copy of that reference). The solution is to *make a copy of the object you wish to return and return a reference to the new object*. Thus, the external class (client) can manipulate this new object without affecting your private internal object. *Figure 8.20* is the properly encapsulated, refactored version of *Figure 8.18*:

```
3     import java.util.Arrays;
4
5     class Seniors {
6         private int[] ages = new int[2];
7         private int num;
8
9         Seniors(){
10            num = 2;
11            ages[0] = 30;
12            ages[1] = 40;
13        }
14        public int getNum() { return num;}
15        public int[] getAges() { // properly encapsulated
16            int newArr[] = Arrays.copyOf(ages, newLength: 2);
17            return newArr;
18        }
19    }
20    public class AdvancedEncapsulation {
21        public static void main(String[] args) {
22            Seniors seniors = new Seniors();
23
24            int[] copyAges = seniors.getAges(); // 'copyAges' and 'ages' refer to 2 different arrays
25            System.out.println(copyAges[0] + ", " + copyAges[1]);// 30, 40
26            copyAges[0] = -9;
27            copyAges[1] = -19;
28            int[] copyAges2 = seniors.getAges();
29            System.out.println(copyAges2[0] + ", " + copyAges2[1]);// 30, 40
30        }
31    }
```

Figure 8.20 – Properly encapsulated code

In the preceding figure, we have replaced the accessor method, getAges, with a new version (lines 15-18). This new version is properly encapsulated. On line 16, instead of simply returning the (reference to the) array instance variable, we are copying the array, ages, into a new array, namely newArr. We achieve this using the Arrays.copyOf method. We return a (copy of the) reference to the new array object.

Now, on line 24, when we initialize copyAges, it is referring to the copy array that was created on line 16. That reference, newArr, has gone out of scope (since we returned from getAges) but the new array object is still on the heap, with copyAges referring to it. The important point here is that on line 25, we have two distinct array references: the ages instance and the local copyAges. These references now refer to two *different* objects.

Line 25 outputs the details of the copy array; 30 for index 0 and 40 for index 1. This is as expected. Lines 26 and 27 change the contents of the copy array indices, 0 and 1, to -9 and -19, respectively. Now, we need to check something: when we changed the contents of the copyAges array, were the contents of the private internal Seniors array's ages changed? To check, on line 28, we can initialize a copyAges2 array with the (copy of the) contents of the private array, ages. When we output the details of copyAges2 on line 29, we get 30 and 40, thereby proving that the private internal array, ages, was *not* changed when we changed the local copyAges array (lines 26-27). Now, Seniors is properly encapsulated.

*Figure 8.21* show this situation in memory as we execute line 29:

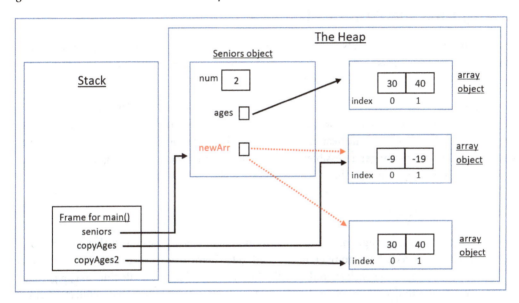

Figure 8.21 – In-memory representation of Figure 8.20

In the preceding figure, just after the Seniors object is constructed (line 22), we have a seniors reference on the stack referring to a Seniors object on the heap. The Seniors object contains a num primitive set to 2 (line 10) and an ages array reference referring to the array object (lines 11-12).

When we call getAges (line 24), the copy array, newArr, is created (line 16) and although not shown here, the new array initially contains the values of 30 and 40 (indices 0 and 1, respectively), as per line 25. When newArr is returned from getAges (line 17), the (copy of the) reference is assigned to copyAges (line 24). As shown in the preceding diagram, the copyAges local variable and the ages instance variable refer to two different array objects. This is what we want. *Any changes made using copyAges will not affect the private array ages.*

This is what the changes on lines 26-27 demonstrate. The changes that were made using the `copyAges` reference are reflected in the diagram. To prove that the changes on lines 26-27 did not affect the `private` array, `ages`, we call `getAges` again. A new array, representing a copy of the `private` array, is again created (line 16) and the (copy of) the new array reference is returned and assigned to the local reference, `copyAges2`. When we output the new array's contents on line 29, we get 30 and 40, demonstrating that the `private` array is unaffected by changes to the local array (lines 26-27).

Now that we understand call by value and advanced encapsulation, we are in an excellent position to discuss the object life cycle.

# Delving into the object life cycle

To understand Java, it is extremely helpful to have an appreciation of what is happening in the background, in memory. This section will help cement what is happening on the stack and the heap when we call methods, declare local/instance variables, and so forth.

Local variables are kept on the stack (for fast access), whereas instance variables and objects live on the heap (a large area of memory). As we know, we use the `new` keyword to create a Java object. The `new` keyword allocates space on the heap for the object and returns the reference to the object. What happens if the object is no longer accessible? For example, the reference may have gone out of scope. How do we reclaim that memory? This is where garbage collection comes into play.

## Garbage collection

As mentioned previously, garbage collection reclaims memory taken up by objects that are no longer being used; as in the objects have no references pointing to them. This garbage collection process is a JVM process that runs in the background. The JVM may decide during an idle time to run garbage collection and then it may not. Simply put, we have no control over when garbage collection runs. Even if we invoke `System.gc()`, this is but a suggestion to the JVM to run garbage collection – the JVM is free to ignore this suggestion. The major advantage of garbage collection is that we do not have to do the tidy-up ourselves; whereas in languages such as C++, we do.

For further detail on Java Memory Management please see our previous book: `https://www.amazon.com/Java-Memory-Management-comprehensive-collection/dp/1801812853/ref=sr_1_1?crid=3QUEBKJP46CN7&keywords=java+memory+management+maaike&qid=1699112145&sprefix=java+memory+management+maaike%2Caps%2C148&sr=8-1`.

# Object life cycle example

A sample program will help at this point. *Figure 8.22* presents a program to suit our purposes:

```
3      class Tag{}
4  ▶   public class Cow {
5          Tag tag;
6          String country;
7
8  ▶       public static void main(String[] args) {
9              Cow cow1 = new Cow();
10             Cow cow2 = cow1;// reassignment
11             cow2.tagAnimal(cow1);
12         }
13 @     void tagAnimal(Cow cow){
14             tag = new Tag();
15             cow.setCountry("France");
16         }
17     void setCountry(String country){
18             this.country = country;
19         }
20 }
```

Figure 8.22 – Sample program to explain an object's life cycle

As this (simple and very contrived) program executes, three methods are pushed onto the stack, namely main, tagAnimal, and setCountry. *Figure 8.23* represents the in-memory representation when we are just about to exit the setCountry method (line 19):

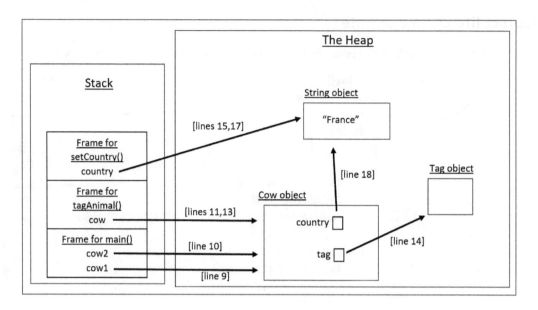

Figure 8.23 – In-memory representation of code in Figure 8.22

Let's look at this in more detail.

### The main method

As can be seen from the previous two figures, line 9 creates the Cow object on the heap, and the local reference, cow1, on the stack in the frame for main, refers to it. The instance variables in the Cow object on the heap, namely tag and country, will be null at this point.

Line 10 assigns the value in cow1 to another local reference in main, namely cow2. Now, at line 11, we have a frame for main on the stack with two local reference variables, namely cow1 and cow2, both referring to the one Cow object on the heap.

Line 11 uses the cow2 reference to execute the instance method, tagAnimal. Thus, when inside the tagAnimal method (during this invocation), the this reference will be referring to whatever cow2 is referring to (which is the Cow object on the heap). In addition, the cow1 reference is passed as an argument to the tagAnimal method. This is not necessary as tagAnimal already has a reference to the Cow object (using this) but this program is just for example purposes.

### The tagAnimal method

As with any method invocation, a stack frame for `tagAnimal` is pushed on the stack. As per call by value rules, `tagAnimal` (line 13) aliases the method parameter `cow` for `cow1` from line 11 (the method call). Thus, the `cow` reference in `tagAnimal` and the `cow1` reference in `main` are pointing at the same `Cow` object, which was created on line 9.

As we know, the `this` reference refers to the object instance responsible for the method call – in this case, `cow2` (line 11). Therefore, the reference to `tag` on line 14 (which is `this.tag` in effect) is referring to the `tag` instance variable that can be accessed via `cow2`. As a result, line 14 creates a new `Tag` object on the heap and stores its reference in the `tag` instance variable of the `Cow` object, overwriting its previous default value of `null`. Note that at this point, given the contrived nature of this example, the `Cow` object is referred to by three different references: `cow1` and `cow2` in `main`; and `cow` in `tagAnimal`.

Line 15 specifies a `String` literal of `"France"`. As `String` literals are objects, a `String` object is created on the heap. Using the `cow` reference, the `setCountry` method is called, passing down the `String` literal, `"France"`.

### The setCountry method

A stack frame for `setCountry` is pushed onto the stack. The `setCountry` declaration aliases the method parameter `country` to refer to the `String` literal, `"France"`, which is passed down in the method call (line 15). Line 18 initializes the `country` instance variable to the argument passed down, namely `"France"`. Line 18 explicitly uses the `this` reference because the parameter name and instance variable have the same identifier, `country`. The *this* reference refers to whatever `cow` is referring to, which is the `Cow` object on the heap. This is because the `setCountry` method call (line 15) was executed on the reference `cow`.

Now that we know how methods are pushed onto the stack, let's examine the memory as we return from these method calls – in other words, as we pop the stack. *Figure 8.24* represents memory after we have exited the `setCountry` method but before we exit the `tagAnimal` method:

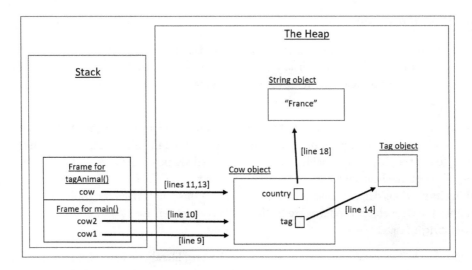

Figure 8.24 – In-memory representation after the "setCountry" method completes

As can be seen from the preceding figure, the setCountry frame has been popped from the stack. However, the String object, "France", remains on the heap because the country instance variable from the Cow instance object still refers to it. Only objects that have no references pointing to them are eligible for garbage collection.

*Figure 8.25* represents the in-memory representation just after tagAnimal finishes but before main completes:

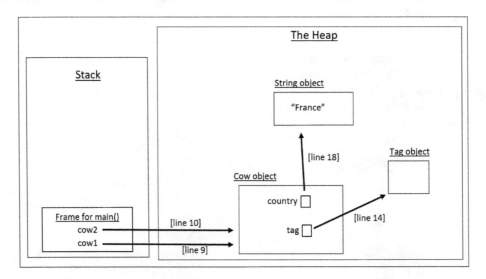

Figure 8.25 – In-memory representation after the 'tagAnimal" method completes

There is very little change in this figure from the previous figure, except that the stack frame for tagAnimal has been popped. The Cow object on the heap cannot be garbage collected because both the references, cow1 and cow2, in main refer to it. In addition, because the Cow object cannot be removed, neither can the Tag or String objects. This is because the Cow instance variables, tag and country, refer to them. This figure represents the situation in memory until main exits, at which point everything can be reclaimed.

That concludes our discussion on an object's life cycle. We will now move on and discuss the instanceof keyword.

# Explaining the instanceof keyword

The instanceof keyword enables us to determine the object type that a reference is referring to. That is why it is so critical to separate the reference from the object. The reference's type and the object's type are often very different. In fact, in most cases, they are different. We will discuss instanceof in greater detail when we cover inheritance (*Chapter 9*) but also when we discuss interfaces (*Chapter 10*).

So, for the moment, we will keep it simple – where the reference type and object type are the same. *Figure 8.26* presents one such code example:

```
3      class Dog{}
4      class Cat{}
5  ▶   public class InstanceOfExample {
6  ▶       public static void main(String[] args) {
7              Dog dog = new Dog();
8              Cat cat = new Cat();
9              if(dog instanceof Dog){ // true
10                 System.out.println("dog referring to a Dog object");
11             }
12             if(cat instanceof Cat){ // true
13                 System.out.println("cat referring to a Cat object");
14             }
15      //       if(cat instanceof Dog){ // Cat and Dog are completely separate classes
16      //           System.out.println("cat referring to a Dog object");
17      //       }
18         }
19      }
```

Figure 8.26 – Basic "instanceof" example

In this figure, line 7 creates a `Dog` object referred to by a `Dog` reference named `dog`. Line 8 creates a `Cat` object referred to by a `Cat` reference named `cat`. Line 9 checks if the object at the end of the `dog` reference is "an instance of" `Dog`. It is, so line 10 executes. Similarly, line 12 checks to see if the object referred to by `cat` is of the `Cat` type. It is, so line 13 executes.

Line 15 is commented out as it generates a compiler error. As `Cat` and `Dog` are completely unrelated classes (lines 3-4), the compiler knows that there is no way a `Cat` reference, namely `cat`, can refer to a `Dog` object. Conversely, a `Dog` reference, such as `dog`, cannot refer to a `Cat` object.

We will come back to `instanceof` later in this chapter. For now, let us move on to our next topic, which is closely related to classes: namely, enumerations.

# Understanding enums

**Enumerations**, or **enums** for short, are a special type of class. Whereas with a class, you can have as many instances (of the class) as you wish; with enums, the instances are predefined and therefore restricted. Enums are very useful for situations where a finite set of values apply – for example, days of the week, seasons of the year, and directions.

This ensures *type-safety* because, with the help of the compiler, only the instances defined are allowed. It is always better to find an issue at compile time than runtime. For example, if you had a method that defined a `String` parameter, namely `direction`, then someone could invoke the method with *"WESTT"* (note the incorrect spelling). The compiler would not catch this error as it is a valid `String`, so the error would manifest at runtime. If, however, the method parameter were an enum instead, the compiler would catch it. We will see this shortly.

There are two types of enums: simple and complex. We will discuss them now.

## Simple enums

A simple enum is named as such because it is, well, simple. This is in the sense that when you look at the enum, there is very little code present. *Figure 8.27* presents code using a simple enum:

```
3    enum Water {
4        STILL, SPARKLING;
5    }
6 ▶  public class SimpleEnums {
7 ▶      public static void main(String[] args) {
8    //        Water stillWater = new Water();// compiler error
9    //        Water stillWater = Water.EXTRA_SPARKLING; // type safety
10
11           Water stillWater = Water.STILL;
12           System.out.println(stillWater == Water.STILL);        // true
13           System.out.println(stillWater.equals(Water.STILL));   // true
14           switch(stillWater){
15               case STILL:
16                   System.out.println("Still water");
17                   break;
18   //            case Water.STILL: // unqualified enum value required
19   //            case 0: // cannot use an int
20           }
21   //       if(Water.STILL == 0){}// Water == int
22           Water sparklingWater = Water.valueOf( name: "SPARKLING");
23           System.out.println(sparklingWater);// SPARKLING
24
25           for(Water water: Water.values()){
26               // Ordinal value of: 0 is STILL
27               // Ordinal value of: 1 is SPARKLING
28               System.out.println("Ordinal value of: "+ water.ordinal() + " is "+ water.name());
29           }
30
31       }
32   }
```

Figure 8.27 – A simple enum

In the preceding figure, the Water enum is defined (lines 3-5). The values of an enum are expressed in capital letters (similar to constants). It is not mandatory to do this but it is common practice. What this enum is saying is that we have an enum named Water and there are only two instances allowed, namely STILL and SPARKLING. In effect, STILL and SPARKLING are references to the only object instances allowed. The semicolon at the end of line 4 is optional for simple enums. The corresponding semicolon for complex enums is mandatory. The enum values are given ordinal values starting at 0. So, for Water, STILL has an ordinal value of 0 and SPARKLING has an ordinal value of 1.

As stated previously, enums are a special type of class. However, there are some differences. One is that enum constructors are private by default. This includes the default constructor generated by the compiler (as in *Figure 8.27* for Water). Contrast this with the default constructor of a class, which has the same access as the class itself. Thus, you cannot instantiate an enum as you would a normal object. This is why line 8 will not compile – the default enum constructor generated by the compiler is private and therefore inaccessible to external types.

So, if we cannot new an enum, how do we create an enum instance? In other words, where are the constructor calls? *The declaration of the enum values, STILL and SPARKLING, (line 4) are the constructor calls!* As they are within the class, they have access to the private constructor. These enum values are initialized only once – that is, when the enum is first used.

So, to create an enum (object), use the relevant enum value. This is done on line 11, where we now have a reference, stillWater, referring to the STILL instance. Contrast line 11 with line 9 (which does not compile). Attempting to use any other value such as EXTRA_SPARKLING will not compile. This is the type safety we discussed previously. Only two instances of Water are allowed, STILL and SPARKLING, and the compiler enforces this rule.

Lines 12 and 13 demonstrate that only one instance of Water.STILL is created. As the equivalence operator and the equals method both return true, there can be only one instance.

> ### Inherited methods
>
> Although inheritance will be discussed in detail in *Chapter 9*, we need to dip into the topic to understand enums. Every class in Java implicitly inherits from a class called Object. This means that there are methods in Object that you get by default. This is how Java ensures every class has certain important methods. You can accept the version from Object or replace it (known as *overriding* the method).
>
> One of these methods that's inherited from Object is equals. The version in Object compares the references to see if they are equal and returns true or false depending on that comparison. Essentially, this is the same as using == to compare the references.
>
> Enums implicitly inherit from the Enum class (and Enum inherits from Object, so there is no escaping Object!). Thus, enums have access to methods such as valueOf, values, ordinal, and name.

The switch statement (lines 14-20) switches on the Water reference, namely stillWater (line 14). The case label is the unqualified enum value (STILL, line 15). Line 18 shows that the qualified enum value is incorrect. Line 19 (and line 21) demonstrate that even though enum values have ordinal values, enums are types and not integers.

Several interesting methods in the Enum type are available to us due to inheritance. Let's start with valueOf(String).

### The valueOf(String) method

This is an implicitly declared method, which, when given one of the enum constant names, returns that enum instance (line 22). Thus, this method provides a quick and easy way to create an enum instance, once you know the constant name.

Let's examine how we can iterate over all the enum instances using the `values()` method.

### The values() method

This is another implicit method. On line 25, we use an enhanced `for` loop to iterate over the enums in the order they are declared on line 4, namely STILL followed by SPARKLING. Once we have an enum instantiated, we can use other methods to get details of that particular enum.

Let's see how the `ordinal()` method provides the ordinal number for the enum.

### The ordinal() method

The `ordinal()` method (line 28) returns the ordinal value of this enum. The initial enum constant is given an ordinal value of 0; therefore, `ordinal()` for STILL returns 0, and `ordinal()` for SPARKLING returns 1.

To determine an enum's name, we can use the `name()` method.

### The name() method

The `name()` method (line 28) returns the name of this enum, exactly as declared in the enum (line 4). For example, `name()` for STILL returns "STILL" and `name()` for SPARKLING returns "SPARKLING". Note that rather than use the `name` method, the better option would be to override the `toString()` method as you can customize the `String` that's displayed (to the user) to be more user-friendly. We will do a lot of this in inheritance (*Chapter 9*).

Now that we have examined simple enums, let's move on and discuss complex enums.

## Complex enums

As stated earlier, enums are a special type of class where the instances are finite. As simple enums are so straightforward, it can be a little harder to see the class/enum relationship. With complex enums, identifying the relationship between an enum and a class is much easier.

Complex enums have instance variables, constructors, and methods, so they are quite similar to classes. *Figure 8.28* presents a complex enum for discussion:

```
3        enum WorkDay {
4            // values must be first
5            MONDAY( hoursOfWork: "9-5"),// constructor calls
6            TUESDAY( hoursOfWork: "9-5"),
7            WEDNESDAY( hoursOfWork: "9-5"),
8            THURSDAY( hoursOfWork: "9-5"),
9            FRIDAY( hoursOfWork: "9-5"),
10           SATURDAY( hoursOfWork: "10-1"){
11               // constant specific class body
12               public String getWorkLocation(){ return "Home";}
13           };// ; required at end
14
15           private String hoursOfWork;
16           WorkDay(String hoursOfWork) {// constructor is 'private'
17               this.hoursOfWork = hoursOfWork;
18           }
19           public String getHoursOfWork() {
20               return hoursOfWork;
21           }
22           public String getWorkLocation() {
23               return "Office";
24           }
25       }
26       public class ComplexEnums {
27           public static void main(String[] args) {
28               WorkDay monday = WorkDay.MONDAY;
29               System.out.println(monday.getHoursOfWork()+", "   // 9-5,
30                   +monday.getWorkLocation());                   // Office
31               System.out.println(WorkDay.SATURDAY.getHoursOfWork() + ", "  // 10-1
32                   +WorkDay.SATURDAY.getWorkLocation());                    // Home
33           }
34       }
```

Figure 8.28 – A complex enum

In this figure, we declare the WorkDay enum (lines 3-25). This enum encapsulates that we work 9 to 5, Monday to Friday at the office and 10 to 1 on Saturday from home. Presumably, we try to rest on Sunday!

The enum constants are declared from lines 5-13. There is a private instance variable called hoursOfWork (line 15), which is initialized by the constructor (lines 16-18). Note that the constructor is `private` by default. The accessor method, `getHoursOfWork` (lines 19-21), is how external classes gain access to the `private` instance variable, `hoursOfWork`. The other accessor method, `getWorkLocation` (lines 22-24), assumes that we work from the office every day (a pre-pandemic assumption for sure!). The SATURDAY constant (lines 10-13) merits discussion and we will come to that shortly.

Let's examine line 5 closely: this is *a constructor call* to the constructor that's declared (lines 16-18). In other words, the `hoursOfWork` instance variable is set to `"9-5"` for MONDAY. The other constants – TUESDAY, WEDNESDAY, THURSDAY, and FRIDAY (lines 6-9) – are initialized similarly.

What about SATURDAY? Since we haven't covered inheritance yet, this may be a little tricky. What we are saying is that for Saturday, we only work from home. To do this, we have to replace ("override") the default `getWorkLocation` method (lines 22-24). The default `getWorkLocation` method returns `"Office"` but our custom `getWorkLocation` (line 12) returns `"Home"` for SATURDAY. The SATURDAY constant defines a "constant specific class body," which starts with the curly brace on line 10 and ends with the curly brace on line 13.

Note that the semicolon on line 13 *is* required at the end of the complex enum constants, regardless of whether they declare a constant specific class body or not. That particular semicolon (line 13) tells the compiler, "We have now finished defining the enum constants, so you can expect instance variables or constructors or methods from here on."

Now that we have defined our enum, let's use it. Line 28 instantiates MONDAY, resulting in the enum constant (line 5) executing the constructor (lines 16-18), thereby initializing `hoursOfWork` for the MONDAY instance to `"9-5"`. Line 29 proves this fact by outputting `"9-5"`. Line 30 calls the (default) version of `getWorkLocation` (lines 22-24), thereby outputting `"Office"` to the screen.

Line 31 instantiates SATURDAY and outputs `"10-1"` for `hoursOfWork` as that is what is passed into the constructor from line 10. Line 32 invokes the constant-specific version of `getWorkLocation` for SATURDAY, which outputs `"Home"` to the screen.

That completes our discussion on enumerations. Let us now discuss a very useful feature, namely records.

# Appreciating records

Records are a special type of class, and are considered "data carriers". They help us avoid typing in copious amounts of boilerplate code. Records are specified using a record declaration where you list the *components* of the record. Implicitly generated in the background are a canonical constructor; `toString`, `equals`, and `hashCode` methods and `public` accessor methods for each of the components specified. The accessor methods take on the same names as the components themselves (as opposed to the more traditional `get` methods). Records are best explained by contrasting them to regular classes. *Figure 8.29* presents a normal class with a lot of boilerplate code:

```
5    public final class Person {
6        private final String name;
7        private final Integer age;
8
9        public Person(String name, Integer age) {
10           this.name = name;
11           this.age = age;
12       }
13       public String name() {
14           return name;
15       }
16       public Integer age() {
17           return age;
18       }
19       @Override
20       public boolean equals(Object obj) {
21           if (obj == this) return true;
22           if (obj == null || obj.getClass() != this.getClass()) return false;
23           var that = (Person) obj;
24           return Objects.equals(this.name, that.name) &&
25                   Objects.equals(this.age, that.age);
26       }
27       @Override
28       public int hashCode() {
29           return Objects.hash(name, age);
30       }
31       @Override
32       public String toString() {
33           return "Person[" +
34                   "name=" + name + ", " +
35                   "age=" + age + ']';
36       }
37   }
```

Figure 8.29 - A class with a lot of boilerplate code

The Person class in the preceding figure is customized somewhat to map to a record more easily. For example, the class itself is final (line 5) and the instance variables, namely name and age (lines 6-7), are also final. The fact that the instance variables are *blank final's* (declared as final but not initialized at declaration time) means that the instance variables must be initialized in the constructor. This is what the constructor does (lines 10-11).

There are two accessor methods for retrieving the instance variables, namely name (lines 13-15) and age (lines 16-18). Note that the method names are deliberately not preceded by get, in other words, getName and getAge. This is because, records use the components identifiers for both naming the instance variables *and* the accessor methods.

In addition, this class also has custom versions of equals, hashCode, and toString, lines 20-26, 28-30 and 32-36 respectively. Each of these methods is overriding an inherited version by providing a specific, custom version. This topic of overriding is discussed in detail in Inheritance (*Chapter 9*). The job of toString is to return a string containing the instance variables values (the component values). The equals method ensures that two records are considered equal if they are of the same type and contain equal component values. The hashCode method ensures that equal objects return the same hashcode value (more on this in *Chapter 13*).

Now let us examine the equivalent record in *Figure 8.30*:

Figure 8.30 - Equivalent record of class from Figure 8.29

Yes – just one line of code! As you can see, this saves us from a lot of boilerplate code. In fact, *Figures 8.29* and *8.30* are equivalent (by the time the compiler is finished). The two parameters are called components and the preceding one liner leads to the following code being generated in the background:

- A final class named after the record (Person in this example).

- private final instance variables, one for each component, named after the components.

- A canonical constructor for initializing the components (instance variables).

- Accessor methods, one for each component, named after the components.

- Custom toString, equals and hashCode methods.

Records are customizable. In other words, we can override (replace) all the default versions if we so wish. *Figure 8.31* presents such a situation.

```
5       public record Person(String name, Integer age) {
6           // compact canonical constructor
7       //     public Person(String name, Integer age)  {
8       //         if(age < 18){
9       //             this.name = "Error"; this.age = -1;
10      //         }
11      //         this.name = name;
12      //         this.age  = age;
13      //     }
14          // compact constructor
15          public Person  {
16              if(age < 18){
17                  name = "Error"; age = -1;
18              }
19          }
20      }
21   ▶  class PersonTest{
22   ▶      public static void main(String[] args) {
23              Person p1 = new Person( name: "Joe Bloggs",  age: 20);
24              System.out.println(p1);                  // Person[name=Joe Bloggs, age=20]
25              System.out.println(p1.name());  // Joe Bloggs
26              System.out.println(p1.age());   // 20
27          }
28      }
```

Figure 8.31 - canonical and compact constructors

In this figure, we are customizing the canonical constructor (lines 7-13) as we want to validate the age component of the person – if they are younger than 18, that is an error and we generate custom error values. Note again that there are better ways to handle error values but for now, this is fine. Otherwise, the components are initialized to the values passed in.

However, this canonical constructor can be written in an even more concise fashion. The compact constructor (lines 15-19) is replacing the canonical constructor. Compact constructors are a variation of the canonical constructor and are specific to records. Note that there is not even a pair of round brackets on line 15 – the components can be inferred from the component list (line 5). Also, there is no need to initialize the components as per lines 11-12; again, the compiler can do this for us.

Lines 23-26 demonstrate how to use the record Person that we have declared. Line 23 declares a Person instance referred to by p1. Line 24 calls the implicit toString provided by the Record class (which every record inherits from). Lines 25-26 invokes the two accessor methods; note their names are name() and age() respectively. The output is in comments on the right of each line (lines 24-26).

As records are so closely related to classes, it is no surprise that records can be used with the `instanceof` keyword. This is what we will examine in record patterns.

## Record patterns

Over the years, the `instanceof` keyword has evolved past the simple `instanceof`-and-cast idiom to support both type patterns and record patterns. Let us first discuss what a "type pattern" is and "pattern matching".

### *Type patterns and pattern matching*

In Java 16, `instanceof` was extended to take a type pattern and perform pattern matching. Prior to Java 16 the following code was commonplace:

```
if(obj instanceof String){ // 'obj' is of type Object
    String s = (String)obj;
    System.out.println(s.toUpperCase());
}
```

This code is checking to see if the `Object` reference `obj` is referring to a `String` object and if so, to (safely) cast the reference to a `String` so we can access the `String` methods. Remember, the methods you can access are based on the reference type. However, if the object at the end of the reference is a `String` object then we can safely cast the reference to a `String` and thus access the `String` methods using the new `String` reference. We will discuss this in more detail in Inheritance (*Chapter 9*).

As of Java 16, we can write the previous code segment more concisely and safely:

```
if(obj instanceof String s){ // "String s" - type pattern
//     String s = (String)obj; // no longer needed
    System.out.println(s.toUpperCase());
}
```

There are two changes to note. The first one is the use of a type pattern `String s` as part of the `instanceof`. Pattern matching occurs at runtime whereby `instanceof` checks the type against the provided type pattern and if there is a match, performs the cast for us as well. The second change is that, as `instanceof` performs the cast on our behalf, we no longer need to do the cast ourselves. This leads to a more declarative style (where you state what you want rather than how to get what you want).

This leads on nicely to record patterns which were introduced in Java 21. Prior to record patterns, the following code was required (assuming the `Person` record from *Figure 8.30*):

```
if(obj instanceof Person p){ // type pattern
    String name = p.name(); // accessor
```

```
    int age    = p.age();  // accessor
    System.out.println(name + "," + age);
}
```

Using record patterns, the previous code can be expressed more concisely:

```
if(obj instanceof Person(String sName, Integer nAge))
    System.out.println(sName + "," + nAge);
}
```

In this code, `Person(String sName, Integer nAge)` is a record pattern. A record pattern consists of a type, a component pattern list (which may be empty) and an optional identifier. A record pattern does two things for us: firstly, it checks to see if the object passes the `instanceof` test and secondly, disaggregates the record instance into its components. So, in our example, assuming `obj` is referring to a `Person` object, then the local variable `sName` will be initialized to the return value of the `name()` accessor method and the local variable `nAge` will be initialized to the return value from the `age()` accessor method. We deliberately used different identifiers for our local variables to highlight the fact that they do not have to match the component identifiers used in *Figure 8.30*. Note however that the order of the types must match; in other words, the record pattern must specify a `String` variable followed by an `Integer` variable, as that is the order of the component list in *Figure 8.30*.

That completes our discussion on records and indeed concludes *Chapter 8*. Now, let's put that knowledge into practice to reinforce the concepts we've learned.

## Exercises

Classes, objects, and enums are great for enhancing our Mesozoic Eden software. In these exercises, you will be creating classes to represent different entities in our park and using enums to define fixed sets of constants:

1.  We have many types of dinosaurs in our park, each with unique characteristics. Define a class called `Dinosaur` with properties such as name, age, and species.

2.  Our park's heart and soul lie in its employees. Create a class called `Employee` that encapsulates properties such as name, job title, and years of experience.

3.  With these classes in place, create some instances of `Dinosaur` and `Employee` and practice manipulating these objects. It's hard for me to provide more details for this exercise, but for example, you could create a new class called `App`. Then, in this class, you could create a few instances of `Dinosaur` and `Employee`. If you want to go wild, you can add a method that takes `Dinosaur` as an argument and then prints the information (such as its name, age, and so on) of this dinosaur. Of course, you could do the same thing for `Employee`.

4.  The "park" itself can be thought of as an object with its own properties and behavior. Design a `Park` class that contains methods for opening and closing the park, adding or removing dinosaurs, and so on. You can also consider giving it an array of employees and an array of dinosaurs.

5.  The food we serve to our dinosaurs varies greatly. Define a class for `Food` with properties such as name, nutritional value, and cost.

6.  As you know, safety is our main priority. For obvious safety reasons, our dinosaurs are housed in different enclosures. Create an `Enclosure` class that contains an array of `Dinosaur` objects.

7.  To add more clarity, let's define an enumeration for dinosaur types, such as herbivore, carnivore, and omnivore.

8.  A park visit isn't complete without a ticket. Create a `Ticket` class with properties such as price, visitor's name, and visit date.

# Project – Mesozoic Eden park manager

In this project, you'll be creating a fully interactive console application known as Mesozoic Eden park manager. This application allows the park manager to oversee and manage the various aspects of the dinosaur park. The park manager can use this application to efficiently manage multiple dinosaurs, park employees, and park tickets. Some of the key features of this system should be as follows:

1.  The ability to create, edit, or remove dinosaur profiles, park employee profiles, and park tickets.

2.  A real-time tracking system that monitors the location and status of the dinosaurs within the park.

3.  A fundamental roster system to organize and manage park employee schedules.

4.  A robust ticketing system to manage guest admissions and ensure the park maintains optimal capacity.

5.  The system should also handle special scenarios such as emergencies or VIP guest visits.

This might sound like a lot. So, here's a step-by-step guide to achieve this:

1.  **Expand the data structures**: Start working from the `Dinosaur` and `Employee` classes. Also, add a class called `Guest`. Each class should include more properties and methods.

2.  **Enhance initialization**: Create the necessary data initialization to support multiple dinosaurs, employees, and ticket types. This could involve creating arrays or lists of `Dinosaur`, `Guest`, and `Employee` objects.

3.  **Implement interaction**: Implement an interactive console-based interface using the `Scanner` class. This interface should provide the park manager with a variety of options to manage the park.

4.  **Enhance menu creation**: The menu should now include options to manage multiple dinosaurs, employees, and tickets. Each option should correspond to a particular function in the program.

5. **Handle actions**: Each menu item should trigger a function. For example, selecting the **Manage Dinosaurs** option could trigger a function to add, remove, or edit dinosaur profiles.

6. **Exit the program**: Provide an option for the user to exit the program.

Here is a starting code snippet:

```java
import java.util.Scanner;

public class Main {
    // Use Scanner for reading input from the user
    Scanner scanner = new Scanner(System.in);


    public static void main(String[] args) {
        Main main = new Main();
        main.start();
    }


    public void start() {
        // This is the main loop of the application. It
          will keep running until the user decides to exit.
        while (true) {
            displayMenu();
            int choice = scanner.nextInt();
            handleMenuChoice(choice);
        }
    }


    public void displayMenu() {
        System.out.println("Welcome to Mesozoic Eden Park
          Manager!");
        System.out.println("1. Manage Dinosaurs");
        System.out.println("2. Manage Park Employees");
        System.out.println("3. Manage Tickets");
        System.out.println("4. Check Park Status");
        System.out.println("5. Handle Special Events");
        System.out.println("6. Exit");
        System.out.print("Enter your choice: ");
    }


    public void handleMenuChoice(int choice) {
```

```
      switch (choice) {
          case 1:
              // manageDinosaurs();
              break;
          case 2:
              // manageEmployees();
              break;
          case 3:
              // manageTickets();
              break;
          case 4:
              // checkParkStatus();
              break;
          case 5:
              // handleSpecialEvents();
              break;
          case 6:
              System.out.println("Exiting...");
              System.exit(0);
      }
    }
  }
```

The commented-out method calls are placeholders for methods you need to implement according to your data structures and functionality.

## Summary

In this chapter, we started our discussion by differentiating objects and classes. Classes are similar to a plan of a house, whereas an object is the (built) house itself. We create an object using the new keyword and manipulate the object using its reference. Differentiating the reference from the object is very important going forward. A useful analogy is that the reference is like a remote control and the object is the TV.

Constructors are special methods that are used when constructing an object. The constructor is a method that has the same name as the class but with no return type. There is always a constructor present – if you don't provide one, the compiler intervenes and inserts the default constructor. The constructor is typically used to initialize the instance variables.

Every object gets a copy of the instance members (variables and methods). Class members are marked as static, and are shared by all instances. When accessing an instance member, we use the reference but when accessing a class member, we use the class name. Dot notation applies to both syntaxes.

The `this` reference is a special reference available to us in instance methods. It refers to the object instance responsible for the method call. Consequently, it is dynamic since its value depends on the reference used to invoke the method. It is not available to class (`static`) methods.

Access modifiers apply at both the top (class/interface/record) level, and the member level. At the top level, `public` or package-private access applies. Package-private is achieved by not specifying any keyword at all and ensures that the top-level construct is visible within the same package only. If the top-level construct is `public`, then it is available everywhere; there are no restrictions.

Members (variables/methods) can, in addition to `public` and package-private (with the same semantics), be `private` and `protected`. `private` means that the member is visible within the class only. `protected` is similar to package-private except that subclasses, regardless of package, can access the member.

Encapsulation is one of the cornerstones of OOP. It means that a class can hide its data from external misuse; this is often called "data hiding." In Java, it is achieved by marking data as `private` and providing `public` accessor/mutator (get/set) methods to manipulate the data. The important concept here is that external code has to access `private` data via your `public` methods. Thus, by using conditional logic in your `public` methods, you can prevent your data from being corrupted.

However, the principle of "private data, public methods" only goes so far. When returning a reference to a `private` object, Java's call by value mechanism returns a copy of that reference. Thus, the `private` object is now *directly* accessible via external code. Advanced encapsulation combats this by copying the `private` object and returning the reference to the copy object. Thus, your `private` object is still private and safe from external interference.

Understanding an object's life cycle is extremely beneficial. Local variables live on the stack, whereas objects and instance variables reside on the heap. When an object no longer has any references referring to it, it is eligible for garbage collection. Garbage collection is an automatic process run by the JVM, at a time of the JVM's choosing. When the garbage collector runs, objects eligible for garbage collection are removed and the heap space is reclaimed.

The `instanceof` keyword enables us to determine the object type that a reference is referring to. This will be very useful going forward.

Enumerations (enums) are closely related to classes in that enums are simply classes, where the number of instances are finite and specified. They are very useful for ensuring type safety, whereby the compiler flags an error as opposed to discovering the error at runtime.

Enums are categorized into two separate types: simple and complex. Simple enums just specify the constant values; the compiler synthesizes the default constructor. All enum constructors are `private` by default. Thus, external classes cannot new them – the constants that are defined are, in fact, the constructor calls. Complex enums look very similar to classes as they have instance variables, (explicit) constructors, and methods.

Records are useful when you have classes with a lot of boilerplate code. The components of the record are specified in the record declaration. The compiler, in the background, generates the instance variables, canonical constructor, accessor methods, `toString`, `equals`, and `hashCode` methods. Records are `final`, as are the instance variables (components). A compact constructor is a more concise variation of the canonical constructor.

That completes our discussion of classes, objects, and enums. We will now move onto another important OOP chapter: inheritance.

# 9

# Inheritance and Polymorphism

In *Chapter 8*, we learned about classes, objects, and enums. Initially, we explored the relationship between classes and objects and the need to separate the reference type from the object type. We contrasted instance versus class members and saw that using the `static` keyword applies class scope to a member. We discussed the `this` reference and demonstrated that inside an instance method, the `this` reference refers to the object instance responsible for the method call. We also covered various access modifiers: `private`, package-private (no keyword), `protected`, and `public`. These modifiers enable us to apply one of the cornerstones of OOP, namely encapsulation. While encapsulation is commonly referred to as "private data, public methods," we demonstrated that this does not go far enough due to Java's call by value mechanism when passing references into and out of methods. We showed how a technique called "defensive copying" can be used to apply proper (advanced) encapsulation. To improve our understanding of what is happening in the background, we detailed the object life cycle and gently touched on garbage collection. We also covered the `instanceof` keyword, which is used to determine the object type a reference is referring to. We covered a variation of a class, namely **enumerations (enums)**. Enums enable us to limit the number of instances created, thereby facilitating type safety. We covered both simple and complex enums. Lastly, we covered another class variation, namely records, which saves us from typing a lot of boilerplate code.

In this chapter, we will explore inheritance, another core principle of OOP. Initially, we will outline the benefits of inheritance and the Java keywords to use. This leads to polymorphism, another core pillar of OOP. We will explain polymorphism and, with the aid of examples, how polymorphism is achieved. As polymorphism requires "method overriding," we will explain how to use `instanceof`, to ensure type safety when downcasting.

We will also contrast method overriding with method overloading. We will explain the `super` keyword and how it is used. As promised in *Chapter 8*, we will revisit `protected`, the most misunderstood of Java's access modifiers.

After that, we will discuss both the `abstract` and `final` keywords and their place in inheritance. We will also show how `sealed` classes enable us to scope inheritance. In addition, we will cover both `static` and instance blocks in an inheritance hierarchy. Lastly, we will discuss upcasting and downcasting the inheritance tree, and how a simple rule-of-thumb helps prevent `ClassCastException` errors.

This chapter covers the following main topics:

- Understanding inheritance
- Applying inheritance
- Exploring polymorphism
- Contrasting method overriding and method overloading
- Exploring the `super` keyword
- Revisiting the `protected` access modifier
- Explaining the `abstract` and `final` keywords
- Applying `sealed` classes
- Understanding instance and `static` blocks
- Mastering upcasting and downcasting

## Technical requirements

The code for this chapter can be found on GitHub at `https://github.com/PacktPublishing/Learn-Java-with-Projects/tree/main/ch9`.

## Understanding inheritance

There are three core pillars in Java: polymorphism, inheritance, and encapsulation (data hiding). It is easy to remember them using the acronym "PIE" (*P*olymorphism, *I*nheritance, and *E*ncapsulation). Let us now examine inheritance.

Inheritance is a code reusability mechanism where common properties between related types are exploited by forming relationships between those types. Inheritance relationships in Java are created by extending from a class or by implementing an interface. We will cover interfaces in *Chapter 10*, so for the moment, we will assume classes throughout. To understand why inheritance in OOP is important, we will examine its advantages (and disadvantages). As we have not covered the terminology used yet, this discussion will be somewhat abstract.

## Advantages of inheritance

One principle advantage of inheritance is code reuse. A new class can be written based on an existing class rather than writing the new class from scratch. In other words, the new class can inherit code that has been already written (and tested). This is called *code reuse* and reduces redundancy.

Inheritance naturally promotes polymorphism, which we discuss later. This feature gives your code flexibility. For example, you could have a method that deals with an `Animal` reference but at runtime, the code executed is in the `Dog` type (or `Cat` or any other type of `Animal` in the hierarchy). In effect, one method works with all `Animal` types.

Inheritance organizes code into a hierarchy. This can improve productivity and simplify the maintenance of code as changes made to inherited code are immediately reflected throughout the hierarchy.

## Disadvantages of inheritance

Despite its advantages, inheritance does have its disadvantages. Tight coupling between the base (source) type and the derived (target) type is one such drawback. Any changes made to the base type affect all the derived types.

Code bloat is another disadvantage. Changes may be made to the base type that many derived types do not need and this can result in an unnecessarily large code base.

Now that we have an appreciation of inheritance and why it is used, let's discuss the nomenclature (terms) used when discussing inheritance.

## Base class

The "base" class is also known as the "super" or "parent" class. This is where the inherited members are defined. As a class is a type, the term *type* is often used interchangeably for class. Note that in Java, the *Object* class is at the top of every hierarchy.

## Subclass

The subclass is also known as the "child" or "derived" class. So, the subclass inherits functionality (and/or data) from the base class. Again, as a class is a type, the term *subtype* is often used interchangeably for subclass. A class can be both a base class and a subclass. Java ensures that *Object* is at the top of every (inheritance) hierarchy. Thus, every class we write is implicitly a subtype already (even if you do not say so).

## The "is-a" relationship

Inheritance generates what is called an *"is-a"* relationship. *Figure 9.1* will help us explain this. We will expand on this diagram as this chapter progresses:

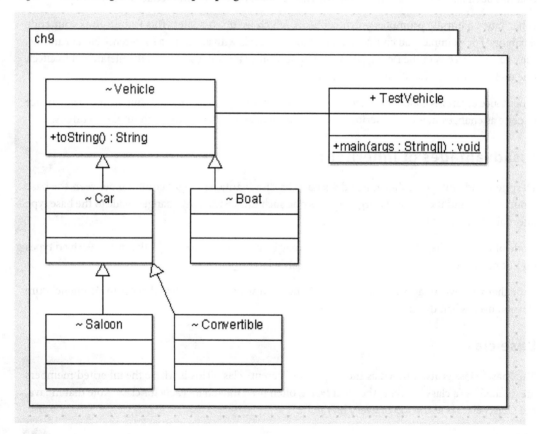

Figure 9.1 – UML diagram for the Vehicle hierarchy

> **Unified Modeling Language (UML)**
>
> UML is a modeling language used in software design availing of the maxim that "a picture speaks a thousand words." UML makes understanding topics such as inheritance very straightforward, so we will present a very brief overview of UML here. Further detail is available here: `https://en.wikipedia.org/wiki/Unified_Modeling_Language`.
>
> With *Figure 9.1* in mind, here is an overview of the symbols used:
>
> - *Package name*: The package name is at the top left (`ch9`)
> - *Classes*: Classes are in boxes with three sections – the top box is the class name; the middle box is for the instance/class variables; the bottom box is for the methods
> - *Access modifiers*: `public` (+), `private` (-), package-private (~), and `protected` (#)
> - *Static*: The underline is used to signify that a member is `static`
> - *Method return type*: The last part of the method signature in UML
> - *Class inheritance*: An arrow with a solid line; for example, `Car` inherits from `Vehicle`
> - *Interfaces*: These are shown in boxes with dashed lines (*Chapter 10*)
> - *Interface inheritance*: An arrow with a dashed line (*Chapter 10*)
> - *Association*: A solid line; for example, `TestVehicle` is associated with `Vehicle` for the simple reason that we will be creating objects based on the `Vehicle` hierarchy in `main()`

As shown in *Figure 9.1*, we have a package, namely `ch9`. There are five classes in the `Vehicle` hierarchy: `Vehicle`, `Car`, `Saloon`, `Convertible`, and `Boat`. In this hierarchy, from a base class viewpoint, `Vehicle` is the base class for `Car` and `Boat`; and `Car` is the base class for `Saloon` and `Convertible`. Interpreting the diagram from the sub-class perspective, `Car` and `Boat` are sub-classes of `Vehicle`, whereas `Saloon` and `Convertible` are sub-classes of `Car`. Regardless of which perspective you use, every `Car` "is-a" `Vehicle`, and every `Boat` "is-a" `Vehicle` too. In addition, every `Saloon` "is-a" `Car`, and every `Convertible` "is-a" `Car`.

It also follows that because `Saloon` "is-a" `Car` and `Car` "is-a" `Vehicle`, `Saloon` "is-a" `Vehicle` as well. The same applies to `Convertible`; in other words, `Convertible` "is-a" `Car`, `Car` "is-a" `Vehicle`; therefore, `Convertible` "is-a" `Vehicle` also.

However, the "is-a" relationship works in one direction only (reading the diagram from the bottom up). For example, while *every* `Car` "is-a" `Vehicle`, *not* every `Vehicle` "is-a" `Car`; some are `Boats`. There is a very good reason for this, which we will explore further when we discuss upcasting and downcasting.

There is one method in `Vehicle`, namely `toString()`, which, because it is `public`, is inherited by all the subtypes; namely, `Car`, `Saloon`, `Convertible`, and `Boat`. Thus, the version of `toString()` in `Vehicle` is available throughout the whole hierarchy. Lastly, the other class, `TestVehicle` contains the `main()` method so that we can test the hierarchy.

Now that we understand the concept of inheritance, let's apply it in code.

## Applying inheritance

As we learned in the previous section, inheritance creates an "is-a" relationship hierarchy. This enables base class functionality to be inherited and therefore available to subclasses, without any extra coding. Java uses two keywords in applying inheritance: `extends` and `implements`. Let's discuss them now.

### extends

This is the principle keyword that's used and relates to both classes and interfaces. Regarding classes, we state that `class Sub extends Base {}`. In this case, all of the non-`private` members from the `Base` class will be inherited into the `Sub` class. Note that `private` members and constructors are not inherited – this makes sense as both `private` members and constructors are class-specific. In addition, Java prohibits multiple class inheritance. This means that you cannot extend from more than one class at a time. Regarding interfaces, we state that `interface ChildInt extends ParentInt {}`.

## implements

While we will discuss interfaces in detail in *Chapter 10*, a brief overview here is appropriate. An interface is a construct that enables Java to ensure that if a class implements an interface, the class is, in effect, signing a contract. The contract states, generally speaking, that the class will have code for the `abstract` methods in the interface. An `abstract` method, which we will discuss in more detail later, is a method that has no implementation code; in other words, no curly braces.

Concerning inheritance, unlike classes, Java allows interfaces to extend from more than one interface at a time. So, for example, `interface C extends A, B {}`, where A, B, and C are all interfaces, is fine. Note that, as of Java 8, both the `default` and `static` methods in interfaces have implementation code.

A class implements an interface using the `class Dog implements Walkable` syntax. With this, the `static` and `default` methods in `Walkable` are available to Dog.

Now, let's look at inheritance in action. *Figure 9.2* shows the Java code for the UML in *Figure 9.1*:

```java
1     package ch9;
2
3     // class Vehicle extends Object
4     class Vehicle{
5         public String toString(){
6             return "Vehicle::toString()";
7         }
8     }
9     class Car extends Vehicle{}
10    class Boat extends Vehicle{}
11    class Saloon extends Car {}
12    class Convertible extends Car {}
13
14    public class TestVehicle {
15        public static void main(String[] args) {
16            Vehicle vehicle = new Vehicle();
17            System.out.println(vehicle.toString()); // Vehicle::toString()
18            Car     car     = new Car();
19            // next line invokes car.toString()
20            System.out.println(car);                // Vehicle::toString()
21            Saloon  saloon  = new Saloon();
22            System.out.println(saloon);             // Vehicle::toString()
23
24            System.out.println(new TestVehicle().toString());// ch9.TestVehicle@378bf509
25        }
26    }
```

Figure 9.2 – Inheritance in action

In this figure, lines 3 and 4 are equivalent. `Vehicle` is at the top of this particular hierarchy and to ensure that `Object` is inherited by every class, the compiler simply inserts `extends Object` after `class Vehicle`, as per line 3. Lines 5-7 are a custom implementation of the `toString()` method inherited from `Object`. This is known as *overriding*, a topic we will discuss in detail shortly. Lines 9-12 represent the rest of the inheritance hierarchy: a `Car` "is-a" `Vehicle`; a `Boat` "is-a" `Vehicle`; a `Saloon` "is-a" `Car`; and a `Convertible` "is-a" `Car`.

On line 16, we create a `Vehicle` object and use a `Vehicle` reference called `vehicle` to refer to it. On line 17, we call the `toString()` method, defined on lines 5-7, outputting `Vehicle::toString()`.

On line 18, we create a `Car` object and use a `Car` reference called `car` to refer to it. On line 20, we simply insert the `car` reference inside `System.out.println()`. When Java encounters a reference like this inside `System.out.println()`, it looks up the object type (`Car`, in this instance) and calls its `toString()`. As every class inherits from `Object`, and `Object` defines a basic (unfriendly) `toString()`, a version of `toString()` will exist. However, in this hierarchy, `Vehicle` has replaced (overridden) `toString()` inherited from `Object` with its own custom one (lines 5-7). This custom one from `Vehicle` is inherited by `Car`. What happens is that Java checks if there is a custom `toString()` defined in `Car`; as there isn't one, Java then checks its parent, namely `Vehicle`. If `Vehicle` has no `toString()`, the version from `Object` would be used. Since `toString()` is defined in `Vehicle`, this is the version inherited by `Car` and used on line 20. Thus, the output is, again, `Vehicle::toString()`.

On line 21, we create a `Saloon` object and use a `Saloon` reference called `saloon` to refer to it. Again, on line 22, we simply insert the `saloon` reference inside `System.out.println()`. As `Saloon` has no custom `toString()` defined, and its parent, `Car`, has no custom version either, the one inherited from `Vehicle` is used. This results in `Vehicle::toString()` being output to the screen.

Line 24 is used to demonstrate the output when the `toString()` method from `Object` is used. On line 24, we are creating an instance of `TestVehicle` and calling its `toString()` method. As `TestVehicle` is not explicitly inheriting from any class (using `extends`), it implicitly inherits from `Object`. In addition, as `TestVehicle` is not overriding `toString()` with its own custom version, the one inherited from `Object` is used. This is demonstrated by the output from line 24: `ch9.TestVehicle@378bf509`. The output from the `toString()` method in `Object` is formatted as `package_name.class name@hash code`. The package name in this case is `ch9` (line 1), the class name is `TestVehicle` (line 24), and the hash code is a hexadecimal number that's used in hashing collections (`Chapter 13`).

Now that we have seen basic inheritance in action, let's move on to another cornerstone of OOP, namely polymorphism.

# Exploring polymorphism

Polymorphism has its origins in the Greek terms poly (many) morphe (forms). Any object that passes more than one "is-a" test can be considered polymorphic. Therefore, only objects of the `Object` type are not polymorphic as any type passes the "is-a" test for both `Object` and itself.

In this section, we will discuss why separating the reference type from the object type is so important. In addition, we will examine method overriding and its critical role in enabling polymorphism.

## Separating the reference type from the object type

Now that we have inheritance hierarchies, we will regularly differentiate the reference type from the object type. The reference type can be a class, record, enum or interface. In other words, we have flexibility with regard to the reference type. The object type is more restrictive: the object type is based on non-abstract classes, records, and enums only. In other words, we cannot create objects based on abstract classes or interfaces.

For example, given the hierarchy in *Figure 9.2*, it is perfectly legal to say the following:

```
Vehicle v = new Car();
```

This is because every `Car` "is-a" `Vehicle` (reading it right to left, as assignment associates right to left). In this instance, the reference, `v`, is of the `Vehicle` type and it is referring to an object of the `Car` type. This is known as *upcasting*, as we are going *up* the inheritance tree (again, reading it from right to left, from `Car` *up* to `Vehicle`). We are upcasting the `Car` reference, created by `new Car()`, and casting it to a `Vehicle` reference, `v`.

Why does this work? This works because, due to inheritance, every inheritable method available to `Vehicle` will exist in `Car`. That is a guarantee. Whether `Car` has overridden (replaced) any/all `Vehicle` methods with its own custom ones is immaterial. Given that the compiler looks at the reference type (and not the object type), the methods we can call using the `Vehicle` reference, `v`, are defined in `Vehicle` (and `Object`) and will be present in `Car` (the object type).

So, that is the first point to keep in mind - the compiler is always looking at the reference type. As we will see shortly, the object type comes into play at runtime. So, a simple but effective rule of thumb is that *a reference can refer to objects of its own type or objects of subclasses*. In effect, a reference can point "across and down" the (UML) hierarchy.

If a reference is ever pointing "up" the hierarchy, that is when you get `ClassCastException` errors. Why is this? Well, a subclass inherits from its parent. In addition to replacing inherited functionality (overriding), the subclass can also add extra methods. So, if you have a reference of the subclass type, you can invoke these *extra* added methods. But if your object is of the parent type, these methods will not exist! This is a serious issue for the JVM and it throws an exception (*Chapter 11*) immediately.

So, the reference type determines the methods that can be called on the object. In addition, while the reference type cannot change, the object type it refers to can.

Now, let's address how to avail of polymorphism.

## Applying polymorphism

Polymorphism applies only to instance (non-static) methods, as only instance methods can be overridden. At compile time, the compiler decides which method signature to bind to; however, the object that will provide the actual method to execute is decided at runtime! That is what polymorphism is. This is why polymorphism is also known as "runtime binding" or "late binding."

> **What if you are accessing a static member?**
>
> A `static` member (method or data) is associated with the class and therefore not involved in polymorphism. The following applies: if you are accessing any type of data (`static` or non-static) or `static` methods, the JVM uses the reference type. Only if it's an instance method is the object type used (polymorphism).

Thus, for polymorphism to work, we need instance methods in the base and subclass where the subclass overrides the base version. For this to happen, the subclass must code a method that has the same signature as the parent.

Okay, that's enough theory – let's look at an example that reinforces everything we've learned thus far.

### Polymorphism in code – example 1

*Figure 9.3* shows the UML for the code to follow:

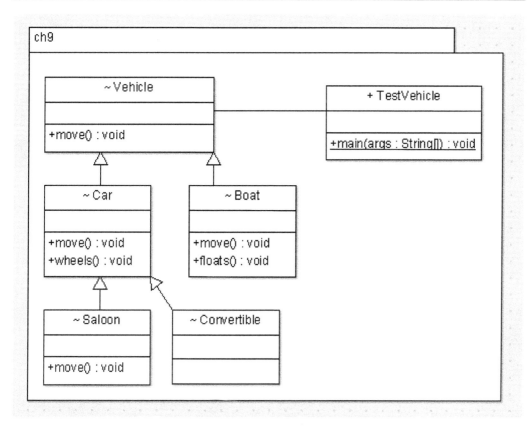

Figure 9.3 – UML for polymorphism example

In this figure, the Vehicle class has a move() method. It is an instance method, with a return type of void. Both Car and Boat extend Vehicle and override move(). Car adds a method called wheels() and Boat adds a method called floats(). Both Saloon and Convertible extend Car. Saloon overrides move() but Convertible does not.

*Figure 9.4* presents the code for this UML and demonstrates polymorphism in action:

**@Override annotation**

An annotation is a form of metadata that provides information about the program that is not part of the program itself. Annotations are preceded in Java with the @ symbol and have several uses. For example, annotations are used by the compiler to detect errors or by the runtime to generate code.

When overriding a base class method, we can insert the @Override annotation just prior to the subclass method. While not mandatory, it is very useful, because, if we apply this annotation, the compiler will ensure that we override the method correctly.

```
 3    class Vehicle{
 4        public void move(){ System.out.println("Vehicle::move"); }
 5    }
 6    class Car extends Vehicle{
 7        @Override public void move(){ System.out.println("Car::move()"); }
 8        public void wheels(){ System.out.println("Car::wheels()"); }
 9    }
10    class Boat extends Vehicle{
11        @Override public void move(){ System.out.println("Boat::move()"); }
12        public void floats(){ System.out.println("Boat::floats()"); }
13    }
14    class Saloon extends Car {
15        @Override public void move(){ System.out.println("Saloon::move()"); }
16    }
17    class Convertible extends Car {}
18
19    public class TestVehicle {
20        public static void main(String[] args) {
21            Vehicle v = new Car();
22            v.move();    // Car::move()
23            v = new Boat();
24            v.move();    // Boat::move()
25    //       v.floats(); // compiler error
26            v = new Saloon();
27            v.move();    // Saloon::move()
28            v = new Convertible();
29            v.move();    // Car::move()
30
31            Saloon s = (Saloon)new Vehicle(); // ClassCastException
32        }
33    }
```

Figure 9.4 – Polymorphism example

In this figure, Car and Boat both extend Vehicle; and Saloon and Convertible both extend Car. Note that the move() method in Vehicle (line 4) is a non-static/instance method and therefore polymorphic. In addition, as move() is non-private, it is inheritable. The move() method from Vehicle is overridden by Car (line 7), Boat (line 11), and Saloon (line 15). To highlight this fact, on each of those lines, we have used the @Override annotation. This means that the parent move() method is overridden by the respective subclass versions.

Line 21 creates a `Car` object and uses a `Vehicle` reference, namely v, to refer to it. It is worth repeating that this upcasting, from `Car` up to `Vehicle`, is only possible because, via inheritance, *every* `Car` "is-a" `Vehicle`. Therefore, any method available to the `Vehicle` reference will exist in `Car`. Consequently, as upcasting is never a risk, it is performed implicitly by the compiler; in other words, you do not need to explicitly state the (up)cast in code, as follows:

```
Vehicle v = (Vehicle) new Car();
```

## Compile time

Line 22 makes the polymorphic `v.move()` call. Every time a method call is in code, there are two perspectives to keep in mind: compile time and runtime. As we know, the compiler concerns itself with the reference type. So, in this case, the compiler checks the reference, v, and determines that it is of type `Vehicle`. The compiler then checks if there is a `move()` method, with that exact signature in the `Vehicle` class, either defined in `Vehicle` or inherited into `Vehicle` (from `Object` in this example). As there is a `move()` method defined in `Vehicle`, the compiler is happy.

## Polymorphism in action

At runtime, as `move()` is a non-static, polymorphic method, the object being referred to by the reference, v, applies. As v is referring to a `Car` object, the `Car` version of `move()` is executed. This is polymorphism in action! We have one method but many implementations of that method. The compiler ensures that the method exists and dynamically, at runtime, polymorphism kicks in and executes the version in the object being referred to. As v is referring to a `Car` object, the output from line 22 is `Car::move()`.

Line 23 reuses the `Vehicle` reference, v (which is perfectly valid), to refer to a `Boat` object. As `Boat` "is-a" `Vehicle`, this is fine. Line 24 makes the same polymorphic call to `v.move()` as was the case on line 22. However, this time, v is referring to a `Boat` object, and as `Boat` has overridden `move()`, the `Boat` version of `move()` is executed at runtime. Therefore the output is `Boat::move()`.

Line 25 demonstrates that the compiler looks at the reference type. As we know, v is of type `Vehicle`. However, `Vehicle` has no `floats()` method; this is a method specific to `Boat`. Therefore, the compiler complains about `v.floats()` on line 25, and hence, the line is commented out.

Line 26 reuses the `Vehicle` reference, v, to refer to a `Saloon` object. As `Saloon` "is-a" `Vehicle`, this is fine. Line 27 makes the same polymorphic call to `v.move()` as was the case on lines 22 and 24. As v is now referring to a `Saloon` object with an overridden `move()` method, the `Saloon` version of `move()` is executed polymorphically at runtime. Therefore, the output is `Saloon::move()`.

Line 28 creates a `Convertible` object and uses v to refer to it. This is not a problem as `Convertible` "is-a" `Vehicle` (indirectly, via `Car`). In other words, because `Convertible` is-a `Vehicle` and `Vehicle` is-a `Car`, `Convertible` is-a `Car` also. Line 29 makes the same polymorphic call, `v.move()`, as was the case on lines 22, 24, and 27. Note, however, that `Convertible` has not overridden `move()`. `Convertible` has an empty class body. Therefore, the methods in `Convertible` are the move() and wheels() methods inherited from Car and the methods inherited from Object, such as toString(). So, at runtime, when v.move() is called, the JVM executes the version of move() in Car, resulting in Car::move(). You can also look at it this way: the runtime looks for move() in Convertible, and finds none; the JVM then checks the parent, Car, and finds one, which it executes. Note that if Car had not provided a move() method, its parent, Vehicle, would have been next in the search. So, there is an "up the hierarchy, one generation at a time" orderly search.

### Why do we get a ClassCastException error?

Line 31 demonstrates downcasting and a ClassCastException error. Exceptions will be discussed in *Chapter 11*, so we won't go into detail here. Downcasting will be discussed in greater detail later in this chapter but this example is too good to pass up! Let's examine line 31 in greater detail:

```
Saloon s = (Saloon) new Vehicle(); // ClassCastException
```

The first thing to note is that the cast (Saloon) *is* required. The compiler will not allow the following:

```
Saloon s = new Vehicle(); // Compiler error
```

This is a compiler error because every Vehicle is not a Saloon class; some are Boats. Indeed, even if the Boat class were not present, this line would still not compile. Why? Because, reading it right to left, you are going *down* the hierarchy from Vehicle to Saloon. As Saloon could (and indeed does) have extra methods not in the Vehicle class, this situation must be prevented. For example, the Saloon reference, s, has access to the wheels() method (inherited from Car), which is not present in Vehicle.

Now, we can override the compiler by using a (down)cast. This is what line 31 has done with the (Saloon) cast. In effect, by inserting the cast and overriding the compiler error, you are saying to the compiler: "Let me proceed, I know what I am doing." So, the code compiles with the cast in place. However, at runtime, the JVM realizes that it has a Saloon reference referring *up* the inheritance tree to a Vehicle object. This is a big no-no because *if* the JVM allowed the Saloon reference s to refer to a Vehicle object, what would it do with a subsequent s.wheels() method call? Remember, we would be looking at a Vehicle object, which has no such method! Hence the JVM generates a ClassCastException error.

Let's refactor this code to demonstrate polymorphism from another angle.

## Polymorphism in code – example 2

*Figure 9.5* shows the refactored code from *Figure 9.4*:

```
3      class Vehicle{
4          public void move(){ System.out.println("Vehicle::move"); }
5      }
6      class Car extends Vehicle{
7          @Override public void move(){ System.out.println("Car::move()"); }
8          public void wheels(){ System.out.println("Car::wheels()"); }
9      }
10     class Boat extends Vehicle{
11         @Override public void move(){ System.out.println("Boat::move()"); }
12         public void floats(){ System.out.println("Boat::floats()"); }
13     }
14     class Saloon extends Car {
15         @Override public void move(){ System.out.println("Saloon::move()"); }
16     }
17     class Convertible extends Car {}
18
19     public class TestVehicle {
20         public static void doAction(Vehicle v){
21             v.move();
22         }
23         public static void main(String[] args) {
24             Vehicle v = new Car();
25             doAction(v);                    // Car::move()
26             doAction(new Boat());           // Boat::move()
27             doAction(new Saloon());         // Saloon::move()
28             doAction(new Convertible());// Car::move()
29         }
30     }
```

Figure 9.5 – Refactored polymorphism example

Note that, in this figure, the inheritance hierarchy remains untouched from *Figure 9.4*. The `TestVehicle` class (lines 19-30) has been refactored though. We have introduced a new method, namely `doAction()` (lines 20-22), that accepts a `Vehicle` reference. In the `doAction()` method, we simply call the `move()` method (line 21). As `Vehicle` has a `move()` method, this is fine.

Line 24 is as before; it creates a `Car` object and upcasts the reference to a `Vehicle` reference, v. Thus, v is referring to a `Car` object. Line 25 invokes the `doAction()` method, passing in the reference, v. This reference, v, which is declared on line 24, is copied into the separate (different scope) but similarly named reference, v, which is declared on line 20. Now, in `doAction()`, we have a local v reference referring to the same `Car` object created on line 24. Thus, when we invoke v.`move()` on line 21, polymorphism kicks in and we get the `Car` version of `move()`, resulting in `Car::move()`.

Line 26 does the same thing in one line of code as was done in the previous two lines of code (lines 24-25). On line 26, the `Boat` object is created, and the method call to `doAction()` results in the upcast to the `Vehicle` reference, v (line 20). After that, line 21 executes polymorphically and we get the `Boat` version of `move()`, resulting in `Boat::move()`.

Line 27 is the same as line 26 except we are creating a `Saloon` object. Thus, the `Vehicle` reference, v, in `doAction()` executes the `move()` method as `Saloon`, resulting in `Saloon::move()`.

Line 28 is the same as line 27 except we are creating a `Convertible` object. Thus, the `Vehicle` reference, v, in `doAction()` attempts to execute the `move()` method in `Convertible`. As there is none, the parent of `Convertible`, namely `Car`, is checked. `Car` does have a version of `move()`, resulting in `Car::move()`.

To be clear about when polymorphism applies and when it does not, we will revisit a callout box presented earlier.

## JVM – object type versus reference type usage

As discussed briefly in a previous callout, if you are dealing with any type of data (`static` or non-static), the reference type applies; when dealing with instance methods, the object type applies (polymorphism). *Figure 9.6* presents a code example:

```
3    class Vehicle{
4        double cost = 100.0;          // instance data
5        static int age = 1;           // class data
6        public void move(){           // instance method
7            System.out.println("Vehicle::move()");
8        }
9        public static void sm() {     // class method
10           System.out.println("Vehicle::sm()");
11       }
12   }
13   class Car extends Vehicle{
14       double cost = 20_000.0;  // hiding
15       static int age = 2;       // hiding
16
17       @Override public void move(){    // overriding
18           System.out.println("Car::move()");
19       }
20       public static void sm() {        // hiding
21           System.out.println("Car::sm()");
22       }
23   }
24   public class TestVehicle {
25       public static void main(String[] args) {
26           Vehicle v = new Car();
27           System.out.println(v.cost); // 100.0
28           System.out.println(v.age);  // 1
29           v.sm();                      // Vehicle::sm()
30           v.move();                    // Car::move()
31       }
32   }
```

Figure 9.6 – When the JVM uses the reference type versus the object type

In this figure, the Vehicle class declares an instance variable, namely cost (line 4), and a class variable, namely age (line 5). In addition, Vehicle also declares an instance method called move() (lines 6-8) and a class method called sm() (lines 9-11). So, in Vehicle, we have both instance and static data and instance and static methods.

The Car class extends from Vehicle (lines 13-23) and simply replicates Vehicle. In other words, Car has the same data and methods as its parent, Vehicle.

In Car, we declare both instance and non-instance variables, namely cost and age, respectively (lines 14-15). These variables in Car have the same types and identifiers as their counterparts in the parent class, Vehicle. In other words, Vehicle has an instance variable called cost, which is a double; and Car also has an instance variable named cost, which is also a double. The same occurs with the age class variable in Vehicle – there is a class variable named age in the Car subclass also. This is known as *hiding* (or *shadowing*).

Vehicle defines the instance method, move() (lines 6-8), which is overridden by the version in Car (lines 17-19). As this is an instance method, polymorphism applies at runtime if move() is called.

Vehicle also defines a class method called sm() (lines 9-11), which is hidden (shadowed) by the version of sm() in Car (lines 20-22).

Line 26 creates a Car object and uses a Vehicle reference, v, to refer to it.

Line 27 outputs v.cost. As cost is data (an instance variable), the reference type applies. Consequently, we get 100.0, which is the cost instance variable in Vehicle (as opposed to 20_000.0, which is the cost instance variable in Car).

> **Using the class name when accessing a static member**
>
> Both lines 28 and 29 present syntax that you should *never* use: using a reference to access a static member. When accessing a static member, you should prefix the member with the class name. For example, line 28 should use Vehicle.age and line 29 should use Vehicle.sm() as this emphasizes the member's static nature. Using references here is confusing as it implies that the member is non-static. We accessed static members using the reference for demo purposes only!

Line 28 outputs v.age. As age is a static member, the compiler checks the type for v (namely Vehicle) and changes v.code to Vehicle.code. Therefore, age from Vehicle is used as opposed to age from Car. In other words, the output is 1, not 2.

Line 29 is the call to v.sm(). As sm() is also static, the compiler translates this into Vehicle.sm() and therefore the output is Vehicle::sm().

Lastly, line 30 is the polymorphic call to move(), and as a result, the object type, Car, is used. This results in Car::move() being output.

Now that we understand polymorphism, let's ensure that we understand the difference between two terms that are often confused, namely method overriding and method overloading.

# Contrasting method overriding and method overloading

These two terms are often confused but in this section, we will compare and contrast both. We will show that concerning method overloading, the method signature must be different; whereas concerning method overriding, the method signature must be the same. Recall that the method signature consists of the method name and the parameter types, including their order. The return type and the parameter identifiers are *not* part of the method signature. So, for example, take the method from *Figure 9.5*:

```
public static void doAction(Vehicle v) {…}
```

The signature is doAction(Vehicle).

With this in mind, we will initially discuss method overloading.

## Method overloading

Recall that the method signature consists of the method name and the parameter types. Method overloading is where you have the same method name but the parameters differ, either in type and/or order. This means that the method signatures are different even though the method names are the same. They have to be – how else will the compiler choose which method to bind to? Thus, method overloading is all about compile time.

### The rules

Bearing in mind that the method signatures *must be different* (apart from the method name), the rules are quite straightforward:

- Overloaded methods must use *DIFFERENT* parameter lists; either the types used must be different or the order of the types must be different
- As the method signature only relates to the method name and the parameter list, overloaded methods are free to change the return type and the access modifier and use new or broader checked exceptions
- An overloaded method can be overloaded in the same type or a subtype

Now, let's look at an example of method overloading in code.

## Method overloading example

*Figure 9.7* presents the example code:

```
2     class Animal{
3         public void eat(){}
4     }
5     class Cow extends Animal{
6         public void eat(){}        // overriding, same signature
7         public void eat(String s){} // overloaded, different signature!
8     }
9     public class OverloadTest {
10        public void calc(int x, double y){} // calc(int, double)
11        public void calc(){}                // calc()
12        public void calc(int x){}           // calc(int)
13        public void calc(double y){}        // calc(double)
14        public void calc(double y, int x){} // calc(double, int)
15
16    //    public void calc(int a, double b){}             // calc(int, double)
17    //    public int calc(int a, double b){ return 1; } // calc(int, double)
18
19        public static void main(String[] args) {
20            Animal aa = new Animal();
21            aa.eat();
22    //        aa.eat("Grass"); // compiler error
23
24            Animal ac = new Cow();
25            ac.eat();
26    //        ac.eat("Grass"); // compiler error
27
28            Cow cc = new Cow();
29            cc.eat();                // inherited
30            cc.eat( s: "Grass");
```

Figure 9.7 – Method overloading

In this figure, we will first discuss the method overloading between lines 10-17. To help, the method signatures are in comments on each line. Line 10 defines a `calc` method that takes in an `int` and a `double`, in that order. Therefore, the signature is as follows:

```
calc(int, double)
```

We are not interested in the return type or the identifiers used for the `int` and `double` parameters. So long as we do not code another `calc(int, double)` method in the *same class*, we are okay. Note that if we coded a method with the same signature in a subtype, this is overriding! As the method signatures between lines 11-14 are different, they are fine.

Let's examine why lines 16 and 17 fail to compile. Line 16 attempts to just change the identifiers used for the parameters. This does not change the method signature. Consequently, this signature is an exact match for the method on line 10 and therefore, the compiler complains. Similarly, line 17 changes the return type (as well as the identifiers in the parameter list). Again, as this signature is a duplicate of the one on line 10, the compiler complains.

The inheritance hierarchy is interesting. We have a parent called `Animal` (lines 2-4) and a subclass class `Cow` (lines 5-8). On line 3, `Animal` defines an `eat()` method. On line 7, `Cow` overloads this method with an `eat(String)` method. The parent `Animal` version accepts no argument, whereas the subtype version accepts `String`. The compiler is happy.

But what about line 6, where `Cow` defines an `eat()` method that accepts no argument? This is overriding the parent version (polymorphism), so there is no conflict. The compiler will bind to the reference type used, be it `Animal` or `Cow`, as both have an `eat()` method. At runtime, depending on the object type, the JVM will execute the relevant code.

Let's examine this process to make sure it is clear. Line 20 creates an `Animal` object and uses an `Animal` reference, aa, to refer to it. Line 21 calls `aa.eat()`. At compile time, the compiler checks if there is an `eat()` method with that exact signature in `Animal`, as `Animal` is the type for aa. As there is, the compiler is happy. At runtime, as the method is an instance method, polymorphism applies and the JVM will execute the `Animal` version (as that is the object type).

Note how line 22 does not compile. This is because there is no `eat(String)` method in `Animal`. Remember, the compiler looks at the reference type only and as aa is of type `Animal`, it checks the `Animal` class.

Lines 24-26 take things one step further. Line 24 creates a `Cow` object and uses an `Animal` reference called ac to refer to it. Line 25 makes the polymorphic call to `eat()`, which will execute the `Cow` version at runtime. Line 26 is interesting and is there to prove that the compiler is looking at the reference type. Even though our object type is `Cow` and `Cow` has an `eat(String)` method, the `ac.eat("Grass")` class still does not compile (because ac is of type `Animal`).

So, how do we get access to the `eat(String)` method? We need a `Cow` reference. This is what lines 28-30 demonstrate. Line 30 successfully invokes `cc.eat("Grass")` using the cc reference declared on line 28.

What this code demonstrates is that an `Animal` reference only has access to the `eat()` method it defined. On the other hand, a `Cow` reference has access to both `eat()` and `eat(String)`. The `Cow` type inherited (and overrode) `eat()` and defined `eat(String)` itself. Note that the `Cow` class did not need to override `eat()` to have access to the inherited version.

## Method overriding

Method overriding occurs when you have the same method signatures in both a parent and subclass. Method overriding is critical for enabling (runtime) polymorphism. Remember, a method must first be inherited to be overridden. For example, methods that are defined as `private`, `static`, or `final` are not inherited because `private` methods are local to the class; `static` methods are not polymorphic and marking a method as `final` is stating that "this method is not to be overridden."

To understand the rules, it is critical to remember that the compiler has compiled the code based on the reference. Therefore, the runtime polymorphic method *must not* behave differently from what the compiler verified. For example, the access modifier on the overriding method cannot be more restrictive.

Before we discuss the rules, we must first explain covariant returns.

### Covariant returns

When you are overriding a parent method in a subclass, if the return type is a primitive, then the overriding method's return type must match. However, if the return type is a non-primitive, then there is one exception to the rule: covariant returns.

What a covariant return means is that if you return a type, X, in the parent method, then you can return X and any subtype of X in the overriding method. For example, if a parent method is returning `Animal`, then the overriding method can return `Animal`, (naturally) as well as any subtype of `Animal`; for example, `Cow`.

### The rules

As we discuss the rules, it is helpful to bear in mind that the compiler checks against the reference type. These overriding rules ensure that the runtime object cannot do something that the compiler (and thus your code) does not expect. The rules are as follows:

- The method signatures must match exactly in the parent and subclass; otherwise, you are just overloading the method.

- The return types must match also, except for covariant returns.

- The access modifier on the overriding method cannot be more restrictive. So, if the parent method defines a method as `public`, the subclass cannot override it with a `private` method. This makes sense, as your code, verified by the compiler, is expecting access to the method. *If*, however, you were allowed to reduce access when overriding, the compiler would have said "It is okay to access this method," whereas the JVM would not! This rule helps keep the compiler and JVM in sync.

- Again, to keep the compiler and JVM in sync, an overriding method cannot throw (generate) new or broader checked exceptions (*Chapter 11*). Briefly, an exception is an error and checked exceptions must have code present to handle them. This is enforced by the compiler. If, at runtime, the overriding method threw/generated an exception for which there was no code to handle it, the JVM would be in trouble. So, the compiler steps in and prevents that from happening.

Now, let's look at an example of method overriding in code.

## Method overriding example

*Figure 9.8* presents the example code:

```
3     import java.io.IOException;
4
5     class Dog{
6         public void walk(){System.out.println("Dog::walk()");};
7         public Dog run() { return new Dog(); }
8     }
9     class Terrier extends Dog{
10    //    public String walk(){ return "Walk the Dog";} // return type should be void
11    //    private void walk(); // access rights cannot be weaker
12    //    public void walk() throws IOException {} // cannot throw new checked exceptions
13        public void walk(int metres){} // an overload, not an override
14        @Override public void walk(){System.out.println("Terrier::walk()");};
15
16    //    @Override public Dog run() {return new Dog();}          // ok
17    //    @Override public Terrier run() {return new Terrier();}   // ok
18        @Override public Dog run() {return new Terrier();}       // ok
19    }
20
21    public class OverridingTest {
22        public static void main(String[] args) {
23            Dog dt = new Terrier();
24            dt.walk();   // Terrier::walk()
25            Dog d = dt.run();
26            if(d instanceof Terrier){
27                System.out.println("Terrier object!");  // Terrier object!
28            }
29        }
30    }
```

Figure 9.8 – Method overriding

The code in this figure demonstrates what you can and cannot do when overriding a method. In the Dog class (lines 5-8), we have a walk() method that returns nothing (void). There is also a run() method that returns Dog.

The Terrier class subclasses from Dog (line 9). Therefore, any Terrier "is-a" Dog. As the two methods in Dog are public, Terrier automatically inherits them.

Let's examine the lines in Terrier in turn.

Line 10 does not compile because, while the method signatures match (both are walk()), the return types are different. The parent return type is void and thus, the overriding return type must match; it does not, it is String, causing the compiler error.

Line 11 does not compile because you cannot weaken the access modifier when overriding. The walk() method in Dog is public, so walk() in Terrier cannot be private. If this was allowed, then when the JVM went to execute the walk() method in Terrier, using a Dog reference (as on line 24), there would be a serious problem. The compiler, looking at the public Dog version, said "All is well;" but the JVM would, polymorphically, encounter the private version in Terrier!

Line 12 fails to compile because the overridden method did not throw any exceptions but the overriding method is attempting to throw a new checked exception (IOException). This is similar to the previous access issue – the compiler will have checked the walk() version in Dog and as it throws no exceptions (errors), no code is present to handle (cater) for these exceptions. If the overriding method was allowed to throw new checked exceptions, what would the JVM do with them (as there is no code in place to handle them)?

Line 13 is simply an overload. Dog defines a walk() method; Terrier defines a walk(int) method. Two separate method signatures means two separate methods. As the methods have the same name, this is method overloading.

Line 14 is a correct method override. We used the @Override annotation to ensure that we have overridden properly (no typos, for example).

Line 16 is an exact duplication of the run() method defined on line 7. We just included it for demonstration purposes.

Line 17 demonstrates covariant returns because it defines a Terrier return type. This is a valid covariant return because Terrier is a subtype of the parent return type, Dog (line 7). The code for the overridden method (line 17) simply returns a Terrier object.

Line 18 is almost identical to line 17 except that the return type is now Dog. Thus, there is an upcast going on in the background. The code for walk() on line 18 is shorthand for the following:

```
Dog d = new Terrier():
return d;
```

Now, let's look at the main() method in OverridingTest.

Line 23 creates a `Terrier` object that can be accessed via a `Dog` reference, `dt`. Line 24 invokes the polymorphic `walk()` method in `Terrier`. As `Terrier` overrode the `walk()` method it inherited from `Dog`, the `Terrier` version is dynamically executed at runtime, resulting in `Terrier::walk()` being output.

Line 25 executes the `run()` method using the `dt` reference created on line 23. As `run()` is an instance method where `Terrier` overrode the version inherited from `Dog`, the version in `Terrier` is executed, resulting in the d reference (line 25) referring to a `Terrier` object (line 18). This is proven by the use of the `instanceof` operator (line 26). As the `Dog` reference, `d`, is indeed referring to a `Terrier` object, the `if` statement is `true`, resulting in *Terrier object* being output to the screen.

That concludes our discussion of method overloading and method overriding. Now, let's examine a keyword that is pivotal in inheritance: `super`.

# Exploring the super keyword

The `super` keyword is used in a subclass in two specific scenarios: to call a parent constructor and to access parent members (typically methods). When an object is constructed, the order of constructor calls is very important. Bearing in mind that we now have the possibility of having many classes in an inheritance hierarchy, *the order of constructor calls is from the top down*. This means that, the parent constructor is *always* called before the subclass constructor. If you have a hierarchy where `Toyota` "is-a" `Car` and `Car` "is-a" `Vehicle`, then when you go to create a `Toyota` object, the order of constructor calls is as follows: `Vehicle` is first, `Car` is second, and `Toyota` is last.

There is a good reason for this. Firstly, remember that the constructor's role is to initialize the instance members of the class. Now, given that the subclass constructor *may use inherited members* from its parent when initializing its own members, it stands to reason that the parent must first get a chance to initialize those members.

Let's discuss the situations where the `super` keyword is very often used. We will then present code, supported by a UML diagram, where both contexts are demonstrated.

## super()

When you use the parentheses after `super`, as in `super()`, you are invoking the parent constructor. If required, you can pass in arguments inside the parentheses as constructors are just (special) methods. There are two rules for the use of `super()`:

- The call to `super()` can only appear inside a constructor and not a regular method
- If present, the call to `super()` must be the very first line in the constructor (there is one exception – see the callout)

We have coded several constructors so far and none of them had a call to `super()` present. How did that work? Well, if you *do not* provide any constructor at all, the default constructor will be synthesized by the compiler for you and its first line of code is `super();`. Please refer back to *Figure 8.1* and *Figure 8.2* for examples of this. If you *do* provide a constructor, then the compiler will also insert `super();` as the first line (unless the first line is already a call to `super()` or `this()`).

> ### The first line of any constructor
>
> The very first line of any constructor is `this()` or `super()`. You cannot have both. A call to `this()` is a call to another constructor in the same class. From the inheritance hierarchy perspective, this is a sideways call. Remember that the parent constructor must be called before the subclass constructor. Regardless of whether `this()` is present or not, the order of constructor calls is from the top down. Now, if the subclass constructor has a `this()` call present, it is only delaying the call to `super()`. At some point, either explicitly or implicitly, the call to `super()` will execute. Note that, as with `super()`, the call to `this()` can contain arguments.

So, `super()` relates only to constructors and must be the first line of code (assuming `this()` is not there already). Now, let's examine the other scenario.

## super.

To access a parent member (not the constructor), you can use the `super.` dot notation syntax. As with the `this` keyword, the `super` keyword relates to instances and thus cannot be used from within a `static` context (`static` methods or `static` blocks). This can be very useful when you want to piggyback on parent functionality. For example, the subclass method can invoke its parent version first and then execute its own version. This is what we will demonstrate in the example.

So, rather than call a parent constructor from a subclass constructor (which is what `super()` is for), `super.` gives us access to the other (non-constructor) members.

## An example of using super

Let's examine both `super()` and `super.` in code. *Figure 9.9* presents the UML inheritance diagram:

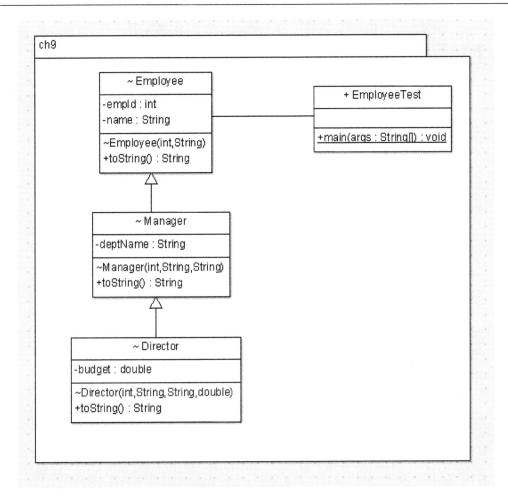

Figure 9.9 – UML for demonstrating super() and super.

In this figure, we have three classes representing a class inheritance hierarchy. Employee is at the top of the hierarchy. Manager "is-a" Employee and Director "is-a" Manager. Indirectly, Director "is-a" Employee also. Each of the classes has private instance variables that its respective constructors will initialize, based on the arguments passed into the respective constructor. For example, the Employee constructor takes in two parameters, int followed by String; these parameters will be used to initialize the Employee instance variables, namely empId (int) and name (String).

EmployeeTest is simply the driver to ensure the code is working as it should. Let's examine the code. *Figure 9.10* is the code for the UML in *Figure 9.9*:

```java
class Employee {
    private int empId;
    private String name;

    Employee(int empId, String name) {
        this.empId = empId;
        this.name = name;
    }
    @Override public String toString() { return "ID: " + empId + ", " + "Name: " + name + ","; }
}
class Manager extends Employee {// a Manager "IS-A" Employee
    private String deptName;    // a Manager "HAS-A" department

    Manager(int empId, String name, String deptName) {
        super(empId, name); // call parent constructor
        this.deptName = deptName;
    }
    @Override
    public String toString() {
        // call the parent toString()
        return super.toString() + " Department: " + deptName + ",";
    }
}
class Director extends Manager {
    private double budget;

    Director(int empId, String name, String department, double budget) {
        super(empId, name, department);
        this.budget = budget;
    }
    @Override public String toString() { return super.toString() + " Budget: " + budget; }
}
public class EmployeeTest {
    public static void main(String[] args) {
        Employee emplDir = new Director( empId: 754, name: "Joe Bloggs", department: "Marketing", budget: 10_000.00);
        System.out.println(emplDir); // ID: 754, Name: Joe Bloggs, Department: Marketing, Budget: 10000.0
    }
}
```

Figure 9.10 – Code demonstrating super

In this figure, the Employee class initializes its instance variables (lines 8-9). The toString() method for Employee (line 11) returns a String outlining the values in the empId and name instance variables. Line 11 also uses the @Override annotation because it is overriding the toString() method inherited from Object.

The Manager class "is-a" Employee (line 13). Manager contains (is composed of) a String instance variable, namely deptName. This is known as composition.

**Composition versus inheritance**

Composition defines a *"has-a"* relationship whereas, inheritance defines an *"is-a"* relationship. Composition is where an object is "composed" of other objects. For example, Car has Engine. In *Figure 9.10*, Manager "is-a" Employee (line 13), but Manager "has-a" department, which is represented by the String instance variable deptName (line 14).

The Manager constructor (lines 16-19) is where things get interesting. Line 17, super (empId, name), is the call to the parent constructor in Employee passing up the employee ID (empId) and employee name (name) that are required by the Employee constructor. That is why the Manager constructor requires those parameters in the first place – it needs the employee ID and employee name so it can invoke its parent Employee constructor. The Manager constructor also requires the department name so that it can initialize its own instance variable, deptName. Thus, when executing a Manager constructor, the Employee constructor is executed first and then the Manager constructor executes.

Note that if line 17 is commented out, the code will not compile. Why? Because the compiler will now insert super (); which is attempting to call the Employee constructor with no-arguments (the no-args constructor, namely Employee ()). There is no such constructor in Employee. Additionally, as Employee has already defined a constructor, the compiler will not insert the default (no-args) constructor.

The Manager classes' toString () method (lines 21-24), overrides the version inherited from Employee. However, Manager can still access the Employee version, which it does by using super.toString() on line 23. Thus, the toString () method in Manager first executes the toString () method in Employee, which returns the employee ID and employee name. The Manager classes' toString () method then appends its own instance variable, deptName, to the overall String to be returned.

The Director class behaves similarly to Manager. The constructor "supers up" (line 30) the required data for the Manager constructor; in turn, the Manager constructor supers up the required data for the Employee constructor. So, when creating a Director object, the order of constructor calls is as follows: Employee is first; Manager is second; Director is last. On line 31, Director initializes its own instance data.

The Director version of toString (), on line 33, first calls the Manager version of toString () using super.toString(). The Manager version (line 23) then calls the Employee classes' toString () method, which is on line 11. So, the employee's ID and name are the first employee details in the string. Next, the manager data (deptName) is appended (after the call to the Employee classes' toString () method returns). Lastly, the Director data (budget) is appended to the string (after the call to the Manager classes' toString () method returns). Note that you cannot bypass a level in the hierarchy; meaning that, super.super. is not allowed.

EmployeeTest is the driver class. In main() on line 39, we create a Director object that can be accessed via an Employee reference of emplDir (implicit upcasting). Using super() as outlined, this results in the Employee constructor being executed first, followed by the Manager constructor, and lastly the Director constructor being executed.

Line 40 passes the emplDir reference to System.out.println(), resulting in a polymorphic call to the Director classes' toString() method. Using super.toString(), Director invokes the Manager classes' toString() method, which also has a super.toString() method resulting in Employee toString() being executed first. Then, the Manager classes' toString() method finishes, and lastly, the Director classes' toString() method finishes. The output shows this:

```
ID: 754, Name: Joe Bloggs, Department: Marketing, Budget:
10000.0
```

Regarding the output, ID: 754, Name: Joe Bloggs is output from Employee toString(), Department: Marketing is output from the Department toString(), and Budget: 10000.0 is output from Director toString().

That concludes our discussion on super. Now that we understand inheritance, as promised in *Chapter 8*, let's return to the protected access modifier.

# Revisiting the protected access modifier

Recall that a protected member is accessible from within its own package and any subclasses outside of the package: *protected = package + children*. On the face of it, this seems very straightforward. However, some nuances lead to confusion. The subclasses that access the protected member (via inheritance), can only do so *in a very specific way*. A subclass from outside the package cannot use a superclass reference to access the protected member! In addition, an unrelated class from outside the package cannot use a reference to the subclass outside the package either to access the protected member. In effect, once the subclass that's outside the package inherits the protected member, that member becomes private to the subclass (and subclasses of the subclass). This is quite tricky and definitely needs an example.

## The UML diagram

*Figure 9.11* shows the UML diagram for this example:

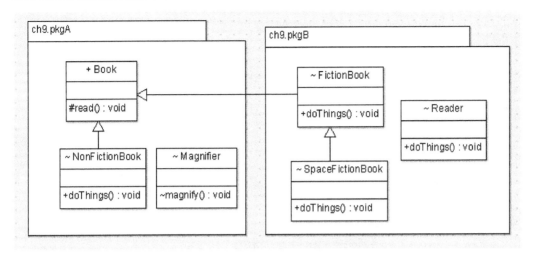

Figure 9.11 – UML for "protected" code

In this figure, we have two packages, namely ch9.pkgA and ch9.pkgB. In ch9.pkgA, we have a Book class and its subclass, NonFictionBook. The read() method in Book is marked with the # symbol, which means it is protected. The Magnifier class is not related to Book and is simply another class in the same package.

In ch9.pkgB, FictionBook subclasses Book from ch9.pkgA and provides a doThings() method, which we will use to demonstrate what is/is not allowed. In addition, SpaceFictionBook subclasses FictionBook and overrides the doThings() method inherited from FictionBook. Lastly, Reader is a completely separate class from the Book hierarchy; its doThings() method is also a sample method for demo purposes.

Recall from the previous chapter that we had not fully completed the access modifiers table (as we had not covered inheritance at that point). *Table 9.1* represents the completed access modifiers table. Bear in mind that the table represents annotating a member in the Book class.

| Access Modifier | Book | NonFictionBook | Magnifier | FictionBook | SpaceFictionBook | Reader |
|---|---|---|---|---|---|---|
| *private* | Y | N | N | N | N | N |
| package-private | Y | Y | Y | N | N | N |
| ***protected*** | Y | Y | Y | Y | Y | N |
| *public* | Y | Y | Y | Y | Y | Y |

Table 9.1 - Access modifiers table with 'protected' row fully filled out

Examining the protected row, we can now see that subclasses, regardless of the package, can access inherited protected members.

Now let us examine the code for each of the packages in turn. Firstly, we will examine the package that defines the `protected` member.

## The package with the protected member

*Figure 9.12* shows the code for the first package, `ch9.pkgA`, from *Figure 9.11*:

```
1    package ch9.pkgA;
2
3    public class Book {
4        protected void read(){}
5    }
6    class NonFictionBook extends Book{
7        public void doThings(){
8            read(); // same package; no problem
9        }
10   }
11   class Magnifier{
12       void magnify(){
13           Book b = new Book();
14           b.read(); // same package; no problem
15       }
16   }
```

Figure 9.12 – Code for "ch9.pkgA" from UML

In this figure, we have a class called Book (lines 3-5) that defines a `protected` `read()` method (line 4). `NonFictionBook` is a subclass of Book and has its own `doThings()` method (lines 7-9). In addition, there is a completely unrelated class to Book, namely `Magnifier`.

The first thing to note is that, as the `read()` method is `protected`, other code in the same package can access it, even if the code is *not* a subclass. This is demonstrated by line 14, where the `read()` method in Book is accessed from `Magnifier`, a completely unrelated class.

Of course, regardless of the package, subclasses can access the `protected` member. This is shown on line 8, where the `NonFictionBook` subclass invokes `read()`. Remember that line 8 is essentially `this.read()`. So, whichever `NonFictionBook` object is used to invoke `doThings()` on line 7 will be used to invoke the inherited (and `protected`) `read()` method on line 4.

The interesting code is in the other package, namely `ch9.pkgB`. Let's examine that now.

# The other package

*Figure 9.13* presents the code:

```
1    package ch9.pkgB;
2
3    import ch9.pkgA.Book;
4
5    class FictionBook extends Book{
6        public void doThings(){
7            read();      // different package, via inheritance; no problem
8            this.read();// different package, via inheritance; no problem
9            FictionBook fb = new FictionBook(); // default ctor created for us
10           fb.read();   // no problem
11
12           // Here, I create an instance of the superclass that has the protected
13           // member. Note that even though FictionBook has access via inheritance
14           // to read(), FictionBook must access it properly.
15           Book b = new Book();
16           b.read();    // not public!
17       }
18   }
19   class SpaceFictionBook extends FictionBook{
20       public void doThings(){
21           read();      // different package, via inheritance; no problem
22           new Book().read();
23           new FictionBook().read();
24           new SpaceFictionBook().read();// ok
25       }
26   }
27   class Reader{
28       public void doThings(){
29           Book b = new Book();
30           b.read();
31
32           // can I access the protected member via the subclass that inherits it?
33           FictionBook fb = new FictionBook();
34           fb.read();
35       }
36   }
```

Figure 9.13 – Code for "ch9.pkgB" from UML

In this figure, we can see that `FictionBook` "is-a" `Book` (line 5) and `SpaceFictionBook` "is-a" `FictionBook` (line 19). For this hierarchy to be possible, the `Book` class needed to be imported from the other package (line 3). We were only able to import `Book` from another package because `Book` is a `public` class. In addition, we have a completely unrelated class called `Reader` (lines 27-36).

Now, for the fun! Let's examine the `dothings()` method in `FictionBook` (lines 6-17). Lines 7 and 8 are essentially equivalent and show that subclasses outside the package, when using *inheritance directly*, can access `protected` members.

Lines 9-10 also show that when inside the subclass outside the package, if you create an instance of that particular subclass (`FictionBook`, in this instance), then all is ok. This makes sense because the two references used to invoke `read()` without issue, namely `this` and `fb`, are both of type `FictionBook`, where the code resides.

Note that line 15, where we instantiate a `Book` object, compiles because the `Book` class (*Figure 9.12*, line 3) is `public`. The `Book` class did not define a constructor, so the default constructor was created for us. This default constructor takes on the same access as the class, namely `public`, and as a result, we can invoke the constructor from a different package.

Line 16, which does not compile, is very interesting. When inside the subclass outside the package, you cannot access the `protected` member using the superclass reference – even though the `protected` member resides in that superclass! Remember that, once outside the package, the `protected` member becomes `private` to subclasses (and their subclasses). In other words, you must use inheritance in a very specific way.

`SpaceFictionBook` (lines 19-26) shows that access is available to subclasses of the subclass outside the package. Line 21 is the same as line 7, except that they are in two separate classes. As this line compiles, it demonstrates that subclasses of the subclass outside the package have access to the `protected` member in the base class.

Lines 22 and 23 both fail to compile. Line 22 tries to access the `protected` member via a `Book` reference and line 23 tries to access it via a `FictionBook` reference. Both fail. Contrast this with line 24, which uses an instance of the current class, namely `SpaceFictionBook`, which works. Note that line 24 is similar to line 21 in that a `SpaceFictionBook` reference is used in both instances (as line 21 is equivalent to `this.read()`). In addition, line 24 is very similar to lines 9-10. Therefore, when in a subclass outside the package, access the `protected` member directly, as on lines 7, 21; or use a reference to the current subclass, as on lines 10, 24.

The `Reader` class (lines 27-36) is a completely separate class from the `Book` hierarchy. Line 30 attempts to access the `protected` member using a reference to the class that defines the `protected` member, namely `Book`, and fails. Line 34 attempts to access the `protected` member using a reference to the subclass outside the package that inherits the `protected` member, namely `FictionBook`, and also fails.

So `protected` is somewhat tricky. While we are revisiting previous topics, it is an ideal opportunity to revisit `switch`. To be more specific, to discuss pattern matching for `switch`.

## Pattern matching for switch

As promised from *Chapter 4*, now that we understand inheritance and polymorphism, we are going to revisit the switch. Given the following code:

```
public static void patternMatchingSwitch(Vehicle v) {
    System.out.println(
        switch(v){
            case Boat b -> "It's a Boat";
            case Train t -> "It's a Train";
            case Car c when c.getNumDoors() == 4  ->
                "Saloon "+ c.onRoad(); // custom Car method
            case Car c when c.getNumDoors() == 2  ->
                "Convertible: " + c.onRoad();
            case null, default -> "Invalid type";
        }
    );
}
```

Assume that Car, Boat, and Train all extend from Vehicle and that Car has a custom method onRoad(). As you can see, in this switch expression, the selector expression, v, can be any reference type (Boat, Train, Car, and so forth). The case labels demonstrate *type patterns and pattern matching*; for example, Boat b.

In addition, both case labels for Car are known as *guarded patterns*. A guarded pattern is a case label protected by a "guard" on the right-hand side of a when clause. A guard is a conditional expression, evaluating to true or false. Note the use of the custom Car method onRoad() and the fact that no cast is required, as the cast is done for us in the background (provided we are dealing with a Car).

The last case label, containing default, ensures exhaustiveness is catered for, thereby keeping the compiler happy. In other words, all possible Vehicles are catered for. Note also the use of null as a valid label and the fact that null and default can be comma separated.

Now, let's examine the effect on inheritance of two particular keywords, namely abstract and final.

# Explaining the abstract and final keywords

As we know, when coding methods, we can apply the access modifier keywords, namely private, protected, public, and package-private (no keyword). Two other keywords have special significance regarding inheritance: abstract and final. Both are opposites of each other, which is why both cannot be applied to a method at the same time. Let's discuss them now, starting with abstract.

# The abstract keyword

The abstract keyword is applied to classes and methods. While abstract classes will be discussed more fully in *Chapter 10*, we will be discussing them here also (for reasons that will soon become obvious). An abstract method has no implementation (code). In other words, the method signature, rather than following it with curly braces, { }, which represents the implementation, an abstract method signature is simply followed by a semi-colon. Marking a method as abstract implies the following:

- The class must be abstract also

- The first concrete (non-abstract) subclass must provide an implementation for the abstract method

Let's discuss this in more detail. When you mark a method (or methods) as abstract, you are saying that this method has no implementation code. As there is something "missing," the class itself must be marked as abstract also. This tells the compiler that the class is incomplete and as a result, you cannot instantiate (create) an object based on an abstract class. In other words, you cannot execute new on an abstract class (although a reference is perfectly ok). The whole rationale for abstract methods (and thus abstract classes) is for them to be overridden by subclasses, where the "missing" implementation code is provided. Now, if the direct subclass does not provide the implementation code for the inherited abstract method, that subclass must also be abstract. Therefore, the first non-abstract (concrete) subclass of an abstract class must provide the implementation code for the abstract method. *Figure 9.14* demonstrates these principles:

```
3    abstract class Pencil{
4        abstract void write(); // no {}
5    }
6    class CharcoalPencil extends Pencil{}
7    abstract class WaterColorPencil extends Pencil{}
8    class GraphitePencil extends Pencil{
9        @Override
10       void write(){
11           System.out.println("GraphitePencil::write()");
12       }
13   }
14
15   public class PencilsExample{
16       public static void main(String[] args) {
17           Pencil pp    = new Pencil(); // cannot "new" a Pencil (abstract)
18           Pencil pdp   = new GraphitePencil();
19           pdp.write();    // GraphitePencil::write()
20       }
21   }
```

Figure 9.14 – The "abstract" keyword in action

In this figure, we have an `abstract` method, namely `write()`, on line 4. Notice how there are no curly braces for the method; we just have the semi-colon immediately after the parentheses. As the `Pencil` class (lines 3-5) contains an `abstract` method, the class itself must be `abstract`; which it is (line 3).

On line 6, `CharcoalPencil` attempts to subclass `Pencil`. But because (a) it does not provide an implementation for the `abstract` method `write()`, which it inherited from `Pencil`, and (b) `CharcoalPencil` *itself* is not abstract, `CharcoalPencil` fails to compile.

Contrast line 6 with line 7. As we saw, line 6 does not compile. However, line 7, `WaterColorPencil`, does compile. Why? Because `WaterColorPencil` is abstract; the fact that it does not provide an implementation for the `abstract` method `write()` is no problem.

---

**Abstract classes do not have to have abstract methods**

As we know, if you have 1 (or more) `abstract` methods, then the class must be `abstract`. However, the opposite is not true. In other words, an `abstract` class does not have to have any `abstract` methods at all! Note that `WaterColorPencil` (line 7 in *Figure 9.14*) is an example of such a class. It is `abstract` and yet has no methods at all. This is fine. This could be a design decision whereby, even if the class contains only concrete methods, you simply want this class to be used as a reference type and not as an object type (as you cannot new it).

---

The `GraphitePencil` class (lines 8-13) is a concrete, non-abstract class. As it `extends` the abstract class, `Pencil`, it must provide an implementation for the `abstract` method `write()`. This is done on lines 10 to 12 and we use the `@Override` annotation to emphasize this.

Line 17 demonstrates that you cannot instantiate an object of an `abstract` class. The reference part of the `Pencil  pp` statement is fine. The issue is with the `new  Pencil()` part.

Line 18 shows what is allowed. Again, we are using a `Pencil` reference but this time, we are referring to a `GraphitePencil` object. `GraphitePencil` is a concrete class (line 8). Line 19 polymorphically calls the `write()` method provided by `GraphitePencil` (lines 10-12). Assuming lines 6 and 17 are commented out (so the code will compile), line 19 outputs `GraphitePencil::write()`.

Now that we understand `abstract` methods and classes, let's examine the `final` keyword.

## The final keyword

The `final` keyword can be applied in various contexts. Inheritance is the main focus here, but we will examine other situations also. We will examine each in turn and then look at code that demonstrates them. We will start with `final` methods.

### final methods

A `final` method cannot be overridden in a subclass. This prevents any unwanted changes by subclasses. We can take this a stage further with `final` classes.

### final classes

A class that is marked `final` cannot be used as a base type. This means you cannot extend from a `final` class. All the methods in the class are implicitly `final`. Java uses this in its API to guarantee behavior. For example, the `String` class is `final` so that nobody can extend it and provide a custom implementation. Therefore, Java always knows how strings behave. Now, we will examine `final` method parameters.

### final method parameters

A `final` method parameter is a parameter that cannot be changed. However, be aware that the semantics are subtly different depending on the parameter type. If the parameter type is a primitive, such as `int`, then you cannot change the value of the `int` parameter.

However, if the parameter in question is a reference (as opposed to a primitive), `final` applies to the reference and therefore, it is the reference that cannot be changed. In other words, the object the reference is pointing to is modifiable, but the reference itself is not. What this means is that, for example, if the method accepts a `Dog` reference, namely `dog`, then using the `dog` reference, you can change the properties of the object, such as `dog.setAge(10)`. You cannot, however, change `dog` to refer to a different object, such as `dog = new Dog()`.

### final (constants)

A constant is a value that cannot change. It is customary and good practice to use capital letters as the identifiers for constants, with each word separated by an underscore. This makes them stand out and developers know they cannot change them. One example from the Java API is the *PI* constant from the `Math` class (in the auto-imported `java.lang` package). It is `final` so that it cannot be changed. To provide easy access, *PI* is also `public` and `static`.

Now, let's look at a code example to re-enforce the use of `final`. *Figure 9.15* presents the code:

```
3     final class Earth{}
4     // cannot extend a 'final' class
5     class SubEarth extends Earth{}
6
7     class Pen{
8         final void write(){}
9         // 'final' and 'abstract' not allowed together
10        // as they have opposite meanings
11    //    final abstract scribble();
12    }
13    class FountainPen extends Pen{
14        // cannot override a 'final' method
15        @Override void write(){}
16    }
17    public class DemoOfFinal {
18        final int ONE_YEAR = 1;
19        void print(final String name, final int age){
20            // primitives
21            age = age + ONE_YEAR;
22            // references - ok to access the object
23            System.out.println(name.toUpperCase());
24            // references - cannot modify the reference
25            name = "Alexander";
26
27            ONE_YEAR = 2; // cannot change a constant
28        }
29    }
```

Figure 9.15 – The "final" keyword in action

In this figure, we have a `final` class called `Earth` (line 3). Line 5 demonstrates, via a compiler error, that you cannot extend from a `final` class.

Line 8 defines a `final` method called `write()` in the `Pen` class. Consequently, the `FountainPen` class encounters a compiler error (line 15) when attempting to override `write()`.

Line 11 shows that you cannot annotate a method as both `abstract` and `final` – `abstract` implies that this method is to be overridden in a subclass; `final` means that this method must not be overridden.

Line 18 declares a constant called `ONE_YEAR` and sets it to 1. Line 27 attempts to change the constant value – as this is not allowed, the compiler complains.

The `print()` method (lines 19-28) outlines what `final` means for method parameters. The method parameters (line 19) are `final String name` and `final int age`, respectively. `String` is a non-primitive type and therefore `name` is a reference. In other words, the value inside `name` is a memory location (reference) of where the object is on the heap. On the other hand, `age` is simply a primitive `int`, whose value is simply a whole number, such as 1. It is easy to understand what you can and cannot do with `final` parameters when you view the *value* as `final`. Thus, if 1 is in `age`, it cannot be changed and neither can the reference (address) in `name`. However, the object referred to by `name` can be modified.

Line 21 is a compiler error and demonstrates that `final` primitives cannot be changed.

Line 23 shows us that the object that the reference is referring to can be accessed (and changed if required). Note that, in this particular example, as `String`s are immutable objects, the `toUpperCase()` method returns the new, uppercase `String`, as opposed to changing the original. We will talk more about `String`s in *Chapter 12*. The important thing to note is that the compiler had no issue with line 23.

Line 25 attempts to change the `String` reference `name` to refer to a different `String`. As the reference is `final`, the compiler complains. Once again, the separation of reference and object makes things much easier to understand.

At this point, we know how to create (unlimited) inheritance hierarchies (using `extends`). We also know that `final` disables inheritance. What if we wanted a "middle ground," where we could customize our hierarchy to certain types? This is what sealed classes enable. Let's discuss them now.

## Applying sealed classes

Sealed classes were introduced in Java 17. What we are going to cover here relates to classes but the same logic applies to interfaces (*Chapter 10*). With inheritance, you can extend from any class (or interface) using the `extends` keyword, unless the class is `final` of course.

> **Note**
> Interfaces cannot be `final` because their whole rationale is to be implemented.

Consider the following scenario: what if you wanted your class to be available for inheritance, but only for certain classes? In other words, you want to scope the subclasses allowed. So far, inheritance, using `extends`, enables every class to become a subclass, whereas `final` prevents a class from having subclasses.

This is where sealed classes are useful – they enable you to specify what subclasses are allowed. Just to reiterate, this also applies to interfaces, where we can specify what classes are allowed to implement the interface.

Before we look at an example, there are some new keywords that we need to understand.

## sealed and permits

These keywords work together. To state that a class is sealed, you can simply specify that it is just that, `sealed`. Once you do that, however, you must specify which classes can extend from this class. To do that, you use the `permits` keyword, followed by the comma-separated list of classes.

## non-sealed

When you start to scope/restrict a hierarchy, you must use certain keywords when specifying the subclasses. A subclass involved in a sealed hierarchy must state one of the following:

- It is also sealed. This means, we have further scoping to perform and therefore we must use the `sealed`/`permits` pairing on this subclass to specify the subclasses allowed.

- It is the `final` class in the hierarchy (no more subclasses allowed).

- It ends the scoping. In effect, you want to open up the hierarchy again for extension. To do this, we use the `non-sealed` keyword as `non-sealed` classes can be subclassed.

Now, let's look at an example.

## Example using sealed, permits, and non-sealed

*Figure 9.16* presents a UML diagram for the code example we will use:

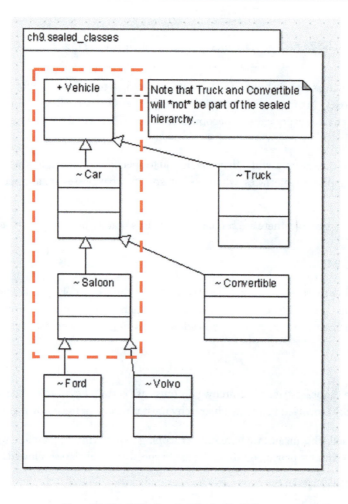

Figure 9.16 – UML diagram for "sealed" classes

In this figure, we have a Vehicle hierarchy. The parts we are going to restrict (seal) are the Vehicle, Car, and Saloon classes. Therefore, the only class that can subclass Vehicle is Car; and the only class that can subclass Car is Saloon. Note that even though the diagram implies Truck "is-a" Vehicle and Convertible "is-a" Car, for this example, we will prevent that in code.

The goal of the code is to ensure that the only Vehicles we are interested in are Cars and the only Cars we are interested in are Saloons. In addition, all Saloons (Ford and Volvo) are of interest. *Figure 9.17* presents the code.

```
3  ●↓   public sealed class Vehicle permits Car{ }    // scoping hierarchy
4  ●↓   sealed class Car extends Vehicle permits Saloon {}
5       //sealed class Truck extends Vehicle {}        // compiler error
6  ●↓   non-sealed class Saloon extends Car{}          // opening up hierarchy again
7       class Volvo extends Saloon{}
8       class Ford extends Saloon{}
9       //class Convertible extends Car{}              // compiler error
```

Figure 9.17 – "sealed" code

In the preceding figure, line 3 states that we have a sealed class called Vehicle and that the only subclass allowed (permitted) is Car. At this point, the Car class must exist; otherwise, the compiler will complain.

Line 4 defines a sealed class called Car as a subclass of Vehicle (which it must do due to line 3) and that the only subclass permitted is Saloon. Note that when we were defining Car, we had to specify that Car was either sealed, non-sealed, or final.

Line 5 is the Truck class attempting to subclass Vehicle. However, as we have sealed Vehicle to only allow Car as a subclass, this generates a compiler error.

Line 6 defines Saloon as a subclass of Car (as expected from line 4). In this instance, we have chosen to open up the hierarchy for further extension (by any class) by stating that Saloon is non-sealed. Lines 7 and 8 demonstrate that Saloon is a non-sealed class by allowing Volvo and Ford to extend from it, respectively.

Lastly, on line 9, Convertible attempts to subclass Car. This is not allowed as line 4 states that the only subclass of Car allowed is Saloon.

Let's move on now and discuss both instance and static blocks.

## Understanding instance and static blocks

As we know, in Java, a block is delimited by curly braces, { }, and these code blocks are no different. What is different about instance and static code blocks is *where* these blocks appear – in other words, their scope. Both of these code blocks appear outside every method but inside the class.

We will discuss each in turn and then present a code example to demonstrate them in operation. We will start with instance blocks.

## Instance blocks

An instance block is a set of braces that appear outside of any method but inside the class. Assuming an instance block is present in a class, every time an object is created (using new), the instance block is executed. Note that the instance block executes *before* the constructor. To be technically accurate, super() is executed first so that the parent constructor has a chance to execute; this is followed by the instance block, after which the rest of the constructor executes. Use the "sic" (*s*uper, *i*nstance block, *c*onstructor) acronym to help remember the order. You can think of the compiler inserting the instance block into the constructor code just after the call to super(). If more than one instance block exists in a class, they are executed in order of appearance, from top to bottom.

As instance blocks execute as part of every constructor, they are an ideal location for inserting code that you want every constructor to have. In other words, code that is common across all constructors should go into an instance block. This saves you from duplicating code across constructors.

As we know, the parent constructor must execute before the child constructor. The same occurs with instance blocks. In other words, the parent instance blocks must execute before the child instance blocks. We will see this in the code example.

## static blocks

A static block is a set of braces, preceded by the static keyword, that appears outside of any method but inside the class. The static block is only executed once, the very first time the class is loaded. This could occur when the first object of the class is created or the first time a static member is accessed. Static blocks execute before instance blocks (as we have to load the class file/bytecode before we can execute a constructor). Once executed, given that the class file is now loaded into memory, the static block is never executed again.

As with instance blocks, if more than one static block exists in a class, they are executed in order of appearance, from top to bottom. Similarly, as with instance blocks, if inheritance is involved, then the parent static blocks execute before the child static blocks.

This will all make a lot more sense with a code example, where we will be able to compare and contrast both types of code blocks in an inheritance hierarchy.

*Figure 9.18* presents the code:

```
3  ●↓   class Parent{
4             // instance initialization block
5             { System.out.println("6. Parent instance init block 1"); }
6             // static initialization block
7             static {System.out.println("2. Parent static init block 1");}
8             Parent() { System.out.println("8. Parent constructor"); }
11            { System.out.println("7. Parent instance init block 2"); }
12            static {System.out.println("3. Parent static init block 2");}
13        }
14     class Child extends Parent{
15            { System.out.println("9. Child instance init block 1"); }
16            static {System.out.println("4. Child static init block 1");}
17            Child() { System.out.println("11. Child constructor"); }
20            { System.out.println("10. Child instance init block 2"); }
21            static {System.out.println("5. Child static init block 2\n");}
22        }
23  ▶  public class InitializationBlocks {
24            static {System.out.println("1. InitializationBlocks static init block");}
25            { System.out.println("InitializationBlocks instance init block"); }
26  ▶       public static void main(String[] args) {
27                System.out.println("---> Creating first Child object...");
28                new Child();
29                System.out.println("\n--->Creating second Child object...");
30                new Child();
31            }
32        }
```

Figure 9.18 – Instance and "static" code blocks example

In this figure, we have a parent class called Parent and a child class called Child (it took a while to come up with those names!). Both classes have two instance initialization blocks, two static initialization blocks, and a constructor. Notice that the static initialization blocks (lines 7, 12, 16, and 21) are all simply blocks of code preceded by the static keyword. Also, note their location/ scope – outside the methods but inside the class. The same is true for the instance initialization blocks (lines 5, 11, 15, and 20), except that the instance blocks have no keyword preceding them.

The main driver class, InitializationBlocks, also has one static and one instance initialization block (lines 24 and 25, respectively).

Each of these blocks simply outputs a tracer message so that we know which block of code is currently executing. The tracer messages are annotated with ascending numbers so we can follow the order of execution more easily. *Figure 9.19*, presents the output from the code in *Figure 9.18*:

```
1. InitializationBlocks static init block

---> Creating first Child object...

2. Parent static init block 1
3. Parent static init block 2
4. Child static init block 1
5. Child static init block 2

6. Parent instance init block 1
7. Parent instance init block 2
8. Parent constructor
9. Child instance init block 1
10. Child instance init block 2
11. Child constructor

---> Creating second Child object...

6. Parent instance init block 1
7. Parent instance init block 2
8. Parent constructor
9. Child instance init block 1
10. Child instance init block 2
11. Child constructor
```

Figure 9.19 – Output from the code in Figure 9.18

> **Note**
>
> To avoid confusion between numbers representing output in *Figure 9.19* with line numbers in *Figure 9.18*, all numbers mentioned here refer to output numbers in *Figure 9.19*. Any line numbers relating to *Figure 9.18* will be explicitly annotated as "line...."

All Java programs start with the main() method. Therefore, the JVM has to find, using the CLASSPATH environment variable, the .class file containing main(), namely InitializationBlocks. class. As the JVM loads the class, if the class has a parent, it loads the parent first. In this example, as InitializationBlocks is not a subclass, this does not apply. However, there is a static block and this gives us our first line of output. Note that the instance block for InitializationBlocks is never executed. This is because no instance of InitializationBlocks was ever created. In other words, there is no new InitializationBlocks() in the code.

Line 27 simply outputs `"---> Creating first Child object..."`. What is interesting to note is that it is not the first line output to the screen – the output from the `static` block is first.

Line 28 creates a `Child` object. Its output is represented by numbers 2-11. As this is the first time a `Child` object has been created (as no `static` member in `Child` has been accessed before this), the class file for `Child` is loaded. During this process, the JVM realizes that `Child` is a subclass of `Parent`, so it loads the `Parent` class first. Therefore, the `static` blocks in `Parent` are executed first, in order of appearance (2 and 3); followed by the `Child` static blocks, also in order of appearance (4 and 5).

Now that the `static` blocks are done, the instance blocks and constructors are executed. First, the superclass `Parent` instance blocks are executed in order of appearance (6 and 7), followed by the `Parent` constructor (8). Then, the subclass `Child` instance blocks are executed in order of appearance (9 and 10), followed by the `Child` constructor (11). That is a lot of processing from a simple `new Child()` line of code.

Line 29 simply outputs `"---> Creating second Child object..."`.

Line 30 creates another `Child` object. As the class was already loaded previously, the `static` blocks will already have run for both `Child` and its superclass, `Parent`. Therefore, they do not run again. So, we run the `Parent` instance blocks (6 and 7), followed by the `Parent` constructor (8). Then, we run the `Child` instance blocks (9 and 10), followed by the `Child` constructor (11).

Note the repetition of line numbers 6-11 when creating a `Child` object. The `Parent` instance blocks are executed in order; followed by the `Parent` constructor. The `Child` instance blocks and constructor follow in a similar fashion.

That covers `static` and instance initialization blocks. Before we conclude this chapter on inheritance, we would just like to delve a little deeper into one of the topics we touched on earlier: upcasting and downcasting.

## Mastering upcasting and downcasting

Earlier, we touched upon why we get `ClassCastException` errors. The rule is that a reference can refer to objects of its own type or objects of subclasses. In effect, a reference can point across and down the inheritance hierarchy, but never up. If a reference does point up the hierarchy, you will get a `ClassCastException` error. Recall that the reason this occurs is that the subclass reference could have extra methods that any superclass object would have no code for. Whether that is the case or not is immaterial, *could have* is enough.

Keep in mind that assignment works from right to left; so, when reading code involving upcasting/downcasting, the direction in the hierarchy is from right to left as well. In addition, remember that the compiler is always looking at the reference type.

Now, let's discuss, with the aid of code examples, both upcasting and downcasting. Let's start with upcasting.

## Upcasting

With upcasting, you are going from a more specific type "up to" a more general type. For example, let's look at the following line of code:

```
Vehicle vc = new Car()
```

Here, we are going from Car *up* to Vehicle. The more specific type (Car) is further down the hierarchy and potentially has extra methods. Due to inheritance, whatever methods the parent reference has access to, the subclass will also have. So, any methods available to the Vehicle reference, vc, will exist in the Car object! Therefore, upcasting is never an issue, and an explicit cast is not required.

*Figure 9.20* presents upcasting in code:

```
3    class Machine {
4        void on(){ System.out.println("Machine::on()"); }
5    }
6    class Tractor extends Machine {
7        @Override void on(){ System.out.println("Tractor::on()"); }
8        void drive() { System.out.println("Tractor::drive()"); }
9    }
10   public class UpcastingAndDowncasting {
11       public static void doAction(Machine machine){
12           machine.on();
13       }
14       public static void main(String[] args) {
15           Machine mt = new Tractor(); // upcasting
16           doAction(mt);                   // polymorphism, Tractor::on()
17           doAction(new Tractor());        // polymorphism, Tractor::on()
18       }
19   }
```

Figure 9.20 – Upcasting in action

In this figure, we have a class called Machine (lines 3-5) and a subclass called Tractor (lines 6-9). The on() method in Tractor (line 7) overrides the on() method in Machine (line 4).

Line 15 involves an implicit upcast. Reading it right to left (as assignment is right to left), we are going from `Tractor` "up to" `Machine`. This is possible because every `Tractor` "is-a" `Machine`. Thus, line 15 results in a `Machine` reference referring to a `Tractor` object.

Line 16 invokes the `doAction()` method while passing in the reference created on line 15, namely `mt`. This `mt` reference is copied (remember Java is call by value) into the `Machine` reference, namely `machine`, on line 11. Thus, the `mt` reference in the `main()` method and the `machine` reference in the `doAction()` method are pointing at the one and same object, which was created on line 15.

Inside the `doAction()` method, we invoke the `on()` method using the `machine` reference (line 12). As the `machine` references type, namely `Machine`, has an `on()` method, the compiler is happy. At runtime, the object that `machine` is referring to, namely `Tractor`, is used. In other words, the `on()` method from `Tractor` is dynamically executed (polymorphically).

Line 17 is just accomplishing in one line what was coded over lines 15 and 16. With the invocation of `doAction()` on line 17, the upcasting is as follows:

```
Machine machine = new Tractor()
```

The `Machine` reference, namely `machine`, is provided by the `doAction()` signature (line 11), and the `Tractor` instance creation comes from line 17.

Both lines 16 and 17 result in the same output: `Tractor::on()`. Now, let's discuss the trickier of the two: downcasting.

## Downcasting

With downcasting, you are going from a more general type "down to" a more specific type. For example, let's look at the following line of code:

```
Car cv = (Car) new Vehicle(),
```

Reading it from right to left, we are going from `Vehicle` *down* to `Car`. Again, the more specific type (`Car`) is further down the hierarchy and potentially has extra methods. The compiler spots this and complains. We can overrule the compiler by inserting a (down)cast, `(Car)`. This is what we have done here. However, at runtime, this line of code results in a `ClassCastException` error. This is because, on the right-hand side of the assignment statement, we are attempting to create a `Car` reference that will point up the inheritance tree at a `Vehicle` object!

*Figure 9.21* presents downcasting in code:

```
3     class Machine {
4         void on(){ System.out.println("Machine::on()"); }
5     }
6     class Tractor extends Machine {
7         @Override void on(){ System.out.println("Tractor::on()"); }
8         void drive() { System.out.println("Tractor::drive()"); }
9     }
10    public class UpcastingAndDowncasting {
11        public static void doAction(Machine machine){
12    //        machine.on();
13
14            // Let us try and call the Tractor-specific method 'drive()'
15    //        machine.drive(); // compiler error
16    //        ((Tractor)machine).drive(); // possible ClassCastException
17            if(machine instanceof Tractor t){
18                t.drive(); // safe
19            }
20        }
21        public static void main(String[] args) {
22            doAction(new Machine());      // outputs nothing
23            doAction(new Tractor());      // Tractor::drive()
24        }
25    }
```

Figure 9.21 – Downcasting in action

The code in this figure is very similar to the code in *Figure 9.20*. The inheritance hierarchy is the same. The changes are in the doAction() and main() methods. Line 12 works normally and we have commented it out to focus on downcasting.

Our goal, as stated on line 14, is to *safely* invoke the Tractor object's drive() method. Note that this method is specific to Tractor. Let's look at the changes in baby steps.

Firstly, as drive() is specific to Tractor (and not Machine), this means that we need a Tractor reference to get the code to compile. The fact that line 15 does not compile demonstrates this – the machine reference is of the Machine type and Machine does not have a drive() method.

Line 16 addresses the compiler error from line 15. Line 16 compiles because it (down)casts the machine reference to a Tractor reference *before* it calls the drive() method. That is why the extra set of parentheses are needed – method invocation has higher precedence than casting, so we change the order of precedence by using parentheses. Without the extra set of parentheses, we have (Tractor) `machine.drive()`, and this does not compile (for the same reason as line 15 does not compile). However, the extra set of parentheses forces the cast from `Machine` to `Tractor` to be performed first, and thus the compiler looks for `drive()` in `Tractor`.

However, we are still not "out of the woods." Yes, the compiler is happy, but the JVM is vulnerable to `ClassCastException` errors at runtime. If line 16 were uncommented, then line 22 would cause a `ClassCastException` error at runtime. This is because line 22 passes in a `Machine` object, so inside the `doAction()` method, the `machine` reference is referring to a `Machine` object. Therefore, on line 16, we would be trying to create a `Tractor` reference to point *up* to the `Machine` object, which is a `ClassCastException` all day long.

Line 17 uses the `instanceof` keyword, in conjunction with a type pattern and pattern matching. Line 17 is only true if the reference `machine` refers to a `Tractor` object; when it is, the cast is done for us in the background and `t` is initialized to refer to the `Tractor` object. This is why line 22 outputs nothing – the `Machine` object passed in, fails the `instanceof` test and therefore line 18 is *not* executed. However, as line 23 passes in a `Tractor` object, it passes the `instanceof` test. This means that line 18 is executed and outputs `Tractor::drive()`.

That completes another hugely important chapter. Now, let's apply what we have learned!

# Exercises

Our park is full of diversity, not just in the species of dinosaurs but also in the roles of our employees. To model this diversity, we will be incorporating the concept of inheritance into our applications:

1.  Not all dinosaurs are the same. Some are small, others big. Some are herbivores, others carnivores. Create at least three subclasses for different types of dinosaurs that inherit from the base `Dinosaur` class.

    If you need inspiration, you can create a `FlyingDinosaur` subclass and an `AquaticDinosaur` subclass from the `Dinosaur` class, each with its unique properties. (This is not the most optimal way to model this, but don't worry about that now.)

2.  Just like our dinosaurs, our employees also have diverse roles. Some are park managers, while others are security officers or veterinarians. Create subclasses for these employee roles that inherit from the `Employee` base class. Come up with at least three subclasses.

3.  Inheritance doesn't just stop at properties and methods. Even the behavior of some methods can be customized in subclasses. Provide a custom implementation of the `toString()` method in the `Dinosaur` and `Employee` classes (from exercises 1 and 2) and their subclasses to display detailed information about each object.

4.  Also, override the `equals()` method in the `Dinosaur` and `Employee` classes to compare objects of these classes.

5.  Create a class called `App` with a `main` method. In there, add functionality to check if an employee is qualified to work in a specific enclosure, considering the employee's role and the enclosure's safety level.

6.  The park offers regular tickets and season tickets. Create a `SeasonTicket` class that extends the `Ticket` class and add properties such as start date and end date.

# Project

You will be developing a more advanced version of the Mesozoic Eden park manager console application. Your task is to implement the concept of polymorphism to handle different types of dinosaurs and employees. By incorporating polymorphism, the application can accommodate an even wider range of dinosaur species and employee roles. The key features of the system should now include the following:

- The ability to manage diverse types of dinosaur profiles, representing a variety of species

- The ability to manage different types of park employee profiles that represent a variety of roles, such as park rangers, janitors, veterinarians, and more

- All previous features, such as editing and removing profiles, real-time dinosaur tracking, employee scheduling, guest admissions, and handling special events, should now accommodate these new varieties

Here's what you need to do, broken down into smaller steps if you need it:

1.  **Extend the data structures**: Extend your `Dinosaur` and `Employee` classes into different subclasses to represent different types of dinosaurs and employee roles. Make sure these subclasses demonstrate the principle of polymorphism.

2.  **Enhance initialization**: Upgrade your data initialization so that it supports different types of dinosaurs and employees. This could involve creating arrays or lists of `Dinosaur` and `Employee` objects, where each object could be an instance of any subclass.

3.  **Update the interaction**: Modify your interactive console-based interface to handle the new types of dinosaurs and employees. You might need to add more options or submenus.

4.  **Enhance menu creation**: Your menu should now handle different types of dinosaurs and employees. Make sure each option corresponds to a particular function in the program.

5.  **Handle actions**: Each menu item should trigger a function that is now able to handle different types of dinosaurs and employees. For example, the "Manage Dinosaurs" option could now trigger a function to add, remove, or edit a profile of any dinosaur species.

6.  **Exit the program**: Ensure your program continues to provide an option for the user to exit the program.

The starting code snippet will remain mostly the same as the previous one. However, when implementing `manageDinosaurs()`, `manageEmployees()`, and other similar functions, you'll need to handle different types of dinosaurs and employees:

```java
public void handleMenuChoice(int choice) {
    switch (choice) {
        case 1:
            manageDinosaurs();  // This function now needs
             to handle different types of dinosaurs
            break;
        case 2:
            manageEmployees();  // This function now needs
             to handle different types of employees
            break;
        case 3:
            // manageTickets();
            break;
        case 4:
            // checkParkStatus();
            break;
        case 5:
            // handleSpecialEvents();
            break;
        case 6:
            System.out.println("Exiting...");
            System.exit(0);
    }
}
```

The `manageDinosaurs()`, `manageEmployees()`, `manageTickets()`, `checkParkStatus()`, and `handleSpecialEvents()` methods now need to be updated to be able to handle the increased complexity.

## Summary

In this chapter, we examined one of the cornerstones of OOP, namely inheritance. Inheritance defines an "is-a" relationship between the sub- and parent classes – for example, `Fox` "is-a" `Animal`, and `Train` "is-a" `Vehicle`. Inheritance promotes code reuse as inheritable base class members are automatically available to subclasses. Class inheritance is enabled via the `extends` keyword and interface inheritance is enabled via the `implements` keyword.

Regarding methods, the subclasses are free to override (replace) the base class implementation. This is how we enable another cornerstone of OOP, namely polymorphism.

Polymorphism is a feature where the instance method from the object is only selected at runtime. Hence, other terms for polymorphism are "late binding," "runtime binding," and "dynamic binding," For polymorphism to work, the signature of the instance method in the subtype must match that of the parent method. The only caveat to that rule is covariant returns, where, in the overriding method, a subtype of the parent return type is allowed. The overriding method, when comparing it with its parent version, must not reduce the access privileges or add extra checked exceptions.

Method overloading, on the other hand, is where the method signatures must be different (apart from the matching method name). Thus, the number of parameters, their types and/or their order, must be different. The return type and parameter names do not matter (as they are not part of the method signature). Method overloading can occur at any level in the hierarchy.

With inheritance, the reference type and object types are often different. As assignment works right to left, when we discuss upcasting and downcasting, we refer to going "up" or "down" the inheritance tree. Upcasting is always safe as the subtype will always have the methods accessible via the supertype reference. Downcasting, however, is not safe and requires a cast for the compiler to be happy. Even at that, if you end up creating a reference that is pointing up the hierarchy tree, you will get a `ClassCastException` error at runtime. Pointing up the hierarchy is not allowed because the subclass reference type could have methods that the parent type object has no code for.

The `super` keyword is used in two situations. The first is to access the parent constructor using `super()`. This call is only allowed as the very first line in any constructor. If not coded explicitly, `super()` will be inserted by the compiler to ensure that the parent constructor executes before the subtype constructor. Construction occurs from the base down because a subtype may rely on parent members and thus, the parent must have a chance to initialize them first. The second scenario is accessing a parent member from subtype code, using `super.parentMember`.

We already know from *Chapter 8*, that the `protected` access modifier ensures members are available within the package and also to any subclasses, regardless of the package. We revisited this and demonstrated that, when accessing a `protected` member from a subclass in a different package, you have to do so, via inheritance, in a very specific way.

An `abstract` method is a method with no code (implementation). Even though a class does not need to have any `abstract` methods to be `abstract` itself; once the class has even one `abstract` method, the class must be `abstract`. Any subclass of an `abstract` class must provide the implementation code for the `abstract` method(s) inherited, or the subclass must also be `abstract`.

Concerning inheritance, a `final` class cannot be inherited from. A `final` method cannot be overridden. Other uses for `final` are for defining constants and ensuring that (the values of) method parameters are constant.

The use of sealed classes enables us to restrict parts of a hierarchy to certain types. Rather than the general `extends`, which allows a class to subclass any base class it wants; and without turning off inheritance altogether using `final`; sealed classes achieve a custom restriction using the `sealed`, `non-sealed`, and `permits` keywords.

Instance and `static` initialization blocks are coded outside the methods but inside the class. The `static` block precedes the block with the `static` keyword. The instance uses no keyword (instance semantics are implied). Both enable initialization at various points. Static initialization occurs just once – the first time a class is loaded. Instance initialization occurs every time a constructor is called. Consequently, instance blocks are perfect locations for inserting code that is common across all constructors.

Lastly, we took a deeper dive into upcasting and downcasting. This helped deepen our understanding as to why upcasting is not an issue, why downcasting needs a cast, and why we get `ClassCastException` errors. In addition, using the `instanceof` operator ensures that we prevent `ClassCastException` errors from occurring.

That completes our discussion on inheritance – this was a big chapter! We will now move on to interfaces and `abstract` classes.

# 10

# Interfaces and Abstract Classes

In *Chapter 9*, we learned about another core pillar of OOP, namely inheritance. We saw that Java uses the extends keyword to define an "is-a" inheritance relationship between the child and the parent class. The subclass inherits functionality from its parent that enables code reuse, a core benefit of inheritance. Java prevents multiple class inheritance by ensuring you can only extend from one class at a time.

We also took a deep dive into the other remaining pillar of OOP, polymorphism. Polymorphism is enabled by subclasses overriding the parent class instance methods. We saw that, regarding the hierarchy, references can point (across) to objects of their own type and (down) to subclass objects. An exception occurs if a reference attempts to point (up) to parent objects in the hierarchy.

Next, we compared and contrasted method overloading and method overriding. In method overriding, the method signatures must match (except for covariant returns). In method overloading, while the method names are the same, the method signatures must be different.

We also discovered that the order of constructor calls is from the top (base class) down. This is facilitated by the super() keyword. To access a parent (non-constructor) member, we can use the super. syntax.

We then revisited the protected access modifier and demonstrated that, for subclasses outside the package to access the protected member, they must do so via inheritance in a very specific manner. In effect, once outside the package, the protected member becomes private to subclasses (of the class containing the protected member).

We then covered two keywords that have an impact on inheritance: abstract and final. As an abstract method has no implementation code, it is intended to be overridden. The first non-abstract (concrete) subclass must provide implementation code for any inherited abstract methods. The final keyword can be applied in several scenarios. Concerning inheritance, a final method cannot be overridden and a final class cannot be subclassed.

Next, we discussed `sealed` classes, which enable us to scope parts of the inheritance tree. Using the `sealed` and `permits` keywords, we can state that a class can only be subclassed by certain other named classes. The `non-sealed` keyword ends the scoping task and thus enables us to subclass as normal.

We examined both `instance` and `static` blocks in an inheritance hierarchy. A `static` block is only executed once when a class is first loaded. An `instance` block, on the other hand, is executed every time an object instance is created, making it an ideal place to insert code common to all constructors.

Lastly, we examined upcasting and downcasting. Whereas upcasting is never an issue, downcasting can lead to an exception. Use of the `instanceof` keyword helps prevent this exception.

In this chapter, we will cover `abstract` classes and interfaces. We will compare and contrast them. Interfaces have had several changes over the years. With the aid of examples, we will examine these changes. Java 8 introduced both `static` and `default` methods for interfaces, thereby enabling code to be present in an interface for the first time. In Java 9, to reduce code duplication and improve encapsulation, `private` methods were introduced to interfaces. Finally, Java 17 introduced `sealed` interfaces, which enable us to customize what classes can implement our interface.

This chapter covers the following main topics:

- Understanding `abstract` classes
- Mastering interfaces
- Examining `default` and `static` interface methods
- Explaining `private` interface methods
- Exploring `sealed` interfaces

## Technical requirements

The code for this chapter can be found on GitHub at `https://github.com/PacktPublishing/Learn-Java-with-Projects/tree/main/ch10`.

## Understanding abstract classes

In *Chapter 9*, we covered the `abstract` keyword. Let's review some key points that we discussed. An `abstract` method is exactly that – it is abstract. It has no code. It doesn't even have curly braces – { }. This is typically a design decision. The class containing the `abstract` method wants subclasses to provide the code. This means that the class itself is "incomplete" and therefore any class defining an `abstract` method must itself be `abstract`. Any subclass of the `abstract` class must either override the `abstract` method or declare that it too is `abstract`. The compiler will complain otherwise.

However, the inverse is not the case – an `abstract` class need not have any `abstract` methods at all. Again, this is a design decision. Since the class is marked as `abstract`, it is considered "incomplete" (even though it may contain code for all the methods). This prevents objects based on `abstract` classes from being instantiated. In other words, you cannot `new` an object based on an `abstract` class. You can, however, have a reference based on an `abstract` type.

Please refer to *Figure 9.14* for a code example of `abstract` methods and classes.

## Mastering interfaces

By default, an interface is an `abstract` construct. Before Java 8, all the methods in an interface were `abstract`. In general, when you create an interface, you are defining a contract for *what* a class can do without saying anything about *how* the class will do it. A class signs the contract when it implements an interface. A class implementing an interface is agreeing to "obey" the contract defined in the interface. "Obeying" here means that, if a concrete (non-abstract) class is implementing an interface, the compiler will ensure that the class has implementation code for each `abstract` method in the interface. As the Oracle tutorials state, "*Implementing an interface allows a class to become more formal about the behavior it promises to provide.*"

In contrast to classes, where you can (directly) inherit from only one other class, a class can implement many interfaces. Thus, interfaces enable multiple inheritance. Let's look at an example:

```
class Dog extends Animal implements Moveable, Loveable {}
```

This line of code states that `Dog` "is-a" `Animal`, `Moveable`, and `Loveable`. Interface names are often adjectives as they often describe a quality of a noun. Thus, interface names often end in "able." For example, `Iterable` and `Callable` are interface names in the Java API.

n the previous line of code, we are limited to extending from one class but we can implement as many interfaces as we like. This flexibility is very powerful as we can link into hierarchies without forcing artificial class relationships. This is one of the core reasons for interfaces – *to be able to cast to more than one base type.*

As with `abstract` classes, given that interfaces are also `abstract`, you cannot new an `interface` type. In addition, similarly to `abstract` classes, you can (and often do) have references that are interface types.

In later sections, we will discuss the `static`, `default`, and `private` methods, all of which have implementation code. Before that, we will deal with the other type of methods we can use in an interface: `abstract` methods. Additionally, we will discuss interface constants.

## Abstract methods in interfaces

Prior to Java 8, all of the methods in an interface were implicitly `public` and `abstract` by default. Back then, you could state that an interface was a "purely abstract class."

Concerning the `public` access modifier, this is still the case, even though Java 9 introduced `private` methods. This means that, you can explicitly mark a method in an interface as `public` or `private`. However, if you do *not* specify any access modifier, `public` is the default.

What about their abstract nature? Well, any method that is *not* denoted as `static`, `default`, or `private` is still `abstract` by default. *Figure 10.1* encapsulates this:

```
3    interface I1{
4        public abstract void m1();
5        void m2();    // public abstract by default
6        private void m3(){};
7    //   protected void m4(); // compiler error
8    }
```

Figure 10.1 – Abstract methods in an interface

In this figure, we can see that the m2 () method is `public` and `abstract`, even though none of those keywords are explicitly coded. The only other valid access modifier is `private`, as shown when declaring m3 () on line 6. The fact that m4 () does not compile (line 7) demonstrates that `protected` is not a valid access modifier on interface methods.

Can we declare variables in an interface? Yes, we can. Let's discuss them now.

## Interface constants

Any variables specified in an interface are `public`, `static`, and `final` by default. In effect, they are constants, and thus, their initial values cannot be changed. By placing these constants in the interface, any class implementing the interface has access to them (via inheritance), but they are read-only. *Figure 10.2* shows some interface constants:

```
9    interface I2{
10       public static final int VALUE1=1;
11       int VALUE2=2; // public static final as well
12   }
```

Figure 10.2 – Interface constants

In the preceding figure, we have two variables, namely VALUE1 and VALUE2. Both are constants. VALUE1 states explicitly that it is public, static, and final, whereas VALUE2 does the same implicitly (no keywords are used).

Now, let's look at an example where a class implements an interface.

*Figure 10.3* represents a class implementing an interface:

```
3    interface Moveable{
4        String HOW="walk";// constant - public static final
5        void move();      // public abstract by default
6    }
7    public class Dog implements Moveable{
8        // MUST be public - cannot assign weaker privileges
9    //   void move(){}
10       @Override
11       public void move(){// MUST be public
12           System.out.println("Dog::move()");
13       }
14       public static void main(String[] args) {
15    //     HOW = "walk"; // cannot change a final variable
16           System.out.println(Moveable.HOW);// walk
17           System.out.println(HOW);          // walk
18           // cannot refer to an instance member from a static context
19    //     move();
20           new Dog().move();                 // Dog::move()
21       }
22    }
```

Figure 10.3 – A class implementing an interface

In this figure, lines 3-6 represent an interface called Moveable that declares a constant, HOW, and a method, move(). The Dog class on line 7 declares that it implements Moveable. Therefore, since Dog is a concrete, non-abstract class, it must provide an implementation for move().

As we know, interface methods are `public` by default. However, this is not the case for classes. In classes, methods are package-private by default; which means, if you do not provide an access modifier on a method in a class, the method is package-private. Therefore, when overriding an interface method in a class, ensure that the method is `public`. As `package-private` (line 9) is weaker than `public` (line 5), we get a compiler error – hence this line is commented out. Line 11 shows that `move()` must be explicitly declared `public` in `Dog`.

Line 15 shows that `HOW`, declared on line 4, is a constant. If uncommented, line 15 gives a compiler error as constants, once assigned a value, cannot change.

Lines 16 and 17 demonstrate both ways we can access the `HOW` constant – either by prepending it with the interface name (line 16) or directly (line 17).

Line 19 shows that once inside a `static` method, which `main()` is, you cannot directly access an instance method, which `move()` is. This is because instance methods are secretly passed a reference to the (object) instance responsible for calling it, namely the `this` reference. Since `static` methods relate to the class and not a specific instance of the class, there is no `this` reference available in `static` methods. Thus, as per line 20, we need to create an instance and then use that instance to invoke `move()`.

When we run this program, lines 16 and 17 both output the value of the `walk` constant. Line 20 outputs `Dog::move()`, the output from the `Dog` implementation of `move()` (line 12).

> **Note**
>
> Since Java 8, code is allowed in `default` methods. As `default` methods are inheritable, the compiler must step in to prevent multiple inheritance in interfaces from causing an issue. We will return to this when we discuss `default` methods in interfaces.

Now, let's look at multiple interface inheritance.

## Multiple interface inheritance

Unlike classes, where multiple inheritance is prohibited in Java, multiple inheritance is allowed in interfaces. Note that the issue with multiple class inheritance is that *if* multiple *class* inheritance was allowed, you could potentially inherit two distinct implementations for the same method.

*Figure 10.4* shows an example of multiple interface inheritance:

```
2      interface MoveableObject{} // tagging interface
3      interface Spherical{
4          void doSphericalThings();
5      }
6      interface Bounceable extends MoveableObject, Spherical{
7          void bounce();
8      }
9      // Concrete class Volleyball must implement all abstract
10     // methods in Bounceable
11     class Volleyball implements Bounceable{
12         @Override public void doSphericalThings(){}
13         @Override public void bounce(){}
14     }
15     // Abstract class Beachball is ok - can implement
16     // some, all or none of the abstract methods in Bounceable
17     abstract class Beachball implements Bounceable{}
18
19     public class InterfaceInheritance {
20     }
```

Figure 10.4 – Multiple interface inheritance

In this figure, the MoveableObject interface on line 2 is an interface with no methods at all. This is known as a tagging interface. A tagging interface is used for type information using instanceof. For example, if you wanted to know if an object is an instance of a class that implements MoveableObject, you would code the following:

```
if (objectRef instanceof MoveableObject) {}
```

Lines 3-5 define an interface called `Spherical`. At this point we could simply define a class that directly implements both of these interfaces as follows:

```
class BallGame implements MoveableObject, Spherical{
    @Override doSphericalThings(){}
}
```

Line 6 is interesting – we can define an interface (`Bounceable` in this instance) that `extends` (inherits) from *both* of the other interfaces, namely `MoveableObject` and `Spherical`. Therefore, `Bounceable` has two `abstract` methods: one it defined itself, called `bounce()`, and one it inherited from `Spherical`, called `doSphericalThings()`.

Since the `Volleyball` class implements `Bounceable` (line 11), it must override both `bounce()` and `doSphericalThings()`. As `Volleyball` does this, it compiles.

Note that on line 17, the `abstract` class, `Beachball`, states that it implements `Bounceable` also. However, as `Beachball` is `abstract`, the "contract" does not have to be obeyed; meaning, `Beachball` is free to implement all, some, or none of the `abstract` methods in `Bounceable`. In this example, none of the `abstract` methods required by `Bounceable` were implemented by `Beachball`.

Now that we understand the implication of `abstract` methods in interfaces for implementing classes, let's examine two of the non-abstract methods in interfaces – the `default` and `static` methods.

## Examining default and static interface methods

Before Java 8, only `abstract` methods were allowed in interfaces. This meant that if you introduced a new `abstract` method to an existing interface, the classes that had already implemented that interface would break. This was inconvenient for not only Java developers but also the designers of Java.

This all changed in Java 8, with the introduction of both `default` and `static` methods. One of the primary drivers for introducing `default` methods was to be able to introduce code into the interface and not break the existing client base. This maintained backward compatibility. In addition, this new code is automatically available to clients implementing that interface.

A primary driver for the introduction of `static` methods was to keep utility code local to the interface rather than having it in a separate class, which was the case before their introduction.

Let's discuss them in turn, starting with `default` methods.

# 'default' interface methods

An interface uses the `default` keyword to mark a method as inheritable by implementing classes. As already stated, if you do not specify an access modifier, they are `public` by default (pardon the pun!). Default methods must have an implementation - a set of curly braces must be present (even if they are empty braces). Classes that implement interfaces inherit any `default` methods. These classes may override the inherited version but this is not necessary.

Let's look at some example code:

```
1     package ch10.defaultMethods;
2
3     interface Moveable{
4     //    default void m(); // missing implementation body
5         default void move () { System.out.println("Moving"); }
8     }
9     class Cheetah implements Moveable{
10        @Override
11        public void move () { System.out.println("Moving very fast!"); }
14    }
15    class Elephant implements Moveable{}
16
17    public class TestAnimal {
18        public static void main(String[] args) {
19            // cannot new an interface type
20            //Moveable m1 = new Moveable();
21            Moveable cheetah = new Cheetah();
22            cheetah.move();// Moving very fast!
23            Moveable elephant = new Elephant();
24            elephant.move();// Moving
25        }
26    }
```

Figure 10.5 – Interface default methods

In this figure, we have an `interface` called `Moveable` (lines 3-8). If line 4 was uncommented, it would not compile since `default` (or `static`) interface methods must have code bodies. Line 5 defines a `default` method called `move()`. As there are no `abstract` methods in `Moveable`, classes implementing `Moveable` are not required to provide any particular methods.

The `Cheetah` class (lines 9-14) implements `Moveable` and overrides `move()`. The `Elephant` class (line 15) implements `Moveable` also but does not override `move()`.

Thus, `Cheetah` objects will have a custom `move()` implementation, whereas `Elephant` objects will use the version inherited from `Moveable`.

Line 20 shows that, as with `abstract` classes, you cannot new an interface type.

Line 21 creates a `Cheetah` object referenced by a `Moveable` reference, namely `cheetah`. This is perfectly okay for two reasons. Firstly, references can be of the `interface` type and in many cases are. Secondly, this will compile so long as the object type implements the interface type, either directly (as is the case here) or indirectly (by inheriting from a class that implements the interface for you). Since the `Cheetah` class implements `Moveable`, all is well.

Line 22 executes the `move()` method from `Cheetah` polymorphically, resulting in `Moving very fast!` being output to the screen.

Line 23 creates an `Elephant` object referenced by a `Moveable` reference, namely `elephant`. Since `Elephant` implements `Moveable`, this is ok.

Line 24 is interesting. Since `Elephant` does not provide a custom version of `move()`, the `default` one from `Moveable` (which `Elephant` implements) is used. Thus, `Moving` is output to the screen.

Now, let's discuss `static` interface methods.

## 'static' interface methods

An interface uses the `static` keyword to mark a method as a utility method. As with `default` methods, `static` methods are `public` by default. Similarly, as with `default` methods, `static` methods must have an implementation. However, classes that implement interfaces do not inherit `static` methods. To access a `static` method, you must use the `InterfaceName.staticMethodName()` syntax.

Let's look at an example in terms of code:

```
1     package ch10.staticMethods;
2
3 ⬇ interface I{
4     //    static void m0(); // missing {}
5         static int m1(){return 3;}
6     }
7 ▶ public class TestStaticMethods implements I{
8 ▶     public static void main(String[] args) {
9     //        System.out.println(m1());    // fails to compile
10            System.out.println(I.m1()); // 3
11        }
12    }
```

Figure 10.6 – Interface static methods

In the preceding figure, we have an interface, I, that has a static method called m1 () on line 5. Note that line 4 is commented out because, as with default methods, the code body must be present for static methods also.

The TestStaticMethods class implements the I interface. As there are no abstract methods in the interface, no particular methods are implemented. Line 9 shows the incorrect syntax to use and thus generates a compiler error. Line 10 shows the correct syntax to use and outputs 3 when run.

Earlier, we referred to multiple interface inheritance having a potential issue regarding default methods. Let's explore that now.

# Multiple interface inheritance

The Diamond of Death (https://en.wikipedia.org/wiki/Multiple_
inheritance#:~:text=The%20"diamond%20problem"%20(sometimes,from%20
both%20B%20and%20C) arises when a class finds that it has inherited two methods of the same name; which one should it work with? This was a concern in C++, where multiple-class inheritance is allowed and was an influencing factor in prohibiting multiple-class inheritance in Java.

However, Java has always allowed a class to implement multiple interfaces. However, now that Java 8 allows `default` methods, which have code bodies that are inheritable, is it not possible for Java 8 to encounter a "Diamond of Death" scenario? Couldn't a class implement two (or more) interfaces that have the same `default` methods? What happens then? The good news is that the compiler steps in and forces your class to override the "offending" `default` method.

So, that just leaves the question, what if we wanted to access each of the `default` methods? For example, let's assume we have a `default` method called `foo()` in interface A and a `default` method called `foo()` in interface B. What if, in our class, we wanted to execute the three different versions of `foo()` – the one from A, the one from B, and the one from our class that the compiler forced us to create?

*Figure 10.7* shows how to do this in code:

```
3    interface A{
4        default void foo(){System.out.println("A::foo");}
5    }
6    interface B{
7        default void foo(){System.out.println("B::foo\n");}
8    }
9    public class TestMultipleInheritance implements A, B{
10       @Override
11       public void foo(){
12           System.out.println("TestMultipleInheritance::foo");
13           A.super.foo(); // A::foo
14 //          A.foo();      // does not compile (foo() assumed 'static')
15           B.super.foo(); // B::foo
16       }
17       public static void main(String[] args) {
18 //          A.super.foo();      // fails to compile
19           new TestMultipleInheritance().foo();
20       }
21    }
```

Figure 10.7 – Accessing multiple default code implementations

In this figure, interface A defines its `foo()` method on line 4, whereas interface B defines its `foo()` method on line 7. The `TestMultipleInheritance` class implements both A and B. As there is `foo()` code coming from both A and B, the compiler has to step in to prevent the "Diamond of Death." Thus, the `foo()` method in `TestMultipleInheritance` (lines 11-16) is mandatory; otherwise, the code will not compile. As `default` methods are instance methods, when we override the interface version of `foo()`, we must ensure it is non-static.

Line 13 shows the syntax to use to invoke `foo()` from A. This syntax is `InterfaceName.super.methodName()`. So in this example, it is `A.super.foo()`. Since `super` is used, the methods must be instance methods. This is because only instance methods have access to (the parent instance using) the `super` reference (and to the current instance using the `this` reference).

Similarly, line 15 invokes `foo()` from B using `B.super.foo()`.

Note that line 14 does not compile and is commented out as a result. This is because, with the `A.foo()` syntax, the compiler is looking for a `static` method named `foo()` in interface A. However, the `foo()` method in A is non-static (line 4).

Interestingly, line 18 fails to compile. This is because, since `main()` is a `static` method (a `static` context), we cannot use `super`.

Line 19 shows how to execute the custom `foo()` method in the class itself. Recall that we need an instance when calling a non-static (instance) method from a `static` method, hence the `new TestMultipleInheritance()`.

With that, we've covered two types of non-abstract methods, namely `default` and `static` methods. There is one more: `private` interface methods.

## Explaining 'private' interface methods

Interfaces can also have `private` methods with code implementations. They were introduced to reduce code duplication and improve encapsulation. These `private` methods can be both `static` and non-static. As they are `private`, they can only be accessed from within the interface. As with classes, you cannot access a non-static method from a `static` method.

Let's have a look at an example in code. Firstly, we will examine code that has code duplication. *Figure 10.8* shows such an interface:

```
1       package ch10.privatemethods;
2
3       interface InefficientTennis{
4           // Lots of code duplication here.
5           static void forehand(){
6               System.out.println("Move into position");
7               System.out.println("Hitting a forehand");
8               System.out.println("Move back into ready position");
9           }
10          default void backhand(){
11              System.out.println("Move into position");
12              System.out.println("Hitting a backhand");
13              System.out.println("Move back into ready position");
14          }
15          default void smash(){
16              System.out.println("Move into position");
17              System.out.println("Hitting a smash");
18              System.out.println("Move back into ready position");
19          }
20      }
```

Figure 10.8 – An interface with code duplication

As this figure shows, lines 6, 11, and 16 are the same. In addition, lines 8, 13, and 18 are also the same. We will refactor this interface to address this code duplication by using private methods. *Figure 10.9* shows the code for this:

```
22      interface EfficientTennis{
23          // encapsulated within the interface
24          private static void hit(String stroke){
25              System.out.println("Move into position");
26              System.out.println("Hitting a "+stroke);
27              System.out.println("Move back into ready position");
28          }
29          default void backhand(){ hit( stroke: "backhand"); }
30          static void forehand(){
31      //          smash();// static to instance not allowed!
32              hit( stroke: "forehand");
33          }
34          private void smash(){ hit( stroke: "smash"); }
35      //    void volley(){ hit("volley"); } // abstract by default
36      }
```

Figure 10.9 – An interface with private methods

In this figure, we have a `private static` method called `hit(String)` that accepts the stroke (shot) to be played. The first thing to notice is that, as with `default` and `static` methods, a code body is expected and is present.

Line 25, which was replicated three times in *Figure 10.8*, now appears only once. The same is true for line 27. Line 26 outputs the stroke being played. Note that `hit(String)` is `static`. This enables the method to be invoked from `static` methods, such as `forehand()` (line 32).

There is a mix of `default`, `static`, and `private` methods to facilitate further discussion. Firstly, line 29 is a `default` method that invokes the `private hit(String)` method, which passes in the backhand string. Note that `default` methods cannot also be marked `private` as they have opposite semantics – `private` methods, as with classes, are not inherited, whereas `default` methods are inherited.

Secondly, the `forehand()` method (lines 30-33) represents invoking `hit(String)` from a `static` context (line 32), passing in `forehand`. Line 31 represents an attempt to call a non-static `private` method called `smash()` from a `static` method. As with classes, this is not allowed and has been commented out as a result.

Lastly, we can call `private` methods from other `private` methods (line 34).

Line 35 is a reminder that methods that are not marked `default`, `static`, or `private` are `abstract` by default, so no code is permitted.

Let's examine how to use the `EfficientTennis` interface from a class that implements it:

```
38      // No abstract methods to implement.
39    ▶ public class SportTest implements EfficientTennis{
40    ▶     public static void main(String[] args) {
41            new SportTest().backhand(); // default method
42            EfficientTennis.forehand(); // static method
43    //        new SportTest().hit("Serve");    // private method
44        }
45    }
```

Figure 10.10 – An interface with private methods

The first thing to notice is that the `SportTest` class has no methods to implement. This is because `EfficientTennis` does not declare any `abstract` methods, only `default`, `static`, and `private` ones.

Line 41 executes the `default` method called `backhand()` and line 42 executes the `static` method called `forehand()`. Note that line 43 attempts to access the `private` method called `hit(String)`. As the method is `private` to the interface, this is not allowed and, as a result, line 43 is commented out. This demonstrates that `hit(String)` is encapsulated from the outside world. In effect, `SportTest` does not know of and is therefore not dependent upon the `hit(String)` method. If `hit(String)` is changed or even deleted, provided that the `backhand()` and `forehand()` methods still work, `SportTest` will not be impacted.

Now, let's move on to our last topic: `sealed` interfaces.

## Exploring sealed interfaces

In *Chapter 9*, we learned that `sealed` classes enable us to scope our inheritance hierarchy by specifying which classes can subtype our class. We used both the `sealed` and `permits` keywords as a pair to do this. Once a class has been sealed, each subclass of that class must be `sealed`, `non-sealed`, or `final` – that is, we continue the sealed hierarchy (`sealed`), end the sealed hierarchy (`non-sealed`), or end the hierarchy altogether (`final`).

It is also possible to seal interfaces. We will use the example from *Chapter 9* with some small changes. Firstly, *Figure 10.11* shows the relevant UML diagram, which will help explain the code:

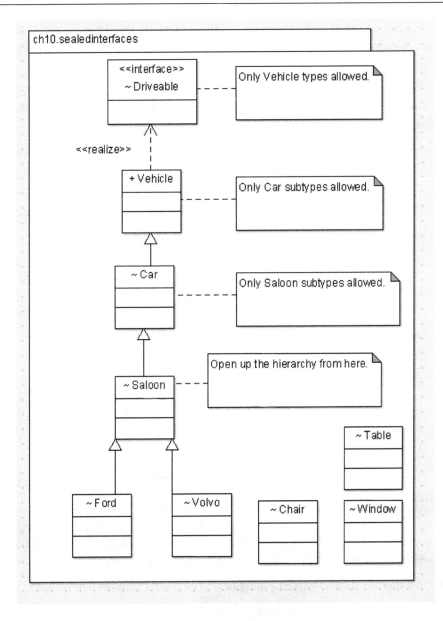

Figure 10.11 – Sealed interface UML diagram

In this figure, we have an interface, indicated by `<<interface>>`, called `Driveable`. In UML, to specify that a class implements an interface, the `<<realize>>` keyword is used (plus the dashed line with an arrow referring to the interface).

In this example, we are going to scope the hierarchy as follows: the only class allowed to implement `Driveable` is `Vehicle`, the only `Vehicle` subclass allowed is `Car`, and the only subclass of `Car` allowed is `Saloon`.

When we get to `Saloon`, we want to open up the hierarchy again – unseal it, if you like. This allows `Ford` and `Volvo` to extend from `Saloon`. Note that this is for demonstration purposes only as any class can now subclass `Saloon`.

The `Chair`, `Table`, and `Window` classes are all unrelated and not part of the sealed hierarchy.

*Figure 10.12* shows some code where a sealed interface is used:

```
1     package ch10.sealedinterfaces;
2
3     sealed interface Driveable permits Vehicle{ } // scoping interface hierarchy
4     public sealed class Vehicle implements Driveable permits Car{ }
5
6     sealed class Car extends Vehicle permits Saloon {}
7     non-sealed class Saloon extends Car{}        // opening up hierarchy again
8     class Volvo extends Saloon{}
9     class Ford extends Saloon{}
10
11    class Window extends Vehicle{}        // Vehicle permits Car only
12    class Chair extends Car{}             // Car permits Saloon only
13    class Table implements Driveable{}    // Driveable permits Vehicle only
```

Figure 10.12 – Sealed interface code

The important lines in this figure are lines 3-4. Line 3 states that the `Driveable` interface is `sealed` and that only one class is allowed to implement it, namely `Vehicle`. `Vehicle` must now implement `Driveable`; otherwise, the code will fail to compile. `Vehicle` does implement `Driveable` (line 4), so all is well. In addition, `Vehicle` is `sealed` and the only subclass permitted is `Car`.

Line 6 states that `Car` subclasses `Vehicle` and that `Saloon` is the only subtype allowed.

Line 7 states that `Saloon` is, as expected, a subclass of `Car`. The fact that `Saloon` is `non-sealed` opens up the hierarchy and enables `Volvo` (line 8) and `Ford` (line 9) to extend from `Saloon`.

Lines 11-13 all fail to compile. Line 11 reminds us that `Vehicle` permits `Car` subtypes only. Similarly, line 12 reminds us that `Car` permits `Saloon` subtypes only. Line 13 shows, as per line 3, that the only class that can implement `Driveable` is `Vehicle`.

That completes our discussion on interfaces and `abstract` classes. Now, let's apply what we have learned!

# Exercises

With interfaces and `abstract` classes, we can improve our application structure even further! Take a look at the following exercises to test your knowledge:

1. Dinosaurs, no matter the exact species, have common behaviors such as eating and moving. Define an interface that encapsulates these behaviors, come up with a logical name for it, and implement it in the `Dinosaur` class.

2. Our park uses different types of vehicles for different purposes. Design an `abstract` class called `Vehicle` and derive concrete classes such as `Jeep` and `Helicopter` from it.

3. Modify the `Vehicle` class so that it includes an `abstract` method called `travel()` that provides different implementations in its subclasses.

4. Make our `Dinosaur` class sortable by implementing the `Comparable` interface to compare dinosaurs based on their age.

5. Similarly, our employees also have common behaviors. Define a `Worker` interface with methods that represent these behaviors and implement it in the `Employee` class.

6. Our dinosaurs are housed in different enclosures. Implement the `List` interface using `ArrayList` to manage dinosaurs for an enclosure.

7. Dinosaurs have different feeding behaviors based on their diet. Create `Carnivore` and `Herbivore` interfaces and implement them in the appropriate dinosaur subclasses.

# Project – unified park management system

In this rather advanced project, you will elevate the Mesozoic Eden Park Manager application to the next level. You'll do so by utilizing the classes you created earlier. You can continue to work on the previous project or start from scratch.

The enhanced system will implement polymorphism so that different types of dinosaurs and employees can be managed. This will increase the versatility and functionality of your park management, allowing for diverse dinosaur species and employee roles. The enhanced system should include the following:

- The capability to manage various dinosaur species profiles, broadening the diversity of your park

- The capacity to manage different types of employee profiles, such as veterinarians, guides, maintenance workers, and security personnel

- All other features should also accommodate these new changes, including editing and removing profiles, tracking dinosaurs, managing employee schedules, managing guest admissions, and handling special events

Here's a step-by-step plan to achieve this:

1.  **Expand data structures**: Extend your `Dinosaur` and `Employee` classes into various subclasses to represent different types of dinosaurs and employees. Make sure you use the principle of polymorphism.

2.  **Enhance initialization**: Upgrade your data initialization so that it supports multiple types of dinosaurs and employees. This might involve creating arrays or lists of `Dinosaur` and `Employee` objects, each of which could be an instance of any subclass.

3.  **Update interaction**: Adapt your interactive console-based interface so that it can handle the new types of dinosaurs and employees. You might need to add new options or submenus.

4.  **Update menu creation**: Your menu should now provide options for managing various types of dinosaurs and employees. Ensure each option corresponds to a particular function in the program.

5.  **Handle actions**: Each menu item should trigger a function that can now handle different types of dinosaurs and employees. For example, selecting the `Manage Dinosaurs` option could now trigger a function to add, remove, or edit profiles for any dinosaur species.

6.  **Exit program**: Provide an option for the user to exit the program.

Your starting code will be very similar to the code shown in the last two chapters. Some methods, such as `manageDinosaurs()` and `manageEmployees()`, will need to be updated and become a bit more complex:

```
public void handleMenuChoice(int choice) {
    switch (choice) {
        case 1:
            manageDinosaurs();   // This method now needs
                to handle different types of dinosaurs
            break;
        case 2:
            manageEmployees();   // This method now needs
                to handle different types of employees
            break;
        case 3:
            // manageTickets();
            break;
        case 4:
            // checkParkStatus();
            break;
        case 5:
            // handleSpecialEvents();
            break;
        case 6:
            System.out.println("Exiting...");
```

```
        System.exit(0);
    }
}
```

The `manageDinosaurs()`, `manageEmployees()`, `manageTickets()`, `checkParkStatus()`, and `handleSpecialEvents()` methods need to handle the added complexity.

## Summary

We started this chapter by examining `abstract` classes. An `abstract` class has zero or more `abstract` methods. However, if any method is `abstract`, then the class must be `abstract`. While an `abstract` class cannot be instantiated, a reference can be of an `abstract` type.

Before Java 8, interfaces consisted of only `abstract` methods (and constants). We started our discussion on interfaces at this point, where all the methods were `abstract`. While a class can only extend from one class, a class can implement many interfaces. This is one of the main reasons why interfaces were introduced – to be able to cast to more than one base type.

A class that implements an interface signs a "contract" to provide code for each of the `abstract` methods (if any) in the interface. If there is an `abstract` method in the interface and the concrete, non-abstract class does not provide code implementation for it, the compiler complains. Therefore, interfaces are a great way of guaranteeing that certain methods will be present in a class. Variables in an interface are constants by default. These constants are available to implementing classes, but are read-only. We noted that multiple interface inheritance, where an interface can inherit from several other interfaces, is allowed. This contrasts with classes, be they `abstract` or concrete, where multiple inheritance is prohibited.

In Java 8, `default` and `static` methods, both with code bodies, were introduced to interfaces. This was the first time code was allowed in interfaces. Regarding inheritance, `default` methods are inherited by implementing classes, whereas `static` methods are not. Thus, accessing both requires different syntaxes. As `default` methods are inherited, they can be overridden by implementing classes. Both types of methods, as with `abstract` methods, are `public` by default.

Next, we saw how the compiler prevents us from experiencing the "Diamond of Death." This issue could arise when two interfaces have the same `default` method name. A class that implements these two interfaces is forced to provide a custom implementation to avoid ambiguity. This led nicely to the syntax (using `super`), which enables us the `default` methods in both interfaces and the custom (non-default) version in the class.

Java 9 introduced `private` interface methods, which also have code bodies. They were introduced to reduce code duplication and improve encapsulation. We detailed an example where we refactored code by introducing `private` interface methods.

We concluded this chapter by discussing `sealed` interfaces, which were introduced in Java 17. Much like `sealed` classes (*Chapter 9*), `sealed` interfaces enable us to scope the hierarchy – that is, when declaring a `sealed` interface, we specify the classes that are permitted to implement it. We presented a UML diagram and some code to explain this in more detail.

That completes our discussion on interfaces and `abstract` classes. In the next chapter, we will cover exceptions.

# 11
# Dealing with Exceptions

Error handling is another fundamental concept of software development. An error happens when the program can't or doesn't know how to react to a certain situation. Error handling allows you to respond to unexpected events in your program gracefully. Without error handling, the application would crash and stop running when the error occurred.

In Java, we have different types of errors. The type of error that we deal with most is called an **exception**. In Java terms that we'll learn later, an Exception is not an Error. This is related to the class hierarchy. However, sticking to daily linguistics it is not weird to think of an exception as some sort of error.

But, instead of talking about errors, we usually talk about exceptions. Errors occur as well, but errors are typically situations your application will not recover from. Your application should be capable of recovering from an exception.

Exception handling in Java allows you to manage problems and unexpected events in your programs. Mastering exception handling will not only improve the robustness of your code but also help you maintain and debug your applications more effectively. By understanding how exceptions work, you can write code that deals with unexpected situations without crashing or producing incorrect results.

Making sure that you have the necessary skills to manage exceptions in your applications is exactly what we're going to learn in this chapter. Here's an overview of what we'll cover:

- Understanding exceptions and their purpose
- Types of exceptions – checked and unchecked
- Basic I/O operations
- Throwing exceptions
- Creating custom exceptions
- The catch or declare principle

- Using try-catch blocks, try-catch-finally, and try-with-resources
- Working with inheritance and exception handling in method signatures

So, let's dive in and explore the world of exceptions!

# Technical requirements

The code for this chapter can be found on GitHub at `https://github.com/PacktPublishing/Learn-Java-with-Projects/tree/main/ch11`.

# Understanding exceptions

In everyday life, we have to execute a lot of processes. And all the time, we have little hiccups that happen, and these should not ruin our day. These hiccups are not considered the happy path of events, but they happen often, and we recover from them and continue business as usual.

There are also more serious problems that can occur, for which we need to have a formal backup plan, such as evacuating a building in case of a fire.

Exceptions in Java are like this. These are things that should not happen; sometimes, we are in control of them happening and sometimes, we are not. In some cases, we are obligated to specify a backup plan, and in other cases, we are not. First, let's talk a bit more about what exceptions are.

## What are exceptions?

Exceptions are events that disrupt the normal flow of the program. They typically arise from errors or unexpected conditions that the program encounters while running. Exceptions in Java are objects. These exceptions are represented by instances of the `Exception` class or its subclasses. The `Exception` class is a subclass of the `Throwable` class.

When an exception occurs, the Java runtime system creates an exception object containing information about the error, such as its type and the state of the program when the error occurred. This process is known as *throwing an exception*. Dealing with an exception is called *catching an exception*.

If the exception is not caught and handled by the program, the Java runtime system will terminate the program, usually displaying an error message and the stack trace. So, let's talk about the need for exception handling.

> **Stack trace**
>
> You might not know this term just yet, but you're likely to have encountered one already. A stack trace shows up when an exception happens. It shows the "path" the code took to get to your error. Here's an example:
>
> ```
> Exception in thread "main" java.lang.ArrayIndexOutOfBoundsException:
> Index 0 out of bounds for length 0
>     at javabook.Example.printFirstValueArray(Example.java:21)
>     at javabook.Example.main(Example.java:8)
> ```
>
> As you can see in this example, the line that eventually triggered the exception is line 21 and the method name was `printFirstValueArray`. That method was called on line 8 in the `main` method.

## Need for exception handling

Since we don't want our program to stop running every time it throws an exception, exception handling is a crucial aspect of programming. We typically separate the code logic from the exception-handling logic. This helps us create an application that is maintainable and resilient. When we have proper exception handling in place, our program can recover gracefully from unexpected situations. This is much more preferred than the program crashing and stopping, or even producing incorrect results.

Since this is so common, Java provides a built-in exception handling mechanism that allows us to catch and handle exceptions. This way, we can recover from the exception and continue executing the program. This mechanism encourages (or even forces) us to think about possible exceptional conditions that the program might encounter and write code to handle these exceptions effectively. Let's talk about some situations in which we need exception handling.

## Common situations that require exception handling

There are many situations in which exceptions can occur. Some of these are within our control, but the most important ones where we absolutely must deal with the possibility of an exception are situations where we are not fully in control. We'll address a few common situations before seeing the exception code.

## File I/O operations

A very common situation that requires exception handling is a piece of logic that deals with file I/O operations. When working with file I/O operations, exceptions can be used to handle situations where a file is not found or cannot be read or written. These are all situations that are not in the programmer's control. Permissions for the program might not be right, a file may have been removed, or a file might already be in use – many other situations out of your control can also happen.

Java has specific subclasses to deal with these types of exceptions. The main subclass to deal with I/O operations is `IOException`. It has its own subclasses, such as `FileNotFoundException`.

## Database operations

Another type of situation where we depend on an external part is all sorts of database operations. A database can be down or altered and that's out of your control as a developer. So, we need to deal with exceptions that can occur while connecting to, querying, or updating a database. For instance, `SQLException` can be thrown when there are issues with a database connection or when an invalid SQL query is executed or when a database constraint (a database specific rule) is violated. Proper exception handling allows your program to recover from these issues, such as by re-establishing the connection or rolling back a transaction.

## User input validation

When your application requires user input, exceptions can be used to handle cases where the input is invalid or does not meet the expected format. For example, `NumberFormatException` can be thrown when attempting to parse a non-numeric string as an integer. Handling this kind of exception well can help your application provide helpful feedback to users and ensure they enter valid data while keeping the core logic separated from error handling.

## Resource management

Your program depends on external resources, such as memory and system resources. These resources can also be third-party services, such as APIs. And in all these situations, exceptions can occur. We need to handle situations where these resources are unavailable or exhausted. For example, when the **Java Virtual Machine (JVM)** cannot find a memory block big enough to allocate a new object, `OutOfMemoryError` will be thrown, and `InterruptedException` can be used to handle cases where a thread is interrupted while waiting for a resource. Proper handling in these scenarios can help your application recover or gracefully degrade its functionality.

What might be striking is that we have an *error* for out-of-memory situations, but so far, we have been talking about *exceptions* instead of errors. Let's have a look at the hierarchy to understand what's going on here.

# Understanding the exception hierarchy

Java is an object-oriented language, and objects can form a hierarchy. In Java, all exceptions are subclasses of the `Throwable` class. Everything that can be thrown by the application in case of a problem is of the `Throwable` type. The `Throwable` class has two main subclasses: `Error` and `Exception`.

*Errors* represent severe issues that occur during the runtime system's operation, and they typically indicate critical problems with the JVM or the application environment. Examples include `OutOfMemoryError` and `StackOverflowError`. Errors are usually not recoverable, and it is *not* recommended to catch and handle them in your code.

On the other hand, the `Exception` class and its subclasses represent exceptional conditions that a program can handle. There are two main categories of exceptions: checked and unchecked exceptions.

## Checked exceptions

**Checked exceptions** are exceptions that can be expected to happen, such as situations where we are dealing with databases or files. When dealt with correctly, these are recoverable exceptions. They must be caught or declared in a method's signature. We are going to learn how to do this in the *catch or declare principle* section. The Java compiler requires you to handle or declare explicitly in your code. Examples include `IOException`, `FileNotFoundException`, and `SQLException`.

Checked exceptions are subclasses of the `Exception` class, excluding `RuntimeException` and its subclasses.

## Unchecked exceptions

**Unchecked exceptions** represent programming errors that do not need to be explicitly dealt with. These exceptions are typically thrown because of programming errors or situations that are not expected to occur during normal program execution.

Since unchecked exceptions usually indicate bugs in the code, the Java compiler assumes that your program should not need to catch or declare them explicitly. However, you can still choose to catch and handle unchecked exceptions. This can come in handy when you want to provide a more user-friendly error message or log the error for debugging purposes.

Examples of unchecked exceptions include `NullPointerException`, `IndexOutOfBoundsException`, and `IllegalArgumentException`. These unchecked exceptions are subclasses of `RuntimeException`. This class is a subclass of `Exception`. Unlike all the other subclasses of `Exception`, `RuntimeException` and its subclasses don't need to be handled. (You can say it's an… exception.)

In *Figure 11.1*, you can see this hierarchy in the form of a diagram:

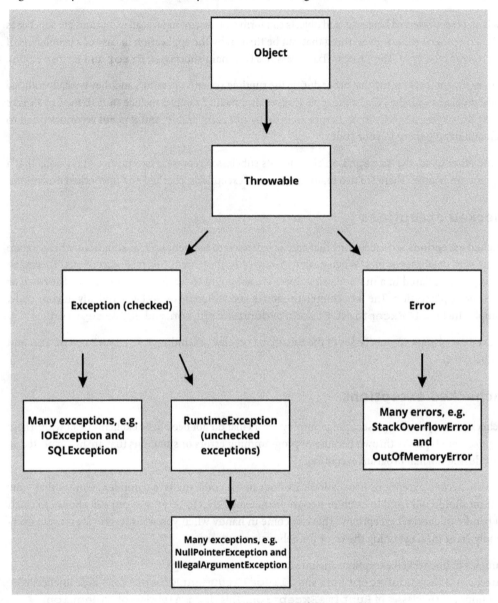

Figure 11.1 – Throwable hierarchy

Understanding the exception hierarchy is essential for effectively handling exceptions. As you can see, there are different types of exceptions. Some of them (checked exceptions) need to be handled, while others do not (unchecked exceptions).

In this chapter, we'll be using I/O operations to demonstrate exceptions. This is something that we haven't seen yet. So, let's introduce I/O operations first.

# Working with basic I/O operations

We'll use I/O operations to illustrate how exceptions work. Therefore, before diving into exception handling, we'll briefly introduce basic I/O operations. There are many ways to do this, but we'll be using `FileReader` and `FileWriter` - `FileReader` and `FileWriter` are classes in the `java.io` package that allow you to read and write characters. We have chosen these two classes because they provide a simple way to work with text files in Java and are commonly used for file I/O operations in the real world as well. First things first, let's read with `FileReader`.

> **Other classes for I/O operations**
>
> It is common to use other classes for I/O operations in common situations. For example, if you're going to read lines from files, you may want to work with `BufferedReader` instead. This is not the focus of this chapter. We just want to understand enough of I/O operations to demonstrate some real situations for exception handling.

## Reading from a file using FileReader

To read from a text file using `FileReader`, you first need to create a `FileReader` object and pass the file path as a parameter. You can then read characters from the file using the `read()` method. After using `FileReader`, you must close it to make sure you don't lock the file and don't use any unnecessary resources. Here's an example of reading a file using `FileReader`:

```java
import java.io.FileReader;
import java.io.IOException;

public class ReadFileExample {
    public static void main(String[] args) {
        try {
            FileReader reader = new
            FileReader("input.txt");
            int character;
            while ((character = reader.read()) != -1) {
                System.out.print((char) character);
            }
            reader.close();
        } catch (IOException e) {
            e.printStackTrace();
        }
}
```

```
        }
    }
```

This code snippet is reading from a file called input.txt. The *try-catch* block is something we'll see later in this chapter; it's for exception handling and you don't need to understand it just yet.

We have created a new FileReader instance and passed it the path of our input file. For the read operation to work, input.txt has been placed in the project folder. For me, it looks like the structure shown in *Figure 11.2*:

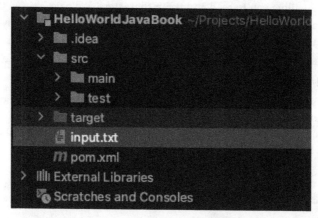

Figure 11.2 – Location of input.txt in the project

The most complicated snippet of the code that reads the file is probably the following one:

```
int character;
while ((character = reader.read()) != -1) {
    System.out.print((char) character);
}
```

FileReader is going to read the input file character by character. The read() method reads a character and moves the cursor. The cursor is the place where it starts reading next. So, we need to store the result of the reading in a variable to not lose the character. When the end of the file is reached, read() will return -1. This means we need to read until we reach -1. And that's exactly what while ((character = reader.read()) != -1) is doing.

Our input.txt file is going to be printed in the output. Of course, we can do more interesting things with the content of the file, but that's not the goal here. All we want to see is how to deal with exceptions. The code will not run when it's just like this:

```
FileReader reader = new FileReader("input.txt");
    int character;
while ((character = reader.read()) != -1) {
```

```
        System.out.print((char) character);
    }
    reader.close();
```

That's how to read a file. Next up, we'll learn how to write to a file.

## Writing to a file using FileWriter

This may sound quite predictable, but to write to a text file, we can use `FileWriter`. The steps are similar to using `FileReader`:

1.  First, you need to create a `FileWriter` object and pass the file path as a parameter.

2.  Next, you can write characters or strings to the file using the `write()` method.

3.  Finally, close `FileWriter`.

Here's an example of writing to a file using `FileWriter`:

```
import java.io.FileWriter;
import java.io.IOException;

public class WriteFileExample {
    public static void main(String[] args) {
        try {
            FileWriter writer = new
              FileWriter("output.txt");
            String content = "I can write!";
            writer.write(content);
            writer.close();
        } catch (IOException e) {
            e.printStackTrace();
        }
    }
}
```

As you can see, first, we created an instance of `FileWriter`. Next, we created a variable of the `String` type called `content`. We wrote this variable to the `output.txt` file with the `write()` method. Again, ignore the try-catch part. We'll get to that soon.

Now that we've covered basic file I/O operations, we can proceed with exceptions and exception handling. We are going to use `FileReader` and `FileWriter` as real-world examples for handling various types of exceptions.

# Throwing exceptions

When something goes wrong, the program *throws an exception*. This is because someone that created Java or the library that you are using, at some point, coded it that way. A lot of the Java library is programmed to throw exceptions, such as in the following situations:

- When you try to access a field or method on a null instance, `NullPointerException`

- When you try to divide by 0, `ArithmethicException`

- When you try to access an index in an array that is not part of the array, `ArrayIndexOutOfBoundsException`

Here's an example of the output of code that throws an exception:

```
int x = 2 / 0;
```

This is the output:

```
Exception in thread "main" java.lang.ArithmeticException: /
by zero
    at ThrowingExceptions.main(ThrowingExceptions.java:3)
```

You can see the name of the exception in the output (`java.lang.ArithmeticException`), as well as the message, stating `/ by zero`.

Underneath the exception, we can see the *stack trace*. A stack trace is the application's steps to get to the exception. The top of the stack trace shows the line that triggered the exception. This is a very tiny stack trace because it went wrong directly in the main method, so we only have one line in there.

A lot of the Java library throws exceptions when problematic situations happen. This is done with the `throw` keyword. In the next section, we're going to see how we can use this `throw` keyword to throw exceptions ourselves.

## The throw keyword

We can throw exceptions explicitly using the `throw` keyword. This is commonly used when your code detects an exceptional condition or when you want to enforce a specific constraint in your code.

Here is the syntax for throwing an exception:

```
throw new IllegalArgumentException("Age cannot be
negative.");
```

We start with the `throw` keyword; after that, there's an instance of `Throwable`. In this case, we throw a new `IllegalArgumentException` instance and specify in the message that age cannot be a negative value.

When an exception is thrown, the normal execution of the program is interrupted, and control goes to the nearest matching catch block. If none are present, the program stops and displays the exception and stack trace.

## Creating and throwing custom exceptions

Java has a lot of built-in exceptions, but in some situations, you may need to have more specific exceptions. Great news – you can also create and throw your own custom exceptions! Custom exceptions are helpful when you want to provide more specific information about the problem that occurred, or when you want to handle certain types of exceptions differently in your catch blocks.

To create a custom exception, you need to define a new class that extends the Exception class or one of its subclasses. Here's an example of a custom exception class:

```java
public class InvalidAgeException extends Exception {
    public InvalidAgeException() {
        super();
    }
    public InvalidAgeException(String message) {
        super(message);
    }

    public InvalidAgeException(Exception e) {
        super(e);
    }
}
```

We overwrite the following three constructors. This is recommended to support conventions:

- The no-args constructor
- The constructor that takes String containing a message
- The constructor that takes another exception

The InvalidAgeException custom class extends the Exception class. Therefore, InvalidAgeException is a checked exception that needs to be handled. If it extended RuntimeException or one of its subclasses, it was an unchecked exception and it didn't need to be handled. Let's talk about catching and handling exceptions.

# The catch or declare principle

The catch or declare principle states that when a method can throw a checked exception, the method must catch the exception with a try-catch statement or declare that it throws the exception in its method signature. This rule ensures that checked exceptions are properly handled or propagated up the call stack so that the calling method can handle them.

## Understanding the principle

The catch or declare principle holds for checked exceptions. If a checked exception is not declared or caught, the code won't compile. For unchecked exceptions, the catch or declare rule does not apply. They are usually caused by programming errors or unexpected situations that cannot be predicted or anticipated. Unchecked exceptions can be caught and handled, but it is not mandatory. Let's see how we can declare exceptions.

Now that we have seen how to declare exceptions, let's have a look at how to deal with exceptions with the try-catch statement.

## Declaring exceptions using throws

The throws keyword is used to declare that a method may throw a certain exception. By using the throws keyword, you can indicate that a method may throw one or more checked exceptions. The method that calls the other method that declares the exception is responsible for handling them.

Declaring an exception is not difficult. You can simply add throws to the method signature followed by the exception type. Here's an example of a piece of code using FileReader:

```
public static void read(String fileName) throws
    IOException {
    FileReader = new FileReader(fileName);
}
```

In this example, the read method declares that it may throw IOException. When another method calls this method, it is responsible for handling the exception. When you know how you want to deal with an exception, you can handle it with the try-catch statement instead of declaring it.

## Handling exceptions with try-catch

When a method declares a checked exception, the calling method is obligated to deal with it. This can be done by catching the exception or by declaring the exception in its own method signature.

Let's have a look at how to deal with exceptions using a try-catch block. Try-catch blocks come in different forms, but we'll start with the most basic.

## Basic try-catch block

A try-catch block is used to handle exceptions that might be thrown during the execution of a specific block of code. The code that might throw an exception is placed inside the `try` block, and the code to handle the exception is placed inside the corresponding `catch` block. Here's the syntax of a try-catch block:

```
try {
    //... code that might throw an exception ...
} catch(SomeException e) {
    //... code that handles the exception ...
}
```

And here's an example of a basic try-catch block that actually has some code that might throw an exception and some basic handling. We saw this when we were learning about `FileReader`:

```
import java.io.FileReader;
import java.io.IOException;

public class ReadingFile {
    public static void main(String[] args) {
        try {
            FileReader fr = new FileReader("input.txt");
            int character;
            while ((character = fr.read()) != -1) {
                System.out.print((char) character);
            }
            fr.close();
        } catch (IOException e) {
            e.printStackTrace();
        }
    }
}
```

In this code, `FileReader` can throw multiple exceptions. For example, when the file does not exist, it will throw `FileNotFoundException`. This exception is an `IOException`, which, in turn, is an `Exception`. Therefore, `FileReader` might throw a checked exception. And checked exceptions need to be handled. Therefore, we must place the code that can throw the exception(s) in the try block. We handle `Exception` in the catch block by printing the stack trace. After handling the exception, the program's execution continues normally.

We can also specify multiple catch blocks if we need to specify specific handling for different kinds of exceptions.

## Multiple catch blocks

A block of code may throw multiple types of exceptions. We can handle different exceptions using *multiple catch blocks*. It's important to have the most specific exception on top. If we were to start by catching Exception, for example, it would always go to that catch block. This is because all exceptions inherit from Exception and would be of type Exception. The catch (Exception e) would catch every possible exception, making the rest of the catch clauses unreachable. Therefore, it doesn't compile if you try to do that.

Here's an example of using multiple catch blocks:

```
public class MultipleCatchExample {
    public static void main(String[] args) {
        try {
            FileReader fr= new FileReader("input.txt");
            int character;
            while ((character = fr.read()) != -1) {
                System.out.print((char) character);
            }
            fr.close();
        } catch (FileNotFoundException e) {
            System.out.println("Not found:" +
                e.getMessage());
        } catch (IOException e) {
            System.out.println("IO error:" +
                e.getMessage());
        }
    }
}
```

In this example, we have two catch blocks – one for FileNotFoundException and one for IOException. If an exception is thrown, the appropriate catch block will be executed based on the exception type.

Sometimes, we want to clean up resources after the catch or perform other sorts of actions. We can do so with the finally block.

## Try-catch-finally

The finally block is an optional block of code that follows a try-catch block. It is executed regardless of whether an exception is thrown or not. The finally block is typically used to clean up resources. These resources could be file streams or network connections that need closing.

Here's an example of using a `finally` block:

```java
public class TryCatchFinallyExample {
    public static void main(String[] args) {
        try {
            // Code that might throw an exception
        } catch (Exception e) {
            System.out.println("Oops: " + e.getMessage());
        } finally {
            System.out.println("This code will always
                run.");
        }
    }
}
```

In this example, the `finally` block is executed after the `try-catch` block, regardless of whether an exception occurred. The only way to not execute the `finally` block is to stop the program completely before it completes the `try-catch` block.

## Use cases for the finally block

The `finally` block can be used to clean up resources. This ensures that they are properly released, even if an exception is thrown. Here's an example of using a `finally` block to close the instance of `FileReader`:

```java
import java.io.*;

public class FileResourceCleanup {
    public static void main(String[] args) {
        FileReader reader = null;
        try {
            reader = new FileReader("input.txt");
            int character;
            while ((character = reader.read()) !=-1){
                System.out.print((char) character);
            }
        } catch (IOException e) {
            System.out.println("Err: " + e.getMessage());
        } finally {
            if (reader != null){
                try {
                    reader.close();
                } catch (IOException e) {
                    System.out.println("Err closing: " +
```

```
                    e.getMessage());
            }
        }
    }
  }
}
```

This example is a little different. Let's start with the most striking difference: we close the `reader` in the finally block now. This ensures that `reader` gets closed, even if an exception occurs in the try block before it gets to that line.

For `reader` to be still in scope in the `finally` block, we have to declare it outside of the `try` block. That's why we have this line on top of the `try` block:

```
FileReader reader = null;
```

We can't initialize it outside of the `try` block because that part needs to be in the `try` block since it may throw an exception.

Here's the flow of the code when no exception occurs:

1.  `try`: Initialize `FileReader` and read the file.
2.  `finally`: Close `reader`.
3.  Continue after the `finally` block with the rest of the code.

And here's the flow of the code when an exception occurs:

1.  `try`: Initialize `FileReader` and read the file.
2.  `catch`: Handle the exception.
3.  `finally`: close the reader.
4.  Continue after the `finally` block with the rest of the code.

So, regardless of whether an exception is thrown, the `finally` block ensures `reader` is closed.

Closing `reader` might throw another exception, which is why we have another try-catch statement in the `finally` block. Arguably, this is not a very pretty syntax. A solution for many of these situations is using the **try-with-resources** statement instead.

## Handling exceptions with try-with-resources

Java 7 introduced the **try-with-resources** statement, which automatically manages resources such as file streams and network connections. This eliminates the need for the `finally` block for resource cleaning for many types of classes. The try-with-resources statement can be used without a catch or `finally` block. The normal `try` statement must have at least one of those.

## What is try-with-resources?

The try-with-resources statement takes care of resource management for you. A resource is a special Java object that opens a channel that needs to be closed in order for the resource to be marked for cleanup by Java. We have seen that the FileReader objects are examples of this.

The resources that are declared within the try-with-resources statement will be automatically closed when the `try` block completes. And of course, just like the `finally` block, it doesn't matter whether or not an exception is thrown. The resources will be closed.

Here's an example of using try-with-resources:

```java
try (FileReader fileReader = new FileReader("input.txt")) {
    int character;
    StringBuilder content = new StringBuilder();
    while ((character = fileReader.read()) != -1) {
        content.append((char) character);
    }
    System.out.println(content.toString());
} catch (IOException e) {
    System.out.println("Oops: " + e.getMessage());
}
```

The resources need to be opened between the parentheses following the `try` block. At the end of the `try` block, the resources will be closed.

You can open multiple ones separated with a semicolon, like this:

```java
try (FileReader fileReader = new FileReader("input.txt");
    BufferedReader bufferedReader = new BufferedReader
      (fileReader);
    FileWriter fileWriter = new FileWriter("output.txt");
    BufferedWriter bufferedWriter = new BufferedWriter
      (fileWriter)) {

    String line;
    while ((line = bufferedReader.readLine()) != null) {
        String uppercaseLine = line.toUpperCase();
        bufferedWriter.write(uppercaseLine);
        bufferedWriter.newLine();
    }
} catch (IOException e) {
    System.out.println("Oops: " + e.getMessage());
}
```

You don't need to understand the details of the code in this example since we did not talk about `BufferedReader` and `BufferedWriter`. These classes are utility classes that provide buffering capabilities for reading and writing text files. With buffering, we can improve the performance of I/O operations by minimizing the number of system calls.

The preceding code snippet uses `FileReader` and `BufferedReader` to read the contents of a file, while `FileWriter` and `BufferedWriter` are used to convert content (all uppercase) into `output.txt`.

The try-with-resources block ensures that all resources are automatically closed after their use. It does so in the opposite order of declaring them, so it starts by closing the last. This is important because, as you can see, we're using `fileWriter` to create `bufferedWriter`. Closing them in a different order may cause issues.

Please don't forget, not all classes can be automatically closed. For Java to be able to automatically close a class, the class needs to implement the `AutoCloseable` interface.

### Implementing the AutoCloseable interface

To be able to use a (custom) class with the try-with-resources statement, the class should implement the `AutoCloseable` interface and override the `close()` method.

We can create our own classes that can be automatically closed. Here's an example of a custom resource that implements `AutoCloseable`:

```java
public class SomeResource implements AutoCloseable {
    public void doSomething() {
        System.out.println("Doing something...");
    }

    @Override
    public void close() {
        System.out.println("Resource closed.");
    }
}
```

This resource can now be used in a try-with-resources statement:

```java
public class SomeResourceExample {
    public static void main(String[] args) {
        try (SomeResource resource = new SomeResource()) {
            resource.doSomething();
        }
    }
}
```

This code opens SomeResource in the try-with-resources statement. We then call the doSomething()
method, which prints a line to the console. At the end of the block, the resource is closed. We print
another line in the close() method that we had to implement for the AutoCloseable interface.

This is the output:

```
Doing something...
Resource closed.
```

As you can see, it prints the line from the doSomething() method. The close() method also
gets triggered. As we can see, the message that it prints in the output as well. We don't trigger the
close() method ourselves, this is done by the mechanism of the try-with-resource statement.

That's the basics of the try-with-resources statement so that you can start working with it. It's now time
for a topic that is often considered to be quite challenging: dealing with inheritance and exceptions.

# Working with inheritance and exceptions

When a class inherits from another class, it can override the methods in this other class. There are
some special rules for dealing with the declared exceptions and overriding methods. It's important
to understand this to successfully override methods that declare exceptions.

## Declaring exceptions in method signatures

When a method can throw a checked exception that isn't dealt with in that method by a try-catch, it is
declared in the method's signature. We have just learned that this is done with the throws keyword,
followed by the exception type(s).

Here's an example:

```
public void readFile(String filename) throws IOException {
    // Read file code
}
```

The readFile method's signature declares that it can throw IOException. When we extend the
class that this method is in, we can override the readFile method. There are some important rules
for how to deal with exceptions that are declared.

## Overriding methods and exception handling

Let's step away from the code for a second here and think of this a little bit more abstractly and
concretely at the same time. Let's say you and I meet up next week to discuss a software application
at your office, and I'm telling you I'll have to bring my young kids due to daycare issues. You know

that certain *exceptions* may occur: tantrums, fights between the kids, random food in your hair and on your clothes, and so on. However, you agree to meet me.

If I'm planning on also bringing my three rottweilers because my dog sitter cancels, I may want to inform you about this beforehand so you can decide whether it's still okay for me to come over with these new conditions. You have incorporated the *kids exceptions* in your decision already, but you haven't decided whether you are also okay with *dog exceptions* yet. This includes muddy paws, drool, dog hair, and potentially accidentally sharing your cookie with one of the gentle giants.

It's probably considered polite to inform you about bringing the cuddly protectors over beforehand. However, if I end up having a babysitter and I come by myself, I probably don't need to mention that in advance because it makes it more convenient. (No, I don't hate my kids.)

Alright – keep this in mind while we make the transition back to Java.

When you override a method in a subclass, the overriding method must follow certain rules regarding exceptions:

- It cannot throw checked exceptions that weren't declared in the signature of the method in the parent class. (We cannot bring the dogs without notice.)

- If the overridden method declares a checked exception, the overriding method can declare the same exceptions, a subclass of that exception, or a subset of the exceptions. (Bringing just one kid instead of two).

- Nothing can also be considered a subset. So, we can also choose not to declare any exception in the child class that overrides the method. (Not bringing the kids.)

Here's an example of an override that declares a subclass:

```
class Parent {
    public void readStuff() throws IOException {
        // Parent implementation
    }
}
class Child extends Parent {
    @Override
    public void readStuff () throws FileNotFoundException {
        // Child implementation
    }
}
```

The Child class overrides the readStuff method from the Parent class. Since the overridden method declares the IOException, the overriding method can declare the same exception or a subclass of it (for example, FileNotFoundException) or not declare any exception at all.

Unchecked exceptions can always be added. They don't have any consequences for the calling code. At the same time, declaring them, in general, doesn't make a lot of sense, since it's not obligated to deal with them.

# Exercises

Let's deal with some common unhappy path scenarios in our app. When these occur, we need our app to be able to recover from them:

1.  When reading and writing the dinosaur data, it is possible that the file cannot be opened due to different circumstances. Perhaps someone moved it, it's in use, or something else. Your task is to simulate a situation where you're trying to read from a file (that may not exist) and deal with the checked exception.

2.  While updating dinosaur data, invalid values could sometimes be provided. Write an `updateDinosaurWeight` method that takes a weight value and a `Dinosaur` object. If the weight value is less than zero, the method should throw `IllegalArgumentException`. Use a try-catch block to handle this exception. The handling can be a simple `System.out.println` for now.

3.  Even in exceptional circumstances, certain operations should always execute. For example, a daily audit of dinosaurs' health should happen, whether an exception occurs (for example due to the weight being too low) or not. Use a `finally` block in your program to demonstrate this. Code the logic so that even if there is an error in updating a dinosaur's health record, a message about the daily audit completion should still be printed.

4.  In our dinosaur park, data about dinosaurs' diets is stored in external resources . In this case, that external resource is a file. Write a program where you use a try-with-resources block to read data from this file, ensuring the file is closed properly after use, even if an error occurs during data retrieval. Here's a sample file called `DinoDiet.txt` that you can use:

    ```
    Tyrannosaurus: Carnivore
    Brachiosaurus: Herbivore
    Triceratops: Herbivore
    Velociraptor: Carnivore
    Stegosaurus: Herbivore
    Spinosaurus: Carnivore
    Ankylosaurus: Herbivore
    ```

5.  If a dinosaur's health score falls below a certain critical value, the program should throw a custom exception, named `CriticalHealthException`. Create this custom exception and use it in your program to handle this specific problematic condition.

## Project – dinosaur care system

Running a dinosaur park is filled with unexpected situations. Some are minor, such as running out of cheese-flavored potato chips. Some are major, such as an escaped T-Rex. The happiness, health, and safety of our dinosaurs and visitors are important, so our system should be able to handle exceptional situations.

Design a "dinosaur care system" for Mesozoic Eden that handles exceptional situations such as a dinosaur falling ill, enclosure breaches, and so on. Use appropriate exceptions to represent various error conditions and handle them properly.

Here are the steps to do this:

1.  Set up your project:

    I.   Create a new Java project in your IDE of choice.

    II.  Create a new package named exception.

2.  Create custom exceptions:

    I.   Create a new class called `DinosaurIllException` inside the exception package. This class should extend the `Exception` class and represent an error condition when a dinosaur falls ill.

    II.  Similarly, create `EnclosureBreachedException` for an error condition where an enclosure has been breached.

3.  Create the dinosaur care system:

    I.   Create a new class called `DinosaurCareSystem`.

    II.  Inside this class, create a method called `handleDinosaurHealth()` that throws `DinosaurIllException`. You can simulate random health conditions for the dinosaur.

    III. Similarly, create a method called `handleEnclosureSecurity()` that throws `EnclosureBreachedException`. Using this, you can simulate the random security status of dinosaur enclosures.

## Summary

We've just explored the importance of exception handling. We now know how it allows us to separate the code logic from the error handling logic. We delved into the two main types of exceptions: checked and unchecked. Checked exceptions are exceptions that require explicit handling, whereas unchecked exceptions are usually caused by programming errors and do not need to be explicitly caught or declared.

We discussed the catch or declare principle, which requires checked exceptions to be caught in a try-catch block or declared in a method's signature. The try-catch block allows us to handle exceptions by executing alternative code when an exception occurs. We also learned about using multiple catch blocks to handle different types.

Next, we saw the `finally` block, which is executed regardless of whether an exception occurs. This block is useful for cleaning up resources and ensuring certain actions are always performed. This `finally` block is less common since Java 7 and try-with-resources is used whenever possible. This simplifies resource management by automatically closing resources when the `try` block finishes executing.

Finally, we examined method exception signatures and how they relate to inheritance while focusing on the rules for checked exceptions when overriding methods.

At this point, you should have a solid understanding of Java exception handling. Now, it's time to learn a little more about the Java core API.

# 12
# Java Core API

In this chapter, we will delve more deeply into popular classes and interfaces from the Java API. We will start with the `Scanner` class, which is commonly used for scanning and parsing text from sources such as the keyboard (the user). We will then examine the very popular `String` and `StringBuilder` classes. We will discuss their differences, which will require contrasting mutable and immutable types. We will also show you how to design immutable types and look at the `List` interface and its popular implementation class, `ArrayList`. Lastly, we will examine the Date API, which was overhauled in Java 8.

For further details on the types covered in this chapter, please refer to the Java Docs API: `https://docs.oracle.com/en/java/javase/21/docs/api/index.html`.

This chapter covers the following main topics:

- Understanding the `Scanner` class
- Comparing `String` with `StringBuilder`
- Designing an immutable type
- Examining `List` and `ArrayList`
- Exploring the Date API

## Technical requirements

The code for this chapter can be found on GitHub at `https://github.com/PacktPublishing/Learn-Java-with-Projects/tree/main/ch12`.

## Understanding the Scanner class

`Scanner` (from the `java.util` package) is a text scanner that can parse primitives and strings using regular expressions. A regular expression is a pattern that enables string manipulation. As it states so eloquently in the Java API: "*A Scanner breaks its input into tokens using a delimiter pattern, which by default matches whitespace. The resulting tokens may then be converted into values of different types using the various next methods."*

These `nextXXX()` methods convert the tokens on the input stream into primitives. For example, if the user has typed in `23`, then `nextInt()` would return an `int` value of `23`; if the user typed in `45.89`, then `nextDouble()` would return a `double` value of `45.89`.

However, if the token on the input stream is not an integer and `nextInt()` is called, an `InputMismatchException` error is thrown. This could occur if the user types in `"abc"` and `nextInt()` is called. To protect against this, each of the `nextXXX()` methods has a corresponding guardian angel method, namely `hasNextXXX()`. For example, `nextInt()` has a corresponding `hasNextInt()` method, `nextDouble()` has a corresponding `hasNextDouble()` method, and so forth. The `hasNextXXX()` methods all take a sneak peek at the input stream for the next token (without consuming it) and check if that token can be successfully converted into the type in question. They return `true` or `false` accordingly. If `true` is returned, then the corresponding `nextXXX()` method can safely be used without causing an exception.

*Table 12.1* shows some of the more important `Scanner` methods. Note that we have just listed one of the `hasNextXXX()` methods, namely `hasNextDouble()`, along with its corresponding `nextXXX()` method, namely `nextDouble()`. All of the following types follow the same pattern: `boolean`, `byte`, `float`, `int`, `long`, and `short`:

| Method Name | Description |
|---|---|
| `Scanner(InputStream source)` | Creates a `Scanner` class that produces values from the specified input stream – for example, the keyboard |
| `Scanner(File source)` | Creates a `Scanner` class that produces values from the specified file |
| `Scanner(String source)` | Creates a `Scanner` class that produces values from the specified string |
| `String next()` | Returns the next token |
| `boolean hasNextDouble()` | Returns `true` if and only if the next token is a valid double value |
| `double nextDouble()` | Scans the next token as a `double` value |
| `String nextLine()` | Returns (the rest of) the line |
| `Scanner useDelimiter(String pattern)` | Sets the Scanner's delimiting pattern according to the argument passed |

Table 12.1 – Sample "Scanner" API methods

Now, let's look at some examples in code.

## Using Scanner to read from the keyboard

The standard input stream can be accessed with `System.in`. Typically, this is the keyboard. When creating our `Scanner`, we must pass the input source (`System.in`, in this case) as an argument of the `Scanner` constructor. *Figure 12.1* shows an example:

```
22        public static void usingKeyboard(){
23            Scanner sc = new Scanner(System.in);
24            System.out.print("Enter age: ");
25            if(sc.hasNextInt()){ // integer ready to be read
26                int age = sc.nextInt();
27                System.out.println(age);
28            }
29            // closes the underlying stream (System.in) which cannot be re-opened
30    //        sc.close();
31    //        Scanner sc1 = new Scanner(System.in);
32    //        System.out.print("Enter another age: ");
33    //        int age = sc1.nextInt();     // NoSuchElementException
34    //        System.out.println(age);
35        }
```

Figure 12.1 – "Scanner" taking input from the keyboard

In this figure, on line 23, we create a `Scanner` object referring to the keyboard by passing `System.in` to the `Scanner` constructor. Line 24 simply prompts the user to type in an age. Line 25 is the guardian angel method to protect against exceptions. If the next token on the input is of the `int` type, then the condition on line 25 will be `true` and we can safely execute `nextInt()` on line 26. Line 27 echoes the integer that was typed on the keyboard.

---

**Closing a Scanner resource**

Closing resources once you are finished with them is prudent as it prevents resource leaks. However, a `Scanner` object wrapped around `System.in` is a little different. In effect, if we close a `Scanner` object that was wrapped around `System.in`, we won't be able to read from standard input again.

This is what lines 30-34 in *Figure 12.1* are demonstrating. If we close the `Scanner` object (line 30), even though lines 31-34 are essentially the same as lines 23-27 (bar `hasNextInt()`), an exception is thrown on line 33. This is because we are attempting to access a closed resource.

Now, let's look at an example that will further explain tokens and delimiters:

```
14      public static void usingKeyboardExtra(){
15          Scanner sc = new Scanner(System.in);
16          System.out.print("Enter name: ");    // Type in Sean Kennedy
17          System.out.println(sc.next());       // Sean
18      }
```

Figure 12.2 – next() delimited by whitespace

In this figure, we are using next() to try and parse Sean  Kennedy from the input stream (keyboard). However, the (default) delimiter is whitespace, and thus, Sean is returned. Note that Kennedy is still there in the input stream. We could invoke next() a second time to consume the extra Kennedy token. However, there is a method that solves this issue: nextLine(). *Figure 12.3* shows nextLine() in action:

```
14      public static void usingKeyboardExtra(){
15          Scanner sc = new Scanner(System.in);
16          System.out.print("Enter name: ");
17          System.out.println(sc.nextLine()); // Sean Kennedy
18      }
```

Figure 12.3 – nextLine() delimited by the end of the line

In this figure, we are using nextLine(), which uses a different delimiter. Rather than whitespace delimiting the tokens (as with next()), the newline character delimits nextLine()). In effect, nextLine() reads a line of text, whereas next() reads words. Line 17 demonstrates this by outputting Sean  Kennedy.

Scanner can be redirected to other sources for input. One such source is a file.

## Using Scanner to read from a file

Let's examine how we can direct `Scanner` to read from a file, as opposed to the keyboard. *Figure 12.4* shows such an example:

```
30    public static void usingFile(){
31        // Relative path built from "current working directory", which is
32        // obtained from user.dir setting -> System.getProperty("user.dir")
33        // Mine was: C:\Users\skennedy\IdeaProjects\JavaFromBeginnerToProfessional
34        try (Scanner sc = new Scanner(
35                        new File( pathname: "out\\production\\" +
36                                "JavaFromBeginnerToProfessional\\ch12\\ages.txt"))) {
37            if(sc.hasNextInt()){
38                int age = sc.nextInt();
39                System.out.println(age);
40            }
41        } catch (FileNotFoundException fnfe) {
42            fnfe.printStackTrace();
43        }
44    }
```

Figure 12.4 – "Scanner" taking input from a file

In the preceding figure, the file in question (`ages.txt`) is a simple text file containing the number 12, followed by a carriage return. We pass the `File` object into the `Scanner` constructor (lines 34-36). The `String` object that's passed into the `File` constructor (lines 35-36) is a relative path. In other words, it is appended to the current working directory (as opposed to an absolute path, which contains the full path from the root). `\\` within `String` is where we are escaping the backslash (`\`). Java converts `\\` into a single backslash internally. Therefore, `"out\\production"` becomes `"out\production"`. The `hasNextInt()` and `nextInt()` methods (lines 37 and 38) work as before.

As we are using try-with-resources, we do not need to remember to explicitly close the `Scanner` or `File` resources (they are closed implicitly for us).

Another possible source for `Scanner` input is a `String` object. Let's look at that now.

## Using Scanner to read from a string

Using `String` as an input `Scanner` source is also possible. *Figure 12.5* shows such an example:

```java
13    public static void usingString(){
14        String input = "Maaike   delim vandelim Putten delim 22";
15        Scanner sc = new Scanner(input).useDelimiter( pattern: "\\s*delim\\s*");
16        System.out.println(sc.next());
17        System.out.println(sc.next());
18        System.out.println(sc.next());
19        System.out.println(sc.nextInt());
20        sc.close();
21    }
```

Figure 12.5 – "Scanner" taking input from a string

In this figure, we declare a `String` object (line 14) and pass it to the `Scanner` constructor (line 15). We then chain the `useDelimiter(String)` method onto the `Scanner` object that is returned. This method accepts `String` as an argument and represents the regular expression pattern required to parse the input. The double backslash is, as before, simply escaping the backslash. In other words, \\ becomes \.

The \s* regular expression translates into *0 or more whitespace characters*. * represents *0 or more* and \s represents *a single whitespace character*. The `delim` string is hardcoded. This means that the input tokens are delimited by 0 or more spaces, followed by the `delim` token, followed by 0 or more spaces.

When we apply this delimiter pattern to the given input string (line 14), the first token returned by `next()` is `Maaike`. This is output by line 16. As `Maaike` has now been consumed from the input stream, the `next()` method call (line 17) returns the `van` token, which is then output. Similarly, the `next()` method on line 18 returns `Putten` to be output. Lastly, line 19 uses `nextInt()` to return `22` as an `int` type, which is then output to the screen.

Now that we know how to obtain input from the user, let's cover two of the most important classes dealing with strings, namely `String` and `StringBuilder`.

# Comparing String with StringBuilder

When dealing with strings, these two classes are your go-to classes. Their primary difference is that `String` objects are immutable, whereas `StringBuilder` objects are mutable. This means that for strings, once you create a `String` object, you cannot ever change that object. Java might make it look like you changed the object but you haven't; a new object, reflecting your changes, has been created. `StringBuilder` objects, on the other hand, are mutable. This means that you are working with one object all the time. We will delve into this with an example later.

> **Why immutability?**
>
> Immutability is attractive from a security perspective as immutable objects cannot be changed. In addition, immutable objects are thread-safe in a multi-threaded environment. In multi-threaded environments, changes to (non-immutable) objects have to be synchronized one at a time so that changes do not interfere with one another Immutable objects are, by definition, protected from that. See *Chapter 17* (Concurrency) for a discussion on multi-threading.

For the moment, let's start with the `String` class.

## String class

The `String` class is in the `java.lang` package and represents a sequence of characters. As the class is in `java.lang`, it is automatically imported for you. The `String` class implements the `Comparable` interface, meaning that a natural ordering is defined when sorting strings. This ordering is alphabetic.

As stated, `String` is an immutable type. Objects of the `String` type, once created, cannot be modified. `String` is also a `final` class, which means that you cannot subclass it. This is deliberate – the Java designers expect strings to behave in a certain way. If we were allowed to subclass `String` and override its behavior, unexpected results would occur. So, making the class `final` prevents this by ensuring predictable string behavior.

All `String` literals are instances of the `String` class. `String` literals are stored in a special area of the heap called the string pool (or string constant pool). This is known as *interning* the string. If another string literal with the same character sequence is encountered, the string in the string pool is reused. This saves on memory. However, if you use the `new` keyword to create your `String` object, a new object with the character sequence is created on the heap, even if such an object is available in the string pool. In other words, the string pool is ignored if `new` is used.

Let's look at an example in code, as well as a supporting in-memory diagram.

## String example (code)

*Figure 12.6* represents the code:

```
3 ▶   public class StringTest {
4 ▶       public static void main(String[] args) {
5             String s1 = "abc";                       // string pool
6             String s2 = "abc";                       // string pool
7             System.out.println(s1 == s2);            // true
8             String s3 = new String( original: "abc"); // heap
9             System.out.println(s1 == s3);            // false
10            System.out.println(s1.equals(s2));       // true
11            System.out.println(s1.equals(s3));       // true
12            s3 = s3.intern();
13            System.out.println(s1 == s3);            // true
14        }
15    }
```

Figure 12.6 – "String" example in code

In this figure, on line 5, we use the s1 string reference to refer to the "abc" string literal. When the JVM encounters a string literal, it first checks if the same string literal exists in the string pool. If it does, it reuses the one from the pool. As line 5 is the first time "abc" is encountered, the String object with "abc" is inserted into the pool. Note that the string pool is simply a special area in the heap.

Line 6 is where the string pool object is reused. Now, we have both s1 and s2 referring to the same String object (in the pool). This is why line 7 outputs true. Recall that when the == operator is used with references, we are comparing the references. In other words, are both s1 and s2 referring to the same object in memory? Yes, they are.

Line 8 uses the new keyword to create a String object. Once new is used, regardless of the same literal "abc" being used, a completely new object is created in a separate part of the heap. As line 8 creates a new object, when we compare s1 and s3 on line 9, the result is false. This is because s1 and s3 refer to two different objects.

The String object's method, equals(), operates differently from the equivalence operator, ==. Rather than compare the references, equals() compares the contents of the objects. As line 10 returns true, it shows that the contents of the objects referred to by s1 and s2 are the same. This should not be a surprise as both s1 and s2 refer to the same object.

Line 11, however, also returns true. Even though s1 and s3 refer to different objects, this demonstrates that equals() compares the object's contents and not the references.

Line 12 is interesting. We can intern a string by using its `intern()` method. What we are saying on line 12 is "Intern in the string pool what s3 is referring to, and make the s3 reference refer to the string pool object." Line 13 returns `true`, demonstrating that both s1 and s3 now refer to the same string object. Note that line 13 is the same code as line 9, which returned `false` previously.

A diagram will certainly help here, so let's examine what is happening in memory.

### String example (diagram)

*Figure 12.7* represents the in-memory representation of the code in *Figure 12.6*:

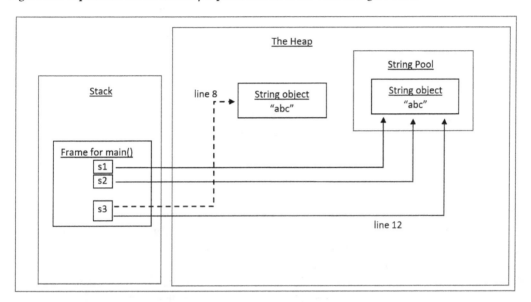

Figure 12.7 – "String" example in memory

As can be seen from the preceding figure, both s1 and s2 refer to the `"abc"` object in the string pool. The dashed line from s3 represents the object that was created by using the new keyword (line 8). Thus, we have two separate string objects: one on the heap and one in the pool (which is also part of the heap).

The solid line from s3 represents the result of the interning operation on line 12. Now, it is straightforward to see why, after line 12, that s1 == s3 returns `true`.

So, when using strings, if you are interested in comparing the contents, use the `equals()` method. Note that `equals()` is case-sensitive. There is a method, namely `equalsIgnoreCase()`, which is case insensitive.

An important property of `String` objects is the fact that they are immutable. Let's discuss that now.

## String immutability

This topic is very important if you want to create immutable types or wish to obtain Java certification. We will discuss how to create a custom immutable type later. Regarding the String class, it is the object that is immutable and not the reference. What this means is that you can change the reference to point to a different string, but you cannot change the contents of the string object itself. Also, note that all the "wrapper" types, such as Integer, Double, Float, and Character, are also immutable.

Let's look at an example in code, with an associated in-memory diagram. *Figure 12.8* represents the code:

```
17          public static void howManyObjectsString(){
18              String s = "The ";
19              s += "quick ";              // s = s + "quick "
20              System.out.println(s);      // The quick
21              s.concat( str: "brown fox");// lost!
22              System.out.println(s);      // The quick
23              s = s.concat( str: "brown fox");
24              System.out.println(s);      // The quick brown fox
25          }
```

Figure 12.8 – "String" immutability (code)

In this figure, on line 18, using the "The  " literal, we create a String object that's referred to by the s reference. As this is a literal, the object goes into the string pool. Line 19 appends "quick " to s using the += operator. As line 20 outputs "The quick ", you would be forgiven for thinking that the string object referred to by s has changed. This is not the case. As String objects are immutable, this is not allowed. What happens is that a new String object is created reflecting the requested changes. Therefore, we have three String objects on line 20: the two literals, "The " and "quick ", are in the string pool, and the newly created "The quick " object is on the heap.

Line 21 is revealing. Many of the String API methods return a String (reference). As String objects are immutable, this String reference that's returned is a reference to the newly created String object. This object is created in the background and reflects the requested changes. As we have not stored the reference on line 21, this object is lost to us and is immediately eligible for garbage collection. When we output s on line 22, you can see that it has not changed; its content is still "The quick ".

Line 23 shows what line 21 should have done. By reinitializing s, we redirect the reference to the newly created object. Consequently, when we output s on line 24, we get the full string – that is, "The quick brown fox".

A diagram representing what is happening in memory will help here. *Figure 12.9* represents the in-memory representation of the code from *Figure 12.8*:

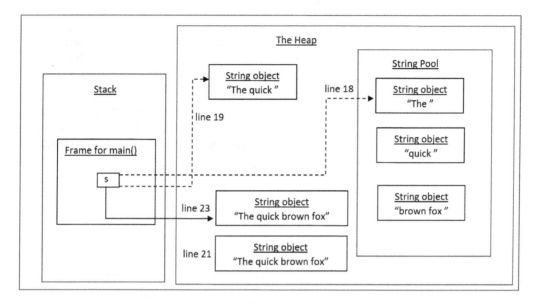

Figure 12.9 – "String" immutability (diagram)

In the preceding figure, dashed lines represent overwritten references. We have six String objects in total – three string literals in the pool and three constructed string objects using both the += operator and the concat() method.

Notice that the string object in the middle (at the bottom), has no reference pointing to it. It never had, hence there is no dashed line pointing to it. This is the object that was created by line 21 but as the reference was never assigned to a variable, it was lost.

On the other hand, line 23 did store the reference to the newly created string object. It overwrote what was in the s reference. This is why s is referring to "The quick brown fox".

When we discuss StringBuilder, we will re-write the code from *Figure 12.8*. For the moment, we will look at the more important methods in the String API. These are reflected in *Table 12.2*:

| Method Name | Description |
|---|---|
| `char charAt(int index)` | Returns the character at the specified index. Indices range from 0 (as per arrays) to `length()`-1. |
| `int compareTo(String anotherString)` | Compares two strings character by character lexicographically (dictionary order). In other words, `this.charAt(k)` - `anotherString.charAt(k)`. For example, `"ace"` comes before `"bat"`, `"and"` comes before `"at"`, and so forth. If all characters match but the two string lengths differ, then the shorter string precedes the longer string. For example, `"bat"` comes before `"battle"`. Let's take a look: <br><br> `"ace".compareTo("bat")` returns `-1`; <br><br> `"and".compareTo("at")` returns `-6`; <br><br> `"bat".compareTo("battle")` returns `-3` |
| `String concat(String str)` | Concatenates the argument string to this string. <br><br> `"abc".concat("def")` returns `"abcdef"`. |
| `boolean endsWith(String suffix)` | Does this string end with the specified suffix? As it uses `equals(Object)`, it is case-sensitive. <br><br> `"abc".endsWith("bc")` returns true. <br><br> `"abc".endsWith("BC")` returns false. |
| `int hashCode()` | Returns a hash code for this string. Hash codes are used to store/retrieve objects used in hash-based collections such as `HashMap`. |
| `int indexOf(String str)` | Returns the index of the first occurrence of the specified substring. It is case-sensitive and overloaded. <br><br> `"abcdef".indexOf("b")` returns 1. <br><br> `"abcdef".indexOf("B")` returns -1. |
| `int length()` | Returns the length of the string. |
| `String substring(int beginIndex)` | Returns the substring of this string, starting at the specified `beginIndex` and proceeding until the end of this string. Indices start at 0. <br><br> `"abcdef".substring(3)` returns `"def"`. |

| Method Name | Description |
|---|---|
| `String substring(int beginIndex, int endIndex)` | Returns the substring of this string. The substring begins at the specified `beginIndex` and extends to the character at `endIndex-1`. Indices start at 0.<br><br>Think: "Give me `endIndex-startIndex` characters, starting at `startIndex`." For example,<br><br>`"Sean Kennedy".substring(3,8)` means "Give me 5 characters, starting at index 3," which returns `"n Ken"`. |
| `String toLowerCase()`<br><br>`String toUpperCase()` | Converts the string to lowercase and uppercase, respectively. |
| `String trim()` | The `trim()` method removes whitespace from both ends of a string – for example,<br><br>`"   lots of   spaces    here      ".trim()` returns `""lots of   spaces    here""` |

Table 12.2 – Sample "String" API methods

Now, let's turn our attention to the `StringBuilder` class.

## StringBuilder class

The `StringBuilder` class is also in the `java.lang` package and represents a mutable sequence of characters. The API for `StringBuilder` is the same as for the `StringBuffer` class. Use `StringBuilder` in a single-thread environment and use `StringBuffer` in a multithreading environment. `StringBuilder` also implements the `Comparable` interface where the natural ordering defined for sorting is also alphabetic.

`StringBuilder` is a mutable type. `StringBuilder` is also a `final` class, which means that you cannot subclass it. Again, this is deliberate as the Java designers wanted to ensure predictable behavior from `StringBuilder` objects.

As promised earlier, we will refactor *Figure 12.8* to use `StringBuilder` instead of `String`. In addition, we will diagram the differences in memory.

## StringBuilder example (code)

*Figure 12.10* represents the code:

```
48    public static void howManyObjectsSB(){
49        StringBuilder sb = new StringBuilder("The ");
50        sb.append("quick ");
51        System.out.println(sb);    // The quick
52        sb.append("brown fox");
53        System.out.println(sb);   // The quick brown fox
54    }
```

Figure 12.10 – "StringBuilder" example in code

In this figure, line 49 creates a new `StringBuilder` object and initializes it to `"The "`. Line 50 uses the `append()` method to append `"quick "` to the object referenced by sb. As `StringBuilder` objects are mutable, we can ignore the reference returned (as we have that reference in sb already). Line 51 outputs `"The quick "`, thereby demonstrating that the (one) `StringBuilder` object was changed. Line 52 appends `"brown fox"` to the `StringBuilder` object and line 53 again shows that there is only one object all the time.

Let's have a look at the in-memory representation of *Figure 12.10*.

## StringBuilder example (diagram)

*Figure 12.11* represents the in-memory representation of the code in *Figure 12.10*:

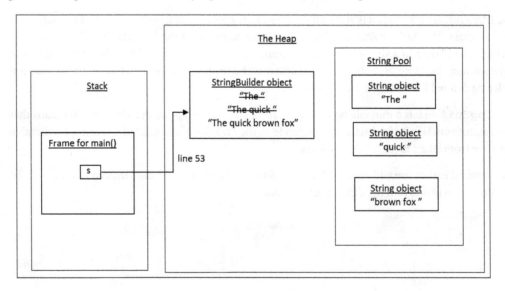

Figure 12.11 – "StringBuilder" example in memory

As can be seen from this figure, apart from the string pool objects (which are there as they are string literals), we only have one `StringBuilder` object. Each time we call `append()`, that one mutable `StringBuilder` object is changed.

Let's have a look at the more commonly used API methods from `StringBuilder`. *Table 12.3* reflects this API:

| Method Name | Description |
|---|---|
| `StringBuilder append(String str)` | Appends the specified string to `StringBuilder`. Overloaded versions are available (see the API). |
| `char charAt(int index)` | Returns the character at the specified index. Indices range from 0. |
| `int indexOf(String str)` | Returns the index of the first occurrence of the specified substring. |
| `StringBuilder insert(int offset, String str)` | Inserts the given string into the `StringBuilder` object at the specified offset, moving any characters above that position upwards. |
| `String substring(int beginIndex)` | Returns a new string, starting at the specified `beginIndex`, and proceeds until the end of this string builder. Indices start at 0. |
| `String substring(int beginIndex, int endIndex)` | Returns a new string, starting at the specified `beginIndex`, and extends to the character at `endIndex-1`. Indices start at 0. |
| `String toString()` | Returns a string representation of the character sequence. |

Table 12.3 – Sample "StringBuilder" API methods

As we have seen, the major difference between `String` and `StringBuilder` is that `String` objects are immutable, whereas `StringBuilder` objects are mutable. Let's look at an example that will help bring that difference into sharp focus.

## String versus StringBuilder example

We will use a sample piece of code to demonstrate this. This code will help highlight both the immutability of `String` objects and the mutability of `StringBuilder` objects. As a bonus, because we are using methods, the code will help us revise the principle of call by value. *Figure 12.12* shows the code:

```
3  ▶    public class StringVersusStringBuilder {
4  @        public static void whatHappens(String s, StringBuilder sb){
5              s = s.concat( str: " there!");
6              sb.append(" there!");
7              System.out.println("whatHappens: "+s);  // Hi there!
8              System.out.println("whatHappens: "+sb); // Hi there!
9          }
10 ▶       public static void main(String[] args) {
11             String s = "Hi";
12             StringBuilder sb = new StringBuilder("Hi");
13             whatHappens(s, sb);
14             System.out.println("main: "+s);  // Hi
15             System.out.println("main: "+sb); // Hi there!
16         }
17    }
```

Figure 12.12 – "String" versus "StringBuilder" code example

In this figure, on line 11, we declare a `String` reference, s, that's referring to `"Hi"` and a `StringBuilder` reference, sb, that contains `"Hi"` also. On line 13, we invoke the whatHappens() method, passing in both s and sb, respectively.

As Java uses call by value, a copy of each reference is made. Thus, the s and sb references in the method declaration (line 4) refer to the same objects that were declared on lines 11 and 12, respectively. While not necessary, keeping the same identifiers, s and sb, helps emphasize this point.

Line 5 then concatenates `" there!"` onto the string referenced by s. As strings are immutable, that object cannot be changed, so the JVM creates a new object with the character sequence (string value) of `"Hi there!"`. Line 7 outputs this new string.

Line 6 appends `" there!"` to the `StringBuilder` object. As it is mutable, the object is simply modified. Line 8 outputs sb after this change.

After the method call on line 13 returns, we output both the values of the string object referred to by s and the string builder object referred to by sb. Remember, because we passed in references and because of call by value, the whatHappens() method had direct access to the objects declared in main() on lines 11 and 12. However, when we output the string object (line 14), we see that it is still `"Hi"`, demonstrating that `String` objects are immutable. On the other hand, when we output the `StringBuilder` object, it has changed to `"Hi there!"`, demonstrating the mutability of `StringBuilder` objects.

A diagram will help here. However, to keep the diagram simple and to focus on mutability/immutability, the string pool has been omitted. *Figure 12.13* is the in-memory representation of the code in *Figure 12.12*:

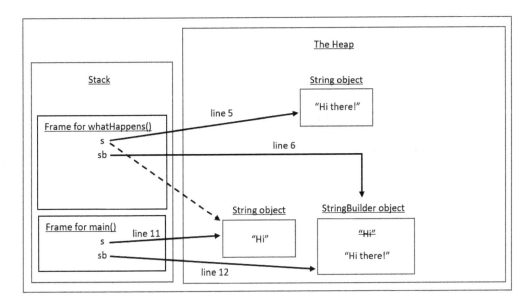

Figure 12.13 - "String" versus "StringBuilder" in memory

This figure represents the picture in memory as we are just about to leave the whatHappens() method (line 9). The dashed arrow is the important arrow. When we entered the whatHappens() method, both s references were pointing at the same String object. Line 5 changes the local s reference to point to the new String object and the original String object was untouched (as it is immutable). The other thing to notice is that the StringBuilder object has been modified (we used a strikethrough to highlight this).

Thus, when we return to main() after calling the method (line 13), the s reference is referring to the untouched String object containing "Hi", whereas the sb reference is referring to the modified StringBuilder object containing "Hi there!".

This discussion on immutable types leads to a natural question, how do I create a custom immutable type? That is the topic of the next section.

## Designing a custom immutable type

In the API, there are mutable types, such as StringBuilder and ArrayList, and immutable types, such as String and Integer. When something is "immutable," it means it cannot change. We can use the final keyword to make a primitive value immutable. When we apply final to a reference, it is the reference that is immutable and not the object.

What if we wanted to create our own type (class) and make it immutable? In other words, we want the *objects* based on our custom class to be immutable. What considerations are involved? That is what we'll discuss in this section.

Before we present the checklist, recall that Java uses call by value when passing arguments to, and retrieving values from, methods. Call by value implies that a copy of the argument is made and that the method works with that copy. For primitives, this means that the called method cannot change the primitive value passed from the caller method. This is analogous to passing a photocopy of a sheet of paper; the photocopied sheet can be written on, without it changing the original. For references, however, the situation is different. Passing a reference to a method means that the called method can change the object that the caller method is looking at. This is analogous to passing a copy of a remote control; the copy-remote can change the TV channel also. This is reflected in the checklist. Let's examine this checklist.

## The checklist

The checklist to apply is as follows:

- Do not provide any "setter" methods
- Make all the fields `private` and `final`
- Prevent subclassing (so that methods cannot be overridden):

  - Make the class `final`
  - Make the constructor `private` and provide a `public static` factory method such as `createNewInstance`

- Regarding instance fields, bear in mind that:

  - Immutable types such as `String` are ok
  - For mutable types such as `StringBuilder`, do *not* share the references – use the advanced encapsulation technique outlined in *Chapter 8*. This technique is also known as "defensive copying".

This checklist is best explained with the aid of a code example. We will start with an example that looks fine but has a subtle issue. We will examine the issue in memory to explain it further. Finally, we will address the issue in code and show why it works in memory.

## Immutable type (breaking encapsulation)

*Figure 12.14* presents such an example:

```
3      import java.util.ArrayList;
4      import java.util.List;
5
6      final class Farm { // cannot subclass this class and all methods are final
7          // private final instance variables
8          private final String name; // String is immutable
9          private final int numAnimals;
10         private final List<String> animals;// mutable
11
12         // private constructor
13         private Farm(final String name, final int numAnimals, final List<String> animals){
14             this.name        = name;
15             this.numAnimals  = numAnimals;
16 //          this.animals     = new ArrayList<String>(animals); // create a new ArrayList
17             this.animals     = animals; // breaking encapsulation!
18         }
19         // factory method to create a Farm
20 @       public static Farm createNewInstance(String name, int numAnimals,
21                                              List<String> animals){
22             return new Farm(name, numAnimals, animals);
23         }
24         // no 'set' methods, only 'get' methods
25         public String getName() { return name; }
28         public int getNumAnimals() { return numAnimals; }
31         public List<String> getAnimals(){
32 //          return new ArrayList<String>(animals);  // return a new object
33             return animals;  // breaking encapsulation!
34         }
35         @Override
36 @       public String toString() {
37             return "Farm{" + "name=" + name + ", numAnimals=" +
38                     numAnimals + ", animals=" + animals + '}';
39         }
40     }
```

Figure 12.14 – A custom immutable type that breaks encapsulation

In this figure, we have an immutable type called `Farm`. The class is `final` (line 6), so it cannot be subclassed. All of the fields are `private` and `final` (lines 8-10). Marking them as `private` ensures no external classes can change their values without our knowledge (basic encapsulation). Marking them as `final` means that once given initial values, those values cannot change. In this example, as they are not given initial values at the point of declaration, they are known as *blank finals*. Blank finals must be initialized before the constructor finishes, which is what we do (lines 14-17).

Our constructor is marked `private` on line 13. Thus, no external class can `new` a `Farm` object directly via this constructor. This is another way to prevent subclassing, as no subclass will have access to this constructor and as we have a constructor coded, the compiler will not insert the default constructor either. We have marked the constructor parameters as `final` also, in case of accidental change.

The `createNewInstance()` factory method (lines 20-23) is how we enable external classes to create `Farm` objects. We provide a `public static` method that calls the `private` constructor on their behalf. Marking it as `public` gives every class access to this method; marking it as `static` ensures that clients do not have to create an object to create a `Farm` (which they can't do directly anyway!).

Note that there are no `set` methods, only `get` methods (lines 25-34). There is one `get` method per instance variable.

Note that this class breaks encapsulation. This is because, in the constructor (line 17), we are storing the reference that was passed in. In addition, our `getAnimals()` method is returning the reference we stored. We will see the implications of this in memory shortly.

However, for now, let's look at a client class utilizing the "supposedly immutable" `Farm` class. *Figure 12.15* highlights an issue:

```
52    public class TestImmutable {
53        public static void main(String[] args) {
54            List<String> animals = new ArrayList<>();
55            animals.add("Cattle");
56
57            Farm farm = Farm.createNewInstance( name: "Small Farm", numAnimals: 25, animals);
58            System.out.println("Created: "+farm); // Created: Farm{name=Small Farm, numAnimals=25, animals=[Cattle]}
59
60            // Get the instance variables
61            String name     = farm.getName();
62            int numAnimals = farm.getNumAnimals();
63            animals        = farm.getAnimals();
64            System.out.println("Retrieved: "+name+" "
65                    +" "+numAnimals+ " "+animals); // Retrieved: Small Farm  25 [Cattle]
66
67            // change what I got back - any affect on the "farm" immutable object?
68            name = "Big Farm";// Strings are immutable so new objects are created in the background => OK
69            numAnimals = 500; // simple primitive i.e. value is just copied back
70            animals.add("Sheep");animals.add("Horses");  // safe or unsafe ?
71
72            // Any change?: Farm{name=Small Farm, numAnimals=25, animals=[Cattle, Sheep, Horses]}
73            System.out.println("Any change?: "+farm);
74        }
75    }
```

Figure 12.15 – A class that uses a weakly encapsulated custom immutable type

In this figure, we declare a `List` (interface) reference, namely `animals`, referring to an `ArrayList` object (line 54). By stating the reference is of the `List<String>` type, we are telling the compiler that only strings are allowed. This gives us type safety, as we cannot, for example, add an `Integer` object to our list. As `ArrayList` is a mutable type, it is perfect for our example. Line 55 adds `"Cattle"` to our `ArrayList`.

Line 57 uses the `createNewInstance()` factory method, passing in `"Small Farm"`, 25, and our `animals` array list. Line 58 proves that the object was created properly.

Lines 61-63 are where we initialize the local variables based on the `Farm` object's state (the values of the instance variables). Lines 64-65 check that they are set as expected.

Lines 68-70 are where we change the *local* variables. This is the acid test. Changing the local variables should *not* affect the state of our `Farm` object. On line 73, we output the instance variables again, via the implicit call to `toString()`. The output is in a comment on the previous line, line 72. As can be seen from the output, the instance's `String` variable name is unaffected (still `"Small Farm"`) and the `numAnimals` instance primitive is also unaffected (still 25). However, the `animals` instance variable has changed! The `ArrayList` object type is the issue here. Originally, the list was just `"Cattle"`; now, it is `"Cattle"`, `"Sheep"`, and `"Horses"`. This change is highlighted by the rectangles. How did this happen? Looking at the situation in memory will reveal the issue.

### In-memory representation (breaking encapsulation)

*Figure 12.16* shows the situation in memory (as we are just about to exit the program). Note that *Figure 12.16* represents the whole program across both figures, namely *Figure 12.14* and *Figure 12.15*.

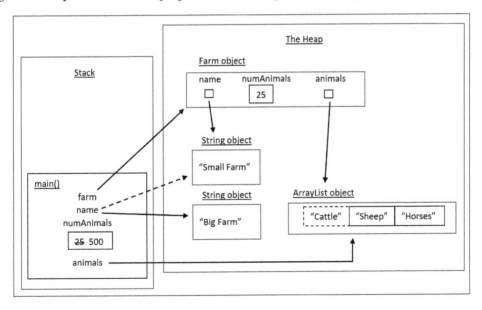

Figure 12.16 – Encapsulation broken by a custom "immutable" type

In the preceding figure, the dashed lines represent original states or values. For example, the dashed line from the `name` variable, on the stack in `main()`, represents line 61 in the code. In contrast, the sold line from the same variable represents line 68.

Let's discuss the stack first. The local `farm` reference refers to the `Farm` object on the heap, which is where the `name`, `numAnimals`, and `animals` instance variables are initialized accordingly. As stated, the local `name` variable in `main()` is initialized (line 61) to refer to the same `String` object that the instance variable in the `Farm` object is looking at. The local `numAnimals` variable is initialized to the value of the instance variable of the same name (line 62). Note that the local copy is represented as a rectangle and not an arrow; this reflects the photocopy of a sheet of paper analogy. Line 63 initializes the local `animals` reference to point to the same `ArrayList` object as the `animals` instance variable in the `Farm` object on the heap. This is the problem, as we shall see very shortly.

Just as we start to execute line 68, both `name` references, the local one on the stack and the instance one on the heap, are referring to the same `String` object. Line 68 changes the name local variable to `"Big Farm"`. However, as `String` objects are immutable, a new `String` object is created on the heap reflecting those changes. In other words, a new `String` object with `"Big Farm"` is created and `name` (on the stack) refers to it. The dashed line, referring to the original `String` object, and the solid line referring to the new `String` object represent this (from `name` on the stack).

Note that the `name` *instance* variable is completely unaffected by this change. That is the strength of immutable types. Other classes are unable to change their values.

Line 69 changes the `numAnimals` local variable (on the stack) to 500. The strikethrough font for the old value and 500 for the new value represent this. Again, the `numAnimals` instance variable is untouched, demonstrating that primitives are fine in custom immutable types.

The issue becomes apparent on line 70, where we add `"Sheep"` and `"Horses"` to the local array list. This should not change the supposedly `private` list that the instance variable is looking at. But it does!

So, we know there is a problem, but how do we fix it?

### Immutable types (properly encapsulated)

The issue here is with the reference to the mutable type being passed in and returned. A custom immutable type should not store or return the reference *directly*. Once you do that, the external class is looking at the same object and as it is mutable, you have no protection from the JVM. That is why lines 17 and 33 are in bold in *Figure 12.16* – they are the lines causing the problem.

So, how do we solve this? Well, the solution is to refer back to what we discussed in *Chapter 8, Mastering Advanced Encapsulation*. In summary, we should use a technique known as "defensive copying" to deal with this situation.

Only two code changes need to be made to our immutable `Farm` type. One is in the constructor; the other is in the relevant `get` method, namely `getAnimals()`. *Figure 12.17* shows the code changes:

```
12          // private constructor
13          private Farm(final String name, final int numAnimals, final List<String> animals){
14              this.name           = name;
15              this.numAnimals     = numAnimals;
16              this.animals        = new ArrayList<String>(animals); // create a new ArrayList
17      //        this.animals        = animals; // breaking encapsulation!
18          }
19          // factory method to create a Farm
20   @      public static Farm createNewInstance(String name, int numAnimals,
21                                                      List<String> animals){
22              return new Farm(name, numAnimals, animals);
23          }
24          // no 'set' methods, only 'get' methods
25          public String getName() { return name; }
28          public int getNumAnimals() { return numAnimals; }
31   @      public List<String> getAnimals(){
32              return new ArrayList<String>(animals);  // return a new object
33      //        return animals;  // breaking encapsulation!
34          }
```

Figure 12.17 – Custom immutable type, properly encapsulated

Rather than present code that has not changed, this figure presents a segment of the class so that we can focus on the changes. Line 16, which was commented out before, is now uncommented and line 17, which has the issue, is now commented out. Contrasting them, we can see that instead of directly storing the reference passed in (line 17), we are now creating a **new** ArrayList object, based on the contents of the list passed in. We then store the reference to the new ArrayList object in our private instance variable.

The other change relates to lines 32 and 33. Line 33, which has the issue, has been commented out, whereas line 32, which has the fix, has been uncommented. Again, rather than returning a copy of our private instance variable (line 33), we are creating a **new** ArrayList object based on the contents of our array list and returning that reference. The contents of the new object can be identical to our private copy, so long as the external class cannot change our private copy. These changes achieve that. Let's look at the situation in memory.

### In-memory representation (properly encapsulated)

In the interests of clarity in the diagram, we have only shown the ArrayList objects and their references. *Figure 12.16* already demonstrated that String objects and primitives were fine, so there's no need to look at those elements again.

*Figure 12.18* shows the situation in memory now (at the end of the program, just before we exit):

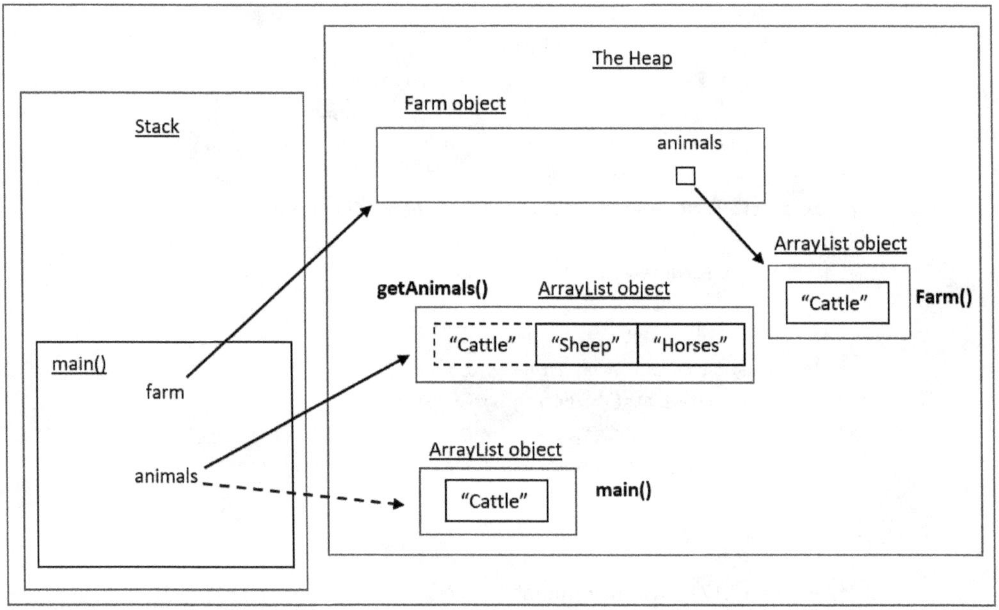

Figure 12.18 - In-memory representation of properly encapsulated custom immutable type

In this figure, the methods where each of the three `ArrayList` objects are created are marked in bold. For example, the bottom `ArrayList` object (marked A) was created in `main()`. Examining that object for a moment, we can see that the `animals` reference on the stack initially (dashed line) refers to it. There is just one `String` in it, `"Cattle"`.

This object is passed via the factory method into the constructor, where its content (`"Cattle"`) is used to create a *new* array list object and initialize the `animals` instance variable so that it points at the new object (line 16). This is represented in the figure by the `ArrayList` object being marked with `Farm()` (and the letter B).

The call to `getAnimals()` also results in a new array list object being created (line 32). This new object is marked by the method name creating it, namely `getAnimals()`, and the letter C. Initially, it just contains `"Cattle"` as this is what the instance variable contains. The dashed rectangle represents this.

Now, however, when we use the local animals reference to insert both "Sheep" and "Horses" into the array list (marked D), the private instance array list is **not** affected. Thus, this class is properly encapsulated.

That completes our coverage on creating a custom immutable type. The next few topics are ones we have touched upon in our recent example, namely `List` and `ArrayList`. Let's discuss both in more detail now.

# Examining List and ArrayList

List is an interface implemented by the ArrayList class. Therefore, any API method in List is automatically in ArrayList. As we know, it is good coding practice to use an interface reference (List) to refer to an object (ArrayList). As the compiler looks at the reference type, this frees you up in the future to use different implementations of List, such as LinkedList.

Both List and ArrayList are in the java.util package. In the API, both are typed generically with E (for Element), which means we are free to specify the type we want to store in our list. Failure to follow the declared type results in a compiler error. We will cover generics in detail in *Chapter 13*.

## List properties

A list is an ordered collection (sometimes called a sequence). We have precise control over where in the list an element is inserted. Indices (as with arrays) start at 0 and duplicate elements are allowed. The order that lists maintain is insertion order. In other words, if you simply add two elements, the second one is positioned after the first one. So, lists maintain order and allow duplicates. *Figure 12.19* shows a small piece of code that captures these properties:

```
10        public static void listProperties() {
11            List<String> list = new ArrayList<>();
12            list.add("J");
13            list.add("A");
14            list.add("V");
15            list.add("A");
16            // insertion order maintained, duplicates allowed
17            System.out.println(list); // [J, A, V, A]
18            list.add( index: 1, element: "O");
19            list.add( index: 3, element: "O");
20            // precise control of where elements are inserted
21            System.out.println(list); // [J, O, A, O, V, A]
22        }
```

Figure 12.19 – Code demonstrating List properties

In this figure, line 11 declares a List reference called list, referring to an ArrayList object. The List reference is typed for strings, meaning that we can only add String objects to the list. As the list is implemented by ArrayList, the properties outlined here apply to ArrayList implementations also.

Lines 12-15 add the J, A, V, and A strings in sequence. When we output the list (line 17), we can see that the insertion order is maintained and that duplicate elements are allowed.

To demonstrate precise control over where elements are inserted, lines 18-19 add "O" to two different locations, namely indices 1 and 3. When we output the list again (line 21), we can see that the strings have been inserted into their correct locations.

Let's look at another example showing other List/ArrayList API calls:

```
25          List<String> list = new ArrayList<>();
26          list.add("Joe"); list.add("Mary"); list.add("Joe");
27          System.out.println(list.contains("Mary"));   // true
28          System.out.println(list.get(0));             // Joe
29          System.out.println(list.indexOf(2));         // -1, no such Object
30          System.out.println(list.indexOf("Joe"));     // 0, first occurrence
31          System.out.println(list.remove( o: "Joe"));  // true, first occurrence
32          System.out.println(list);                    // [Mary, Joe]
33          list.remove( index: 0);
34          System.out.println(list);                    // [Joe]
35          list.set(0, "Paul");
36          System.out.println(list);                    // [Paul]
```

Figure 12.20 – Code demonstrating "List" and "ArrayList"

In this figure, we have several API calls and their respective output is in commented form on the right-hand side of each line. In this figure, our list contains "Joe", "Mary", and "Joe" in that order. We have the following sequence of API calls:

- **Line 27**: contains(Object o) checks if "Mary" is in the list. This returns true.

- **Line 28**: get(int index) returns the element at index 0, namely "Joe".

- **Line 29**: indexOf(Object o) returns the index of the first occurrence of 2. This will be boxed as an Integer type, which "is-a" Object. However, as there is no such object in the list, -1 is returned.

- **Line 30**: Returns 0 as this is the index of the first occurrence of "Joe" in the list.

- **Line 31**: remove(Object o) removes the first occurrence of the object from the list and returns true/false depending on whether the object was found or not. As "Joe" was present in the list, true is returned.

- **Line 32**: Outputs the list, which is now "Mary" and "Joe".

- **Line 33**: remove(int index) removes the object at index 0, which is "Mary".

- **Line 34**: Outputs the list, which is now just "Joe" (the second "Joe").

- **Line 35**: set(int index, E element) changes the contents of the given index to the object passed. Therefore, "Paul" is now in index 0.

- **Line 36**: This shows that line 35 operated as expected.

Now that we have discussed some of the API methods, let's discuss some others. *Table 12.4* presents this information:

| Method Name | Description |
|---|---|
| `void add(int index, E element)` | Adds the element at the specified index |
| `boolean add(E e)` | Adds the element to the end of the list |
| `void clear()` | Removes all the elements from the list |
| `boolean contains(Object o)` | Returns `true` if the object is in the list |
| `E get(int index)` | Returns the element at the specified index |
| `boolean isEmpty()` | Returns `true` if the list is empty |
| `int indexOf(Object o)` | Returns the index of the first occurrence of the specified element; its returns -1 if no such element exists in the list |
| `E remove(int index)` | Removes the element at the specified index |
| `boolean remove(Object o)` | Removes the first occurrence of the specified object |
| `E set(int index, E element)` | Replaces the element at the specified index with the given element |
| `int size()` | Returns the number of elements in the list |

Table 12.4 – Sample "List" and "ArrayList" API methods

That concludes this section on examining `List` and `ArrayList`. For further reading please see the JavaDocs at `https://docs.oracle.com/en/java/javase/21/docs/api/index.html`. Now, let's move on to exploring the Date API.

# Exploring the Date API

The `java.time` package was introduced in Java 8 and was designed to replace the previous `java.util.Date`, `java.util.Calendar`, and `java.text.DateFormat` classes. The classes in `java.time` represent dates, times, timezones, instants, periods, and durations. The ISO calendar system is followed, which is the de facto world calendar (following Gregorian rules). All the classes are immutable and thread-safe.

It is a large API (`https://docs.oracle.com/en/java/javase/21/docs/api/java.base/java/time/package-summary.html`) with a large number of classes for dealing with dates, with relatively fewer classes dealing with times. Thankfully, despite the large number of methods available, the consistent use of method prefixes makes this manageable. We will look at these API prefixes shortly. But before we do that, let's discuss the more important date and time classes.

> **Coordinated Universal Time (UTC)**
>
> UTC is the standard by which the world regulates clocks and time. It is effectively a successor to **Greenwich Mean Time (GMT)**. UTC makes no adjustment for daylight savings time.
>
> The time zone uses UTC+/-00:00, which is sometimes denoted by the letter Z – a reference to the equivalent nautical time zone (GMT). Since the NATO phonetic alphabet word for Z is "Zulu", UTC is sometimes referred to as "Zulu time."

## Dates and times

There are five important classes here. Let's examine each in turn:

- `Instant`: An instant is a numeric timestamp. It is useful for logging and persistence. Historically, `System.currentTimeMillis()` would have been used. `System.currentTimeMillis()` returns the number of milliseconds since the "epoch day" (Jan 1st, 1970 at 00:00:00 UTC). The epoch is a fixed time from which all timestamps are calculated.

- `LocalDate`: Stores a date without a time. This is useful for representing birthdays such as 2000-10-21. As it follows ISO-8601, the format is year-month-day.

- `LocalTime`: Stores a time without a date. This is useful for representing opening/closing hours such as 09:00.

- `LocalDateTime`: Stores a date and time such as 2000-10-21T17:00. Note the "T" used as a date and time separator. This is useful for representing the date and time of a scheduled event, such as a concert.

- `ZonedDateTime`: Represents a "full" date-time with a time zone and resolved offset from UTC. For example, 2023-02-14T16:45+01:00[Europe/Zurich] is the date-time for the Europe/Zurich time zone and is 1 hour ahead of UTC.

## Duration and Period

In addition to dates and times, the API also represents durations and periods of time. Let's look at these now.

- `Duration`: An amount of time, represented in seconds (and nanoseconds); for example, "54 seconds."
- `Period`: Represents an amount of time in units more meaningful to humans, such as years or days. For example, "3 years, 6 months, and 12 days."

## Additional interesting types

Other types are interesting also. Let's examine some of these now.

- `Month`: Represents a month on its own; for example, JANUARY.
- `DayOfWeek`: Represents a day-of-week on its own; for example, FRIDAY.
- `YearMonth`: Represents a year and month, without a day or time; for example, 2025-12. This could be useful for a credit card expiry date.
- `MonthDay`: Represents a month and day, without a year or time; for example, --08-09. This could be useful for an annual event, such as an anniversary.
- `ZoneOffset`: Represents a time zone offset from GMT/UTC, such as +2:00.

As stated earlier, there are a large number of methods across the classes. However, as the prefixes are consistently applied, this is manageable. *Table 12.5* represents these prefixes.

| Method Prefix | Description |
| --- | --- |
| | Note: `1d2` and so forth used in these examples are related. |
| `of` | A static factory method for creating instances – for example, <br><br>`LocalDate ld1 = LocalDate.of(2023, 3, 17);` |
| `parse` | A static factory method for creating instances – for example, <br><br>`LocalDate ld2 = LocalDate.parse("2023-03-17");` |
| `get` | Gets the value of something – for example, <br><br>`int dayOfMonth = ld2.getDayOfMonth(); // 17` |
| `is` | Checks if something is true – for example, <br><br>`boolean isLeapYear = ld2.isLeapYear(); // false` |

| Method Prefix | Description |
|---|---|
| | Note: ld2 and so forth used in these examples are related. |
| with | The immutable equivalent of a setter method – for example,<br><br>`LocalDate ld3 = ld2.withDayOfMonth(25); // 2023-03-25` |
| plus | Adds an amount to an object – for example,<br><br>`LocalDate ld4 = ld3.plusDays(2); // 2023-03-27` |
| minus | Subtracts an amount from an object – for example,<br><br>`LocalDate ld5 = ld4.minusMonths(2); // 2023-01-27` |
| at | Combines this object with another – for example,<br><br>`LocalDateTime ldt1 = ld5.atTime(13, 45, 10); //`<br>`2023-01-27T13:45:10` |

Table 12.5 – Date API method prefixes

Now that we have had a look at the prefixes in the API, let's look at some sample code to reinforce them. *Figure 12.21* shows some code for manipulating dates and times:

```
13    LocalDate nowDate = LocalDate.now(); // get current date from system clock
14    LocalTime nowTime = LocalTime.now();
15    LocalDateTime nowDateTime2 = LocalDateTime.now();   // one way
16    LocalDateTime nowDateTime = LocalDateTime.of(nowDate, nowTime);// another way
17    System.out.println(nowDateTime);// 2023-07-09T13:28:00.322907600
18
19    // Setting St. Patricks Day, 2025
20    LocalDate ld1 = LocalDate.of( year: 2025,  month: 3,  dayOfMonth: 17);// one way
21    LocalDate ld2 = LocalDate.parse( text: "2025-03-17");// another way
22    System.out.println(ld2.getDayOfWeek());// MONDAY
23    LocalDate ld3 = ld2.withMonth(5);
24    System.out.println(ld3);// 2025-05-17
25    LocalDate ld4 = ld3.plusYears( yearsToAdd: 1);
26    System.out.println(ld4);// 2026-05-17
27    LocalDate ld5 = ld4.minusDays( daysToSubtract: 5);
28    System.out.println(ld5);// 2026-05-12
29    LocalDateTime ldt1 = ld5.atTime( hour: 13,  minute: 45,  second: 10);
30    System.out.println(ldt1);// 2026-05-12T13:45:10
```

Figure 12.21 – Code for manipulating dates and times

In this figure, line 13 creates `LocalDate` using the factory `now()` method. This creates a `LocalDate` object based on the system clock setting for the default locale. Also, using the `now()` method, lines 14-15 create `LocalTime` and `LocalDateTime` objects, respectively. Line 16 shows another way to create `LocalDateTime` objects by using the `of()` factory method to pass in both `LocalDate` and `LocalTime` objects. Line 17 shows the output of the `LocalDateTime` object to be `yyyy-mm-ddThh:mm:ss:nnnnnnnnn`. The date part comes first, then `"T"`, which separates the date from the time, where n in the time part represent nanoseconds.

Next, we want to create `LocalDate` values representing St. Patrick's Day (March 17), 2025. Line 20 uses the `of()` factory method and passes in numeric values for the year, month, and day. Note that the months start at 1 and not 0. Thus, March is represented as 3.

Line 21 uses an alternative factory method, namely `parse(String)`, which accepts a `String` and creates a `LocalDate` accordingly. If the string cannot be parsed, an exception will occur.

Line 22 outputs what day of the week, March 17, 2025, occurs (which is a Monday). Line 23 "modifies" the months, changing it from 3 to 5 (March to May). As the Date API types are immutable, the change is made to a new object in the background (`ld2` is untouched). The `ld3` reference refers to this new object (`2025-05-17`).

Line 25 adds a year, so we now have 2026-05-17. Line 27 subtracts 5 days, so we now have 2026-05-12. Lastly, on line 29, we "change" our `LocalDate` to `LocalDateTime`. As we already have a date, we just provided the time elements. The nanoseconds, which are not provided, are set to 0 and are not displayed as a result.

Now, let's look at a `ZonedDateTime` example in *Figure 12.22*:

```
34    LocalDateTime flightDepTime  = LocalDateTime.of( year: 2023,
35                                           Month.NOVEMBER,
36                                           dayOfMonth: 24,
37                                           hour: 13,
38                                           minute: 00);
39    ZonedDateTime flightDepTimeZ = flightDepTime.atZone(ZoneId.of( zoneId: "Europe/Dublin"));
40    System.out.println(flightDepTimeZ);// 2023-11-24T13:00Z[Europe/Dublin]
41
42    ZonedDateTime arrivalTimeZ  =
43           flightDepTimeZ.withZoneSameInstant(ZoneId.of( zoneId: "Europe/Paris"))
44                 .plusHours(1)
45                 .plusMinutes(45);
46
47    System.out.println(arrivalTimeZ); // 2023-11-24T15:45+01:00[Europe/Paris]
48    System.out.println(arrivalTimeZ.getHour()+":"+arrivalTimeZ.getMinute()); // 15:45
```

Figure 12.22 – ZonedDateTime example

In this figure, a flight leaves Dublin for Paris at 1 PM local time. The flight duration is 1 hour 45 minutes. We are trying to calculate the local time in Paris when the flight lands. The solution presented here is one option.

Lines 34-38 create a `LocalDateTime` object for the departure date and time (November 24th, 2023, at 1 P.M.). Line 39 zones the date-time object using the `atZone()` method by passing in the relevant time zone (a `ZoneId`). To get the time zone `ZoneId` object, simply call the factory `of()` method while passing in the relevant time zone string. In this example, it is `"Europe/Dublin"`. Line 40 shows the format of the `ZonedDateTime` object. Note `"Z"` for Zulu time (UTC). At that time of year, as summertime has ended, Dublin is in line with UTC.

Lines 42-45 represent the calculation of the local arrival time in Paris. Line 43 calculates what time is it in Paris when the flight leaves Dublin using the `withZoneSameInstant()` method. Now, all we have to do is add on the flight time of 1 hour and 45 minutes.

Line 47 shows the `ZonedDateTime` for the arrival time. The time and zoned offset elements are interesting. The local time allows for the fact that Paris is 1 hour ahead of Dublin. This time difference is reflected in the offset of `+1:00`. Thus, Paris is 1 hour ahead of UTC.

Now, let's look at some code that uses `Period` and `Duration`. *Figure 12.23* presents an example:

```
56          // Period
57          LocalDate startDate = LocalDate.of( year: 1861,  month: 4,  dayOfMonth: 12);
58          LocalDate endDate   = LocalDate.of( year: 1865,  month: 4,  dayOfMonth: 9);
59          Period howLongP     = Period.between(startDate,endDate);
60          System.out.println(howLongP);              // P3Y11M28D, weeks not represented
61          System.out.println(howLongP.getYears());   // 3
62          System.out.println(howLongP.getMonths());// 11
63          System.out.println(howLongP.getDays());   // 28
64
65          // Duration
66          LocalTime lt1 = LocalTime.of( hour: 12, minute: 0,  second: 20);
67          LocalTime lt2 = LocalTime.of( hour: 14, minute: 45,  second: 40);
68          Duration howLongD2 = Duration.between(lt1, lt2);
69          System.out.println(howLongD2);// PT2H45M20S
```

Figure 12.23 – An example using Period and Duration

In this figure, both `Period` and `Duration` are demonstrated. `Period` is suited for time blocks of greater than 1 day; for example, 2 years, 5 months, and 11 days. `Duration` is more suited to blocks of time of less than 1 day; for example, 8 hours and 20 seconds.

Lines 57-63 calculate and output the number of years, months, and days the American Civil War lasted. Firstly, we create `LocalDate` objects for the start and end dates (lines 57-58). Line 59 creates a `Period` object using the static `Period.between()` method, passing in the relevant start and end dates. Line 60 outputs the period object, `P3Y11M28D`, which represents a `Period` of 3 years,

11 months, and 28 days (weeks are represented in days). Lines 61-63 output the years, months, and days values separately.

Next, we will look at `Duration`. In this case, we use two `LocalTime` objects; one representing 12:00:20 (line 66) and the other representing 14:45:40 (line 67). Line 68 calculates the time difference between both and line 69 outputs the result. Note that there is no Y, M, or D (years, months, or days) as there was on line 60 (`Period`). Now, on line 69, we have a `Duration` of PT2H45M20S representing 2 hours, 45 minutes, and 20 seconds.

Lastly, let's look at how to format dates and times.

## Formatting dates and times

A formatter can work in both directions: formatting your temporal (time-related) object as a string or parsing a string into a temporal object. Both approaches work with formatters. This is represented by the following code from the API:

```
LocalDate date = LocalDate.now();
String text = date.format(formatter);
LocalDate parsedDate = LocalDate.parse(text, formatter);
```

We will focus on how to create formatters for the `format()` method. However, as formatters are common to both formatting and parsing, what we say for one applies to the other.

We have a lot of flexibility in how we specify the format for our dates and times. Firstly, there are pre-defined standard formats available for us. In addition, we can specify custom formats. When specifying custom formats, the letters A-Z and a-z are reserved and have specific semantics. Importantly, the number of format letters is important – for example, MMM formats the month to Aug, whereas MM produces 08.

There are two common approaches to formatting your dates and times. One is to use `format(DateTimeFormatter)` in the `LocalDate`, `LocalTime`, `LocalDateTime`, and `ZonedDateTime` temporal classes. Its signature accepts a parameter of the `DateTimeFormatter` type. The other approach is to use `format(TemporalAccessor)` in the `DateTimeFormatter` class itself. `TemporalAccessor` is an interface that's implemented by the temporal classes just mentioned.

Before we look at some example code, we must cover the more popular pre-defined formatters and format patterns. There are quite a few and we encourage you to look up the API for further details.

### Pre-defined formatters

The easiest way to access these formatters is to use the constants in the `DateTimeFormatter` class or by calling the factory "of" methods in `DateTimeFormatter`. *Table 12.6* presents an overview of the more popular ones. Please see the API for further details. Note that **ISO** stands for **International Organization for Standardization**:

| Formatter | Description | Example |
|---|---|---|
| ofLocalizedDate (dateStyle) | Formatter with the date style from the locale | This depends on the style that's passed in. An example is "Monday 10 July 2023". |
| ofLocalizedTime (timeStyle) | Formatter with the time style from the locale | This depends on the style that's passed in. An example is "15:47". |
| ofLocalizedDateTime (dateTimeStyle) | Formatter with the date and time styles from the locale | This depends on the style that's passed in. An example is "3 July 2018 09:19". |
| ISO_DATE | ISO date (may contain offset) | "2023-07-10", "2023-07-10+01:00". |
| ISO_TIME | ISO time (may contain offset) | "15:47:13", "15:47:13+01:00". |
| ISO_LOCAL_DATE | ISO local date (no offset) | "2023-07-10". |
| ISO_LOCAL_TIME | ISO local time (no offset) | "16:00:03". |
| ISO_ZONED_DATE_TIME | Zoned date time | "2023-07-12T09:33:03+01:00 [Europe/Dublin]". |

Table 12.6 – Date API pre-defined formatters

Now, let's examine some code that uses pre-defined formatters.

*Figure 12.24* presents code that uses these pre-defined formatters:

```
74          LocalDate date = LocalDate.now();
75          DateTimeFormatter isoDate = DateTimeFormatter.ISO_DATE;
76          System.out.println(date.format(isoDate));        // 2023-07-10
77          DateTimeFormatter fullDateStyle =
78                  DateTimeFormatter.ofLocalizedDate(FormatStyle.FULL);
79          System.out.println(date.format(fullDateStyle));  // Monday 10 July 2023
80
81          LocalTime time = LocalTime.now();
82          DateTimeFormatter isoTime = DateTimeFormatter.ISO_TIME;
83          System.out.println(time.format(isoTime));         // 15:47:13.3961956
84          DateTimeFormatter shortTimeStyle =
85                  DateTimeFormatter.ofLocalizedTime(FormatStyle.SHORT);
86          System.out.println(time.format(shortTimeStyle));   // 15:47
```

Figure 12.24 – Code example using pre-defined formatters

In this figure, we represent the current date (line 74) and the current time (line 81) in various formats, based on the pre-defined formats available in `DateTimeFormatter`. First up is `ISO_DATE` (line 75). Its output (in comments on line 76) is `2023-07-10`, which is in yyyy-mm-dd format.

Line 78 uses the `ofLocalizedDate()` factory method to create a format. By passing in the `FormatStyle.FULL` enum constant, we are requesting as much detail as possible. As a result, this format outputs (line 79) `Monday 10 July 2023`. As can be seen, this is more detailed than the `ISO_DATE` format.

Line 82 creates an `ISO_TIME` formatter and applies it (line 83) to the time object that's already been created (line 81). Line 85 uses the `ofLocalizedTime()` factory method. The `FormatStyle.SHORT` enum returns the fewest details, typically numeric.

That covers the pre-defined formatters. Now, let's discuss how to specify custom formatters.

## *Custom formatters*

Custom formatters are defined using pattern letters, where the number of letters used is significant. Let's discuss the most commonly used pattern letters first and then present some code that utilizes them. *Table 12.7* presents a summary of the pattern letters:

| Letter | Description | Examples |
|---|---|---|
| y | Year | 2023; 23 |
| M | Month | 8; 08; Aug; August |
| d | Day of the month | 16 |
| E | Day of the week | Wed; Wednesday |
| D | Day of the year | 145 |
| h | Hour of the day; 12-hour clock (1-12) | 10 |
| H | Hour of the day; 24-hour clock (0-23) | 19 |
| m | Minute of the hour | 32 |
| s | Second of the minute | 55 |
| a | A.M. or P.M. | PM |
| z | Timezone | GMT |
| G | Era | AD |

Table 12.7 – Date API pattern letters overview

This table is best explained with the aid of an example. *Figure 12.25* presents an example that uses the pattern letters from *Table 12.7*:

```
91    ZonedDateTime zdt = ZonedDateTime.now();
92    System.out.println(zdt);        // 2023-07-11T09:05:50.792542600+01:00[Europe/Dublin]
93    DateTimeFormatter dateFormatter = DateTimeFormatter.ofPattern("yy-MMM-dd E D");
94    System.out.println(zdt.format(dateFormatter));// 23-Jul-11 Tue 192
95
96    DateTimeFormatter timeFormatter1 = DateTimeFormatter.ofPattern("hh:mm:ss a z G");
97    System.out.println(zdt.format(timeFormatter1));// 09:05:50 a.m. IST AD
98
99    // how to insert text
100   DateTimeFormatter dateFormatter2 =
101        DateTimeFormatter.ofPattern("'Year: 'yyyy'. Month: 'MMMM'. Day: 'dd'.'");
102   System.out.println(zdt.format(dateFormatter2));// Year: 2023. Month: July. Day: 11.
103
104   // parse
105   String dateTimeString = "2023-07-10 22:10"; // last night
106   DateTimeFormatter timeFormatter2 = DateTimeFormatter.ofPattern("yyyy-MM-dd HH:mm");
107   LocalDateTime ldt = LocalDateTime.parse(dateTimeString, timeFormatter2);
108   System.out.println(ldt);       // 2023-07-10T22:10
```

Figure 12.25 – Code example using pattern letters

In this figure, line 91 gets the current date and time for this timezone, which is **Irish Standard Time (IST)**.

---

**Irish Standard Time (IST)**

This is the timezone that's used in Ireland. In Ireland, we utilize daylight savings time ("summertime"). This means that during the summer months, we advance the clocks forward 1 hour so that darkness falls at a later clock time. Therefore, in March, we put the clocks forward 1 hour, and in October, we put the clocks back 1 hour.

There is no "summertime" in UTC. Because of this and the fact that it is July right now, IST is +1:00 hours ahead of UTC.

---

The output for line 92 is in a comment to the right. The date and time are separated, as usual, by "T." The zone offset is "+1:00," indicating that this zoned time is 1 hour ahead of UTC. The zone ID is "[Europe/Dublin]."

We will first look at a date-related formatter. Line 93 creates a formatter using the yy-MMM-dd E D pattern. The output it generates is 23-Jul-11 Tue 192 (line 94). Thus, the current year of 2023 is output as 23 because we only provided yy in the format (as opposed to yyyy). Note that, had it been yyyy in the format, 2023 would have been output. This is why the number of pattern letters is important. The capital M is for the month. M produces 7, MM produces 07, MMM (as in the pattern) produces Jul, and MMMM produces July. Again, this demonstrates that the number of pattern letters is important.

The dd pattern outputs the day of the month. This gives us 11 for the 11th. E gives us the day of the week, which is Tue. Note that EEEE returns Tuesday. D represents the day of the year; the 192nd in this example.

Note that the dashes and spaces are simply inserted into the output. This is because, unlike letters, they are not reserved. We will learn how to insert words (containing letters) into the output without causing exceptions shortly.

Now, let's examine a time-related formatter. Line 96 creates a formatter using the hh:mm:ss a z G pattern, which generates the output (line 97) of 09:05:50 a.m. IST AD. The hh:mm:ss pattern returns the current time in hours (12-hour clock), minutes, and seconds format. a returns whether it is A.M. or P.M. Right now, it is the morning, so am is returned. The z pattern letter returns the abbreviated zone name, IST. Expanding this to zzzz returns Irish Standard Time. Lastly, G returns the era, AD (Anno Domini).

Now, let's learn how to insert text into our formatter. As we know, the letters a-z and A-Z are reserved. So, how do we insert letters as regular letters and not pattern letters? To do this, we must surround the regular letters with single quotes. Line 101 specifies a pattern that uses both regular letters and pattern letters. The pattern is "'Year: '*yyyy*'. Month: '*MMMM*'. Day: '*dd*'.". The pattern letters are in italics. Any other characters are enclosed in single quotes.

Year: 2023. Month: July. Day: 11. is generated as output.

As we can see, the year value, 2023, is preceded by the text "Year: ". This was achieved by surrounding the text with single quotes: 'Year: '. Following the year pattern yyyy, the regular text '. Month: ' is inserted. Thus, the capital M is treated as simply a capital M, instead of a month pattern letter. After that, '. Day: ' is inserted to precede the day of the month, which is 11. Lastly, a period is inserted at the end by enclosing it in single quotes also. Note that the period without single quotes is also fine as it is not a reserved character.

Lastly, let's look at an example of parsing where we can create temporal objects from String values. Line 105 declares a string of "2023-07-10 22:10". Line 106 then declares a pattern that will be able to parse this string. The pattern is "yyyy-MM-dd HH:mm". Note that "HH" represents the 24-hour clock. This will enable us to parse the time of "22" in the string.

Line 107 creates a LocalDateTime object by parsing the string according to the pattern provided. Line 108 outputs the LocalDateTime object, producing "2023-07-10T22:10", which is what the string represents.

That completes our discussion on custom formatters and concludes *Chapter 12*. Now, let's put that knowledge into practice to reinforce the concepts we've covered.

# Exercises

We've learned so many fun new things in this chapter. It's time to enlighten the users of the Mesozoic Eden software with some new features that have been built with our new skills:

1. Manage the birthdays of the dinosaurs in our park. Add the `birthday` property to the `Dinosaur` class.

2. The park operates on a strict schedule. Create a simple system to log events such as feeding times, cleaning, and emergency drills in the park using the Date API.

3. In Mesozoic Eden, we have a very strong safety-first policy. Regular inspections help us maintain our high standards of safety. Create a program that calculates how many days are left until the park's next safety inspection, based on the date of the last safety inspection. Safety inspections need to happen every 45 days.

4. We have a newborn Theropod. The guests were asked to submit names for our youngest inhabitant of Mesozoic Eden. 10 names were picked. Create a list for these 10 names.

5. We want to create a string with the newborn's full name. Use `StringBuilder` to append every name to its new name, and then convert it into a string when you're done. (Hint: Use a loop combined with `StringBuilder`.)

# Project – dinosaur care system

We'll continue to work on our "dinosaur care system" by adding functionality to log daily care activities for dinosaurs using the Java Core API. This includes features to accept user input, maintain a history of activities, and store dinosaur health data over time. Don't worry – we'll break this down for you step by step.

**Step 1: Add additional Java classes:**

- Create a new package named `coreapi`.

- Inside this package, create a class named `Dinosaur`. This class should have properties such as name, species, health status, and so on.

- Also, create a class named `Activity` with properties such as name, date, dinosaur, and so on.

**Step 2: Extend the dinosaur care system:**

- In your `DinosaurCareSystem` class, create a `List` to hold `Dinosaur` objects, and another `List` to hold `Activity` objects.

- Create a method called `addDinosaur()` that takes user input to create a new `Dinosaur` object and add it to the list of dinosaurs.

- Create a method called `logActivity()` that also takes user input to create a new `Activity` object (including selecting a dinosaur from the list) and add it to the list of activities.

Here is some sample code to get you started with this step:

```java
import java.util.*;

public class DinosaurCareSystem {
    private List<Dinosaur> dinosaurs;
    private List<Activity> activities;

    public DinosaurCareSystem() {
        dinosaurs = new ArrayList<>();
        activities = new ArrayList<>();
    }

    public void addDinosaur(Dinosaur dinosaur) {
        dinosaurs.add(dinosaur);
    }

    public void logActivity(Activity activity) {
        activities.add(activity);
    }

    //... existing methods for handling exceptions here
}
```

**Step 3: Interact with the system:**

- In your main class, create a `DinosaurCareSystem` object and use a loop to continuously ask the user what they want to do (add a dinosaur, log activity, and so on). Use a `Scanner` object to get input from the user.

Here's some code to get you started:

```java
import java.util.Scanner;

public class Main {
    public static void main(String[] args) {
        DinosaurCareSystem system = new
            DinosaurCareSystem();
        Scanner scanner = new Scanner(System.in);

        while (true) {
            System.out.println("What would you like to
```

```
            do?");
            System.out.println("1. Add a dinosaur");
            System.out.println("2. Log an activity");
            System.out.println("3. Exit");

            int choice = scanner.nextInt();
            scanner.nextLine();  // consume newline

            if (choice == 1) {
                // add dinosaur
            } else if (choice == 2) {
                // log activity
            } else if (choice == 3) {
                break;
            }
        }
    }
}
```

As always, feel free to expand on this and let your creativity run free!

## Summary

In this chapter, we looked at popular classes from the Java Core API. We started with Scanner, a useful class for reading input. Scanner can be directed to read from a file, a String object, or the keyboard. Reading from the keyboard is particularly useful for dealing with user input.

We examined the String class and its API. We saw how String literals use the string constant pool to save on memory. We examined an important property of String objects, namely immutability. A String object, once created, cannot be changed.

Next, we examined StringBuilder and its API. We discussed that StringBuilder is a mutable type and thus, there is only ever one object in memory.

Given that String is immutable but StringBuilder is mutable, we presented a detailed example with both code and supporting diagrams to compare and contrast String and StringBuilder.

This led to a discussion on how to create our own custom immutable types. We examined a checklist of steps you must perform to ensure that your class is immutable. We then showed an example where, very subtly, Java's call by value principle broke encapsulation (and hence immutability). We discussed how to fix such an issue using defensive copying. Effectively, for our private instance mutable types, we had to ensure that the references passed in to initialize them were not stored directly; we must copy them first. In addition, we had to ensure that we did not return the references to our private instance mutable types either; we must copy them first also.

From there we examined the `List` and `ArrayList` APIs. `List` is an interface and `ArrayList` is an implementation of `List`. `ArrayList` is essentially an expandable array. It maintains the order of insertion and allows duplicates.

Then, we examined the Date API, which was overhauled in Java 8. We discussed `Instant`, `LocalDate`, `LocalTime`, `LocalDateTime`, `ZonedDateTime`, `Period`, and `Duration`. All of these types are immutable, meaning we can use factory methods (such as `now()` and `of()`) to create instances. In a large API, the consistency of method prefix names is helpful.

Finally, we discussed how we can format a temporal object for output and also how we can parse a string into a temporal object. We examined the pre-defined formatters available and in addition, we designed custom formatters using reserved pattern letters.

That completes our discussion on the Java Core API. We will move on to generics and collections in the next chapter.

# Part 3:
# Advanced Topics

In this part, we will take a look at some of the more advanced topics in Java. We will start with the Java Collection framework. This will include several of its popular interfaces and their common implementations. We will discuss sorting in Java and how to work with generics. We then move on to lambda expressions and their relationship to functional interfaces. We will look at popular functional interfaces from the API and also method references. We will then discuss streams over two chapters, both the fundamentals and advanced topics. The fundamentals will cover topics such as the stream pipeline, stream laziness, and terminal operations. The advanced chapter will discuss intermediate operations, primitive streams, `Optional`s, and parallel streams. Lastly, we will discuss concurrency, where we will explain multi-threading, data races, `ExecutorService,` and concurrent collections.

This section has the following chapters:

- *Chapter 13, Generics and Collections*
- *Chapter 14, Lambda Expressions*
- *Chapter 15, Streams: Fundamentals*
- *Chapter 16, Streams: Advanced Concepts*
- *Chapter 17, Concurrency*

# 13

# Generics and Collections

Organizing data is another important software development topic. Java hands us collections to deal with various data structures. It also gives us generics to achieve type safety and avoid duplicate code in our applications. We cannot say we're masters of Java without understanding how to use collections and generics.

That's why we devoted this chapter to the Java collections framework. In this chapter, we'll cover the following topics:

- The collections framework and its interfaces – `List`, `Set`, `Map`, and `Queue`
- Several implementations of each collection type and their basic operations
- Sorting collections using natural ordering and the `Comparable` and `Comparator` interfaces
- Working with generics
- Basic hashing concepts and their relevance

By the end of this chapter, you will have a solid understanding of the Java collections framework and generics, and you'll be ready to manage data and use collections in your programs.

## Technical requirements

The code for this chapter (*Exercise* section) can be found on GitHub at: `https://github.com/PacktPublishing/Learn-Java-with-Projects/tree/main/ch13/exercises`.

## Getting to know collections

**Collections** are worth getting to know. Collections are a much more elegant way of dealing with multiple values in one variable than arrays. A common example of a collection would be a list.

Writing any proper Java application without collections would be very complicated. You'd probably start by creating some classes that will act like Java's built-in collections. They play a vital role in software development as they provide a means to manage and organize data.

There are many reasons why we need them, but let's just list (collection pun) a few:

- **Managing large amounts of data**: As applications grow in complexity, they often need to deal with large amounts of data. Collections help store and manage these datasets. They also come with helpful methods that make it easier to perform typical operations on data, such as searching and filtering.

- **Storing and manipulating various data structures**: Different data structures have unique characteristics and are suited for specific tasks. Collections provide a diverse set of data structures. This way, we get to choose the most appropriate one for our requirements.

- **Ensuring efficient data management and access**: Collections offer a wide range of functionality. This helps us optimize data management and data access in our applications.

Since there are different data structures, we also need to have different collection types. Let's have a look at them.

## Overview of different collection types

The Java collections framework offers quite a few different collection types. This ensures that developers don't go ahead and build custom data structure classes for all sorts of problems. This would make it very hard for different applications to communicate and there would be a lot of boilerplate code necessary for so many tasks. It's a good thing Java comes with these built-in collection interfaces and implementations. Let's have a look at the main interfaces first. You don't need to understand the tiniest details of the coding examples; we'll explain all of it in more detail after.

### List

One of the most common data structures is the list. **Lists** are ordered and indexed collections that allow duplicate elements. They are useful when the order of elements is important, and you need to access elements based on their index.

Here's an example of a list where we are storing a sequence of student names in a class, where the order of names is significant. This is a list that only holds elements of the `String` type. As you can see, `List` is an interface. When we instantiate it, we need to choose a class that implements `List`. In this case, we're choosing `ArrayList`. This is a very common choice, but there are other options as well, such as `LinkedList`. There are a few important differences, but we won't dive into those here:

```
List<String> studentNames = new ArrayList<>();
studentNames.add("Sarah-Milou");
studentNames.add("Tjed");
studentNames.add("Fahya");
```

With that, we have seen that `List` can hold strings, but collections can hold any type of object, including custom objects. Let's say we have a `Person` object. This is what that may look like:

```
List<Person> personNames = new ArrayList<>();
personNames.add(new Person("Sarah-Milou", 4));
personNames.add(new Person("Tjed", 6));
personNames.add(new Person("Fahya", 8));
```

For simplicity, we'll mostly use `String` for our examples but do keep in mind that this could be any object (and that includes other collections).

There are unordered collections that don't allow duplicates as well. These are of the `Set` type. Let's have a look at them.

## Sets

**Sets** are (commonly) unordered collections that do not allow duplicate elements. They are useful when you need to store unique elements but don't need to care about their order.

Let's say we need a data structure for all the email addresses we need to send a newsletter to. We don't want to have any duplicates present because that would result in duplicate mail for the receiver:

```
Set<String> emailAddresses = new HashSet<>();
emailAddresses.add("sarahmilou@amsterdam.com");
emailAddresses.add("tjed@amsterdam.com");
emailAddresses.add("fahya@amsterdam.com");
```

You don't need to worry about adding duplicates, nothing happens if you try to do that. You'll see different implementations of `Set` later, including two types that maintain a particular order of their elements. But let's have a look at another data structure first: maps.

## Maps

**Maps** store key-value pairs and provide lookups based on the key. They are useful when you need to associate values with unique keys, such as storing user information based on their usernames:

```
Map<String, String> userInfo = new HashMap<>();
userInfo.put("Sarah-Milou", "Sarah-Milou Doyle");
userInfo.put("Tjed", "Tjed Quist");
userInfo.put("Fahya", "Fahya Osei");
```

As you can see, maps use different methods. Even though `Map` is part of the collections framework, it's a bit of an odd one. Map is the only main interface that doesn't extend the `Collection` interface. `List`, `Set`, and `Queue` do.

Sometimes, we need an ordered collection that only allows access to the beginning and/or the end of the collection. We can use queues for this.

## *Queues and deques*

**Queues** allow you to add elements to the beginning of the queue and access elements at the ends. There's a special queue that allows insertion and removal at both ends. This is known as a **deque**. Deque stands for double-ended queue. So, queues follow the **First-In, First-Out (FIFO)** principle, while deques can be used as both a queue (FIFO) and a stack, which follows the **Last-In, First-Out (LIFO)** principle.

They are useful for tasks that require processing elements in a specific order, such as when implementing a task scheduler. Here's an example of a print job queue where tasks are processed in the order they are received:

```
Queue<String> printQueue = new LinkedList<>();
printQueue.add("Document1");
printQueue.add("Document2");
printQueue.add("Document3");
String nextJob = printQueue.poll(); // "Document1"
```

Let's look at these interfaces in a bit more detail, starting again with `List`.

# List

So, the `List` interface is a part of the Java collections framework and it is used to represent an ordered collection of elements. Elements in a `List` interface can be accessed by their position (index) and can include duplicates. Since `List` is an interface, it cannot be instantiated. Two commonly used implementations of the `List` interface are `ArrayList` and `LinkedList`. Since these are implementation classes, they can be instantiated. Let's explore what they are.

## ArrayList

`ArrayList` is a resizable array-backed implementation of the `List` interface. It provides fast random access to elements and is efficient for read-heavy operations. Random access means directly reaching any item using its index quickly.

`ArrayList` dynamically resizes itself when elements are added or removed. Adding and removing elements is somewhat slower. `LinkedList` is optimized for this.

## LinkedList

`LinkedList` is an implementation of the `List` interface based on a doubly linked list data structure. Not only does it implement `List` but it also implements `Queue` and `Deque`. It provides fast insertion and deletion of elements at the beginning and end of the list, as well as efficient traversal in both directions. However, accessing elements by index can be slower in `LinkedList` compared to `ArrayList` as elements must be traversed from the head or tail of the list.

The upcoming examples could be happening on both an `ArrayList` and a `LinkedList` in the same way. The difference is the performance (which is not a significant difference for the small amounts of data in these examples).

## Exploring the basic operations for lists

We can add, remove, alter, and access items on lists. Let's have a look at how to perform these everyday operations. There are a lot of other useful methods for lists, but we'll stick to the must-haves and start with adding elements to a list.

### Adding elements to a list

We can add elements to a `List` interface using the `add()` method. The `add()` method has two forms: `add(E element)` and `add(int index, E element)`. The first one adds the element to the end of the list, while the second one adds the element at the specified index. This will shift all the other elements that follow one index up. Here, E is the placeholder for the actual type. If it's a list of the `String` type, we can only add strings to the list.

Let's have a look at a simple example that uses a list of names:

```
List<String> names = new ArrayList<>();
names.add("Julie"); // Adds "Julie" at the end of the list
names.add(0, "Janice"); // Inserts "Janice" at index 0
```

First, we create an instance of `ArrayList`. This is a list of the `String` type, as we can see by the word `String` between the angle (`<>`) brackets. We then go ahead and add `Julie` to the list. After that, we specify the position. Instead of adding `Janice` after `Julie`, we add `Janice` at index 0. This makes `Julie` change from index 0 to index 1.

After this, we have a list with two `String` elements in it. Let's see how we can access these elements.

### Getting elements from a list

You can get elements from a `List` interface using the `get()` method, which takes an index as an argument. We'll continue from our previous example. Here's how to do it:

```
String name = names.get(1);
```

This will get the element at index 1, which is `Julie`, and store it in a variable called `name`. We can also alter the elements in a list. This can be done with the `set()` method.

## Changing elements in a list

We can change elements in a List interface using the set() method, which takes an index and a new element as arguments. We're going to alter the element at index 1 here:

```
ames.set(1, "Monica");
```

With that, we have updated the value of Julie to Monica. If we want, we can also remove elements from a list.

## Removing elements from a list

We can use the remove() method to remove elements. The remove() method has two forms: remove(int index) and remove(Object o). The first one removes an element at a certain position, while the second one removes an element with a certain value:

```
names.remove(1); // Removes the element at index 1
names.remove("Janice"); // Removes the first occurrence
```

At this point, the list is empty again, because we've removed both elements. We removed Monica by using index 1 and we removed Janice by looking for an element with that value.

## Iterating through a list

There are different ways to iterate through a list. We're going to have a look at the two most common ways of doing this.

Firstly, we can use a regular for loop to iterate through a list. In this case, we're iterating over the list names. Let's assume we didn't remove both elements just now and it still has Janice and Monica in there:

```
for (int i = 0; i < names.size(); i++) {
    System.out.println(names.get(i));
}
```

The output will be as follows:

```
Janice
Monica
```

We can also achieve this same output by using a for-each loop:

```
for (String name : names) {
    System.out.println(name);
}
```

The difference between the regular for and for-each loop is that we have access to the index with the regular for. The for-each loop makes it easier to access the elements since we don't need to make sure we stay within the bounds, use the index, and update the index.

There are quite a few more methods available, but these are the most important ones to get you started. Now, let's have a look at the `Set` interface.

> **Note**
>
> You can find more information about all the collection in the official documentation here: `https://docs.oracle.com/en/java/javase/21/docs/api/java.base/java/util/doc-files/coll-overview.html`.

## Set

The `Set` interface is part of the Java collections framework and represents a generally unordered collection of unique elements. This means that an element can only be in the set once. The commonly used implementations of the `Set` interface are `HashSet`, `TreeSet`, and `LinkedHashSet`. Let's have a quick look at each.

### HashSet

Let's look at the most popular set first: `HashSet`. This is a widely used implementation of the `Set` interface based on a hash table. A hash table stores data in key-value pairs, enabling fast lookup by computing an item's key hash. It provides constant-time performance for basic operations such as `add`, `remove`, and `contains` (checking whether a `Set` interface contains a certain value).

*Constant-time complexity* means that the time it takes to perform these operations does not increase when the number of elements in the set grows, assuming that the hash function used to distribute the elements among the buckets does its job well. We'll cover hashing and bucket distribution in more detail at the end of this chapter, but hashing is pretty much the process of turning a certain value into another value – for example, turning a string into a number.

Please note that hash-based data structures such as `HashSet` do not guarantee any specific order of the elements stored in them. This is because the elements are placed in the set based on their hash values, which might not be related to any meaningful order to humans such as ascending or chronological order.

## TreeSet

TreeSet is an implementation of the Set interface based on a tree. It maintains elements in a sorted order according to their natural ordering or according to a custom comparator provided during instantiation. TreeSet provides logarithmic time performance for common operations such as add, remove, and contains.

*Logarithmic time complexity* means that the time it takes to perform these operations increases logarithmically with the size of the input, making TreeSet an efficient choice for reasonably large datasets.

As opposed to hash-based data structures such as HashSet, which do not maintain any specific order of elements, TreeSets are an excellent choice when you need a set that maintains elements in sorted order. This can be useful for tasks such as maintaining a list of unique items in sorted order, finding the smallest or largest element in a set quickly, or performing range queries on a set of data.

---

**Tree explained**

A *tree* in computer science is not something you'd have in your backyard. In computer science, a tree is a hierarchical data structure that represents relationships between different nodes. Each node is a data point. The first node, called the root, has no parents. Every other node descends (directly or indirectly) from the root along a single path. The nodes at the very ends of the paths, which have no children, are called *leaf nodes*. This structure is ideal for representing hierarchical relationships because each node has a parent (except for the root) and potentially many children, much like the branches and leaves of a natural tree.

In a tree, you can think of a path from the root to any node as a journey. Each step in the path represents a relationship between parent and child nodes. The *height* of a tree is the number of steps in the longest path from the root to a leaf. The *depth* of a node is the number of steps in the path from the root to that node. Trees with small heights relative to the number of nodes they contain are often efficient at finding nodes or adding and removing them. They are valuable for several use cases, such as organizing files in a filesystem or storing sorted data for efficient lookups, such as in TreeSet.

---

## LinkedHashSet

LinkedHashSet is an implementation of the Set interface that maintains elements in the order they were inserted and it is backed by a combination of a hash table and a doubly-linked list. LinkedHashSet provides constant-time performance for basic operations while preserving insertion order.

You would typically choose this implementation when the insertion order is important and the elements don't need to be sorted. And, since it's a Set, of course, the elements need to be unique (otherwise, List might be more logical). An example of a use case for LinkedHashSet would be maintaining a list of unique items in the order they were visited, such as web page browsing history or a playlist of unique songs in the order they were added. Another example is tracking events or user actions in an application in the order they occurred while ensuring that each event or action is processed only once.

To do all this, we do need to be able to perform some basic operations. So, let's have a look at how to do this.

## Performing basic operations on a set

The operations on a `Set` interface are very similar to the operations on `List`. Of course, we don't work with the index for the methods on `Set`. We'll start by learning how to add to sets.

### Adding elements to a set

Just like we did for `List`, we can add elements to a `Set` interface using the `add()` method. Here's how to do it:

```
Set<String> names = new HashSet<>();
names.add("Elizabeth");
names.add("Janie");
```

Sets cannot contain duplicate values. Adding the same value twice won't give an error and won't add the value another time.

With the same ease, we could have created a `LinkedHashSet` class, as follows:

```
Set<String> names = new LinkedHashSet<>();
```

We could have also created a `TreeSet` class:

```
Set<String> names = new TreeSet<>();
```

The operations on these sets would be the same.

### Changing the elements in a set

We cannot change elements in a `Set` directly. To modify an element, we must remove the old element and add the new one. So, let's learn how to remove elements.

### Removing elements from a set

We can remove elements from a `Set` interface using the `remove()` method. We cannot remove by index like we can for `List`, because the elements don't have an index:

```
names.remove("Janie");
```

After this, the set will only have one value, namely `Elizabeth`. Since sets don't have indexes, accessing the elements works a bit differently for them as well. We can access elements via iteration.

### Iterating through a set

We can iterate through a set using a `for-each` loop. We can't use a regular `for` loop since we don't have an index.

Here's an example:

```
for (String name : names) {
    System.out.println(name);
}
```

After the removal, our `Set` interface only has one name left. So, this `for-each` loop will output the following:

```
Elizabeth
```

And that's it for `Set`. Now, let's explore the `Map` data structure.

## Map

Another member of the collections framework is the `Map` interface. This interface represents a collection of key-value pairs. Keys are unique, while values can be duplicated. That's why we use the key to add and access the key-value pairs in a map. The commonly used implementations of the `Map` interface that we'll discuss are `HashMap` and `TreeMap`.

## HashMap

Probably the most popular one is `HashMap`. This is a widely used implementation of the `Map` interface that's based on a hash table. Just like `HashSet`, it provides constant-time performance for basic operations. However, it does not guarantee any specific order of the keys. `HashMap` is suitable for situations where you need fast lookups and modifications, such as storing configuration settings or counting word occurrences in a piece of text. When the order is important, we can use `TreeMap`.

## TreeMap

`TreeMap` is an implementation of the `Map` interface that's based on a tree. It maintains key-value pairs in a sorted order according to their natural ordering or a custom comparator provided during instantiation. We'll look at custom comparators soon as well, but it's pretty much a way of specifying the order in which it needs to be sorted.

`TreeMap` provides logarithmic time performance for common operations such as getting elements from the map and adding elements to the map. `TreeMap` is useful for scenarios where you need to maintain a sorted collection of key-value pairs, such as managing a leaderboard or tracking time-based events.

## LinkedHashMap

LinkedHashMap is another implementation of the Map interface. It combines the strengths of HashMap and TreeMap by providing constant-time performance for basic operations, similar to HashMap, while also maintaining the insertion order of key-value pairs. This order is the sequence in which keys are added to the map.

LinkedHashMap is essentially a HashMap implementation with an additional linked list that connects all entries, which allows it to remember the order of insertion. This is particularly useful in scenarios where the sequence of data matters, such as caching operations or maintaining a record of user activities.

Its usage is very similar to the other two implementations. We won't be showing all the implementations here because the basic operations are the same for each implementation. The only difference is that they have a specific order when you iterate over them, but iterating over them is done in the same way.

# Basic operations on maps

Map is quite different from the other collections. Let's learn how to perform the basic operations on Map.

### Adding elements to a map

There is no add() method for Map. We can add elements to a Map interface using the put() method:

```
Map<String, Integer> gfNrMap = new HashMap<>();
gfNrMap.put("Ross", 12);
gfNrMap.put("Chandler", 8);
```

This adds two key-value pairs to Map. Let's see how we can get the values out again.

### Getting elements from a map

We can get elements from a Map interface using the get() method. This is how we can get the Integer value associated with the Ross key:

```
int rossNrOfGfs = gfNrMap.get("Ross");
```

We can also use the key to modify the values of the map.

### Changing the elements of a map

We can change the elements in a Map interface using the put() method with an existing key:

```
gfNrMap.put("Chandler", 9);
```

The preceding code changes the value of 8 to 9 for the Chandler key. We cannot change the key. If we need to do this, we need to remove the key-value pair and add a new one.

## Removing elements from a map

The key is also used for removing elements from a map. We can do this with the remove () method.

```
gfNrMap.remove("Ross");
```

At this point, our map only contains one key-value pair. We can iterate through a map as well. This is a bit different than what we did for List and Set.

## Iterating through a map

We can iterate through the key-value pairs, the values, and the keys with a for-each loop. We need to call different methods on our map object to achieve this. We can use the entrySet (), keySet (), and values () methods for this.

Let's assume that we still have two key-value pairs in our map, with Ross and Chandler as keys. The following code snippet loops through the key-value pairs using the entrySet () method:

```
for (Map.Entry<String, Integer> entry : gfNrMap.entrySet()) {
    System.out.println(entry.getKey() + ": " +
        entry.getValue());
}
```

entrySet () provides a set of Map.Entry objects. On this object, we can use the getKey () and getValue () methods to get the key and the value, respectively. This will output the following:

```
Ross: 12
Chandler: 9
```

We can also loop through the keys:

```
for (String key : gfNrMap.keySet()) {
    System.out.println(key + ": " + gfNrMap.get(key));
}
```

This will output the following:

```
Ross: 12
Chandler: 9
```

You might be surprised that this is the same output as the previous snippet and contains the values as well, but this is because we are using the key to obtain the value. This is not possible when we loop through the values. Here's how we can do this:

```
for (Integer value : gfNrMap.values()) {
    System.out.println(value);
}
```

This will output the following:

```
12
9
```

Now, we can only see the values, since that is what we're looping through. Next, let's have a look at the last main interface: Queue.

# Queue

The last in line is the Queue interface. It's part of the Java collections framework and allows FIFO data storage. The head of the queue is the oldest element, and the tail is the newest element. Queues are useful for processing tasks in the order they are received. There is also a sub-interface called Deque, which is a special type of queue that allows you to get elements from both the head and the tail of the queue. This is why it can also be used for LIFO systems.

We'll only briefly deal with the different types of queues since this is the collection that's typically least used in the wild.

## Queue implementations

The Queue interface extends the Collection interface. There are several implementations, with some of the most common ones being PriorityQueue, LinkedList, and ArrayDeque. The Deque interface, which extends the Queue interface, adds support for double-ended queues, allowing the insertion and removal of elements from both ends of the queue. LinkedList and ArrayDeque are Deque implementations.

## Basic operations on the Queue interface

The basic operations on the Queue interface are a bit special because the elements can only be accessed at the ends of the queue.

## Adding elements to a queue

We can add elements to a queue using the add() or offer() methods. If a queue is at its maximum capacity, the add() method throws an exception when it cannot add to the queue. offer() would return false if it cannot add the element to the queue. Looking at the verbs it seems logical; *offer* is without obligation and the queue can turn down the offer when it's full, hence there is no exception if it's full. It simply returns false if it cannot append it to the queue. Whereas *add* really intents to add, if it doesn't work an exception will be thrown.

Here's how we can use both for LinkedList:

```
Queue<String> queue = new LinkedList<>();
queue.add("Task 1");
queue.offer("Task 2");
```

For objects of the Deque type, adding to the beginning of the queue works with different methods. LinkedList so happens to be of the Deque type. The add and offer methods add to the end of the queue, and so do the Deque type's special methods, addLast() and offerLast():

```
Deque<String> queue = new LinkedList<>();
queue.addLast("Task 1"); // or add
queue.offer("Task 2"); // or offerLast
```

Here's how to add to the beginning:

```
queue.addFirst("Task 3");
queue.offerFirst("Task 4");
```

The order of the elements in the queue is now (from head to tail) *Task 4, Task 3, Task 1, Task 2*.

## Getting elements from a queue

We can get the element at the head of a Queue interface using the peek() or element() method. They just return the value, without removing it from the queue.

Here's how to get the head of the queue with the peek() method:

```
String head = queue.peek();
```

The value of head becomes *Task 4*. The element() method throws an exception when it cannot return a value, while the peek() method doesn't. The peek() method returns null when the queue is empty.

For Deque, we can get elements at both the head and the tail. For the head, we can use getFirst() and peekFirst(). For the tail, we can use getLast() and peekLast(). Please note that getFirst() is the Deque equivalent of Queue's element(), even though these differ in name quite a bit.

You may wonder, why do we have two methods that do the same for all of these. They don't do the same, there's an important difference. The getFirst(), getLast(), and element() methods attempt to retrieve an end of the queue, but if the queue is empty, it throws a NoSuchElementException. In contrast, the peek(), peekFirst(), and peekLast() methods also retrieve the ends of the queue but return null if the queue is empty, thus they will not throw an exception.

## Changing the elements in a queue

We cannot change elements in a Queue interface directly. To modify an element, we must remove the old element and add the new one. So, let's see how to remove elements.

## Removing elements from a queue

We can remove elements from a queue using the remove() or poll() methods. These methods do two things:

1. Return the head of the queue.
2. Remove the head of the queue.

Here's an example:

```
String removedElement = queue.poll();
```

This is going to store *Task 4* in removedElement. At this point, the values in the queue will be *Task 3, Task 1, Task 2*.

This may not surprise you, but for Deque, we can remove elements from both ends. For the head, we use removeFirst() and pollFirst(). For the tail, we can use removeLast() and pollLast().

Again, the difference is in how they deal with null values:

- remove(), removeFirst(), and removeLast() throw a NoSuchElementException if the queue is empty.
- poll(), pollFirst(), and pollLast() return null without throwing an exception, signaling that the queue was empty.

Now that we know how to remove elements, let's learn how to iterate through a Queue interface.

## Iterating through a queue or deque

We can iterate through a queue or deque using a for-each loop. This doesn't remove theiterating through" elements from the queue:

```
for (String element : queue) {
    System.out.println(element);
}
```

This will output the following:

```
Task 3
Task 1
Task 2
```

The reason it's not printing *Task 4* is that we removed it in the previous section.

We have now covered the basics of the four main interfaces and some of the most common implementations. We can do more with collections, such as sorting them. Let's have a look at how to do that.

# Sorting collections

So far, we've learned how to create collections and how to perform basic operations on them. They have a lot of useful built-in methods, and one of them helps us sort collections. The reason we are paying attention to this one is because it's not as straightforward as some of the others.

Some types have a natural order, such as numbers. They can be easily sorted from small to large. The same goes for strings – we can sort them A-Z. But how do we sort a collection that contains custom objects of the `Task` type?

Stick with me – soon, you'll be able to do both natural ordering and custom ordering while using the `sort` method that's built into collections.

## Natural ordering

When we talk about natural ordering, we mean the default sorting order for a particular data type. For example, numbers are sorted in ascending order, while strings are sorted lexicographically. But still, Java wouldn't know this without us telling them that's what we want. That's why Java's built-in classes, such as `Integer` and `String`, implement the `Comparable` interface. This is what tells Java what the natural order is. Two interfaces are relevant for ordering: `Comparable` and `Comparator`. We will cover these next.

## The Comparable and Comparator interfaces

When a class implements the `Comparable` interface, we need to implement the `compareTo()` method. Here's an example of how a class would implement that interface:

```
public class Person implements Comparable<Person> {...}
```

The code is omitted, but as you can see it implements the interface. Now it needs to override the `compareTo` method.

This method defines how to sort two objects of the same type. The `compareTo()` method takes another object of the same type as an argument and returns a negative, zero, or positive integer based on how the two objects compare.

This is what the outcomes mean:

- 0 if the two objects are equal
- A positive value if the object is greater than the passed-in object
- A negative value if the object the method is called on is less than the passed-in object

The `Comparator` interface does something similar but is not meant to be implemented by a class. This interface is used for creating a custom `Comparator` on the fly and is typically implemented with a Lambda expression. We haven't seen Lambda expressions yet, but we will in the next chapter. `Comparator` can be passed to the `sort` method, to tell the `sort` method how to sort the items.

`Comparator` is not for natural sorting orders but for "one-off" sorting orders. It contains one method, `compare()`. This method takes two objects as arguments and returns a negative, zero, or positive integer based on the comparison. Here are what the values mean for the result of compare:

- 0 if the two objects are equal.
- A positive value if the first object is greater than the second (hence they are in the wrong order).
- A negative value if the first object is less than the second (hence they are in the right order).

Alright, enough talking. Let's see some implementations of `Comparable` and `Comparator`.

### Implementing compareTo()

So, there are roughly two options when we want to sort our custom types:

- Give them a natural order by making them implement `Comparable`.
- Implement `Comparator` and pass this to the `sort` method.

Let's start with the first one. We're going to give our `Person` class a natural order. To implement the natural ordering for a custom class, we need to implement the `Comparable` interface and the `compareTo()` method. Here's how to do that:

```
public class Person implements Comparable<Person> {
    int age; // not private to keep the example short
    String name;

    public Person(String name, int age) {
        this.name = name;
        this.age = age;
```

```
        }

    @Override
    public int compareTo(Person other) {
        return Integer.compare(this.age, other.age);
    }
}
```

Here, the Person class is given a natural order by implementing the Comparable interface.

The Person class now implements Comparable<Person>. This means that Person objects can now be compared to each other based on a natural ordering, which is determined by the compareTo() method. This method takes one input parameter. And it is always going to compare that one to the instance the compareTo() was called. It should return 0 if the objects are equal, a positive value if the object the method is called on is greater than the input parameter, and a negative value if the input parameter is bigger.

The Person class has two attributes: age (an integer) and name (a string). The constructor initializes these attributes with the given values. The compareTo() method is defined to compare Person objects based on their age, but we could also have chosen the length of the name to just give an example. In this compareTo() method, we use the Integer.compare() method to perform the comparison. It takes two integer values as arguments and returns the following:

- 0 if the two integers are equal
- A positive value if the first integer is greater than the second
- A negative value if the first integer is less than the second

In the context of the compareTo() method, this means the following:

- If two Person objects have the same age, the method will return 0 .
- If the current Person object's age is greater than the other object's age, the method will return a positive value.
- If the current Person object's age is less than the other object's age, the method will return a negative value.

These return values determine the natural ordering of the Person objects when they're sorted. In this case, the objects will be sorted by their age. Let's have a look at how to do this:

```
List<Person> personList = new ArrayList<>();
personList.add(new Person("Huub", 1));
personList.add(new Person("Joep", 4));
personList.add(new Person("Anne", 3));
Collections.sort(personList);
```

Before sorting, the elements have the order they were added in. After sorting, they are sorted from age low to high, so we get Huub, Anne, and Joep.

But again, since we wrote it, we could have chosen anything. And whatever we choose determines the natural order. Natural order is, for example, to sort strings A-Z and numbers 0-9. What the natural order for your custom class is, is up to you. It depends on how you implement the compareTo() method.

Sometimes, we'll need a different order than specified in the compareTo() method. For example, sorting strings by the length of the word. Luckily, we can also create an order that is not connected to the class. Let's have a look at how to do custom sorting next.

## Implementing compare()

There are several ways to implement custom ordering using the Comparator interface:

- Create a separate class (not typical)
- Use an anonymous inner class (better)
- Implement it with a Lambda expression (most common)

For example, to sort a list of Person objects by their names, we can create this anonymous class:

```
Comparator<Person> nameComparator = new
  Comparator<Person>() {
    @Override
    public int compare(Person p1, Person p2) {
        return p1.getName().compareTo(p2.getName());
    }
};
```

Here, we created a new Comparator object called nameComparator that implements the Comparator interface. This custom comparator will be used to compare Person objects based on their names. The compare() method is implemented within the anonymous inner class. Inside the compare() method, we use the compareTo() method of the String class to perform a lexicographic comparison between the names of the two Person objects.

The compare() method in the Comparator interface follows the same rules for return values as the compareTo() method in the Comparable interface:

- If the two objects being compared are equal, the method will return 0.
- If the first object is greater than the second, the method will return a positive value.
- If the first object is less than the second, the method will return a negative value.

To use the custom comparator to sort a list of `Person` objects, we can pass the `nameComparator` object as an argument to the `Collections.sort()` method, like this:

```
List<Person> personList = new ArrayList<>();
personList.add(new Person("Huub", 1));
personList.add(new Person("Joep", 4));
personList.add(new Person("Anne", 3));
Collections.sort(personList, nameComparator);
```

In this example, `personList` will be sorted according to the names of the `Person` objects in alphabetical order, as specified by nameComparator. If we don't specify nameComparator, it will use the natural order and sort by age. Before sorting, the elements have the order they were added in. After sorting, they are sorted by name, A-Z, so we get Anne, Huub, and Joep.

---

**Implementing Comparator with a Lambda expression**

It is more common to use a Lambda expression to implement the `Comparator` interface. This way, we have a shorter syntax for creating a comparator without the need for an anonymous inner class. You don't need to understand this yet, but here's an example of using a Lambda expression to create a comparator that sorts Person objects by their names:

```
Comparator<Person> nameComparatorLambda = (p1, p2) ->
    p1.getName().compareTo(p2.getName());
```

This works the same. We can pass it as an argument to the `Collections.sort()` method:

```
Collections.sort(personList, nameComparatorLambda);
```

Since we now have custom comparators, we can create as many as we can think of. Here's another example of sorting `Person` objects by the length of their names using a Lambda expression:

```
Comparator<Person> nameLengthComparator = (p1, p2) ->
    Integer.compare(p1.getName().length(),
        p2.getName().length());

Collections.sort(personList, nameLengthComparator);
```

Here, nameLengthComparator compares `Person` objects based on the length of their names. personList will be sorted in ascending order of the name lengths. Our names all have a length of four, and therefore they will remain in the order they were added.

---

The advantage of using `Comparator` over the natural order defined by the `Comparable` interface is that you can define multiple custom orderings for the same class without modifying the class itself. In addition, we can easily change the ordering criteria at runtime by providing a different `Comparator` object to the `Collections.sort()` method.

Which option we choose depends on what we need. If we want to give our object a natural order, we have to implement the `Comparable` interface. If we don't have access to the class directly, or we want to specify an order that should not be the natural order, we can use `Comparator`.

We can also use comparators when we create `TreeSets` and `TreeMaps`. This will determine how the values in these collections are going to be sorted.

## TreeSets and TreeMaps

`TreeSet` and `TreeMap` are sorted collections that use the natural order of their elements or a custom comparator for sorting. This is why we cannot create `TreeSets` or `TreeMaps` for objects that don't have a natural order (they don't implement the `Comparable` interface) without providing a custom comparator during the creation of `TreeSet` or `TreeMap`. Let's see how to do this for each of them.

## The order of elements in TreeSet

As a quick reminder, `TreeSet` is a `Set` implementation that stores elements in sorted order. That's why the elements in `TreeSet` must implement the `Comparable` interface or a custom comparator must be passed along during the construction of `TreeSet`.

Here's an example of creating a `TreeSet` class of `Person` objects using the natural order:

```
TreeSet<Person> personTreeSet = new TreeSet<>();
personTreeSet.add(new Person("Huub", 1));
personTreeSet.add(new Person("Joep", 4));
personTreeSet.add(new Person("Anne", 3));
```

In this example, the `Person` class implements the `Comparable` interface, so `TreeSet` will use the natural order defined by the `compareTo()` method in the `Person` class (this was sorted by age).

If you want to create a `TreeSet` class with a custom comparator, you can pass the comparator as an argument to the `TreeSet` constructor, like this:

```
Comparator<Person> nameComparator = (p1, p2) ->
    p1.getName().compareTo(p2.getName());
TreeSet<Person> personTreeSetByName = new
    TreeSet<>(nameComparator);
personTreeSetByName.add(new Person("Huub", 1));
personTreeSetByName.add(new Person("Joep", 4));
personTreeSetByName.add(new Person("Anne", 3));
```

In this example, `TreeSet` will be sorted by the names of the `Person` objects, as specified by `nameComparator`. We can do something similar for `TreeMap`.

### The order of elements in TreeMap

In case you've forgotten, `TreeMap` is a `Map` implementation that stores key-value pairs in a sorted order based on the keys. That's why the keys in `TreeMap` must implement the `Comparable` interface or we should send in a custom comparator when we create `TreeMap`.

Let's start with a `TreeMap` class of `Person` objects as keys and their ages as values using the natural order:

```
TreeMap<Person, Integer> personTreeMap = new TreeMap<>();
personTreeMap.put(new Person("Huub", 1), 1);
personTreeMap.put(new Person("Joep", 4), 4);
personTreeMap.put(new Person("Anne", 3), 3);
```

In this example, the `Person` class implements the `Comparable` interface, so `TreeMap` will use the natural order defined by the `compareTo()` method in the `Person` class.

If you want to create a `TreeMap` class with a custom comparator, you can pass the comparator as an argument to the `TreeMap` constructor, like this:

```
Comparator<Person> nameComparator = (p1, p2) ->
    p1.getName().compareTo(p2.getName());
TreeMap<Person, Integer> personTreeMapByName = new
    TreeMap<>(nameComparator);
personTreeMapByName.put(new Person("Huub", 1), 1);
personTreeMapByName.put(new Person("Joep", 4), 4);
personTreeMapByName.put(new Person("Anne", 3), 3);
```

Now, this `TreeMap` will be sorted by the names of the `Person` objects, as specified by `nameComparator`.

So, `TreeSet` and `TreeMap` are sorted collections that use either the natural order of their elements or a custom comparator to sort their contents.

By using the `Comparable` interface and custom comparators, you can define multiple orderings for your custom classes and easily control the sorting behavior of your collections.

## Working with generics

We have been working with generics in this chapter. Generics are flexible and used for (amongst others) collections. We were passing in values to these collections by the specified type between the angle brackets. We can create a collection with a type parameter like this:

```
List<String> names = new ArrayList<>();
```

This is because the `List` interface and the `ArrayList` class are created with a type parameter (generic). This makes the class a lot more flexible, while still ensuring type safety. Let's have a look at how this was done before generics to understand why they are so great.

## Life before generics – objects

When we didn't have generics, all collections would have objects. You'd have to manually check to make sure the item in the list was of the type you hoped it was. And if it was, you'd have to cast it to this type to use this, much like this:

```
List = new ArrayList();
list.add("Hello");
list.add("World");
list.add(123); // Integer inserted in a List of strings.
               //  Allowed, but not logical.

for (int i = 0; i < list.size(); i++) {
    Object item = list.get(i);
    if (item instanceof String) {
        String strItem = (String) item; // Type casting
                                         //  required
        System.out.println(strItem);
    } else {
        System.out.println("Item is not a String");
    }
}
```

In the preceding code, we created a list without specifying any type. This creates a list of the `Object` type. And as you probably remember, all Java objects are of the `Object` type. Then, we added two strings and an integer to it. This is technically allowed since the list accepts objects of any type, but it can lead to logical errors in your code.

Later, when we iterate over the list, we must manually check the type of each item with `instanceof` before we can safely cast it to a string with `(String) item`. If we try to cast an item of the wrong type, the code will throw a `ClassCastException` error at runtime. This can be time-consuming and error-prone, which is one of the main reasons why generics were introduced.

Let's have a closer look at generics and see them outside of the collection use case. We'll learn how to create a class with a generic and why we would do that.

## Use case of generics

Let's start by creating two types that we are going to be putting in a bag class. We'll do this first without generics.

Here is a public `class` called `Laptop`:

```
public class Laptop {
    private String brand;
    private String model;

    public Laptop(String brand, String model) {
        this.brand = brand;
        this.model = model;
    }

    // Getters and setters omitted
}
```

And here is a public `class` called `Book`:

```
public class Book {
    private String title;
    private String author;

    public Book(String title, String author) {
        this.title = title;
        this.author = author;
    }

    // Getters and setters omitted
}
```

A book and a laptop are typical things to store in a bag. Let's write the Java code to do this. Without generics, we would need two classes. The first will be for `Laptop`:

```
public class LaptopBag {
    private Laptop;

    public LaptopBag(Laptop laptop) {
        this.laptop = laptop;
    }

    public Laptop getLaptop() {
```

```
            return laptop;
        }

        public void setLaptop(Laptop laptop) {
            this.laptop = laptop;
        }
    }
```

The second will be for Book:

```
public class BookBag {
    private Book;

    public BookBag(Book book) {
        this.book = book;
    }

    public Book getBook() {
        return book;
    }

    public void setBook(Book book) {
        this.book = book;
    }
}
```

Now, we have two custom classes, Laptop and Book, and two bag classes, LaptopBag and BookBag, each holding a specific type of item. However, there is a lot of duplicate code in the LaptopBag and BookBag classes. We could solve this by, instead of making Bag specific for one type, allowing it to hold Object types, like this:

```
public class ObjectBag {
    private Object;

    public ObjectBag(Object object) {
        this.object = object;
    }

    public Object getObject() {
        return object;
    }

    public void setObject(Object object) {
        this.object = object;
```

```
        }
    }
```

This class allows us to add a `Laptop`, `Book`, or `Person` class. Pretty much anything – it doesn't care. But that comes with some disadvantages as well. Since the `ObjectBag` class can store any type of object, there is no way to ensure type safety at compile time. This can lead to runtime exceptions, such as `ClassCastException`, if we accidentally mix different types of objects in our code.

Very much related to this is the casting we need to do when retrieving an object from `ObjectBag`. To get access to all its methods and fields, we need to explicitly cast it back to its original type. This adds verbosity to our code and increases the chances of getting a `ClassCastException` error.

Luckily, generics come to the rescue! Generics offer a way to create flexible and type-safe classes that can handle different types without the disadvantages associated with using an `Object` type. So, let's see how we can rewrite the `ObjectBag` class using generics.

## Syntax generics

Generics are used by specifying a type parameter within angle brackets, such as `<T>`, where T represents a type. Here's a generic solution that uses a single `Bag` class:

```java
public class Bag<T> {
    private T content;

    public Bag(T content) {
        this.content = content;
    }

    public T getContent() {
        return content;
    }

    public void setContent(T content) {
        this.content = content;
    }
}
```

By using the generic type parameter, `<T>`, we can now create a more flexible Bag class that can hold any type of item, such as `Laptop` or `Book`. At the same time, we can ensure type safety and avoid the need for explicit casting. Here's how we can use the Bag class:

```java
Bag<Laptop> laptopBag = new Bag<>(new Laptop("Dell", "XPS
    15"));
Bag<Book> bookBag = new Bag<>(new Book("Why Java is fun",
    "Maaike and Seán"));
```

To conclude, generics add flexibility when you're creating reusable classes, all while maintaining type safety. However, sometimes, we may want to restrict the types that can be used with a generic class. This is where bounded generics come into play. Let's take a look.

## Bounded generics

Without bounded generics, we may run into situations where we need to call methods specific to a certain type or its subclasses within the generic class. We cannot do that directly as the generic class knows nothing about the specific methods of the types it handles. Here's a short example to illustrate the need for bounded generics.

Let's suppose we have an interface called `Measurable`:

```
public interface Measurable {
    double getMeasurement();
}
```

We want to have a class that is a lot like Bag, but only accepts generics that implement the `Measurable` interface. That's why we need to create a generic `MeasurementBag` class that can only hold objects that implement the `Measurable` interface. We can use bounded generics to achieve this:

```
public class MeasurementBag<T extends Measurable> {
    private T content;

    public MeasurementBag(T content) {
        this.content = content;
    }

    public T getContent() {
        return content;
    }

    public void setContent(T content) {
        this.content = content;
    }

    public double getContentMeasurement() {
        return content.getMeasurement();
    }
}
```

By using `<T extends Measurable>`, we specify that the generic type, T, must be a class that implements the `Measurable` interface. This ensures that only objects of types that implement `Measurable` can be used with the `MeasurementBag` class. That's why we can safely call the getMeasurement() method within the MeasurementBag class – since we know that T is guaranteed to implement the Measurable interface.

So, these bounded generics allow us to restrict the types that are used in the generic class and ensure that they share a common set of methods. That's why it's safe to call those methods within the generic class. Does this sound familiar to what collections do? For example, Collections.sort() requires a collection with objects that implement Comparable when we only pass in one argument (the collection). Generics and bounded type parameters are actually very common in Java's own code.

We have now seen bounded generics that specify an upper bound (a superclass or interface) for the generic type. This ensures that only objects of that type or its subclasses can be used with the generic class. There are also lower bounds, but these are out of scope here. You may run into these in the Java source code, but it's not very likely you'll be working with these yourself.

Let's dive into another concept that's important for using custom objects with HashMap and HashSet.

# Hashing and overriding hashCode()

Hashing is an important concept in Java. It is used to efficiently store and retrieve data in various data structures, such as HashMaps and HashSets. It's also a very interesting topic. You'll get quite far without understanding what this does, but at some point, you may wonder about the horrible performance of your HashMap class. And understanding what is going on is not possible without understanding hashing. So, let's discuss the basic concepts of hashing, the role of the hashCode() method in collections, and best practices for overriding the hashCode() method in your custom classes.

## Understanding basic hashing concepts

Hashing is a method that transforms data into a piece of code called a hash code. Think of it like taking a huge pile of books and assigning each book a unique number. A good hash function should give different books different numbers and spread them evenly. This makes it easy to find and organize the books. All objects in Java have a hashCode() method.

## hashCode() and its role in collections

The Object class has the hashCode() method defined. Since all classes inherit from Object (indirectly), all the objects have the hashCode() method. This method returns an integer value. Two objects that are the same should have the same hash code.

When you use an object in a `HashMap` or `HashSet` class, its `hashCode()` is used to decide its position in the data structure. When we create custom classes, we sometimes need to override `hashCode()`.

## Overriding hashCode() and best practices

When we create a custom class and plan to use it as a key in a `HashMap` class or an element in a `HashSet` class, we need to override the `hashCode()` method. This ensures that our class has a consistent and efficient hash function.

Here are some best practices for overriding `hashCode()`:

- Include all fields that are used in the `equals()` method. This way, equal objects have the same hash code.
- Use a simple algorithm to combine the hash codes of individual fields, such as multiplying by a prime number and adding the hash codes of the fields.

Here's an example of `hashCode()` implemented in our `Person` class:

```
public class Person {
    private String name;
    private int age;

    // Constructor, getters, and setters

    @Override
    public int hashCode() {
        int result = 17;
        result = 31 * result + (name == null ? 0 :
          name.hashCode());
        result = 31 * result + age;
        return result;
    }
}
```

As you can see, the `hashCode()` method has been added.

**Explaining hashCode() in more detail**

The numbers 17 and 31 are used as part of the hash code calculation for the Person class. These are both prime numbers and using prime numbers in hash code calculations helps to produce a better distribution of hash codes and reduces the likelihood of hashcode collisions. 17 is used as the initial value for the result variable. It's an arbitrary prime number that helps ensure that the hash code calculation starts with a non-zero value.

By doing so, it reduces the likelihood of generating similar hash codes for different objects, which, in turn, helps minimize collisions. 31 is used as a multiplier in the hashcode calculation. Multiplying the current result by a prime number (31, in this case) before adding the next field's hash code helps mix the hash codes of individual fields more effectively. This results in a better distribution of hash codes across the possible range. 31 is often chosen because it can be computed efficiently using bitwise operations (that is, x * 31 is the same as (x << 5) - x)).

## Using hashCode() in custom generic types

When creating custom generic classes, we may need to use the hashCode() method of the objects being stored. To do this, we can simply call the hashCode() method on the object or use the Objects.hashCode() utility method, which handles null values gracefully:

```java
public class Bag<T> {
    private T content;

    // Constructor, getters, and setters

    @Override
    public int hashCode() {
        return Objects.hashCode(content);
    }
}
```

Understanding hashing and the hashCode() method is important when working with Java collections, especially when using custom classes combined with hashed collections. If we follow best practices for overriding hashCode() and using it in custom generic types, we can achieve better performance when adding and accessing elements in our collections.

# Exercises

You may not have noticed directly, but we've been longing for this! We can finally add collections and generics to the applications of our apps. Life will get easier. Let's look at some exercises:

1.  Our park has an assortment of dinosaurs and their related data. Implement a List interface that stores a custom dinosaur class.

2.  We need to ensure that the most dangerous dinosaurs are taken care of first. Write a PriorityQueue class that sorts dinosaurs based on a custom Comparator interface, such as their danger level.

3.  Generics can make our code more reusable. Create a class called Crate with a generic for the thing you'd like to store in there. This could be food or drinks for the restaurant, but also dinosaurs if we need to relocate them.

4.  Create three instances of your Crate class with different classes in your program – for example, Dinosaur, Jeep, and DinosaurFood.

5.  Hashing is essential for efficient data handling. Override the hashCode() method in your dinosaur class.

6.  Challenging: We have some issues with finding personnel for the restaurants. Let's automate the ordering at the ice cream store in our park. Write a program that does the following:

    *   Ask how many ice creams the guest would list.

    *   For every ice cream, ask what flavor they would like (come up with a few choices for flavors, make them dinosaur-themed if you dare) and how many scoops.

    *   For simplicity, let's assume that each guest can only order every flavor once. Add all the ice creams and their descriptions to a List interface that contains maps. These maps will represent the ice creams and the amount of scoops.

7.  Challenging: Elaborate on *Exercise 13.6*. Print the order (loop over the list!) and say it will be ready at the current time plus 10 minutes (you need to calculate this, not print that literally!)

## Project – advanced dinosaur care system

As the number of dinosaurs in our park increases, the need for a more sophisticated data management system becomes apparent. Generics and collections to the rescue!

We will continue to build on the dinosaur care system. The system should handle collections of dinosaurs, allowing functionalities such as sorting dinosaurs based on various parameters, ensuring the uniqueness of dinosaurs, and so on.

Here are the steps we're going to take.

**Step 1: Add additional Java classes:**

- Create a new package named `collections`.

- Inside this package, create a class named `DinosaurComparator`. This class should implement `Comparator<Dinosaur>`. Override the `compare()` method to sort dinosaurs based on various parameters, such as age, size, and so on.

> **Note**
> Normally you don't create a class for comparator, but we don't see lambdas until the next chapter.

**Step 2: Extend the dinosaur care system:**

- Change the `List` interface in the `DinosaurCareSystem` class that holds the `Dinosaur` objects to a `Set` interface. This will ensure the uniqueness of the dinosaurs.

- Create a method called `sortDinosaurs()` that sorts the `Dinosaur` set using `DinosaurComparator`.

Here is some sample code to get you started:

```java
import java.util.*;

public class DinosaurCareSystem {
    private Set<Dinosaur> dinosaurs;
    private List<Activity> activities;

    public DinosaurCareSystem() {
        dinosaurs = new HashSet<>();
        activities = new ArrayList<>();
    }

    public void addDinosaur(Dinosaur dinosaur) {
        dinosaurs.add(dinosaur);
    }

    public void logActivity(Activity activity) {
        activities.add(activity);
    }

    public List<Dinosaur> sortDinosaurs() {
        List<Dinosaur> sortedDinosaurs = new
            ArrayList<>(dinosaurs);
```

```
        Collections.sort(sortedDinosaurs, new
          DinosaurComparator());
        return sortedDinosaurs;
    }


    //... existing methods for handling exceptions and
        other functionalities here
}
```

And here's the DinosaurComparator class that you could use:

```
import java.util.Comparator;

public class DinosaurComparator implements
  Comparator<Dinosaur> {
    @Override
    public int compare(Dinosaur d1, Dinosaur d2) {
    // assume Dinosaur has a getSize() method
        return d1.getSize().compareTo(d2.getSize());        }
}
```

**Step 3: Interact with the system:**

- In your main  class, you can interact with the DinosaurCareSystem object similar to what did in the previous steps, but now, add the functionality to sort the dinosaurs based on the parameters.

Do you want more? You can expand on this by adding more functionalities, such as sorting based on different parameters, searching for dinosaurs based on their properties, and more.

## Summary

Alright, you've made your way through another tough chapter. In this chapter, we explored the fundamentals of collections and generics in Java. We began by discussing the need for collections in programming and provided an overview of the different collection types available in Java, including List, Set, Map, Queue, and Deque. We examined the specific implementations of each collection type, such as ArrayList, LinkedList, HashSet, TreeSet, HashMap, TreeMap, and more, along with their differences and appropriate use cases. We also covered basic operations, such as adding, removing, and iterating through elements in each collection.

Then, we moved on to sorting collections. We made the distinction between natural ordering and custom ordering with the use of the `Comparable` and `Comparator` interfaces. We learned how to implement the `compareTo()` and `compare()` methods, as well as how to sort lists, sets, and maps using `Collections.sort()` and the `TreeSet` and `TreeMap` classes.

We then delved into generics, explaining their importance in providing type safety. The syntax and basic usage of generics were demonstrated, including the use of the `extends` keyword in bounded generics.

Next, we proceeded to learn how to create custom generic types by defining generic classes. We also covered the implications of not having generics, and how to create instances of generic types.

Lastly, we discussed basic hashing concepts and the role of the `hashCode()` method in collections. We provided guidelines for overriding `hashCode()` and best practices for its implementation, emphasizing its significance in custom generic types.

At this point, you should have gained a solid understanding of the differences between `List`, `Set`, `Map`, and `Queue`, as well as have basic knowledge of working with generics and hashing. You are now ready for the next exciting topic: Lambda expressions.

# 14

# Lambda Expressions

In this chapter, we will cover lambda expressions, which is one of my favorite features. Introduced in Java 8, lambda expressions (*lambdas*) brought functional programming to Java. First, we will define a *functional interface* and its relationship with lambdas. We will demonstrate both custom and API-based lambda expressions. We will also explain the concept of "final or effectively final" concerning local variables used inside a lambda expression.

After that, we will cover method references. We will discuss and present example code showing bound, unbound, static, and constructor method references. Lastly, we will explain the critical nature of context in understanding method references.

This chapter covers the following main topics:

- Understanding lambda expressions
- Exploring functional interfaces from the API
- Mastering method references

## Technical requirements

The code for this chapter can be found on GitHub at `https://github.com/PacktPublishing/Learn-Java-with-Projects/tree/main/ch14`.

## Understanding lambda expressions

Lambda expressions save on keystrokes and therefore make your code more concise and hence, more readable and maintainable. For this to work, the compiler has to be able to generate the code that you no longer type in. This brings us to our first topic: functional interfaces. To understand lambdas, we must first understand functional interfaces.

## Functional Interfaces

Recall that an interface has `default`, `static`, `private`, and `abstract` methods. A concrete (non-abstract) class that implements an interface must provide code for all of the `abstract` methods. *A functional interface is an interface with just one abstract method* – `default`, `static`, and `private` methods do not count. Neither do any methods inherited from `Object`. This one `abstract` method is known as the *functional method.*

## Lambda expressions

*A lambda expression is an instance of a class that implements a functional interface.* The lambda is boiled down to its bare essentials. Lambdas look a lot like methods (and indeed in some quarters are called "anonymous methods"). However, a lambda is an instance with everything, but the method stripped away.

Let's start with a sample functional interface and how a regular class would implement it:

```
interface SampleFI{
    void m();
}
class SampleClass implements SampleFI{
    @Override
    public void m(){System.out.println("m()");}
}
```

Now, let us examine the lambda version which does the same thing:

```
        SampleFI lambda = () -> System.out.println("m()");
        lambda.m();
```

The preceding two lines of code can appear in any method. The first line declares/defines the lambda and the second line executes it. Note that, when defining the lambda, there is no mention of a class implementing the functional interface `SampleFI` and also, there is no mention of the functional method `m()`. In fact, in the lambda declaration, the `()` is the parameter list for `m()`, which takes in nothing; the `->` token separates the method header from the method body and the `System.out.println("m()")` is the code for the method `m()`. Don't worry, we will explain lambda syntax in detail very shortly with further code examples.

Bear in mind that lambdas save us from typing unnecessary code. For this to happen, the compiler must generate the (missing) code for us in the background. That is why lambdas are only applicable to functional interfaces – the compiler can infer a lot from the interface definition, due to the presence of only one abstract method. The compiler sees the one abstract method and knows immediately the signature required in the lambda. So, to recap:

- Lambdas make your code more concise
- Lambdas only work with functional interfaces
- A lambda expression is an instance of a class that implements a functional interface

Now let us look at some examples.

### Lambda expressions – example 1

*Figure 14.1* presents a custom lambda with an associated functional interface:

```
3    @FunctionalInterface // a functional interface
4    interface I{
5        // one abstract method
6        void m();
7    }
8    public class BasicLambdas {
9        public static void main(String[] args) {
10           // define the lambda
11           I lambda1 = () -> {
12               System.out.println("First lambda!");
13           };
14           // execute the lambda
15           lambda1.m(); // First lambda!
16
17           I lambda2 = () -> System.out.println("Second lambda!");
18           lambda2.m(); // Second lambda!
19
20       }
21    }
```

Figure 14.1 – A functional interface with a lambda expression

In this figure, we define a functional interface SomeFunctionalInterface.

```
interface SomeFunctionalInterface {
    void m();
}
```

It has one abstract method, named m(). As coded, this functional interface, SomeFunctionalInterface, can now be used in lambda expressions.

Lines 11-13 define the first lambda expression, namely `lambda1`:

```
SomeFunctionalInterface lambda1 = () -> {
    System.out.println("First lambda!");
};
```

The reference type is of the `SomeFunctionalInterface` type, our functional interface type. The `lambda1` reference is assigned (to refer to) the instance of the class that implements `SomeFunctionalInterface`.

On the right-hand side of the assignment are round brackets, `()`. These are for the `m()` method in the interface, `SomeFunctionalInterface`. No parameters have been defined in the method declaration in the interface, so there are no parameters being passed in. As there are no parameters, `()` is required. Note that there is no need to mention the method name – this is because, as `SomeFunctionalInterface` is a functional interface, the compiler knows the only abstract method is `m()`. And as `m()` defines no parameters, the lambda header is simply `()`.

The arrow token, `->`, separates the method header (the parameters coming in, if any) from the method body. In this instance, the method body is a block of code; in other words, there are curly braces `{ }`, as there would be in a normal method. Once you specify a block of code, the usual rules with a block are followed – meaning, the compiler backs off and does nothing for you. For example, if you wanted to `return` something from the block, you must do this yourself. In the next example, we will see that the compiler will do the `return` for you, provided you do not use a code block.

The lambda in this example is simply outputting `"First lambda!"` to the screen. The semi-colon on line 13 is the normal end of statement token. Lines 11-13 simply *define* the lambda. No code has been executed at this point.

Line 15, `lambda1.m()` executes the lambda referred to by `lambda1`, resulting in `"First lambda!"` being output to the screen.

Line 17 defines a similar lambda except that it is even more concise:

```
SomeFunctionalInterface lambda2 = () ->
    System.out.println("Second lambda!");
```

This lambda, `lambda2`, takes advantage of the fact that the compiler can do even more work for us. If you have only one statement to execute, then, as with other constructs such as loops, a set of curly braces is not necessary. As we are only executing `System.out.println()`, we do not need the curly braces, `{ }`. The semi-colon at the end of line 17 is actually for the end of the assignment statement and not the end of `System.out.println()`. In other words, the semi-colon at the end of line 17 is the same semi-colon at the end of line 13 (and not the semi-colon at the end of line 12).

Again, line 17 only defines the lambda and no code has been executed. Line 18, `lambda2.m()` executes the lambda, resulting in `"Second lambda!"` being output to the screen.

Note, the @FunctionalInterface annotation (line 3 in *Figure 14.1*). This annotation ensures that the interface defines only one abstract method. Although optional, it is good practice to use it, as it highlights to other developers our intention with this interface. In addition, use of this annotation enables the compiler to step in if we fail to provide exactly one abstract method.

Let's look at another example. This time, the functional method will accept a parameter and return a value.

### Lambda expressions – example 2

*Figure 14.2* presents an example that will enable us to discuss further nuances:

```
5        // Functional Interface
6        @FunctionalInterface
7    ⓘ↓  interface Evaluate<T> {
8    ⓘ↓      boolean check(T t);
9        }
10   ▶   public class TestPredicate {
11   ▶       public static void main(String[] args) {
12               Evaluate<Integer> isItPositive = (Integer n) -> {return n > 0;};
13               System.out.println(isItPositive.check( t -1));//false
14               System.out.println(isItPositive.check( t +1));//true
15
16               Evaluate<String> isMale = s -> s.startsWith("Mr.");
17               System.out.println(isMale.check( t "Mr. Sean Kennedy"));//true
18               System.out.println(isMale.check( t "Ms. Maaike van Putten"));//false
19           }
20       }
```

Figure 14.2 - A more complex functional interface with a lambda expression

In this figure, the Evaluate function interface is generically typed for <T>. This means that we can use it for various types, such as Integer (line 12) and String (line 16). The check functional method (line 8) takes in a parameter of type T, namely t, and returns a boolean value. This particular functional interface is very similar to one we will look at later from the Java API, namely Predicate. By way of contrast, the first lambda (line 12) is coded quite differently from the second lambda (line 16).

On line 12, we declare an Evaluate reference, namely isItPositive, that is typed for integers only. With lambdas, context is key. As we have typed isItPositive for Integer, this means that the identifier, n, in round brackets is of the Integer type! We have explicitly specified the type for n in this example, but this is not necessary since the compiler can figure it out from the context. In other words, we could have just used (n) or simply n in the lambda and it would have worked. We just left it as (Integer n) so that the relationship between the lambda (line 12) and the check (T t) functional method (line 8) is clearer.

The right-hand side of = on line 12 we have `(Integer n) -> {return n>0;}`. This is the code for the `check(T t)` method in the class implementing `Evaluate`. Therefore, one parameter is required, typed for `Integer` due to the `Evaluate<`*Integer*`>` declaration, and a `boolean` value must be returned.

We have the `->` token again to separate the method header from the method body.

On line 12, as with all lambdas, the right-hand side of the `->` token is the method body. In this case, we have `{return n>0;}`. As we have used curly braces, we must follow regular syntax rules when inside a code block. Given that the `check(T t)` method has a `boolean` return type, we must return a `boolean` value from the code block. Also, the `return` statement requires a closing semi-colon as usual. The overall assignment statement requires a closing semi-colon also. This is why there are two semi-colons near the end (line 12). What we are saying in this lambda is that if the `Integer` type passed in is greater than 0, we return `true`; otherwise, we return `false`.

Line 13, `isItPositive.check(-1)` executes the lambda, passing in `-1`, which returns `false`. Line 14, `isItPositive.check(+1)` also executes the lambda, this time passing in `+1`, which returns `true`.

Line 16 is: `Evaluate<String> isMale = s -> s.startsWith("Mr.");`. This defines an `Evaluate` lambda, typed for `String`, referred to by the `isMale` reference. As we typed the lambda for `String`, the parameter this time coming in, namely `s`, is of type `String`. Remember, what we are defining on line 16 is effectively the code for the `check(T t)` method. Notice that this time, we have not specified the type for `s` as the compiler figures it out from the context (`Evaluate<String>`). Also, as there is just one parameter and we have not specified the type, we can leave out the round brackets, `()`. However, as we have seen already, if you have no parameters at all, you must specify `()`.

Also, on line 16, note that as we have not used a code block, we do not need an explicit `return` statement as the compiler will do that for us. As `s` is a `String`, we can call `String` methods; which is why we have no issue calling `startsWith("Mr.")`. The semi-colon at the end of the line is for the overall assignment statement and not for the lambda (as none is required). In this lambda, we just evaluate the string passed in to see if it begins with "Mr." and if it does, `true` is returned; otherwise, `false` is returned.

With the lambda now defined, we can execute it. Line 17, `isMale.check("Mr. Sean Kennedy")` returns `true` and line 18, `isMale.check("Ms. Maaike van Putten")` returns `false`.

As you can see, the compiler infers a lot, saving us a lot of typing. It takes a while to get used to lambdas but once you do, you will love them. *Table 14.1* summarizes the syntax:

| Functional Interface | Sample Lambda Expressions |
|---|---|
| ```
interface FI{

    void m();

}
``` | ```
FI fi1 = () -> System.out.
println("lambda");

fi1.m(); // outputs "lambda"

FI fi2 = () -> { System.out.
println("lambda"); } ;

fi2.m(); // outputs "lambda"
``` |
| ```
interface FI{

    int m(int x);

}
``` | ```
FI fi3 = (int x) -> { return x * x;};

System.out.println(fi3.m(5)); // 25

FI fi4 = x -> x * x;

System.out.println(fi4.m(6)); // 36
``` |
| ```
interface FI{

    String m(String a,
String b);

}
``` | ```
FI fi5 = (s1, s2) -> s1 + s2;

// next line returns 'Sean Kennedy'

System.out.println(fi5.m("Sean", "
Kennedy"));


FI fi6 = (String s1 , String s2) ->
{return s1 + s2; };

// next line returns 'Sean Kennedy'

System.out.println(fi6.m("Sean", "
Kennedy"));
``` |

Table 14.1 – Examples of functional interfaces and associated lambda expressions

The longer syntax, with the parameter types, code blocks, and `return` statements, is syntactically similar to regular methods (except the method name is omitted). The shorter, more concise syntax, demonstrates just how much the compiler can infer from the surrounding context. This is possible as there is only one `abstract` method in a functional interface. Lambdas cannot and do not work with interfaces that have more than one `abstract` method. As interfaces can inherit from each other, be wary of inheriting an `abstract` method and then trying to define your own – that will not work for lambdas.

Now that we understand functional interfaces and how to implement them using lambda expressions, let's examine why local variables must be `final` or "effectively final."

## final or effectively final

Recall that by declaring a variable final, you are making it a constant, which means that the value of the variable, once assigned, cannot be changed. "Effectively final" means that even though the final keyword is not used in the variable declaration, the compiler makes it *effectively final* by ensuring that if you try to change its value, you get a compiler error. Note that this rule of final or "effectively final" relates only to local variables and does not apply to instance or class variables.

*Figure 14.3* presents code demonstrating the use of final or "effectively final". We will first explain the code and then explain why the local variable is "effectively final."

```
7    public class LambdaEffectivelyFinal {
8        public static void main(String[] args) {
9            ArrayList<String> people = new ArrayList<>();
10           people.add ("Mr. John Bloggs");people.add ("Ms. Ann Bloggs");
11           people.add ("Mr. Mike Bloggs");people.add ("Ms. Mary Bloggs");
12
13           String title="Mr."; // final or effectively final
14           int y = 0;
15           y++; // no issue, 'y' is not used in lambda
16
17           // Lambdas take a snapshot/picture of local variables; these local
18           // variables MUST NOT change. Only setting up lambda here.
19           Predicate<String> lambda = str -> {
20               //title = "Miss;
21               return str.startsWith(title); // "Mr."
22           };
23
24           // If 'title' was allowed to change, then the method and the lambda would
25           // have 2 different views of 'title'!
26           //title = "Ms";
27           filterData(people, lambda);// lambda views 'title' as "Mr."
28
29           //title = "Ms";
30           filterData(people, lambda);// lambda views 'title' as "Mr."
31       }
32       public static void filterData(List<String> list, Predicate<String> lambda){
33           list.removeIf(lambda); // only executing lambda here!
34       }
35   }
```

Figure 14.3 – "final" or "effectively final" code example

In this figure, the algorithm removes any names from the list that begin with `"Mr. "`. Lines 9-11 declare and populate an `ArrayList` list.

Line 13 declares a local `String` variable named `title`. This variable is used in the lambda (line 21) and therefore, as it is not explicitly declared `final`, it is "effectively final."

Lines 14-15 declare and change a local `int` variable, `y`. As `y` is not used in the lambda expression, this is fine.

Lines 19-22 present the lambda expression:

```
Predicate<String> lambda = str -> {
    return str.startsWith(title);
};
```

The lambda is a `Predicate`, typed for `String`. `Predicate` is an API functional interface, which we will discuss in detail in the next section. The functional method for `Predicate` is `boolean test(T t)`. As we have typed the `Predicate` for `String`, both `T` and consequently `str` are `String`'s. The lambda returns `true` or `false` depending on whether `str` begins with `"Mr. "`, thereby matching the return type of the `test` functional method. This is an important point – the lambda has taken a snapshot of the value in the local variable `title`; which is `"Mr. "`.

Both lines 27 and 30 invoke `filterData(people, lambda)`. This is one of the real advantages of lambdas – they can be passed around! But remember, the value of `title` in the lambda is `"Mr. "`.

Lines 32-34 show the `filterData()` method:

```
public static void filterData(List<String> list,
                              Predicate<String> lambda) {
    list.removeIf(lambda);
};
```

The lambda is passed to the `default` method, `removeIf(Predicate)`, which is inherited from `Collection`. `Collection` is a parent interface of `List`. `removeIf(Predicate)` removes all elements from the list that satisfy the predicate (lambda) passed in. In this example, any names that begin with `"Mr. "` are removed.

Now, you can see why the value of `title` (line 13) must never be allowed to change – the lambda uses `"Mr. "` (line 21). If we were allowed to change `title`, either in the lambda (line 20) or in the method (lines 26 or 29), then the value of `title` in the method and the value of `title` in the lambda would not match! This must not happen. Therefore, any changes to `title`, either in the method or in the lambda, are prohibited. This is why lines 20, 26, and 29 are all commented out. Uncommenting any of them results in a compiler error.

# Exploring functional interfaces from the API

Now, let's examine some popular functional interfaces defined in the API. Interestingly, the two sorting interfaces from *Chapter 13*, namely `Comparator` and `Comparable`, are both functional interfaces. `Comparable` defines one `abstract` method, namely `int compareTo(T o)`, and `Comparator` defines two `abstract` methods, namely `int compare(T o1, T o2)` and `boolean equals(Object o)`. Remember, however, that methods inherited from `Object` do not count when you're deciding if an interface is a functional interface or not. As `boolean equals(Object o)` is inherited from `Object`, this means that `Comparator` is a functional interface.

In this section, we will concentrate on the functional interfaces defined in the `java.util. function` package (`https://docs.oracle.com/en/java/javase/21/docs/api/ java.base/java/util/function/package-summary.html`). This package has a large number of general-purpose functional interfaces that are used by the JDK and are available to us also. *Table 14.2* presents the most commonly used ones. Please refer to the API for further details. We will examine these functional interfaces and their lambda expressions in code shortly:

| Functional Interface | Functional Method | Description |
| --- | --- | --- |
| `Predicate<T>` | `boolean test(T t)` | Useful for testing |
| `BiPredicate<T, U>` | `boolean test(T t, U u)` | This is a two-arity (two parameters) specialization of `Predicate` |
| `Supplier<T>` | `T get()` | Useful for when you want values without providing input |
| `Consumer<T>` | `void accept(T t)` | Useful for when you pass in input but do not care about a return value |
| `BiConsumer<T, U>` | `void accept(T t, U u)` | This is a two-arity specialization of `Consumer` |
| `Function<T, R>` | `R apply(T t)` | Transforms the input into an output (types can be different) |
| `BiFunction<T, U, R>` | `R apply(T t, U u)` | This is a two-arity specialization of `Function` |
| `UnaryOperator<T>` | `T apply(T t)` | The same as `Function` except the types are the same |
| `BinaryOperator<T>` | `T apply(T t1, T t2)` | The same as `BiFunction` except the types are all the same |

Table 14.2 – Popular functional interfaces in the API

Now, let's examine each of the preceding functional interfaces and their associated lambdas in code. Let's start with `Predicate` and `BiPredicate`.

## Predicate and BiPredicate

A predicate is a boolean-valued function (a function that will return `boolean`). *Figure 14.4* presents `Predicate` and `BiPredicate`:

```
31      public void predicate() {
32          // Predicate<T> is a functional interface i.e. one abstract method:
33          //      boolean test(T t);
34          Predicate<String> pStr = s -> s.contains("City");
35          System.out.println(pStr.test( t: "Vatican City"));//true
36
37          // BiPredicate<T, U> is a functional interface i.e. one abstract method:
38          //      boolean test(T t, U u);
39          BiPredicate<String, Integer> checkLength = (str, len) -> str.length() == len;
40          System.out.println(checkLength.test( t: "Vatican City",  u: 8));//false (length is 12)
41
42      }
```

Figure 14.4 – Predicate and BiPredicate in code

In this figure, we would first like to discuss the relationship in the API between the generic types of functional interfaces and their functional methods. Understanding this relationship is key to understanding the examples and creating the context used by the compiler. This context will be very important when we discuss method references later.

As the comments on lines 32-33 indicate, there is a direct relationship between the generic types and both the parameter and return types used by the functional method. In this case, `Predicate` is generically typed for T (line 32), and the functional methods input parameter is also typed for T (line 33). Therefore, if we type our `Predicate` for `Integer`, then the parameter in the functional method will be `Integer`. We cannot pass `Cat`, `Dog`, `String`, or any other type as an argument. Now, let's look at the example.

Line 34 defines a `Predicate`, generically typed for `String`, namely isCityInName. cityName -> cityName.contains("City") is the code for the `boolean test(T t)` functional method. As the generic type is `String`, T is now `String` for this functional method, meaning that the parameter type is `String`. Thus, the cityName variable on line 34 represents a `String` variable. This is why the compiler has no issue with cityName.contains("City") in the lambda expression. As cityName.contains("City") is a simple expression, we do not need { } or a `return` statement – the compiler will fill all that in for us. Bear in mind that the expression we use must return a `boolean` value as the `boolean test(T t)` functional method returns `boolean`. The `String` method, `boolean contains(CharSequnce)`, does exactly that, so we are fine. So, with our lambda expression defined, let's execute it.

Line 35 executes the isCityInName lambda defined on line 34. Note that the method that's invoked using the isCityInName reference is the boolean test(T t) functional method. As we have generically typed isCityInName to String, the argument we pass must be a String argument. This is what we do, passing in "Vatican City". This means that the cityName parameter in our lambda (line 34) becomes "Vatican City" and thus the code in the boolean test(T t) method becomes "Vatican City".contains("City"). Consequently, line 35 outputs true.

Line 39 defines a BiPredicate, generically typed for String, Integer; namely checkStringLength Again, the comments (lines 37-38), demonstrate the close relationship between the functional interface's generic types and the parameters for the functional method. BiPredicate is simply an extension of Predicate except that there are now two (input) parameters for the functional method, instead of one. The functional method name is still test and the return type is again boolean.

As checkStringLength is defined as BiPredicate<String, Integer>, the signature for the functional method is now boolean test(String str, Integer len). The lambda then checks if the length of the string passed in as the first parameter, is equal to the number passed in as the second parameter.

On line 40, we test BiPredicate, passing in "Vatican City" and 8 in that order. The lambda returns false as the length of the "Vatican City" string is 12 (and not 8).

As discussed earlier, both Predicate and BiPredicate are generically typed for T. This means that their functional method consumes a type, T, such as String, Integer, and so forth. This is in contrast to predicates that consume primitives. The following table, *Table 14.3*, presents the functional interfaces defined in the API for predicates that wish to consume primitives:

| Functional Interface | Functional Method | Example |
|---|---|---|
| DoublePredicate | boolean test(double value) | DoublePredicate p1 = d -> d > 0; |
| IntPredicate | boolean test(int value) | IntPredicate p2 = i -> i > 0; |
| LongPredicate | boolean test(long value) | LongPredicate p3 = lg -> lg > 0; |

Table 14.3 – Primitive testing specializations of Predicate in the API

As can be seen from the table, there are no generic types, such as <T> in the names of the functional interfaces. The functional methods have primitive parameters (instead of generic types). As we are dealing with primitives, the lambdas cannot invoke methods on the arguments (as primitives are just simple types and have no methods).

Now, let's discuss the Supplier functional interface.

# Supplier

*Figure 14.5* presents code that demonstrates `Supplier`:

```
45          // Supplier<T> is a functional interface i.e. one abstract method:
46          //      T get()
47          Supplier<StringBuilder> supSB = () -> new StringBuilder();
48          System.out.println(supSB.get().append("SK"));// SK
49
50          Supplier<LocalTime> supTime = () -> LocalTime.now();
51          System.out.println(supTime.get());   // 11:00:50.769271700
52
53          Supplier<Double> sRandom = () -> Math.random();
54          System.out.println(sRandom.get());   // 0.13482391499981883
```

Figure 14.5 – Supplier in code

The `Supplier` functional interface is very useful when you want a new object. The generic type determines the result supplied. In other words, line 47 types `supSB` for `StringBuilder`, where the functional method, `get()`, returns `StringBuilder`. Line 47 also demonstrates that if you have no parameters at all, you must specify the round brackets, `()`.

Line 48 executes the lambda expression defined on line 47. Note that we chain `append("SK")` onto the return of the `get()` method. This will only work if the `get()` method returns a `StringBuilder` object, which it does.

Line 50 defines a `Supplier` functional interface, typed for `LocalTime`, called `supTime`. The lambda returns the local time. Line 51 executes it by invoking the functional method for `Supplier`, namely `T get()`. The output from a sample run is included in a comment on the right-hand side.

Line 53 defines a `Supplier` functional interface typed for `Double` called `sRandom`, which returns a random number. `Math.random()` returns a `double` value greater than or equal to 0.0 and less than 1.0. Line 54 executes it with sample output in a comment on the right.

The generically typed `Supplier` functional interface also has variants to cater to primitives. *Table 14.4* shows these:

| Functional Interface | Functional Method | Example |
| --- | --- | --- |
| `BooleanSupplier` | `boolean getAsBoolean()` | `BooleanSupplier bS = () -> LocalDate.now().isLeapYear();` |
| | | `System.out.println(bS.getAsBoolean());` |
| `DoubleSupplier` | `double getAsDouble()` | `DoubleSupplier dS = () -> Math.random();` |
| | | `System.out.println(dS.getAsDouble());` |
| `IntSupplier` | `int getAsInt()` | `IntSupplier iS = () -> (int)(Math.random()*20);` |
| | | `System.out.println(iS.getAsInt());` |
| `LongSupplier` | `long getAsLong()` | `LongSupplier lgS = () -> (long)(Math.random()*100);` |
| | | `System.out.println(lgS.getAsLong());` |

Table 14.4 – Primitive-producing specializations of Supplier in the API

In this table, the functional interface name identifies the primitive type being generated. For example, `BooleanSupplier` produces a `boolean` primitive type. The functional method follows accordingly; for example, `BooleanSupplier` has a `boolean getAsBoolean()` method. The other functional interfaces follow a similar pattern.

Now, let's discuss the `Consumer` and `BiConsumer` functional interfaces.

## Consumer and BiConsumer

We will start with `Consumer`, which, as per the API, "*represents an operation that takes in a single input and returns no result.*" *Figure 14.6* presents code demonstrating the use of `Consumer`:

```
66        // Consumer<T> is a functional interface i.e. one abstract method:
67        //      void accept(T t)
68        Consumer<String> printC = s -> System.out.println(s);// lambda
69        printC.accept( t: "To be or not to be, that is the question");
70
71        List<String> names = new ArrayList<>();
72        names.add("Maaike");names.add("Sean");
73        names.forEach(printC);   // Maaike, Sean
```

Figure 14.6 – Consumer in code

In this figure, line 67 (a comment) outlines that the void accept (T t) functional method does exactly as per the API: it takes in a single input and returns nothing (void). Consumers are very useful for outputting collections. In this example, Consumer (line 68) takes in a String, s, and echoes it to the standard output (the screen). We execute the lambda (line 69), passing in the string we want displayed. So, the "To be or not to be, that is the question" string is the argument to the void accept (T t) functional method. Here, the s parameter (line 68) takes on the string value, which is then output.

> **The Iterable interface**
>
> The Iterable interface is inherited by many other popular interfaces, such as List and Set, and consequently, implemented by a large number of classes. Before Java 8, interfaces only had abstract methods – there were no default, static, or private methods (they all came in later releases of Java). This meant that if you changed an interface (method signature or added a new method), the existing code base would break. One of the main reasons for introducing default methods was for the Java designers to introduce the default method, forEach(Consumer<? super T> action), into Iterable without breaking the existing code base. The default implementation is to execute the Consumer lambda on each element in the collection.

Now, let's examine how the Java API utilizes consumers. Line 71 declares an ArrayList of strings, namely names. Line 72 adds "Maaike" and "Sean" to the list.

Line 73 is very interesting. We execute the forEach() method on the list, passing in the consumer lambda, printC, that was created on line 68. The forEach() method loops through each String in the list and invokes the Consumer lambda, printC, on each String. In effect, the following happens in the background:

```
printC.accept("Maaike");
printC.accept("Sean");
```

Now, let's look at an example of a `BiConsumer` interface in action. *Figure 14.7* presents an example:

```
75          Map<String,String> mapCapitalCities = new HashMap<>();
76          // BiConsumer<T, U> is a functional interface i.e. one abstract method:
77          //       void accept(T t, U u)
78          // Note: Object put(k,v) - return value ignored.
79          //       This Consumer has a side-effect.
80          BiConsumer<String, String> biCon = (key, value) ->
81                                  mapCapitalCities.put(key, value);
82          biCon.accept( t: "Dublin",  u: "Ireland");
83          biCon.accept( t: "The Hague",  u: "Holland");
84          System.out.println(mapCapitalCities);// {Dublin=Ireland, The Hague=Holland}
85
86          BiConsumer<String, String> mapPrint = (key, value) ->
87                                  System.out.println(key +
88                                      " is the capital of: "+value);
89          mapCapitalCities.forEach(mapPrint); // Dublin is the capital of: Ireland
90                                              // The Hague is the capital of: Holland
```

Figure 14.7 – BiConsumer in code

In this figure, on line 75, we declare a `Map<String, String>`, namely `mapCapitalCities`, implemented by a `HashMap`. Both the key and the value in the map are strings. The `BiConsumer` `biCon` is declared on lines 80-81. The functional method, `void accept(T t, U u)`, requires two parameters – we have called them `key` and `value`. Both are strings due to the context (the declaration of `biCon`). The lambda on line 81, is simply inserting the `key` and `value` into the map. This is known as a "side effect" (see the callout). Lines 82-83 populate the map using the lambda and line 84 outputs the map.

---

**Side effects**

In Java, lambda expressions are considered a functional style of programming. While functional programming is outside the scope of this book, functions adhering to the functional programming style should not generate side effects. A side effect is a change to the program state not reflected in the function's output. `Consumers`, unlike most other functional interfaces in Java, are expected to operate via side effects (as the return type for the functional methods is `void`). For further detail please see: `https://en.wikipedia.org/wiki/Functional_programming`

Is there a forEach() method for Map? Thankfully, there is. It is a default method defined in the Map interface and its signature is default void forEach(BiConsumer<? super K, ? super V) action). Lines 86-88 set up the lambda expression to output the decorated string, stating that key is the capital of value (depending on the key/value pairs). Line 89 executes forEach(), passing in our BiConsumer. The forEach() method loops through each entry in the map and invokes the BiConsumer lambda, mapPrint, on each entry. In effect, the following happens in the background:

```
mapPrint.accept("Dublin", "Ireland");
mapPrint.accept("The Hague", "Holland");
```

The generically typed Consumer functional interface also has variants to cater for primitives. *Table 14.5* shows these:

| Functional Interface | Functional Method | Example |
|---|---|---|
| DoubleConsumer | void accept(double value) | DoubleConsumer dc = d -> System.out.println(d); |
| | | dc.accept(2.4); |
| IntConsumer | void accept(int value) | IntConsumer ic = i -> System.out.println(i); |
| | | ic.accept(2); |
| LongConsumer | void accept(long value) | LongConsumer lc = lg -> System.out.println(lg); |
| | | lc.accept(8L); |

Table 14.5 – Primitive-accepting specializations of Consumer in the API

Again, the primitive name is embedded into the functional interface name. Note that the parameter type passed into the accept() functional method is a primitive each time

Now, let's discuss the Function and BiFunction functional interfaces.

## Function and BiFunction

A function accepts one argument and produces a result. *Figure 14.8* presents some code demonstrating the use of both `Function` and `BiFunction`:

```
101    // Function<T, R> is a functional interface i.e. one abstract method:
102    //      R apply(T t)
103    Function<String, Integer> fn2 = s -> s.length();
104    System.out.println("Function: " + fn2.apply( t: "London"));// 6
105
106    // BiFunction<T, U, R> is a functional interface i.e. one abstract method:
107    //      R apply(T t, U u)
108    BiFunction<String, String, Integer> biFn =
109            (s1, s2) -> s1.length() + s2.length();
110    System.out.println("BiFunction: " +
111            biFn.apply( t: "William",  u: "Shakespeare"));// 18
112
113    BiFunction<String, String, String> biFn2 =
114            (s1, s2) -> s1.concat(s2);
115    System.out.println("BiFunction: " +
116            biFn2.apply( t: "William ",  u: "Shakespeare"));// William Shakespeare
```

Figure 14.8 – Function and BiFunction in code

In this figure, the comments on lines 101-102 show how the `Function` functional interface and its functional method appear in the API. `Function` is generically typed, with the first type, `T`, representing the input type and the second type, `R`, representing the output type. What this means is that, when, on line 103, we declare `Function<String, Integer>`, the functional method is `Integer apply(String s)`. This is reflected in the lambda expression on line 103, where we accept a string, s, and return its length. Note that the string's `length()` method returns an int type but Java will auto-box this to an `Integer` type for us.

Line 104 executes the lambda, passing in `"London"`, which returns 6.

The `BiFunction` functional interface represents a function that accepts two arguments and produces a result. The comments on lines 106-107 shows its signature in the API, namely `BiFunction<T, U, R>`, and that of its functional method, which is `R apply(T t, U u)`. Therefore, the first two types are inputs and the last type is the output type.

Lines 108-109 define a `BiFunction` interface where we are accepting in two `String`s and returning an `Integer` type. The lambda implementing it takes in two `String` parameters, namely `s1` and `s2`, and returns the sum of their lengths.

Line 111 invokes the lambda while passing in the `"William"` and `"Shakespeare"` strings. Their lengths are 7 and 11, respectively, resulting in 18 being returned by the lambda.

Lines 113-114 define a `BiFunction` interface where we are accepting in two `Strings` again, but this time, we return a `String`. The lambda (line 114) simply concatenates the second `String` onto the first `String` and returns the result. Line 116 executes the lambda while passing in the same two strings, `"William"` and `"Shakespeare"`. This time, the result is the concatenation of the two, which is `"William Shakespeare"`.

The generically typed `Function` functional interface also has variants to cater to primitives. *Table 14.6* presents a subset of them:

| Functional Interface | Functional Method | Example |
|---|---|---|
| DoubleFunction<R> | R apply(double value) | DoubleFunction<String> df = (double dbl) -> "" + Math.pow(dbl, 2); |
| | | df.apply(2.0); // "4.0" |
| DoubleToIntFunction | int applyAsInt(double value) | DoubleToIntFunction dtoif = dbl -> (int) Math.round(dbl); |
| | | dtoif. applyAsInt(4.2);// 4 |
| DoubleToLongFunction | long applyAsLong(double value) | DoubleToLongFunction dtolf = (dbl) -> Math.round(dbl); |
| | | dtolf. applyAsLong(4.0);// 4 |

Table 14.6 – Double (primitive) specializations of Function in the API

There are many more functional interfaces than those presented in *Table 14.6*. Please refer to the API for further details. They can be daunting but remember that there is a pattern in the functional interface names and their associated functional method names. This helps in understanding what they do.

For example, in *Table 14.6*, the `double` primitive type is catered for with `DoubleFunction<R>`, `DoubleToIntFunction`, and `DoubleToLongFunction`. There are corresponding functional interfaces for `int` and `long`.

The int functional interfaces are `IntFunction<R>`, `IntToDoubleFunction`, and `IntToLongFunction`. These int-related functional interfaces do the same thing as their `double` counterparts (as outlined in *Table 14.6*), except the input is `int` and not `double`. The relevant functional method names will depend on the result type. For example, the functional method for `IntToDoubleFunction` will be `double applyAsDouble(int value)`.

The same is true for the `long` primitive. The `long` functional interfaces are `LongFunction<R>`, `LongToDoubleFunction`, and `LongToIntFunction`. Their functional method names follow the same pattern as `int` and `double`.

Let's finish our discussion on functional interfaces by examining `UnaryOperator` and `BinaryOperator`.

## UnaryOperator and BinaryOperator

Both of these functional interfaces are specializations of other interfaces. Let's discuss `UnaryOperator` first.

### *UnaryOperator*

In the API, the `Function` functional interface is defined as `Function<T, R>`. T represents the input to the function and R represents the output from the function. The fact that the letters are different is important. This means that, while the types can of course be the same, they can also, and often are, different.

`UnaryOperator` is a specialization of `Function` where both the input and output types are the same. In the API, `UnaryOperator` is defined as `UnaryOperator<T> extends Function<T, T>` and its functional method is `T apply(T t)`.

*Figure 14.9* presents an example in code:

```
126    // UnaryOperator<T> extends Function<T, T>
127    //      T apply(T t)
128    UnaryOperator<String> unaryOp = name -> "My name is "+name;
129    System.out.println("UnaryOperator: " +
130        unaryOp.apply( "Sean"));// My name is Sean
```

Figure 14.9 – UnaryOperator in code

In this figure, line 128 defines a `UnaryOperator` typed for `String`. This means that both the input and output are now strings. The name identifier is a `String` and we are just pre-pending "My name is " to name.

Line 130 executes the lambda by passing in "Sean". The return String of "My name is Sean" is output to the screen.

Now, let's examine BinaryOperator.

### BinaryOperator

The BinaryOperator functional interface is to BiFunction what UnaryOperator is to Function. In other words, BiFunction allows us to specify two input parameters and an output result, all of which could be different types. BinaryOperator, which extends BiFunction, mandates that the two input types and the output type must be the same.

In the API, BinaryOperator is defined as BinaryOperator<T> extends BiFunction<T, T, T>, and its functional method is T apply(T t1, T t2).

*Figure 14.10* presents an example in code:

```
132        // BinaryOperator<T> extends BiFunction<T, T, T>
133        //     T apply(T t1, T t2)
134        BinaryOperator<String> binaryOp   = (s1, s2) -> s1.concat(s2);
135        System.out.println("BinaryOperator: " +
136            binaryOp.apply( t: "William ",  u: "Shakespeare"));// William Shakespeare
```

Figure 14.10 – BinaryOperator in code

In this figure, line 134 defines a BinaryOperator typed for String. This means that both the input parameters and the result are now strings. The s1 and s2 identifiers are strings and we are just returning the result of concatenating s2 onto s1.

Line 136 executes the lambda by passing in "William" and "Shakespeare". The return String of "William Shakespeare" is output to the screen.

## Mastering method references

Now, let's move on to another important topic concerning lambda expressions, and that is method references. As concise as lambdas are, in certain situations, they can be even more concise! This is where method references apply. If all your lambda does is call one method, then this is an opportunity for a method reference. In addition, if a lambda parameter is simply passed to a method, then the redundancy of specifying the variable twice can also be removed.

Let's look at an example:

```
List<String> names = Arrays.asList("Maaike", "Sean");
names.forEach(name -> System.out.println(name); // lambda
names.forEach(System.out::println); // method reference
```

In this code, we declare a list of strings by invoking the `Arrays.asList()` method. The first `forEach(Consumer)` shows how to output the list using a lambda expression. Recall that the functional method of `Consumer` is `void accept(T t)`.

The second `forEach(Consumer)` shows the method reference syntax. Note the double-colon operator, `::` (or method reference operator), and the fact that there are no round brackets, `()`, after the method name, as in `println`.

Keep in mind at all times that the code has to be generated at some point. If we have all the code specified, then the compiler has nothing to do. However, if we have availed of lambdas and/or method references, the compiler must step in and generate the omitted code. The compiler can only do so when it understands the *context*. This is crucial to making sense of method references given that there is so much code omitted. Moreover, the functional interface, with its functional method, is critical for providing context.

There are four different types of method references:

- Bound

- Unbound

- Static

- Constructor

These are best explained with examples in code. Regarding the examples, to make them easier to understand, we have coded both the lambda and method reference versions for each example. The lambda variables use the `"L"` suffix and the method reference variables use the `"MR"` suffix. In addition, in the comments, just before each example, are the signatures of the functional interfaces and their associated functional methods.

Now, let's start with the first method reference type: bound method references.

## Bound method references

Bound references get their name from the fact that the reference is bound to an instance of a particular object. A bound method reference is sometimes referred to as a "reference to an instance of a particular object." Let's use an example to explain this further. *Figure 14.11* presents a bound method reference example:

```
21    String name = "Mr. Joe Bloggs";
22    // Supplier<T>
23    //     T get()
24    Supplier<String> lowerL   = () -> name.toLowerCase();    // lambda
25    Supplier<String> lowerMR  = name::toLowerCase;           // method reference
26
27    // No need to say which instance to call it on - the supplier is bound to name
28    System.out.println(lowerL.get()); // mr. joe bloggs
29    System.out.println(lowerMR.get());// mr. joe bloggs
30
31    // Predicate<T>
32    //     boolean test(T t)
33    // Even though startsWith is overloaded, boolean startsWith(String) and
34    // boolean startsWith(String, int), because we are creating a Predicate which
35    // has a functional method of test(T t), the startsWith(String) is used.
36    // This is where "context" is important.
37    Predicate<String> titleL  = (title) -> name.startsWith(title);
38    Predicate<String> titleMR = name::startsWith;
39
40    System.out.println(titleL.test( t: "Mr.")); // true
41    System.out.println(titleMR.test( t: "Ms."));// false
```

Figure 14.11 – Bound method reference example

In this figure, line 21 declares a `String` variable called name, initialized to `"Mr. Joe Bloggs"`. Lines 22-23 outline the `Supplier` functional interface and the signature of its functional method, `T get()`, in the API. Line 24 declares a `Supplier` lambda that converts name into lowercase. This is the same name variable declared on line 21. Hence, this lambda is *bound* to the name variable at compile time. As the lambda is simply calling one method, this is an opportunity to introduce a method reference.

Given the lambda on line 24, line 25 outlines the equivalent method reference. Note the use of the name variable; the method reference operator `::` and the omission of the round brackets `()` after the method name. Also, note that name is a `String` and that the `toLowerCase()` method is a method in the `String` class.

Lines 28 and 29 execute the lambda and method reference versions, respectively, returning `"mr. joe bloggs"` on both occasions.

The first example in *Figure 14.11* is using the `Supplier` functional interface, which did not require an input parameter. What if we wanted to pass in a value? A `Supplier` functional interface will not work as its functional method is `T get()`, which does not accept parameters. However, a `Predicate` will work as its functional method, `boolean test(T t)`, does accept an input parameter. The second example in *Figure 14.11* shows this in action.

Line 37 is the lambda version. As `Predicate` is typed for `String`, `title` is a `String`. Again, we bind to `name` and execute the `String` method, `startsWith()`, passing in the input parameter. We can see the redundancy in the lambda given that `title` is mentioned twice. Couple this with the fact that the lambda is simply calling one method, we have another opportunity to introduce a method reference.

Line 38 is the method reference version of the lambda on line 37. This method reference requires a bit more explanation however because, in the `String` class, the `startsWith()` method is overloaded. The overloaded versions are `boolean startsWith(String, int)` and `boolean startsWith(String)`. How does the compiler decide which version of `startsWith()` to use? This is where context is important! We are defining a `Predicate` and the functional method for `Predicate` is `boolean test(T t)`   - given that this method accepts just one parameter, the compiler selects the `startsWith()` method with one parameter, namely `boolean startsWith(String)`.

Line 40 executes the lambda version, passing in `"Mr."` This results in the lambda executing `"Mr. Joe Bloggs".startsWith("Mr.")`, which is true.

Line 41 executes the method reference version, passing in `"Ms."`. As the compiler translates the method reference into a lambda in the background, this results in the lambda executing `"Mr. Joe Bloggs".startsWith("Ms.")`, which is false.

Now, we will examine unbound method references.

## Unbound method references

Unbound method references do not bind to a variable. Instead, the instance to use is provided at runtime. An unbound method reference is sometimes referred to as a "reference to an instance of an arbitrary object of a particular type." *Figure 14.12* present an example in code:

```
44    public static void unboundMethodReferences(){
45        //   Function<T, R>
46        //      R apply(T)
47        //          String apply(String)
48        Function<String, String> upperL  = s -> s.toUpperCase();
49        Function<String, String> upperMR = String::toUpperCase;
50        // The function is unbound, so you need to specify which instance to call it on
51        System.out.println(upperL.apply( t: "sean"));    // SEAN
52        System.out.println(upperMR.apply( t: "sean"));   // SEAN
53
54        //   Function<T, U, R>
55        //      R apply(T t, U u)
56        //          String apply(String, String)
57        BiFunction<String, String, String> concatL   = (s1, s2) -> s1.concat(s2);
58        BiFunction<String, String, String> concatMR = String::concat;
59        System.out.println(concatL.apply( t: "Sean ",  u: "Kennedy"));// Sean Kennedy
60
61        // 1st parameter is used for executing the instance method
62        // "Sean ".concat("Kennedy")
63        System.out.println(concatMR.apply( t: "Sean ",  u: "Kennedy"));// Sean Kennedy
64    }
```

Figure 14.12 – Unbound method reference example

In this figure, we define a lambda on line 48. This lambda is of the Function<String, String> type, meaning that the functional method is String apply(String). Thus, s is a String and we can invoke the String method, toUpperCase(). Note that s is not a variable from the method's scope. In *Figure 4.11*, we were bound to the name variable declared in the method. Now, however, s has the scope of the lambda expression only. This means that the method reference is *unbound*. The lambda parameter, s, will be bound to at runtime (when the apply() method is called), as on line 51.

As the lambda has just one method call and there is redundancy with s on both sides of the -> token, we can use a method reference. Line 49 represents the method reference version of the lambda on line 48. Note the use of the method reference operator :: and the absence of () after the method name, toLowerCase. As toLowerCase is a String method, String precedes the :: operator in the method reference. The method reference on line 49 is semantically equivalent to the lambda on line 48.

Line 57 declares a BiFunction lambda. Recall that BiFunction takes in two inputs and returns a result. In this case, all are String types. The parameters that are passed in are concatenated and returned. Again, we have only one method call in the lambda and redundancy of variables, so we can code a method reference.

Line 58 represents the method reference version of the lambda on line 57. Again, context is going to be key in figuring out the method reference. `BiFunction<String, String, String>` and `String::concat` inform the compiler that this is an unbound method reference that will take in two `String` arguments and concatenate them.

There is one other bit of information implied here – the first argument provided in the `apply()` method call is the instance to be used for the `concat()` method; the second argument is to be passed into the `concat()` method as an argument. What this means is as follows:

```
concatMR.apply("Orange", " Juice");
```

This translates into the following:

```
"Orange ".concat("Juice");
```

This can be seen on lines 62 and 63. The execution of the method reference on line 63 translates into the code in comments on line 62. Both the lambda and method reference invocations (lines 59 and 63, respectively) result in `"Sean Kennedy"` being returned.

Now, let's explore static method references.

## Static method references

A `static` method reference is also considered unbound as we do not bind to a variable from the outer scope. The method being invoked is `static`, hence the name. Let's examine a `static` method reference in code. *Figure 14.13* shows such an example:

```
104    // Static method references are considered UNBOUND also. An example static method
105    // is Collections.sort(List)
106    // Consumer<T>
107    //      void accept(T t)
108    //          void accept(List<Integer>)
109    // NB: Consumer takes one parameter => sort(List) is used, as opposed to sort(List, Comparator)
110    Consumer<List<Integer>> sortL  = list -> Collections.sort(list);
111    Consumer<List<Integer>> sortMR = Collections::sort;
112
113    List<Integer> listOfNumbers = Arrays.asList(2,1,5,4,9);
114    sortL.accept(listOfNumbers);// execution
115    System.out.println(listOfNumbers);  // [1, 2, 4, 5, 9]
116
117    listOfNumbers = Arrays.asList(8,12,4,3,7);
118    sortMR.accept(listOfNumbers);// execution
119    System.out.println(listOfNumbers);  // [3, 4, 7, 8, 12]
```

Figure 14.13 – Static method reference example

In this figure, we define a `Consumer` lambda (line 110) that takes in a `List<Integer>` list. As we know, `Consumers` take in one argument and do not return anything. The side effect is to call the `static Collections` method, `sort`, passing in the list to be sorted. As our lambda has just one method call and we have redundancy (`list` on both sides of the `->` token), we can re-write the lambda even more concisely as a method reference.

Line 111 is the method reference version of the lambda that was coded on line 110. The `Collections.sort()` method is overloaded – one version is `sort(List)` and the other is `sort(List, Comparator)`. Context decides which one the compiler selects. As the `Consumer` lambda's functional method is `void accept(T t)`, which takes just one parameter, the `sort()` with one parameter, namely `sort(List)`, is used.

Line 113 generates a `List<Integer>` using the `Arrays.asList()` method. Lines 114 and 115 execute and output the lambda version.

Line 117 re-generates a `List<Integer>`, again using the `Arrays.asList()` method. Lines 118 and 119 execute and output the method reference version.

Our last method reference type is constructor method references. Let's discuss them now.

## Constructor method references

Constructor method references are a special type of method reference in that, rather than calling a (regular) method, the `new` keyword is used and an object is instantiated. Suppliers are a natural fit for constructor method references. *Figure 14.14* presents an example in code:

```
73    // Supplier<T>
74    //      T get()
75    Supplier<StringBuilder> sbL  = () -> new StringBuilder();  // lambda
76    Supplier<StringBuilder> sbMR = StringBuilder::new;         // method reference
77    StringBuilder sb1 = sbL.get(); sb1.append("lambda version"); System.out.println(sb1);
78    StringBuilder sb2 = sbMR.get(); sb2.append("method reference version"); System.out.println(sb2);
79
80    // Function<T, R>
81    //      R apply(T)
82    //          List<String> apply(Integer)
83    // ArrayList(int initialCapacity)
84    Function<Integer, List<String>> alL  = x -> new ArrayList(x);
85    Function<Integer, List<String>> alMR = ArrayList::new;
86    List<String> ls1 = alL.apply( t 100);  // initial capacity 100
87    ls1.add("21");
88    System.out.println(ls1);//[21]
89    List<String> ls2 = alMR.apply( t 200);  // initial capacity 200
90    ls2.add("88");
91    System.out.println(ls2);//[88]
```

Figure 14.14 – Constructor method reference example

In this figure, line 75 defines a `Supplier<StringBuilder>` lambda. The `Supplier` lambda's functional method is `T get()`, so we do not pass anything in. As we typed `sbL` for `StringBuilder`, the lambda code is `new StringBuilder()`. As we have only one method invocation in the lambda, a method reference version can be coded.

The method reference on line 76 is the constructor method reference equivalent of the lambda defined on line 75. Note the use of the `new` keyword after the `::` operator in the syntax.

Lines 77 and 78 invoke the lambda and method references, respectively. In addition, the `StringBuilder` objects that were created are populated and output.

As stated already, `Supplier` is a perfect fit for constructor method references. But what if you wanted to pass an argument in? Suppliers do not accept parameters (`T get()`). We need a functional interface that will accept a parameter and return a result. `Function` will do nicely for this use case.

The second example in *Figure 14.14* presents a `Function`-based constructor method reference. The `ArrayList` constructor is overloaded – one of the versions accepts an `int` type, which is used to specify the initial capacity.

Line 84 defines a `Function`-based lambda, which accepts an `Integer` type and returns a `List<String>` list. The lambda takes an `Integer` type, `x`, and constructs an `ArrayList` with an initial capacity of `x`. The value of `x` will be obtained from the lambda invocation (for example, 100 on line 86).

As we have only one method call in the lambda and as `x` is replicated on both sides of the `->` token (redundancy), we can write an equivalent method reference.

Line 85 is the method reference equivalent of the lambda that was coded on line 84. `ArrayList` is specified to indicate which implementation of `List` we want to return. The `::new` syntax is unique to constructor method references. Line 89 shows how the method reference is executed – invoke the `apply()` method while passing in 200 in this example.

That concludes our discussion on the four different types of method references. However, before we leave method references, we would like to discuss an example outlining just how important context is when trying to understand method references.

## Method references and context

This example will present three lambdas with their corresponding method references. *Figure 14.15* shows the code example:

```
 7    class Person{
 8 @      public static Integer howMany(Person... people){
 9            return people.length;
10        }
11    }
12 ▶  public class MethodRefsAndContext {
13 ▶      public static void main(String[] args) {
14            // No Person being passed in => Supplier
15            Supplier<Integer> lambda1 = () -> Person.howMany();
16            Supplier<Integer> mr1     = Person::howMany;
17            System.out.println(lambda1.get()); // 0
18            System.out.println(mr1.get());     // 0
19
20            // One Person to be passed in => Function
21            Function<Person, Integer> lambda2 = person -> Person.howMany(person);
22            Function<Person, Integer> mr2     = Person::howMany;
23            System.out.println(lambda2.apply(new Person()));  // 1
24            System.out.println(mr2.apply(new Person()));      // 1
25
26            // Two Person's to be passed in => BiFunction
27            BiFunction<Person, Person, Integer> lambda3 = (p1, p2) -> Person.howMany(p1, p2);
28            BiFunction<Person, Person, Integer> mr3     = Person::howMany;
29            System.out.println(lambda3.apply(new Person(), new Person()));  // 2
30            System.out.println(mr3.apply(new Person(), new Person()));      // 2
31        }
32    }
```

Figure 14.15 – Method references and context

In this figure, lines 7-11 define a class called Person. Line 8 defines a static howMany() method that returns the number of objects in the Person array. Recall that varargs is represented by ... and within the method, it is treated as an array (hence the length property). Given that the people parameter is a varargs parameter, we can invoke howMany() with 0 or more arguments.

The first scenario is calling howMany() with no Person object at all and getting back the count of objects passed, which will be 0. Supplier fits nicely as we will not be passing anything into the lambda, but will be getting back an Integer result. Line 15 is the lambda for this scenario. We accept in nothing and return an Integer count, which is the count of the number of Person objects passed to howMany(). This is, of course, 0.

Line 16 is the method reference equivalent for the lambda on line 15. We will return to discuss this shortly.

The second scenario is calling howMany() with one Person object and getting back the count of objects passed, which will be 1. Function fits nicely as we will be passing in one Person object to the lambda and receiving the Integer count. Line 21 is the lambda for this scenario. We accept one Person and return an Integer, representing the number of Person objects passed to howMany(). This is 1.

Line 22 is the method reference equivalent for the lambda on line 21. Again, we will return to discuss this shortly.

The third scenario is calling howMany() with two Person objects and getting back the count of objects passed, which will be 2. BiFunction fits nicely as we will be passing in two Person objects to the lambda and receiving the Integer count. Line 27 is the lambda for this scenario. We accept two Person objects and return an Integer representing the number of Person objects passed to howMany(). This is 2.

Line 28 is the method reference equivalent for the lambda on line 27.

Now, let's discuss the method references (lines 16, 22, and 28). Notice how they are all the same! Again, this is where context is key. The compiler can generate the relevant lambdas based on the functional interfaces and the generic types specified. Here's an example:

```
Supplier<Integer> mr1 = Person::howMany;
```

Firstly, as howMany() is a static method in Person, the compiler knows that the lambda will be Person.howMany(). But how many objects should be passed? As it is a Supplier interface, whose functional method is T get(), the compiler knows there will be no parameter input, so it knows to pass nothing to howMany(). Concerning what to return, Supplier is typed for Integer, which matches the return type for howMany().

What if we want to pass one object to howMany()? Let's examine the second method reference:

```
Function<Person, Integer> mr2     = Person::howMany;
```

The one difference here is that we are declaring a Function as opposed to the previous Supplier. Functions take in one parameter and return a result. We know Integer must be the return type, as that is the return type of howMany(). So, what the compiler does here is take the input and pass it to the howMany() method. The equivalent lambda (line 21) shows what is happening in the background.

Lastly, what if we want to pass in two objects to howMany()? The last method reference demonstrates how to do this:

```
BiFunction<Person, Person, Integer> mr3     =
    Person::howMany;
```

The compiler sees BiFunction and realizes that BiFunction requires two inputs, so it will pass the two inputs to howMany(). And of course, this particular BiFunction return type of Integer matches the return type of the method howMany().

So, we have three equivalent method references that map to three different lambdas because of the three different contexts. Method references can be tricky. Check the context and if possible, map the method reference to its equivalent lambda expression. Once in lambda form, it is easier to interpret.

That completes our discussion on method references and concludes *Chapter 14*. Now, let's put that knowledge into practice to reinforce the concepts we've learned.

# Exercises

1.  Dinosaur care tasks are often very similar, but not identical. To make our code cleaner, we can use lambda expressions. Create a custom functional interface called DinosaurHandler with a method called handle(Dinosaur dinosaur). Implement it in a lambda expression that sets a dinosaur to be asleep or awake (first, add a property to your Dinosaur class if needed).

2.  Lambda expressions are extremely useful with the java.util.function interfaces. Let's use them to manage dinosaurs:

    - Write a Predicate<Dinosaur> lambda that checks if a dinosaur is a carnivore

    - Write a Supplier<Dinosaur> lambda that returns a new dinosaur

    - Write a Consumer<Dinosaur> lambda that prints a dinosaur's name

    - Write a Function<Dinosaur, String> lambda that returns a dinosaur's diet

3.  Lambda expressions have specific rules about variable usage. We're going to create an example of a lambda expression that modifies an "effectively final" variable. Add a variable that tracks the number of dinosaurs and create a lambda expression that increases this count.

4.  Method references can make our code more readable. Write examples of using method references in the context of your park:

    - **Bound instance method**: Use System.out::println to print dinosaur names.

    - **Unbound instance method**: Use Dinosaur::getName (assume the Dinosaur class has a getName() method) to get the name of each dinosaur.

    - **Static method**: Use Collections::sort to sort a list of dinosaur names.

    - **Constructor reference**: Use Dinosaur::new to create a new dinosaur (assume the Dinosaur class has an appropriate constructor)

# Project – agile dinosaur care system

Our park is growing, and so are the tasks that need to be accomplished. Lambda expressions can simplify our code and improve the efficiency of operations. Let's integrate them into our system!

Incorporate lambda expressions into your "dinosaur care system" for sorting, filtering, and performing actions on collections of dinosaurs. Furthermore, design a notification system using method references to alert park staff about various events, enhancing communication and responsiveness within our park.

Here are the steps. We assume certain methods exist. You'll have to create those methods according to your `Dinosaur` class's design:

1.  **Set up your project**: If you haven't already done so in the previous chapter, create a new Java project in your IDE. Make sure you have a `Dinosaur` class defined with properties such as name, species, `healthStatus`, and so on. You'll also want to have a `DinosaurCareSystem` class where the main functionalities of handling dinosaurs are implemented.

2.  **Incorporate lambda expressions**: lambda expressions can be very handy when dealing with collections. Let's incorporate them into the system:

    - **Sorting**: Suppose you have a list of `Dinosaur` objects and you want to sort them by their name. Use the `sort` method of the `List` interface with a lambda expression. Here's an example: `dinosaurs.sort((d1, d2) > d1.getName().compareTo(d2.getName()))`.

    - **Filtering**: To filter out dinosaurs that are ill, you could use the stream method with a filter and a lambda. Here's an example: `List<Dinosaur> illDinosaurs = dinosaurs.stream().filter(d > d.isIll()).collect(Collectors.toList())`.

3.  **Design a notification system using method references**: Method references can simplify our code when the lambda expression is calling a method directly. In your `DinosaurCareSystem` class, create a method called `sendNotification(String message)`. Then in another method where you are checking dinosaur health status, for example, use a method reference to call `sendNotification` each time a dinosaur is found to be ill. The code may look something like this: `dinosaurs.stream().filter(Dinosaur::isIll).forEach(d > sendNotification(d.getName() + " is ill."))`.

4.  **Perform actions on collections**: lambda expressions are great for performing actions on collections. For instance, you may want to increase the health of all healthy dinosaurs as part of a `healthboosting` program. With lambdas, you can do this directly on the list: `dinosaurs.forEach(d > d.increaseHealth(10))`.

# Summary

In this chapter, we learned that lambda expressions make your code more concise. We saw that a functional interface is an interface with just one `abstract` method. Lambda expressions are classes that implement functional interfaces with everything but the bare minimum remaining.

The terms `final` and "effectively final" refer to local variables used inside lambda expressions. Any non-`final` local variable used by a lambda must not change its value, either in the method or the lambda itself. The compiler enforces this, thus making the local variable "effectively final." This is to ensure that the method's view of the local variables value is consistent with the lambda's view (of the local variable's value). This does not apply to instance or `static` variables or local variables *not* used inside lambdas.

We took a deep dive into functional interfaces from the API. We examined predicates (which test a condition), such as `Predicate<T>` and `BiPredicate<T, U>`, plus their primitive consuming counterparts, `DoublePredicate`, `IntPredicate`, and `LongPredicate`.

We also examined `Supplier<T>` (which gives you something) and its primitive consuming specializations, which are `BooleanSupplier`, `DoubleSupplier`, `IntSupplier`, and `LongSupplier`.

We explored consumers (which take but do not give back), `Consumer<T>` and `BiConsumer<T, U>`, and their primitive consuming specializations, `DoubleConsumer`, `IntConsumer`, and `LongConsumer`.

We also looked at functions (which both take and give back), `Function<T, R>` and `BiFunction<T, U, R>`, and their primitive consuming counterparts.

Lastly, we examined variations of functions. `UnaryOperator<T>` is a variation of `Function`, where both the input and output types are the same. Similarly, `BinaryOperator<T>` is a variation of `BiFunction`, where the two input types and the output type are all the same.

To make your code even more concise, in certain situations, you can use method references instead of lambda expressions. If your lambda is just invoking one method and there is redundancy concerning parameters, a method reference can be written.

There are four different types of method references: bound, unbound, static, and constructor. A bound method reference is bound to an existing variable in the method, outside of the lambda's scope. An unbound method reference relies on the instance to be passed at runtime. A static method reference is also considered unbound and executes a `static` method. Lastly, a constructor method reference creates objects using the `::new` syntax.

We also had a look at the importance of context in understanding method references. We saw an example where the same method reference was generating three different lambdas (in the background) due to the three different contexts.

That completes our discussion on lambda expressions. They will be very important as we move on to our next two Stream-related chapters.

# 15

# Streams – Fundamentals

In *Chapter 14*, we learned about lambda expressions. Lambda expressions enable us to write more concise code. Be aware, however, that the compiler is, in the background, inserting the code we omit. For that to work, the compiler must have no decisions to make. This is where "functional interfaces" come into play. A functional interface is an interface with just one `abstract` method; this is known as the "functional method." Lambda expressions can only be used with functional interfaces.

We saw that if a local variable is used in a lambda expression, that variable must be `final` or "effectively final." This keeps both views (method and lambda) of the variable's value in sync. In other words, both the method and the lambda have the same value for the variable at all times.

We also examined the more popular functional interfaces in the API, namely, `Predicate`, `BiPredicate`, `Supplier`, `Consumer`, `BiConsumer`, `Function`, and `BiFunction`. There are many other functional interfaces in the API, including variants that cater to primitives (as opposed to objects).

Next, we discussed method references, which can make your code even more concise than lambdas. A method reference is a shorthand for a lambda expression. For the compiler to generate the lambda from the method reference, the context is key. The context factors in the functional interface declared and the generic types used.

We also explored the four types of method references: bound, unbound, static, and constructor. Bound method references bind, at compile time, to a variable from the method, whereas unbound rely on the object to be passed in at runtime. Static method references are unbound and invoke a `static` method. Constructor method references use the `::new` syntax to create objects.

We finished the chapter by discussing an example where the same method reference was used in three different contexts. Each of the method references resulted in a different lambda due to the differing contexts. This demonstrated the importance of context when examining method references.

In this chapter, we will start our coverage of streams. This is a large and important topic, requiring two chapters. Java 8 introduced both lambdas and streams to enable a more functional style of programming. This can lead to cleaner, more expressive code as we are not bogged down in how to do something; we just say we want it done.

We will start by discussing the stream pipeline. We will then discuss stream "laziness" before moving on to show ways of creating streams. Lastly, we will, with the aid of code examples, examine terminal operations.

This chapter covers the following main topics:

- Understanding stream pipelines
- Exploring stream laziness
- Creating streams
- Mastering terminal operations

# Technical requirements

The code for this chapter can be found on GitHub at `https://github.com/PacktPublishing/Learn-Java-with-Projects/tree/main/ch15`.

# Understanding stream pipelines

A *stream* in Java is a sequence of data that can be processed by operations. Streams are not another way to organize data, such as using an array or `Collection`, because streams do not hold data. Streams are all about efficiently processing data that is flowing by.

Let's look at the stream pipeline.

## Stream pipeline

A *stream pipeline* is a set of operations that run on a stream to produce a result. At a minimum, a stream pipeline consists of a source, zero or more intermediate operations, and a terminal operation, in that order. A pipeline is similar to an assembly line in a factory. Let's look at an example.

### Assembly line analogy

Let's assume we have a task of sharpening and stamping pencils that are currently sitting in a box (which contains 100 pencils). Stamping them means marking the pencil type on the pencil, such as 2B, 2H, and so forth. The pencils must be sharpened, stamped, and finally packed away, in that order. Declaring a stream is the same as giving instructions to the supervisor. In this assembly line, Java is the supervisor. Nobody does anything until the supervisor shouts "Start." The supervisor examines the instructions and sets up workstations with workers – one to take pencils from the box, one to sharpen the pencil, one to stamp the sharpened pencil, and one to pack away the finished pencil.

The worker taking pencils from the box is the pipeline *source*. The pencils are the data. Sharpening and stamping the pencils are the *intermediate operations*. The last operation, packing away the pencils, is the *terminal operation*. The terminal operation is very important as the supervisor will not shout "Start" until they see the terminal operation. Upon seeing it, however, the supervisor will shout "Start" and the process will begin.

Let's examine this process.

The first worker takes a pencil out of the box and hands it to the second worker, who sharpens it. The second worker hands the sharpened pencil to the next worker, who stamps it and hands it to the final worker in the assembly line, who packs the pencil away.

Note that pencils (and data) can only proceed in one direction – once the worker passes on the pencil, they can't get it back. From a Java perspective, this makes streams different from arrays and collections (where you can access the data at any time).

In addition, there is a principle of "lazy evaluation" in streams that we must be aware of here. We will discuss lazy evaluation in greater detail in the next section but for now, understand that data is *not* generated up front; it is only created *as and when needed*. This improves performance as you scale the amount of data you wish to process. Concerning our assembly line example, this means that the second pencil is not retrieved until required. What would be the point in having extra pencils sharpened and stamped if all you needed was one pencil? The supervisor, having the overall instructions, would be aware of this and ensure that the second pencil is never started.

Let's get back to our analogy where, at this point, we have one pencil packed away. Let's say we only want two pencils sharpened and stamped. This will require a new worker to be on the assembly line to keep count. The supervisor will place this new worker after the worker who stamps the pencils. The new worker's job is to count the pencils as they pass by (to be packed) and to inform the supervisor when two pencils have passed. The supervisor then instructs the first worker to take the second pencil out of the box. This pencil is sharpened and stamped. The new worker sees this second pencil pass by to be packed and informs the supervisor of this fact. The supervisor lets the last worker finish packing the second pencil and shouts "Stop." Therefore, the other 98 pencils are never taken out of the box, as they were not needed. This is a lazy evaluation.

Now, let's discuss what makes up a stream pipeline.

### Elements of a stream pipeline

A stream pipeline consists of the following:

- **Source**: This is where the stream comes from; this could be an array, a collection, a file, or a `varargs`.

- **Intermediate operations**: They transform the stream into another stream. We can have as many or as few as we like (zero or more). Due to lazy evaluation, they do not run until the terminal operation runs.

- **Terminal operation**: This is required to start the whole process and produce a result. Streams can only be used once – after the terminal operation completes, the stream is no longer usable (regenerate the stream if necessary).

Let's discuss the pipeline with the aid of an example. *Figure 15.1* presents a sample pipeline:

```
7     var temps = Arrays.asList(98.4, 100.2, 87.9, 102.8);
8     long count = temps.stream()
9             .peek(System.out::println) // 98.4, 100.2, 87.9, 102.8
10            .filter(temp -> temp > 100)
11            .peek(System.out::println) //     100.2,      102.8
12            .count();
13    System.out.println(count);   // 2
```

Figure 15.1 – A sample pipeline

> **The var keyword**
>
> The var keyword is known as **local variable type inference (LVTI)**. LVTI enables us to omit a local variables type as the compiler can infer it from the context. In this example, temps is a List<Double>.

The output from the previous figure is as follows:

```
98.4
100.2
100.2
87.9
102.8
102.8
2
```

In this figure, we are counting the number of temperatures > 100. As streams do not hold data, pipelines specify how we want to manipulate the source. The first thing we do is to create a List<Double> list represented by temps:

```
var temps = Arrays.asList(98.4, 100.2, 87.9, 102.8);
```

We then stream the list – in other words, the list is our source:

```
temps.stream()
```

Next, we use the `peek(Consumer)` intermediate operation, which is useful for debugging a pipeline and also for demonstrating what data is where in the pipeline:

```
.peek(System.out::println)
```

At this point, we want to filter *in* temperatures that are greater than 100. In other words, only temperatures > 100 will make it past the filter:

```
.filter(temp -> temp > 100)
```

Now that we have a temperature > 100, we use `peek(Consumer)` again to ensure our filter is working properly:

```
.peek(System.out::println)
```

Lastly, we have the terminal operation, `count()`, which starts off the whole process:

```
.count();
```

Let us discuss how the streaming process works here. Firstly, 98.4 is streamed. As 98.4 fails the filter, it is removed from the stream. Next, 100.2 is streamed; it passes the filter and Java sets the count to 1. The next value 87.9, is then streamed but it fails the filter. Lastly, 102.8 is streamed, which also passes the filter, thereby increasing the count to 2. Therefore, the count of temperatures that are > 100 is 2 (100.2 and 102.8). Notice the order in which the values come out of the stream is demonstrating stream laziness.

We will discuss the various operations from this example in due course. For the moment, we would like to cover stream laziness in more detail.

## Exploring stream laziness

The principle of lazy evaluation is that you get what you need, only when you need it. For example, if shopping websites such as Amazon were to display 10,000 records to a user, the principle of lazy evaluation would be to retrieve the first 50 and while the user is viewing these, retrieve the next 50 in the background. An eager evaluation would be to retrieve all 10,000 records in one go. With regards to streams, this means that nothing happens until the terminal operation gets called.

The pipeline specifies what operations we want performed on the source and in what order. As nothing happens until the terminal operation runs, Java is aware of the full pipeline. This enables Java to introduce efficiencies whenever possible. For example, why run an operation on a piece of data if that operation is not required? This could arise in the following situations:

- We have already found the data item we are looking for

- We may have a limit set of the number of elements (as in the pencils analogy)

Let's examine an example where the order of processing elements from the source demonstrates lazy evaluation. *Figure 15.2* (Laziness.java) shows this:

```
20          List<String> names = Arrays.asList("April", "Ben", "Charlie",
21                      "David", "Benildus", "Christian");
22      names.stream()
23              .peek(System.out::println)
24              .filter(s -> {
25                  System.out.println("filter1 : "+s);
26                  return s.startsWith("B") || s.startsWith("C"); } )
27              .filter(s -> {
28                  System.out.println("filter2 : "+s);
29                  return s.length() > 3; } )
30              .limit( maxSize: 1) // intermediate operation   Stream<T> limit(long)
31              .forEach(System.out::println);   // terminal operation
```

Figure 15.2 – Lazy evaluation – stream pipeline example

The algorithm in this figure obtains the first name that begins with 'B' or 'C' that is longer than 3 characters. In this example, we initially create a List<String> called names:

```
List<String> names = Arrays.asList("April", "Ben",
            "Charlie","David", "Benildus", "Christian");
```

As Java does not do any streaming until the terminal operation is encountered; nothing happens in this example until the forEach(Consumer) operation (line 31). This means that the code names. stream() at the start, is merely creating an object that knows where to go for the data when the streaming starts.

The first thing we do in this pipeline is output the current string, representing the person's name using the peek(Consumer) intermediate operation:

```
.peek(System.out::println)
```

Next, we use the `filter(Predicate)` intermediate operation to filter in names that begin with "B" or "C.":

```
.filter(s -> {
    System.out.println("filter1 : "+s);
    return s.startsWith("B") || s.startsWith("C"); } )
```

Immediately following that, we filter in names that are longer than three characters:

```
.filter(s -> {
    System.out.println("filter2 : "+s);
    return s.length() > 3; } )
```

After that, we use the `limit(long)` intermediate operation to keep track of how many names have passed the second filter:

```
.limit(1)
```

In this example, once one name passes by, the JVM is informed and no other name will be streamed from the source. Lastly, we provide the (required) terminal operation:

```
.forEach(System.out::println);
```

*Figure 15.3* shows the output from the code in *Figure 15.2*, which is very revealing:

```
34    /* Output:
35    April                   - peek
36    filter1 : April         - filter1 removes April
37    Ben                     - peek
38    filter1 : Ben           - filter1 passes Ben on
39    filter2 : Ben           - filter2 removes Ben
40    Charlie                 - peek
41    filter1 : Charlie       - filter1 passes Charlie on
42    filter2 : Charlie       - filter2 passes Charlie on
43    Charlie                 - forEach()
44
45    Note: limit(1) means David, Benildus or Christian are not
46          processed at all i.e. none of them appear in the output
47          via "peek()"
48    */
```

Figure 15.3 – Output from Figure 15.2 (with comments on the right)

Line 35 shows the first name, `April`, being streamed from the list. `April` makes it to the first filter and is removed (as `April` does not start with "B" or "C").

Line 37 shows the next name, `Ben`, being streamed. `Ben` passes the first filter and makes it to the second filter. However, as the length of `Ben` is only 3 characters, it is removed by the second filter.

Line 40 shows the next name, `Charlie`, being streamed. `Charlie` passes the first filter (as `Charlie` begins with "C") and is passed to the second filter. `Charlie` also passes this filter as the length of `Charlie` is > 3 characters long. So, `Charlie` is passed to the `limit(long)` intermediate operation, which notes that this is the first name passing by. As the limit is set to 1, the JVM is informed. `Charlie` is processed by the `forEach(Consumer)` terminal operation printing out `Charlie` (line 43) and the stream is shut down.

Note that none of the other names – `David`, `Benildus`, or `Christian` – are streamed at all. This is a small example but you can imagine the efficiencies of scale when you are dealing with millions of data items.

We will now move on to discussing how to create streams.

# Creating streams

Streams, both finite and infinite, can be generated from various sources. For example, sources such as arrays, collections, `varargs`, and files can be used. Let's examine these in turn. For the moment, we will deal with non-primitive types; all the streams will be serial (non-parallel). Both primitive and parallel streams will be discussed in *Chapter 16*.

## Streaming from an array

We will use `Stream<T> Arrays.stream(T[] array)` for this. This `static` method accepts an array of type T and returns `Stream<T>`. *Figure 15.4* (`CreatingStreams.java`) presents an example:

```
80        Double[] numbers = {1.1, 2.2, 3.3};
81        Stream<Double> stream1 = Arrays.stream(numbers);
82        long n = stream1.count();
83        System.out.println("Number of elements: "+n);// 3
```

Figure 15.4 – Streaming an array

In this figure, we declare a `Double` array (note that this is not a primitive `double` array). The stream object is created using the `Arrays.stream(T[] array)` method call. We start the stream off using the terminal operation `count()`. Lastly, we output the number of elements in the array. Note that this is just an example and that there is a more straightforward way (using the `length` property) of outputting the number of elements in an array.

Let's examine how we stream from a collection.

## Streaming from a collection

By *collection*, we mean the `Collection` interface hierarchy. The `Collection` interface has a default `Stream<E> stream()` method. *Figure 15.5* (`CreatingStreams.java`) presents code that generates a stream from a collection:

```
58    List<String> animalList = Arrays.asList("cat", "dog", "sheep");
59    // using stream() which is a default method in Collection interface
60    Stream<String> streamAnimals = animalList.stream();
61    System.out.println("Number of elements: "+streamAnimals.count()); // 3
62
63    // stream() is a default method in the Collection interface and therefore
64    // is inherited by all classes that implement Collection. Map is NOT one
65    // of those i.e. Map is not a Collection. To bridge between the two, we
66    // use the Map method entrySet() to return a Set view of the Map (Set
67    // IS-A Collection).
68    Map<String, Integer> namesToAges = new HashMap<>();
69    namesToAges.put("Mike", 22);namesToAges.put("Mary", 24);namesToAges.put("Alice", 31);
70    System.out.println("Number of entries: "+
71            namesToAges
72                .entrySet() // get a Set (i.e. Collection) view of the Map
73                .stream()   // stream() is a default method in Collection
74                .count());  // 3
```

Figure 15.5 – Streaming a collection

In this figure, we initially create a `List<String>` using `Arrays.asList(T... a)`:

```
List<String> animalList = Arrays.asList("cat", "dog", "sheep");
```

We then use the `Collection stream()` method to create the stream object:

```
Stream<String> streamAnimals = animalList.stream();
```

To start the stream off, we use the terminal `count()` operation:

```
System.out.println("Number of elements: "+streamAnimals.count()); // 3
```

What if you had a *Map* and wanted to stream it? Remember that Map is not a `Collection` as it does not implement it. This is what the second example shows. Firstly, let us declare and populate the map:

```
Map<String, Integer> namesToAges = new HashMap<>();
namesToAges.put("Mike", 22);
namesToAges.put("Mary", 24);
namesToAges.put("Alice", 31);
```

To bridge across from a Map to a `Collection` we will do the following:

```
namesToAges.entrySet()
```

The `entrySet()` method in Map returns a `Set` view of the entries in the map. As Set is a sub-interface of `Collection`, Set "is-a" `Collection`. At this point, we can now stream the collection as normal:

```
.stream()
```

Finally, we start off the process using the terminal operation, count(), which returns 3, showing that the stream worked.

Now, let's look at the `Stream.of()` method.

## Stream.of()

`static <T> Stream<T> of(T... values)` is a very useful method. While its signature can seem a little confusing, it is very straightforward to use. It is a `static` method that is generically typed, hence `<T>`. Thus, the compiler does not complain about the use of T in the signature. It returns `Stream<T>` and T depends on what is passed in. For example, if you pass in strings, then you get back `Stream<String>`. The parameters are a `varargs` list, which is very flexible.

Let's look at some examples. *Figure 15.6* (BuildStreams.java) presents the code:

```
15          String[] cities = {"Dublin", "Berlin", "Paris"};
16          Stream<String> citiesStream = Stream.of(cities);
17          System.out.println(citiesStream.count()); // 3
18
19          Stream<Integer> streamI = Stream.of( ...values: 1,2,3);
20          System.out.println(streamI.count()); // 3
21
22          Stream<String> streamS = Stream.of( ...values: "a", "b", "c", "d");
23          System.out.println(streamS.count()); // 4
24
25          Stream<Dog> streamD = Stream.of(new Dog());
26          System.out.println(streamD.count()); // 1
```

Figure 15.6 – Stream.of() examples

In this figure, we initially declare an array of strings:

```
String[] cities = {"Dublin", "Berlin", "Paris"};
```

Using the `Stream.of()` method, we declare the stream source to be the array:

```
Stream<String> citiesStream = Stream.of(cities);
```

Once declared, we start the stream using the `count()` terminal operation:

```
System.out.println(citiesStream.count()); // 3
```

Next, `Stream.of()` sources the stream from a `varargs` of integers passed in (boxed as `Integer`s):

```
Stream<Integer> streamI = Stream.of(1,2,3);
```

We start the streaming process as before, using the `count()` terminal operation:

```
System.out.println(streamI.count()); // 3
```

Following that, `Stream.of()` sources the stream from a `varargs` of strings and stream them:

```
Stream<String> streamS = Stream.of("a", "b", "c", "d");
System.out.println(streamS.count()); // 4
```

Lastly, we source the stream from a `varargs` of Dog (just one), and stream them:

```
Stream<Dog> streamD = Stream.of(new Dog());
System.out.println(streamD.count()); // 1
```

Now, let's examine how to stream from a file.

## Streaming from a file

To stream a file, we can use the `Files.lines()` method. Its signature is `public static Stream<String> lines(Path path) throws IOException`.

The `Path` parameter refers to the file we want to process. This file needs to be delimited; for example, using the forward slash (/) character. The file we will use contains the following lines:

```
Fido/Black
Lily/White
```

The returned `Stream<String>` refers to the lines from the file, one `String` for each line in the file. We can process the returned stream using the `forEach(Consumer)` terminal operation defined in the `Stream` interface. Inside the consumer block of code, each line from the file (a `String`) could be parsed into `String[]` using the `split()` method from the `String` class – where we pass in the delimiter and get back a `String[]` of the elements. Once we have this `String[]`, we can easily create our object and add it to a collection, such as `ArrayList`. This is an example of a `Consumer` side effect.

Assuming a `Cat` class with `name` and `color` instance variables and an associated constructor (ProcessFile.java), we could do the following:

```
try(Stream<String> stream =
  Files.lines(Paths.get(filename))){
      stream.forEach(line -> {
          String[] catsArray = line.split("/");
          cats.add(new Cat(catsArray[0], catsArray[1]));
      });
} catch (IOException ioe) {
          ioe.printStackTrace();
}
```

> **forEach(Consumer) versus forEach(Consumer)**
>
> In the Java API, these two versions of `forEach()` look very similar but they are in fact from two very different hierarchies. One is a `default` method in the `Iterable` interface (which `Collection` inherits). The other is a terminal operation in the `Stream` interface.

## Infinite streams

Infinite streams can easily be created using two `static` methods from the `Stream` interface, namely `generate()` and `iterate()`. Let's examine these in turn.

### Stream<T> generate(Supplier<T> s)

As per the API, it "returns an infinite, sequential unordered stream where each element is generated by the provided `Supplier`." *Figure 15.7* (`InfiniteStreamsGenerate.java`) presents some code that we can discuss:

```
48          // infinite stream of random unordered numbers
49          // between 0..9 inclusive
50          //    Stream<T> generate(Supplier<T> s)
51          //       Supplier is a functional interface:
52          //            T get()
53          Stream<Integer> infStream = Stream.generate(() -> {
54              return (int) (Math.random() * 10);
55          });
56          // keeps going until I kill it.
57          infStream.forEach(System.out::println);
```

Figure 15.7 – Creating an infinite stream using generate()

As this figure shows, the `Supplier` provided produces random numbers between 0 and 9 inclusive:

```
() -> (int) (Math.random() * 10);
```

We start the streaming process using the `forEach (Consumer)` terminal operation:

```
infStream.forEach(System.out::println);
```

`Consumer` accepts a method reference to output the numbers generated. This stream will keep going until we terminate the application (for example, from within the IDE).

> **Math.random()**
> Recall that `Math.random()` returns a `double` type between `0.0 <= x < 1.0`. In other words, a number between 0 and less than 1. When we multiply this number by `10` and subsequently cast that number to an `int` type, we are, in effect, scaling it to `0 <= x < 10`.

Now, let's discuss the other method for generating infinite streams, namely `iterate()`.

### Stream<T> iterate(T seed, UnaryOperator<T> fn)

This method gives you more control over the numbers generated. The first argument is the seed, which is the first number in the stream. The second parameter is a `UnaryOperator` (a `Function` where the input and output are the same type). This `UnaryOperator` function is a lambda that accepts the previous value and generates the next value. *Figure 15.8* (`InfiniteStreamsIterate.java`) presents a code example for us to discuss this further:

```
23          // infinite stream of ordered numbers
24          //    2, 4, 6, 8, 10, 12 etc...
25          // iterate(T seed, UnaryOperator<T> fn)
26          //    UnaryOperator is-a Function<T, T>
27          //       T apply(T t)
28          Stream<Integer> infStream = Stream.iterate( seed: 2, n -> n + 2);
29
30          // keeps going until I kill it.
31          infStream.forEach(System.out::println);
```

Figure 15.8 – Creating an infinite stream using iterate()

As this figure shows, the seed is 2 and the lambda expression generates the next even number after 2 and so forth. Thus, this stream generates 2, 4, 6, 8, and so on, until we kill the application.

What if we wanted only so many numbers? For example, what if we wanted only the even numbers up to 20 (starting at 2)? There is an overloaded version of iterate () that caters to this – its second parameter is a Predicate, which states when to finish. *Figure 15.9* (InfiniteStreamsIterate. java) presents an example:

```
49          // finite stream of ordered numbers
50          // 2, 4, 6, 8, 10, 12, 14, 16, 18, 20
51          Stream
52                  .iterate( seed: 2,              // seed
53                           n -> n <= 20,    // Predicate
54                           n -> n + 2)      // UnaryOperator
55                  .forEach(System.out::println);
```

Figure 15.9 – Creating an infinite/finite stream using iterate() and Predicate

The Predicate condition:

```
n -> n <=20
```

is the important line here. that specifies when this stream stops. Thus, this is one way of creating a finite stream from an infinite stream. If the Predicate condition keeps returning true, the stream will keep generating numbers until you kill the application.

In this figure, 2, 4, 6, 8, 10, 12, 14, 16, 18, and 20 all pass the `Predicate` condition and are output. Once 22 is generated and the `Predicate` fails, the stream stops.

Another way of turning an infinite stream into a finite stream is to use the `limit()` intermediate operation. *Figure 15.10* (`InfiniteStreamsIterate.java`) presents this scenario:

```
36              // finite stream of ordered numbers
37              // 2, 4, 6, 8, 10, 12, 14, 16, 18, 20
38              Stream
39                  .iterate( seed: 2, n -> n + 2)
40                  // limit() is a short-circuiting stateful
41                  // intermediate operation
42                  .limit( maxSize: 10)
43                  // forEach(Consumer) is a terminal operation
44                  .forEach(System.out::println);
```

Figure 15.10 – Creating a finite stream using limit()

In this figure, we restricted the numbers generated to 10 by using the `limit()` intermediate operation. We will discuss intermediate operations in *Chapter 16*. In this example, once the 10[th] number has passed by, `limit()` informs the JVM of this fact, and no further numbers are generated.

Now that we know how to create streams, let's examine terminal operations.

# Mastering terminal operations

As we discussed earlier, no streaming happens until the terminal operation executes. This gives the JVM an overall picture of the stream pipeline, thereby enabling efficiencies to be introduced in the background.

A terminal operation can be performed without any intermediate operation but not the other way around. *Reductions* are a special type of terminal operation where all of the contents of the stream are combined into a single primitive or *Object* (for example, a *Collection*).

*Table 15.1* represents the terminal operations we will be discussing in this section:

## Stream terminal operations

| Method | Return value | Reduction[1] |
|---|---|---|
| count() | long | Yes |
| min(), max() | Optional<T>    - stream may be empty | Yes |
| findAny(), findFirst() | Optional<T> | No – may not look at all of the elements |
| allMatch(), anyMatch(), noneMatch() | boolean | No – may not look at all of the elements |
| forEach() | void | No (as it does not return anything) |
| reduce() | varies | Yes |
| collect() | varies | Yes |

[1] Reductions are a special type of terminal operation where ALL of the contents of the stream are combined into a single primitive or Object e.g. long or Collection.

Table 15.1 – Terminal operations

Before we discuss them in turn, a brief discussion regarding the table. Remember, a reduction must look at all elements in the stream and then return a primitive or `Object`.

Some of these terminal operations, such as `allMatch(Predicate)`, may not look at all of the elements in the stream. For example, let's say we had the following code:

```
List<String> names = Arrays.asList("Alan","Brian","Colin");
Predicate<String> pred = name -> name.startsWith("A");
System.out.println(names.stream().allMatch(pred)); // false
```

The `Predicate` condition fails on `"Brian"`, as it does not start with `"A"`, and `allMatch()` returns `false`. Therefore, `"Colin"` is never examined and hence, `allMatch()` is not a reduction.

We will discuss `Optionals` later but for the moment, `Optionals` were introduced in Java 8 to replace `null` return values (and thereby help to reduce the number of `NullPointerExceptions`). If the stream is empty, an empty `Optional` is returned (and not `null`). Therefore, an `Optional` object either has a non-`null` value or is empty. One way of ending up with an empty stream is by filtering out all of its elements before calling the terminal operation.

Let's deal with the operations in turn.

# count()

We have already encountered count (), so a quick example has been provided in *Figure 15.11* (TerminalOperations.java):

```
152              long count = Stream.of( ...values: "dog", "cat")
153                              .count();
154           System.out.println(count); // 2
```

Figure 15.11 – count() in code

The count () method works with finite streams as it will never terminate for an infinite stream. In this example, the two strings, "dog" and "cat", are streamed and a count of 2 is returned. Note that count () is a reduction as it looks at each element in the stream and returns a single value.

# min() and max()

Like count (), both min () and max () work with finite streams and hang on infinite streams (in case another value might be the minimum or maximum value). Both are reductions as they return a single value after processing the whole stream. Given that the stream could be empty, *Optional* is the return type.

*Figure 15.12* (TerminalOperations.java) presents some code using min () and max ():

```
163      // Optional<T> min(Comparator)
164      // Optional<T> max(Comparator)
165      Optional<String> min = Stream.of( ...values: "deer", "horse", "pig")
166                              .min((s1, s2) -> s1.length()-s2.length());
167      min.ifPresent(System.out::println);// pig
168
169      Optional<Integer> max = Stream.of( ...values: 4,6,2,12,9)
170                              .max((i1, i2) -> i1-i2);
171      max.ifPresent(System.out::println);// 12
172
173      Optional<Object> noMin = Stream.empty().min((x1, x2) -> 0);
174      System.out.println(noMin.isEmpty());// true
175      System.out.println(noMin.isPresent());// false
```

Figure 15.12 – min() and max() in code

In this example, we initially define a custom `Comparator` that sorts the list of strings into ascending length-of-string order. This `Comparator` is then passed into the `min()` method, where `"pig"` is returned to `Optional`:

```
.min((s1, s2) -> s1.length()-s2.length())
```

We then use the functional-style `Optional` method, `ifPresent()`, to determine if there is a non-`null` value in `Optional`. As `"pig"` is there (present)), it is output:

```
min.ifPresent(System.out::println);// pig
```

Next up is a different custom `Comparator` that sorts the list of numbers into ascending numeric order. This is then passed into the `max()` method, where `12` is stored in the `Optional` variable `max`:

```
.max((i1, i2) -> i1-i2)
```

Again, we use the `ifPresent()` method to determine if there is a non-`null` value in max. As `12` is present, it is output:

```
max.ifPresent(System.out::println);// 12
```

Lastly, we demonstrate that you can use `Stream.empty()` to create an empty stream:

```
Optional<Object> noMin = Stream.empty().min((x1, x2) -> 0)
```

In this example, as the stream is empty, the comparator `(x1, x2) -> 0` is never called and as a result, there is no value in `Optional`. Thus, `isEmpty()` returns true and `isPresent()` returns false:

```
System.out.println(noMin.isEmpty());// true
System.out.println(noMin.isPresent());// false
```

## findAny() and findFirst()

These terminal operations are not reductions as they do not process the entire stream. As its name suggests, `findAny()` will return any element – typically, the first one is returned but this is not guaranteed. On the other hand, `findFirst()` does just that – it returns the first element. Not surprisingly, these methods can work with infinite streams (as they don't process all of the stream). An *Optional* is returned in both cases (as the stream may be empty when they are called).

A *short-circuiting* terminal operation is defined as an operation that, when presented with infinite input, may terminate in finite time. Given that these operations can return before processing all of the stream, they are considered short-circuiting.

*Figure 15.13* (TerminalOperationsFindAnyFindFirst.java) presents their use in code:

```
135         // Optional<T> findAny()
136         // Optional<T> findFirst()
137         // These are terminal operations but not reductions
138         // as they can return without processing all
139         // the elements in the stream. Reductions reduce the
140         // entire stream into one value.
141         Optional<String> any = Stream.of( ...values: "John", "Paul")
142                             .findAny();
143         any.ifPresent(System.out::println);// John (usually)
144
145         Optional<String> first = Stream.of( ...values: "John", "Paul")
146                             .findFirst();
147         first.ifPresent(System.out::println);// John
```

Figure 15.13 – findAny() and findFirst() in code

In this figure, we execute findAny() on the stream of strings "John" and "Paul". This returns "John" usually but is not guaranteed; whereas when we execute findFirst() on the same stream, "John" is returned all the time. As this example demonstrates, neither operation processes "Paul" and therefore they are not considered reductions.

## anyMatch(), allMatch, and noneMatch()

These three terminal operations all accept a Predicate condition and return a boolean value. Like the "find" methods, they are not reductions either as they may not look at *all* of the elements. Depending on the data, these operations may or may not terminate when presented with infinite streams. That said, they are considered short-circuiting as they may terminate. *Figure 15.14* (TerminalOperations.java) presents an example:

```
125         // boolean anyMatch(Predicate)
126         // boolean allMatch(Predicate)
127         // boolean noneMatch(Predicate)
128         List<String> names = Arrays.asList("Alan", "Brian", "Colin");
129         Predicate<String> pred = name -> name.startsWith("A");
130         System.out.println(names.stream().anyMatch(pred)); // true ("Alan")
131         System.out.println(names.stream().allMatch(pred)); // false ("Brian")
132         System.out.println(names.stream().noneMatch(pred));// false ("Alan")
```

Figure 15.14 – anyMatch(), allMatch(), and noneMatch() in code

In this figure, we define a finite stream of `String` names as follows:

```
List<String> names = Arrays.asList("Alan", "Brian", "Colin");
```

A predicate is defined to see if a name begins with `"A"`:

```
Predicate<String> pred = name -> name.startsWith("A");
```

We then stream the (source) list of names and check, using `anyMatch()`, if any of the names begin with `"A"` – as `"Alan"` does, `true` is returned:

```
names.stream().anyMatch(pred); // true ("Alan")
```

Next, we re-stream the list and check, using `allMatch()`, if all of the names begin with `"A"` – as `"Brian"` does not, `false` is returned:

```
names.stream().allMatch(pred); // false ("Brian")
```

We then re-stream the list and check, using `noneMatch()`, if none of the names begin with `"A"` – as `"Alan"` does, `false` is returned:

```
names.stream().noneMatch(pred);// false ("Alan")
```

Notice that we have to re-stream the source twice (for `allMatch()` and `noneMatch()`). This is because, once a terminal operation is performed, a stream is considered consumed and can no longer be used. If you need the same data, then you must return to the source and get a new stream. This is what we have done here. Attempting an operation on a closed source generates an `IllegalStateException` error.

Let's delve a little deeper into the short-circuiting nature of these operations when presented with infinite data. The following example (*Figure 15.15*) presents code (`TerminalOperations.java`) where each of these operations, given an infinite stream, may or may not terminate. Whether they terminate or not is determined by the data (and the predicate being tested against that data):

```
134    Stream<String> infStr = Stream.generate(() -> "abc");
135    Predicate<String> startsWithA = s -> s.startsWith("a");
136    Predicate<String> startsWithB = s -> s.startsWith("b");
137    System.out.println(infStr.anyMatch(startsWithA));    // true, short-circuit
138    System.out.println(infStr.anyMatch(startsWithB));    // forever...
139
140    System.out.println(infStr.noneMatch(startsWithA));   // false
141    System.out.println(infStr.noneMatch(startsWithB));   // forever...
142
143    System.out.println(infStr.allMatch(startsWithA));    // forever...
144    System.out.println(infStr.allMatch(startsWithB));    // false, short-circuit
```

Figure 15.15 – Short-circuiting nature of anyMatch(), allMatch(), and noneMatch() in code

In this figure, we generated an infinite stream of `"abc"` strings and defined two predicates; one checks if the string begins with `"a"` and the other checks if the string begins with `"b"`. Note that, as explained previously, a closed stream must be reopened before being used. Therefore, lines 137-144 are *mutually exclusive* – you can only use one of them at a time. We have left them all uncommented as this aids the clarity of the diagram. When we run the code, we must comment out five of the six lines.

`infStr.anyMatch(startsWithA)` checks if any of the strings start with `"a"` – as the first one does, it short-circuits with `true`.

`infStr.anyMatch(startsWithB)` checks if any of the strings start with `"b"` – the first one does not, so it checks the next one; it does not either, and so on. We had to kill the program in this instance.

`infStr.noneMatch(startsWithA)` checks if none of the strings start with `"a"` – as `"abc"` begins with `"a"`, `noneMatch()` short-circuits with `false`.

`infStr.noneMatch(startsWithB)` checks if none of the strings start with `"b"` – the first one does not, so it checks the next one; it does not either, and so on. This goes on forever, so we had to kill the program. So, when does `noneMatch()` return `true`? If you have a finite stream where none of the elements match the given predicate.

`infStr.allMatch(startsWithA)` checks if all the strings begin with `"a"`. In this instance, this will go on forever as we keep generating strings that do begin with `"a"`, ensuring `allMatch()` needs to check the next one and so on.

`infStr.allMatch(startsWithB)` can short-circuit as `"abc"` does not begin with `"b"`, enabling `allMatch()` to return `false`.

## forEach()

As `forEach(Consumer)` has no return value (returns `void`), it is not considered a reduction. As it returns nothing, any changes you wish to make must occur inside `Consumer` as side effects. We covered several examples of `forEach()` already, so *Figure 15.16* (TerminalOperations.java) shows just a simple one:

```
109          // void forEach(Consumer)
110          // As there is no return value, forEach() is not a reduction.
111          // As the return type is 'void', if you want something to
112          // happen, it has to happen inside the Consumer (side-effect).
113          Stream<String> names = Stream.of( ...values: "Cathy", "Pauline", "Zoe");
114          names.forEach(System.out::print);//CathyPaulineZoe
```

Figure 15.16 – The forEach() terminal operation in code

In this example, we are streaming a list of *strings*, representing peoples' names and echoing them to the screen.

## reduce()

The reduce() method combines a stream into a single object. As it processes all the elements, it is a reduction. There are three overloaded versions. We will discuss them in turn with examples.

### T reduce(T identity, BinaryOperator<T> accumulator)

This is the most common way of doing a reduction – start with an initial value (identity) and keep merging it with the next value. As well as the identity being the initial value, it is also the value returned if the stream is empty. This means that there will always be a result and thus Optional is not the return type (in this version).

The accumulator combines the current result with the current value in the stream. As it is a BinaryOperator, this means it is a function where the two inputs and the return type are all the same type.

*Figure 15.17* (TerminalOperations.java) presents some examples to help explain this:

```
82        // T reduce(T identity, BinaryOperator<T> accumulator)
83        //      BinaryOperator<T> functional method:
84        //          T apply(T, T);
85        String name = Stream.of( ...values: "s", "e", "a", "n")
86                        .reduce( identity: "", (s1, s2) -> s1 + s2);
87        System.out.println(name);// sean
88
89        String name2 = Stream.of( ...values: "s", "e", "a", "n")
90                        .filter(s -> s.length()>2)
91                        .reduce( identity: "nothing", (s1, s2) -> s1 + s2);
92        System.out.println(name2);// nothing
93
94        Integer product = Stream.of( ...values: 2,3,4)
95                        .reduce( identity: 1, (n1, n2) -> n1 * n2);
96        System.out.println(product);// 24
```

Figure 15.17 – T reduce(T identity, BinaryOperator<T> acc) in code

Let us examine the first reduction in this figure:

```
String name = Stream.of("s", "e", "a", "n")
                .reduce("", (s1, s2) -> s1 + s2);
System.out.println(name);// sean
```

This reduction defines the empty string as the identity. This is both the string we start with and the string returned if the stream is empty. The accumulator takes in two strings, namely, s1 and s2. The first time round, s1 is "" and s2 is "s", resulting in "s". The next time round, s1 is the result from the previous run, which is `"s"`, and s2 is `"e"`, resulting in `"se"`. After that, s1 is `"se"` and s2 is `"a"`, resulting in `"sea"`. Finally, s1 is `"sea"` and s2 is `"n"`, resulting in `"sean"`. That's how accumulators work.

The second reduction starts by re-streaming the source:

```
String name2 = Stream.of("s", "e", "a", "n")
                .filter(s -> s.length()>2)
                .reduce("nothing", (s1, s2) -> s1 + s2);
System.out.println(name2);// nothing
```

However, a filter intermediate operation is applied. This filter ensures only strings with a length of > 2 are kept, resulting in an empty stream for `reduce()`. Thus, `reduce()` returns the `"nothing"` identity.

The last reduction gives another example of an identity and an accumulator in action:

```
Integer product = Stream.of(2,3,4)
                    .reduce(1, (n1, n2) -> n1 * n2);
System.out.println(product);// 24
```

The sequence of values is n1 is 1, n2 is 2, and the result is 2; n1 is 2, n2 is 3, and the result is 6; n1 is 6, n2 is 4 and the result is 24.

### Optional<T> reduce(BinaryOperator<T> accumulator)

This is very similar to the first version except that no identity is provided. As no identity is provided, `Optional` is the return type (given that, the stream may be empty before this method is called). There are three possible returns:

1.  An empty stream – results in an empty `Optional`

2.  One element in the stream – that element is returned (in `Optional`)

3.  Multiple elements in the stream – the accumulator is applied

Why are there two versions that are so similar? Why not just have the first version, with its identity? Well, there may be a situation, however unlikely, that the accumulator returns with the same value as the identity. In that scenario, you would not know whether the stream was empty (identity returned) or not (accumulator applied). This second version, with its use of `Optional`, ensures that you know when the stream is empty.

Now, let's examine the third version of `reduce()`.

### *<U> reduce(U identity, BiFunction accumulator, BinaryOperator combiner)*

This version is used when we are dealing with different types where intermediate reductions are created that are combined at the end. This version is useful in parallel streams as the stream can be decomposed and reassembled by different threads. *Figure 15.18* (`TerminalOperations.java`) presents an example in code:

```
37      // <U> U reduce (U identity,
38      //                  BiFunction accumulator,
39      //                  BinaryOperator combiner)
40      Stream<String> stream = Stream.of( values: "car", "bus", "train", "aeroplane");
41      int length = stream.reduce( identity: 0,  // identity
42                                  (n, str) -> n + str.length(), // n is Integer
43                                  (n1, n2) -> n1 + n2); // both are Integers
44      System.out.println(length);// 20
```

Figure 15.18 - U reduce(U identity, BiFunction accumulator, BinaryOperator combiner) in code

In this example, we are streaming a list of strings and we want to total the overall number of characters in all of the strings. The `reduce()` method is coded as follows:

```
stream.reduce( 0,  // identity
              (n, str) -> n + str.length(), // n is Integer
              (n1, n2) -> n1 + n2); // both are Integers
```

and has 3 elements:

- 0 is the identity, which represents our starting value.

- `(n, str) -> n + str.length()` is the `BiFunction` accumulator. In this case, the first parameter is `Integer` and the second parameter is `String`. The return type matches the first parameter – in other words, `Integer`. We did not highlight this in the method signature as all the letters can sometimes confuse the issue. This accumulator adds the length of the current `String` to the current total.

- `(n1, n2) -> n1 + n2` represents the combiner `BinaryOperator` (a function where the types are the same). Its lambda simply adds the two numbers and returns the sum. This function adds the intermediate results from the accumulators.

Thus, with parallel streams, one thread could return the accumulated value of 6, which is the sum of the lengths of `"car"` and `"bus"`, whereas another thread could return the accumulated value of 14, which is the sum of the lengths of `"train"` and `"aeroplane"`. These two values are then combined by the combiner, resulting in 20.

Now, we will move on to a powerful terminal operation, namely `collect()`.

# collect()

This is a special type of reduction called a mutable reduction because we are using the same mutable object while accumulating. This makes it more efficient than regular reductions. Common mutable objects include `StringBuilder` and `ArrayList`.

This operation is extremely useful for getting data **out** of streams and putting it into other forms, such as a `Map`, `List`, or `Set`.

There are two versions – one that gives you complete control over the collecting process and another that gives you predefined collectors from the API. We will start with the first one, where you can specify everything yourself.

## collect(Supplier, BiConsumer, BiConsumer)

This method is best explained with a code example, see *Figure 15.19*, which is taken from `TerminalOperations.java` on the repo.

```
20      public static void doCollect1(){
21
22          // StringBuilder collect(Supplier<StringBuilder> supplier,
23          //                       BiConsumer<StringBuilder,String> accumulator
24          //                       BiConsumer<StringBuilder,StringBuilder> combiner)
25          StringBuilder word = Stream.of( ...values: "ad", "jud", "i", "cate")
26                  .collect(() -> new StringBuilder(),        // StringBuilder::new
27                          (sb, str) -> sb.append(str),       // StringBuilder::append
28                          (sb1, sb2) -> sb1.append(sb2));    // StringBuilder::append
29          System.out.println(word);// adjudicate
```

Figure 15.19 – The collect(Supplier, BiConsumer, BiConsumer) operation in code

In this figure, we are building up one long word from a list of smaller words. Note that the equivalent method references (to the lambdas used), are in comments on the right-hand side of each line.

The first argument to `collect()` is a `Supplier` which specifies that we want to work with a `StringBuilder`:

```
() -> new StringBuilder()
```

The accumulator adds the current `String` to the `StringBuilder`:

```
(sb, str) -> sb.append(str)
```

The combiner takes the two `StringBuilder`'s and merges them:

```
(sb1, sb2) -> sb1.append(sb2)
```

This is useful in parallel processing, where different threads can perform accumulations and have their results combined. In this example, thread 1 could return `"adjud"`, the result of accumulating `"ad"` and `"jud"`; and thread 2 could return `"icate"`, the result of accumulating `"i"` and `"cate"`. These two results combine into `"adjudicate"`.

Now, let's look at the version of `collect()` where we pass in pre-defined API collectors.

## collect(Collector)

This is the version that accepts a pre-defined API collector. We access these collectors via `static` methods in the `Collectors` class. These collectors do nothing on their own – they exist to be passed into the `collect(Collector)` method.

We will examine many of them, particularly the ones that help us extract data out of the stream into collections for subsequent processing. In addition, we will look at how to group and partition information. Let's start with some of the more basic collectors.

### Collectors.joining(CharSequence delimiter)

This collector returns a `Collector` that concatenates the input elements, separated by the specified delimiter. The order of the stream is maintained. *Figure 15.20* presents an example (taken from CollectorsExamples.java on the repo).

```
187         String s = Stream.of( ...values: "cake", "biscuits", "apple tart")
188                     .collect(Collectors.joining( delimiter: ", "));
189         System.out.println(s);   // cake, biscuits, apple tart
```

Figure 15.20 - Collectors.joining() in code

In this example, the strings are appended together and delimited by `", "`.

### Collectors.averagingInt(ToIntFunction)

This returns a `Collector` that produces the average of the integers produced by the function supplied. *Figure 15.21* (CollectorsExamples.java) presents an example:

```
196         Double avg = Stream.of( ...values: "cake", "biscuits", "apple tart")
197                     // averagingInt(ToIntFunction) functional method is:
198                     //      int applyAsInt(T value);
199                 .collect(Collectors.averagingInt(s -> s.length())); // String::length
200         System.out.println(avg);   // 7.333333333333333
```

Figure 15.21 – Collectors.averagingInt(ToIntFunction) in code

In this example, we are streaming strings, representing desserts. Each string has a length and we want to calculate the average of the lengths. The function, `s -> s.length()` takes in a `String`, namely `s`, and returns its integer length. The method reference version is in a comment on the right. The average is then output.

Now, let's examine how we can extract the stream contents into a `List`, `Set`, or `Map`. We will start with `List`.

## Collectors.toList()

This returns a `Collector` operation that accumulates the elements into a new `List`. There is no guarantee on the type of `List`. For example, there is no guarantee that the `List` is an `ArrayList` or a `LinkedList`. To gain that level of control, you must use the `toCollection(Supplier)` method (which we will be using in the `Set` example). *Figure 15.22* presents the `Car` type (`CollectorsExamples.java`) that we will use in the next few examples:

```java
6     class Car{
7         private String brand;
8         private int year;
9         public Car(String brand, int year) {
10            this.brand = brand;
11            this.year  = year;
12        }
13        public String getBrand() {
14            return brand;
15        }
16        // other methods omitted
17    }
```

Figure 15.22 – The Car class

*Figure 15.23* presents an example of `Collectors.toList()` in code (from `CollectorsExamples.java` in the repo):

```java
40    var cars = new ArrayList<Car>();
41    cars.add(new Car( brand: "Tesla",  year: 2021));
42    cars.add(new Car( brand: "Ford",   year: 2022));
43    cars.add(new Car( brand: "Audi",   year: 2018));
44    List<String> list = cars.stream()
45            .map(car -> car.getBrand())// Car::getBrand
46            .collect(Collectors.toList());
47    System.out.println(list);// [Tesla, Ford, Audi]
```

Figure 15.23 – Collectors.toList() in code

In this example, we added three `Cars` to our `List`. Recall that `Lists` maintain insertion order. The `map(Function)` method is an intermediate operation that takes in one stream and transforms it into another stream. We will discuss the `map()` method in more detail in *Chapter 16*, but for now, realize that there is `Stream<Car>` coming into `map()` and `Stream<String>` coming out. This is because `brand` in `Car` is a `String`. Now, we have a `Stream<String>` for `collect()` to extract in `List` format.

As stated earlier, the implementation type is not guaranteed. What if we wanted a specific implementation and not just that, but an implementation that sorted the elements as they were added? `TreeSet` will do this. Let's look at that now.

### Collectors.toSet() and Collectors.toCollection(Supplier)

`Collectors.toSet()` returns a `Collector` that accumulates the elements into a new `Set`. There is no guarantee on the type of `Set`. In this example, however, we want a specific `Set`, namely `TreeSet`. We can use `Collectors.toCollection(Supplier)` when we want a specific implementation. *Figure 15.24* presents the code (`CollectorsExamples.java`):

```
28    var cars = new ArrayList<Car>();
29    cars.add(new Car( brand: "Tesla",  year: 2021));
30    cars.add(new Car( brand: "Ford",  year: 2022));
31    cars.add(new Car( brand: "Audi",  year: 2018));
32    Set<String> treeSet = cars.stream()
33            .map(car -> car.getBrand())// Car::getBrand
34            .collect(Collectors.toCollection(TreeSet::new));
35    System.out.println(treeSet);// [Audi, Ford, Tesla]
```

Figure 15.24 – Collectors.toCollection(Supplier) in code

In this example, the cars have been deliberately added to our `ArrayList` in unsorted brand order. The following line is where the magic happens:

```
.collect(Collectors.toCollection(TreeSet::new));
```

We are passing in a `Supplier` method reference to create a `TreeSet` that is, in turn, passed to the `Collectors.toCollection()` method. This results in a `TreeSet` implementation. When we output `treeSet` we get:

```
[Audi, Ford, Tesla]
```

Notice that the brands are now sorted alphabetically (the default sort order for strings). We can also extract data out of a stream into a `Map`. Let us examine that now.

## Collectors.toMap(Function keyMapper, Function valueMapper)

This returns a `Collector` that gathers elements into a `Map` where the keys and values are the result of applying the provided mapping function to the stream elements. Again, there are no guarantees of the type of `Map` returned. *Figure 15.25* presents an example in code (`CollectorsExamples.java`):

```
175         // We want a map: dessert name -> number of characters in dessert name
176         // Output:
177         //   {biscuits=8, cake=4, apple tart=10}
178         Map<String, Integer> map =
179                 Stream.of( ...values: "cake", "biscuits", "apple tart")
180                     .collect(
181 //                      Collectors.toMap(s -> s,             // lambda key
182 //                                       s -> s.length()) // lambda value
183                         Collectors.toMap(String::toString,  // Function for the key
184                                          String::length)    // Function for the value
185                     );
186         System.out.println(map);
```

Figure 15.25 – Collectors.toMap(Function keyMapper, Function valueMapper) in code

In this example, we are streaming a list of desserts (as strings). The declared `Map` states that our key is a `String` type and that the value is an `Integer` type. This is because we want to set up a `Map` so that the dessert name is the key and the number of characters in the dessert name is the value.

The keys in the `Map` are set up using the following `Function`:

```
String::toString  // Function for key, same as: s -> s
```

Recall that `Function<T, R>` takes in one parameter of type T and returns a result of type R. In this example, our function will be `Function<String, String>` as we are streaming a dessert (`String`) and this dessert is what we want to use as the key. We can simply use the lambda `s -> s` or use the `String::toString` method reference. Either version will work.

The values in the `Map` are set up using the following `Function`:

```
String::length      // Same as: s -> s.length()
```

Our function in this case is `Function<String, Integer>` as we want our function to return the length of the dessert. We can use the lambda `s -> s.length()` or the `String::length` method reference.

The output that's generated is:

```
{biscuits=8, cake=4, apple tart=10}
```

Before we present the next version, let's look at an example that generates an exception. *Figure 15.26* presents the example in code (CollectorsExamples.java):

```
176    // We want a map: number of characters in dessert name -> dessert name.
177    // However, 2 of the desserts have the same length (cake and tart).
178    // As length is our key and we can't have duplicate keys, this leads to an
179    // exception as Java does not know what to do...
180    //    IllegalStateException: Duplicate key 4 (attempted merging values cake and tart)
181    Map<Integer, String> map =
182        Stream.of( ...values: "cake", "biscuits", "tart")
183            .collect(
184                Collectors.toMap(String::length,    // length is the key
185                                 String::toString) // dessert name is the value
186            );
187    System.out.println(map);
```

Figure 15.26 – The Collectors.toMap(Function keyMapper, Function valueMapper) exception

In this figure, we are trying to set up a Map where the key is the length of the dessert name and the value is the dessert name itself. Note that the dessert names are subtly different from the previous figure. Now, instead of `"apple tart"`, we have `"tart"`. This is going to lead to problems. Maps cannot have duplicate keys and both `"cake"` and `"tart"` are 4 characters long. This leads to an `IllegalStateException` error.

To fix this issue, we need to use the second version of `toMap()`.

### Collectors.toMap(Function, Function, BinaryOperator mergeFunction)

This collector operates similarly to the previous collector, except when we encounter duplicate keys. In that scenario, the merge function is applied to the *values*. The merge function is a `BinaryOperator<T,>`, which is-a `BiFunction<T, T, T>`. In other words, there are two inputs and one result, and they are all the same type. *Figure 15.27* presents the code (`CollectorsExamples.java`) with the merge function present to handle duplicate keys:

```
156    // To get around the duplicate keys issue, we can supply a merge function,
157    // whereby we append the colliding keys values together.
158    Map<Integer, String> map =
159        Stream.of( ...values: "cake", "biscuits", "tart")
160            .collect(
161                Collectors.toMap(s -> s.length(),// length is the key
162                                 s -> s,          // dessert name is the value
163                                 (s1, s2) -> s1 + "," + s2)// Merge function - what to
164                                                  // do if we have duplicate keys
165                                                  //   - append the values
166            );
167    System.out.println(map);// {4=cake,tart, 8=biscuits}
```

Figure 15.27 – Collectors.toMap(Function, Function, BinaryOperator)

In this example, the only difference is the merge function:

```
(s1, s2) -> s1 + "," + s2)
```

The merge function takes in `s1` and `s2`, the values for the two colliding keys. In this example, the values are appended with a comma between them.

The output generated is:

```
{4=cake,tart, 8=biscuits}
```

The colliding key was 4 and their values were `"cake"` and `"tart"`, resulting in `"4=cake, tart"`.

The next version enables us to specify the `Map` implementation we desire.

### Collectors.toMap(Function, Function, BinaryOperator, Supplier mapFactory)

As we know, the `Map` implementations that are returned are not guaranteed. You could get a `HashMap` or `TreeMap` implementation. This `toMap()` version is very similar to the previous one except there is an extra argument where we can specify our implementation type. *Figure 15.28* presents the code (`CollectorsExamples.java`) with the constructor method reference used to ensure a `TreeMap` implementation:

```
139        // The maps returned are not guaranteed. What if we wanted
140        // a TreeMap implementation so our keys would be sorted. The last argument
141        // caters for this.
142        TreeMap<String, Integer> map =
143                Stream.of( ...values: "cake", "biscuits", "apple tart", "cake")
144                .collect(
145                    Collectors.toMap(String::toString, // dessert name is the key
146                                     String::length,   // length is the value
147                                     (len1, len2) -> len1 +len2, // what to do if we have
148                                                                 // duplicate keys:
149                                                                 //    - add the *values*
150                                     TreeMap::new ));   // Supplier
151        System.out.println(map);// {apple tart=10, biscuits=8, cake=8} Note: cake maps to 8
152        System.out.println(map.getClass());// class java.util.TreeMap
```

Figure 15.28 – Collectors.toMap(Function, Function, BinaryOperator, Supplier)

In this figure, the dessert name is the key and the length of the dessert name is the value. `"cake"` is in the source twice, causing a duplicate keys issue and a reason to invoke the merge function. In this instance, the values for the duplicate keys are to be added. As `"cake"` appears just twice, this means that `"cake=8"` will be in `Map`.

In this example, we want a `TreeMap` implementation. To ensure this, we specify an extra argument, the following `Supplier`:

```
TreeMap::new
```

Thus, our keys will be sorted. When we output our map we can see that the keys are alphabetically sorted, as expected:

```
{apple tart=10, biscuits=8, cake=8}
```

Also, note that `"cake"` maps to 8 (4 + 4).

We can also use the `getClass()` method to prove that we have indeed a `TreeMap` implementation:

```
System.out.println(map.getClass());// java.util.TreeMap
```

Now, let's examine the `groupingBy` terminal operations.

### Collectors.groupingBy(Function classifier)

The `groupingBy()` operation tells `collect()` to group all the elements into a `Map` implementation. The `Function` parameter determines the keys in `Map`. The values are a `List` (the default) of all entries that match that key. Having the values returned as a `List` can, as we shall see, be changed. There is no guarantee as to the `Map` or `List` implementations used. *Figure 15.29* presents an example in code, taken from `CollectorsExamples.java` in the repo:

```
127    Stream<String> names = Stream.of( ...values: "Martin", "Peter", "Tom", "Tom", "Ann");
128    Map<Integer, List<String>> map =
129        names.collect(
130            // passing in a Function that determines the
131            // key in the Map
132            Collectors.groupingBy(String::length) // name -> name.length()
133        );
134    System.out.println(map);// {3=[Tom, Tom, Ann], 5=[Peter], 6=[Martin]}
```

Figure 15.29 – Collectors.groupingBy(Function) in code

In this example, we are streaming a list of names and are extracting a `Map<Integer, List<String>` from the stream (as per the declaration). The `Function` parameter `String::length` that's passed into `groupingBy()`, tells `collect()` that the key in the map is the length of the `String` (in effect, the number of characters in the name). The values are organized into a `List`, and each entry in the list is a `String` where the length of the `String` matches the key. For example, as per the output:

```
{3=[Tom, Tom, Ann], 5=[Peter], 6=[Martin]}
```

5 maps to `"Peter"` and 6 maps to `"Martin"`. Note that in the output, `"Tom"` appears in the list twice. This is because lists allow duplicates.

What if we wanted "Tom" to appear only once in the output list? There is an overloaded version of groupingBy() that will help us here.

### Collectors.groupingBy(Function keyMapper, Collector downstreamCollector)

Recall that a Set implementation does not allow duplicates, so using a Set implementation for the values, as opposed to the default List, will solve this. The second parameter here is known as a *downstream collector*. The function of a downstream collector is to do something special with the *values*. In this example, we want the values organized as a Set implementation. *Figure 15.30* presents the code (CollectorsExamples.java) adjustments:

```
116         Stream<String> names = Stream.of( ...values: "Martin", "Peter", "Tom", "Tom", "Ann");
117         Map<Integer, Set<String>> map =
118             names.collect(
119                 Collectors.groupingBy(
120                     String::length,      // key Function
121                     Collectors.toSet()) // what to do with the values
122             );
123         System.out.println(map);// {3=[Ann, Tom], 5=[Peter], 6=[Martin]}
124         System.out.println(map.getClass());// class java.util.HashMap
```

Figure 15.30 – Using Collectors.groupingBy(Function, Collector) for a Set implementation

In this example, the type for the values in the Map is Set<String> and not List<String>. The downstream collector:

```
Collectors.toSet()
```

states that we want the values organized as a Set. The output shows that "Tom" is now listed only once:

```
{3=[Ann, Tom], 5=[Peter], 6=[Martin]}
```

Note that the implementation type for our Map happens to be a HashMap implementation:

```
System.out.println(map.getClass());// java.util.HashMap
```

This implementation is not guaranteed. What if we wanted to guarantee a TreeMap implementation? There is an overloaded version to help us here also.

### Collectors.groupingBy(Function, Supplier mapFactory, Collector)

This version accepts a Supplier as its second parameter. This Supplier returns the implementation that you desire.

*Figure 15.31* presents the code adjustments (`CollectorsExamples.java`):

```
103        Stream<String> names = Stream.of( ...values: "Martin", "Peter", "Tom", "Tom", "Ann");
104        Map<Integer, List<String>> map =
105            names.collect(
106                Collectors.groupingBy(
107                    String::length,
108                    TreeMap::new,        // map type Supplier
109                    Collectors.toList())// downstream collector
110            );
111        System.out.println(map);// {3=[Tom, Tom, Ann], 5=[Peter], 6=[Martin]}
112        System.out.println(map.getClass());// class java.util.TreeMap
```

Figure 15.31 – Using Collectors.groupingBy(Function, Supplier, Collector) for a TreeMap implementation

In this example, we are reverting to a `List` type for the values:

```
Map<Integer, List<String>> map
```

To extract the stream data as a `List` type, we must use the appropriate downstream collector:

```
Collectors.toList()
```

As can be seen from the output:

```
{3=[Tom, Tom, Ann], 5=[Peter], 6=[Martin]}
```

`"Tom"` is now duplicated again (as lists allow duplicates).

We also pass a `Supplier` argument to `groupingBy()`, stating we want a `TreeMap` implementation:

```
TreeMap::new
```

The `map.getClass()` call outputs:

```
java.util.TreeMap
```

showing that we have a `TreeMap` implementation.

We will now look at a special case of grouping, called partitioning.

## Collectors.partitioningBy(Predicate)

Partitioning is a special case of grouping where there are only two groups – true and false. Thus, the keys in the `Map` implementation will be of the `Boolean` type. The values will default to a `List` type. There is no guarantee as to the `Map` or `List` implementations returned.

*Figure 15.32* presents a code example (CollectorsExamples.java):

```
93          Stream<String> names = Stream.of( ...values: "Thomas", "Teresa",
94                                                "Mike", "Alan", "Peter");
95          Map<Boolean, List<String>> map =
96              names.collect(
97                      // pass in a Predicate
98                      Collectors.partitioningBy(s -> s.startsWith("T"))
99              );
100         System.out.println(map);// {false=[Mike, Alan, Peter],
101                                  // true=[Thomas, Teresa]}
```

Figure 15.32 – Collectors.partitioningBy(Predicate) in code

In this figure, we are extracting data from the stream into a Map<Boolean, List<String>`. The keys will be true and false. The values will be the elements in the stream that are either true or false based on the predicate provided.

Using the following line of code, we tell `collect()` to partition the stream based on whether the String name begins with "T":

```
Collectors.partitioningBy(s -> s.startsWith("T"))
```

As can be seen from the output:

```
{false=[Mike, Alan, Peter, Alan], true=[Thomas, Teresa]}
```

the true partition contains "Thomas" and "Teresa" and the false partition contains all the other names. Note that "Alan" is in the false partition twice, as lists allow duplicates.

There is an overloaded version of `partitioningBy()` that enables us to pass in a downstream collector.

### Collectors.partitioningBy(Predicate, Collector downstreamCollector)

A downstream collector is useful for specifying a different collection for our values. For example, instead of a `List` view, we may want a `Set` view so that duplicates are automatically removed. *Figure 15.33* presents a code example (CollectorsExamples.java):

```
59          Stream<String> names = Stream.of( ...values: "Alan", "Teresa", "Mike",
60                                            "Alan", "Peter"); // "Alan" here twice
61          Map<Boolean, Set<String>> map =
62                  names.collect(
63                      Collectors.partitioningBy(
64                          s -> s.length() > 4,// predicate
65                          Collectors.toSet()    )
66                  );
67          System.out.println(map);// {false=[Mike, Alan], true=[Teresa, Peter]}
```

Figure 15.33 – Collectors.partitioningBy(Predicate, Collector) in code

In this example, note that the name "Alan" is in the source twice:

```
Stream.of("Alan", "Teresa", "Mike", "Alan", "Peter");
```

In addition, we are collecting data into a Map<Boolean, *Set*<String>>.

We also changed the predicate just to do something different:

```
s -> s.length() > 4,// predicate
```

Thus, if the number of characters in the string is > 4, the string is placed in the true partition; otherwise, the string is placed in the false partition.

We specify the required downstream collector as follows:

```
Collectors.toSet()
```

This means that the values are to be returned as a Set. As can be seen in the output, "Alan" appears only once (in the false partition):

```
{false=[Mike, Alan], true=[Teresa, Peter]}
```

That completes our discussion on the terminal operations section and also concludes *Chapter 15*. Now, let's put that knowledge into practice to reinforce the concepts we've learned.

## Exercises

1.  Create a stream of dinosaur names (use a List or an array). Use the filter method to create a new stream that only includes the names of carnivorous dinosaurs. Then, use the forEach method to print out these names..

2.  Demonstrate stream laziness by creating a stream from a list of dinosaur ages. Use the filter method to filter out ages greater than 100, and then use a map method to increase each remaining age by 10. However, do not use any terminal operation. Explain why nothing is printed or no operation is performed until a terminal operation (like forEach) is called..

3. Using a stream of dinosaur weights (as doubles), count the number of dinosaurs that weigh more than 5000 kg using the filter and count terminal operations.

4. Given a stream of dinosaur species names (String), use the `findFirst` terminal operation to retrieve the first name on the list.

# Project – dynamic dinosaur care system

Integrate the Stream API into your dinosaur care system to process large volumes of dinosaur data, such as health records, feeding schedules, and so on. The system should also incorporate `Optional` and parallel streams where appropriate, optimizing data processing and minimizing potential null pointer exceptions.

Here are the steps to get you there:

1. **Set up your project**: If you haven't done so already, create a new Java project in your IDE of choice. You should have a `Dinosaur` class with properties such as `name`, `species`, `healthStatus`, and so on. There should also be a `DinosaurCareSystem` class for implementing the main functionalities.

2. **Use streams to process dinosaur data**:

   I. **Health records**: Suppose you have a list of health records for each dinosaur and you want to find records where a dinosaur's health status was below a certain threshold. You could create a `Stream` from the list of records and use the `filter` method to get these records. Here's an example: `List<HealthRecord> criticalRecords = records.stream().filter(r -> r.getHealthStatus() < CRITICAL_THRESHOLD).collect(Collectors.toList())`.

   II. **Feeding schedules**: Maybe you want to find out all the feeding schedules within a certain period. Again, you can use a `Stream` to filter the schedules. Here's an example: `List<FeedingSchedule> morningFeeds = schedules.stream().filter(s -> s.getTime().isBefore(LocalTime.NOON)).collect(Collectors.toList())`.

3. **Use Optional to avoid** `NullPointerException` **errors**: Let's say each dinosaur has a trainer field that could be null. When trying to access the trainer's name, use `Optional` to avoid a `NullPointerException` error. Here's an example: `Optional.ofNullable(dinosaur.getTrainer()).map(Trainer::getName).orElse("No trainer assigned")`.

4. **Use parallel streams to process large amounts of data**: If the number of health records or feeding schedules is very large, you could use parallel streams to speed up the processing. This is as simple as replacing `stream()` with `parallelStream()` in the previous examples. Be aware, though, that not every problem is suitable for parallel processing. If the tasks have dependencies or need to be processed in a specific order, stick with regular streams.

# Summary

In this chapter, we explored the fundamentals of streams and stream terminal operations. Streams (along with lambda expressions) enable a style of programming known as functional-style programming, where you state what you want to solve rather than how to solve it (imperative style). Functional-style programming tends to be easier to read because, with imperative programming, the details of how to solve the problem can get mixed up in the implementation.

We discussed stream pipelines using the analogy of an assembly line. A stream pipeline consists of a data source, zero or more intermediate operations, and a terminal operation, in that order. Streams are lazily evaluated, which means that data is only provided as and when needed. This is possible because the JVM has an overall view of the pipeline, as nothing happens until the terminal operation is executed.

Stream sources can vary from arrays (`Arrays.stream(arrayToUse)`), collections (`collectionToUse.stream()`), and files (`Files.lines(Path)`) to a variable number of arguments (`Stream.of(varargs)`). Infinite streams can be generated using two `static` methods from the Stream API: `Stream.generate()` and `Stream.iterate()`.

Terminal operations kickstart the whole pipeline and every pipeline must have a terminal operation. Once a terminal operation executes on a stream, the stream is closed and must be re-streamed to be reused. Popular terminal operations include `forEach()`, `count()`, `min()`, `max()`, `findAny()`, `findFirst()`, `allMatch()`, `anyMatch()`, `noneMatch()`, `reduce()`, and `collect()`.

A reduction is a special type of terminal operation where all of the stream items are combined into one primitive or `Object`. The `reduce()` method has overloaded versions to facilitate this. The `collect()` method is very useful for extracting data out of the stream and into a collection, such as a `List` or `Map` delete The `collect()` method accepts collectors, which you can define yourself, or you can simply use one of the many pre-defined collectors in the API.

That completes our discussion on the fundamentals of streams. In the next chapter, we will expand into more advanced streaming concepts.

# 16
# Streams: Advanced Concepts

In *Chapter 15*, we learned about the fundamentals of streams. We started by discussing what a stream pipeline is by using an analogy of an assembly line. We saw that items only make their way onto the assembly line as and when needed. This is the principle of lazy evaluation. In this analogy, there are several operators that operate on the data (pencils) under the supervision of a supervisor (Java). The supervisor will not allow any work to start until the terminal operation in place. As Java is now aware of the full pipeline, efficiencies can be introduced. Once a pencil has passed an operator, the operator cannot get that pencil back. Thus, streams are different to arrays or `Collections` in that manner. The pencils can be processed by as many operators as necessary but only one operator is the terminal operation. The other operators represent intermediate operations (a topic in this chapter).

We examined how to create streams. Streams can be created from various sources: arrays, collections, files, and varargs. We created both finite and infinite streams. Infinite streams are created using `Stream.generate()` and `Stream.iterate()`.

We took a deep dive into terminal operations. Nothing happens until a terminal operation executes and once executed the stream is considered closed and must be re-streamed if you want to use it again. A reduction is an operation that examines all of the stream and produces a single output (primitive or `Object`). One of the terminal operations is the overloaded `reduce()` method which performs reductions on the stream. The `collect()` terminal operation is extremely useful for extracting data out of the stream (into a `Map` for example) for later use.

In this chapter, we will continue our coverage of streams. We will, with the aid of code examples, examine intermediate operations. Following that, we will discuss primitive streams and how to map streams. We will also discuss `Optional`s and lastly, we will finish with parallel streams.

This chapter covers the following main topics:

- Examining intermediate operations
- Delving into primitive streams
- Mapping streams

- Explaining `Optionals`
- Understanding parallel streams

# Technical requirements

The code for this chapter can be found on GitHub at `https://github.com/PacktPublishing/Learn-Java-with-Projects/tree/main/ch16`.

# Examining intermediate operations

As we know, a stream pipeline consists of a source, followed by zero or more intermediate operations, followed by a terminal operation. While the terminal operation is mandatory, intermediate operations are not. That said, intermediate operations are where pipelines get their real power as they transform the stream data as it flows by. Unlike terminal operations, intermediate operations produce a stream as a result. Let us start with `filter()`, which is taken from IntermediateOperations.java on the repo:

## filter(Predicate)

The `filter()` operation returns a stream containing the elements matching the given predicate. *Figure 16.1* presents a code example (from `IntermediateOperations.java` on the repo):

```
146        public static void doFilter() {
147
148            // Stream<T> filter(Predicate)
149            // The filter() method returns a Stream with the elements that
150            // MATCH the given predicate.
151            Stream.of( ...values: "Canada", "Ireland", "Spain")
152                    .filter(country -> country.length() > 5)
153                    .forEach(System.out::print);// CanadaIreland
154
155        }
```

Figure 16.1 - The filter(Predicate) intermediate operation in code

In this figure, the countries whose names are longer than 5 characters are output.

## distinct()

The `distinct()` operation returns a stream with duplicate elements removed. Internally, `distinct()` uses the `equals()` method from `Object` when comparing.

It is a *stateful* intermediate operation which means it needs to keep some state to operate effectively. This state enables `distinct()` to operate as follows: if this is the first time `distinct()` has seen this object, it passes it on but remembers it; if `distinct()` has already seen this object, it filters it out.

*Figure 16.2* presents a code example (from `IntermediateOperations.java` on the repo):

```
134    public static void doDistinct() {
135
136        // Stream<T> distinct()
137        // distinct() is a stateful intermediate operation
138        // Output: Before: eagle, After: eagle
139        //         Before: eagleBefore: EAGLE, After: EAGLE
140        Stream.of( ...values: "eagle", "eagle", "EAGLE")
141            .peek(s -> System.out.print("Before: "+s))
142            .distinct()
143            .forEach(s -> System.out.print(", After: "+s + "\n"));
144
145    }
```

Figure 16.2 - The distinct() intermediate operation in code

In this figure, we are streaming a list of strings, where `"eagle"` is duplicated. We are using the very useful `Stream<T> peek(Consumer)` intermediate operation. This `peek()` operation executes the consumer on the data as it passes by. This is a great help as it enables us to view the data flowing by. The `distinct()` operation is in our pipeline and the `forEach()` terminal operation starts the streaming.

When run, this code generates the following output:

```
// Output: Before: eagle, After: eagle
//         Before: eagleBefore: EAGLE, After: EAGLE
```

The first `"eagle"` is streamed into the pipeline, where `peek()` echoes it to the screen, with the decoration `"Before: "`. Then `peek()` passes `"eagle"` on to `distinct()`. As this is the first time `distinct()` has seen `"eagle"`, it passes it on but remembers it. Lastly, `forEach()` takes `"eagle"` and outputs it prepended with the string `", After:"`, followed by a newline.

Now the second `"eagle"` is streamed. The `peek()` operation outputs the details and passes `"eagle"` on. However, `distinct()` remembers that it has seen this element already and filters it out. This is why `", After: eagle"` appears only once in the output.

Lastly, `"EAGLE"` is streamed. This proceeds just as the first `"eagle"` did.

# limit(long)

The limit() operation is a short-circuiting, stateful intermediate operation. We saw its short-circuiting nature put into good effect by transforming an infinite stream into a finite stream in *Chapter 15*. Obviously, it needs to maintain some state in order to keep a count of the elements that have passed by. *Figure 16.3* presents a code example (IntermediateOperations.java):

```
119    public static void doLimit() {
120
121        // Stream<T> limit(long maxSize)
122        // limit is a short-circuiting stateful intermediate operation.
123        // Lazy evaluation - 66, 77, 88 and 99 are not streamed as they
124        // are not needed (limit of 2 i.e. 44 and 55).
125        // Output:
126        //   A - 11 A - 22 A - 33 A - 44 B - 44 C - 44 A - 55 B - 55 C - 55
127        Stream.of( ...values: 11,22,33,44,55,66,77,88,99)
128                .peek(n -> System.out.print(" A - "+n))
129                .filter(n -> n > 40)
130                .peek(n -> System.out.print(" B - "+n))
131                .limit( maxSize: 2)
132                .forEach(n -> System.out.print(" C - "+n));
133    }
```

Figure 16.3 - The limit(long) intermediate operation in code

In this example, we are streaming a list of numbers. This example is a good example of lazy evaluation. The output is:

```
A - 11 A - 22 A - 33 A - 44 B - 44 C - 44 A - 55 B - 55 C - 55
```

Let us examine what happens here.

- 11 is streamed, first peek() outputs it prepended with "A - " and passes it to filter() where it fails (as 11 is not > 40)

- 22 is streamed and behaves just as 11 did

- 33 is streamed and operates in a similar fashion to 11 and 22

- 44 is streamed, passes the filter, hence "B - 44" is output; 44 is passed to limit() which records that this is the first element it has seen, before passing it on; forEach() outputs 44 prepended with "C - ".

- 55 is streamed and operates as 44 except that `limit()` informs Java that this is the second element it has passed and the limit is 2. Java lets `forEach()` finish and the stream is closed.

- Note that the first `peek()` never outputs `"A - 66"`, `"A - 77"`, `"A - 88"`, or `"A - 99"`. Therefore, 66, 77, 88, and 99 are never streamed - as they are not needed. This is another example of lazy evaluation.

Now let us look at `map()`.

## map(Function)

The `Stream<R> map(Function<T, R>)` operation is for transforming data. It creates a one-to-one mapping between elements in the stream and elements in the new stream returned. *Figure 16.4* presents a code example (`IntermediateOperations.java`):

```
111        public static void doMap() {
112
113            // <R> Stream<R> map(Function<T,R> mapper)
114            //      Function's functional method: R apply(T t);
115            Stream.of( ...values: "book", "pen", "ruler")
116                   .map(String::length) // s -> s.length()
117                   .forEach(System.out::print);// 435
118        }
```

Figure 16.4 - The map(Function) intermediate operation in code

The `map()` operation takes in a `Function` which, takes in one type and returns another, possibly different type. In this example, the lambda used, takes in a `String` namely s, and returns the `Integer` length of that `String`. The `forEach()` outputs the lengths of the `Strings` streamed: `"book"` is 4, `"pen"` is 3 and `"ruler"` is 5.

## flatMap(Function)

The `flatMap()` operation "flattens" a stream. In other words, multiple collections/arrays are merged into one. For example, if we were streaming `List<String>` elements, they would be flattened into a stream of `Strings`, which "removes" or hides each individual `List`. This is helpful when combining lists or for removing empty elements (which `flatMap()` also does). *Figure 16.5* presents a code example (`IntermediateOperations.java`):

```
97         public static void doFlatMap() {
98             List<String> nothing = List.of();
99             List<String> list1 = Arrays.asList("Sean");
100            List<String> list2 = Arrays.asList("Maike", "van", "Putten");
101            Stream<List<String>> streamOfLists = Stream.of(nothing, list1, list2);
102            streamOfLists.forEach(System.out::print); // [][Sean][Maike, van, Putten]
103            System.out.println(); // blank line to separate outputs
104
105            // flatMap(Function(T, R)) IN:T OUT:R
106            // flatMap(Function(List<String>, Stream<String>))
107            streamOfLists = Stream.of(nothing, list1, list2);
108            streamOfLists.flatMap(list -> list.stream())
109                    .forEach(System.out::print);// SeanMaikevanPutten
110        }
```

Figure 16.5 - The flatMap(Function) intermediate operation in code

In this example, we are going to contrast two streams - one with flatMap() and the other without flatMap(). Let us start with the non-flatMap() stream.

Firstly, we create the lists, the first of which is an empty list:

```
List<String> nothing = List.of();
List<String> list1 = Arrays.asList("Sean");
List<String> list2 = Arrays.asList("Maike", "van", "Putten");
```

We then stream the three lists:

```
Stream<List<String>> streamOfLists = Stream.of(nothing, list1,
list2);
```

We then stream and output our streamOfLists using forEach():

```
streamOfLists.forEach(System.out::print);
```

This outputs:

```
[] [Sean] [Maike, van, Putten]
```

Note that each element is a list (reflected by the square brackets [ ] ) and that the empty list is present.

As the stream has been processed by a terminal operation (forEach()), the stream is closed. To avoid an exception, we must re-stream the source. This is what we do:

```
streamOfLists = Stream.of(nothing, list1, list2);
```

This second pipeline contains the flatMap() operation:

```
streamOfLists.flatMap(list -> list.stream())
```

The signature for flatMap() is as follows:

```
Stream<R> flatMap(Function(T, R))
```

Therefore, flatMap() takes in a Function. The function input T, is a List<String> and the function output R, is a Stream<String>.

Using forEach() again to both start off the streaming and output the elements in the stream, we get the following:

```
SeanMaikevanPutten
```

Note that they are all just Strings (no Lists) and that the empty element has been removed. The String elements that were in the Lists are now top-level elements in the stream. This is the flattening process explained earlier.

## sorted() and sorted(Comparator)

The overloaded sorted() operation returns a stream with the elements sorted. Just like sorting arrays, Java uses natural ordering unless we provide a Comparator. For example, natural ordering for numbers is ascending numeric order; natural ordering for Strings is alphabetic. This operation is a stateful intermediate operation which means that sorted() needs to see all of the data before it can sort it. Both sorted examples are based on IntermediateOperations.java in the repo. *Figure 16.6* presents a code example of sorted(Comparator).

```java
59      public static void doSorted2() {
60
61          // Stream<T> sorted(Comparator<T> comparator)
62          // Output:
63          //    Person{name=John, age=23}Person{name=Mary, age=25}
64          Person john = new Person( name: "John",  age: 23);
65          Person mary = new Person( name: "Mary",  age: 25);
66          Stream.of(mary,john)
67                  .sorted(Comparator.comparing(Person::getAge)) // p -> p.getAge()
68                  .forEach(System.out::print);
69
70      }
```

Figure 16.6 - The sorted(Comparator) intermediate operation in code

In this example, assume the existence of a Person class that has both String name and Integer age instance variables. We start by streaming the Person objects; "Mary" is first, age 25 and "John" is second, age 23.

The sorted(Comparator) line is interesting:

```
.sorted(Comparator.comparing(Person::getAge)) // p -> p.getAge()
```

The Comparator.comparing(Function keyExtractor) static method is a very useful way of generating a Comparator. It accepts in a Function that extracts a Comparable sort key - as in, a key whose type implements the Comparable interface. In this example, the Function input is a Person and the Function return is an Integer (the age of the person). As Integer implements Comparable, this is fine. The method then returns a Comparator that compares by that sort key. This pipeline is short and does not clearly demonstrate the stateful nature of sorted(). The next example will do that.

When we output the stream, "John" comes out first and "Mary" second (the reverse of the order in which they were streamed). This is because we are sorting by age and "John", at 23, is younger than "Mary", who is 25.

Now let us look at another sorted() example. This one will demonstrate the stateful nature of sorted() and at the same time, highlight lazy evaluation. *Figure 16.7* presents the code.

```
42    public static void doSortedOther() {
43
44        // Stream<T> sorted()
45        // Stream<T> sorted(Comparator<T> comparator)
46        // Output:
47        // 0.Tim 1.Tim 0.Jim 1.Jim 0.Peter 0.Ann 1.Ann 0.Mary 2.Ann 3.Ann 2.Jim 3.Jim
48        Stream.of( ...values: "Tim", "Jim", "Peter", "Ann", "Mary")
49            .peek(name -> System.out.print(" 0."+name))    // Tim, Jim, Peter, Ann, Mary
50            .filter(name -> name.length() == 3)
51            .peek(name -> System.out.print(" 1."+name))    // Tim, Jim, Ann
52            .sorted()                                      // Tim, Jim, Ann (stored)
53            .peek(name -> System.out.print(" 2."+name))    // Ann, Jim
54            .limit( maxSize: 2)
55            .forEach(name -> System.out.print(" 3."+name));// Ann, Jim
56
57    }
```

Figure 16.7 - The stateful nature of sorted()

In this example, we are streaming a list of Strings (names). Names that are of length 3 pass the filter:

```
.filter(name -> name.length() == 3)
```

The `sorted()` operation is stateful - it needs to see *all* of the data before it can sort that data. We also have a `limit(2)` operation which is both stateful and short-circuiting. It will short-circuit after 2 names have passed by. Lastly, the terminal operation `forEach()` starts off the streaming process and outputs the names as they arrive.

The output is as follows:

```
0.Tim 1.Tim 0.Jim 1.Jim 0.Peter 0.Ann 1.Ann 0.Mary 2.Ann 3.Ann
2.Jim 3.Jim
```

Let us examine what happens here. Note that the comments on the right of the pipeline (lines 49-55) indicate what stage each name gets to.

- "Tim" is streamed and passes the filter. "Tim" makes its way to `sorted()` where it is stored. Java tells `sorted()` that there is more data to be streamed and not to sort yet. This results in "0. Tim 1. Tim" in the output.

- "Jim" is streamed next and behaves exactly as "Tim", with `sorted()` keeping a record that it will have to sort both "Tim" and "Jim". Again, Java tells `sorted()` that there is more data to come and not to sort yet. Thus, we have "0. Jim 1. Jim" in the output.

- "Peter" is then streamed but fails the filter (just "0. Peter" and no "1. Peter" in the output).

- "Ann" is streamed next and behaves exactly as "Tim" and "Jim", with `sorted()` keeping a record that it will have to sort "Tim", "Jim", and "Ann". Again, Java tells `sorted()` not to sort yet. Thus, we have in "0. Ann 1. Ann" in the output.

- "Mary" is the last name to be streamed. "Mary" fails the filter also (just "0. Mary" and no "1. Mary" in the output).

- As the stream is now empty, Java tells `sorted()` that it can sort the data. The sorted names are "Ann", "Jim", and "Tim". So "Ann" now makes its way out of `sorted()` and onto the next stage of the stream pipeline.

- The `peek()` after `sorted()` outputs "2. Ann" showing "Ann" got here.

- The `limit()` operation passes "Ann" on but records that it has handled one name.

- The terminal operation `forEach()` which kick-started the whole streaming process, outputs "3. Ann" to show that "Ann" got as far as here.

- "Jim" now makes its way out of `sorted()`. "Jim" is peeked ("2. Jim") and passes through `limit()`. However, `limit()` short-circuits as this is the second name it has handled. Java is informed of this fact.

- The `forEach()` operation is allowed to finish outputting `"3. Jim"`.

- Note that `"Tim"` never gets out of `sorted()` and into the last `peek()` - there is no `"2. Tim"` in the output.

That completes this section on intermediate operations. Let us now examine primitive streams.

# Delving into primitive streams

Thus far, all our streams have been for `Object` types. For example, a `Stream<Integer>` caters for the wrapper class `Integer`. Java also has classes specifically tailored for streams of primitives. For example, assuming a stream of `int` primitives, rather than `Stream<Integer>`, we use `IntStream`. As we shall see shortly, primitive streams have some really useful methods for processing numeric data, such as `sum()` and `average()`.

*Table 16.1* introduces the primitive stream classes.

| Wrapper stream | Primitive stream | Primitives catered for |
|---|---|---|
| Stream<Integer> | IntStream | int, short, byte, char |
| Stream<Double> | DoubleStream | double, float |
| Stream<Long> | LongStream | long |

Table 16.1 - Primitive stream classes

In this table, the first column lists the wrapper type streams; the second column lists the corresponding primitive stream and the last column, enumerates the primitives catered for by the primitive stream from column two.

Let us examine how to create primitive streams.

## Creating primitive streams

As with creating `Object` streams, we can easily create primitive streams as well. *Figure 16.8* presents sample code creating primitive streams (based on code from PrimitiveStreams.java in the repo).

```
37        public static void creatingFinitePrimitiveStreams(){
38            int[] ia    = {1,2,3};
39            double[] da = {1.1, 2.2, 3.3};
40            long[] la   = {1L, 2L, 3L};
41
42            IntStream iStream1       = Arrays.stream(ia);
43            DoubleStream dStream1    = Arrays.stream(da);
44            LongStream lStream1      = Arrays.stream(la);
45            System.out.println(iStream1.count() + ", " +
46                    dStream1.count() + ", " + lStream1.count());// 3, 3, 3
47
48            IntStream iStream2       = IntStream.of( ...values: 1, 2, 3);
49            DoubleStream dStream2    = DoubleStream.of( ...values: 1.1, 2.2, 3.3);
50            LongStream lStream2      = LongStream.of( ...values: 1L, 2L, 3L);
51            System.out.println(iStream2.count() + ", " +
52                    dStream2.count() + ", " + lStream2.count());// 3, 3, 3
53        }
```

Figure 16.8 - Creating primitive streams

In this example, we create arrays of differing primitive types:

```
int[] ia        = {1,2,3};
double[] da     = {1.1, 2.2, 3.3};
long[] la       = {1L, 2L, 3L};
```

Using the overloaded `Arrays.stream()` method, we create an `IntStream`, `DoubleStream` and `LongStream` respectively:

```
IntStream iStream1       = Arrays.stream(ia);
DoubleStream dStream1    = Arrays.stream(da);
LongStream lStream1      = Arrays.stream(la);
```

For example, the `Arrays.stream(ia)` takes in an `int []` and returns an `IntStream` with the specified array as its source.

We then execute the `count()` terminal operation on each of the streams. Each returns 3 as there are 3 primitives in each array source:

```
System.out.println(iStream1.count() + ", " + dStream1.count() + ", " +
lStream1.count()); // 3, 3, 3
```

The `of()` method should look familiar from how we created a regular stream using the `Stream` class. There is an equivalent method in `IntStream`, `DoubleStream` and `LongStream`. The values in the streams are specified in the varargs arguments:

```
IntStream iStream2      = IntStream.of(1, 2, 3);
DoubleStream dStream2   = DoubleStream.of(1.1, 2.2, 3.3);
LongStream lStream2     = LongStream.of(1L, 2L, 3L);
```

Again, we execute the `count()` terminal operation on each of the streams. As before, 3 is returned each time, as there are 3 primitives in each of the streams:

```
System.out.println(iStream2.count() + ", " + dStream2.count() + ", " +
lStream2.count()); // 3, 3, 3
```

We can of course create infinite streams of primitives. *Figure 16.9*, from PrimitiveStreams.java in the repo, shows them being used and their equivalent names in the `Stream` class are familiar, namely `generate()` and `iterate()`.

```
24      public static void creatingInfinitePrimitiveStreams(){
25          // DoubleStream generate(DoubleSupplier)
26          //     DoubleSupplier is a functional interface. Its
27          //     functional method is: double getAsDouble()
28          DoubleStream random    = DoubleStream.generate(() -> Math.random());
29          random.limit( maxSize: 5).forEach(System.out::println);
30
31          // IntStream iterate(int seed, IntUnaryOperator f)
32          //     IntUnaryOperator is a functional interface. Its
33          //     functional method is: int applyAsInt(int)
34          IntStream even = IntStream.iterate( seed: 2, (n) -> n + 2);
35          even.limit( maxSize: 5).forEach(System.out::println);
36      }
```

Figure 16.9 - Infinite primitive streams

In this example, we start out with the following two lines of code:

```
DoubleStream random    = DoubleStream.generate(() -> Math.
random());
    random.limit(5).forEach(System.out::println);
```

The `DoubleStream.generate(DoubleSupplier)` method has equivalent versions in `IntStream` and `LongStream`. Its parameter `DoubleSupplier` is a functional interface where it produces a `double`. Thus, it is a `double` primitive version of `Supplier<T>`. Its functional method `double getAsDouble()` reinforces this fact. We use `limit(5)` to limit the infinite flow of numbers to 5 and each is output by the terminal operation `forEach()`.

We follow that with the next two lines of code:

```
IntStream even = IntStream.iterate(2, (n) -> n + 2);
even.limit(5).forEach(System.out::println);
```

The `IntStream.iterate()` method has equivalent versions in `DoubleStream` and `LongStream`. It takes two arguments, an `int` seed (the starting value) and an `IntUnaryOperator` function. This `IntUnaryOperator` function takes in an `int` and returns an `int`. It is the `int` primitive specialization of `UnaryOperator<T>`. The stream of numbers generated are even numbers, starting at 2. As the sequence of numbers is infinite, we apply a limit of 5 numbers (2, 4, 6, 8, 10).

Let us now examine common primitive stream methods.

## Common primitive stream methods

The methods just presented, namely `of()`, `generate()` and `iterate()` are common to `Stream<T>` as well. *Table 16.2* presents commonly used methods that are unique to primitive streams.

| method | | primitive stream |
|---|---|---|
| OptionalDouble | average() | IntStream |
| | | LongStream |
| | | DoubleStream |
| OptionalInt | max() | IntStream |
| OptionalLong | | LongStream |
| OptionalDouble | | DoubleStream |
| OptionalInt | min() | IntStream |
| OptionalLong | | LongStream |
| OptionalDouble | | DoubleStream |
| int | sum() | IntStream |
| long | sum() | LongStream |
| double | sum() | DoubleStream |

Table 16.2 - Common primitive stream methods

This table has two columns: the name of the method (including its return type) and the primitive streams. Each of the methods listed are reductions and terminal operations. Recall that a reduction produces a single summary result by repeatedly applying an operation to a sequence of input results. We saw the general form of reductions with the `reduce()` and `collect()` methods in the `Stream<T>` interface. The reductions in this table are specialized for primitives.

Let us first examine the `sum()` method. Notice that it does not return an `Optional` whereas all the other methods do. This is because 0 is a valid value to return for the sum of an empty stream. In other words, if the stream is empty when you execute `sum()` - perhaps all of the data has been filtered out - then 0 is a valid return. The other methods in the table, however, would need to return an empty `Optional` in that scenario. The `IntStream` for `sum()` returns an `int`, the version in `LongStream` returns a `long` and the version in `DoubleStream` returns a `double`.

Regarding `min()` and `max()`, both `IntStream` versions return an `OptionalInt`; both `LongStream` versions return an `OptionalLong` and both `DoubleStream` versions return an `OptionalDouble`.

The `average()` method is a little different because of the possibility of decimal places regardless of the type being totaled. So all three primitive stream types, namely `IntStream`, `LongStream`, and `DoubleStream` return an `OptionalDouble`.

Let us examine them in code (PrimitiveStreams.java in the repo). Firstly, *Figure 16.10* presents `min()`, `max()` and `average()`.

```java
64    public static void maxMinAverage(){
65
66        OptionalInt max = IntStream.of( ...values: 10, 20, 30)
67                .max(); // terminal operation
68        max.ifPresent(System.out::println);// 30
69
70        OptionalDouble min = DoubleStream.of( ...values: 10.0, 20.0, 30.0)
71                .min(); // terminal operation
72        // NoSuchElementException is thrown if no value present
73        System.out.println(min.orElseThrow());// 10.0
74
75        OptionalDouble average = LongStream.of( ...values: 10L, 20L, 30L)
76                .average(); // terminal operation
77        System.out.println(average.orElseGet(() -> Math.random()));// 20.0
78    }
```

Figure 16.10 – The min(), max() and average() operations in code

In this figure, we start with the following code:

```
OptionalInt max = IntStream.of(10, 20, 30)
         .max(); // terminal operation
max.ifPresent(System.out::println);// 30
```

Firstly, we create a stream of `int` primitives. We then execute the terminal operation `max()`, which starts the stream and calculates the maximum number in the stream, which is 30. No need for any `Comparator` or accumulator here! We then use the `ifPresent(IntConsumer)` from `OptionalInt` (there are equivalents for `OptionalDouble` and `OptionalLong`). What this method means, is that, if there is a value *present* in the `OptionalInt`, output it. If the optional is empty, nothing is printed.

The next code segment of interest is:

```
OptionalDouble min = DoubleStream.of(10.0, 20.0, 30.0)
         .min(); // terminal operation
// NoSuchElementException is thrown if no value present
System.out.println(min.orElseThrow());// 10.0
```

In this code segment, we create a `DoubleStream` based on the values provided in the varargs argument. Using `min()`, we stream the values and calculate the minimum value. The `orElseThrow()` method means: if there is a value present, return that value; otherwise throw a `NoSuchElementException`.

The last code segment is:

```
OptionalDouble average = LongStream.of(10L, 20L, 30L)
         .average(); // terminal operation
System.out.println(average.orElseGet(() -> Math.random())); // 20.0
```

Here, we create a `LongStream` based on the values provided in the varargs argument. This is followed by executing `average()`, which both streams the values and calculates their average. The `orElseGet(DoubleSupplier)` method means: if there is a value present, return that value; otherwise return the value from the supplying function (a random number).

Let us now examine `sum()`. It is easy to see why primitive streams are useful in the next example, *Figure 16.11*.

```
90          public static void usingSum(){
91
92              IntStream is = IntStream.of( ...values: 4, 2, 3);
93              System.out.println(is.sum());// 9
94
95              // 1. Using Stream<T> and reduce(identity, accumulator)
96              Stream<Integer> numbers = Stream.of( ...values: 1,2,3);
97              System.out.println(numbers.reduce( identity: 0, (n1, n2) -> n1 + n2));// 6
98
99              // 2. Using IntStream and sum()
100             // IntStream mapToInt(ToIntFunction)
101             //    ToIntFunction is a functional interface:
102             //       int applyAsInt(T value);
103             Stream<Integer> sInteger = Stream.of( ...values: 1,2,3);
104             IntStream intS           = sInteger.mapToInt( n -> n);// unboxed
105             System.out.println(intS.sum());// 6
```

Figure 16.11 - The sum() primitive operation

In this figure, we start out with the following:

```
IntStream is = IntStream.of(4, 2, 3);
System.out.println(is.sum());// 9
```

This code creates an `int` primitive stream directly using the `IntStream.of()` method and uses the `sum()` terminal method to stream the numbers and return the sum, which is 9.

The rest of the example code, contrasts `reduce()` from `Stream<T>` and `sum()` from `IntStream`. Let us focus on `reduce()` first:

```
Stream<Integer> numbers = Stream.of(1,2,3);
System.out.println(numbers.reduce(0, (n1, n2) -> n1 + n2)); // 6
```

Initially, we stream a list of `Integers` into a `Stream<Integer>` and them sum them up by passing an accumulator function argument to `reduce()`.

Now we will focus on how to do the same thing using `sum()`:

```
Stream<Integer> sInteger = Stream.of(1,2,3);
IntStream intS           = sInteger.mapToInt( n -> n); // unboxed
System.out.println(intS.sum()); // 6
```

Firstly, we stream the same numbers as a `Stream<Integer>` again - we do not have a stream of primitives at this point. The second line shows how easy it is to convert from a `Stream<Integer>`

to a `Stream` of `int` primitives. Using the `Stream` interfaces `mapToInt()` function; we pass in our function, which takes in an `Integer` and returns the `int` primitive wrapped by that `Integer`. In this code, we are availing of auto-unboxing by simply specifying the identifier n on both sides of the arrow token in the lambda. Now that we have an `IntStream` object we can use the `sum()` method - which streams the integers and returns the sum of 6. Note that we have deliberately left the return types visible in the code. This helps explain what is happening in the pipeline. In reality, you would code it much more concisely as follows:

```
int sum = Stream.of(1,2,3)
                         .mapToInt(n -> n)
                         .sum();
System.out.println(sum); // 6
```

With each of the primitive streams, you can get summarizing statistics (summary data about the elements in the stream). Let us look at these in action. *Figure 16.12* presents `IntSummaryStatistics`.

```
54 @      public static void stats(IntStream numbers){
55             IntSummaryStatistics intStats =
56                   numbers.summaryStatistics();        // terminal operation
57             System.out.println(intStats.getMin());    // 5 (2147483647 if nothing in stream)
58             System.out.println(intStats.getMax());    // 20 (-2147483648 if nothing in stream)
59             System.out.println(intStats.getAverage()); // 12.5 (0.0 if nothing in stream)
60             System.out.println(intStats.getCount());   // 4 (0 if nothing in stream)
61             System.out.println(intStats.getSum());     // 50 (0 if nothing in stream)
62        }
```

Figure 16.12 - IntSummaryStatistics in code

In this example, the streams are being passed in via the following method calls:

```
stats(IntStream.of(5, 10, 15, 20));
stats(IntStream.empty());
```

The first invocation passes in a valid stream of integers whereas the second stream is empty. Once inside the `stats()` method, the terminal operation `summaryStatistics()` is executed on the `IntStream` passed in. The resultant `IntSummaryStatistics` object is now available to inspect for summary data:

```
IntSummaryStatistics intStats = numbers.summaryStatistics();
// terminal op.
```

The output for the first stream (5, 10, 15 and 20) is:

```
5
20
12.5
```

```
4
50
```

5 is output by getMin(); 20 is output by getMax(); 12.5 is output by getAverage(); 4 is output by getCount() and 50 is output by getSum().

The output for the empty stream is:

```
2147483647
-2147483648
0.0
0
0
```

2147483647 (which is Integer.MAX_VALUE) is output by getMin(); -2147483648 (Integer.MIN_VALUE) is output by getMax(); 0.0 is output by getAverage(); 0 is output by getCount() and 0 is output by getSum().

With primitive streams there are now extra functional interfaces that we need to be aware of.

## New primitive stream interfaces

There are many new functional interfaces to be aware of. Thankfully, they follow a consistent naming pattern. *Table 16.3* outlines the more common ones. For further details please see the JavaDocs at: https://docs.oracle.com/en/java/javase/21/docs/api/java.base/java/util/function/package-summary.html.

| | | | | |
|---|---|---|---|---|
| Supplier<T> | T get() | | Function<T, R> | R apply(T) |
| DoubleSupplier | double getAsDouble() | | BiFunction<T,U,R> | R apply(T, U) |
| IntSupplier | int getAsInt() | | DoubleFunction<R> | R apply(double) |
| LongSupplier | long getAsLong() | | IntFunction<R> | R apply(int) |
| Consumer<T> | void accept(T) | | LongFunction<R> | R apply(long) |
| BiConsumer<T, U> | void accept(T, U) | | UnaryOperator<T> | T apply(T) |
| DoubleConsumer | void accept(double) | | BinaryOperator<T> | T apply(T, T) |
| IntConsumer | void accept(int) | | DoubleUnaryOperator | double applyAsDouble(double) |
| LongConsumer | void accept(long) | | IntUnaryOperator | int applyAsInt(int) |
| Predicate<T> | boolean test(T) | | LongUnaryOperator | long applyAsLong(long) |
| BiPredicate<T,U> | boolean test(T, U) | | DoubleBinaryOperator | double applyAsDouble(double, double) |
| DoublePredicate | boolean test(double) | | IntBinaryOperator | int applyAsInt(int, int) |
| IntPredicate | boolean test(int) | | LongBinaryOperator | long applyAsLong(long, long) |
| LongPredicate | boolean test(long) | | | |

Tables 16.3 (a) and (b) - New primitive stream functional interfaces

In this figure, table A is on the left, with table B on the right. Each table has two columns - one for the functional interface name and one for its functional method.

We have deliberately included the generically marked functional interfaces encountered earlier. This is to help contrast them with their primitive counterparts. The previous functional interfaces that we came across are: `Supplier<T>`, `Consumer<T>`, `BiConsumer<T, U>`, `Predicate<T>`, `BiPredicate<T, U>`, `Function<T, R>`, `BiFunction<T, U, R>`, `UnaryOperator<T>` and `BinaryOperator<T>`. Note the generic types in them all. Very few primitive functional interfaces use generics, as they are typed for a particular primitive.

We have color-coordinated the interfaces in order to group them. So for example, in table A the yellow colored interfaces are the suppliers. `Supplier<T>` with its `T get()` functional method - as stated, this is included for comparison purposes. `DoubleSupplier` is the interface for generating `double` primitives. Its functional method is `getAsDouble()` and its return type is a `double`. The `IntSupplier` and `LongSupplier` interfaces follow the same pattern.

Still in table A, the consumers are next, in green. `DoubleConsumer` "accepts" a `double` primitive and returns nothing. `IntConsumer` accepts in an `int`, returns nothing; and `LongConsumer` accepts in a `long`, returns nothing. All the functional methods are called `accept()`. Note the pattern for naming: suppliers use `DoubleSupplier`; consumers use `DoubleConsumer`.

This naming convention continues with the predicates (blue). We have `DoublePredicate` that "tests" a `double` and returns a `boolean`. `IntPredicate` and `LongPredicate` behave in a similar manner - a primitive type parameter and a return type `boolean`. All the functional methods are called `test()`.

In table B, we have the functions, in yellow. We have `DoubleFunction<R>` that "applies" a `double` and returns the type R. The functions are a case where generics are used to represent the type being returned. However, the primitive being applied is the important aspect here. `IntFunction<R>` and `LongFunction<R>` behave in a similar manner - a primitive type parameter and a return type R. All the functional methods are called `apply()`.

Lastly, in table B, we have the primitive versions of `UnaryOperator<T>` and `BinaryOperator<T>`. The `double` primitive version of `UnaryOperator<T>` is `DoubleUnaryOperator` (note the word `Double` at the start again). Recall that unary functions are functions that accept in one parameter and return a value; where both types are the same. Therefore, `DoubleUnaryOperator` has a `double` parameter and a `double` return type. `IntUnaryOperator` and `LongUnaryOperator` follow the same pattern.

The `DoubleBinaryOperator`, `IntBinaryOperator` and `LongBinaryOperator` interfaces only differ from their unary counterparts in the number of parameters they take in. Therefore, `DoubleBinaryOperator` takes in two doubles, `IntBinaryOperator` takes in two ints and `LongBinaryOperator` takes in two longs.

There are other ways to create streams and that is by mapping from other streams. Let us examine that now.

## Mapping streams

Again, there are many new functional interfaces to be aware of; and again, thankfully, they follow a consistent naming pattern. *Table 16.4* outlines the more common ones.

| Source stream class | To create Stream<T> | To create DoubleStream | To create IntStream | To create LongStream |
|---|---|---|---|---|
| Stream<T> | map( Function<T,R> )<br>R apply(T value) | mapToDouble(ToDoubleFunction<T>)<br>double applyAsDouble(T value) | mapToInt( ToIntFunction<T> )<br>int applyAsInt(T value) | mapToLong( ToLongFunction<T> )<br>long applyAsLong(T value) |
| DoubleStream | mapToObj(DoubleFunction<R>)<br>R apply(double value) | map( DoubleUnaryOperator )<br>double applyAsDouble(double) | mapToInt(DoubleToIntFunction)<br>int applyAsInt(double) | mapToLong(DoubleToLongFunction)<br>long applyAsLong(double) |
| IntStream | mapToObj( IntFunction<R> )<br>R apply(int value) | mapToDouble( IntToDoubleFunction )<br>double applyAsDouble(int) | map( IntUnaryOperator )<br>int applyAsInt(int) | mapToLong( IntToLongFunction )<br>long applyAsLong(int) |
| LongStream | mapToObj( LongFunction<R> )<br>R apply(long value) | mapToDouble(LongToDoubleFunction)<br>double applyAsDouble(long) | mapToInt( LongToIntFunction )<br>int applyAsInt(long) | map( LongUnaryOperator )<br>long applyAsLong(long) |

Table 16.4 - Mapping streams

In this table, the rows represent the source stream class and the columns represent the target stream class. Again, we use color to help organize our explanations. The yellow boxes represent situations where the source and target classes are the same. So, for example, if you are going from a `DoubleStream` to another `DoubleStream`, the method is `map(DoubleUnaryOperator)`. The functional method is also listed - so for this example, `DoubleUnaryOperator`'s functional method is `double applyAsDouble(double)`.

Let us examine the brown boxes. Each of these uses a `mapToObj()` method as the source is a primitive stream and the target is a stream of objects. The source stream hints at the function to be used. For example, if the source is a `DoubleStream` then the `DoubleFunction` interface applies, as you are mapping from a `double` primitive to a type R. This is specified in the functional method `R apply(double value)`.

Next the green boxes. The target stream is `DoubleStream` and hence the method name is `mapToDouble()`. If the source stream is a stream of objects then the interface is `ToDoubleFunction<T>`. Its functional method is `double applyAsDouble(T value)`, so a type T is input and a `double` primitive is output. Just what you would expect, when going from an object of type T to a primitive `double`.

Staying with the target stream of `DoubleStream`, if the source was an `IntStream`, then the primitives involved are in the name of the interface: `IntToDoubleFunction`. No surprise that its functional method is `double applyAsDouble(int)`. If the source was a `LongStream`, then the primitives involved are again in the name of the interface: `LongToDoubleFunction`. No surprise either that its functional method is `double applyAsDouble(long)`.

The blue boxes represent a target stream of `IntStream`. The method name is `mapToInt()`. The functional interfaces used as parameters and their functional methods, follow the same naming pattern as outlined for `DoubleStream`.

Lastly, the grey boxes represent a target stream of `LongStream`. The method name is `mapToLong()`. A similar naming pattern is again applied to the functional interfaces and their functional methods as shown in `DoubleStream` and `IntStream`.

Let us look at some code examples. We will start with mapping from streams of objects.

## Mapping from Object streams

The first example will have a `Stream<String>` as the source and map to the various other streams accordingly. *Figure 16.13* represents the code (`MappingStreams.java` in the repo).

```
13    public static void mappingObjectStreams(){
14        // Stream<T> to Stream<T>
15        Stream.of( ...values: "ash", "beech", "sycamore")
16            // map(Function<T,R>)
17            //    Function<T,R> => Function<String, String>
18            //        String apply(String s)
19            .map(tree -> tree.toUpperCase())
20            .forEach(System.out::println);// ASH, BEECH, SYCAMORE
21
22        // Stream<T> to DoubleStream
23        DoubleStream dblStream = Stream.of( ...values: "ash", "beech", "sycamore")
24            // mapToDouble(ToDoubleFunction<T>)
25            //    ToDoubleFunction<T> is a functional interface:
26            //        double applyAsDouble(T value) => double applyAsDouble(String tree)
27            .mapToDouble(tree -> tree.length()); // upcast in background
28        dblStream.forEach(System.out::println); // 3.0, 5.0, 8.0
29
30        // Stream<T> to IntStream
31        IntStream intStream    = Stream.of( ...values: "ash", "beech", "sycamore")
32            // mapToInt(ToIntFunction<T>)
33            //    ToIntFunction<T> is a functional interface:
34            //        int applyAsInt(T value) => int applyAsInt(String tree)
35            .mapToInt(tree -> tree.length());
36        intStream.forEach(System.out::println); // 3, 5, 8
37
38        // Stream<T> to LongStream
39        LongStream longStream = Stream.of( ...values: "ash", "beech", "sycamore")
40            // mapToLong(ToLongFunction<T>)
41            //    ToLongFunction<T> is a functional interface:
42            //        long applyAsLong(T value) => long applyAsLong(String tree)
43            .mapToLong(tree -> tree.length()); // upcast in background
44        longStream.forEach(System.out::println); // 3, 5, 8
45
46    }
```

Figure 16.13 - Mapping Object streams

In this figure, we are mapping a `Stream<String>` to all the other stream types, including `Stream<String>` itself. The first example is:

```
// Stream<T> to Stream<T>
Stream.of("ash", "beech", "sycamore")
        // map(Function<T,R>)
        //    Function<T,R> => Function<String, String>
        //        String apply(String s)
        .map(tree -> tree.toUpperCase())
        .forEach(System.out::println);// ASH, BEECH, SYCAMORE
```

In this case, the `map(Function<T,R>)` maps from `String` to `String`. The function converts the string to uppercase. The `forEach()` terminal operation starts the streaming process and outputs the strings.

The second example is:

```
// Stream<T> to DoubleStream
DoubleStream dblStream = Stream.of("ash", "beech", "sycamore")
        // mapToDouble(ToDoubleFunction<T>)
        //    ToDoubleFunction<T> is a functional interface:
        //        double applyAsDouble(T value) => double
applyAsDouble(String tree)
        .mapToDouble(tree -> tree.length()); // upcast in background
dblStream.forEach(System.out::println); // 3.0, 5.0, 8.0
```

This time the `Stream<String>` is mapped to a `DoubleStream` (of `double` primitives). Notice that we must re-stream the source as the previous `forEach()` closed it. This pipeline uses the `mapToDouble(ToDoubleFunction<T>)` to map from a `String` to a `double` primitive. The function this time use the `length()` of the `String` which is an `int`. This `int` is upcast to a `double` in the background. The `forEach()` starts the stream and outputs the `double` values.

The third example is:

```
// Stream<T> to IntStream
IntStream intStream    = Stream.of("ash", "beech", "sycamore")
        // mapToInt(ToIntFunction<T>)
        //    ToIntFunction<T> is a functional interface:
        //        int applyAsInt(T value) => int applyAsInt(String tree)
        .mapToInt(tree -> tree.length());
intStream.forEach(System.out::println); // 3, 5, 8
```

This time the `Stream<String>` is mapped to an `IntStream`. Again we must re-stream the source. This pipeline uses the `mapToInt(ToIntFunction<T>)` to map from a `String` to an `int` primitive. We again use the `length()` function of `String`. As this is an `int`, no upcasting is required in the background. The `forEach()` terminal operation is used to start the stream and output the `int` values.

The last example is:

```
// Stream<T> to LongStream
LongStream longStream = Stream.of("ash", "beech", "sycamore")
        // mapToLong(ToLongFunction<T>)
        //   ToLongFunction<T> is a functional interface:
        //      long applyAsLong(T value) => long applyAsLong(String
tree)
        .mapToLong(tree -> tree.length()); // upcast in background
longStream.forEach(System.out::println); // 3, 5, 8
```

Here, the `Stream<String>` is mapped to a `LongStream`. This pipeline uses the `mapToLong(ToLongFunction<T>)` to map from a `String` to a `long` primitive. As the `length()` of `String` returns an `int`, upcasting is done in the background. The `long` values are output as part of the `forEach()` terminal operation.

Now let us examine code examples mapping from streams of primitives.

## Mapping from primitive streams

In this example, we are mapping from streams of primitives to other stream types. *Figure 16.14* presents the code (`MappingStreams.java`).

```java
47    public static void mappingPrimitiveStreams(){
48
49        // IntStream to Stream<T>
50        Stream<String> streamStr = IntStream.of( ...values: 1, 2, 3)
51                // mapToObj(IntFunction<R>)
52                //    IntFunction is a functional interface:
53                //       R apply(int value)
54                .mapToObj(n -> "Number:"+ n);
55        streamStr.forEach(System.out::println);// Number:1, Number:2, Number:3
56
57        // IntStream to DoubleStream
58        DoubleStream dblStream = IntStream.of( ...values: 1, 2, 3) // re-open closed stream
59                // mapToDouble(IntToDoubleFunction)
60                //    IntToDoubleFunction is a functional interface:
61                //       double applyAsDouble(int value)
62                .mapToDouble(n -> (double)n); // cast NOT necessary
63        dblStream.forEach(System.out::println); // 1.0, 2.0, 3.0
64
65        // IntStream to IntStream
66        IntStream intStream = IntStream.of( ...values: 1, 2, 3)
67                // map(IntUnaryOperator)
68                //    IntUnaryOperator is a functional interface:
69                //       int applyAsInt(int)
70                .map(n -> n*2);
71        intStream.forEach(System.out::println);// 2, 4, 6
72
73        // IntStream to LongStream
74        LongStream longStream = IntStream.of( ...values: 1, 2, 3)
75                // mapToLong(IntToLongFunction)
76                //    IntToLongFunction is a functional interface:
77                //       long applyAsLong(int value)
78                .mapToLong(n -> (long)n); // cast NOT necessary
79        longStream.forEach(System.out::println); // 1, 2, 3
80
81    }
```

Figure 16.14 - Mapping primitive streams

In this example, we are streaming `int` primitives using `IntStream.of()`, and converting the `IntStream` to a `Stream<String>`, `DoubleStream`, `IntStream` and `LongStream` in turn.

Here is the first example:

```
// IntStream to Stream<T>
Stream<String> streamStr = IntStream.of(1, 2, 3)
        // mapToObj(IntFunction<R>)
        //    IntFunction is a functional interface:
        //       R apply(int value)
        .mapToObj(n -> "Number:"+ n);
streamStr.forEach(System.out::println);// Number:1, Number:2, Number:3
```

This code represents a sample pipeline for streaming `int` primitives and mapping them to a stream of `String` objects. The `mapToObj()` method is important here. It's signature is: `Stream<R> mapToObj(IntFunction<R>)`. The lambda passed in is easier to understand when we look at the functional method of the functional interface `IntFunction<R>`. The functional method is `R apply(int value)`. In our example, the `int` primitive is passed in as n and the `String` returned (represented by R in the method signature) is the string formed by prepending `"Number: "` in front of the `int`. Recall that when you have a string on the left or the right side (or both) of a + the result is a `String`. The `forEach()` streams the `int` primitives and outputs the `Stream<String>`.

The next example is:

```
// IntStream to DoubleStream
DoubleStream dblStream = IntStream.of(1, 2, 3) // re-open closed
stream
        // mapToDouble(IntToDoubleFunction)
        //    IntToDoubleFunction is a functional interface:
        //       double applyAsDouble(int value)
        .mapToDouble(n -> (double)n); // cast NOT necessary
dblStream.forEach(System.out::println); // 1.0, 2.0, 3.0
```

This code is mapping from an `IntStream` to a `DoubleStream`. The `mapToDouble()` method is important here. It's signature is:

`DoubleStream mapToDouble(IntToDoubleFunction)`. The functional method for `IntToDoubleFunction` is `double applyAsDouble(int value)`. Thus, our lambda passes in an `int` and returns a `double`. The cast is not necessary and it just there to emphasize that a `double` primitive is returned.

Here is the next example:

```
// IntStream to IntStream
IntStream intStream = IntStream.of(1, 2, 3)
        //  map(IntUnaryOperator)
```

```
            //      IntUnaryOperator is a functional interface:
            //          int applyAsInt(int)
         .map(n -> n*2);
  intStream.forEach(System.out::println);// 2, 4, 6
```

Here we are mapping an `IntStream` to another `IntStream`. The method `IntStream` `map(IntUnaryOperator)` is used. Its functional method is:

`int applyAsInt(int value)` so we pass in an `int` and get back an `int`. Our lambda is simply multiplying the `int` coming in by 2 and returning the result.

And the last example:

```
  // IntStream to LongStream
  LongStream longStream = IntStream.of(1, 2, 3)
          // mapToLong(IntToLongFunction)
          //   IntToLongFunction is a functional interface:
          //       long applyAsLong(int value)
          .mapToLong(n -> (long)n); // cast NOT necessary
  longStream.forEach(System.out::println); // 1, 2, 3
```

This code maps an `IntStream` to a `LongStream`. The method `LongStream` `mapToLong(IntToLongFunction)` is used. Its functional method is:

`long applyAsLong(int value)` so we pass in an `int` and get back a `long`. Again, the cast is not necessary, it is simply emphasizing that a `long` primitive is returned.

That completes our coverage of mapping streams. Let us now move on to examining `Optionals`.

## Explaining Optionals

An `Optional` can be thought of as a container that may or may not be empty. As per the API, the container "may or may not contain a non-null value". An `Optional` is primarily used as a method return type where there is a real need to represent "no result" and when returning `null` could cause errors. Before Java 8, programmers would return `null` but now, since Java 8, we can return an *empty* `Optional` instead. This has several advantages:

- Reduces the risk of `NullPointerExceptions`
- By using `Optional` as the return type, the API can now clearly state that there may not be a value returned
- The `Optional` API facilitates the functional programming style

As well as `Optional<T>`, there are `Optionals` for the primitive types also; namely: `OptionalInt`, `OptionalDouble` and `OptionalLong`. We will examine them later.

Let us first look at how to create `Optionals`.

## Creating Optionals

The API provides several `static` methods for this purpose. Let's start with `Optional.of(T)`.

```
Optional<T> Optional.of(T value)
```

The `value` parameter is wrapped in an `Optional`. The `value` passed must be a non-`null` value. If `null` is passed in, a `NullPointerException` results.

Now, let us look at `Optional.empty()`. This is how you create an empty Optional instance.

```
Optional.empty()
```

Lastly, we will examine `Optional.ofNullable(T)`.

```
Optional.ofNullable(T value)
```

If the given `value` is non-`null`, this method returns the wrapped `value` in an `Optional`. If `null` is passed in, an empty `Optional` is returned. If we examine the following code:

```
Optional opt1 = Optional.ofNullable(value);
Optional opt2 = (value == null) ? Optional.empty() : Optional.of(value);
```

Both of these lines do the same thing. The first line is shorthand for the ternary operator on the second line. The ternary operator is expressing the following: if `value` is `null`, `opt2` is assigned an empty `Optional`; otherwise, `opt2` is assigned the wrapped `value`.

*Figure 16.15* presents them in code (`Optionals.java` in the repo).

```
16        public static void createOptionals(){
17            Optional opt1 = Optional.empty();
18    //        System.out.println(opt1.get()); // NoSuchElementException
19            opt1.ifPresent(o -> System.out.println("opt1: "+o)); // no exception
20
21            Optional opt2 = Optional.of( value: 23);
22    //        Optional.of(null); // NullPointerException
23            opt2.ifPresent(o -> System.out.println("opt2: "+o)); // opt2: 23
24
25            Optional opt3 = Optional.ofNullable( value: 23);
26            opt3.ifPresent(o -> System.out.println("opt3: "+o)); // opt3: 23
27
28            Optional opt4 = Optional.ofNullable( value: null);
29            opt4.ifPresent(o -> System.out.println("opt4: "+o));
30            if(opt4.isEmpty()){
31                System.out.println("opt4 is empty!");            // opt4 is empty!
32            }
33        }
```

Figure 16.15 - Creating Optionals

The first example here creates an empty Optional:

```
        Optional opt1 = Optional.empty();
//          System.out.println(opt1.get()); // NoSuchElementException
        opt1.ifPresent(o -> System.out.println("opt1: "+o));
        // no exception
```

We use the Optional.empty() method to create an empty Optional. The next line is commented out because if you execute get() on an empty Optional, you will get a NoSuchElementException exception. The last line shows the functional style ifPresent(Consumer). If a value is present, the given consumer is applied to the value; otherwise it does nothing. In this case, it does nothing as the Optional is empty.

The next example creates a non-empty Optional:

```
        Optional opt2 = Optional.of(23);
//          Optional.of(null); // NullPointerException
        opt2.ifPresent(o -> System.out.println("opt2: "+o));
        // opt2: 23
```

This time we create an Optional using Optional.of(), with the value 23. The second line shows that you will get a NullPointerException if you pass null to Optional.of(). The ifPresent() now executes the consumer passed, which outputs "opt2: 23".

The next example uses `Optional.ofNullable()`:

```
Optional opt3 = Optional.ofNullable(23);
opt3.ifPresent(o -> System.out.println("opt3: "+o)); // opt3: 23
```

Here we create an `Optional` using `Optional.ofNullable()`, also with the value 23. As the `Optional` is not empty, the consumer passed to `ifPresent()` outputs "opt3: 23".

Here is the last example:

```
Optional opt4 = Optional.ofNullable(null);
opt4.ifPresent(o -> System.out.println("opt4: "+o));
if(opt4.isEmpty()){
    System.out.println("opt4 is empty!");            // opt4 is empty!
}
```

In this example, we use `Optional.ofNullable()` again, but this time, we pass in `null`. Rather than getting an exception (which is what `Optional.of(null)` would generate), we get an **empty** `Optional`. As the `Optional` is empty, the `ifPresent()` does nothing. The `isEmpty()` proves that the `Optional` is in fact empty resulting in "opt4 is empty!" being output.

Now that we know how to create `Optionals`, let us explore the API methods available.

## Using the Optional API

*Table 16.5* represents the instance methods in `Optional`.

| Method | What happens if Optional is empty | What happens if Optional has a value |
|---|---|---|
| get() | Throws NoSuchElementException | Returns the value |
| isPresent() | Returns false | Returns true |
| ifPresent(Consumer) | Does nothing | Executes Consumer with value |
| orElse(T otherValue) | Returns otherValue | Returns the value |
| orElseGet(Supplier) | Returns result of executing Supplier | Returns the value |
| orElseThrow() | Throws NoSuchElementException | Returns the value |
| orElseThrow(Supplier) | Throws exception returned by Supplier. However, if Supplier is null, throws a NullPointerException | Returns the value |

Table 16.5 - Optional instance methods

Many of these methods enable us to write code in a more concise and expressive manner. ifPresent(Consumer) is a very good example - rather than having in if-else statement, ifPresent(Consumer) removes the need to code the else part. Additionally, ifPresent(Consumer) helps us express our intent more clearly - if a value *is present*, do this; otherwise do nothing.

*Figure 16.16* presents methods from the Optional API in code.

```java
64        public static void doOptionalAPI(){
65            Optional<Double> valueInOptional = Optional.ofNullable( value: 60.0);
66            if(valueInOptional.isPresent()){
67                System.out.println(valueInOptional.get()); // 60.0
68            }
69            valueInOptional.ifPresent(System.out::println);// 60.0
70            System.out.println(valueInOptional.orElse(Double.NaN)); // 60.0
71
72            Optional<Double> emptyOptional = Optional.ofNullable( value: null);
73            System.out.println(emptyOptional.orElse(Double.NaN)); // NaN
74            System.out.println(emptyOptional.orElseGet(() -> Math.random())); // 0.8524556508038182
75            System.out.println(emptyOptional.orElseThrow()); // NoSuchElementException
76    //         System.out.println(emptyOptional.orElseThrow(() ->
77    //                             new RuntimeException())); // RuntimeException
78        }
```

Figure 16.16 - Optional methods in code

In this example, we will use both a non-null Optional and an empty Optional to test the various methods. Let us start with a valid non-null Optional.

### *Optional with a value*

Firstly, we create an Optional wrapped around the Double 60.0:

```java
Optional<Double> valueInOptional = Optional.ofNullable(60.0);
```

We then use isPresent() to ensure it is safe to execute the get() method, as executing get() on an empty Optional results in an exception:

```java
if(valueInOptional.isPresent()){
    System.out.println(valueInOptional.get());   // 60.0
}
```

As isPresent() returns true, it is safe to execute get(), which returns 60.0 and this is output to the screen.

The next 2 lines are:

```
valueInOptional.ifPresent(System.out::println);// 60.0
System.out.println(valueInOptional.orElse(Double.NaN)); // 60.0
```

In this code segment, as there is a non-null value in `valueInOptional`, the consumer argument to `ifPresent()` is executed, and `60.0` is output to the screen. In addition, as we have a value in `valueInOptional`, the `orElse(T value)` method is not executed; meaning that `60.0` is output to the screen.

### *Empty Optional*

Firstly, we create an empty `Optional` by passing in `null` to `ofNullable()`:

```
Optional<Double> emptyOptional = Optional.ofNullable(null);
```

We then have:

```
System.out.println(emptyOptional.orElse(Double.NaN)); // NaN
System.out.println(emptyOptional.orElseGet(() -> Math.random()));
// 0.8524556508038182
```

The `orElse(T value)` returns NaN and `orElseGet(Supplier)` executes the `Supplier` which is to generate a random number. Note that the `Supplier` must return a `Double` as that is the type of `emptyOptional`.

Lastly, we have:

```
System.out.println(emptyOptional.orElseThrow());
// NoSuchElementException
// System.out.println(emptyOptional.orElseThrow(() -> new
RuntimeException()));
```

Both lines execute `orElseThrow()` and are mutually exclusive. What this means is that, to see the exception on the second line, comment out the first line. As the `Optional` is empty, the first line throws a `NoSuchElementException`. Assuming we comment out the first line and uncomment the second line, the `Supplier` passed in to `orElseThrow()` will return a `RuntimeException`. Note that we do not use the keyword `throw` in our `Supplier`. The `orElseThrow()` method will do that for us - our job is to give it, via the `Supplier`, an exception object to throw.

Our last section regarding `Optionals`, are primitive `Optionals`.

# Primitive Optionals

As stated earlier, there are Optionals for the primitive types also; namely: OptionalInt, OptionalDouble and OptionalLong. We will look at them now.

*Table 16.6* highlights the more commonly used primitive stream methods.

| OptionalInt | OptionalDouble | OptionalLong |
|---|---|---|
| int getAsInt() | double getAsDouble() | long getAsLong() |
| ifPresent(IntConsumer) <br><br> void accept(int) | ifPresent (DoubleConsumer) <br><br> void accept(double) | ifPresent(LongConsumer) <br><br> void accept(long) |
| OptionalInt of(int) | OptionalDouble of(double) | OptionalLong of(long) |
| int orElse(int other) | double orElse (double other) | long orElse(long other) |
| orElseGet(IntSupplier) <br><br> int getAsInt() | orElseGet (DoubleSupplier) <br><br> double getAsDouble() | orElseGet(LongSupplier) <br><br> long getAsLong() |
| IntStream stream() | DoubleStream stream() | LongStream stream() |

Table 16.6 - Commonly used primitive stream methods

This table contrasts the more commonly used methods across the primitive streams. Where appropriate, the functional method is also listed, beneath the functional interface. For example, examining the ifPresent(IntConsumer) for OptionalInt shows that IntConsumer's functional method is void accept(int).

Note that the return types for the orElseGet() methods can be deduced from the functional methods just below. For example, examining the orElseGet() for OptionalInt shows that IntSupplier's functional method is int getAsInt(). Therefore, the return type for orElseGet(IntSupplier) is also int.

Let us examine some of these in code. *Figure 16.17* is the example (Optionals.java):

```
35    public static void doOptionalPrimitiveAverage(){
36        OptionalDouble optAvg = IntStream.rangeClosed(1, 10).average();
37        optAvg.ifPresent(d -> System.out.println(d));// 5.5
38        System.out.println(optAvg.getAsDouble());// 5.5
39        double dblAvg = optAvg.orElseGet(() -> Double.NaN);
40        System.out.println(dblAvg);// 5.5
41
42        OptionalInt optInt = OptionalInt.of( value: 35);
43        int age = optInt.orElseGet(() -> 0);
44        System.out.println(age);// 35
45        System.out.println(optInt.getAsInt());// 35
46
47
48    }
```

Figure 16.17 - Primitive stream methods in code

In this figure, we start out as follows:

```
OptionalDouble optAvg = IntStream.rangeClosed(1, 10).average();
optAvg.ifPresent(d -> System.out.println(d));// 5.5
```

This first line uses the IntSream method rangeClosed() to generate a stream of integers from 1 to 10 inclusive, in steps of 1. The average() method then calculates the average of these numbers, which is 5.5 (55/10). Note that the type for optAvg is OptionalDouble.

The second uses the now familiar ifPresent() method. This time the consumer argument is a DoubleConsumer, which means the functional method is void accept(double). This is what we are doing - the value of the OptionalDouble is used (namely d) and output.

We then have:

```
System.out.println(optAvg.getAsDouble()); // 5.5
```

which uses getAsDouble() to return the double value. If no value is present, this method (like get() in Optional<T>) generates a NoSuchElementException.

The next two lines are:

```
double dblAvg = optAvg.orElseGet(() -> Double.NaN);
System.out.println(dblAvg);// 5.5
```

The first line uses the `orElseGet()` method. We pass in a `DoubleSupplier`, which means there is no input argument (hence the `()` in the lambda) and a `double` returned (`Double.NaN`). As the `OptionDouble` has a value, the value is used to initialize `dblAvg` and the `DoubleSupplier` is ignored. We then output the variable `dblAvg`.

The following code segment completes the example:

```
OptionalInt optInt = OptionalInt.of(35);
int age = optInt.orElseGet(() -> 0);
System.out.println(age); // 35
System.out.println(optInt.getAsInt()); // 35
```

The first line creates an `OptionalInt` using the static `OptionalInt.of()` method. The second line uses the `orElseGet()` method. We pass in a `IntSupplier`, meaning we pass in nothing and get back in `int` (which is 0). As `optInt` has a value, the value is used to initialize `age` and the `IntSupplier` is ignored. The third line outputs the variable `age`. The last line uses `getAsInt()` to return the `int` value. If no value is present in the optional, this method would also, like `getAsDouble()`, generate a `NoSuchElementException`. However, as `optInt` contains a value (of 35), it is returned and output.

That complete the `Optionals` section. Our least section in this chapter is parallel streams.

# Understanding parallel streams

All of the streams so far have been serial streams where the results are ordered. With serial streams, a single thread processes one entry at a time. A parallel stream is processed by multiple threads executing concurrently (running on multiple CPUs). The stream elements are split into substreams, which are processed by multiple instances of the stream pipeline being executed in multiple threads. These partial substream results are then combined into a final result. To execute the substreams in parallel, the streams use the support of Java's fork/join framework for thread management.

## Creating parallel streams

To make a stream a parallel stream is very straightforward. We have two options: we can use the `parallelStream()` method from the `Collection` API or the `parallel()` intermediate operation from the `Stream` API.

Here are examples of both methods:

```
Stream<String> parallelFarmAnimals =
    List.of("sheep", "pigs", "horses").parallelStream(); // Collection
API
Stream<String> parallelHouseAnimals =
    Stream.of("cats", "dogs").parallel(); // Stream API
```

Let us look at an example contrasting a sequential stream with a parallel stream to show how easy it is to create a parallel stream. *Figure 16.18* is the code (`ParalledStreams.java` in the repo):

```
100    public static void sequentialAddition() {
101        int sum = Stream.of( ...values: 10, 20, 30, 40, 50, 60) Stream<Integer>
102                        .mapToInt(Integer::intValue) IntStream
103                        .sum();
104        System.out.println("Sum == "+sum); // 210
105    }
106    public static void parallelAddition() {
107        int sum = Stream.of( ...values: 10, 20, 30, 40, 50, 60) Stream<Integer>
108                    .parallel() // Stream<T> method
109                    .mapToInt(Integer::intValue) IntStream
110                    .sum();
111        System.out.println("Sum == "+sum); // 210
112    }
```

Figure 16.18 - Creating a parallel stream

Let us examine the sequential stream first:

```
int sum = Stream.of (10, 20, 30, 40, 50, 60)
                        .mapToInt (Integer::intValue)
                        .sum();
System.out.println("Sum == "+sum);   // 210
```

We initially generate a stream of `Stream<Integer>`. The second line uses the `mapToInt()` function to map the `Stream<Integer>` to an `IntStream`. In other words, map from a stream of `Integer` objects to a stream of `int` primitives. This is so we can use the `sum()` method in `IntStream`. The result, 210 is then output.

The parallel version is:

```
int sum = Stream.of (10, 20, 30, 40, 50, 60)
                        .parallel()   // Stream<T> method
                        .mapToInt (Integer::intValue)
                        .sum();
System.out.println("Sum == "+sum);   // 210
```

The only difference is the call to `parallel()` on the second line. This is a `Stream` method. This is abstraction at its finest! The data partitioning and thread management are handled by the API and the JVM.

# Parallel decomposition

Creating parallel streams is the easy part. Things get interesting when performing *parallel decomposition* - where a task is broken down (decomposed) into smaller tasks that are executed concurrently, and their results assembled afterwards.

With serial streams, results are ordered and therefore predictable. With parallel streams and parallel decomposition, this is not the case, as order is not guaranteed and therefore, results are unpredictable. This is because the threads take the subtasks in any order and return the results in any order.

Let us look at a simple code example demonstrating this. *Figure 16.19* presents the code (`ParalledStreams.java`):

```java
73    public static int dbAction(int x){
74        try {
75            Thread.sleep( millis: 1000);
76        } catch (InterruptedException e) {
77            throw new RuntimeException(e);
78        }
79        return x;
80    }
81    public static void orderedSerialStreams(){
82        long atStart = System.currentTimeMillis();
83        List.of(10, 20, 30, 40, 50) List<Integer>
84            .stream() Stream<Integer>
85            .map(i -> dbAction(i))
86            .forEach(i -> System.out.print(i + " "));
87        long howLong = (System.currentTimeMillis() - atStart) / 1000;
88        System.out.println("\nOperation took: "+howLong+" seconds.");
89    }
90    public static void unorderedParalleltreams(){
91        long atStart = System.currentTimeMillis();
92        List.of(10, 20, 30, 40, 50) List<Integer>
93            .parallelStream() Stream<Integer>
94            .map(i -> dbAction(i))
95            .forEach(i -> System.out.print(i + " "));
96        long howLong = (System.currentTimeMillis() - atStart) / 1000;
97        System.out.println("\nOperation took: "+howLong+" seconds.");
98    }
```

Figure 16.19 - Ordering in serial streams and lack of ordering in parallel streams

This figure presents a `dbAction()` method that mimics a database action by sleeping the thread for 1 second. When the `orderedSerialStreams()` method executes, the output is predictable:

```
10 20 30 40 50
Operation took: 5 seconds.
```

The integers are ordered as per the source and the operation took 5 seconds, 1 second for each value.

The unorderedParallelStreams() method is the same as the serial version except that we are now creating a parallel stream. Let us examine its output:

```
40 20 30 50 10
Operation took: 1 seconds.
```

One can see the obvious performance benefit of parallel processing: 1 second versus 5 seconds. Note that this performance gain depends on the number of CPUs available - if this code is run on a machine with fewer processors, the gain would be less.

However, the output is now unordered as both map() and forEach() are applied concurrently. Instead of forEach(), we could use the forEachOrdered() terminal operation. This operation ensures the consumer is applied to the elements in their *encounter order* as they left the source. In our example, this would be 10, 20, 30, 40, and 50. *Figure 16.20* shows it in code (ParalledStreams. java).

```
90    public static void unorderedParalleltreams(){
91        long atStart = System.currentTimeMillis();
92        List.of(10, 20, 30, 40, 50) List<Integer>
93            .parallelStream() Stream<Integer>
94            .map(i -> dbAction(i))
95            .forEachOrdered(i -> System.out.print(i + " "));
96 //        .forEach(i -> System.out.print(i + " "));
97        long howLong = (System.currentTimeMillis() - atStart) / 1000;
98        System.out.println("\nOperation took: "+howLong+" seconds.");
99    }
```

Figure 16.20 - The forEachOrdered() method

In this figure, the terminal operation is no longer forEach() but is forEachOrdered(). The output from this figure is as follows:

```
10 20 30 40 50
Operation took: 1 seconds.
```

Now the integers are ordered and the performance gain is still significant due to map() being applied concurrently.

# Parallel reductions using reduce()

As order is not guaranteed with parallel streams, the results of parallel reductions can be unexpected. A reduction combines a stream into a single result. Recall that the overloaded reduce() operation accepted three parameters: an identity, an accumulator and a combiner. The combiner function is used in a parallel environment for combining the accumulator results. What the following examples are going to demonstrate is that the *accumulator and combiner must work regardless of the order in which they are executed*. They must be associative.

> **Associativity**
>
> An operator or function is considered associative if the following holds:
>
>    (a op b) op c == a op (b op c).
>
> For example, addition is associative:
>
>    (2 + 3) + 4 == 2 + (3 + 4) == 9
>
> However, subtraction is not associative:
>
>    (2 - 3) - 4 == -5 whereas 2 - (3 - 4) == 3
>
> This is really important in parallel processing. For example:
>
>    a op b op c op d == (a op b) op (c op d)
>
> If op is associative then (a op b) and (c op d) can be evaluated in parallel; and op then performed on the results.

Let us first examine a serial reduction:

```
int result = Stream.of(1,2,3,4,5)
                        .reduce(0,
                                (n1, n2) -> n1 - n2);
System.out.println(result); // -15
```

As this is a serial reduction, there is no need for a combiner. The result is -15. Let us now examine the parallel version to see do we get the same result. *Figure 16.21* represents the code (ParallelStreams.java).

```
43        public static void parallelReduction1(){
44            int result = Stream.of( ...values: 1,2,3,4,5)
45                    .parallel()
46                .reduce( identity: 0,
47                    (n1, n2) -> { // accumulator
48                        System.out.print(n1 + ", " + n2 + "\n");
49                        return n1 - n2;
50                    },
51                    (subTask1, subTask2) -> { // combiner
52                        System.out.print("\t" +subTask1 + ", " + subTask2 + "\n");
53                        return subTask1 - subTask2;
54                    });
55            System.out.println(result); // 5
```

Figure 16.21 - A parallel reduction using reduce()

In this figure, we have expanded both the accumulator and the combiner to show the values as they appear:

```
(n1, n2) -> { // accumulator
    System.out.print (n1 + ", " + n2 + "\n");
    return n1 - n2;
},
(subTask1, subTask2) -> { // combiner
    System.out.print ("\t" +subTask1 + ", " + subTask2 + "\n");
    return subTask1 - subTask2;
}
```

The output is as follows (with the combiner subtask values tabbed in):

```
0, 1            // (identity, 1) == -1        // line 1
0, 3            // (identity, 3) == -3        // line 2
0, 5            // (identity, 5) == -5        // line 3
0, 2            // (identity, 2) == -2        // line 4
0, 4            // (identity, 4) == -4        // line 5
    -1, -2      // (line 1, line 4)           // line 6
    -4, -5      // (line 5, line 3)           // line 7
    -3, 1       // (line 2, line 6)           // line 8
    1, -4       // (line 7, line 8)           // line 9
5               // line 9
```

Notice that the final result is 5, which is incorrect. This is because subtraction is not associative. Interestingly, in the parallel process the identity is applied to multiple elements in the stream, giving us unexpected results.

# Parallel reductions using collect()

The collect() method, like reduce() has a three-argument version, which accepts an accumulator and a combiner. For the first argument, rather than an identity, collect() uses a Supplier. The same rule applies here too - the accumulator and combiner operations must be able to perform in any order.

One should use a concurrent collection, in order to avoid concurrent threads causing ConcurrentModificationExceptions. Another consideration is the target collection - if it is ordered (a List for example), then the background processing required to maintain that order may reduce performance. *Figure 16.22* presents an example of a concurrent collection, namely ConcurrentMap in code (ParallelStreams.java).

```
26    public static void concurrentCollection(){
27        var names = Stream.of( ...values: "John","Mary","Mike", "Paula")
28                .parallel();
29        ConcurrentMap<Character, String> map =
30                names.collect(Collectors.toConcurrentMap(
31                        name -> name.charAt(0),  // key
32                        name -> name,            // value
33                        (name1, name2) -> name1 + ", "+ name2));// key collisions
34        System.out.println(map); // {P=Paula, J=John, M=Mike, Mary}
35        System.out.println(map.getClass()); // class java.util.concurrent.ConcurrentHashMap
36    }
```

Figure 16.22 - collect() returning a concurrent collection

The output from the code is:

```
{P=Paula, J=John, M=Mike, Mary}
class java.util.concurrent.ConcurrentHashMap
```

Therefore, the ConcurrentMap implementation here is a ConcurrentHashMap. This is not guaranteed but some implementation of the ConcurrentMap interface is guaranteed.

The key in our map is the first letter in the name:

```
name -> name.charAt(0),  // key
```

The value associated with the key is the name itself:

```
name -> name,            // value
```

If more than one name starts with the same letter, the names are appended, with a comma between the names:

```
(name1, name2) -> name1 + ", "+ name2));// key collisions
```

That completes our discussion on parallel streams and indeed concludes *Chapter 16*. Let us now put that knowledge into practice to reinforce the concepts.

## Exercises

1.  To keep the park running smoothly, we need to keep track of the health of all dinosaurs. We need to identify any ill dinosaurs. Using a stream of `Dinosaur` objects, filter out dinosaurs that are ill (assuming the `isIll()` method exists the in `Dinosaur` class), map them to their names, and collect the results in a list. Lastly, print out this list of names of the dinosaurs that need immediate attention.

2.  Managing a dinosaur park of this size involves handling large amounts of data. To make an announcement in the park about dinosaur feeding times, create a list of dinosaurs, convert it into a stream, and use the `map()` function to get a list of dinosaur names. Then, use the `forEach` terminal operation to print out a message for each dinosaur's feeding time.

3.  Keeping track of the total food required for all the dinosaurs can be tricky. Suppose you have an array of weights of all dinosaurs. Convert it into an `IntStream` and use the `sum` method to get the total weight of all dinosaurs in the park. This could help you estimate the total food requirements.

4.  When dealing with data about dinosaurs or employees, we may encounter null references. To avoid a `NullPointerException` error, use `Optional` when retrieving a dinosaur by its name from a map of dinosaurs. If a dinosaur with the provided name doesn't exist, `Optional` should return a message indicating the dinosaur hasn't been found.

5.  Calculating the average weight of dinosaurs can be a time-consuming operation, especially when dealing with a large number of dinosaurs. To speed up the process, use parallel streams. Convert a list of dinosaur weights into a parallel stream and use the average method to calculate the average weight.

## Project – dynamic dinosaur care system

Integrate the Stream API into your dinosaur care system to process large volumes of dinosaur data, such as health records, feeding schedules, and so on. The system should also incorporate `Optional` and parallel streams where appropriate, optimizing data processing and minimizing potential null pointer exceptions.

Here are the steps to get you there:

1.  **Set up your project**: If you haven't done so already, create a new Java project in your IDE of choice. You should have a `Dinosaur` class with properties such as `name`, `species`, `healthStatus`, and so on. There should also be a `DinosaurCareSystem` class for implementing the main functionalities.

2.  **Use streams to process dinosaur data**:

    I.   **Health records**: Suppose you have a list of health records for each dinosaur and you want to find records where a dinosaur's health status was below a certain threshold. You could create a `Stream` from the list of records and use the `filter` method to get these records. Here's an example: `List<HealthRecord> criticalRecords = records.stream().filter(r -> r.getHealthStatus() < CRITICAL_THRESHOLD).collect(Collectors.toList())`.

    II.  **Feeding schedules**: Maybe you want to find out all the feeding schedules within a certain period. Again, you can use a `Stream` to filter the schedules. Here's an example: `List<FeedingSchedule> morningFeeds = schedules.stream().filter(s -> s.getTime().isBefore(LocalTime.NOON)).collect(Collectors.toList())`.

    III. **Use Optional to avoid**: `NullPointerException` **errors**: Let's say each dinosaur has a trainer field that could be null. When trying to access the trainer's name, use `Optional` to avoid a `NullPointerException` error. Here's an example: `Optional.ofNullable(dinosaur.getTrainer()).map(Trainer::getName).orElse("No trainer assigned")`.

3.  **Use parallel streams to process large amounts of data**: If the number of health records or feeding schedules is very large, you could use parallel streams to speed up the processing. This is as simple as replacing `stream()` with `parallelStream()` in the previous examples. Be aware, though, that not every problem is suitable for parallel processing. If the tasks have dependencies or need to be processed in a specific order, stick with regular streams.

# Summary

In this chapter, we explored advanced streaming concepts. We started by exploring intermediate operations, which are powerful, as they transform the stream into another stream. Popular intermediate operations are: `filter()`, `distinct()`, `limit()`, `map()`, `flatMap()`, and `sorted()`. Some of these are known as *stateful* as they need to maintain some state to operate effectively. Examples are `limit()` and `sorted()`. The `limit()` method is also *short-circuiting* as it can cause the pipeline to shut down even if there is more data available in the source.

We then examined the primitive stream types in the API, namely `IntStream`, `LongStream` and `DoubleStream`. These types have some very useful methods for operating on numeric types, such as `sum()` and `average()`. We also explained the patterns behind the names of the new primitive stream functional interfaces and their functional methods.

We can create streams by mapping from another stream. There are many methods to do this but they follow a pattern in their naming. We examined these and explained the patterns.

Optionals are boxes that may or may not be empty. They are mainly used as a method return type where there is a real need to represent "no result". Rather than returning null (with its pitfalls), we can return an empty Optional. We can create Optionals using Optional.of, Optional.empty() and Optional.ofNullable(). The Optional API supports functional-style programming; for example, ifPresent() lets us state clearly what we want without the need for an else statement. We also examined the primitive Optionals, namely OptionalInt, OptionalLong and OptionalDouble.

Lastly, we looked at parallel streams, which can be easily created using the Collection API method parallelStream() or the Stream API method parallel(). While serial streams are ordered, parallel streams are not. This is due to parallel decomposition where tasks are broken down and re-assembled later. In a parallel multi-threaded environment, threads can take sub-tasks in any order and return the results in any order. This is fine for an associative task such as addition but not suitable for subtraction.

If you are using the parallel reduction methods reduce() and collect(), ensure that the accumulator and combiner functions are associative; as they must work correctly regardless of the order they are executed in.

That completes our discussion on streams. The next chapter, Concurrency will further solidify the last section here on parallel streams.

# 17

# Concurrency

In the previous chapter, we explored the nuances of streamlined data manipulation and parallelized operations that utilize the power of modern multi-core processors. This was already a little introduction to this chapter's topic: concurrency!

Concurrency allows applications to perform multiple tasks at the same time. This makes the system more efficient. Any available resources can be utilized more efficiently, and this leads to overall improved performance. In order to do multiple things at the same in Java, we need to know quite a bit. That's what this chapter is for!

Here's what we'll cover:

- A definition of concurrency
- Working with threads
- Atomic classes
- The synchronized keyword
- Using locks for exclusive thread access
- Concurrent collections
- Using `ExecutorService`
- Common threading problems and how to avoid them

This is often a dreaded (or threaded?) topic, especially for new developers, so don't despair if you need to go over parts of this chapter twice. I'm going to try my best to carefully walk you through all the concepts you need to know. Unlike your applications, focus solely on this chapter and don't do other things simultaneously. Let's get started!

## Technical requirements

The code for this chapter can be found on GitHub at `https://github.com/PacktPublishing/Learn-Java-with-Projects/tree/main/ch17`.

# Understanding concurrency

Have you ever wondered how many tasks a computer can truly run simultaneously? It's tempting to say *several*, yet, in reality, a single-core computer can only execute one process at a given instant. This might appear as simultaneous due to the impressive speed at which CPUs switch between processes, thus creating the illusion of simultaneous multitasking.

Concurrency is the concept of executing multiple tasks or threads at the same time, rather than sequentially. In a sequential system, tasks are executed one after the other, with each task waiting for its predecessor to complete before starting.

For our Java applications, concurrency refers to executing different segments of a program, simultaneously. The term *simultaneously* might be a little ambiguous here, as it could mean multiple things – and that is because concurrency can occur at the hardware level, such as in multi-core processors, or at the software level. An OS could schedule threads to run on different cores.

Which one we mean exactly depends on the type of concurrency being employed. An overview of them can be found in *Figure 17.1*. These can be any of the following:

- Multiprocessing
- Multitasking
- Multithreading

First off, let's discuss multiprocessing.

## Multiprocessing

In the context of **multiprocessing**, the simultaneous execution of diverse processes is facilitated by the presence of multiple CPUs. Each CPU independently executes its own process. To draw a parallel from our daily life, consider two individuals managing a household where one person is occupied with childcare, while the other is out for grocery shopping. They are both a "CPU," each taking care of a unique task concurrently.

## Multitasking

The next concept is **multitasking**, where the term "simultaneous" obtains a slightly different connotation. It implies rapid alternating execution rather than literal simultaneous execution. Imagine a scenario where a person is cooking and intermittently stepping out to hang laundry while the pot is cooking (safely away from the kids, of course). They are the "CPU," continuously switching between two (or more) tasks, giving the illusion of simultaneous progression. This, however, doesn't exactly constitute parallel execution, but it is a very efficient use of resources for sure.

# Multithreading

Last but not least, we have **multithreading** – and that happens to be our primary focus. Multithreading involves different sections of the program running on different threads of execution. This can take place in both single- and multi-CPU environments. Both previously mentioned everyday scenarios can exemplify multithreading.

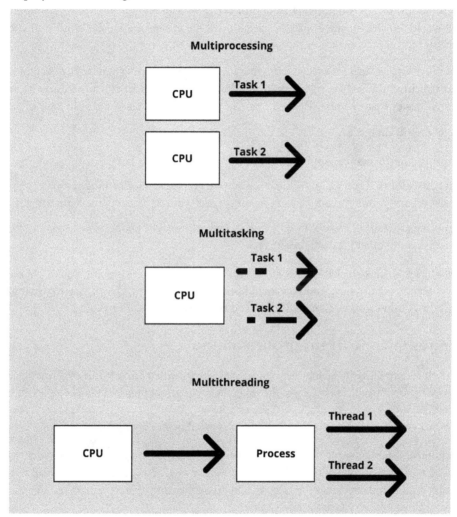

Figure 17.1 - Schematic overview of multiprocessing, multitasking, and multithreading

We will delve deeper into the concept of threads shortly. Let's first talk about why we need to have concurrency in our applications (or lives actually!).

## Importance of concurrency in modern applications

To help you visualize concurrency in computing, consider the way your computer runs multiple programs at the same time. You might have a browser, an email client, a text editor, a code editor, and Slack running concurrently. This kind of operation demands the ability to manage multiple processes concurrently. It's also seen within applications, such as an IDE processing your input while executing code. Without some sort of concurrency, stopping a script with an infinite loop would be impossible, as the IDE would be too consumed with the execution of the infinite loop to deal with your click on the button.

And let's think of web services for a second; imagine a web server processing hundreds, even thousands, of requests concurrently. Such an operation would be unfeasible without concurrency, so it's safe to say that concurrency is an essential aspect of our day-to-day computer use and even daily life!

Let's sum up the advantages:

- **Improved performance**: Applications can complete operations faster

- **Responsiveness**: Applications remain responsive even when performing resource-intensive tasks (as background threads can handle these tasks without blocking the main thread)

- **Resource utilization**: More efficient use of system resources by taking advantage of multi-core processors and other hardware resources

Advantages like this, make real-time execution use cases possible. At this point, you might be very enthusiastic about concurrency. And you should be! However, employing concurrency in our Java applications does come with its own set of costs and complexities. Let's talk about it.

## Challenges in concurrent programming

I've said it before, and I'll say it again: every magic trick comes with a price. While concurrency offers many benefits, it also introduces challenges that can make concurrent programming complex and even error-prone. We even have some errors that are unique to concurrent environments. We'll mention them in more detail later, but it's good to keep these in mind before diving in:

- **Data race**: When multiple threads access the same memory location in a non-synchronized manner and at least one of these threads performs a write. For example, one thread wants to read the value and concludes the value is 5, but the other thread increments to 6. This way, the former thread doesn't have the latest value.

- **Race condition**: A problem that occurs due to the timing and order of events. This problematic order of events can influence the correctness of the outcome. A race condition typically requires external input, from the OS, hardware, or even user. It can, for example, happen when two users try to sign up with the same username at the same. When not handled well, this can lead to unpredictable and undesirable results.

- **Deadlocks**: When two or more threads are waiting for each other to release a resource, a deadlock can occur, causing the application to become unresponsive. For example, when you think your friend will call you and you wait until they do, and your friend thinks you'll call them and they wait until you do, nothing happens, and the friendship is stuck.

- **Livelocks**: Similar to deadlocks, livelocks occur when two or more threads are stuck in a loop, unable to progress due to constantly changing conditions. Let's say you and your friend said you'd meet up at a church in the city center. You are at church *a*, and your friend is at church *b*. You wonder whether your friend is at church *b* and you walk there. Your friend wonders if you are at church *a* and walks there. (And you take a different path and don't bump into each other.) You don't find each other at the church and keep on walking from church *a* to church *b*. Not a very effective use of resources (but all the walking is probably great for your health!).

Starvation: When a thread is unable to obtain the resources it needs to progress, it can experience starvation, leading to poor application performance and inefficient use of resources. A real-life example could be a busy bar where multiple people are trying to acquire a drink from the bartender. There are a lot of people at the bar; the people represent threads. The bartender is serving the people who shout the loudest (comparable to threads with higher priority). The shy person that doesn't stand out experiences "starvation" (or thirst) because he doesn't get access to the shared resource (the bartender).

Challenges are there to be overcome! Java provides various concurrency constructs and tools, which we will explore throughout this chapter. I will refer to these aforementioned problems every now and then. At the end of the chapter, you'll even see some examples of how to break things! But first, let's talk about a key concept of concurrency: threads!

# Working with threads

Let's finally get to explaining *threads*. Threads are sequences of executed instructions, representing the most fundamental units of execution. Each thread follows a certain path through the code. The threads perform specific tasks within processes. A process is typically composed of multiple threads.

To give you an example, the programs we've created so far had one user-created thread (and the user in this case is the developer). The thread went through the lines of code in a certain order; for example, when a method was called, the thread would execute that method before continuing with the code that was directly on the next line after the method call. This is the path of execution of the thread.

When multiple threads are running, multiple paths of execution are being walked through your code, and that's why multiple things are happening at the same time.

In order to make this possible, we'll need duplicates of certain Java constructs. For example, we cannot have two threads using the same stack. That's why every thread has its own stack. We will not dive into the details of the Java memory model here. However, it helps to at least realize that while each thread has its own stack, they share the heap with other threads.

In order to make this digestible for your brain, we'll explain the theory with some not-too-interesting but easy-to-follow examples.. We'll start with threads. There are multiple ways to create and start a thread. Let's see how we can create a thread using the `Thread` class.

## The Thread class

Possibly the simplest way to create a thread is by extending the `Thread` class. The `Thread` class provides an entry point for your thread's execution through the `run()` method. To create a custom thread, you need to define a subclass of `Thread` and override the `run()` method with the code that the thread should execute. Here's a silly example to demonstrate this:

```
class MyThread extends Thread {
    @Override
    public void run() {
        System.out.println("Hello from MyThread!");
    }
}
```

And then in some other class (or even in the same but that might be confusing), we can create a new `MyThread` and kick off the thread execution with the `start()` method:

```
public class Main {
    public static void main(String[] args) {
        MyThread myThread = new MyThread();
        myThread.start(); // starts the new thread
    System.out.println("Hello from Main!");
    }
}
```

This will output the following two lines, but we cannot be sure about the order:

```
Hello from MyThread!
Hello from Main!
```

The `start()` method is part of the `Thread` class that we inherited from and it is used to start a new thread. You could also execute the content of the `run()` method by calling `myThead.run()`, but that would not start a new thread! That would be the same thread as the one executing the `main` method, which would be executing the content of the `run()` method.

We started with this way to create a thread because it is easiest to understand. It's definitely not the most common way. It's more common to implement the `Runnable` interface. Let's see how to do that.

## The Runnable interface

An alternative approach to creating threads is by implementing the Runnable interface. This is a built-in functional interface that can be used to create threads in Java. The Runnable interface has a single method, run(), that you must implement in your class when you extend this interface. Instead of extending the Thread class, you pass an instance of your Runnable implementation to a Thread object. Here's an example:

```
class MyRunnable implements Runnable {
    @Override
    public void run() {
        System.out.println("Hello from MyRunnable!");
    }
}
```

And again, we can now instantiate MyRunnable at another spot. The second step is different though; we are going to instantiate the Thread class and pass our instance of MyRunnable to its constructor. This way, when we start the instance of the thread, whatever we specified in the run() method of the Runnable instance will be executed:

```
public class Main {
    public static void main(String[] args) {
        MyRunnable myRunnable = new MyRunnable();
        Thread thread = new Thread(myRunnable);
        thread.start(); // starts the new thread
    }
}
```

This will output the following:

```
Hello from MyRunnable!
```

And again, to execute what is in MyRunnable's run method, we could have written myRunnable. run(), but this also would not have started a new thread! Let's prove that we actually start a new thread. Every thread has a unique ID. By outputting the ID of the thread in the run method, we can prove it's a different thread. Here's the adjusted example for that:

```
class MyRunnable implements Runnable {
    @Override
    public void run() {
        System.out.println("Hello from thread: " + Thread.
          currentThread().threadId());
    }
```

```
    }
```

And here's our adjusted `Main` class:

```java
public class Main {
    public static void main(String[] args) {
        System.out.println("Hello from main: " + Thread.
          currentThread().threadId());
        MyRunnable myRunnable = new MyRunnable();
        Thread thread = new Thread(myRunnable);
        thread.start(); // starts the new thread
    }
}
```

This will print the following:

```
Hello from main: 1
Hello from thread: 22
```

Please note that the IDs might be different for you, but they will also be two different threads. The thread IDs remain consistent across multiple executions due to some background threads started by Java such as the garbage collector. Say we change the `start()` method to `run()`, like this:

```java
public static void main(String[] args) {
        System.out.println("Hello from main: " + Thread.
          currentThread().threadId());
        MyRunnable myRunnable = new MyRunnable();
        Thread thread = new Thread(myRunnable);
        thread.run(); // doesn't start a new thread
    }
```

The IDs are the same; this is the result:

```
Hello from main: 1
Hello from thread: 1
```

This is already a bit more common, but more often we don't create a class for `Runnable` and rather implement `Runnable` with a lambda expression. As you might be able to recall from the Lambda expression *Chapters 15* and *16*, we can implement any functional interface with a lambda expression. Let's see how that is done.

## Lambda expressions with Runnable

Since the Runnable interface is a functional interface with a single method, you can use lambda expressions to create and run threads more concisely. Here's an example using a lambda expression:

```
public static void main(String[] args) {
    Runnable myRunnable = () -> System.out.println("Hello
      from a lambda Runnable!");
    Thread thread = new Thread(myRunnable);
    thread.start(); // starts the new thread
}
```

As you can see, we don't need a separate class for Runnable anymore. We can just do it *on the fly*. Here's the output:

```
Hello from a lambda Runnable!
```

And as I mentioned a few times before, if you use run() instead of start(), you are getting the same output in this case, but this is not done by a new thread.

These are the basics of how to create threads. Let's see how we can control the execution with sleep() and join(). So, join me for some sleep!

# Thread management – sleep() and join()

This might be a weird statement, but threads can go to *sleep*. This means that the execution of the thread gets paused for a short while. Before we dive into how to do this, it is worth noting that this is something that is often considered to be a code smell. This means that it can be a problematic solution to, for example, a data race or a challenge with loading times. However, sometimes you will need this – for example, to slow down a background thread. Just make sure to proceed with caution here. Let's see how we can make our threads go to sleep now.

## The Thread.sleep() method

The Thread.sleep() method is a static method that causes the currently executing thread to go to sleep. That means pausing its execution for a specified period. It is useful for simulating delays, allowing other threads to execute, or performing time-based operations. The sleep() method takes a single argument, the duration of the sleep in milliseconds. Here's an example:

```
public class Main {
    public static void main(String[] args) {
        Thread t = new Thread(() -> {
            try {
    // Next two lines represent the same Java line
```

```
            System.out.println("Thread will go to sleep
              for 2 seconds...");
            Thread.sleep(2000);
            System.out.println("*Yawn...* I'm awake!");
        } catch (InterruptedException e) {
            e.printStackTrace();
        }
    });
    t.start();
  }
}
```

We need the try/catch block here because sleep() can be interrupted. This interrupt would result in the checked exception, InterruptedException, being thrown.

## Handling InterruptedException

Imagine if the main thread decides that the execution is taking too long and wants to end the program. It can suggest the secondary thread stops by using the interrupt method. If the instance is called t, this can be done with t.interrupt(). Interrupting a sleeping thread throws InterruptedException.

This is a checked exception that you must handle if you use the Thread.sleep() method. We can also make our thread wait for another thread to be done. This is done with the join() method.

## Using the join() method

Threads can wait until another thread is done. The join() method allows the calling thread to wait until the specified thread has finished its execution. This is useful when you need to ensure that a particular thread has completed its work before proceeding. Here's an example where the main thread is waiting for thread t1:

```
public class Main {
    public static void main(String[] args) {
        Thread t1 = new Thread(() -> {
            System.out.println("t1 started");
            try {
                Thread.sleep(2000);
            } catch (InterruptedException e) {
                e.printStackTrace();
            }
            System.out.println("Thread finished!");
        });
```

```
        t1.start();

        try {
            System.out.println("Main thread will be waiting
               for other t1 to be done...");
            t1.join();
            System.out.println("Main thread continues...");
        } catch (InterruptedException e) {
            e.printStackTrace();
        }
    }
}
```

This will output the following:

```
Main thread will be waiting for other t1 to be done...
t1 started
t1 finished!
Main thread continues...
```

So, as you can see, t1.join() is called. This makes the main thread wait until t1 is done executing (and that includes 2 seconds of sleep) before the main thread continues. The main thread can also wait for a specified amount of time, for example, 1 second, by calling t1.join(1000) instead. This is a bit safer because our program would get stuck if t1 for some reason hung indefinitely. You should go ahead and try to remove join() and run the program a few times to inspect the behavior and see if you can get it to hang indefinitely.

As you can see, we also need to catch InterruptedException when we use the join() method. This is in case the calling thread gets interrupted while waiting for the other thread to be done.

Let's have a look at how to avoid (or solve) some common issues with read and write operations in concurrent environments.

## Atomic classes

Data integrity can easily be a problem in a concurrent program. Imagine two threads reading a value, and then both changing it and overwriting each other's change right after. This could, for example, result in a counter that ends up being only one higher, while it should be two higher. Data integrity gets lost! This is where atomic classes come in.

Atomic classes are used for atomic operations. That means that the read (getting a value) and write (changing a value) are considered one operation instead of two separate ones. This avoids the problems with data integrity that we just demonstrated. We'll briefly discuss how to use AtomicInteger, AtomicLong, and AtomicReference.

## AtomicInteger, AtomicLong, and AtomicReference

There are several atomic classes for basic data types. We have `AtomicInteger` to represent an integer value and support atomic operations on it. Similarly, we have `AtomicLong` for the `Long` type. We have `AtomicReference` for references to an object and to support atomic operations on it.

These atomic classes provide methods for performing atomic operations, such as `get`, `set`, `compareAndSet`, and various arithmetic operations. Let's have a look at an example that would be problematic without `AtomicInteger`:

```java
public class ExampleAtomicInteger {
    private static AtomicInteger counter = new
      AtomicInteger(0);

    public static void main(String[] args) throws
      InterruptedException {
        Thread thread1 = new Thread(() -> {
            for (int i = 0; i < 10000; i++) {
                counter.getAndIncrement();
            }
        });

        Thread thread2 = new Thread(() -> {
            for (int i = 0; i < 10000; i++) {
                counter.getAndIncrement();
            }
        });

        thread1.start();
        thread2.start();

        thread1.join();
        thread2.join();

        System.out.println("Counter value: " + counter);
    }
}
```

This code will print the following output:

```
Counter value: 20000
```

Without `AtomicInteger`, the value of the `counter` at the end of the program would differ. It could be 14387, 15673, 19876, and so on. (It could not be more than 20000). This is because multiple threads would read it at the same time (so reading the same value) and then update it in the next operations, thereby potentially writing a lower value than the current value of the `counter`.

To illustrate, picture this. You're in a room with two friends. On the table is a hat with a piece of paper in it. The piece of paper is folded and has a number on it, the number 4. All three of you need to increment the value by 1. If your friend reads the value, then puts the number back in the hat, and then starts to search the house for a piece of paper and a pen. Your other friend might read the value right after, before your friend had a chance to increment the number. The other friend has a piece of paper and pen available (quite a friend to not share with the other friend) and replaces the piece of paper with the new value 5. You then go next, read the value, see that it is 5, get your piece of paper and pen, write down the number 6 and put it in the hat. The other friend then finally comes back, and updates the piece of paper with the new value, which, according to his knowledge from when he was reading, should be 5. The final value in the hat is then 5. Even though it has been 6 before, it went back down. You and your friends behave like threads that treat reading and writing as two different operations.

Let's say that you are not just friends, but you are atomic friends. This would mean that you would treat reading and writing as one action. So instead of putting the piece of paper back in the hat right after reading it, you would not put it back before updating it with the new value. So now, if you would all have to increment it by 1, there would be no confusion and the value would end up being 7.

We have a Java way of doing this with the atomic classes. In the snippet above, the `getAndIncrement` method ensures that two threads cannot access the counter at the same time and guarantees that the counter will have the correct value. This is because getting and incrementing are not two separate operations, but one atomic operation. This is why atomic classes are particularly useful in multi-threaded environments where you need to ensure consume shared resources without using explicit synchronization. However, we can always work with explicit synchronization. Let's explore the `synchronized` keyword next.

# The synchronized keyword

As we've just seen, working with many threads can bring potential new problems, such as data integrity. The **synchronized** keyword is a Java keyword that uses a lock mechanism to achieve synchronization. It is used to control access to critical sections of code for different threads. When a thread is inside a synchronized method or block, no other thread can enter any of the synchronized methods for the same object.

To understand the need for synchronization, let's consider another simple concurrent counting scenario where unexpected outcomes can occur. We have a class named Count with a static counter variable. This class also has a method, incrementCounter, which increments the value of counter by one:

```java
public class Count {
    static int counter = 0;

    static void incrementCounter() {
        int current = counter;
        System.out.println("Before: " + counter + ",
          Current thread: " + Thread.currentThread()
            .threadId());
        counter = current + 1;
        System.out.println("After: " + counter);
    }
}
```

This program, when run in a for loop 10 times in a single-threaded environment, will behave as expected, incrementing the counter sequentially from 0 to 10. The value of the id of the thread would also be the same since it's a single thread.

```
Before: 0, Current thread: 1
After: 1
Before: 1, Current thread: 1
After: 2
Before: 2, Current thread: 1
After: 3
Before: 3, Current thread: 1
After: 4
Before: 4, Current thread: 1
After: 5
Before: 5, Current thread: 1
After: 6
Before: 6, Current thread: 1
After: 7
Before: 7, Current thread: 1
After: 8
Before: 8, Current thread: 1
After: 9
Before: 9, Current thread: 1
After: 10
```

Now, imagine instead of a single-threaded environment, we have 10 threads, and each thread is tasked to increment the `counter`:

```
public class Main {
    public static void main(String[] args) {
        for (int i = 0; i < 10; i++) {
            new Thread(Count::incrementCounter).start();
        }
    }
}
```

And now we have a problem! Here's the output I got (yours might be different!):

```
Before: 0, Current thread: 26
Before: 0, Current thread: 29
Before: 0, Current thread: 22
Before: 0, Current thread: 30
Before: 0, Current thread: 25
Before: 0, Current thread: 31
Before: 0, Current thread: 23
Before: 0, Current thread: 24
Before: 0, Current thread: 27
Before: 0, Current thread: 28
After: 1
After: 1
After: 1
After: 1
After: 1
After: 1
After: 1
After: 1
After: 1
After: 1
```

The output becomes unpredictable because of a phenomenon called *thread interference*. In a multithreaded environment, multiple threads may read and increment the value of `counter` concurrently. This concurrent modification can lead to unexpected results, causing a loss of data integrity. This is again due to a race condition. We have seen how to solve that by using an atomic class, but we could also solve it by synchronizing the method. The best option would be the one that allows multiple threads in most part of the code, without creating data integrity problems. For this case, that would be the atomic classes. However, this is a great example to demonstrate how the `synchronized` keyword is working.

## Using synchronized methods

To create a synchronized method, you simply add the synchronized keyword before the method definition. This ensures that only one thread at a time can execute the method for a given object instance. Here's the updated example:

```
public class Count {
    static int counter = 0;

    static synchronized void incrementCounter() {
        int current = counter;
        System.out.println("Before: " + counter + ",
          Current thread: " + Thread.currentThread()
            .threadId());
        counter = current + 1;
        System.out.println("After: " + counter);
    }
}
```

In this case, if multiple threads call the incrementCounter() method simultaneously, the synchronized keyword ensures that only one thread at a time can access the method. This prevents race conditions. Without any changes to the Main class, this will be the output (your thread IDs might differ):

```
Before: 0, Current thread: 22
After: 1
Before: 1, Current thread: 31
After: 2
Before: 2, Current thread: 30
After: 3
Before: 3, Current thread: 29
After: 4
Before: 4, Current thread: 28
After: 5
Before: 5, Current thread: 27
After: 6
Before: 6, Current thread: 26
After: 7
Before: 7, Current thread: 25
After: 8
Before: 8, Current thread: 24
After: 9
Before: 9, Current thread: 23
After: 10
```

You can imagine that synchronizing an entire method can be inefficient. Since this makes all the threads wait outside of the method and it creates a possible bottleneck for your performance. It is very possible that part of the code in the method can be executed by multiple threads at the same time without being a threat (sorry) to data integrity. Sometimes, you only need to synchronize a part of the method. This can be done with a synchronized block.

## Using synchronized blocks

In some cases, you may want to synchronize only a portion of a method, rather than the entire method. To do this, you can use a *synchronized block*. A synchronized block requires an object to lock on, and the code inside the block is executed while holding the lock. Here's an example:

```
class Counter {
    private int count;

    public void increment() {
        synchronized (this) {
            count++;
        }
    }

    public int getCount() {
        synchronized (this) {
            return count;
        }
    }
}
```

In this code snippet, the increment() and getCount() methods use synchronized blocks instead of synchronized methods. The result is the same – the count variable is accessed and modified safely in a multi-threaded environment.

## Synchronized methods versus synchronized blocks

It's a best practice to minimize the scope of synchronization to improve performance and reduce contention among threads. This concept is closely related to **lock granularity**, which refers to the size or scope of the code that is being locked. The finer the granularity, the smaller the locked section, allowing more threads to execute in parallel without waiting for each other.

Synchronizing large sections of code or entire methods is considered coarse-grained locking and can lead to poorer performance. In this scenario, multiple threads may be queued up, waiting for a single lock to be released, which can create a bottleneck. While coarse-grained locking might be necessary for ensuring data integrity, it should be used with caution and only if there is no other option.

On the other hand, fine-grained locking involves using synchronized blocks to limit the scope of synchronization to the smallest possible critical section. This allows for better concurrency, as threads are less likely to be blocked waiting for a lock, thereby improving the system's throughput.

So, to achieve optimal performance without compromising data integrity, aim for fine-grained locking by using synchronized blocks whenever possible. This aligns well with the principle of minimizing the scope of synchronization. The `synchronized` keyword provides a low-level mechanism for synchronization. For more complex scenarios, consider using higher-level concurrency constructs, such as the `Lock` interface or concurrent collections. Let's see the `Lock` interface next!

# The Lock interface

Let's talk about the `Lock` interface. This is an alternative to the `synchronized` keyword for handling concurrency control. While synchronized helps us achieve thread safety, it also introduces some drawbacks:

- Threads are blocked while waiting for a lock, potentially wasting processing time
- There's no mechanism to check whether a lock is available or to time out if a lock is held for too long

If you need to overcome these limitations, you can use the built-in `Lock` interface with implementations that offer more control over synchronization. We will discuss one of the most common implementations: `ReentrantLock`.

## ReentrantLock

The `ReentrantLock` class is a popular implementation of the `Lock` interface. `ReentrantLock` is used to protect a section of code similar to `synchronized` but provides additional features through its methods:

- `lock()`: This method locks the lock
- `unlock()`: This method releases the lock
- `tryLock()`: This method attempts to acquire the lock and returns a boolean indicating whether the lock was acquired
- `tryLock(time, unit)`: This method attempts to acquire the lock for a specified duration

Let's update the example we used to demonstrate the synchronized keyword with `ReentrantLock`:

```
import java.util.concurrent.locks.Lock;
import java.util.concurrent.locks.ReentrantLock;

public class Count {
```

```
        static int counter = 0;
        static Lock lock = new ReentrantLock();

        static void incrementCounter() {
            try {
                lock.lock();
                int current = counter;
                System.out.println("Before: " + counter + ",
                  Current thread: " + Thread.currentThread()
                    .threadId());
                counter = current + 1;
                System.out.println("After: " + counter);
            } finally {
                lock.unlock();
            }
        }
    }
}
```

In the preceding code snippet, we replace the synchronized block with ReentrantLock.
We lock the Lock before the critical section and unlock it afterward in the finally block. This
unlocking in the finally block is of utmost importance; otherwise, the lock won't be released when
an exception occurs.

The Main class remains the same:

```
public class Main {
    public static void main(String[] args) {
        for (int i = 0; i < 10; i++) {
            new Thread(Count::incrementCounter).start();
        }
    }
}
```

And this works like a charm. Here is the output:

```
Before: 0, Current thread: 22
After: 1
Before: 1, Current thread: 23
After: 2
Before: 2, Current thread: 24
After: 3
Before: 3, Current thread: 25
After: 4
Before: 4, Current thread: 26
After: 5
```

```
Before: 5, Current thread: 27
After: 6
Before: 6, Current thread: 28
After: 7
Before: 7, Current thread: 29
After: 8
Before: 8, Current thread: 30
After: 9
Before: 9, Current thread: 31
After: 10
```

But what if the block was locked already? We want to avoid waiting indefinitely. In that case, it may be better to use `tryLock`. If the lock is unavailable, the thread can continue with other tasks. This is one of the benefits compared to using the `synchronized` keyword! Here's the updated code:

```
public class Count {
    static int counter = 0;
    static Lock lock = new ReentrantLock();

    static void incrementCounter() {
        if (lock.tryLock()) {
            try {
                int current = counter;
                System.out.println("Before: " + counter +
                    ", Current thread: " + Thread.
                    currentThread().threadId());
                counter = current + 1;
                System.out.println("After: " + counter);
            } finally {
                lock.unlock();
            }
        } else {
            System.out.println("Thread didn't get the lock
                and is looking for a new task.");
        }
    }
}
```

As you can see, we surround the `try` block with `tryLock()`. If the lock is not available, the thread proceeds to do other work. We could also have used the `tryLock(time, unit)` method to wait for the lock for a specific duration.

We won't go into detail due to the scope of this book, but there are other locks available – for example, the `ReadWriteLock` interface. It separates read and write operations, allowing multiple concurrent reads but exclusive writes. This can improve performance in read-heavy workloads.

## Best practices for working with locks

When working with the `Lock` interface, it's important to keep a few best practices in mind:

- Always unlock in a `finally` block to ensure the lock is released even in the case of an exception.

- Use `tryLock()` for non-blocking operations, which can help avoid deadlocks and improve performance.

- Even though we didn't discuss it in detail, consider using `ReadWriteLock` for read-heavy workloads. This allows concurrent reads and exclusive writes. This improves the throughput of your application.

Enough about locks! Let's talk about the another key tool for working with concurrency in Java: concurrent collections!

# Concurrent collections

Multi-threaded environments are important for performance, but in any multi-threaded environment, data integrity becomes an issue to consider. Imagine a situation where you have several threads interacting with a shared data structure, such as an `ArrayList` or `HashMap`. While one thread might be trying to read data from the structure, another could be writing to it. This can lead to data inconsistency and other types of errors.

One common problem that arises in such situations is known as a concurrent modification exception. This occurs when one thread is iterating over a data structure, and another thread attempts to modify it. Java recognizes that this can cause inconsistencies and throws an exception to prevent this dangerous operation.

Consider the following example, where a `HashMap` is being used:

```
Map<String, String> languageMap = new HashMap<>();
languageMap.put("Maaike", "Java");
languageMap.put("Seán", "C#");

for (String key : languageMap.keySet()) {
    System.out.println(key + " loves coding");
    languageMap.remove(key);
}
```

In this example, we're trying to iterate over HashMap and remove an entry during the process. This will throw ConcurrentModificationException.

You might have guessed it; this is exactly why we have concurrent collections. A concurrent collection, such as ConcurrentHashMap, is a thread-safe alternative to HashMap, which means it can handle simultaneous reading and writing from multiple threads. With ConcurrentHashMap, you can modify the map while looping over it:

```
ConcurrentMap<String, String> languageMap = new
  ConcurrentHashMap<>();
languageMap.put("Maaike", "Java");
languageMap.put("Seán", "C#");

for (String key : languageMap.keySet()) {
    System.out.println(key + " loves coding");
    languageMap.remove(key);
}
```

We don't get ConcurrentModificationException this time. ConcurrentHashMap allows us to remove items while iterating.

And that's not even all! Concurrent collections offer another advantage. They allow us to lock on a per-segment basis. This means that multiple threads can have read access simultaneously, which can enhance the performance without compromising data integrity.

## Concurrent collection interfaces

Within the java.util.concurrent package, there are several interfaces designed to facilitate concurrent operations on collections. The two primary ones we will discuss are ConcurrentMap and BlockingQueue.

### ConcurrentMap

ConcurrentMap is a sub-interface of the standard java.util.Map. It provides atomic operations for adding, removing, and replacing key-value pairs, enhancing thread safety. The two primary implementations of ConcurrentMap are ConcurrentHashMap and ConcurrentSkipListMap. It works very similarly to a regular Map:

```
ConcurrentMap<String, String> map = new
  ConcurrentHashMap<>();
map.put("Nadesh", "PHP");
String language = map.get("Nadesh");  // Returns "PHP"
```

ConcurrentHashMap is a thread-safe Map implementation that provides better performance than Hashtable (an older thread-safe alternative). It allows concurrent reads and writes with minimal contention.

### BlockingQueue

BlockingQueue is another interface, a subtype of Queue, optimized for multi-threaded operations. Unlike standard queues, BlockingQueue will block or time out when attempting to add an element to a full queue or retrieve an element from an empty queue:

```
BlockingQueue<String> queue = new LinkedBlockingQueue<>();
queue.offer("Maria");
String name = queue.poll();
```

These interfaces provide additional functionality that becomes invaluable when working in a multi-threaded environment, enhancing both performance and data integrity.

There are quite a few other concurrent implementations of collections that you might work with in the future, they work very similarly to their non-concurrent counterparts. We'll talk about two categories: SkipList and CopyOnWrite collections.

## Understanding SkipList collections

ConcurrentSkipList collections represent naturally ordered collections, which means they maintain their elements in a sorted manner. ConcurrentSkipListSet and ConcurrentSkipListMap are the two most common ConcurrentSkipList collections. They work very similar to the collections that we're used to.

### ConcurrentSkipListSet

Using ConcurrentSkipListSet is the same as using TreeSet, but it's optimized for concurrent usage. Let's take a look at an example:

```
Set<String> set = new ConcurrentSkipListSet<>();
set.add("Gaia");
set.add("Jonas");
set.add("Adnane");

for (String s : set) {
    System.out.println(s);
}
```

In the preceding code block, when you print the set, the elements will be displayed in their natural order: Adnane, Gaia, and Jonas.

### ConcurrentSkipListMap

ConcurrentSkipListMap works similarly to TreeMap, but it's designed for concurrent operations. Like ConcurrentSkipListSet, the map entries are maintained in the natural order of their keys:

```
Map<String, String> map = new ConcurrentSkipListMap<>();
map.put("Flute", "Nabeel");
map.put("Bass", "Job");
map.put("Piano", "Malika");

for (String s : map.keySet()) {
    System.out.println(s + ": " + map.get(s));
}
```

In this code, the map entries are printed in the alphabetical order of the keys: Bass, Flute, and Piano.

## Understanding CopyOnWrite collections

CopyOnWrite collections, as the name suggests, make a fresh copy of the collection every time it is modified. This means they perform well when there are more read operations than write operations but can be inefficient when there are more writes. Let's discuss the common implementations.

### CopyOnWriteArrayList

CopyOnWriteArrayList works just like a regular ArrayList but creates a new copy of the list every time it gets modified:

```
List<String> list = new CopyOnWriteArrayList<>();
list.add("Squirrel");
list.add("Labradoodle");
list.add("Bunny");

for (String item : list) {
    System.out.println(item);
    list.add(item);
}

System.out.println(list);
```

Even though we're modifying the list during iteration, it doesn't result in ConcurrentModificationException because a new copy of the list is created when it's modified.

### CopyOnWriteArraySet

CopyOnWriteArraySet is similar to HashSet, but it creates a new copy every time the set is modified:

```
Set<String> set = new CopyOnWriteArraySet<>();
set.add("Dog");
set.add("Cat");
set.add("Horse");

for (String s : set) {
    System.out.println(s);
    set.add(s);
}

System.out.println(set);
```

In the preceding code, the size of the set remains the same after the loop because the set only contains unique objects.

## Synchronized collections

*Synchronized collections* are a different way to use collections in a multithreaded environment. The Collections class provides several static methods for returning synchronized versions of regular collections such as List, Set, and Map. Here's an example for List:

```
List<String> regularList = new ArrayList<>();
List<String> syncList =
    Collections.synchronizedList(regularList);
```

In this example, syncList is a thread-safe version of regularList. These synchronized collections are a good choice when you need to turn an existing collection into a thread-safe one, but if you know a collection will be used in a multithreaded environment upon creation, it's better to use concurrent collections as they perform better.

The most important difference between synchronized and concurrent collections is that synchronized collections cannot be modified in a loop as they will throw ConcurrentModificationException. They are otherwise safe to use and don't lead to issues with data integrity when used with multiple threads. Managing a lot of threads by hand would be quite a daunting task. Luckily, there is a special interface, ExecutorService, to help us with that!

# ExecutorService and thread pools

Java's `ExecutorService` is a mechanism for executing tasks asynchronously. As a part of the `java.util.concurrent` package, `ExecutorService` is an interface used to manage and control thread execution in a multithreaded environment. We have seen so far how we can manually control threads, and we'll now see how we can use `ExecutorService` instead. We'll see the details of `ExecutorService` and its implementations, such as `SingleThreadExecutor` and `ScheduledExecutorService`. Let's see `SingleThreadExecutor` first.

## Executing tasks using SingleThreadExecutor

Firstly, let's start with `SingleThreadExecutor`. This `ExecutorService` has one single worker thread to process tasks, guaranteeing that tasks are executed in the order they're submitted. It's useful when we need sequential execution.

Consider a scenario with an election where votes are being counted. To mimic this process, we'll represent each vote as a task. For simplicity, let's assume we're counting votes for one candidate.

Here's how we can do that:

```java
import java.util.concurrent.ExecutorService;
import java.util.concurrent.Executors;

public class VoteCounter {
    public static void main(String[] args) {
        ExecutorService executor = Executors.
          newSingleThreadExecutor();

        // Submitting tasks
        for(int i=1; i<=4; i++) {
        // We must create a new variable to use in the
        // lambda, because variables in lambdas must be
        // effectively final. And i is not.
            int voteId = i;
            executor.execute(() -> {
                System.out.println("Vote " + voteId + "
                  counted by " + Thread.currentThread().
                    threadId());
            });
        }

        // Remember to shutdown the executor
        executor.shutdown();
```

```
        }
    }
```

In the preceding code block, we first create a `SingleThreadExecutor` instance. We then submit four tasks, each representing a vote being counted. Notice that we use `executor.execute()`, passing a `Runnable` lambda function as an argument. This function prints the vote number and the thread ID handling it. At the end, we shut down `ExecutorService` using `executor.shutdown()`. This is crucial to terminate the non-daemon thread of the executor and failing to do so will prevent your application from terminating. A non-daemon thread is one that prevents the program from ending. When you forget to do that, you'll see that once you run the program, it will not stop. The stop button will stay visible.

This is what it outputs (for me):

```
Vote 1 counted by 22
Vote 2 counted by 22
Vote 3 counted by 22
Vote 4 counted by 22
```

As you can see, it will count four votes, printing the corresponding vote number and the same thread ID each time since all tasks are processed by a single thread. We can actually also invoke multiple tasks at the same time. Before we can do that, we need to understand `Callable` and `Future`. So, let's see what that means first – is the future calling us?

## The Callable interface and Future

While the `Runnable` interface enables you to execute code concurrently, it does not return a result. In contrast, the `Callable` interface allows concurrent tasks to produce a result. It has a single `call` method that returns a value. So, it's a functional interface too.

`ExecutorService` not only executes `Runnable` tasks but also `Callable` tasks, which return a result. The `submit()` method is used to execute `Callable` tasks. This `submit()` method returns a `Future` object, which can be used to retrieve the result once it's ready. If you'd like to think of a non-code example, you can compare it to placing an order at a restaurant: you receive a token (`Future`) and you can use it to collect your order (the result) when it's ready.

The `Future` object represents the result of an ongoing computation—a placeholder of sorts. When you submit a `Callable` task to `ExecutorService`, it returns a `Future` object. You can use this `Future` object to check whether the computation is complete, wait for its completion, and retrieve the result. It's time to see an example!

## Submitting tasks and handling results

Let's simulate counting votes and maintaining a tally using `Callable` tasks. Here, we'll use the `submit()` method, which returns a `Future` object.

The code might look like this:

```java
import java.util.concurrent.*;

public class VoteCounter {
    private static final ExecutorService executorService =
      Executors.newSingleThreadExecutor();

    public static void main(String[] args) {
        try {
            Future<Integer> vote1 = getRandomVote(1);
            Future<Integer> vote2 = getRandomVote(2);
            Future<Integer> vote3 = getRandomVote(3);
            Future<Integer> vote4 = getRandomVote(4);

            // wait until all tasks are done
            while (!(vote1.isDone() && vote2.isDone() &&
              vote3.isDone() && vote4.isDone())) {
                Thread.sleep(10); // sleep for 10ms then
                                  //    try again
            }

            int totalVotes = vote1.get() + vote2.get() +
              vote3.get() + vote4.get();
            System.out.println("Total votes: " +
              totalVotes);
        } catch (InterruptedException |
          ExecutionException e) {
            e.printStackTrace();
        } finally {
            executorService.shutdown();
        }
    }

    public static Future<Integer> getRandomVote(int i) {
        return executorService.submit(() -> {
            Thread.sleep(1000); // simulate delay
            System.out.println("Vote " + i + " counted by "
              + Thread.currentThread().threadId());
```

```
        return 1; // each vote counts as 1
    });
  }
}
```

And here is what it will output:

```
Vote 1 counted by 22
Vote 2 counted by 22
Vote 3 counted by 22
Vote 4 counted by 22
Total votes: 4
```

We are still using `SingleExecutorService` in the preceding code. To our `ExecutorService`, we submit four `Callable` tasks using `executorService.submit()` in the `getRandomVote` method. Each task waits for one second (simulating vote counting) and then returns 1 (representing one vote). Each submission returns a `Future` object, which is stored in `vote1`, `vote2`, `vote3`, and `vote4`, respectively.

Then, we wait in a loop until all `Future` objects report they're done. Once all votes are counted (all `Future` objects are done), we retrieve the results using the `get()` method on each `Future` object. This is wrapped in a `try/catch` block to handle potential exceptions. Finally, we add all the votes and print the total votes. Before we continue, let's talk a bit more about the methods on the `Future` class.

## Future objects and their methods

The `Future` object provides several methods to handle the results of asynchronous computations. We already used `isDone()` to check whether the task was done and the result was in. And we already used `get()` to get the result of the task when it was done. This `get()` method waits until the task is done executing. Here are some other methods that are important to know:

- `get(long timeout, TimeUnit unit)`: Retrieves the result only if it's ready within the provided timeout duration
- `isCancelled()`: Checks whether the computation was canceled
- `cancel(boolean mayInterruptIfRunning)`: Attempts to cancel the task

In the latest example, we submitted the four tasks one by one, but we can also submit multiple tasks at the same time. Let's see how that is done.

## Invoking multiple tasks and handling the results

We can submit multiple tasks and handle their results. For this, we'll use the `invokeAny()` and `invokeAll()` methods, and represent tasks as `Callable` tasks instead of `Runnable` tasks.

The `invokeAny()` method takes a collection of `Callable` objects and returns the result of a successfully executed task (the first one to finish), canceling all others. Conversely, `invokeAll()` executes all tasks and returns a list of `Future` objects representing the results.

Consider the following code, which is counting our votes again. In this case, people can vote for option 1 or option 2. Counting is now implemented with the use of `Callable` and `Future`. We will demonstrate the use of `invokeAny` (not very democratic) and `invokeAll` in this code snippet:

```java
import java.util.Arrays;
import java.util.List;
import java.util.concurrent.*;

public class VoteCounter {
    public static void main(String[] args) {
        ExecutorService executor = Executors.
            newSingleThreadExecutor();
        List<Callable<Integer>> callables = Arrays.asList(
                () -> { Thread.sleep(1000); return 1; },
                () -> { Thread.sleep(2000); return 2; }
        );

        try {
            // Invoking any task and printing result
            Integer result = executor.invokeAny(callables);
            System.out.println("Result of the fastest task:
              " + result);

            // Invoking all tasks and printing results
            List<Future<Integer>> futures = executor.
                invokeAll(callables);
            for (Future<Integer> future : futures) {
                System.out.println("Task result: " +
                    future.get());
            }
        } catch (InterruptedException |
            ExecutionException e) {
            e.printStackTrace();
        }
    }
```

```
        executor.shutdown();
    }
}
```

And this is what the code outputs:

```
Result of the fastest task: 1
Task result: 1
Task result: 2
```

In the code, we start by defining a list of `Callable` tasks. Each `Callable` returns an `Integer` after a certain sleep period (simulating the work done by the task). We then invoke the tasks using the `invokeAny()` and `invokeAll()` methods, displaying the results accordingly. The `try/catch` block is needed to handle potential exceptions that may arise during task execution.

This example gives us a good understanding of invoking tasks and handling results using `ExecutorService`. So far, we've only seen `SingleThreadExecutor`. There are also `ExecutorService` available that use multiple threads. That's going to make it a lot more interesting (and complicated, so stay focussed!). Let's see these next.

## Thread pools and task execution

Thread pools are a key concept of concurrent programming. Thread pools can be compared to a crew of workers—multiple threads waiting for tasks. When a task is available, each thread can pick it up from the queue, execute it, and wait for new tasks rather than being destroyed. This is a lot more efficient compared to creating a new thread for every task.

There are different `ExecutorServices` to manage thread pools, and each has its specific use case. Let's explore `FixedThreadPool` first.

### FixedThreadPool

`FixedThreadPool` maintains a fixed number of threads. If a task is submitted and all threads are active, the task waits in a queue until a thread becomes available.

So far, we've had a single thread do all the vote counting for us. Instead, consider an election scenario where you have three polling stations to count the votes from all 100 voting stations:

```
public static void main(String[] args) {
    ExecutorService executorService = Executors.
      newFixedThreadPool(3);

    for (int i = 0; i < 100; i++) {
        final int stationId = i;
        executorService.submit(() -> {
```

```
            try {
                System.out.println("Counting votes from
                    station: " + stationId + ", Thread id: "
                        + Thread.currentThread().threadId());
                Thread.sleep((int) (Math.random() * 200));
            } catch (InterruptedException e) {
                e.printStackTrace();
            }
        });
    }
    executorService.shutdown();
}
```

This will output something like this:

```
Counting votes from station: 1, Thread id: 23
Counting votes from station: 2, Thread id: 24
Counting votes from station: 0, Thread id: 22
Counting votes from station: 3, Thread id: 23
Counting votes from station: 4, Thread id: 23
[part omitted]
Counting votes from station: 97, Thread id: 22
Counting votes from station: 98, Thread id: 23
Counting votes from station: 99, Thread id: 24
```

Every time you run the program, it will be somewhat different! The count for each vote is carried out asynchronously, as demonstrated by the randomly assigned sleep times. This is because we're simulating a scenario in which each of the three threads (in this case with id 22, 23, and 24) corresponds to a polling station that starts counting the votes. Even if there is a large number of votes, there will still only be three threads (polling stations) performing the counting.

As you can see, the order of the voting stations is no longer the same. This is because multiple threads are working simultaneously. And that's not a problem, as it doesn't influence the end result.

### CachedThreadPool

CachedThreadPool, on the other hand, creates new threads as needed and reuses previously constructed threads if they are available. Threads in this pool that haven't been used for a certain amount of time are terminated and removed from the cache.

Imagine an election with numerous mobile polling stations that move around to different locations and count votes as needed:

```java
public static void main(String[] args) {
    ExecutorService executorService = Executors.
        newCachedThreadPool();

    for (int i = 0; i < 100; i++) {
        final int stationId = i;
        executorService.submit(() -> {
            try {
                System.out.println("Counting votes at
                    station: " + stationId + ", Thread id: "
                        + Thread.currentThread().threadId());
                Thread.sleep((int) (Math.random() * 200));
            } catch (InterruptedException e) {
                e.printStackTrace();
            }
        });
    }
    executorService.shutdown();
}
```

This code can output the following:

```
Counting votes at station: 5, Thread id: 27
Counting votes at station: 19, Thread id: 41
Counting votes at station: 24, Thread id: 46
Counting votes at station: 3, Thread id: 25
Counting votes at station: 6, Thread id: 28
Counting votes at station: 0, Thread id: 22
[middle omitted]
Counting votes at station: 97, Thread id: 125
Counting votes at station: 98, Thread id: 126
Counting votes at station: 99, Thread id: 127
```

In this case, CachedThreadPool creates as many threads as needed to process the votes simultaneously, leading to faster vote counting. However, this comes at the cost of system resources since an uncontrolled number of threads could be created.

Another option that we have is to schedule commands to run after a given delay or to execute periodically. This is done with ScheduledExecutorService. Let's see how we can schedule tasks to run after a certain delay or periodically.

## ScheduledExecutorServices

Now, we're going to take a look at `ScheduledExecutorService`. As the name suggests, `ScheduledExecutorService` allows you to schedule tasks to be executed after a certain delay, or to be executed periodically. This is incredibly useful when you need a task to be executed at regular intervals without having to manually reschedule it each time.

To use `ScheduledExecutorService`, you first create one using the `Executors` class. There are multiple options, but we'll only use `newScheduledThreadPool()`.

Let's see some example code. Assume that we are building a simple voting system where we need to schedule a task to close the voting process after a certain period, say 1 hour. Here's how we can do that:

```java
import java.util.concurrent.Executors;
import java.util.concurrent.ScheduledExecutorService;
import java.util.concurrent.TimeUnit;

public class VotingSystem {

    private static final ScheduledExecutorService scheduler
      = Executors.newScheduledThreadPool(1);

    public static void main(String[] args) {
        // Open voting
        System.out.println("Voting started!");

        // Schedule voting to close after 1 hour
        scheduler.schedule(VotingSystem::closeVoting, 1,
          TimeUnit.HOURS);
    }

    private static void closeVoting() {
        // Close voting
        System.out.println("Voting closed!");

        // Shut down the scheduler
        scheduler.shutdown();
    }
}
```

This outputs the following:

```
Voting started!
Voting closed!
```

We create `ScheduledExecutorService` with a single thread. We then use the `schedule()` method to schedule the `closeVoting()` method to be executed after 1 hour. The `schedule()` method takes three arguments: the method to execute, the delay before execution, and the time unit of the delay.

This is a simple example. You could also schedule tasks to be executed periodically. For example, if you wanted to remind voters every 15 minutes that voting will close soon, you could do this:

```
// Schedule reminders every 15 minutes
  scheduler.scheduleAtFixedRate(VotingSystem::remindVoters,
  15, 15, TimeUnit.MINUTES);


// ...

private static void remindVoters() {
    // Remind voters
    System.out.println("Remember to vote! Voting will close
      soon!");
}
```

In this code, we use the `scheduleAtFixedRate()` method to schedule the `remindVoters()` method to be executed every 15 minutes. The `scheduleAtFixedRate()` method takes four arguments: the method to execute, the initial delay before execution, the period between executions, and the time unit of the delay and period.

And this is what it outputs with these modifications:

```
Voting started!
Remember to vote! Voting will close soon!
Remember to vote! Voting will close soon!
Remember to vote! Voting will close soon!
Remember to vote! Voting will close soon!
Voting closed!
```

Remember, when you are done with your `ScheduledExecutorService`, don't forget to shut it down. This will stop any new tasks from being accepted and allow the existing tasks to complete. If you don't shut down `ScheduledExecutorService`, your application might not terminate because the non-daemon threads in the pool will keep it running.

And that's all you need to know to get started with `ScheduledExecutorService`. Let's explore the data race problem in a bit more detail before moving on to other Java tools, such as atomic classes for dealing with concurrency.

# Data races

Instead of starting by explaining atomic classes, let's start with explaining a problem called a data race with an example. We already have seen how to fix this problem with the use of atomic classes, synchronized keyword, and locks. Can you spot the problem in the following code snippet?

```java
public class Main {

    private static int counter = 0;

    public static void main(String[] args) throws
      InterruptedException {
        Thread thread1 = new Thread(() -> {
            for (int i = 0; i < 10000; i++) {
                counter++;
            }
        });

        Thread thread2 = new Thread(() -> {
            for (int i = 0; i < 10000; i++) {
                counter++;
            }
        });

        thread1.start();
        thread2.start();

        thread1.join();
        thread2.join();

        System.out.println("Counter value: " + counter);
    }
}
```

We have a static `int` counter that is being incremented 10,000 times by two threads. You'd expect the counter to be 20,000 then, right? Yet, if we print the value of the counter, this is what we get:

```
Counter value: 12419
```

And if we run it again, this is what we get:

```
Counter value: 13219
```

A third time? This is what we get:

```
Counter value: 15089
```

Long story short, we have a problem! But why? Well, we are looking at the result of a data race. A data race occurs when two or more threads access shared data simultaneously, and at least one of them modifies the data. So, in our case, thread1 reads the value and wants to increase it, but at the same time, thread2 read the value and increases it too. Let's say the value was 2,000 at the time. Both thread1 and thread2 increase it to 2,001. There are a few other variations possible, for example, thread1 writing 4,022, and then thread2 overwriting the value with a much lower value, such as 3,785.

This happens because these ++ and -- operators are not atomic operators. This means that getting the value and increasing it are two separate operations, allowing it to be intersected by another thread. In order to avoid this, we can work with atomic classes. As we have seen, for atomic classes, getting and modifying the value is just one single operation, avoiding this issue.

---

**A non-code data race**

Let's tell you a true story to give you a non-code example (and a first-world problem) about a data race I had to experience myself. I love it when my friends have wish lists for their birthdays so that I can get them something they want instead of spending lots of time thinking about what to get them. So apparently, I and another friend saw that the kid of one of our friends wanted an inflatable bouncy unicorn. So, we both checked the list at almost the same time and we saw that the bouncy unicorn was still an available gift option. We both crossed it off and got the unicorn. (Okay, to be honest, I remember that I had to cross it off twice actually, but I figured it was a glitch.)

Turns out that we were looking at that list, at the very same time, ordering the unicorn and crossing it off. Can't say it ended up being a real problem, because what is better to a 6-year-old than one inflatable bouncy unicorn? Yup, two inflatable bouncy unicorns!

---

Let's see the common problems such as the data race mentioned here before we wrap up this chapter.

# Threading problems

When working with concurrency, we have the opportunity to increase performance! However, with great power comes great responsibility; things can go awfully wrong as well. Therefore, we must be aware of several potential problems that can arise due to incorrect or inefficient synchronization. Let's discuss four common threading problems: data races, race conditions, deadlocks, livelocks, and starvation.

## Data races

We have just talked quite a bit about data races already. They occur when two or more threads access shared data concurrently, and at least one of them modifies the data, leading to unpredictable results. Here's an example of an innocent-looking snippet of code that can lead to a data race in multithreaded environments:

```
class Counter {
    private int count = 0;

    public void increment() {
        count++;
    }

    public int getCount() {
        return count;
    }
}
```

If multiple threads call the `increment()` method simultaneously, the `count` variable's value may not be updated correctly, resulting in an incorrect final count.

### Strategies to prevent data races

To prevent data races, you can use various synchronization techniques as we have seen in this chapter, such as the following:

- Using the `synchronized` keyword on methods or blocks of code
- Using atomic classes, such as `AtomicInteger`, `AtomicLong`, and `AtomicReference`
- Using locks, such as `ReentrantLock` or `ReadWriteLock`

## Race conditions

A race condition is a situation in concurrent programming where the program's outcome can change based on the sequence or timing of thread scheduling and execution. It is a flaw that occurs when the timing or order of events affects the program's correctness. Unlike a data race, where concurrent access to shared data is the issue, a race condition is about multiple threads sequencing their operations incorrectly.

Here's an example code snippet to illustrate the problem:

```
class Flight {
    private int seatsAvailable;
```

```java
    public Flight(int seats) {
        this.seatsAvailable = seats;
    }

    public void bookSeat() {
        if(seatsAvailable > 0) {
            try {
                // Simulate the time needed
                Thread.sleep(100);
            } catch (InterruptedException e) {
                Thread.currentThread().interrupt();
                throw new RuntimeException(e);
            }
            seatsAvailable--;
            System.out.println(Thread.currentThread().
                getName() + " successfully booked a seat.
                Remaining seats: " + seatsAvailable);
        } else {
            System.out.println("Sorry, " + Thread.
                currentThread().getName() + ". The flight is
                fully booked.");
        }
    }

    public int getSeatsAvailable() {
        return seatsAvailable;
    }
}
```

If two threads (representing two customers) called the bookSeat method at the same time when only one seat is left, they could both pass the if(seatsAvailable > 0) check before either of them had the chance to decrement seatsAvailable. As a result, two customers might book the last seat, which is a race condition.

This situation is an example of a race condition because the order of operations (checking the availability and then decrementing the number of seats) matters for correctness. Specifically, there is a critical section of code (if(seatsAvailable > 0) and seatsAvailable--;) that needs to be executed atomically (without interruption) to prevent errors.

To make sure that we understand the difference from a data race, a data race specifically involves simultaneous access to shared data where at least one operation is a write operation. A data race could occur in our example if multiple threads attempted to decrement seatsAvailable at the same time, potentially leading to one thread reading the value of seatsAvailable before another thread had finished decrementing it.

### Strategies to prevent race conditions

To avoid these types of problems, we need to ensure that the critical section of code is executed atomically, which can be achieved by synchronization. For instance, we can use the `synchronized` keyword to prevent multiple threads from executing the critical section simultaneously. You should consider these general strategies:

- **Synchronization**: Use synchronization mechanisms such as the `synchronized` keyword or explicit locks to ensure that only one thread can execute a critical section at a time.

- **Atomic operations**: Use atomic operations that are completed in a single step without the possibility of being interrupted.

- **Sequential design**: Design your program so that thread access to shared data is sequenced or coordinated in a manner that eliminates the timing or order of events as a factor, reducing the chance of race conditions

- **Higher-level concurrency abstractions**: We haven't talked about it here, but the `java.util.concurrent` package provides higher-level synchronization utilities such as `Semaphores`, `CountDownLatches`, and `CyclicBarriers`, which can be used to coordinate operations between threads and thus prevent race conditions.

## Deadlocks

A deadlock occurs when two or more threads wait for each other to release a resource, resulting in a circular waiting pattern. Here's an example of a deadlock:

```java
Object resourceA = new Object();
Object resourceB = new Object();

Thread thread1 = new Thread(() -> {
    synchronized (resourceA) {
        try {
            Thread.sleep(100);
        } catch (InterruptedException e) {
            e.printStackTrace();
        }
        synchronized (resourceB) {
            System.out.println("Thread 1: Locked
                ResourceB");
        }
    }
});

Thread thread2 = new Thread(() -> {
```

```
        synchronized (resourceB) {
            try {
                Thread.sleep(100);
            } catch (InterruptedException e) {
                e.printStackTrace();
            }
            synchronized (resourceA) {
                System.out.println("Thread 2: Locked
                    ResourceA");
            }
        }
    }
});

thread1.start();
thread2.start();
```

So, please mind the problem here is the incorrect use of the `synchronized` keyword! The `thread1` variable acquires a lock on `resourceA` and `thread2` acquires a lock on `resourceB`. Then, both threads attempt to acquire a lock on the other resource, leading to a deadlock. Meaning that both threads are stuck indefinitely.

### Strategies to prevent and resolve deadlocks

To prevent and resolve deadlocks, you can employ the following strategies:

- **Avoid nested locks**: Ensure that you only lock one resource at a time, or acquire locks in a specific order.
- **Use lock timeouts**: Set a timeout for acquiring locks and release them if the timeout expires.

## Livelocks

A livelock occurs when two or more threads are stuck in a loop, repeatedly releasing and re-acquiring resources, without making any progress. Here's a silly example of a livelock:

```
public class ExampleLivelock {
    public static void main(String[] args) {
        run();
    }
    public static void run(){
        final PhoneCall buddy1 = new PhoneCall("Patricia");
        final PhoneCall buddy2 = new PhoneCall("Patrick");

        final HangUpButton s = new HangUpButton(buddy1);
```

```
        new Thread(new Runnable() {
            public void run() { buddy1.callWith(s, buddy2); }
        }).start();

        new Thread(new Runnable() {
            public void run() { buddy2.callWith(s, buddy1); }
        }).start();
    }

    static class HangUpButton {
        private PhoneCall owner;
        public HangUpButton(PhoneCall d) { owner = d; }
        public PhoneCall getOwner() { return owner; }
        public synchronized void setOwner(PhoneCall d) {
            owner = d;
        }
        public synchronized void use() {
            System.out.printf("%s has hang up!",
                owner.name);
        }
    }

    static class PhoneCall {
        private String name;
        private boolean isDone;

        public PhoneCall(String n) {
            name = n; isDone = true;
        }
        public String getName() { return name; }
        public boolean isDone() { return isDone; }

        public void callWith(HangUpButton hangUpButton,
          PhoneCall buddy) {
            while (isDone) {
                if (hangUpButton.owner != this) {
                    try {
                        Thread.sleep(1);
                    }catch(InterruptedException e) {
                        continue;
                    }
```

```
                    continue;
            }

            if (buddy.isDone()) {
                System.out.printf(
                        "%s: You hang up, buddy %s!%n",
                        name, buddy.getName());
                hangUpButton.setOwner(buddy);
                continue;
            }
        }
    }
}
```

In this example, two PhoneCall objects, Patricia and Patrick, are trying to hang up a phone call using a shared hangUpButton object. The hangUpButton object can have only one owner at a time. Patricia and Patrick both seem to have the rule that if they own hangUpButton and the other person hasn't hung up yet, they will pass hangUpButton to the other person. This leads to a situation where the two of them are perpetually passing hangUpButton back and forth to each other because they're always seeing that the other person hasn't hung up yet, which is a livelock situation.

Please note that in this particular silly code, there is no mechanism to break out of the livelock (the infinite while loop in the callWith method). In real-world scenarios, a mechanism to detect and recover from the livelock should be implemented.

### Strategies to prevent and resolve livelocks

To prevent and resolve livelocks, consider the following strategies:

- **Use a backoff algorithm**: Introduce a (very small) random delay or an exponential backoff before retrying an operation to minimize the chances of livelock.

- **Prioritize resources or threads**: Assign priorities to resources or threads to avoid contention and ensure that higher-priority tasks can proceed.

- **Detect and recover from livelocks**: Monitor the application for livelocks and take corrective action, such as restarting threads or reassigning priorities.

A livelock is a special case of resource starvation. It's a condition where two or more processes continuously change their state in response to changes in the other process(es) without doing any useful work. Let's talk about starvation next.

## Starvation

Starvation occurs when a thread is unable to access shared resources for an extended period, hindering its progress. This usually happens when higher-priority threads monopolize resources, causing lower-priority threads to be starved. Here's an example of starvation:

```java
Object sharedResource = new Object();

Thread highPriorityThread = new Thread(() -> {
    synchronized (sharedResource) {
        try {
            Thread.sleep(10000);
        } catch (InterruptedException e) {
            e.printStackTrace();
        }
    }
});
highPriorityThread.setPriority(Thread.MAX_PRIORITY);
highPriorityThread.start();

Thread lowPriorityThread = new Thread(() -> {
    synchronized (sharedResource) {
        System.out.println("Low priority thread accessed
            the shared resource.");
    }
});
lowPriorityThread.setPriority(Thread.MIN_PRIORITY);
lowPriorityThread.start();
```

In this example, the high-priority thread monopolizes the shared resource for a long time, causing the low-priority thread to be starved. Please mind that thread priorities are only hints of how to the scheduler. It's up to the OS implementation to decide.

### Strategies to prevent and resolve starvation

To prevent and resolve starvation, you can employ the following strategies:

- **Fairness**: Ensure fair access to shared resources by using data structures or synchronization mechanisms that provide fairness guarantees, such as `ReentrantLock` with the `fair` parameter set to `true`.

- **Monitor resource usage**: Keep track of resource usage and adjust thread priorities or access patterns to avoid monopolization.

- **Use time-sharing**: Limit the time for which a thread can hold a resource or ensure that each thread gets a chance to access the resource periodically.

And that's it for now! There's a lot more to know about concurrency in fact, we could write an entire book on it – but this will be enough to get you started. Time to roll up your sleeves and get started with the hands-on part!

# Exercises

1.  **Create threads**: Create two classes, FeedingActivity and CleaningActivity. Make FeedingActivity extend the Thread class and CleaningActivity implement the Runnable interface. In both, override the run method to print out the activity's name and a message indicating that the activity is happening.

2.  **Use sleep() and join()**: Create a ParkOperations class with two threads, one for feeding and another for cleaning. Start both threads and then use sleep() to simulate a time delay for the feeding activity. Use join() to ensure cleaning only happens after feeding is complete.

3.  **Use ExecutorService**: Create a TaskAssigner class where you use ExecutorService to assign tasks to employees. Tasks could be represented as Runnable or Callable objects, and employees could be represented as threads.

4.  Solve race conditions in the following code snippet. updater1 and updater2 both are trying to update the status of the same dinosaur object. Since they run concurrently, it might lead to inconsistent outputs. Use the synchronized keyword or AtomicReference to prevent data inconsistency:

```
class Dinosaur {
    private String status;

    public Dinosaur(String status) {
        this.status = status;
    }

    public String getStatus() {
        return status;
    }

    public void setStatus(String status) {
        this.status = status;
    }
}

class DinosaurStatusUpdater implements Runnable {
    private Dinosaur;
    private String newStatus;

    public DinosaurStatusUpdater(Dinosaur dinosaur,
```

```
            String newStatus) {
            this.dinosaur = dinosaur;
            this.newStatus = newStatus;
        }

        @Override
    public void run() {
        dinosaur.setStatus(newStatus);
        System.out.println("Dinosaur status set to: "
            + dinosaur.getStatus());
        }
    }

public class Main {
    public static void main(String[] args) {
        Dinosaur dinosaur = new Dinosaur("Healthy");

        Thread updater1 = new Thread(new
          DinosaurStatusUpdater(dinosaur, "Feeding"));
        Thread updater2 = new Thread(new
          DinosaurStatusUpdater(dinosaur, "Resting"));

        updater1.start();
        updater2.start();
        }
    }
```

# Project – Park Operations System – the calm before the storm

While our park thrives with lively dinosaurs and excited visitors, our behind-the-scenes operations must run concurrently and seamlessly. The use of concurrency can ensure that tasks such as feeding dinosaurs, tracking dinosaur movements, and scheduling staff shifts are handled efficiently.

However, despite our best efforts, things start to go awry. A few dinosaurs become restless, security systems begin to glitch, and staff reports mysterious occurrences. Could this be the calm before the storm, and will we relive what happened in a famous competing park they made a movie about?

Update the following *Park Operations System* so that it concurrently safely handles different park operations. Use low-level threading, `ExecutorService`, atomic classes, synchronized blocks, and the `Lock` interface to manage concurrent access to shared resources. Prevent and handle race conditions, deadlocks, livelocks, and starvation scenarios to keep things under control as tensions rise.

Here's the problematic code that causes the issues:

```java
import java.util.concurrent.*;

class ParkStatus {
    private int foodStock;
    public ParkStatus(int foodStock) {
        this.foodStock = foodStock;
    }
    public int getFoodStock() {
        return this.foodStock;
    }
    public void reduceFood(int amount) {
        this.foodStock -= amount;
    }
}

class FeedingDinosaurs implements Runnable {
    private ParkStatus parkStatus;
    public FeedingDinosaurs(ParkStatus parkStatus) {
        this.parkStatus = parkStatus;
    }
    @Override
    public void run() {
        while (true) {
            parkStatus.reduceFood(1);
            System.out.println("Food stock after feeding: "
                + parkStatus.getFoodStock());
        }
    }
}

class TrackingMovements implements Runnable {
    private ParkStatus parkStatus;
    public TrackingMovements(ParkStatus parkStatus) {
        this.parkStatus = parkStatus;
    }
    @Override
    public void run() {
        while (true) {
            System.out.println("Current food stock: " +
                parkStatus.getFoodStock());
        }
    }
}
```

```
    }

public class Main {
    public static void main(String[] args) {
        ParkStatus parkStatus = new ParkStatus(100);

        Thread feedingThread = new Thread(new
          FeedingDinosaurs(parkStatus));
        Thread trackingThread = new Thread(new
          TrackingMovements(parkStatus));

        feedingThread.start();
        trackingThread.start();
    }
}
```

As you can see, there is a race condition when accessing and modifying `foodStock`. Additionally, these threads will run indefinitely, creating the potential for starvation of other threads in the system.

Here are some hints for modifications:

- **Solving race condition**: To solve the race condition, you could use a synchronized block, the `Lock` interface, or an atomic class. Remember, the goal is to ensure that the `reduceFood()` method and the reading of `foodStock` happen atomically.

- `ExecutorService`: Rather than creating threads directly, you could use `ExecutorService` to manage the threads. This provides more flexibility and utility methods for handling threads.

- **Preventing indefinite looping**: Currently, the `run` methods of `FeedingDinosaurs` and `TrackingMovements` run indefinitely. You could use conditions to control these loops and ensure `ExecutorService` shuts down after the operations are complete.

- **Deadlocks, livelocks, and starvation**: To simulate and prevent these, consider adding more shared resources and threads, and experiment with different locking orders, lock-releasing mechanisms, and thread priorities.

Remember to be cautious when modifying the code to prevent and handle these concurrency issues. Incorrect modifications could cause more problems than they solve. Thank you for saving the day!

# Summary

Concurrency is a fundamental concept in modern software development, allowing applications to perform multiple tasks simultaneously, and efficiently utilizing system resources. In this chapter, we explored various aspects of concurrent programming in Java, from basic thread creation and management to advanced techniques for handling synchronization and shared data.

We started by introducing concurrency and its importance, followed by walking through creating threads using the `Thread` class, the `Runnable` interface, and implementing the `Runnable` interface with lambda expressions. We then moved on to two thread management methods: `sleep()` and `join()`. Next, we talked about `ExecutorService`, which provides a higher level of abstraction for managing thread execution and made our lives a little easier (after making it harder first).

A crucial aspect of concurrent programming is avoiding data races. We demonstrated a data race example and discussed strategies to resolve them, including the use of atomic classes and the `synchronized` keyword. We also explore the `Lock` interface as an alternative to the `synchronized` keyword. This gave us more flexibility and control.

Concurrent collections, such as `ConcurrentHashMap`, `CopyOnWriteArrayList`, and `ConcurrentLinkedQueue`, provide thread-safe alternatives to standard Java collections. We briefly mentioned their benefits and use cases and saw some examples of their usage.

Finally, we examined common threading problems, including data races, race conditions, deadlocks, livelocks, and starvation. We provided examples and strategies to prevent and resolve these issues. By this point, you should have a solid understanding of concurrent programming in Java and be equipped with the skills to deal with multi-threaded applications.

# Index

## Share Your Thoughts

Now you've finished *Learn Java with Projects*, we'd love to hear your thoughts! Scan the QR code below to go straight to the Amazon review page for this book and share your feedback or leave a review on the site that you purchased it from.

https://packt.link/r/1837637180

Your review is important to us and the tech community and will help us make sure we're delivering excellent quality content.

www.ingramcontent.com/pod-product-compliance
Lightning Source LLC
Chambersburg PA
CBHW060635060326
40690CB00020B/4412